P9-BID-735

for HEARST
and MORGAN

THE GEORGE
LOORZ PAPERS

by TAYLOR COFFMAN

FOREWORD BY KEVIN STARR

BERKELEY HILLS BOOKS

BERKELEY, CALIFORNIA

2003

Copyright © 2003 by Taylor Coffman
All Rights Reserved

Berkeley Hills Books
P.O. Box 9877
Berkeley, CA 94709
www.berkeleyhills.com

Building for Hearst and Morgan is a revised and much-expanded successor
to *The Builders Behind the Castles: George Loorz & the F. C. Stolte Co.*,
published in 1990 by the San Luis Obispo County Historical Society,
with whose kind permission this newer book has been produced.

Several of the photographs used, dating from 1973 through 1976, were
taken by the author at Hearst Castle during his employment there.

Linda Trujillo prepared the new set of maps on pp. xx–xv, taking up where
Charles Collins and especially Jan French left off in the former book.

Library of Congress Cataloging-in-Publication Data

Coffman, Taylor.
  Building for Hearst and Morgan : voices from the George Loorz papers /
by Taylor Coffman ; foreword by Kevin Starr.
    p. cm.
Includes bibliographical references and index.
  ISBN 1-893163-52-0 (alk. paper)
  1. Historic buildings — California. 2. Architecture — California — 20th
century. 3. Architects — California — Correspondence. 4. Loorz, George —
Correspondence. 5. Hearst, William Randolph, 1863–1951 — Homes and
haunts — California. 6. Morgan, Julia, 1872–1957. I. Title.
F862.C595   2003
728.8'09794'78 — dc21   2002026297

Printed in the United States of America

Contents

Photographs follow pages 86, 214, 326, and 454

Foreword

Most great construction projects, at least in modern times, have engendered an equally impressive amount of documentation. With the rise of architectural history and librarianship, collections of these documents have increasingly found their way into public archives. Fortunately for the history of American architecture, for the social and cultural history of California, and for a more complete understanding of the life and times of William Randolph Hearst, one such collection — housed at the San Luis Obispo County Historical Museum — is the George Loorz Papers.

From 1932 through 1937, George Loorz worked as year-round construction superintendent for Hearst and his architect, Julia Morgan, in the ongoing development of San Simeon, dominated by the famous hilltop castle, Casa Grande. Loorz kept meticulous records and wrote an abundance of letters, many of them pertaining to this renowned project; still other documents pertain to Wyntoon, a concurrent Hearst-Morgan production in northern California (this one more directly involving Loorz's partner, Fred Stolte). With almost equal energy, Taylor Coffman has meticulously studied these records and correspondence, sifting and combing them for their revealing moments.

The result is this important and elegantly presented contribution to architectural and cultural history, at once the legacy of Loorz's keen observations and near-mania for documentation and Coffman's patient scholarship and narrative skills. In *Building for Hearst and Morgan*, Coffman has freed from archival boxes not only the voice of George Loorz but the voices as well of Hearst, the great man, Morgan, the equally great architect, and a host of skilled craftsmen and other workers — members of the last generation of its kind — whose testimony might otherwise have been lost.

The strength of this book comes from an intersection of client, architect, and builder — Hearst, Morgan, and Loorz — and the twin projects, San Simeon and Wyntoon. That intersection is in and of itself an intriguing moment in American cultural history, especially in its California variation. No one, after all, can fully appreciate California without reference to Hearst and the Spanish castle he built overlooking the sundown sea.

Hearst Castle, as it is now called, remains a primary icon of the state's identity. Powerful psychological and cultural forces brought it into being. As a boy, Hearst spent long months in Europe, traveling with his mother, Phoebe Apperson Hearst, one of the most impressive women of her generation. A native of Missouri, she was largely self-educated; she revered culture and the life of the mind with the pent-up energy that came in part from her isolated girlhood on the frontier. In 1862, she married the mining baron George Hearst (another native Missourian) and soon became one of the wealthiest women in San Francisco and the Far West. Phoebe Hearst spent the rest of her life using that wealth to promote the arts and education, both for herself and her adopted state of California. The letters she wrote home during her first European trips, now in the Bancroft Library, tell of how she and her son encountered European culture in the 1870s. For William Randolph Hearst, its continued pursuit—which for him meant the collecting of paintings, statuary, and objects of art; the acquisition of rare books and manuscripts; and even the wholesale appropriation of European buildings, ultimately including two monasteries shipped over from Spain—would always be linked to a profound memory, the memory of how he had once had his mother all to himself and how they had embraced the Old World in those happy times.

Hearst did not begin developing San Simeon until 1919, the year his mother died. The project would become, in many ways, his monument to her. Meanwhile, he had already discovered the talents of Julia Morgan, a graduate of the Ecole des Beaux-Arts and the first woman licensed to practice architecture in California. Working closely together over the next quarter-century (Hearst only half-jokingly referred to himself as Morgan's assistant architect), they created Casa Grande and other great buildings, which have always loomed as Hearst's tribute to his beloved mother and have endured as something equally compelling about California itself. Through the 1920s (that most prosperous of decades, during which Americans seemed incapable of building a bad building) and into the 1930s, Morgan created for Hearst—and Hearst helped create for Morgan—an architectural embodiment of the California dream, steeped in the Spanish Revival spirit of the era. Here was California as an enchanted city on a hill, a place apart, rich with associations of Spain and Latin America, of blue sky, sunlight, and roses against creamy white walls. From this perspective the main building, Casa Grande, was the ultimate fantasy of that period, the heroic counterpart of all the mansions and even humbler homes that were simultaneously rising in Santa Barbara, Pasadena, San Marino, San Clemente, Rancho Santa Fe, La Jolla, and elsewhere: homes expressive of California as a second Spain, a second Italy, an American Mediterranean shore.

By the time George Loorz began working at San Simeon in 1932 the estate had been under development for some twelve years. The Depression had slackened the pace, but construction still continued: on the indoor Roman Pool, for example, and on the outdoor Neptune Pool, undoubtedly the the most stunning and lavish structure of its kind in the country. What did young Loorz bring to his assignment? A degree in civil engineering from the University of California, for one thing; and behind that, a sturdy upbringing in rural Nevada and service in France during the First World War. But there was more. Loorz wrote clear, direct American prose and had a passion for documenting construction and related matters. His reliance on writing, linked to a powerful impulse to document events, was more characteristic of an earlier day. The art of writing would decline, moreover, as the century wore on, with more and more people doing business by telephone; indeed, Loorz himself curtailed his incessant efforts in the 1940s. But for several busy years — perhaps sensing that Hearst, Morgan, and San Simeon were part of history — Loorz observed and wrote, wrote and observed, then wrote some more (as did many of his friends and colleagues), and those writings are the basis of this book.

Because Loorz was so observant, so little given to exaggeration — he was, remember, a builder, an engineer! — his observations are as lasting as the marble used in the Neptune Pool. His papers are essential to the understanding of San Simeon and its sister project, Wyntoon; for it was through these documents, whether as instructions from Hearst or Morgan, or as queries from Loorz himself, that the young builder guided construction. Since Loorz saw things with a disciplined and accurate eye, his papers — so skillfully arranged by Taylor Coffman into sequential narrative, which is further enhanced by documents from related holdings — offer us a minutely detailed, behind-the-scenes view of events. This is an important breakthrough, given the exaggerations, the hearsay, the myths and outright fabrications surrounding William Randolph Hearst.

Largely because of the film *Citizen Kane*, for example, Hearst survives in folkloric memory as a remote, foreboding, even sinister figure, ensconced in paranoid isolation at Xanadu. One of Coffman's more interesting excerpts reveals another side of Hearst entirely. Noting the poor condition of the workers' quarters at San Simeon, Hearst wrote to Loorz in detail about renovations and improvements. "How about baths and showers?" Hearst asked. "Would it not be well to put a toilet, basin and shower between each two cabins, so that the men can have access to these bathrooms without going into the outer air?"

The entertaining that Hearst did at San Simeon has long since passed into American legend. Yet he was also a businessman while in residence, a working executive who maintained dozens of telephones on the property to keep in constant touch with his far-flung interests. He was a shy man who became more withdrawn

in the 1930s and, politically, more and more alienated from the Roosevelt Administration and the New Deal. But he always loved a party, from his Hasty Pudding
days at Harvard in the 1880s to the times, half a century later, when he and Marion Davies gave stunning masquerade balls at their beachfront mansion in Santa
Monica, a setting that also figures in this story.

The Loorz Papers reveal, furthermore, that Hearst's entertaining often drove
construction at San Simeon and his other estates. Early on, in 1934, Loorz received
orders to complete all the rooms in the Recreation Wing of Casa Grande, if only
temporarily, for a large weekend party to be held just ten days later. San Simeon
ever remained a work in progress. Hearst was first and foremost a journalist, but
the requirements of a party could be just as urgent as the details of a late-breaking
news story.

The very fact of sudden and unexpected deadlines posed by "the Chief"—
and there are several in this compilation—dispels the myth that life at San Simeon
was rigid or subject to obsessive protocol. Time and again Loorz had to respond to
new situations, to changing whims, often conveyed by Hearst's memos and letters.
Trees should be moved. A better bear grotto should be built. (Its walls could be low,
Hearst wrote, because bears don't jump.) As late as 1939, Morgan, on Hearst's behalf, was still sending lists of construction priorities to Loorz.

George Loorz admired Julia Morgan. The Lady, he called her—and not facetiously. The diminutive Miss Morgan constantly amazed him by her attention to
and grasp of detail and, though nearly thirty years older than Loorz, by her tireless
energy. She often took the evening train to San Luis Obispo, arrived at San Simeon
the next morning, worked a full day, and then returned that night to her concurrent
practice in San Francisco. She was not only a gifted architect, she also loved materials and craftsmanship and the practical aspects of construction. A deep friendship developed between these two people. At one point, Loorz thought of leaving
his job at San Simeon but then reconsidered—precisely because he didn't want to
disappoint Morgan. "She has been awfully good to me," Loorz told a friend. "I owe
her a lot."

Loorz also admired William Randolph Hearst. The Chief rarely appears as a
villain or even as a genuinely unpleasant figure in these pages. Even when Hearst
lost his temper with the workmen, as happened on one occasion, Loorz believed he
was just play-acting, putting on a show, like a tough city editor chewing out wayward reporters. In contrast, Loorz also wrote of occasions on which Hearst strove
to keep workmen employed through lean times. Loorz further depicted Hearst in
some private moments, sitting, for instance, in the large Assembly Room of Casa
Grande with Marion Davies, his son John and John's wife, and his friend and confidant Arthur Brisbane. When Loorz finally left San Simeon after 1937 (however,

he did some further work for Hearst and Morgan in the years that followed), Hearst sent him a much-deserved letter of recommendation, which, as Coffman notes, Loorz treasured for the rest of his life.

Soon after Loorz received that letter in 1938, Hearst not only brought construction at San Simeon and Wyntoon to a virtual halt, he also began selling off much of his land holdings. A huge parcel of ranch property north of Hearst Castle went to the federal government in 1940, becoming part of the new Hunter Liggett Military Reservation. Before long, those pastoral acres resounded with the movements of troops in training, engaged in war games. The real thing, triggered by Pearl Harbor, lay just a year ahead.

Earlier, in 1937, during his last full year on the job, Loorz witnessed the opening of Highway 1 through Big Sur, right up the coast from San Simeon. The public in its own cars—the you and I of that time—could now enjoy scenic landscapes previously reserved for elites like Hearst and his Hollywood friends. Two decades later, some of those same people would be among the first to visit Hearst San Simeon State Historical Monument, awed by the great Spanish castle Hearst had created to externalize his compelling dream. With the opening of the new highway, one California yielded to another. Loorz, in fact, had already prefigured this transition, this process of democratization. While supervising work on the Neptune Pool in 1934, he was also building a small swimming pool for his sons next to his home on San Simeon Bay. The pool, a mere thirty feet long and barely four feet deep, was dug mostly by hand. A far cry from the breathtaking Neptune Pool on The Enchanted Hill, Loorz's homemade counterpart nonetheless made its own California statement.

There was, after all, something overwrought about San Simeon and, to a lesser extent, Wyntoon. The dreams and fantasies of one powerful man had played themselves out to their logical limit both on the rolling hills of the coast and in the deep forests of the north. The California which William Randolph Hearst and Julia Morgan had glimpsed in such grand, epic terms would soon, following the Second World War, be democratized into a paradigm for the middle class. A place like San Simeon could not, in the long run, function successfully as a home; its maintenance, both as buildings and grounds and as a setting for Hearst's royal life, had been daunting enough even before the Depression took hold.

In the midst of those bygone days Hearst told Loorz in 1934 that the fireplace in the East Room of Casa Grande was drafty and that, at night, noises reverberated in both towers—almost as though the great building were haunted. "Whenever there is any kind of a wind," he wrote his trusted builder, "even a stiff breeze, the moans and groans in the tower are pitiful to hear. . . . If we can get these two things fixed up—the fireplace and the ghosts—the house will be much more habitable."

While Loorz was meeting these and other challenges, San Simeon was already becoming—like Cornelius Vanderbilt's Breakers in Newport, Rhode Island, like Phillip II's Escorial in Spain—a museum, a monument of an earlier and perhaps more heroic era. It was also the embodiment of an old man's memory, realized as architecture, of those happy days of boyhood when Hearst wandered about Europe with his mother, the two of them enchanted by the beauty around them—sharing experiences that, from then on, imbued them with the long, long daydream of art and grandeur.

KEVIN STARR
State Librarian of California

Prefaces Old and New

Preface to the former book on the George Loorz Papers,
The Builders Behind the Castles:
George Loorz & the F. C. Stolte Co. (1990)

April 23, 1988, was a Saturday, an ordinary Saturday that found me working in my study. Early that afternoon the phone rang. The caller was Bill Loorz, the second of George Loorz's three sons. (I knew that George Loorz, during the 1930s, had been Julia Morgan's construction superintendent on the San Simeon job for William Randolph Hearst.) My ears perked up because I had long been wondering about the George Loorz Papers, which I knew were still being held by the Loorz family. And it was about those papers that Bill Loorz was calling. Mr. Loorz said that he and his brothers wanted to do right by their father's papers, that they felt the time to act had come, and that I might like to see some of the papers before any final decisions were made regarding their disposition. I naturally jumped at the chance. Two months later I was driving home from Los Angeles, with a few boxes of papers that Bill Loorz had entrusted to me for archival processing.

The project grew. By the end of 1988, I had been entrusted with nearly twenty boxes of George Loorz's papers—enough to keep me busy in my spare time for many months.

On June 26, 1989, Bill Loorz wrote me one of his typically encouraging notes. "I don't know exactly how these things work," he said, "but if you think there is enough in here of interest to Hearst-Morgan-San Simeon buffs, maybe we could underwrite your efforts to write a small book or pamphlet on the Loorz papers." I assured him that the papers contained more than enough information—largely untapped, unsuspected information—to warrant a book. I also assured him that a small book was the least we should consider, a pamphlet being too limited for the extensive, richly detailed Loorz Papers.

The idea of a small book also grew. Late in 1989, I completed several years of historical work for the Hearst Corporation and was free to pursue the Loorz project full time. Bill Loorz authorized me to proceed—to process an additional twenty boxes of his father's papers, to write a narrative based on the roughly forty boxes all told, and, as a culminating step, to direct the publication of a full-scale book befitting the subject. And so *The Builders Behind the Castles* was launched. I will be forever grateful to Bill Loorz and his brothers for having trusted me to carry out this challenging assignment.

A related assignment was to find a good home for the George Loorz Papers. That home proved to be the San Luis Obispo County Historical Museum, which is operated by the San Luis Obispo County Historical Society.

No one can act alone in writing a book like *The Builders Behind the Castles*. Bill Loorz, of course, was especially helpful from the very start. Later on I met Bill's older brother, Don, and his younger brother, Bob, both of whom likewise deserve my thanks; Don Loorz was most helpful, for instance, in discussing how his father and Fred Stolte became associated in 1928. Maurice McClure, a good friend of the Loorz family, deserves a special word of thanks. He was the one who mentioned me to Bill Loorz and urged him to sound me out. Few other "old timers" besides Maurice McClure are still with us from George Loorz's era. One of them, Conrad Gamboni, read the manuscript and made helpful suggestions. Another old timer, the late Carl Daniels, also read it.

Among my colleagues who read the manuscript were Shirley Shewmaker Wahl, who provided important information on Hearst's Wyntoon estate; Sara Holmes Boutelle, who had interviewed George Loorz and Fred Stolte while writing her biography of Julia Morgan; Lynn Forney Stone, whose mother was Miss Morgan's longtime secretary; Dan Krieger and Mark P. Hall-Patton, who represented the San Luis Obispo County Historical Society; and of course John Porter, who has been my chief editor for several years.

This book is largely an edition of letters, and any such book requires a comment on editorial technique. George Loorz, the principal correspondent, typed nearly all his letters—and he usually typed them fast, with little if any fussing over misspellings and the like. I have preserved these quirks, these irregularities, within reason; I have "followed copy" more often than not. Some bracketed insertions have been necessary, and a very occasional "*sic*" crops up; however, I have tried to keep these devices to a tolerable minimum. Loorz was not alone in making slips in his writing. Julia Morgan certainly made some in hers. So did many of the others whose letters I have quoted. I hope the reader will enjoy seeing their words, their punctuation (or lack thereof), and their sometimes erratic phrasing, however flawed these elements may seem.

MAY 1990

POSTSCRIPT: On July 22, 1990, Bill Loorz called me from Los Angeles. We both thought we had located all of George Loorz's surviving papers, but three more boxes had just surfaced—less than two weeks before *The Builders Behind the Castles* was slated to go to press. The three boxes were labeled "Burnett Road for 1932," "1933 Miscellaneous," and "F.C.S. 1936." Bill Loorz sent me the boxes the next day; I quickly confirmed that their historical value was comparable to that of the other boxes I had processed. The box from 1936, for example, threw much light on George Loorz's "outside work" for the F. C. Stolte Co. and on his dealings with Julia Morgan and William Randolph Hearst that same year. Would that I had had those papers at my disposal six months earlier! Yet just as sportsmen say that records are made to be broken, editors must concede that history is made to be rewritten—or at least amplified. The users of the George Loorz Papers will find endless grist for their mills in that regard. I wish them well in their efforts.

Preface to the present book,
Building for Hearst and Morgan:
Voices from the George Loorz Papers (2003)

After it went through its first small printing of 1990, the former book on the Loorz Papers was reprinted in 1992. Not long after that, and despite its being favorably reviewed in the magazine *California History* (Winter 1991/92), *The Builders Behind the Castles* dropped from sight. True, it remained familiar to employees at Hearst Castle, San Simeon (for whose torchbearing I've always been grateful). But otherwise the book was soon forgotten. Few libraries outside San Luis Obispo County had a copy; few historians or collectors knew it even existed. And in the brief heyday of the book, the *Castles* portion of its title was often mistaken for *Castle*. The writing was on the wall—rather than on the printed page before a larger audience.

The book needed several things: better design, better distribution, and certainly a better title. Hence *Building for Hearst and Morgan*, which shifts the focus somewhat from *builders* as a group of people to *building* as an activity of that group—an activity likewise pursued by the client and the architect, William Randolph Hearst and Julia Morgan. But the lead still belongs to the same player, George Loorz, whose *papers* provide words and music for a full chorus of distinctive *voices*.

All such imagery aside, to reconstruct the book required a good deal of time—and an ample budget. Fortunately, an unquenchable optimist, a steadfast believer, a perennial patron was still at hand in Bill Loorz. (The former book, though nominally published by the San Luis Obispo County Historical Society, owed its existence to Bill Loorz above all.) Late in 1996, Bill and I agreed to resume efforts. We made no wasteful haste, set ourselves no frantic deadlines. Eight months passed before I started revising and expanding the former book (a work not only written but also designed and printed in as little time).

By then I was conferring with Patrick O'Dowd, who urged the recruiting of someone noteworthy from California's literary-historical pool—preferably Kevin Starr, the State Librarian of California. In joining us, Dr. Starr did more than simply applaud our enterprise. Through his spirited foreword he embraced the multiplicity of the Hearst-Morgan-Loorz saga with rare command.

From the outset I relied on John Porter, my editor for more than twenty years now. Another man named John—John Tucker of Norfleet Press in New York, an independent book producer—worked closely with us in 1997 and 1998.

A prime contributor was archival: the Loorz Papers themselves, namely, the three boxes described in the postscript to my older preface. I'd always thought those belated documents would be grist for someone's mill. Almost providentially, they became so for *my* mill. In June 1997 I went back to the San Luis Obispo County Historical Museum. The main body of the Loorz Papers had been little touched since the Loorz family's gift of them in 1990; and the three late-surfacing boxes were the least touched of all. Voilà! With the help of Catherine Trujillo, I secured the needed copies. In addition, Bill Loorz found letters that belonged with the original files; he also lent me postcards from his own collection. These are among the archival addenda cited in the footnotes (a component lacking in the former book).

John Tucker and I began designing the new book late in 1997, working with Brush & Associates in Santa Barbara. Midway through 1998, I struck forth as sole producer on the project, under Bill Loorz's wing as always, accompanied by Patrick O'Dowd and of course John Porter. Scott Freutel, who designed one of my previous books, made a firm recommendation upon seeing the initial layouts: go a step further by working with typographers as skillful as Wilsted & Taylor in Oakland. I did so, and my dealings with Leroy Wilsted, Christine Taylor, and their staff have been a high point for me. *Building for Hearst and Morgan* is as much Wilsted & Taylor's triumph as it is that of everyone else involved.

Richard Longstreth, Judith Robinson, David Nasaw, and Sara Holmes Boutelle (who died in 1999) pored over the manuscript before writing thoughtful endorsements. For her part, Judith Robinson also secured information for me in the San Francisco Bay Area. Carole Adams of Cambria, near San Simeon, was likewise helpful. At Cal Poly State University in San Luis Obispo, whose Julia Morgan Collection is overseen by Nancy Loe, her assistant Michael Line fielded every request I made. My out-of-state sources included David King Dunaway, Dolores

Swekel, Louis Pizzitola, Carol Everingham, and the Honolulu Information Service.

Thus equipped, the book stood ready for printer's ink as 1999 drew to a close. And then came an unforeseen, ultimately welcome event—one signaling that most bets were off, that so many convenient assumptions, mine among them, would soon be dashed.

Lynn Forney McMurray (formerly Lynn Forney Stone), whom I'd long known and whose late mother, Lilian, I'd also known, came forth with some astonishing items: detailed office records that Lilian Forney, Julia Morgan's secretary, retained after Morgan's death in 1957. In 1977, Lynn and her mother had shown me records of a different kind; they pertained mostly to Hearst as a collector and to Morgan's tie-in with that rarefied activity. And now late in 1999 I saw for the first time some items that reflected the other side of the historical coin. As the recent heir of her family's Morgan-Forney Collection, Lynn McMurray was putting architectural and construction records at my disposal, documents whose down-to-earth nature was wholly compatible with the George Loorz Papers. We asked ourselves: could a valid link be made between the Loorz and the Morgan-Forney holdings? Could the prospective book be a fitting vehicle for both, with the Morgan-Forney Collection supplementing and complementing the Loorz Papers?

The verdict—in favor of broadening the scope of the book more than ever before—wasn't long in coming. The George Loorz Papers were uniquely suited to provide the structure, the time line, the archival framework to carry the Hearst-Morgan story through most of the thirties decade and even through some of the adjoining years. The Morgan-Forney Collection could also accentuate things uniquely. On certain points, for that matter, so could the William Randolph Hearst Papers at the Bancroft Library and the Julia Morgan Collection at Cal Poly. And there were other holdings, public and private, that could be included as part of a comprehensive blend.

Fine in theory. Yet that old saying "Back to the drawing board" clung to my efforts from early in 2000 until the book went to press through John Strohmeier of Berkeley Hills Books late in 2002. So much to unlearn and then learn anew; so much to write and rewrite, and then to write and rewrite again—plus so much to wrestle with mathematically—surely more, it seemed, than in the usual course of bookish events. That was precisely the point, though: to discover once and for all what the term "nonfiction" could really mean.

Along the way, I incurred new debts, a post-1999 group of them that I gratefully acknowledge. Peter Hanff and his colleagues at the Bancroft Library deserve my thanks, as do Waverly Lowell and her staff at the Environmental Design Archives, likewise on the U.C. Berkeley campus. The Hearst Castle Curatorial Staff and other Castle employees should also be mentioned; so should Friends of Hearst Castle, led by David Gray through most of this period.

Others who helped me in various ways include Marc Wanamaker, William Apperson, Ben Procter, Ron Clarke, Ora Marie Lambert, Eleanor Weinstein, Judy Bellis, Michael Yakaitis, Bob Board, Kathe Tanner, Dennis Judd, Ellen Easton, Margaret Burke, Richard Orsi, Charlene Woodcock, Mark Swope, Marian Abrecht, Allison Pennell, William Kostura, Thomas Eastham, Malcolm Margolin, Carol Stolte Paden, Bryan Stevens, Anthony Bruce, Michael Quinn, Amy Boothe Green, and Winton "Woody" Frey. Meanwhile, Judith Robinson, David Nasaw, Louis Pizzitola, Michael Line, and the late Shirley Shewmaker Wahl were among those whose help carried over into this phase of full-scale reinvention, a period surpassing everything done before the year 2000.

Through all the changes, all the growth and improvement surrounding the book these past three years, certain people were uncommonly devoted, untiringly patient. My editor, John Porter, is one such person. So is Lynn Forney McMurray. As always, Bill Loorz was in my corner and, increasingly toward the end, so was his older brother, Don. Will Hearst III is another whose belief in me helped assure the renewal process.

My closing thoughts are not only with these key people but also with my wife and her parents, with our two daughters, with my mother and sister (and my late father, who much admired my former book on the Loorz Papers), and with everyone else — friends, co-workers, colleagues (far too many of them now gone) — who encouraged me to follow the muse that first beckoned me at San Simeon in 1972.

EDITORIAL NOTE: This greatly revised, much-expanded book remains largely an edition of letters, and George Loorz remains the principal correspondent. What I pointed out in 1990 bears repeating here — that Loorz typed nearly all his letters and that he usually typed them fast, seldom fussing over occasional misspellings or other errors. As before, I've preserved most of these "accidentals," as textual editors often call them. Meanwhile, the longer gestation of *Building for Hearst and Morgan* has yielded more bracketed insertions, and devices like *sic* have increased somewhat. Loorz, as I said in 1990, was by no means alone in making writer's slips (Fred Stolte's use of "sitiation" and "personnally" on p. 264 of this new book comes readily to mind). Hearst and Morgan themselves made their share of slips, as did many of the other people whose writings I've worked from. I'm as hopeful now as I was before that my readers will appreciate seeing the original syntax, punctuation (or often lack of it), and other quirks that humanize the pages ahead.

Maps of San Simeon

and Wyntoon

———

*The ranch lands surrounding Hearst Castle remain in private hands;
so does the forest acreage at Wyntoon. This book's inclusion of those
subjects is for historical purposes only. The prospect of public access is
not implied by the author, nor is it allowed by the private property owner.*

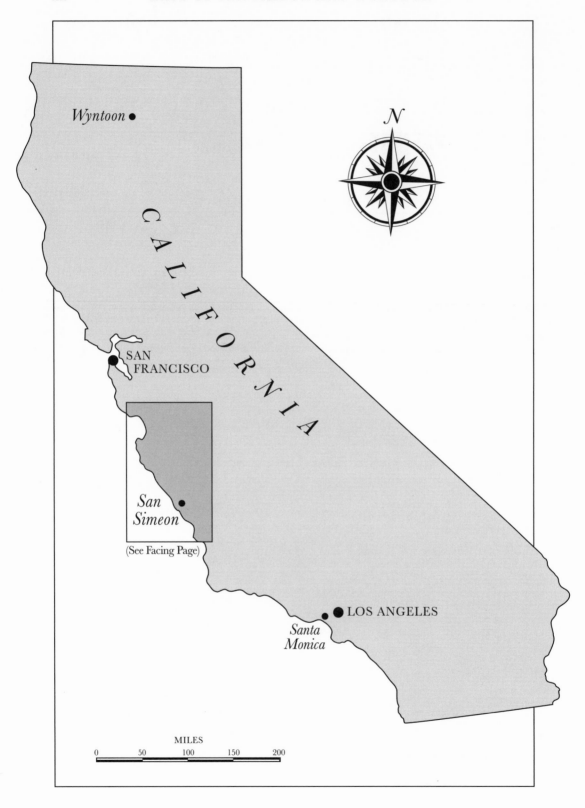

Wyntoon ●

C A L I F O R N I A

SAN
FRANCISCO

*San
Simeon* ●

(See Facing Page)

● LOS ANGELES

*Santa
Monica*

MILES

0   50   100   150   200

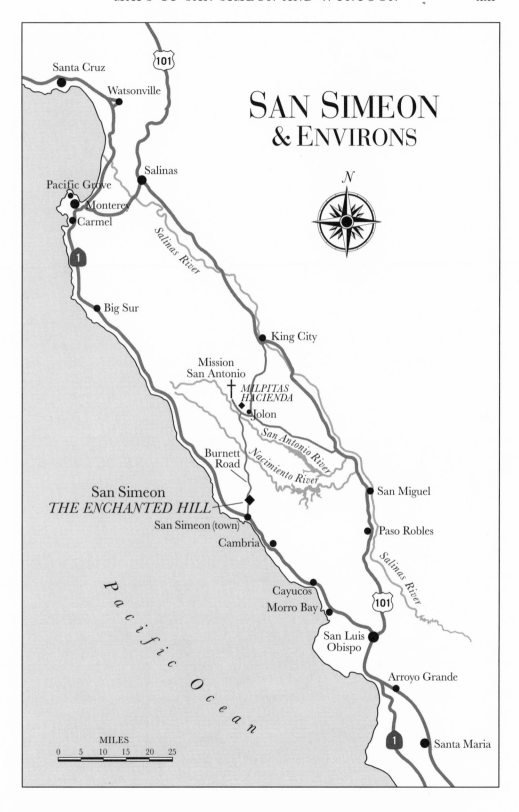

SAN SIMEON
& ENVIRONS

N

Santa Cruz

Watsonville

Salinas

Pacific Grove
Monterey
Carmel

Salinas River

Big Sur

King City

Mission
San Antonio
MILPITAS HACIENDA
Jolon

San Antonio River

Burnett
Road

Nacimiento River

San Simeon
THE ENCHANTED HILL

San Miguel

San Simeon (town)

Cambria

Paso Robles

Salinas River

Cayucos
Morro Bay

101

San Luis
Obispo

Arroyo Grande

Pacific Ocean

MILES
0   5   10   15   20   25

1   Santa Maria

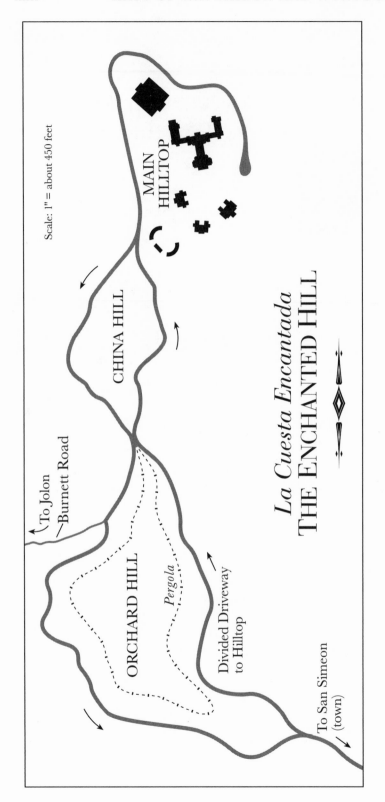

Scale: 1" = about 450 feet

To Jolon
Burnett Road

CHINA HILL

MAIN HILLTOP

ORCHARD HILL

Pergola

Divided Driveway
to Hilltop

To San Simeon
(town)

La Cuesta Encantada
THE ENCHANTED HILL

Above:
Hearst's Enchanted Hill encompasses not only
the castle and its grounds but also the areas
called China Hill and Orchard Hill.

Facing Page:
Detail of castle and grounds.

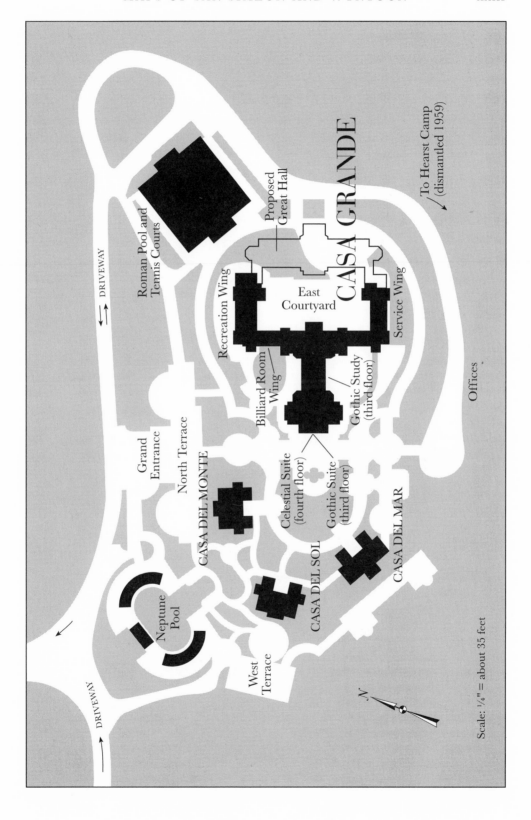

Proposed Great Hall

CASA GRANDE

To Hearst Camp (dismantled 1959)

Roman Pool and Tennis Courts

DRIVEWAY

Recreation Wing

East Courtyard

Service Wing

Offices

Billiard Room Wing

Gothic Study (third floor)

Grand Entrance

North Terrace

CASA DEL MONTE

Celestial Suite (fourth floor)

Gothic Suite (third floor)

CASA DEL SOL

CASA DEL MAR

Neptune Pool

West Terrace

DRIVEWAY

N

Scale: ¼" = about 35 feet

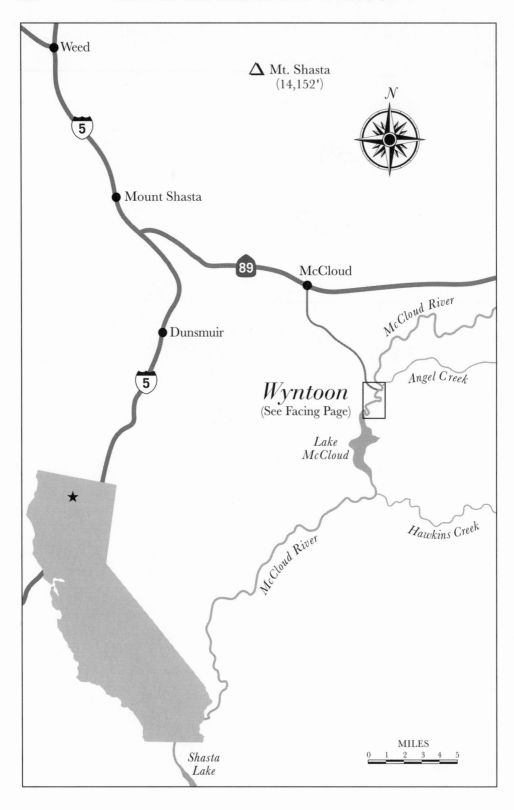

Weed

△ Mt. Shasta
(14,152')

N

5

Mount Shasta

89   McCloud

McCloud River

Angel Creek

Dunsmuir

5

Wyntoon
(See Facing Page)

Lake
McCloud

Hawkins Creek

McCloud River

MILES
0 1 2 3 4 5

Shasta
Lake

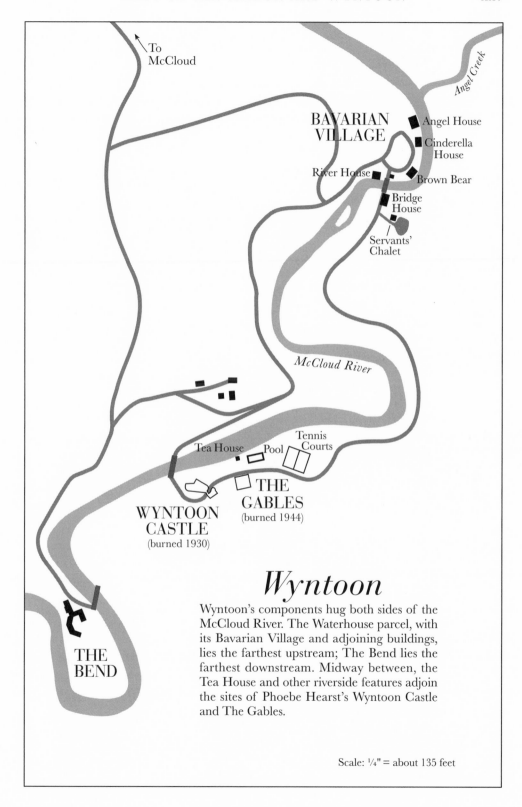

To
McCloud

Angel Creek

BAVARIAN
VILLAGE

Angel House

Cinderella
House

River House

Brown Bear

Bridge
House

Servants'
Chalet

McCloud River

Tennis
Courts

Tea House   Pool

THE
GABLES
(burned 1944)

WYNTOON
CASTLE
(burned 1930)

THE
BEND

Wyntoon

Wyntoon's components hug both sides of the
McCloud River. The Waterhouse parcel, with
its Bavarian Village and adjoining buildings,
lies the farthest upstream; The Bend lies the
farthest downstream. Midway between, the
Tea House and other riverside features adjoin
the sites of Phoebe Hearst's Wyntoon Castle
and The Gables.

Scale: ¼" = about 135 feet

Monetary Note

This book on the Loorz Papers contains many references to the money of a bygone era, a time when "a dollar was a dollar," as people like to say. True, the money of the 1920s through the 1940s differs greatly from the legal tender of 2003. But not consistently so. In general terms, we can regard the 1920s dollar as the equivalent of ten or eleven dollars today. For the late 1940s the equivalence presently stands at eight or nine dollars. The biggest difference lies in relating the 1930s to 2003: as a product of a sharply deflationary period whose weakened currency prevailed till the early 1940s, a single Depression dollar often equates with as many as thirteen of today's dollars, closer to fourteen at times.

In the years ahead—in 2005 or 2010, in 2020 or well beyond— such disparities will most likely become greater, as they have ever since World War II.

These dollar amounts rely on a book first published in 1992 and then updated in 2001. Compiled by John J. McCusker, a historian and economist, its short title is How Much Is That In Real Money? *A fuller citation appears in the bibliography of* Building for Hearst and Morgan, *pp. 556–57.*

Introduction

EARLY IN 1938, six years after George Loorz had begun working at San
Simeon as construction superintendent, he received the following letter
from William Randolph Hearst:

> I shall be very happy to have you refer anyone to me regarding the high quality of
> your construction work at San Simeon.
>
> I have had the most complete satisfaction with everything that you have super-
> vised and executed.
>
> You have been most careful, not only about the quality of the construction, but
> about the cost.
>
> I cannot imagine it possible for anyone to be more competent and conscien-
> tious, and I am glad to testify to that effect.

Generosity was one of Hearst's winning traits, but the diehard publisher, soon
to be seventy-five, stopped short of bestowing undeserved praise. The only way one
could have warranted that glowing a statement from Hearst was to earn it. By almost every indication, both through the written word of those days and through
long-standing oral tradition, Loorz did exactly that.

Hearst's letter of February 4, 1938, has come down to us as part of the George
Loorz Papers, a choice collection of documents on which *Building for Hearst and
Morgan* is principally based. Loorz was a packrat in the best sense, a man who saved
his correspondence and other types of records in pasteboard file boxes. As one
of his sons later quipped, "The old man never needed a wastebasket."[1] In reality,
many documents that passed through Loorz's hands have long since vanished. But
about twenty-two thousand have survived. By 1990 half of them had been archivally processed and catalogued, with most of the Hearst, Morgan, and kindred

---

1. Conversation with Bill Loorz, November 27, 1989 (while touring the warehouse of Stolte
Inc. in Oakland, California, with him and retrieving numerous letter boxes and other files kept by
George Loorz).

I

items being among them.[2] (The bulk of the unprocessed items stem from government jobs that Loorz and his colleagues worked on during World War II.) The eleven thousand processed items—the cream of the collection—date mainly from the 1930s. Of those documents, close to eight thousand are letters, at least half of which pertain to San Simeon and other subjects covered in this book.

Along with the Loorz Papers, which the San Luis Obispo County Historical Museum has had since 1990, some related archives also pertain to the San Simeon of Hearst's time. They include the Julia Morgan Collection, housed since 1980 at California Polytechnic State University, San Luis Obispo; the William Randolph Hearst Papers, which have been in use at the University of California, Berkeley (the Bancroft Library), since 1977; and the Morgan-Forney Collection, originally held by Morgan's secretary, Lilian Forney, and now held by Mrs. Forney's daughter, Lynn Forney McMurray, who made job ledgers and related items available for this book in 1999 and 2000.[3]

These other archives figure at times in *Building for Hearst and Morgan*, supplementing its discourse on social, cultural, and, above all, architectural themes. The Morgan-Forney Collection, for instance, has yielded two appendices that show how essential a patron Hearst was for Morgan, and how strategic Morgan was for Hearst, especially in the very part of the 1930s that saw Loorz working for them at San Simeon. But the correspondence in the George Loorz Papers remains the heart and soul of the book. From that source do the "voices" so often emerge: from letters, for the most part, though also from notes and memos, from lists and reports, and at times from the merest jottings. The same is true of the Loorz Papers' crosstown relation in San Luis Obispo—the Julia Morgan Collection at California Polytechnic—whose Hearst-Morgan correspondence flows steadily through

---

2. In April 1990, after processing that foremost half of the collection, I compiled "The George Loorz Papers: Storage List and Finding Aid" for the Loorz family; the San Luis Obispo County Historical Museum has a copy of the list. Its thirty-one pages predate the surfacing in July 1990 of three more letter boxes, as described in the postscript to my older preface (p. xv in this volume).

3. Meanwhile, portions of the Morgan-Forney material that focus on Hearst's collecting had been at my disposal since 1977. Other private holdings that pertain to San Simeon and the like include those of Don Loorz, George Loorz's oldest son. The heirs of Joseph Willicombe, Hearst's secretary, have several key items; some are now at the Bancroft Library. The Shewmaker Collection, the Vanderloo Collection, and the Warren McClure Papers are also in private hands.

In the public sector, other holdings are the Edward Bright Hussey, Bernard Maybeck, and Walter T. Steilberg collections in UC Berkeley's Environmental Design Archives [College of Environmental Design, at times hereinafter simply EDA]. In addition, EDA has a small Julia Morgan Collection, as does the Bancroft Library, where the Elizabeth M. Boyter Papers and the James Rankin & Sons Records are also held. (Regarding the three identically named holdings of Morgan material, this volume's use of "Julia Morgan Collection" or simply "Morgan Collection" denotes the preeminent one: Cal Poly's holdings in San Luis Obispo, unless it's otherwise stated.)

much of the 1920s, providing crucial insight into San Simeon's emergent, formative years. Unfortunately, the Morgan Collection at Cal Poly starts thinning to a trickle in the mid-1930s (as does the Bancroft Library's coverage of San Simeon). Thank heaven, therefore, for the George Loorz Papers. Likewise rich in correspondence, the Loorz stream forms a near torrent from its outset in 1932, just as the Morgan Collection is about to run dry. And the Loorz Papers flow plentifully right through the late thirties; in fact, they keep going until the mid-forties.[4]

The six years of George Loorz's full-time tenure, 1932–37, overlapped with the middle and end of San Simeon's glittering heyday, a period that began in the late 1920s and lasted almost till the outbreak of World War II. Meanwhile, Loorz's tenure coincided even more closely with a time of much wider significance, the period called the Roosevelt Revolution by a leading historian.[5]

Elsewhere in California during those years, William Randolph Hearst had another country retreat, a less-renowned alternative to famous San Simeon. It was a place called Wyntoon, hidden deep in the Cascade Range along the McCloud River, some sixty-five miles south of the Oregon border and twenty miles south of Mt. Shasta. Because the Loorz Papers treat richly of Wyntoon as well, and because Wyntoon, unlike San Simeon, has been obscure for so long, the Loorz Papers are virtual Dead Sea Scrolls on that subject. (In turn, the Morgan-Forney Collection provides a Rosetta Stone for Wyntoon, hence the importance of its supportive role in the book, in concert with the roles played by Cal Poly's Julia Morgan Collection and the Bancroft's William Randolph Hearst Papers.) Although San Simeon has been portrayed for years as "Hearst Castle"—to the exclusion of Wyntoon and the other residences Hearst owned in this country—Wyntoon has features as striking, in many ways as castle-like, as those at San Simeon. Indeed, Hearst's medieval inclination is even more pronounced at the Teutonic, richly forested Wyntoon than it is at the Mediterranean, often sun-drenched San Simeon.

---

4. For all their mind-numbing extent, the encyclopedic William Randolph Hearst Papers at the Bancroft Library are fragmentary, and not just regarding San Simeon. On that and related subjects, they collate neatly at times with the "Hearst/Morgan Correspondence" in the Morgan Collection at Cal Poly: an original letter is in one collection, its carbon copy is in the other. The years 1927, 1931, 1932, and 1937 are the best represented in this dovetailing regard. But gaps occur in those stretches, too.

As to collations with the Hearst-Loorz exchanges in the Loorz Papers, the Hearst Papers provide few (and the Morgan Collection, having almost no Morgan-Loorz items, fewer still). Pending more processing of the Hearst Papers, and because the Morgan Collection becomes so spotty in the 1930s, the Loorz Papers rule the archival roost for most of the years and subjects they cover. They may prove to do so indefinitely.

5. "The six years from 1933 through 1938 marked a greater upheaval in American institutions than in any similar period in our history, save perhaps for the impact on the South of the Civil War." From William E. Leuchtenburg, *Franklin D. Roosevelt and the New Deal, 1932–1940* (New York, 1963), p. xv.

During his six years in residence at San Simeon, Loorz lived just downhill from that southern castle, on the edge of San Simeon Bay. Greater San Simeon—the grand buildings on "The Enchanted Hill,"[6] the vast Hearst Ranch hinterland, the quaint old town of San Simeon alongside the bay —remained prominent in his correspondence throughout that period. During the first year, 1932, greater San Simeon (of which the palatial hilltop always commanded center stage) was the leading subject. Wyntoon, whose name more narrowly denoted the Hearst compound on the McCloud River, attained equal stature in the Loorz Papers in 1933. The two "castles," San Simeon and Wyntoon, shared the spotlight from then on; in the process, the plot thickened considerably. Loorz's business partner, Fred Stolte, oversaw Wyntoon's expansion through most of the 1933–37 period while Loorz kept busy at San Simeon.

The Loorz Papers also contain a good deal of local history, most of it pertaining to San Luis Obispo County, within which lie San Simeon, Cambria, Cayucos, Arroyo Grande, and other rural towns of past years whose names figure in the pages to come. Certain places in Monterey County, such as Big Sur, and in other parts of California figure as well. Beyond the state line, no less a setting than the Grand Canyon has also left traces, thanks to the work Hearst was about to launch there in 1936. Loorz and his many correspondents interwove these secondary details with their discussions of San Simeon and Wyntoon, increasingly so as the years unfolded. Had lesser scribes conveyed them, these details might have paled next to those concerning the mythical Hearst. But Loorz and his friends — most of them forthright, hard-working men—held the art of letter writing in high esteem, regardless of the subject.

GEORGE LOORZ was a native of Lovelock, Nevada, where he was born on a small farm on October 13, 1898. His hometown lay halfway between Reno and Winnemucca on the Humboldt River, whose desert traces pointed many a pioneer toward California once James Marshall discovered gold there in 1848. Did young Loorz ever reflect upon that historic event, that momentous find preceding his birth by half a century? He may well have done so. And in later years he must surely have thought of Nevada's own Comstock Lode and one of the investors in its silver mines, George Hearst, who passed the site of Lovelock in 1850 on his way from Missouri to California—and to the establishment of a great family fortune. The wealth that George Hearst amassed and left to his wife, Phoebe, stemmed from both precious

---

6. *La Cuesta Encantada*, the formal Spanish name since 1924 of Hearst's hilltop estate, has often been rendered both orally and in print as "The Enchanted Hill." I've chosen to use this English version of the name throughout my interspersed narration in *Building for Hearst and Morgan*.

and common metals. It was wealth that their son, William Randolph Hearst, would in turn lavish on newspapers, on art objects, on land holdings, and—of the utmost importance to George Loorz—on complex building projects.

Loorz was a senior at Lovelock High School when this country went to war in April 1917. That spring he enlisted in the aviation branch of the Army (he and other volunteers his age were granted their diplomas a month early). He served for two years, mostly in England and France. Right after the armistice in 1918, he severely injured one of his hands while defusing a grenade. He bore the mark of that incident permanently, though few would ever guess he was in any sense disabled. For Loorz was a tall, robust man who was every bit as strong and forceful as he was warm and gregarious. He was the perfect embodiment, in fact, of the "hail-fellow-well-met" personality. (He resembled more pointedly, both in appearance and in demeanor, the homespun screen idol James Stewart, who was born ten years after him.) While in England during World War I, Loorz adopted the jaunty British expression "Cheerio," which he used the rest of his life. "Cheerio" and George Loorz—the two seemed made for each other.

Loorz entered the University of California, Berkeley, in the fall of 1919, right before he turned twenty-one. (At that very moment, William Randolph Hearst was poised at age fifty-six to break ground at San Simeon.) Loorz completed a degree in mathematics in 1923 and another in civil engineering in 1924. He began doing construction work around the San Francisco Bay Area; and in 1925 he married a fellow Nevadan, Grace Sullivan, a native of Virginia City. Destiny soon crossed his path. While Loorz was working on the Hills Brothers Building in San Francisco, designed by George Kelham, Julia Morgan visited the jobsite and, in the process, met the younger George—George Loorz, that is.[7] Long recognized as one of California's best architects, even more so than the respected Kelham, Miss Morgan was fifty-three then (she was born in January 1872) and already had numerous buildings to her credit. She took an immediate liking to Loorz. Her sentiments were at once professionally motivated and instinctively maternal, and they led to a lasting friendship with Loorz and his family. She regarded Loorz, as his wife recalled years later, as something of a "prodigy" and as someone she could count on "any time she

---

7. This sentence is offered as a plausible recounting of an episode in 1925. When she was ninety-one, Loorz's widow recalled that Morgan designed the Hills Brothers Building and that Loorz worked for Morgan during its construction. (I adopted Mrs. Loorz's version in my former book on the Loorz Papers, *The Builders Behind the Castles: George Loorz & the F. C. Stolte Co.* [San Luis Obispo, 1990], p. 17; but I'm now certain that Morgan had no professional bearing on the Hills Brothers project, which was Kelham's design entirely—and one predating 1933, a year cited in some sources.) From an interview with Grace Loorz, taped in Alameda, California, on June 9, 1988, by Bill Loorz and his secretary, Kathie Strong; privately held by the Loorz family.

needed anything.''[8] Few other builders or colleagues were ever as warmly embraced by Morgan—or as deeply touched by her quiet humor and, above all, her
abiding sense of humanity.

Loorz's trail through the mid-1920s remains faint, despite his providential
association with Morgan. He is known, however, to have worked for Bay Area contractors like McClaren and later Dyer Brothers. Loorz also worked for King Parker, one of Morgan's favorite contractors, on the Phoebe Apperson Hearst Memorial Gymnasium for Women. The Gym had been commissioned for the Berkeley
campus by William Randolph Hearst, after his mother's death in 1919 and his
inheritance of the San Simeon ranch—and of much else constituting Phoebe
Hearst's dynastic fortune. For the moment, though, it probably meant more to
George Loorz and his budding career that the Hearst Gynmnasium was being designed by Julia Morgan and her former mentor, Bernard Maybeck.

The summer of 1927 found Loorz working on another of Morgan's many jobs
for Hearst. This was in Santa Monica, just west of Los Angeles, where Hearst was
building a residence for the actress Marion Davies (and for himself as well), a mansion nonchalantly called the Beach House.[9] Hearst had started there in 1926
through William Flannery, a young designer in the Hollywood film colony, rather
than through a veteran architect like Julia Morgan (or through one like Joseph Urban, who was the same age as Morgan, whose settings enriched Hearst's motion
pictures from 1920 to 1925, and who had recently designed the "bungalow" that
Hearst and Miss Davies maintained near Santa Monica, on the Metro-Goldwyn-
Mayer lot in Culver City).[10] But problems soon cropped up at the Beach House un-

---

8. Taped interview with Grace Loorz, as in note 7.

9. Despite its informality, *Beach House* was indeed the name of the Hearst-Davies showplace
in Santa Monica; it also went by its address: 415 Ocean Front. The more formal-sounding *Ocean
House* postdates the sale of the Beach House in 1947; the building began operating as a private club
under that new name in 1948. John Tebbel's *Life and Good Times of William Randolph Hearst* (New
York, 1952) had Marion Davies purportedly saying "Ocean House" in regard to the Hearst-Davies
era (p. 17 only; Tebbel himself always wrote "beach house" or "beach place"). This muddling of usage and context has endured. See also pp. 515–16 in this volume, plus their notes 27 and 28.

Miss Davies was almost thirty-four years younger than Hearst, who was born in April 1863; in
fact, she was nearly as young as George Loorz. She was born in January 1897, not quite two years
before Loorz's birthdate in the fall of 1898.

10. Long assumed to have been a "Julia Morgan," the bungalow (more properly the West
Coast headquarters of Hearst's Cosmopolitan Productions) was first worked on by Morgan in 1933.
At that point, Hearst had her begin adding a projection room to Joseph Urban's original building;
most of that new work took place in 1934. See pp. 541 and 542 in Appendix A, compiled from the
Morgan-Forney Collection; see also pp. 148–49 in this volume, plus their notes 82 and 84. For perspective on the long-overlooked Urban (despite the authors' not citing the Cosmopolitan bungalow),
see Randolph Carter and Robert Reed Cole's *Joseph Urban: Architecture, Theatre, Opera, Film* (New
York, 1992). See also David Nasaw, *The Chief: The Life of William Randolph Hearst* (Boston, 2000),
p. 347; Nasaw is the first author to have associated Urban with the bungalow.

der Bill Flannery. By the middle of 1926 Hearst began falling back on Morgan; and now a year later came Loorz's turn to oversee a job that, after Flannery's departure, would remain among Morgan's active accounts through the 1930s (see Appendix A on pp. 531–45 in this volume). For Loorz, the assignment in Santa Monica was short-term, lasting only through the spring of 1928.[11] As for Hearst, his aloofness during that stretch was no doubt what Loorz was speaking of when he later told a friend, "I worked for him under the roof where he lived for 8 months without meeting him." Despite those circumstances, Loorz had received "many orders in writing thru another party from him" at the Beach House, a harbinger of things to come in the 1930s at San Simeon.[12]

Midway through 1928 Loorz headed to Wyntoon, where Hearst and Morgan launched the first in a long series of projects. Some of these efforts —like those at San Simeon—would reach well into the 1940s. For Loorz, though, it was another temporary job: the building of a swimming pool and tennis courts close to the fairy-tale castle, German in spirit, that Hearst's mother had built through Bernard Maybeck soon after 1900. Loorz's pool and courts lay closer to The Gables, a smaller house on the grounds of Wyntoon Castle that likewise dated from early in the century.[13]

By 1929, Hearst and Morgan were about to embark on grander efforts along the McCloud River. Certain plans called for using part of an ancient English barn in Wyntoon Castle; others called for elongating the Castle enough to incorporate The Gables, which stood nearly 150 feet distant. And then a new factor arose, a new

---

11. The Morgan-Forney Collection includes three loose-leaf account ledgers, maintained from the mid-1920s onward by Morgan's secretary, Lilian Forney. The Beach House gave rise to eleven accounts, reflecting the period 1926 through 1938. The first of these, comprising the years 1926 through 1929, mentions Loorz's name twice—initially under August 26, 1927, and then under April 24, 1928.

12. Both excerpts regarding the Beach House are from the same letter: Loorz to Cliff Bright, January 30, 1934. These and most other excerpts in this book are from the George Loorz Papers; the departures from that rule are indicated.

True, the "8 months" in Loorz's letter coincides perfectly with the span indicated above in note 11. But Loorz later referred to what must have been a longer stint for him on the Beach House job (by the end of which he may finally have met Hearst): Loorz wrote of having spent "a year and a half under Julia Morgan, Architect, as superintendent of W. R. Hearst work at Santa Monica and McCloud [Wyntoon]." From a typescript headed "Geo. C. Loorz," submitted to the Northern California chapter of Associated General Contractors for its annual meeting in December 1949; courtesy of Don Loorz, May 29, 1990. The wording in the typescript is important, as are some earlier references that George Loorz made to those two jobs: by his last years (the 1970s), he was thinking of his stint at Wyntoon as having *preceded* the one in Santa Monica.

13. After Wyntoon Castle arose in 1902–03 and before Phoebe Hearst died in 1919, Maybeck went on to design The Gables—presumably. The Maybeck Collection in Berkeley's Environmental Design Archives leaves the matter unclarified. Some references may await detection in the Phoebe Apperson Hearst Papers in the Bancroft Library.

opportunity presented itself for Hearst and Morgan, one having ramifications for Loorz and others in the years ahead: Wyntoon Castle went up in flames.[14]

When that fire struck early in 1930, Loorz had been focusing on new prospects for a year or so. In fact, it was late in 1928, soon after his brief stint at Wyntoon, that he began working for Ferdinand C. Stolte, an Oakland contractor. Fred Stolte, as he was usually called, had been active in the Bay Area and elsewhere in California since about 1914. He succeeded in both commercial and residential work, especially after World War I and before the Great Crash of 1929. In a brief "mug book" account of his life and career, coincidentally published in 1928, the same year he first employed Loorz, Stolte was thus portrayed:

> As a builder of fine homes no contractor in Oakland takes precedence over Ferdinand C. Stolte, whose operations have been large in volume and of a character

---

14. Phoebe Hearst had left her Wyntoon holdings to her niece, Anne Apperson Flint, rather than to her son, who bought the property from Mrs. Flint in 1924 (interview with William Apperson, July 9, 2000); however, Judith Robinson cites the date 1925 in *The Hearsts: An American Dynasty* (Newark, Delaware; 1991), p. 381. The former date seems likelier: Hearst made his first architectural overtures for Wyntoon in 1924—yet they were false starts that yielded only $2.98 in office expenses for Morgan (meanwhile, her travel expenses to Wyntoon that August were assigned to the main San Simeon account).

The first of eight Wyntoon accounts in the Morgan-Forney ledgers, simply headed "Wyntoon," begins on this minuscule note of $2.98 in September 1924; it then skips to June 1928, to a subheading of "Swimming Pool & Tennis Court." Morgan and Loorz visited that new job on July 4, 1928. Loorz's name appears nowhere else in the account, which soon encompassed other (unspecified) work; this same general account remained active through March 1930. In the meantime, Maybeck visited Wyntoon with Morgan on October 30–31, 1929.

A separate account headed "Wyntoon: Additions to Gables, etc." dates from May 1930, followed by another one headed "Wyntoon Gables" as of February 1931.

Still another account—"Wyntoon Castle (new)"—addressed the remodeling of Phoebe Hearst's former showplace and, before long, its proposed replacement. The opening entries date from early in 1929 and then skip to August 1930—without mentioning the fire that intervened on January 18, 1930 (a brief reference appears in one of the other accounts). "Wyntoon Castle (new)" also contains entries for the latter part of 1930 and for some of 1931 and 1932, the last of them coinciding with Loorz's first year at San Simeon. One entry indicates that Morgan went to Wyntoon on August 11, 1932.

My former book on the Loorz Papers, *The Builders Behind the Castles*, gave a flawed recounting of Wyntoon from 1928 through 1932, largely because the Loorz Papers postdate most of that period. For her part, my late colleague Sara Holmes Boutelle ascribed undue importance to a letter Hearst sent Morgan on August 2, 1924, from Wyntoon (Boutelle saw a copy in the Hearst Corporation files in New York); Hearst seemed ready to make improvements there on a scale that, in reality, lay some years ahead. See Sara Boutelle's *Julia Morgan: Architect* (New York, 1988), p. 247 (note 1 under "Wyntoon and Other Hearst Projects") and p. 259 (under 1924–43 in the appendix "Buildings by Julia Morgan" [p. 260 in the revised and updated edition of 1995, exclusively cited hereinafter]). Others have embraced Boutelle's dates of 1924 and 1925 for Hearst's earliest structures at Wyntoon; see, for example, Robert T. Packard and Balthazar Korab's *Encyclopedia of American Architecture* (New York, 1995 [second edition]), p. 439.

that has gained him an enviable reputation as a reliable and capable builder and business man. Mr. Stolte was born in Portland, Oregon, October 24, 1889, and when a year old was brought to Oakland by his parents. He secured his education in the public schools of this city and then learned the carpenter trade under Ben O. Johnson, with whom he remained for a few years and then embarked in the contracting business on his own account, going to Dixon [near Sacramento], where he spent three years, during which period he built a number of good residences. Since that time he has confined his operations to the East Bay district, in which he has erected many of the best homes now standing here, and in Berkeley and Piedmont, ranging in cost from thirty thousand to one hundred and fifty thousand dollars. These include the residences of H. R. Jackson, Mrs. Hills, Fritz Henshaw and Henry Patterson, together with a number of the leading apartment houses, and he recently completed a three story garage for Lloyd Brothers, one of the best in Oakland. He is painstaking in the fulfillment of his contracts, employs none but expert workmen and the work done by him has been uniformly satisfactory to those who have employed him.

. . . Mr. Stolte enlisted for service in the World war and was assigned to engineering construction work in the state of Washington, where he remained until the close of the war. He is a member of the American Legion, the Castlewood Country Club, Sequoia Club and the Athens Club and is deservedly popular among his associates.[15]

In 1951 Loorz recounted how he and Stolte became connected in 1928—actually, early in 1928 rather than late, to hear Loorz tell it, if indeed he had all the details straight. (But the birthdate of his second son in June 1928 may well have preceded rather than followed the episode described.)[16] Nevertheless, Loorz recalled things this way:

I took stock of my total assets and found I had a Model A, all paid for, a small down payment on a very small home in Berkeley [on Allston Way], about $400 cash, a wife, a baby [born February 1926] and another one coming [born June

---

15. From Frank Clinton Merritt, *History of Alameda County California* (Chicago, 1928), pp. 256–57. The Castlewood Country Club was formerly the Hacienda del Pozo de Verona, Phoebe Hearst's estate near Pleasanton, fifteen to twenty miles southeast of Oakland. "Mrs. Hills," which Merritt also mentioned, brings the Hills Brothers Building to mind; see p. 5, plus its note 7.

16. Only one item in the Loorz Papers survives from 1928, a letter from Loorz to Stolte dated December 18 of that year. The future partners had yet to become well acquainted, for Loorz addressed Stolte as "Dear Sir" and confined himself to some dryly worded business details.

Loorz's earliest known letters, likewise from 1928, are in the James Rankin & Sons Records in the Bancroft Library. With his more familiar exuberance, Loorz wrote on August 29 and September 6 to "Jimmie" Rankin (a favorite plumber of Morgan's and an old standby at San Simeon); Rankin's reply of September 11 to Loorz's second letter is part of the same collection. The three letters help pinpoint Loorz's role and presence at Wyntoon in 1928.

1928]. It was necessary to get with someone who had some dough [some financial resources] and liked contracting. I made a list of four people with Mr. Stolte's name at the top. I had met him. He had chiseled me out of one low bid, giving the job to my competitor. He at least had a good name, did good work and I thought he had some money.

Well, when I talked to him in the *little out-house office* in his back yard on Laguna Avenue in Fruitvale [an Oakland neighborhood] I nearly took his breath. Imagine my audacity when you think of my assets. To think that I offered to work for him for nothing until I proved to him what I could do. When I proved *that*, we were to sit down and decide on a fair division of the profits and eventually to become an actual partner. After two hours I found him very interested but I couldn't get him to say any more than that *he would have to think it over* since he had never before entertained the idea of sharing his business with anybody. I showed him my list [of contractors' names] and said I was in no position to wait so I was proceeding to visit number two and walked down his driveway to my car. About the time I opened the car door I heard him address me from the top of the drive ramp behind me. He said, "O.K. Loorz, I don't see how I can lose on that proposition—let's give it a trial." I said, "When?" He said, "*Tomorrow*, if you want."

That was 23 years ago, gentlemen [of the Rotary group Loorz was addressing in 1951], and we are still good partners and enjoy being around each other very much, either working, traveling or playing. We're as different as the two poles. He is an introvert and I'm an extreme extrovert. He's quiet and I'm loquacious. He makes good money on his farm in Linden [near Stockton] and I lose on my 200 acres out of Hayward [in the East Bay].[17]

Stolte and Loorz were indeed a perfect example of that old saying "Opposites attract." As Loorz said of the two of them in his Rotary speech, he was garrulous and outgoing, whereas Stolte was quiet and retiring. One thing Stolte had over Loorz was age (he was nine years older). Otherwise, Loorz was easily the more dynamic of the two. The F. C. Stolte Co. owed its name to Fred Stolte, but it increasingly owed its success to George Loorz. That became true as the two endured the early years of the Depression and incorporated as partners in 1932; it remained true once the Depression began to ease in the mid-1930s and they hit their full stride.[18] Nonetheless, the two maintained a close friendship throughout this period

---

17. From "Self Introduction—Rotary," an undated typescript [1951] privately held by the Loorz family; courtesy of Don Loorz, May 29, 1990.

18. Three years after they incorporated, Loorz disclosed that he then held fifty percent of the company to Stolte's forty-eight percent, with their attorney holding the remaining two percent. See pp. 175–76 in this volume: Loorz to Armand Brady, March 8, 1935. The Loorz Papers have several other documents from the early and mid-1930s that consistently show Loorz's share as fifty percent, whereas Stolte's share is set forth either as forty-eight percent or as forty-nine percent.

and for years to come, a rapport based on mutual respect and concern. Their part-nership often seemed to have sprung from the pages of a storybook.

ANOTHER PARTNERSHIP — the term is figurative here — that at times seemed equally idyllic (and one also comprising a nine-year age difference) was that of William Randolph Hearst and Julia Morgan. "Fellow architects," they were once called, Morgan herself supposedly having used the expression.[19] In their best moments they indeed had an uncanny rapport; yet at times they obviously got on each other's nerves. In any event, by 1932, when Loorz hired on at San Simeon, they had been equally committed to their roles as patron and architect for many years. Before San Simeon began in 1919, Morgan had worked for Hearst on lesser projects such as his Grand Canyon property in Arizona and, much more notably, on his Los Angeles Examiner Building. She and Hearst carried their commitment into the pulsating 1920s, on through the nerve-wracking 1930s, and even into the restrictive 1940s. The extent of her work for Hearst over seventeen of those years, from the outset of 1924 to the end of 1940, is now precisely known. (And it's nearly as well known for several of the years flanking that span.) Loorz's debut year of 1932, for example, saw nearly sixty percent of Morgan's work stemming from her San Simeon and other Hearst ac-counts;[20] San Simeon, along with the others, had averaged more than fifty per-cent over the past several years as it was. In 1933 that inclusive figure jumped to nearly eighty percent, and it soon went even higher, as Appendix A on pp. 531–45 shows. During Loorz's years at its helm, the San Simeon job alone repre-sented almost forty percent of Morgan's total activity; and if combined with Wyntoon, almost seventy percent. For the 1930s overall, the figures are smaller, mostly because of Hearst's cutting back on those two jobs in 1938 and 1939. But San Simeon still represented thirty-five percent of Morgan's efforts in that de-cade as a whole; and if combined once more with Wyntoon, fifty-five percent.

---

19. As quoted by Hearst's authorized biographer, Mrs. Fremont Older, in her rhapsodic yet often insightful *William Randolph Hearst: American* (New York, 1936), p. 531. The passage also has Morgan saying reverently of Hearst (although in a brusque staccato unknown in her letters): "He supplies vision, critical judgment. I give technical knowledge and building experience. He loves ar-chitecting. If he had chosen that career he would have been a great architect. San Simeon is Mr. Hearst."

20. Not just for 1932 but for the entire period from 1924 through 1940, "other Hearst ac-counts" means those besides San Simeon and Wyntoon, like the Phoebe Hearst Memorial Gym. It also means those involving Marion Davies — the Beach House, the Marion Davies Clinic, the Bev-erly Hills (1700 Lexington) house, the Cosmopolitan bungalow — and those involving George Hearst, the oldest of Hearst's five sons. By themselves, the Davies accounts represent eight percent of the grand Hearst total of $418,703 (as tallied in Appendix A, p. 536) and the George Hearst accounts not quite two percent.

The data (courtesy of the Morgan-Forney Collection) can be endlessly analyzed, their salient points emphasized, their finer points compared and pondered. Nonetheless, they invariably portray Morgan as an architect whose
great career, now in its second half, rose and fell decisively with the whims and
fortunes of Hearst—far more so than with those of any other client, past or
present.

And thus for Loorz and others in the construction field, to build for Hearst
was usually to build for Morgan; and to build for Morgan was quite often to
build for Hearst. That was true not only of the main years recounted in this
book but also of several other years adjoining them.

The astounding extent of Morgan's work for Hearst brings to mind what
can be called the "Morgan myth." Arising in the 1960s—Morgan had died in
1957—the myth portrayed her as having been so prolific, so widely in demand,
that her efforts on Hearst's part represented a mere ten percent or, at the most,
twenty percent of her work. Exactly what period this applied to and how much
it pertained to San Simeon are moot questions; the Morgan-Forney Collection
has deflated the myth in all but its stubbornest guises. Exaggeration has always
been part of "Hearstiana," a kind of yellow-journalism legacy stemming no
less from Hearst's building projects than from his newspaper ventures. The cult
of the biggest, the boldest, the brightest likewise embraced the circumspect
Morgan, giving rise to such notions as these: she designed two thousand buildings; she regarded Hearst and his endless demands as a tolerable nuisance; best
of all, she pursued San Simeon as a virtual moonlight job, stealing time from
her hectic schedule to drop in when she could. Ironically, the Morgan myth
stemmed mostly from a man who frowned on loose talk and puffery, a man who
was close to Morgan and to whom this book is much indebted—Walter Steilberg. Steilberg, who was both an architect and an engineer, urged people to look
beyond San Simeon, beyond the factor of Hearst alone. His point was well
taken. It was a point, though, that became etched in stone through Steilberg's
part in *The Julia Morgan Architectural History Project* (Berkeley, 1976), two volumes
of interviews conducted by Suzanne B. Riess and others, mostly in the early
1970s—whose publication Steilberg didn't live to see. The Riess volumes provided a firm supportive voice in Morgan North, Julia Morgan's nephew; his
quantifying of the Hearst-Morgan output was consistent with, and no doubt influenced by, Steilberg's. But in 1976, when the volumes appeared, four years remained before the Julia Morgan Collection arrived at Cal Poly, fourteen years
before the George Loorz Papers reached the San Luis County Museum, and
even longer before the Morgan-Forney Collection made its present debut. The

larger perspective that Steilberg championed is one whose rightful time is only now at hand.[21]

For whatever reason, the Loorz Papers tell little about Morgan's growing reliance on the fountainhead that was Hearst. Loorz himself must have been aware of it, along with Fred Stolte and certain members of Morgan's own staff. Gaps, omissions, and blind spots like this epitomize the danger of relying too much on correspondence in historical work, no matter the subject. Even in the hands of a devoted practitioner like George Loorz, correspondence can be a

---

21. When he was much younger, Walter Steilberg produced a landmark article on Morgan's earlier efforts, before Hearst began dominating her practice. "Some Examples of The Work of Julia Morgan" appeared in *The Architect and Engineer of California* (November 1918), pp. 38–107. Other writings on Morgan appeared over the following decades. For example, Morgan North's wife, Flora, profiled his aunt in "She Built for the Ages," *Kappa Alpha Theta Journal* (Spring 1967), pp. 9–11, reproduced in *The Julia Morgan Architectural History Project*, Vol. II ("Julia Morgan, Her Office, and a House"), pp. 170a–170c. The Norths were book publishers. Their company brought out Elinor Richey's *Eminent Women of the West* (Berkeley, 1975); its chapter on Miss Morgan ("Architect with Empathy"), pp. 237–63, was briefly deemed authoritative but then lost favor. In any event, it was Flora North who gave the Julia Morgan Collection to Cal Poly after her husband died in 1978.

Earlier in the 1970s the more scholarly Richard Longstreth sought to redefine Morgan's career. By 1975, when he passed the torch as the leading Morgan researcher to Sara Holmes Boutelle, he believed that Morgan had designed six to eight hundred buildings all told, the majority being residences. (Longstreth's booklet on the subject, *Julia Morgan: Architect*, appeared afterward [Berkeley, 1977], bearing a dedication to the late Steilberg.)

Sara Boutelle developed a good sense of how varied Morgan's work for Hearst became. In her identically titled but much longer book, *Julia Morgan: Architect*, p. 169, she mentioned many lesser-known projects (beyond San Simeon and Wyntoon)—almost as if she had seen the Morgan-Forney data that help anchor *Building for Hearst and Morgan*. But she hadn't. What she concluded instead was that the full range of greater Hearst projects, from Phoebe Hearst's Hacienda near Pleasanton on through San Simeon and all the others, constituted "only a fraction of the total output from Morgan's office." Surely in saying "a fraction," she meant a small portion, not a large one (and concerning the second half of Morgan's career, it was in truth a very large one—almost sixty percent overall). Such was the inadvertent legacy of the best-intentioned Steilberg.

Longstreth and Boutelle were preceded by a researcher who shared some rare insights with Mrs. Boutelle. James T. Maher, whose *Twilight of Splendor: Chronicles of the Age of American Palaces* (Boston, 1975) remains a classic, wrote to Boutelle that same year:

> It is quite clear to me now that Miss Morgan occupies a unique place in the history of American architecture for many reasons. Let me cite just one: I do not believe that any architect ever had the tremendous amount of work [number of projects] for domestic works from a single client that she handled for Hearst.

From Boutelle's *Julia Morgan*, p. 247 (note 15 under "The Hearsts and San Simeon"). Maher had still more to say, relying in part on what he knew of the future Julia Morgan Collection—which Morgan and Flora North had privately shown him. Boutelle, though, seems not to have caught Maher's full meaning. Neither did I or most others who pored over her book when its first edition appeared in 1988.

frustratingly imprecise and at times even misleading medium; its stature as a "primary" source — never mind as an infallible primary source — requires constant weighing and reassessment. Reports, lists, memos, and other non-letter items, in which the Loorz Papers also abound, are quite often a saving grace, but not automatically so; their weighing and analysis must also be kept fresh and current.

Nonetheless, the Loorz Papers reveal a multitude of details about Hearst and Morgan — quite often more, in fact, than one finds in the Morgan Collection at Cal Poly, justly renowned for its correspondence between Hearst and Morgan themselves. In contrast, the Loorz Papers offer a greater range of voices and, frequently, more intimacy and realism, characteristics often lacking in the Morgan Collection. Loorz, after all, could be a good deal less guarded in writing to a fellow supporting player than he could be in writing to Hearst or Morgan. (So much so that, in one instance in 1935, he referred to Hearst as "his Highness"; and in another instance in 1936, he spoke of San Simeon as "this Bastile on the hill.")[22] The same kind of candor was true of the supporting players when they wrote to Loorz. Occasionally, in writing to Loorz, Morgan herself dropped her guard long enough to qualify as one of those players. Hearst, on the other hand, seldom broke character. Whether he was writing to Morgan, Loorz, or anyone else, he would politely but unmistakably say what he thought. Without hesitation, he took it as a great man's prerogative to do so.

Julia Morgan was the one who recruited George Loorz for San Simeon at the outset of 1932. They had stayed in touch all along; moreover, the F. C. Stolte Co. had worked at Wyntoon in recent years, helping to remodel The Gables in 1930 and 1931.[23] Loorz's predecessor at San Simeon, Camille Rossi, had been

---

22. Loorz to George Wright, January 15, 1935, and Loorz to Louis Reesing, September 17, 1936 (see pp. 162–63 and 270–71 for the full excerpts). As my older preface stated, misspellings and textual quirks — such as Loorz's rendering in 1936 of *Bastille* with a single *l* — have been retained within reason. If a bracketed *sic* does not appear in these instances, the reader may safely assume that errors or irregularities have been allowed to stand.

23. The F. C. Stolte Co. may also have been active at Wyntoon during the fair-weather months of 1929. Come the winter of 1929–30, some carpenters — quite possibly a Stolte crew — installed storm windows in Wyntoon Castle, working on the very Saturday, January 18, whose evening saw the Castle burn.

Concerning George Loorz himself, his résumé for these first years with the Stolte Co. remains hard to fill in. So does Fred Stolte's for the same period. Sara Boutelle, after interviewing Stolte in 1975, associated him with a Morgan job of 1929–31, the Berkeley Women's City Club; she also identified Stolte as the "engineer in charge of the project"; see *Julia Morgan*, p. 246 (note 11 under "The Women's Network"). Neither assertion bears out. Stolte was not an engineer; his name (and Loorz's) are absent from Morgan's record of that job, preserved in the Morgan-Forney Collection. Instead, the City Club account lists King Parker (late of the Phoebe Hearst Gym) as the contractor, Walter Steilberg (another Morgan stalwart) as the engineer, and Herbert Washburn (a carryover from the San Simeon of 1919–22) as the superintendent.

there since 1922 and had been prolific as construction superintendent. During those ten years on The Enchanted Hill, Rossi had completed the three earliest houses, such as Casa del Mar; had begun the main building, Casa Grande, and had enlarged it greatly; had built two versions of an outdoor swimming pool (the eventual Neptune Pool); had built the indoor Roman Pool, which he nearly finished before he left; and had also made great strides in the landscape architecture. Oh, but for those big-budget days of the 1920s before the Depression took hold! (That prosperous romp of Hearst's, which saw him expanding his newspapers and all his other holdings, both paralleled and encouraged Morgan's success. The size of her office staff in San Francisco, the range of her pursuits, and the height of her earnings increased steadily through the decade, reaching their peak in 1928, a year before the Wall Street crash.)

Camille Rossi, however, despite being an expert engineer, kept running afoul of his superiors, especially Miss Morgan. He was too headstrong, too dictatorial toward the workmen under him. He was also highly inventive: at some point in the vibrant twenties, he began calling one of Hearst's antiques the "Cardinal Richelieu Bed," a name enshrined ever since in San Simeon folklore. Rossi persisted in digging his own grave, even as the new decade cast its cheerless pall. Morgan hoped to fire him; Hearst kept granting him reprieves. Morgan finally reached her limit and, armed at last with Hearst's approval, sent Rossi packing once she lined up Loorz.[24]

Morgan was sure that Loorz, who was all of thirty-three in 1932, was equal to the challenge. Without question he was, but things had changed since the days when he worked for her at Santa Monica and on his first outing at Wyn-

---

24. Rossi hoped that with Morgan's help he might go to Elsah, Illinois (near St. Louis, Missouri), where Principia College was under construction. The job was Bernard Maybeck's, with Morgan and her staff providing drafting-room support; she had visited the job early in January 1932. Rossi's thoughts about Principia, after an eleventh-hour plea for his life at San Simeon, are in a letter he wrote Morgan on January 18. Morgan enclosed Rossi's letter with one she wrote Hearst on January 20, firmly denouncing Rossi and promoting Loorz (though not by name) as a replacement: "I think the man we discussed Friday [January 15] would do. He is equally good as an engineer [as good as Rossi], is experienced, has left a record for good work and good will behind wherever he has been and is in demand even in these times."

The letters of January 18 and 20, 1932, are in the William Randolph Hearst Papers, Bancroft Library, carton 15 (under "Morgan, Julia"); copies of each, plus an original letter from Rossi to Hearst on January 18 (annotated by Hearst and then forwarded to Morgan), are in the Hearst/Morgan Correspondence, Morgan Collection, Cal Poly. As for Rossi's prospects in Illinois, the Maybeck Collection at EDA covers the Principia job extensively. Rossi's name appears nowhere in the payrolls, correspondence, or other files. However, I've not checked the separate Maybeck Collection at Principia itself, an archives said to be "unusually large for a private institution." See Charles B. Hosmer, Jr., *Bernard Maybeck and Principia College: The Historic District* (Elsah, Illinois; 1988), p. 39. The same booklet, p. 33, cites Morgan's visit to Principia in 1932.

toon. Loorz had Fred Stolte to consider now and the welfare of their contracting business in Oakland. In Loorz's absence the business might falter, might even go under with the Depression deepening. Furthermore, the proposal was that Loorz hire on independently, not on behalf of his company. Morgan and her office staff would continue to act in the extra capacity of general contractor, just as they had for San Simeon from the outset in 1919; Loorz would simply be her superintendent on site, just as he had been on the Hearst jobs back in 1927 and 1928. (In contrast, the F. C. Stolte Co. *was* brought in as general contractor for a new, expanded phase of work that began at Wyntoon in 1933—but only at Wyntoon, not at San Simeon.)[25]

Despite certain drawbacks, Morgan's offer was too enticing to ignore. Loorz was promised a substantial $100 a week—equal to roughly $1,300 in today's economy—a beachfront house in San Simeon at no charge, and a car for good measure. He needed only to rent out his house in Berkeley, pack up his wife and two young boys, and wave the Bay Area and the Depression good-bye. Of course it wasn't quite that simple. He *had* to make sure Fred Stolte was ready to go it alone, even though he would be helping him out as much as possible, moonlighting from faraway San Simeon. Loorz's skill as an estimator—he excelled in "figuring" jobs—would remain essential for the company to secure its most important work.

Loorz made his arrangements; and with nothing more to count on at San Simeon than a single season's work, he went ahead and took what he rightly felt was a daring plunge.

---

25. The uncommon situation of Morgan-as-contractor at San Simeon—stemming not only from the job's remoteness but also from Hearst and Morgan's belief that no one else could do certain things quite to their liking—was spelled out by Morgan early in the game. She told Hearst:

> I have been charging you as usual 6% on the costs of the work [the standard architect's commission of the period], but partly because of its nature, and partly because we are providing unusual service which circumstances brought gradually on us, 6% does not cover the actual cost expenses. You see my office has been buying practically everything from cooks and dishwashers to glue size, marble and cement, following up and sending things onto boats, checking, auditing, etc.,—all work which is generally a contractor's, and which Mr. Washburn [Herbert Washburn, the first construction superintendent] has been unable to attempt to do from San Simeon.

From Morgan to Hearst, December 15, 1920; Hearst/Morgan Correspondence, Morgan Collection. A commission of 8.5% (six percent for the prevailing standard plus 2.5% for Morgan's extra efforts) proved more fitting. Once adopted, it remained in force till the late 1930s. See Appendix B on pp. 546–50 in this volume. The 8.5% rate also applied to Morgan's work on Wyntoon in the 1930s, despite the F. C. Stolte Co.'s general-contractor status and the commissions (albeit smaller) that Hearst paid that firm.

1932

Digging in at San Simeon

GEORGE LOORZ ARRIVED at San Simeon during the first week of February 1932. He soon wrote to Julia Morgan at her office in the Merchants Exchange, a grandly classical building on California Street, deep in San Francisco's financial district. Thus began a stream of correspondence with Morgan and many others—Hearst among them—that would flow steadily through most of the thirties decade. Loorz had had a chance to look over the job at San Simeon before he wrote that first letter, dated February 6. He told Morgan he was "very pleased with the definite and complete layout of the present construction program." He also had this to tell her:

> I can offer no alibi's if I fail to make progress. Your assured cooperation in regards to the personel[1] and the few kindly words that you must have used in conversing with others is already showing effects. I look forward to very sudden cooperation on the part of every craftsman in camp.

The camp Loorz mentioned was Hearst Camp, a virtual company town situated a short distance from Casa Grande on The Enchanted Hill; the camp was occupied by laborers, artisans, and various other workers. Loorz spoke with nearly everyone in Hearst Camp during his first days on the job. He also convened the foremen and addressed them from a statement he had prepared:

> We are all working directly under the architect and thru her for Mr. Hearst. At present we are all in good standing in her office, and will remain so as long as we obtain results, satisfactorily and harmoniously. Her personal friendship, in your case and my case, is purely from a business point of view.
>
> I want your cooperation and thru you the cooperation of your men, in keeping our work and our camp, clean and tidy at all times. There are exceptions but most

---

1. As the introduction states on p. 14, note 22, original misspellings and similar "accidentals" (such as *alibi's, personel,* and, a Loorz standard, *dont*) have been retained within reason throughout this book.

of us can improve. Anything that I can do in the way of repairs and equipment in this respect, I will take up with those over me and do what I can. I'm an awful crank on good scaffolding, and safety precautions.[2]

Loorz was rarely formal. He obviously had to assert himself at the outset, though, especially in the wake of Camille Rossi's dismissal and the discord that was Rossi's legacy. (As the gatekeeper and aspiring writer Ray Swartley later said of Loorz, he brought out "excellence where only mediocrity reigned before.")[3] Loorz had a gift for making friends quickly and keeping them. Indeed, most of the men he addressed on that winter day in 1932—men like the labor foreman, Frank Souza, and the carpentry foreman, Pete Petersen—soon became his close friends.

Loorz and Morgan had known each other for the past six or seven years. Now that he was on the job, she had someone she could depend on implicitly, someone she knew would keep her closely apprised—above all, someone she knew would promote harmony in the ranks and efficiency on the job. San Simeon needed a strong dose of those qualities in the winter of 1932. She also had in George Loorz someone who shared her penchant for work. Sundays, for instance, weren't necessarily days of rest, not when there was a task to be done.

It was on a Sunday, in fact, February 7, that Loorz next wrote to Morgan, telling her about the mosaic decoration in progress at the indoor Roman Pool. An imposing structure that stood by itself at the northeast corner of the hilltop complex, the Roman Pool was one of many projects that had felt the pinch of the Depression since the Great Crash of 1929 and that Morgan, and now Loorz as well, would push to completion for Hearst by the end of 1932.[4] But first Loorz needed to make sure his views on the Roman Pool—and, in turn, on any other matter he might air with the architect—would meet with her favor:

> Now Miss Morgan this has been a lengthy description and I ask you to pass frank judgment upon it. If it is of no use then I have wasted two hours and do not want to repeat it. Or if the idea is alright and my execution poor please say so, for it

2. Typewritten by Ray Van Gorden of Hearst Camp (perhaps as dictation from Loorz) but left undated.

3. From an essay entitled "On Personality," by Royal L. Swartley, signed and dated May 30, 1934. The original typescript remains with the Loorz family; courtesy of Don Loorz, May 29, 1990. A few months after George Loorz went to San Simeon, Julia Morgan spoke equally well of the young builder, describing him as "simple, direct and capable," and as a person "with a natural manner." See Morgan to Hearst, July 13, 1932; William Randolph Hearst Papers, Bancroft Library, carton 15 (under "Morgan, Julia")—hereinafter simply Hearst Papers but with its cartons and file names still cited, pending more archival processing and the refining of those units.

4. "The Hearst work has been small this year, funds difficult to move. But in spite of that the place [San Simeon] keeps on developing slowly into finishedness." Morgan conveyed those words to Elizabeth Boyter after returning from Principia College in January 1932, a brief trip that was per-

seems to me that this, more than anything else, is where I can best serve in connection with the several segregated crafts [like the mosaic tile-setting at the pool], those I mean that do not come directly under me.

Loorz had more to tell Morgan about the mosaic work the next day, February 8. He also mentioned the blustery winter weather, undoubtedly without knowing how recurrent a subject it would prove to be:

> We are in the midst of the hardest wind and rainstorm they have had here for many years, according to the old timers. The glass is broken in several of the storm windows and we have braced several more. Leaks are plentiful but we have had no complaints as they are not serious. The telephone lines we[re] out of order due to poles blown over. I let [the electrician Louis] Schallich and his men help Mr. [Marks] Eubanks repair them as they were not able to work this afternoon anyway.

A letter that Morgan sent Loorz on February 9 may have crossed with this latest one of his, for she said nothing about the storm; instead, she assured Loorz that he was on the right track regarding the Roman Pool, that his comments of Sunday the seventh were welcome:

> I like people to express their own frank opinions and to make suggestions for betterments. It never hurts my feelings,—am glad people trust me enough to do so,—then it is up to me in the end to decide what solution is nearest best. There is no disloyalty if the opinion is contrary to mine, and no lack of appreciation on my part, if the opinion is not used. Let us all work on this basis.

The Roman Pool wasn't the only thing that the Depression, now in its third year, had slowed at San Simeon. Several other projects had likewise felt the budgetary cutbacks Hearst periodically made as the nation's economy worsened. But the carillon of bells he had ordered for Casa Grande —for the twin towers of the huge "castle" itself—had been withheld from installation for another reason. The towers already contained tanks of water (for a gravity-flow supply throughout Casa Grande); and Hearst feared that the heavy tanks, along with the weight of the carillon, would prove excessive — especially during an earthquake. He even considered selling the carillon.

Hearst, however, had recently done what came so naturally to him: he had changed his mind. And thus on February 15 Morgan notified Loorz, "We have news today that the Carillon *is* to go in. The bells will be on this week's boat—the men [to install them] will appear any day." She was referring to the regular supply run out of San Francisco Bay, courtesy of steamers like the *Daisy Freeman* that still plied the California coast in the 1930s (much as they had since the late 1800s). In his extreme isolation at San Simeon, Hearst had depended heavily on coastal shipping ever since he began developing his ranch property in 1919.

The "bell men" that Morgan spoke of were from Tournai, Belgium, where Hearst's carillon had been cast in solid bronze. Loorz told Morgan on the last day of February, "I enjoy their Belgian humor [yet] they take up so much of my time that I am anxious to get this installation completed." Speaking of the hilltop work in a larger context, he also told her: "It is surprising how much there is to be done on up-keep alone." She knew all too well about matters at San Simeon that fell outside architectural bounds but that required her close attention just the same.

Ever the diplomat, Loorz paused long enough on March 9 to write to the deposed Camille Rossi, who at the moment was in Needles, California—collecting his thoughts, no doubt, before seeking new prospects in Los Angeles (his hopes of working under Bernard Maybeck in Illinois having fizzled).[5] Loorz was deferential, almost to a fault:

> For the present at least things are going quite smoothly but the job and conditions are such that I'm certain I would not have as much patience as you had. Sorry we did not meet and talk before you left for I feel certain that you could and would give me a lot of downright good advice.
>
> I want to say without hesitancy that you left the job in first class condition structurally and it has been very easy for me [to] pick up and continue. I find the crew you had to be the best possible for this job and I have, to date, not hired a single new man, though I have and still am employing some 50 to 100 men continually in my business elsewhere. For this I am grateful and if you will accept, let me compliment you.

So much for graciousness and kind words. In writing on March 12 to his partner,[6] Fred Stolte, Loorz was more candid in describing the job that first winter—

---

5. See p. 15, note 24. Shortly before Loorz wrote to Rossi, Morgan alluded to the Principia job when she told Hearst, "As explained the other day, the Christian Science work payments have come in regularly each month [since February 1931] in cash, which has carried our office comfortably through these difficult days." But that source would soon dry up, she added, and she'd be forced to seek back payments on the Wyntoon, Beach House, and San Simeon jobs. See Morgan to Hearst, February 17, 1932; Hearst Papers, carton 15 (under "Morgan, Julia"); a carbon copy is in the Morgan Collection, Cal Poly. Henceforth in these dual situations, the original alone will be cited unless otherwise warranted.

6. "Partner" is used here in a general sense. Aside from his new position at San Simeon, Loorz technically was still an employee and associate of Stolte, rather than a partner in full standing. They became the principal shareholders in the newly incorporated F. C. Stolte Co. some three weeks

and in speaking of William Randolph Hearst himself, the man whose quest for grandeur kept the whole enterprise going:

> The Big Boss here raised hell with everyone in General yesterday but left me out of it. Maybe it pays to be big [like Loorz]. These people seldom say anything back so it is easy for him to let loose. It's all bluff for he never gets mad enough to lay them off. I dont blame him for they have worked for about two years and haven't completed a single extra bedroom for him.[7] He has some 47 guests coming this week end and [his] need [for] another suite or two was the cause of the eruption. We managed to arrange one for occupancy although the decorating in them is about 5 months from being completed. It does seem impossible that it should take so long to decorate but with all of the feature painting and gold leaf work it is almost impossible to get men who can do the work.

It was Casa Grande that bore witness to Hearst's "eruption." Within that main building — the centerpiece of the hilltop kingdom — Loorz's crew needed to finish as many as eight bedrooms; all of them were slated, as Loorz told Stolte, to house Hollywood celebrities and other famous guests of the kingly Hearst and the glamorous Marion Davies. (In replying on March 15, Stolte added: "Well, I guess this [company news] doesn't interest you any more — now that you are associating with newspaper *magnets* and movie stars. *Ha Ha*.")[8] Besides the bedrooms Loorz

---

later, on April 5; the deal rested on Loorz's having invested $3,273 in the company — half its "net value" early in 1932 of $6,546 (Loorz to Stolte, February 28).

Two months before the incorporation, which must have been imminent for some time, Loorz portrayed the matter as a fait accompli in his first surviving letter to Morgan, the one dated February 6, 1932. He also told her, "In line with our conversation before coming down here I would deeply appreciate it if you could when the opportunity arises give Mr. Stolte a chance to figure [bid on] or do any kind of construction work, however small."

7. Loorz was referring to a new phase of work that, in reality, had begun as recently as the summer of 1931 — during which the mid-section of Casa Grande was boldly enlarged while Hearst was abroad with Marion Davies and a group of their friends. In letters written months later in 1932, Loorz was still confusing the work of 1931 with some additions made to the north side of Casa Grande in 1929 and 1930 (where the interiors also remained to be finished).

8. A photograph taken in front of Casa Grande about 1927 and later published in King Vidor's Hollywood memoir, *A Tree is a Tree* (New York, 1953) — and later still in *Life* magazine — portrays such screen idols as Greta Garbo, John Gilbert, Buster Keaton, Aileen Pringle, and Norma Shearer; several producers and directors, one of them Vidor, plus some Metro-Goldwyn-Mayer studio executives, are also included. Hearst and Davies — he as an independent film lord, she as the leading lady in his Cosmopolitan Productions — had been affiliated with Louis B. Mayer and MGM since the mid-twenties. In turn, the idolized "Metro crowd" dominated many a gathering at San Simeon until late in 1934, when Hearst and Davies allied themselves with Warner Bros.

The group photograph is more captivating in its magazine version; see p. 81 in "A Unique Tour of San Simeon," *Life* (August 26, 1957), pp. 68–84 overall. The caption speaks of "Hollywood luminaries who were frequent San Simeon guests in the late '20s and early '30s." Another photograph (p. 84) dates from 1924, harking back almost to the beginnings of the estate; it shows Hearst

mentioned, the job included an equal number of adjoining bathrooms, hallways, and, for the Celestial Suite, a sitting room as well. The Celestial Suite was perched in the twin towers at the front of the west-facing mansion, right above Hearst's own Gothic Suite. The other rooms helped flesh out the back side of Casa Grande, where they formed a virtual maze—albeit a symmetrical one—of narrow passageways and staggered floor levels. Spatially, this cluster of guest rooms (which overlooked the unfinished east courtyard) constituted the most intricate part of a building to which complexity and an air of mystery were already second nature. Here were the North Deck and South Deck bedrooms; adjoining them were the two North Duplex suites and the corresponding South Duplexes.

Hearst's reduced budget was strained by these eight rooms alone, and had been for some time, to say nothing of the other projects he hoped to wrap up soon, like the Roman Pool. The landscape architecture for the hilltop was also making demands on the budget. Loorz, always the skillful estimator, projected on March 18 a cost of $4,400 to bring in fifteen palm trees from San Luis Obispo, some fifty miles away. On top of that, he figured $700 for the replacement of four laggard palms in front of Casa Grande with some of the new ones from San Luis. In addition, he figured $800 more for the moving of some Italian cypresses to the outdoor swimming pool (the future Neptune Pool)[9] from the adjoining West Terrace, their places also to be taken by palms from the San Luis group. His total projected cost: $5,900. With the Depression holding fast, Hearst was counting pennies now as never before. Many a proposed job at half that price or less had to be delayed or even abandoned during this period. Yet the moving of the palm trees from San Luis Obispo was important to Hearst, and the job was one of the larger new expenditures he approved in 1932.

LOORZ WAS JOINED at San Simeon by his wife, Grace, and their two sons, Don and Bill, shortly after he arrived. The young family moved into the stucco and tile-

---

with John Hylan, mayor of New York. This memorable, commanding feature in *Life* gives the distinct impression that San Simeon's heyday coincided more with the Jazz Age or the Roaring Twenties, as popular usage might put it, than with anything as unfestive as the Great Depression. In truth, the 1930s (nearly to their end) saw Hearst spending more time at San Simeon and entertaining larger groups—if only because it took him that long to complete enough guest rooms for his purposes.

9. A letter of Morgan's dated March 16, 1932, and addressed to both Louis Reesing (the head gardener) and George Loorz, refers to the existing pool as "the Neptune Pool." Indeed, the name had been in use for some time, although terms like "outdoor pool" and "outside pool" were being used just as often, if not more so. Throughout my interspersed narration, I'll be using "Neptune Pool" to mean one thing only: the full-scale, colonnaded version of the outdoor pool that emerged in the mid-1930s and that superseded its previous, less palatial versions.

roofed house vacated by Camille Rossi, one of a small group of such buildings designed by Julia Morgan in recent years next to San Simeon Bay. That idyllic setting remained the Loorzes' home, as things turned out, until the San Simeon job slowed to a crawl after the 1937 season and the family moved to the Monterey Peninsula early in 1938. Loorz described his good fortune to Fred Stolte, the partner he'd left behind in Oakland, in a letter dated March 21, 1932:

> We certainly do like it there on the beach. Spent three hours frolicking up and down, jumping rope (seaweed) rolling old tires in the sand and gathering beachwood logs for the fireplace. You see we combined business with pleasure. . . .
>
> Everybody here has shown a great deal of interest and pleasure at our arrival. I have a cellar full of all kinds of vintage and cooling waters. One brought some nice fish caught yesterday and yet another promised some large Red Abalone for today. We visit all of them from laborer to Marble carver so we have laid the foundation for quite a pleasant sojourn.

Three hours were about as many as Loorz could devote to frolicking. Hearst had improvements in mind elsewhere on his sprawling ranch, not just on his Enchanted Hill with its gleaming white castle. The time had come, for instance, to improve the landing field—a field consisting of little more than what, years later, was recalled as a "graded strip in a pasture."[10] The field lay immediately west of today's private tree-lined drive that enters the Hearst Ranch from State Highway 1. Among its other drawbacks, the field was too close to a row of utility poles. Both Hearst and some of his guests, and Morgan as well, had landed on the field and knew its limitations. Morgan had done so as a passenger of Hearst's oldest son, George, who was a pilot and had his own plane. As she told Loorz on March 30:

> Mr. George Hearst's objection to the high tension poles is that it is necessary to begin to fall to the landing field only after passing them and that it shortens an already too short field by that amount. I've gritted my teeth several times thinking we would crash through the fence, so know it is fact.

She asked Loorz to help Warren McClure, George Gillespie, and Arch Parks correct the problem. (McClure, a draftsman, was Morgan's "representative" at San Simeon; Gillespie was in charge of fence work on the Hearst Ranch; Parks was the ranch superintendent.)

Before long, though, the idea of merely moving the obstructing poles had blossomed into something larger, as Hearst's ideas so often had a way of doing. Hearst

---

10. Letter from Maurice McClure to author, November 11, 1989 (a different McClure from the one first mentioned elsewhere on this page; see also note 37, below).

opted for an entirely new landing field, one having both north-south and east-west runways; the chosen site, roughly a mile east of the old field, is partly covered today by the Hearst Castle Visitor Center. Several months passed, during which more pressing matters intervened. It was September 26 before Loorz could brief Hearst on how the job was progressing:

> Mr. Parks has worked splendidly with me in clearing the new airport site. I am at present making a heavy railroad iron drag to smooth up the small irregularities of the surface. We will use horses to pull it as Mr. Parks says they need to be exercised. We hope to have the runway ready for Ray [Crawford, Hearst's pilot] to make a few trial landings and take-offs when he comes tomorrow. He will then be more able to pass judgment. The cost so far has not been more than $200.

The cost soon exceeded $200, of course, especially when the lighting equipment was moved over from the old field and reinstalled. But Loorz watched the expenditures as closely as he could, a virtue never lost on Hearst.

Loorz also tried his hand at animal husbandry during his debut at San Simeon. Hearst's bull terrier, Buddy, needed a new dog house. Marianne the elephant needed an elephant house. On a more urgent note, Hearst told Loorz and Carey Baldwin, the ranch zookeeper, to "do everything possible to protect the remaining giraffe." That was back on April 26. A giraffe had died the previous day, and another had died earlier that month—"a loss amounting to some $20,000," Loorz told Morgan on May 10, hence "the hasty order for quarters."

LIKEWISE IN THE SPRING of 1932—on April 6, to be exact—Loorz notified Alexander T. Sokolow, a lawyer who was also Hearst's controller in Los Angeles, that he had received "written orders from Mr. Hearst to proceed immediately with a bridge across the Creek in the ravine to the north where the Burnet[t] road crosses." The orders to Loorz took the form of an undated, hand-scrawled memorandum in which Hearst assured him, "Just a plank bridge will do for the present." And he said in a postscript, "We did more damage to the cars today than the bridge would cost."

Here again was the germ of another expansive idea. For Hearst meant to do more than simply build a bridge across his backyard creek. He meant to extend the Burnett Road across the rugged Santa Lucia Range that bordered his Enchanted Hill. And thus would that road, now just a few miles long, go on to link the main coastal portion of his ranch kingdom with the uppermost, inland portions more than twenty miles north—the portions surrounding Mission San Antonio and the remote settlement of Jolon in Monterey County.

Hearst and Morgan had recently finished the Milpitas Hacienda near Jolon, a sprawling structure in its own right, portions of which Loorz would remodel a few years later.[11] In contrast to how the major work at San Simeon was handled (usually "in house" through Morgan and her trusted circle), the Milpitas job had been allotted to an outsider, to a general contractor in San Luis Obispo named W. J. Smith—under the watchful eye, of course, of the Morgan office and with plenty of support from Morgan regulars like the plumber James Rankin. W. J. Smith had also built the "Chicken House" (the poultry unit) on the Hearst Ranch and the bayside houses that now included the Loorz residence; in addition, Smith had built the concrete, mission-like warehouse in San Simeon village that matched those picturesque homes.

As for remote Milpitas, the only ways thus far of getting there from San Simeon were problematic at best, and yet they were richly scenic ways in that era of sparkling skies and wide-open spaces. Once or twice, Hearst and his guests had motored down to San Luis Obispo, looped back over the historic Cuesta Grade into the Salinas Valley, and purred north past Atascadero, Paso Robles, and San Miguel en route to Jolon and Milpitas—a meandering jaunt of more than a hundred miles. The trip also entailed a retracing of these lengthy steps, for there was scarcely any other way for cars to cross the Santa Lucias south of the Carmel Valley-Arroyo Seco route in Monterey County. The sole exceptions in 1932 were steep, winding roads that could be tough on engines: the forerunner of today's State Highway 41 (from Atascadero to Morro Bay); the Old Creek route (from the Paso Robles area to Morro Bay's neighboring town of Cayucos); and the York Mountain route (likewise from the Paso Robles area, but to Cambria).

At times, Hearst and a few others had also taken a daring shortcut to Milpitas from the coastal side of his property, making a quick flight to a landing field at Jolon—a field as spartan as the one he'd decided to replace at San Simeon. The Jolon field was likewise slated for improvement in the near future.

Although *Jolon* was a local Indian name, and one said to mean "valley of dead trees,"[12] it nonetheless evoked California's romanticized past, as much as an Old

---

11. The Milpitas Hacienda dated from 1929 and 1930; by then a vibrant and eclectic style—the Spanish Colonial Revival—had held sway among the Mediterranean-minded for several years. Much later, though, some of the foremost historians of California architecture said Milpitas hailed from the preceding, stylistically narrower period: "a splendid Mission Revival building designed in the early 1900s by Julia Morgan." They offset their error by also saying, with equal enthusiasm, that Milpitas conveyed "many very personal almost idiosyncratic views of the style." From David Gebhard et al., *A Guide to Architecture in San Francisco & Northern California* (Santa Barbara, 1973), p. 443. The revised editions of 1976 and 1985 contain the same wording.

12. As defined by Nellie Van de Grift Sanchez in *Spanish and Indian Place Names of California: Their Meaning and Their Romance* (San Francisco, 1914), p. 159, and then by Erwin G. Gudde in *California Place Names: A Geographical Dictionary* (Berkeley, 1949, p. 168; plus two later editions). However, the revised and enlarged fourth edition of Gudde (1998), edited by William Bright, cites on p. 186 the

World name like *San Simeon* did; but *Jolon* was also a name that could be puzzling. In 1933, Loorz received some "weekly notices to airmen" from the Department of Commerce. The typewritten envelope had been carefully addressed to the "Jolson Airport." Maybe the thought of Hearst the Hollywood impresario—and of the stars like Al Jolson that he entertained—had played on someone's mind in Washington.[13]

The proposed lengthening of the Burnett Road, meanwhile, a road named for the creek that drained the western flank of the Santa Lucias, was first and last an engineering job and thus right down Loorz's alley. As such, the job fell outside Morgan's accustomed bounds, as diverse as her role at San Simeon had been since 1919 and would continue to be for several more years. (As part of the "Morgan myth" described earlier, Morgan was once vaguely regarded as an engineer—as though this architect were also a civil engineer, as though a task like large-scale road building might naturally fall within her ken. It never had; it never would. Nor did she ever assume the more kindred role of a structural engineer.)[14]

Indian word *xolon*, which is thus defined: "it leaks; a leak; a channel where water cuts through." Bright also cites a colloquialism from Jolon's wild-west phase, when stagecoaches in that lawless district could fall prey to highwaymen: "Hol' on! Hol' on!" went the bandits' cry.

13. The "Jolson" envelope and its notices are from "Misc. 1933," one of three boxes now appended to the George Loorz Papers. Having surfaced in July 1990, the boxes (still unprocessed) were excluded from my compilation of earlier that year, "The George Loorz Papers: Storage List and Finding Aid"; see p. 2 in this volume, note 2. They were also excluded from my book of later that year, *The Builders Behind the Castles*.

For the most part, these and some other appendants to the Loorz Papers are the only ones whose provenance I'll be citing in *Building for Hearst and Morgan*; the exceptions include items in the Morgan Collection and in the Hearst Papers that I've quoted. Since April 1990 the processed portions of the Loorz Papers have been arranged chronologically in three record groups; it has thus been possible to locate among them, by date and context, the excerpts that appear in *The Builders Behind the Castles*. The same is true (and more readily so) of the excerpts in this newer book.

14. The idea of Morgan as engineer rested on her having gone to the University of California when its College of Engineering (from which she graduated, class of 1894) was still a fledgling department. An aspiring architect could do no better on the West Coast at that time. In the 1970s, Richard Longstreth liked to play off the term "pre-med" by saying Morgan's curriculum at Berkeley had been "pre-architecture" in spirit. The training that truly counted, that truly made her an *architect* (as she regarded herself), awaited her at the Ecole des Beaux-Arts in Paris.

Had she gone to Berkeley a decade or two later—or three, when Loorz did—her life's work might have been different. By the early 1900s the curriculum had been strengthened enough to produce graduates like Walter Steilberg (class of 1910), who majored in architecture and minored in structural engineering. It was Steilberg, in fact, who became a bona fide architect-engineer, an uncommon dual calling that some identified with Morgan. Instead, she focused on design and planning throughout her career, often delegating her engineering needs—which could be extensive— to Steilberg and especially to Walter Huber, some of whose papers adjoin the Morgan Collection at Cal Poly.

Besides the Burnett Road, another job outside Morgan's bounds (and in this case Rossi's and

Loorz told Hearst they should bring in a bona fide road contractor, someone with the right equipment and the men to operate it, rather than limp along with the equipment on hand and day labor out of Hearst Camp. At intervals since 1928, that approach had been tried under F. W. Slattery in cutting the first few miles of the road to Jolon: down the back side of The Enchanted Hill and up the lower reaches of Burnett Creek. (Slattery preceded Arch Parks as the Hearst Ranch superintendent.) Loorz knew that to continue higher up the creek—a job Camille Rossi had hoped to inherit—then to cross the Santa Lucias themselves, and finally to bridge a much larger watercourse, the Nacimiento River, would require a new tack. Hearst agreed.

By June 4, Loorz could write the following words to his partner back home, Fred Stolte:

> We hear a lot about shortage of money here but they still spend thousands like water. I am letting a road contract to Tieslau Bros. [of Berkeley] for eight miles of pleasure road back thru the mountains here for some $30,000 so I guess all of the money is not buried as yet.

Stolte replied with "just a few lines" to let Loorz know he was "still doing business at the same peanut stand"—a stock phrase in many of his early letters (and in this instance an undated one). "Seems strange to hear of someone who is spending real money. A $30,000 pleasure road must be some job."

It was, and the eight miles Loorz had mentioned were merely the first phase of a renewed project, a matter of taking up where Slattery had left off in 1930. Surveyors had kept busy on the proposed route in 1931, but no construction had been done that year. Come the end of the 1932 season, Tieslau Brothers completed its eight miles, as specified. By then the road ran as far as the crest of the Santa Lucias above Burnett Creek and a little beyond. To get from there to Jolon, through a torturous canyon leading down to the Nacimiento River, would require two further seasons of work. And it was work that, because of a more strained budget come 1933, Loorz and Hearst would decide to tackle with their "own crew and equipment,"[15] rather

---

Loorz's too) was the landscaping and forestation that Charles Gibbs Adams of Los Angeles had been overseeing since about 1930; the work required large crews at times and was mostly done on Orchard Hill, Reservoir Hill, and elsewhere on the Hearst Ranch away from the main hilltop itself. Adams wrote to Morgan on July 25, 1932, hoping she might intercede: Hearst was more than $1,100 in arrears, an amount she could carry but that few others could. Her reply of July 27 began with "On nearly all work these days a slowness of payments has caused much inconvenience and worry." She ended by telling Adams that she hoped he and the Hearst interests had "arrived at a happy settlement." Hearst Papers, carton 57 (both items under "Julia Morgan").

15. Loorz to Alexander T. Sokolow, April 21, 1933 (from "Burnett Road for 1932," another of the three belated boxes mentioned in note 13, above; the box also contains items from 1933).

than through an outside contractor. They realized by then that they could pay their labor costs and buy their own bulldozers and other road machinery for less than what a new contract would entail.

DURING THIS PART of spring 1932, Morgan paid a visit to San Simeon that, along with a new financial strategy of Hearst's, resulted in a remarkable document — or rather a remarkably misconstruable one that falls outside the George Loorz Papers. (Instead, the document is part of the Morgan Collection at Cal Poly.) Sunday, May 22, found Morgan conferring on the hilltop with Hearst, who planned to leave for Los Angeles that evening; she herself had just been in Los Angeles on Friday and Saturday, May 20–21. On the first of those days, and possibly on the second one also, she divided her time between the Beach House in Santa Monica and a job that dated from March 1931, the Marion Davies Clinic in West Los Angeles.[16]

The document, at any rate, was a list of "Bills Payable," dated May 27, 1932. It went to John Francis Neylan, Hearst's foremost attorney and, until recently, a manager of the principal construction funds for San Simeon, at the Crocker Bank Building in San Francisco; Morgan's covering letter to Neylan bore the date May 31, a Tuesday.

Morgan, however, was on the hilltop again at that moment in May 1932 (on that Tuesday); and thus dictation she'd already given her secretary, Lilian Forney, may have been postdated. Morgan began by telling Neylan:

> Last Sunday [actually May 22, not May 29], in talking budget with Mr. Hearst, I told him that if we could proceed at about the rate we are now going, and he could allow us $25,000 a month for the season, we could handle the outstanding accounts [payable] without any large down-right sum at this time as most of the people will be satisfied with small payments, if regular.

The round figures Morgan used in the letter typify the amounts that, until the end of 1931, Neylan had periodically disbursed to her on Hearst's behalf: a check

---

16. Morgan wrote to Hearst in this period, saying she would be in Los Angeles "on Friday" (May 20); his secretary, Joseph Willicombe, annotated the letter, "HAVE NOTIFIED MISS MORGAN THAT MR HEARST IS AT RANCH UNTIL SUNDAY NIGHT [MAY 22]." After hearing the news, Morgan wired Willicombe, "Will be at ranch Sunday as have to be Los Angeles Saturday. Kindly tell George [Loorz]." See Morgan to Hearst, May 17, 1932, and Morgan to Willicombe, May 20, 1932; Hearst Papers, carton 15 (under "Morgan, Julia").

Morgan's whereabouts and activities in the May 19–21 period are further discernible from the account ledgers in the Morgan-Forney Collection. These cite May 19 (perhaps as an en-route, evening-before-visit date) for the Marion Davies Clinic, charged to Hearst as $15 in travel expenses; they also cite May 19 for the Beach House, charged as $20. The combined amount — $35 — is on par with what Morgan normally charged him for a visit to San Simeon.

for $10,000 here, one for $15,000 or $20,000 there, and so on up the dizzying scale. As of the current year, such round-figure disbursements were being made through Alexander Sokolow's office in Los Angeles; and as of May 15, 1932, those amounts would further involve the Piedmont Land & Cattle Company, a Hearst subsidiary in San Francisco. That was Hearst's new strategy, his latest tribute to convoluted bookkeeping. All the while, the separate commission payments Morgan received, reflecting 8.5% of diverse and varied construction costs, had been the diametric opposite of the amounts sent by Neylan and Sokolow. Odd sums like $1,074.09 and $1,548.91, which appear on the Bills Payable list of May 27, had long been the norm.

In this same letter to Neylan, Morgan alluded to her architectural firm in the Merchants Exchange; she did so while touching on the subject of compensation for services rendered by Morgan et al. "We are much behind on payments of our own commission as we can not draw for ourselves under the circumstances."[17]

---

17. From Morgan to Neylan, May 31, 1932 (covering letter for the Bills Payable list dated May 27, 1932); Hearst/Morgan Correspondence, Morgan Collection, Cal Poly. One could easily side here with the Morgan myth, with its portrayal of Hearst the skinflint and Morgan his pawn; one could even conclude that Miss Morgan had been going without commission payments since late in the 1920s. No less a San Simeon expert than Victoria Kastner has done so in *Hearst Castle: The Biography of a Country House* (New York, 2000), p. 151. Without the Morgan-Forney ledgers at her disposal, Kastner had no ready means of deciphering these two entries on the Bills Payable list: "Invoices Special Fund Jan. 31, 1928, Sept. 30/[19]29, Nov. 30/[19]29, Dec. 31/[19]29, Dec. 31/[19]30, Dec. 31/[19]31," followed by "Regular fund invoices Oct. 31, 1931 to April 30, 1932."

The wording on the Bills Payable list must be scrutinized to the last syllable: a Special Fund existed, and so did a Regular Fund. The Belgian carillon, for example, was obtained through the Special Fund. As Morgan had explained to Hearst five years earlier:

You have two San Simeon accounts in our care — one [the Regular Fund] in which we deposit the money received through Mr. Neylan, and one "Special Fund" account for money you provide for definite purposes. Both funds are audited by the auditor from Mr. Neylan's office, but no accounting is made to him of the special funds.

From Morgan to Hearst, April 18, 1927; Hearst/Morgan Correspondence, Morgan Collection. A related letter from Morgan to Hearst on September 5, 1927, is in the Hearst Papers, carton 5 (under "Morgan, Julia," filed with Hearst to Morgan, September 13, 1927). The Morgan Collection lacks the item of September 5 — the more important of the two — but has the incoming original of the one dated September 13.

The list of May 27, 1932, also has this adjoining entry: "J. M. Commissions 8075.95." That amount can't be handily reconciled with the Special Fund invoices of January 31, 1928, through December 31, 1931 (equaling $4,369.94 and finally paid in June 1933). Nor can it be reconciled with the Regular Fund invoices of October 31, 1931, through April 30, 1932 (equaling $11,066.76). Yet in the most general sense, $8,075.95 suggests a year-to-date figure as of May 31, 1932 — a figure commensurate with the $20,060 (reflecting Special and Regular funds combined) in Morgan's "Commission Account" for 1932 as a whole. Appendix B on pp. 546–50 shows that, in the full scheme of things, Hearst often lagged a bit in his commission payments (overall, his paid-up status averaged 94.4%). Morgan, however, made more than $100,000 in profit on San Simeon by the late 1930s (the $427,843

In her own way, Morgan could be as much a shoot-from-the-hip writer as the fast-typing Loorz: for both of them, their recipients would know well enough in most cases what the intended meaning was. Her letter of May 31 is far from her only one that begs careful decoding and deep interpretation. In short, she seems to have been juggling money—robbing Peter to pay Paul for the greater good of San Simeon. She'd been a juggler before and, when conditions required it, would be one again in the years to come. Her letter to Neylan was all in a day's work, a timely clearing in 1932 of the financial air. And yet its attached list of Bills Payable stands out with unusual salience in the Morgan Collection at Cal Poly, and it does so mostly because of its rarity. Few other documents like it survive in the Morgan Collection; it's a type of document that, long ago, may have been common among the woman's extensive office records. (Dozens of such lists *do* survive in the Loorz Papers.) But this particular communication of Morgan's—prompted not just by her having discussed the budget with Hearst on May 22 but also by his having made a related decision a week earlier—lies in wait for historians, tempting them decades later to misinterpret it.

ON JUNE 10, 1932, which was a Friday, Morgan wrote to Loorz from her Merchants Exchange office in San Francisco: "Mr. Hearst will be up for next week end [June 18–19]—and wants all rooms possible." She also told Loorz she planned to see him at San Simeon on the following Monday, June 13.

Whereas the 1920s had found Morgan making so many of her visits on Sundays, this new decade would increasingly find her appearing on Mondays. Either way, the trend had long been for her to check on the job as the weekend waned. The other days of the week were also fair game; but overall, she was less likely to show up then. Hence the frequent portrayal, verging on folklore, of San Simeon as a weekend job for Morgan or even as a moonlight job, a job that a one-day visit was enough to perform, almost offhandedly. Yet with so much of her work in recent years having been for Hearst (see Appendix A on pp. 531–45), cannot her many weekend—and immediate post-weekend—trips be viewed differently? When Hearst was on hand, as he increasingly was after the mid-twenties, cannot Morgan be seen as having gone to San Simeon to receive the latest marching orders for the days just ahead? Even in his absence her staffing, budgeting, and other decisions were greatly influenced by the headway at San Simeon and on her other Hearst projects.

---

in Appendix B, p. 550, minus the lion's share of $312,028 in Appendix A, note on p. 536). The inconveniences she bore were grandly offset by a job whose munificence kept her steadily prosperous. And thus she could—and often did—take certain other jobs on a break-even basis or even at a loss (beyond the non-Hearst jobs that *were* profitable).

Morgan usually left San Francisco by train on the preceding afternoon or evening and, upon reaching San Luis Obispo, stayed at the Anderson Hotel. That was
the calmer way, the more prevalent way. At times, though, she had to leave San
Francisco (or somewhere else that her work had taken her) in the dead of night, a
red-eye schedule made possible by an era whose passenger trains ran more frequently than they do now. In any event, she was driven to San Simeon in the morning; she could thus get in a solid session before returning to San Luis by the evening and, later still, to San Francisco, although she sometimes stayed in San Luis
for a second night and caught an early train. She upheld this often grueling pattern through most of Loorz's tenure, seldom remaining overnight at San Simeon
itself.[18]

By appearing on Sundays or Mondays, Morgan and her office staff had most
of the new week to act on Hearst's wishes. And if her next visit lay more than a week
ahead, there was still more time, precious time, to be productive. The Sunday-
Monday trend had another advantage: Morgan could better avoid the movie stars
and their fellow notables (perhaps even Al Jolson) who enlivened many a weekend—especially a Saturday—at the fabled "ranch." With the fun having sub-
sided, and if Hearst remained on hand, she could gain a better audience with
that uncommonly busy client. But regardless of when she appeared, and whether

18. The Julia Morgan Collection has records of Morgan's trips to San Simeon; all told, 590
trips from 1919 through 1939 are cited, mostly by single dates, such as June 12, 1932. (The records of
the earliest years, when longer visits were more common, contain several clustered dates, such as
April 16–19, 1923.) The San Simeon accounts in the Morgan-Forney ledgers corroborate the Morgan Collection and disclose a final trip in 1940, bringing the recorded total to 591. To compare those
two archives with the Loorz Papers is revealing: from 1932 through 1937 (Loorz's full-time tenure),
both the Morgan Collection and the Morgan-Forney entries reflect either the date Morgan embarked for San Simeon or the date (and sometimes dates) she actually spent on the job; the same may
be true of the years before and after Loorz. Through the Loorz collation, certain Saturdays prove to
have preceded a Sunday visit, certain Sundays a Monday visit, and so on; thus does June 12, 1932,
pertain to Morgan's appearance on Monday, June 13. Other patterns—and certain discrepancies—can also be cited. The subject invites much more probing and interpretation (the entries show,
for instance, that 1931 was a banner year, in which Morgan visited the job nearly fifty times; 1928 was
almost as active for her, with forty-five visits; also, the Loorz Papers indicate she made two unrecorded visits in September 1932, and there are known to have been others).

This analysis stems from an appendix in Carol J. Everingham's summary of the Hearst/
Morgan Correspondence (the record series in the Morgan Collection that pertains mostly to San
Simeon). The Everingham summary is entitled "Dateline: San Simeon 1919–1939: A Chronological
Development of Ideas, Plans, Drawings, and Actual Construction Starting in 1919 at the William
Randolph Hearst Estate in San Simeon" (San Simeon, 1981). Everingham's travel dates have been
closely checked (and amended in places) against a smaller record series in the Morgan Collection—
a series identified as "San Simeon Financial Records" in *Descriptive Guide to the Julia Morgan Collection*
(San Luis Obispo, n.d. [compiled by Nancy E. Loe, 1985]), pp. 57–58. Those data, in turn, have been
checked against the San Simeon account ledgers in the Morgan-Forney Collection.

Hearst was in residence (and whether his guest list was large or small), she normally had plenty to do.

Loorz took detailed notes whenever he conferred with Miss Morgan on the jobsite. Within a few days of her latest visit he would type out his notes and send her a copy for her corrections and approval, much like a secretary submitting minutes of a meeting. These notes could be fairly detailed, could run to multiple pages with closely spaced entries. Loorz usually called each of his write-ups a "Recapitulation of Architect's Interview."

His notes dated June 17, based on Morgan's visit of Monday, June 13, contained this entry: "As soon as plan of Great Hall arrives, stake it out for approval of Mr. Hearst." Hearst had proposed the Great Hall quite recently. The name was no exaggeration. Conceived as a link between the east ends of Casa Grande's Recreation Wing and Service Wing, the Great Hall was to be part exhibit hall, part ballroom, part banqueting hall—the most spectacular room of its kind in this country, Hearst had written Morgan. (In doing so on April 26, he had begun with "I have an idea which I have outlined to Mr. [Warren] McClure. I think it should provide the crowning glory of our Hilltop." The details followed in short, rapid-fire paragraphs: managerial Hearst in his daily-newspaper mode. "That is the scheme," he exclaimed upon ending. "Isn't it a pippin?" Morgan had wired back to her "assistant architect"—Hearst's self-description in signing off—saying his proposed room was a pippin indeed.)[19] Hearst's grand idea had its drawbacks, though, not the least of them budgetary. The Theater, which occupied the ground floor of the Recreation Wing on the north side of Casa Grande, practically defied the abutting of a new structure. Hearst and Morgan could have juggled the aesthetics successfully enough, but to join the Theater and the Great Hall structurally and spatially was another matter. And then there were the big oak trees that grew smack dab in the path of the Great Hall—ancient, native oaks that could be moved, as certain others had been in recent years, but only at much risk and expense. We may never know which of these obstacles was most responsible for finally thwarting Hearst's proposal. For the time being, his dream of a Great Hall on the east side of Casa Grande remained alive.

19. Hearst to Morgan, April 26, 1932; Hearst/Morgan Correspondence, Morgan Collection. Morgan to Hearst, April 28, 1932; Hearst Papers, carton 15 (under "Morgan, Julia"). Carol J. Everingham's "Dateline" summarizes these letters and many others (both originals and copies) in the Morgan Collection. See also *Descriptive Guide to the Julia Morgan Collection*, pp. 47–56, for its list of the Hearst/Morgan Correspondence (mostly regarding San Simeon) from 1919 to 1945. Certain other Hearst-Morgan letters are filed elsewhere in the Morgan Collection; see, for example, pp. 63–64 in the *Descriptive Guide* for the separately designated Hearst/Morgan Babicora Correspondence, dating from 1943–44.

Morgan had told Loorz that Hearst would be at San Simeon over the weekend of June 18–19. On Thursday, June 16, however, Hearst wrote to Loorz from Los Angeles, saying he didn't think he could "get to the ranch before the last of the month." Mid-July proved to be more like it. The distinction is important because on Friday, July 1, Hearst played the most fateful political card in his life—that of maneuvering the California delegation at Chicago's Democratic National Convention, threatened with deadlock, in favor of Franklin Delano Roosevelt. Hearst's deal-making in the 1932 convention is well known. What is less known is that it was from Los Angeles that he played his hand in Roosevelt's behalf. Hearst's authorized biographer, Mrs. Fremont Older, placed him in Los Angeles for that historic gesture, the Morgan Collection at Cal Poly virtually confirms his whereabouts, and the Loorz Papers (plus the Hearst Papers at the Bancroft Library) reinforce that fact still more. The popular account, though, has long been that he was at San Simeon when he opted for Roosevelt—a choice he was destined to regret for years to come.[20]

While Hearst was still in Los Angeles, Loorz wrote to E. E. Boss, the caretaker of Wyntoon, whom he had met while working there in 1928. Ever since that first year of concerted effort along the McCloud River, Wyntoon had been an open-ended venture, just as San Simeon had been since 1919. The remodeling of The Gables was among the tangible results; a new version of Wyntoon Castle had also been taking shape, even before the fire in 1930, though mostly in Hearst's imagina-

---

20. See Mrs. Older's *William Randolph Hearst: American*, pp. 552–53. The influential—but mistaken—account of Hearst's whereabouts on July 1, 1932, descends mostly from Edmond D. Coblentz's compilation, *William Randolph Hearst: A Portrait in His Own Words* (New York, 1952), pp. 124–40. Late in 1951, George Rothwell Brown, a "political analyst for the Hearst newspapers," provided Coblentz (a fellow Hearst veteran) with the "inside story" of Hearst's role in the Chicago convention. Brown portrayed Hearst's secretary, Joseph Willicombe, as having been in Chicago at the crucial moment in 1932 and Hearst as having been at San Simeon; the two men stayed in constant touch by telephone. In turn, the Coblentz-Brown account has conjured a fond picture of Hearst that is architecturally errant as well: an image of "the Chief" giving Roosevelt the nod from within the sumptuous Gothic Study—a portion of Hearst's private suite in Casa Grande that was not ready for use till the mid-1930s.

But long before Coblentz, the following appeared in another book: "The impression was widespread at the convention, and it has been given currency since then, that publisher William Randolph Hearst was primarily responsible for breaking the deadlock." (The *potential* deadlock, the passage would better have said.) From *Behind the Ballots: The Personal History of a Politician*, by James A. Farley (New York, 1938), p. 149; Farley also recounted a telephone call that he and Willicombe made to Hearst at San Simeon (pp. 131–32). *Jim Farley's Story: The Roosevelt Years* (New York, 1948) likewise mentioned the call—which Farley said reached Hearst "at his San Simeon, California, ranch" (p. 24). However, Mrs. Fremont Older (as cited above) recounted that Farley placed his call in Roosevelt's behalf to San Francisco—to John Francis Neylan, Hearst's chief attorney and "political representative in California." Neylan, in turn, relayed Farley's urgent appeal to Hearst, "who was in Los Angeles," as Mrs. Older said on p. 552 (probably at the Beach House in Santa Monica).

tion and on Morgan's drafting board.[21] Boss had written to Loorz on June 10, 1932, telling him how tight the budget was at Wyntoon that season; the old bridge, for example, had "about seen its last days" and no money seemed forthcoming from Hearst to repair it. Boss assumed Hearst was having difficulties "along with the rest of the world."

Loorz told Boss on June 24, "Like yourself we are forced to run short handed this year." Boss had hoped a man he laid off at Wyntoon could hire on with Loorz at San Simeon. But Loorz told him, "Honestly I have so many applications daily that plead so for work that it certainly gives me an unhappy feeling to turn them down." Loorz could make no exception for Boss's man. What extreme, improbable contrasts—between Hearst's proposed Great Hall for San Simeon and the decrepit bridge at Wyntoon, between Hearst's maneuvering on the highest political level and Boss's agonizing over the humblest employee.

Although the San Simeon of 1932 discouraged most job seekers, a certain amount of turnover did occur. Back in May, Loorz wrote to Henry and Gus Tieslau, the Berkeley contractors who were about to start work on the new segment of the Burnett Road. "I had one hell of [a] time here yesterday morning," he told the Tieslaus. Three carpenters had "reported to work drunk," leaving Loorz with no choice but to lower the boom.[22] The situation was one that his predecessor, Camille Rossi, might have relished. But not Loorz himself. He knew that loneliness and isolation were facts of life for the men in Hearst Camp, despite the ample food and, by Depression standards, adequate pay. And to think that a stone's throw away stood a majestic castle, its opulent rooms awaiting the next influx of merrymakers from that dreamland called Hollywood.

With Hearst remaining in Los Angeles, a large group in San Luis Obispo got to visit The Enchanted Hill on July 9. On these infrequent (and no doubt coveted) occasions, visitors saw the gardens and other outdoor areas. The interiors were normally off limits, yet memories lasting a lifetime could still be had. A near tragedy befell the San Luis group when, contrary to orders, it entered the Roman Pool compound to marvel at the intricate tile work, then approaching completion. Hoping to get a closer look, dozens of people crowded onto a small wooden scaffold— whose framework crumpled like matchsticks on the hard concrete. Luckily, no one was killed. But some people had to be hospitalized. The incident is all but unknown, never having established itself in San Simeon's boundless lore. Both the

21. See pp. 7–8 in this volume, plus their notes 13 and 14.

22. The letter is dated "Saturday" only—probably meaning May 28, 1932 (from "Burnett Road for 1932"; see notes 13 and 15, above).

Hearst Papers and the Morgan Collection contain little on the subject. The Loorz Papers, however, give it sufficient play, as do some old newspapers.[23] Loorz told Stolte on Friday, July 15, "No doubt you read about the accident here. I was not on the hill at the time as it happened [last] Saturday afternoon." Loorz further absolved himself by saying of the scaffold, "As it was built long before my time and I did not take them in there, they have not figured me in on it [the negligence] at all." Good thing: for even in a lean year like 1932, and even with the tile work at the Roman Pool being partly outside his jurisdiction, Loorz kept finding that he had more and more to oversee.

HEARST WAS AT SAN SIMEON again in late July. He and Loorz toured the hilltop on July 28, inspecting the progress to date. Morgan got a three-page summary from Loorz, compiled on Friday, July 29. (Loorz timed it to reach her before she left San Francisco on Saturday, bound for San Simeon and a Sunday meeting with Hearst. She knew Loorz planned to be gone from Saturday afternoon until later the next day, and thus this short message she sent him on Friday: "Certainly go on, and don't try to get back Sunday at all. I will leave you copious notes!")[24]

"In general regarding the construction in the Castle," went Loorz's report, "he was well pleased with everything completed, and *very* well pleased with the nearness to completion of the Duplexes. His own statement was, after walking around, 'Well, things are beginning to finish up quickly, aren't they.'" Loorz also told Morgan, "He glanced into the South Deck Room as we walked by to the South Duplex and said, 'All ready to move into' and after a moment's hesitation, 'I like it better than the other one.'" Hearst's allusion was to the corresponding North Deck bedroom.

---

23. The subject also figures in a local-history book, though oddly so in regard to context and to some of the details recounted. Under "Wartime Recreation," the author portrays the accident as having occurred ten years later—in the midst of World War II. (This is a switch: Hearstiana abounds in stories set several years *before* their rightful time.) The author went as far astray in describing what, in reality, was the artisans' simple platform: "Hearst's generous hospitality included a grandstand constructed over the pool for the occasion [the visit]." From Rose McKeen, *Parade Along the Creek: San Luis Obispo Memories of the 1920s through '60s* (San Luis Obispo, 1988), p. 94. More recently, the subject has appeared in Victoria Kastner's *Hearst Castle*, p. 226, note 44.

24. Loorz may, in fact, have returned to meet with Morgan on Sunday, July 31, at least briefly; a one-page "Recapitulation of Architect's Interview" exists for that date, typed in his usual style and with some quick notes of hers attached.

On Monday, August 1, Morgan headed farther south. She checked on the Marion Davies Clinic in West Los Angeles, a job now in its late stages. (These details typify what the Morgan-Forney account ledgers reveal; among other facts, Morgan's trips from 1924 through 1940, in behalf of Hearst and all other clients, are minutely recorded.) Meanwhile in 1932, Morgan wrote to Loorz on August 3: "This is Wednesday and I am only just back in San Francisco." She went to San Simeon

Deep in the cavernous back reaches of Casa Grande, Loorz and Hearst surprised two artisans while on that tour of July 28, resulting in a long paragraph for Morgan to read:

> Unfortunately when we walked into the Lower North Duplex Mr. [Camille] Solon and Mr. [Frank] Gyorgy were in the midst of [a] very unpleasant argument in quite loud voices. I waited just a second hoping they would look down [from the bedroom loft or from scaffolding] and see us and stop but I had to raise my voice and stop them, which they did promptly of course. Naturally it was a bit disturbing and his [Hearst's] reaction to the ceiling was perhaps made hastily. He stated that he thot it would be alright [but it] wasn't far enough along to really judge as yet. I'm not quite certain but I think he expects to see a lot more color, well glazed over and toned down a lot of course. He mentioned the Alhambra samples being [the] idea with lots of color but of course toned as above stated for he didn't think the original [is] as bright as the samples. He liked the woodwork. He says the carved corbels look alright and that we better leave them.

Morgan had as much to pore over regarding other rooms, among them the Celestial Suite, whose Captain's Bridge (the adjoining walkway) would soon regale guests with its majestic views of land and sea. She also learned from Loorz's report that the two men had discussed the pergola—the columned arbor on Orchard Hill, just west of the higher knoll dominated by Casa Grande and its adjacent buildings.[25] Hearst had decided to add to the existing row of columns on Orchard Hill and extend it around that lower knoll. Nigel Keep, his orchard man since 1922, had been standing by for some time, eager to plant the grape vines the new columns would require; Hearst knew as well as Keep did that it would be years before the vines matured. The placement of the columns, meanwhile, had to be just so in the eyes of the perfectionist Hearst.

Loorz had more to tell Morgan on Thursday, August 11, about the "pergola continuation." He included a glimpse of the activities that Hearst's entourage was enjoying:

> Most of the guests have gone [for the moment]. They are all on a picnic way up the coast this afternoon. It was rumored that they might go down [to Los Angeles] for a few days during the week but that is apparently out. Have had no complaints so I assume all is well, have not talked to him.

---

again on August 7, to Wyntoon on August 11, to San Simeon once more on August 17—and to the Marion Davies Clinic for another inspection right after that.

25. I think of The Enchanted Hill in the largest sense as comprising three adjacent knolls. These surmount the same ridge—which stands apart, island like, from the Santa Lucia Range be-

Four days later, on August 15, Loorz had further details to share with Morgan about Orchard Hill:

> Mr. Hearst has been down to the Pergola twice and is taking an active part in the location of the line to follow. We are now setting up a few poles to the finished height of the Pergola on the supposed course to see how it will look from the Castle above and from the road [the main driveway] below.

As for new headway within the castle itself—within Casa Grande, that is—Hearst's entertaining could cause delays. "It certainly handicaps us with the carpentry when we cannot hammer until noon," Loorz told Morgan in that same letter of August 15. "He has so many guests that any hammering in the forenoon bothers. I have plenty of work previously outlined that they can do but it does not permit real visible progress in any one room." The subject of noise had cropped up before. So had the subject of "visible progress." With broader strokes, Morgan herself had painted a similar picture in writing to Hearst a few months earlier.[26]

The pergola remained a priority as fall approached. Loorz brought Hearst up to date (somewhat clumsily at one point) on September 19:

> We have the road machine working on the pergola extension. There are two fairly large pine trees which come directly in the proper location of the roadbed. The cost of moving and attempting to save these trees would be around $60 if they could simply be moved down the hill a short distance. Mr. Keep looked at them with me and said that the chances of trees as old as they were would very likely die if moved. Said he could replace the trees with smaller ones for less than $50 each and thot it might not be advisable to attempt to move them. What would you advise?

"Move 'em," said Hearst.[27]

In writing to Hearst in Los Angeles on October 10, Loorz related that "the pine trees on the Pergola road were moved quite successfully at a cost of about $55 each, net."

---

hind it. The three are Orchard Hill, China Hill, and the main hilltop area itself, the last being the domain of the "castle" and its architectural brethren. See the map on p. xxii.

26. "I am sorry we are so slow, but the place grows larger and larger and in comparison [with past years] the workers are less and less able to make any startling impression." From Morgan to Hearst, March 24, 1932; Hearst Papers, carton 15 (under "Morgan, Julia").

Loorz struck a similar note in writing to the plumber James Rankin on September 27, 1932. "We are scattering affections all over the hill-top and surrounding country and pushing as hard as we can. So much so that we can hardly make an impression on anything, particularly the Castle."

27. Penciled on Loorz's letter of September 19, Hearst having returned the original as a reply.

Hearst was actually in Cleveland, Ohio, in early October, not Los Angeles, having throat surgery. 'Twas the season for the movers and shakers to pause a moment and reflect. The following April, Hearst would turn seventy. Morgan, now sixty, had undergone surgery several weeks before Hearst had—in her case for a mastoid condition—at Stanford Memorial Hospital in San Francisco.

During her absence (she last saw San Simeon on August 17), Loorz wrote to the electrician Louis Schallich on September 9: "Will welcome the lady back on the job. Dont seem to realize how important she is until she fails to show up."

Morgan herself wrote an undated letter to Loorz from the hospital, probably a few days later:

> Am having a longer stay than expected,—probably will not see the Hill for two weeks yet,—but maybe at the *end* of two weeks. . . . In their effort to save me, the office only brought up the questions on the West Terrace today—& do hope it has not delayed you.[28]

Apparently it had, though, for in writing to Stolte on September 14 Loorz said, "Boy how I wish she was here. No one to select or approve anything, design or detail or whatnot. It keeps me humping to do some things way ahead hoping I can guess how she will want it."

Hearst was still in residence on September 14; he hadn't left yet for Los Angeles or Cleveland. Might not he have made the selections or given the approvals Loorz sought? The letter Loorz wrote Morgan the next day is illuminating:

> I think he was a little peeved because I did not set up the mantel taken from the North Lower Duplex in the South Upper Duplex.[29] I hesitated because of our conversation up there and knowing that it was too large for such a shallow firebox as we can get there. I wanted him to look at one of the small ones [mantels] that you sent photos of. Since he insists I'm proceeding today which I hope you approve of in this case.
>
> . . . So yesterday afternoon [Frank] Frandolich had little [work] ahead so I had him set up temporarily, one of the small ones in the North Lower Duplex, hoping Mr. Hearst would see it for we believed it to be very good and certainly the correct size. Anyway he saw it and said to set it permanently and wondered why it had not

---

28. Another undated item from this period—a card from Morgan to Hearst—expressed thanks for "the kind telegram and the beautiful flowers." She also told Hearst, "Am coming on finely, although this 'plastic surgery' is not to be forced, it seems,—& at least heard how things were progressing today during a call from Geo. Loorz.—My thoughts cannot ever be very far from the Hill." Hearst Papers, carton 15 (under "Morgan, Julia").

29. The more logical names of these rooms, frequently inverted, are the Lower North Duplex and the Upper South Duplex. In keeping with the symmetrical floor plan in its mid-section, Casa Grande also has an Upper North Duplex and a Lower South Duplex.

been used in the first place. . . . You will please speak frankly to me regarding such action but I feel that my job is to build and finish things even more than just to please. In this case you sent the photos of the small ones and he only carelessly glanced at them so by putting it up he was virtually forced to observe carefully and we're certain he likes it. . . .

Several times he has mentioned or requested changes from things you have approved and when he mentions them to me I tell him what you had planned and explain the reason and nearly always he agrees with your ideas. When he requests these changes of anyone else I usually stall until I can talk with him about them or until I can write and consult you about them. The result is that, though he has never criticized or shown outward displeasure he knows that I consult you before proceeding with anything he requests in connection with architecture.

In time I may lose his confidence because I do not do what he requests immediately and say "Yes" like a parrot. I do it for your sake and for the good of the job for he really asks for more things done than we could do with double the crew. If I kept jumping from job to job as fast as he requested, just to make an impression I would never get anything finished and he repeatedly remarks that he likes to get things finished.

Loorz ended that letter of September 15 with "No doubt you're a bit disappointed in being detained longer at the hospital but it may be just the enforced rest that will do you a lot of real good."

Historically, some real good came of the situation through James LeFeaver, Morgan's office manager and virtual third eye, who soon wrote a key letter regarding this moment in her career. Edward Hussey was the recipient. Hussey was a young architect who in 1926–27 had overseen the construction of Morgan's YWCA building in Honolulu, who had gone from there to another YWCA project in Tokyo, and who now, as part of Bernard Maybeck's camp, was finishing a second year of supervising the Principia College job in Illinois. LeFeaver told Hussey, "Miss Morgan was out of the office for nearly two months and just at that time we were finishing up the 3 Y.W.C.A.s here in San Francisco so I was in the throes of the usual details — only more so." The three buildings were the Chinese Y on Clay Street, the Japanese Y on Sutter Street, and, the most prominent of them, the YWCA "Residence" hotel on Powell Street. LeFeaver also told Hussey about Morgan's current staff, much reduced lately, even with the Hearst work continuing. Ray Carlson, for example — who had helped oversee the Milpitas Hacienda job — was vacationing in Florida and other eastern states. "Only ones left in [the] office are Dick [Nusbaum], Jack [Wagenet], Mrs. [Lilian] Forney and myself." LeFeaver also said that Hathaway Lovell — a former San Simeonite — "is up in the redwood country building an outdoor fireplace for us." The setting was near the town of

Scotia in Humboldt County, where the California Federation of Women's Clubs had commissioned a rustic monument called "the Hearthstone."[30]

Twice in late September, Morgan felt well enough to visit the job at San Simeon by flying in, availing herself of Hearst's plane and pilot on both occasions, both of them Tuesdays. On her doctors' orders she stayed just a few hours each time before being whisked back to San Francisco. Part of the Morgan myth may have sprung from these minor events: that of Morgan the pioneer jet-setter, the architect who raced from one job to the next in her own plane. Morgan's nephew, Morgan North, tried to clarify the matter in *The Julia Morgan Architectural History Project*. In 1974 he told the editor, Suzanne Riess, that Miss Morgan didn't own a plane but rather chartered one "on a steady basis for several years," mainly for covering "Wyntoon and San Simeon and Santa Monica and way points." Despite its air of plausibility, and its grasp of Hearst's dominance, North's assertion is overblown. It sounds levelheaded, though, next to his wife's earlier claim that Julia Morgan had "her own plane and pilot to check on her ever-widening sphere of operations."[31] In

---

30. LeFeaver to Hussey, October 25, 1932; Edward Bright Hussey Collection, Environmental Design Archives. Five years earlier (November 28, 1927), a letter to Hussey in Japan from Thaddeus Joy of Morgan's office showed how much larger her staff had once been. "The office force at present," wrote Joy in San Francisco, consisted of "Miss Morgan, Jim LeFeaver, Harriet DeMari, Mrs. Forney, Eleanor Joy, Elizabeth Boyter, Ray Carlson, Jack Wagenet, Ehrling Olausen, Shirley Davidson, Camille Solon, Dick Nusbaum, Walter Clifford," and Joy himself. The excerpt here (whose commas are mine) is from *The Julia Morgan Architectural History Project*, Vol. II, pp. 75a–75d. The Morgan office made preliminary drawings for the Tokyo YWCA. See Hussey to Morgan, n.d. [July 1927?]; Julia Morgan Collection, Bancroft Library. But Baker, Vogel & Roush of Seattle—for whom Hussey worked in Japan—was the architectural firm of record.

The name "Hearthstone" for the fireplace near Scotia is from Sara Boutelle, *Julia Morgan*, pp. 125–27, wherein the date 1928 is assigned to that job for the women's group. In his letter to Hussey, LeFeaver called the project a "big job"; Morgan paid her sole visit to Scotia late in March 1932. The $943 the job accrued in office expenses in 1932 made it the fifth largest non-Hearst undertaking for the year, surpassed by the three YWCA buildings LeFeaver mentioned and by Principia College; the Monday Club in San Luis Obispo was the sixth largest.

A few months before he wrote to Hussey in October 1932, LeFeaver shared the spotlight with Morgan in this important passage:

Mr. LeFeaver is an ex-engineer who has been Miss Morgan's right hand man for many years and is now her associate. She [Miss Morgan] told me once that she could not possibly have put over what she has without his help. They have done work from Japan to New York [for the YWCA in these two instances] and have had a particularly large experience in what is called "institutional" work, in which class Principia belongs.

From Annie Maybeck (Mrs. Bernard Maybeck) to Frederic Morgan, director of Principia College, May 4, 1932; Bernard Maybeck Collection, EDA.

31. *Morgan Architectural History Project*, Vol. II, p. 166 (for Morgan North's portion). Flora D. North's portion appears in "She Built for the Ages" (*Kappa Alpha Theta Journal*, Spring 1967), p. 11 (reproduced in the *Morgan Project*, Vol. II, p. 170c). See also p. 504 in the present volume, wherein Loorz alludes to his company's use of its own plane and pilot in the 1940s.

any case, the instances in September 1932 of Miss Morgan's trips to San Simeon went unrecorded in her account ledgers: Hearst's arrangements had offset the thirty-five dollars she normally charged for visits involving a long train trip, a stay-over in San Luis Obispo, and related expenses.

It was October 5 (a Wednesday this time, right after a trip to the Beach House) before she returned to the hilltop in her accustomed way, Loorz sharing the good news with Stolte:[32]

> Miss Morgan is here today and though still unwell is very much on her toes and is a great help. Work is rushing at present in a vain effort to get the Roman Pool, showers, lounges etc ready by the 1st of December. We are concentrating on exterior terrace changes etc that should get underway immediately to be cleaned up when the rainy season starts. So you can bet your Uncle Dudley is a busy boy.
>
> Wish I had time to tell you about my hike over thru the mountains to Jolon [on] the other ranch and my visit to the ruins of the old San Antonio Mission and the remnants of its old irrigation system.[33] I enjoyed it immensely although the purpose of the trip was to locate the new road course.

Loorz's outing took him beyond the eight-mile stretch on the Burnett Road that Tieslau Brothers was about to finish. A good deal of cutting, blasting, and grading still lay ahead before the link to Jolon would be complete; that phase awaited the coming season, plus another one after that. Meanwhile, among the jobs on the hilltop that Loorz spoke of, the "exterior terrace changes" pertained to the West Terrace — often called C Terrace today — which Morgan had mentioned in her letter from Stanford Hospital. Some of the palms shipped earlier in the year from San Luis Obispo were earmarked for the West Terrace, to replace its former row of Italian cypresses. But first the terrace was to be enlarged. So much for Hearst's misgivings lately about tackling any new, grand-scale projects in reinforced concrete, a method prone to be an expensive one. The West Terrace warranted a healthy splash of red ink.

---

32. Both the Morgan-Forney account ledgers and the Morgan Collection at Cal Poly cite October 5 (this time the actual date of the visit, not the eve thereof). But Loorz's letter to Stolte, with its clear citing of "today" and its other wording in the present tense, is dated October 4 — a typographical error, undoubtedly.

Morgan stopped twice again at the Beach House in October 1932, in conjunction with visits to the Marion Davies Clinic. Besides the combined visit she'd made on May 19 to the Beach House and the Davies Clinic (as in note 16, above), Morgan also stopped at the Beach House alone on May 3, having been at San Simeon the day before.

33. Mission San Antonio de Padua (founded in 1771) lies a short distance from Hearst and Morgan's Milpitas Hacienda, which, at first glance, is often mistaken for the old mission compound. In 1948 the William Randolph Hearst Foundation provided $50,000 for San Antonio's long-needed repair. Concerning Morgan's possible role in that work — in its proper context of the forties decade — see p. 512 in this volume, note 20.

Loorz told Hearst on October 10 that his crew was almost ready to pour the augmented terrace. The job was going to require lots of gravel. The old gravel bed on the ranch had played out, and Loorz had found a new source at the mouth of Little Pico Creek, just below San Simeon Bay:

> The road formerly used was washed out during the heavy rains last winter and the new bridge will cross it anyway so I asked the State Engineer on the new road if he would not make us a good road down. He gave it promptly and a very good one. I made arrangements with the Road Contractor to scrape up a lot of material with his tractor while there so we will have a supply out of reach of the tides for all of the present needs. With his machine right there it was more economical than using a team for a fairly long haul.

State roadwork of the type Loorz described to Hearst was bringing the twentieth century to the great man's doorstep, after years of isolation for San Simeon at the northwest corner of San Luis Obispo County. Farther up the coast, in adjoining Monterey County (where Hearst's guests had recently picnicked), the roadwork had become one of the most stunning projects in California—the building of the Big Sur portion of the Carmel-San Simeon highway, with all its sweeping curves and daring bridges (epitomized by the breathtaking span over Bixby Creek, just north of Point Sur). It was a project whose rising drama would captivate Loorz over the next few years, culminating in the grand opening of the highway in June 1937.

For now, though, Hearst's Enchanted Hill commanded center stage for Loorz. As he told Hearst in that same letter of October 10, 1932, "If I can continue on this wall [the West Terrace] with the majority of the present crew we should complete the concrete work within four weeks."[34] He did so, through his labor foreman, Frank Souza, whose men used some thirty tons of reinforcing steel in the process.

At least one other big project was under way in these final months of 1932—the completion of the Billiard Room on the ground floor of Casa Grande. This passageway between the centrally placed Morning Room and the Theater, which occupied the north side of the building, had long promised to become the Music Room. Now it was to be completed as the Billiard Room instead. The first step was to install the rare Spanish ceiling Hearst and Morgan had selected for it from a bur-

---

34. Morgan told Hearst a week later, "The new West Terrace boxing and steel work is progressing well,— equal to quite a building really. The sense of space is fine." From Morgan to Hearst, October 17, 1932 (sent to New York, versus another letter she wrote him that day that went to Cleveland, where he was still recuperating from surgery); Hearst Papers, carton 15 (under "Morgan, Julia").

geoning stockpile of antiquarian treasures.[35] Hearst had been gathering centuries-old architectural elements and related objects since the early 1900s; he had done so at a heightened pace, in fact compulsively, ever since he launched San Simeon in 1919; as of 1932, the end of his royal buying spree was nowhere in sight—the Depression be damned. Concerning the Spanish ceiling for the new Billiard Room, Loorz told Morgan on September 8 that W. R. Williams, the manager of the San Simeon warehouses, would find the crates amid the rows and rows of Old World treasures he cared for. "He will open the beam one at least and determine the size so I can put the men on preparing the splices on the ends." In other words, the ancient ceiling required some skillful alteration before it could be installed.

Loorz had told Stolte back on March 12 that it was "almost impossible" to find men who could do the highly skilled work that San Simeon often demanded. But only "almost impossible"—not entirely so. Morgan had the magic touch in recruiting artisans who excelled at these virtually lost trades. For his part, Loorz proved adept at handling these sometimes quirkish, temperamental souls, at coaching these rarest of players and cheering them on to victory.

In writing to Stolte during the fall itself—"October Last" was how Loorz described that year's Halloween Monday—he told his partner about work as well as play. He said in the latter regard, "Gee but the weather has been wonderful here. Went out digging clams yesterday for an hour and got plenty of the large Pismo clams for supper." Radiantly clear and perhaps windless, the Sunday the Loorzes enjoyed on that idyllic, uncrowded beach, with the afternoon tide at alluring ebb, can readily be imagined by all who know the California coast in its autumn prime.

He also said to Stolte, "We are expecting the Chief any day and want to have a few things completed and cleaned up before his arrival if possible for [otherwise] things look messy for him and his guests."

NOVEMBER SAW HEARST returning to San Simeon after his surgery in Cleveland.[36] By the twenty-second Loorz could tell Morgan, "Mr. Hearst looks much

35. The "Barbastro" ceiling (from a town by that name in northeastern Spain); Hearst acquired the ceiling in 1930 through Arthur Byne, an American architect and exporter based in Madrid.

36. *The New York Times* had found the episode newsworthy, printing no fewer than five articles on Hearst's surgery, from his arrival at the hospital in early October until his departure three weeks later. The same paper may have missed its chance to administer the last rites; but before 1932 ended, Hearst was back in *The Times* on another score, by way of its editorial page. With the nation's financial woes in mind, Hearst had sent a "10-point" Christmas message from San Simeon to his own *New York American*. *The Times* quoted the first point on December 27, p. 12 (under "Topics of

better than when he first came back. In fact, I have never seen him looking better. I have conversed with him at length but once and I found him to be in very splendid Humor." Hearst's lilting step may have stemmed from politics as much as from brisker health, at least momentarily. For the Presidency had been captured earlier that month by Franklin D. Roosevelt.

On that same day that Loorz wrote to Morgan, November 22, Hearst sent a long memorandum to Loorz and Warren McClure—better known as "Mac"— a draftsman who, intermittently, had been on the job on Morgan's behalf since 1930.[37] A year older than Loorz (and thus the same age as Marion Davies), Mc-Clure had risen quickly in the eyes of Hearst and Morgan, first by working on the Beverly Hills home of Miss Davies (at 1700 Lexington Road) and then on the Beach House in Santa Monica. That was in 1929. By the winter of 1930, McClure was ready for the ultimate test—San Simeon. He passed, which meant that, for starters, he successfully replaced Hathaway Lovell of Morgan's office as an on-site representative. As best he could at San Simeon, Mac McClure also replaced Thaddeus Joy, Morgan's top draftsman. "Hatch" Lovell and Thad Joy had both served there as on-site men; but Joy, much more than Lovell, had long been indispensable to Morgan on that job and on many others. She so esteemed Joy that his name sometimes appeared next to hers and Jim LeFeaver's on her office letterhead. It was Joy, in fact, who brought McClure to Hearst and Morgan's attention. And then

---

The Times: Precept and Practice"): "Buy American and spend American. See America first. Keep American money in America and provide employment for American citizens."

The high-minded *Times* hastened to pillory Hearst for his simplism—and for what many regarded as his do-as-I-say, not-as-I-do attitude:

> What a refreshing contrast this makes to what one has read about the palatial California residence of a famous American publisher! The magnificent castle does not, alas, represent 100 per cent American employment and wages. American masons, stone-carvers, chimney builders, carpenters, wood-carvers, sculptors, painters and other craftsmen and artists could have easily supplied all the comforts and conveniences that any man could ask for. But the owner chose instead to bring over from every country and every clime not only costly furnishings of every sort, but actual construction material—ancient timbers, old staircases, superb stone fireplaces.

The editorial ignored the art market that had long flourished in New York itself (to Hearst's constant benefit) as much as it did the roles played by Morgan, Loorz, and other "American citizens" in building San Simeon. The parting shot was similar: "Counting the artistic treasures which authentic report ascribes to this American publisher in his other residences and in many storage warehouses, he must have sent out of the country millions upon millions of American dollars."

37. From here on, I'll usually identify Warren McClure either as Mac McClure or, as his friends and colleagues did, simply as Mac—the better to distinguish him from Maurice McClure (cited on page 23, note 10, and mentioned in later chapters as well), a younger man to whom Mac was unrelated.

cruel fate intervened. Joy contracted typhoid on the Beach House job in 1929, as
did McClure and a few others; but Joy was never himself again. By 1932, when
Loorz signed on at San Simeon, Mac McClure was starting his third year as the
sole on-site representative of Julia Morgan. Hatch Lovell had since been reassigned
and Thad Joy had proved unable to continue—in the on-site capacity or in any
other. This sad transition, so unlike the contentious one that saw Loorz replacing
Rossi, has been overlooked, indeed virtually forgotten. What if Joy had stayed active in Morgan's practice? He was only in his mid-forties when stricken. What if he,
rather than McClure, had tackled the new projects that began at Wyntoon in 1933?
Would their outcome have been any different? Would Joy and Loorz have become
the close friends, the confidants, that McClure and Loorz became? Would the
Loorz Papers be the richer for it? Such questions aside, Mac McClure proved a
worthy successor not only to Hatch Lovell but also to Thad Joy. Mac became in-
extricably part of the Hearst-Morgan sphere for many years—and humbly, self-
effacingly so, eluding posterity's prying eyes for a long, long time. Miss Morgan
would have been proud.[38]

A memo like the one Hearst sent Mac and Loorz on November 22 could chain
both men to their writing desks; Mac, it turns out, not just Loorz, was keeping in
close touch with the Morgan office. On August 20, Loorz had told LeFeaver, "Carpenters etc are making real evident progress with ceilings etc but [I] will not go

---

38. Mac's name makes its debut in July 1929 in one of the Beach House accounts (Morgan-
Forney ledgers). His name is absent from the Davies-Lexington account, whereas Thad Joy's name
appears under April and May 1929. But many years later, by his mentioning a "big Beverly Hills"
house, Mac seemed to have been there before going to Santa Monica; see p. 524 in this volume. The
odd thing is that Mac thought Joy died in the early 1930s; see p. 527.

In reality, Thad Joy hung on till 1942, yet in the meantime he "couldn't do any work" for Morgan or anyone else. We owe this excerpt to Alex Rankin, a son of the plumber James Rankin. The
younger Rankin said his brother, James, Jr., and Joy "got Encephalitis at the Chicken ranch" (San
Simeon's poultry unit). James Rankin, Jr., was also incapacitated for the rest of his life, not dying
until 1964. Whether the scourge was in fact typhoid, as Morgan told Hearst on December 30, 1929
(Hearst/Morgan Correspondence, Morgan Collection), and whether the setting was the Beach
House or the Chicken Ranch are questions that need further answering. Both excerpts here are from
Alex Rankin's handwritten memoir (misattributed to James Rankin, Sr.) in the James Rankin &
Sons Records, Bancroft Library.

Hatch Lovell put in many hours at San Simeon from 1927 through 1929, sometimes overlapping with Thad Joy as on-site representative. At one point in that stretch, Morgan explained why she
was using both men in that capacity. (Back then a larger budget afforded more latitude in such matters, but other factors were also involved.) She told Walter Steilberg on October 7, 1928: "T. J. has had
to spend considerable time at S. S. on acct of Mr Rossi's not having been friendly of late—& I've had
to keep Hathaway Lovell there as a companion to TJ [to] keep him from getting dispirited." From a
letter reproduced in *The Julia Morgan Architectural History Project*, Vol. I ("The Work of Walter Steilberg and Julia Morgan," etc.), pp. 61c–61f.

into detail knowing that Mac is again back on the job with his daily reports." Alas, those documents are not among the archival living. Hearst's memo, at any rate, aired several points with the two men, among which were these:

> I do not know about the elephant pond. That is beyond me. I should think an elephant hose [for bathing the elephant] would be pretty good. If we have a puddle of some kind I do not see that it need be ornamental. . . .
>
> Any additions to the Roman pool building are a matter of the distant future. The next building to be built will be the proposed great hall.

Dream on, Mr. Hearst, they must have thought. Hearst closed his memorandum on a more pragmatic note:

> I realize we have bills to pay and that is the reason I want to reach the irreducible minimum point as soon as possible and pay the bills.
>
> We will, of course, keep some men at work during the winter. The unfinished duplexes should be finished, and so should the so-called music room [the Billiard Room].[39]

Julia Morgan was technically the architect, Mac McClure her on-site representative, and George Loorz the construction superintendent. Yet each of them had to be ready at a moment's notice to assume duties above and beyond the usual. It fell to Loorz, for instance, as the 1932 season drew to a close, as Hearst Camp battened down its hatches for a winter recess, to do some financial tallying. On December 12 he wrote to Alexander Sokolow, Hearst's controller in Los Angeles, "One has to be somewhat of a contortionist to keep a completed, balanced record of accounts that are so mixed up as many of these have been but we have a real system and record that is of great value to me as regards to costs and exact information." Make no mistake about it, Loorz would far rather have been pouring concrete (a particular passion of his) than tapping on his adding machine.

Would Loorz be back for another season at San Simeon? Having just turned thirty-four he was hardly ready to retire. And the business he had left behind in Oakland in Fred Stolte's hands was scarcely setting the world ablaze. (Loorz

---

39. Daily reports (like those mentioned just before the Hearst memo) were common to Morgan's distant jobs whose size or complexity required on-site representation. The Honolulu YWCA was among them. It made a devoted writer of Edward Hussey; his typed reports of 1926–27 survive in the Morgan Collection, EDA (under "YWCA Commissions"). In contrast, Mac McClure's San Simeon reports were probably in his preferred longhand. A few others by him from 1943 (mostly concerning Wyntoon) are filed in the Hearst/Morgan Babicora Correspondence, Morgan Collection, Cal Poly; see pp. 490–91 in this volume.

Regarding the November 22 memorandum, a copy of it was sent to Morgan by Joseph Willicombe; it bears a later date, November 28. Hearst/Morgan Correspondence, Morgan Collection.

grossed a mere $140 from the F. C. Stolte Co. in 1932—his earnings in January, before he went to San Simeon. Despite the formal partnership he'd entered into in April, he would have no further income from the company until 1934, when it could afford to pay him $1,100.)[40]

Fortunately, Morgan had reassuring words for Loorz on December 14 of the current year:

> Your vacation plans I am sure will be acceptable, and I will write Mr. Hearst today explaining them, so that you can bring up the details with him as may seem necessary, and you come back when your vacation is over whether any number of men are put on immediately after the holidays or not—as it gives a chance to catch up on detail, as well as to be on hand in emergency.[41]

Loorz stayed on till December 21. The next day he and his family drove to San Francisco (still having to go the long way around, through San Luis Obispo and Paso Robles). Upon reaching the Bay Area, they picked up Loorz's younger

---

40. See note 6, above. Nineteen thirty-three would find Loorz telling a man named C. R. Price, "My business in Oakland certainly died down to a minimum. Here it is May [fourteenth] already and we have done just a little over 20,000 dollars worth of work. In four years [1929 through 1932?], I never failed to average that much every single month." (Loorz was speaking of total construction costs, on which the Stolte Co.'s percentage was based.) And on June 5, 1933, he told his friend Charlie Badley that the company's work "in the past" had amounted to "3 to 500,000 per year" (a reference again to total, percentage-yielding costs).

Loorz supplemented his annual salary at San Simeon in 1933 by monitoring a tide gauge in San Simeon Bay; he earned $149 in his sporadic efforts for the U. S. Coast & Geodetic Survey.

41. Morgan wrote the promised letter the next day. See Morgan to Hearst, December 15, 1932; Hearst Papers, carton 15 (under "Morgan, Julia"). Hearst replied by wiring his approval of Loorz's plans. See Hearst to Morgan, December 17, 1932; Hearst/Morgan Correspondence, Morgan Collection. In contrast, Morgan also told Loorz on December 14 that the artisan John Vanderloo—a favorite of hers whom on March 2 she'd called "a fine youth"—would be returning "on a salary cut," of which Jim LeFeaver could alert Vanderloo "in advance."

LeFeaver broke the news on February 9, 1933, telling Vanderloo that the Morgan office needed "to put all men on the new wage basis":

> Most of the craftsmen had their pay adjusted last year, taking cuts from fifteen to twenty-five percent. In the case of the old employees like yourself, we have put this off as long as possible, but, in fairness to the owner and the other men as well, it will be necessary, as much as we regret it, to put all men on the new scale.
>
> In your own case, we feel that $11.00 per day would be a fair wage. This, plus the meals which you take in camp, will give you a net income of at least $11.40 per day.

Vanderloo Collection (1933 excerpt); all such examples in this volume are courtesy of Judy Bellis, a granddaughter of John Vanderloo. The adjusted wage was on par with what craftsmen like Camille Solon and Frank Gyorgy were earning; it was nearly three times higher than common laborers' wages on the hilltop. Yet it was still a good deal less (by at least $5.00 per day) than Loorz's salary.

brother, Claude. Then they set out for Lovelock, Nevada, their family home, which George hadn't visited since the pivotal year for him of 1928.

Before leaving San Simeon, Loorz had written to Stolte on the twenty-first: "Of course things look dull for you there next year, just as it has to us each year for the past four at this time of the year. Cheer up it cannot last this way forever." Then he told his partner about the trip he'd be making to Nevada and about how Hearst had said he could be gone more than two weeks if he wished. Loorz added, "It certainly has been a pleasure to work with him."[42]

That last line said it all. The 1932 season, like each of its predecessors over the past dozen years or so, had been unforgettable for everyone closely connected with Hearst and his incredible dream at San Simeon.

_____

42. Immune so far to the pay cuts that John Vanderloo and others were sustaining, Loorz had conveyed equally agreeable words to his friend Cliff Bright on June 3, 1932: "I must add that I consider Mr. Hearst personally the most considerate and appreciative employer that I have ever come in contact with."

1933

Brother, Can You Spare a Million?

THE SAN SIMEON of 1932 recalled *The Great Gatsby*—as though in a time warp, to be sure. So did the San Simeon of 1933—but it also foreshadowed *The Grapes of Wrath*. The contrast between those two years was pronounced, especially through the first part of 1933. True, the Depression had nipped at Hearst during 1932. Yet he'd still achieved some spectacular results at San Simeon that year. By the time Loorz got back from Nevada, the Depression was more than just nipping at Hearst; it was threatening to swallow him whole. The Hoover Administration was the lamest of ducks come 1933, and the economy nearly ground to a halt.

Loorz resumed work at San Simeon in the second week of January. Morgan was right in thinking there might be few others on the job for a while; she was also right in assuming Loorz would have plenty to do. Indeed, his letter of January 12 to her second-in-command, Jim LeFeaver, included this paragraph:

> As fast as I get caught up with my paper work here in the office I will personally start doing the many miscellaneous items that have been requested. Then I can work with Marks [Eubanks, the resident electrician] and complete the lighting of the airport when the party leaves and we can be away from the hilltop.

The relocated airport needed another feature besides lights: a hangar. The new season would see its construction, but that episode lay months ahead. Until then, the prospect of putting up a hangar as big as Hearst wanted, some five thousand square feet, would simply have to wait. And who could tell right now when its moment would come—or if it would come at all? Roosevelt had yet to take office, his "Hundred Days" had yet to jump-start the sputtering nation.

LeFeaver got further details in a letter dated January 17. The anticipated calm that Loorz and Eubanks needed for the airport job hadn't descended. "We have been continually hearing that they are leaving," Loorz reported, "even Mr. Hearst said they would be going down [to Los Angeles] soon, but——I've noticed more guests walk across the patio [behind Casa Grande] going to the tennis court this afternoon, than at any time since I returned." The nerve of that man and his friends, Loorz could have muttered; you'd think they would need to get back to MGM or *somewhere*; after all, it's mid-month now; but since it's already Tuesday, they may hang on for the coming weekend . . .

Just the same, January 17 also found Loorz writing to Henry and Gus Tieslau, veterans of the Burnett Road. A jewel-studded castle may have loomed nearby, yet the young builder wasn't about to put on airs. He told the Tieslaus he was "back doing business at the same old peanut stand":

> Been as busy as a fly on a hot skillet even though I have hardly a man to tell what to do. I am Butcher, Baker and Candlestick maker, on the job now. Ray Van [Gorden, the Hearst Camp timekeeper] is away and will be for some time so its up to me, but I like it, no chance to grow stale.[1]

In finishing some of the financial tallying he had wrangled with in December, Loorz compared notes with Jim LeFeaver in San Francisco, who was also counting beans at this juncture—likewise to satisfy Hearst's controller in Los Angeles. In talking shop with Loorz, LeFeaver laughed and said that, of all Morgan's clients, Hearst (through his underlings) was the only one who kept finding discrepancies. Thus went Loorz's description of things for Henry Tieslau on February 6. Hearst's accounting office comprised "about seven men that do nothing but check bills," Loorz also told Tieslau. "The depression is surely on."[2]

Yes, the Great Depression was giving Hearst fits. But certainly not paralyzing him. The new season at San Simeon could therefore get under way soon, although cautiously.

On Monday, February 13, Loorz wrote to the electrician Louis Schallich, who (unlike San Simeon's home-town electrician and maintenance man, Marks Eubanks) was holed up in the Crest Hotel in San Francisco. "Well we are starting up

---

1. From "Burnett Road for 1932" (one of three boxes appended in 1990 to the main body of the Loorz Papers; see p. 26, note 13). "Burnett Road for 1932" also contains items from 1933; Loorz's letter to the Tieslaus (misdated January 17, 1932) is one of several examples.

2. From "Burnett Road for 1932" (see note 1, regarding items from 1933 in this box). Loorz's reference to LeFeaver's humorous side is a prime example of how useful these belated documents of 1990 have proved to be.

More recent insights on the financial side of Hearst and Morgan's association have come from the Morgan-Forney Collection. Portions of that material (concerning Hearst's art and book acquisitions) were at my disposal as early as 1977; but the Morgan-Forney "Distribution of Expenses" sheets and job-by-job account ledgers first came to my attention in 1999. Appendix A on pp. 531–45 is based on the newer material; it shows that Hearst indeed had much to keep track of—much more than any other client of Morgan's.

tomorrow with a small crew of about six or seven men," said Loorz. "The intention is to finish the two [South] Duplexes and the Billiard Room." Unfortunately for Schallich, his services would not be needed just yet. Loorz told him to "keep a stiff upper lip."

That same day, similar tidings went to Los Angeles—to King Walters, who operated a Caterpillar for Tieslau Brothers on the Burnett Road in 1932. "There will certainly be no work on the road before April 1st or 15th," Walters learned from Loorz. "At that time we will likely start up but will use but one cat."

These tidbits of discouraging news paled next to what hit the local area on February 16. A shock wave had been rolling ever since Black Tuesday in 1929, leaving wreckage in its wake. Nationwide, some five thousand banks had failed; the crisis became especially acute in these waning days of Hoover's presidency. Michigan declared a "bank holiday" for February 14. Almost every other state quickly followed suit. It was too late, though, for a little town in California, a town that had long been a sister community to the bayside hamlet of San Simeon on the Hearst Ranch. Loorz gave Stolte the details on February 17:

> The Cambria Bank closed its doors yesterday with a little over $100 of my cash and some $1200 to $1500 of Mr. Hearst's in my name depending upon how many checks issued have gone thru. It certainly did hit the natives here for most of them had a lot of confidence in it and had most of their savings in the bank.

So did "most of the boys on the hill," Loorz said in sharing the same news with Henry Tieslau three days later. Among the bona fide natives, such as the fence builder George Gillespie, several had been in Hearst's employ for many years. Their stability mattered greatly to "the Chief," who was sometimes gone from his ranch for months on end. Indeed, the loyalty and dependability of the local people meant as much to Hearst as his continued solvency—his ability to keep providing work—meant to them. With the failure of the Cambria Bank, hard times now gripped the surrounding area. In speaking of Cambria itself, Loorz doffed his cap in that letter to Tieslau, written on Monday, February 20: "She was certainly a thrifty community up until last Wednesday."[3]

By Saturday the twenty-fifth Loorz had brighter news, much more customary news, which he conveyed to Stolte. "We expect Mr. Hearst with a party of 50 here for the coming week. He will see lots of things that he wants and we no doubt will have to step on things a bit, even if we are right up to the budget at present."

Hearst's visit revolved around the wedding of his third son, John, on March 4. "Talk about an array of new cars, musicians, floral pieces etc.," Loorz wrote that

---

3. From "Misc. 1933" (another of the three appended boxes, as mentioned in note 1).

day to Jack and Irma Hall, some college friends in Berkeley. "I wonder if it really is *wonderful* to be rich."

Stolte, meanwhile, didn't have to wonder for a minute. He told Loorz that same March 4, "Well, we apparently are in the midst of a real tough time and we thought two or three years ago was bad." He went on to explain, "The jobs that we have had are showing a fair profit—about 10% but there is no volume to speak of."

Loorz wrongly assumed that Hearst would want him to "step on things a bit." Hearst returned to Los Angeles soon after his son's wedding, and he called Loorz on March 8, telling him to "cut down to the absolute minimum."[4]

The job limped along for two more weeks; and on March 22 Loorz had these words for Camille Solon, an artisan who lived in the Bay Area town of Mill Valley (and who had many San Simeon credits to his name):

> Suppose you are aware that there is very little doing here at present. The Upper South Dulex is completed and that is all that has been done [thus far in 1933]. I put on a few men about a month ago and have laid most of them off since. I think I have fewer than ten counting laborers and all. It is lonesome around here especially with Mr. Hearst and his guests not here.

Ah, so even when Loorz was chafing to start, say, on the airport lighting, the presence of Hearst and his party was more often a boon than a detriment. Even the much calmer Mac McClure—no back slapper like Loorz—could languish when those people were away. (Two years earlier, Mac wrote to a woman named Julian Mesick, who had long been making architectural models for the Morgan office; he told her with regard to Hearst and The Enchanted Hill, "I am glad he is returning as the presence of guests here is a welcome relief from the lonesomeness of the closed house.")[5]

Hearst came back to San Simeon on March 24. He lost no time in telling

---

4. These were Loorz's words in writing to Jack and Irma Hall for the second time in a week, on March 9, 1933. This time he recounted what Hearst had said "just yesterday."

5. McClure to Mesic (a variant spelling), February 5, 1931; Morgan Collection, Environmental Design Archives. The letter was saved by Mesick, whose surviving papers are part of EDA's Morgan holdings. Miss Mesick's surname usually bears the final *k* in those papers, as it also does in the Morgan-Forney ledgers on San Simeon—in which "Julian Mesick Model" and similar entries appear as early as 1921. Soon after Mac's letter to her of ten years later, Mesick contributed the article "Berkeley Women's City Club" to *The Architect and Engineer* (April 1931), pp. 25–34 (but under Julian C. Mesic). Sara Boutelle believed the correct form was C. Julian Mesic, with the *C* standing for Charlotte; see *Julia Morgan*, pp. 44, 46, and especially 86.

Mesick's article on the City Club (a recent Morgan building) referred on p. 32 to "the fine work Miss Morgan has done at La Cuesta Encantada, San Simeon, California." Mesick quoted Morgan as having told her, "Few *can* have the opportunity of working with real things such as are part of San Simeon, belonging to the best art of the ages."

Loorz more emphatically than ever before that times were bad. Loorz, in turn, lost no time in spreading the latest news among his pen pals the next day. Meanwhile, on the twenty-fourth itself (sometime before Hearst arrived),[6] Loorz wrote to Henry Tieslau in Berkeley; in doing so, he disclosed another factor in the thickened plot:

> We have slowed up to a snail's pace, with but ten men. Mostly because Miss Morgan still is unable to come down and pass judgment upon what she wants done. We made up full sized details etc of everything hoping she would O.K. them and let us go ahead but she still has them [at home in San Francisco].[7]

Although her mastoid operation had been performed six months earlier (and then re-performed in the meantime), Morgan had yet to make a full recovery. All of a sudden, though, her absence seemed immaterial, for Hearst's financial worries took precedence. Thus did Loorz spell things out for Fred Stolte, King Walters, and Henry and Gus Tieslau in the letters he sent them on March 25. The one he wrote the Tieslaus ended with his saying of Hearst, "apparently like the rest of us, his income has hit the toboggan."[8] In the one to Stolte, Loorz included these details:

> Well the hatchet has fallen at last. Mr. Hearst notified me yesterday that I should arrange to complete the rooms I am working in at present as soon as possible and shut the camp down for a couple of months at least. He says times are a little too tough for him to keep on spending as we have been.
>
> So for a while yet I will be here as usual. After that I am not so certain. In any case Fred, because I now have so few men and expect to have fewer for the next

---

6. The afternoon before Hearst left for San Simeon, he had wired similar news from Los Angeles to Miss Morgan in San Francisco. See Hearst to Morgan, March 23, 1933; Hearst/Morgan Correspondence, Morgan Collection, Cal Poly.

7. From "Burnett Road for 1932" (see note 1, above). Several letters between Loorz and Morgan in the first half of 1933 bear the address 2211 Divisadero Street, San Francisco; in fact, that number appears in the Loorz Papers as late as May 1938. However, Sara Boutelle cites 2229 Divisadero Street as Morgan's home address as of the mid-1920s (she also cites 2231 Divisadero as an adjoining house Morgan owned; see *Julia Morgan*, pp. 160–61 and 260, the latter under "c. 1925"). For their part, the Morgan-Forney ledgers list some minor work done at both 2209 and 2211 Divisadero in 1929.

A perusal of San Francisco and of Oakland city directories (the latter because Morgan lived in the East Bay for many years) yields further data; they concern her business addresses and her residential ones also. But the Sanborn maps of 1929 and 1950 throw definitive light on the house numbers on Divisadero Street—numbers, it turns out, that the city changed about 1940.

In sum, Morgan owned a duplex house on Divisadero from the mid- or late 1920s onward. Originally numbered 2211 (2209 was a neighbor's place), the duplex was renumbered 2229 (but not 2231 as well). San Francisco directories give Morgan's address as 2229 for the first time in 1941.

8. From "Burnett Road for 1932." Loorz was hardly going downhill in earning $5,200 per year at San Simeon. Yet he was no doubt careful about whom he told of his good fortune.

few weeks I have taken a reduction in pay which will mean that I will likely not average the $75.00 [per week] which is the mithycal [mythical] amount we hoped for. I took this [pay cut] voluntarily but presume that they would have suggested it sooner or later if I hadn't. $100 per week was certainly too much for so small a crew. . . .

Will let you know as soon as I know definitely what is going to happen. As long as things are as tough as they are there [in the Bay Area] I might even try to work for Mr. Hearst in some other capacity.

Stolte replied in a lighthearted vein on March 27, saying Hearst could "*probably get along* on the building that is finished." But Stolte also said, "Personally I feel that he has been quite a sport to continue up to the present." Loorz and the few others who were still on the payroll undoubtedly felt the same.

THINGS CHANGED BY THE MINUTE with the quixotic, imperious, at times impetuous William Randolph Hearst. They always had; they always would. He soon decided to forge ahead at San Simeon, Depression or no; and by March 31 Loorz had better news for his partner in Oakland:

For the present at least I am definitely located here. I will spend but $4000 or $5000 per month.[9] That means just 10 men with the expensive materials they use. I am to complete two more rooms which will take at least three months, with all of the modeling, casting and figure decorating. I refuse to worry about time beyond that limit, it may never get here. I am assured that I will not be cut below $75 per [week in personal salary], which is quite fair with 10 men.[10]

Loorz also referred to the Victory Highway Garage in Lovelock, Nevada, a building he had figured for the F. C. Stolte Co. in his spare time. (The bid was unsuccessful, yet Loorz was hoping to retain the client's "good will in the home town.")

There was more in that same letter of March 31, providentially more. Acting again on behalf of the F. C. Stolte Co., Loorz had begun figuring some of the latest work that Hearst and Morgan were planning for Wyntoon. San Simeon's counterpart was near the little town of McCloud in northern California, not far from the

---

9. Whence was such money to come, despite its being small change by Hearst's usual standards? At least partly through more belt-tightening in his newspaper operations. As Loorz told a friend named Robert Dorsey on this same date, March 31: "I have overheard him calling his papers in N. Y. and elsewhere, requesting them to cut salaries and reducing the number on their payrolls."

10. Upon going to San Simeon in 1932, Loorz and Stolte agreed that Stolte would draw a weekly salary from the company of $75; Loorz would bridge the gap between his $100 and Stolte's $75 by preparing estimates for jobs. Despite this reference and others Loorz made early in 1933 to his reduced earnings, his tax return for the year indicates he received his full compensation of $5,200.

towns of Dunsmuir and Mount Shasta; the jobsite hugged the forested banks of the McCloud River. Through the four years since 1928, when Loorz built a swimming pool and tennis courts there, further work had been done. The Stolte Co. played a role, and so did Wyntoon's original architect, Bernard Maybeck. Repairs and remodeling began in Wyntoon Castle itself in January 1929, a full year before fire claimed that grand vestige of Phoebe Hearst. Not one to lose momentum, her son turned to The Gables (another of Mrs. Hearst and Maybeck's buildings, which stood nearby), improving that smaller, outlying guest house for short-term purposes. For even before the fire, Hearst had meant above all to enlarge the Castle, had meant to enrich and embolden it beyond anything his mother and Maybeck had done. (As early as February 1929—eleven months before the fire broke out—Hearst announced in a letter to Morgan, with a photograph attached, "Here is the famous Bradenstoke barn, which I hope to use for the dining room at Wyntoon." He discussed the attributes of the barn, adding that he didn't think there was "anything finer of this character to be had in England." The barn dated from medieval times. A kindred item was the Bradenstoke abbey; Hearst owned that as well, but he had other plans for it. "This is not available for Wyntoon," he said of the abbey. "I am using it at St. Donats [in Wales]." The abbey's ceiling beams and rafters remain in that Welsh castle to this day, in a room called Bradenstoke Hall. Its similarities to the Bradenstoke barn recall what Hearst once envisioned for his sylvan stronghold in California.)[11]

But in the Loorz Papers no reference appears just yet to such large-scale work,

---

11. The Bradenstoke excerpts are from Hearst to Morgan, February 23, 1929; Morgan Collection, EDA. The letter is a unique (sole) copy; no carbon copy or transcription exists in the Morgan Collection at Cal Poly or anywhere else. As missing links go in the Hearst-Morgan saga, this one is crucial. Without it, early references by Hearst and Morgan to large-scale work at Wyntoon can be puzzling; so can certain Morgan drawings (and sometimes Maybeck drawings) at EDA and in other hands. Through local publicity and word of mouth, the Bradenstoke barn—more properly the Bradenstoke tithe barn—has long been known to be stored in San Luis Obispo, Alex Madonna (of the Madonna Inn) having bought its crated remains from the Hearst San Simeon warehouses in 1960. Few, though, have known of the key that the tithe barn holds to Wyntoon's past.

Even Walter Steilberg, no stranger to Wyntoon, seemed unaware of any link between the barn and that northern estate—this from an interview with Sally Woodbridge in *The Julia Morgan Architectural History Project*, Vol. I, p. 42. Twenty-two years after Madonna acquired the barn, it figured in a portrayal of St. Donat's Castle, with the author reporting that the barn had "simply disappeared" from England. See Clive Aslet, *The Last Country Houses* (New Haven, 1982), pp. 207–10. The barn has since resurfaced through *Hearst's Other Castle*, by Enfys McMurry (Bridgend, Wales; 1999), pp. 35–37, and through *The Chief*, by David Nasaw (New York, 2000), pp. 403–04—thanks to both authors' having cited San Luis Obispo as the barn's resting place. Yet some confusion stems from their accounts and from Aslet's, mostly nomenclatural. Hearst's letter of 1929 helps clarify things. He spoke of the barn and the abbey separately, inasmuch as each was a discrete part of a larger complex, the Bradenstoke priory. And thus *priory* should not be regarded as synonymous with either of those components.

past or present. For the time being in 1933, Loorz was addressing only one aspect of a project that would soon become as multi-faceted as the work at San Simeon. He put it this way in his letter of March 31 to Stolte:

> I am going over an alteration job at McCloud that we will get if it goes ahead. I'd guess about $20,000. I want to make certain the money will be available. I am now six weeks behind in paying the men and I dont like to mention how many thousands for materials. If it does go ahead Fred I thot you could meet Miss Morgan up there and arrange to handle the work. It will be a rush job and you would have to be there quite a bit yourself, leaving some old reliable like Mr. Carlson,[12] or someone equally loyal and pleasant, and real active [in charge in Oakland]. I will let you know when and if it turns up.

Stolte assured Loorz on April 4 that he would be pleased to work with Miss Morgan at Wyntoon, that he would "make a special effort to make the job easy for her," and that he would hope for the best on Hearst's coming through for all concerned. "Business here is just the same," he added, "a few new beer buffets have come to stay, however I can't figure that people are going to buy much beer at 15¢ per glass." The beer in question was of the 3.2 variety, President Roosevelt having urged its legalization soon after he took office in March. Not until December would prohibition be fully repealed.

Through the rest of April 1933, the subject of Wyntoon is barely detectable in the Loorz Papers. In writing to Morgan on the twenty-second, for instance, Loorz ended by saying, "Mac [McClure] mentions that Mr. Hearst is still quite enthused about Wyntoon. Do hope he meets your present budget before proceeding with it." But little else crops up in this stretch. We can be sure, though, from what had been done "up north" in recent years and from what new approaches were soon taken there that Hearst — and Morgan — were giving it plenty of thought.[13]

IN THE MEANTIME, the Billiard Room and the South Duplexes, especially the Lower South Duplex, saw continued work at San Simeon. These rooms fairly dom-

---

12. Ray Carlson, an architect for many years in Morgan's office (first mentioned on p. 39 in this volume), is also mentioned in later chapters. But he most likely was not the "old reliable" that Loorz spoke of here.

13. The Morgan-Forney ledgers include an account called "Wyntoon new" that began in April 1933; coincidentally, its earliest entry bears the same date as Loorz's letter to Morgan: April 22, a Saturday. The account cites $40 in drafting expenses for the six-day workweek that ended then. These renewed efforts, possibly intermittent, were made in behalf of Wyntoon Castle. For the week ending on April 29, the new account shows initial costs similar to the first week's: another $40 in drafting-room time and $25 for Walter Steilberg's engineering services. (An earlier, separate account called "Wyntoon Castle (new)" had started in February 1929 and had resumed after the fire of January 1930; it lapsed after September 1932 but then gained a belated, final entry in June 1936.)

inated the periodic consultations between Loorz and Morgan, according to each "Recapitulation of Architect's Interview" he compiled. Loorz also typed out notes and questions in advance for Morgan. For her visit of April 10, for example, he submitted this question: "Just how much do you wish the decorators to do in livening up the antique ceiling of the Billiard Room?"

Her answer in part, as Loorz recorded it, was to "do more antiqueing on woodwork of panels and beam soffits before going ahead with any more decorating on the new section of the ceiling." She had more to say about the same matter on April 27: "Continue cracks in ceiling beam sides thru patches at ends so as to match in character the original beam sides." No such detail was too trifling to be considered. (Nor were certain other details overlooked. Hearst's seventieth birthday was about to fall with perfect timing on Saturday, April 29; and Loorz spent $13.33 on a covered wagon for the Old West costume extravaganza, of which the Chief and Miss Davies would be the hosts.)

After the first of those two visits by Morgan, Loorz wrote on April 15 to Camille Solon, the artisan from Mill Valley whom he'd been in touch with a few weeks before. Solon had been the chief designer of the mosaic tile work for the indoor Roman Pool, which was now completed, and he was eager to see the building. Loorz knew, though, that Solon was none too keen about bumping into Hearst:

> He is here at present and may be for a long time but you know he is not around until afternoon and you could have most of your *snooping* completed by the time he gets around. . . .
>
> The pool is still clear but not quite as nice as last week. We have to date added thirteen tons of salt and have five more to add later. At first the salt made it a bit dirty but it is now clearing up again. Who said we couldn't have ocean water without waiting years for the proposed pipe lines from San Simeon?[14]

The water in the Roman Pool may have been clearing, but the eighteen tons of salt soon played havoc with the plumbing system. It had to be revamped entirely. Tons of salt were also added to the outdoor pool in 1933. Hearst was about to re-

---

14. Although the pipelines were never installed—and despite Hearst's reverting to fresh water for the Roman Pool—a story long endured that the pool was filled with seawater pumped five miles uphill from the Pacific.

In writing to the plumber James Rankin a year earlier (April 7, 1932), Loorz said this about the Roman Pool: "Miss Davies is still asking for salt walter, what have you heard? The chief has not made a formal request for it." But Hearst did so by the first part of 1933. His secretary, Joseph Willicombe, pursued the matter and learned it would take half again the eighteen tons that apparently got used—an eye-smarting "27 tons of salt to turn a 200,000 gallon pool of fresh water into sea water." See H. O. Hunter to Willicombe, January 24, 1933, plus its attachment of the same date, sent by the Leslie California Salt Co. to Hunter; Hearst Papers, carton 17 (under "1933 Samples").

model that pool at the northwest corner of the estate—a job that would yield the dazzling Neptune Pool—now that the indoor Roman Pool was completed. (He had avoided working on both pools concurrently so that he and his guests could always swim in one or the other.) As Loorz said in some notes he made on the outdoor pool, "Pool pipes were not originally intended for salt water and will corrode. As pool will be changed this may not matter."[15]

James Rankin, a sub-contractor from Oakland in charge of plumbing at San Simeon, was an old and very close friend of Loorz's and a fellow member of the Exchange Club in that Bay Area city. Loorz wrote to him on April 18:

> Well no doubt Alex [Rankin, one of Rankin's sons] is keeping you posted on the job. Some crew with about nine men total. I thot you would be down roughing in [the plumbing] for the bedrooms upstairs over the Billiard Room by this time.[16] I asked the lady [Miss Morgan] about it last week. . . . She said, "Oh that won't be ready for a long time and I'm not quite sure the arrangement Mr. Hearst wants." She added that she would take it up with him on her next visit. I again reminded her about it in my written notes and she answered that she'd see him soon. If you chance to be talking to her just cry a little bit about hard times and she'll let you come on down for a little vacation.

Hard times at San Simeon—the idea is almost too improbable. Yet compared with the high-flying 1920s, when Hearst's monthly budget often ran in the tens of thousands, these *were* hard times.

Nonetheless, Hearst had recently approved the resumption of work on the Burnett Road. Henceforth, the work would be done directly under Loorz, rather than by contract with Tieslau Brothers, although Henry Tieslau would be part of the new crew. So would King Walters and one or two others from the previous year. Loorz wrote to Walters in Los Angeles on April 26:

> This is the brief fact. If you can move just $3/4$ as much dirt per hour as you moved last year the net cost to me will still be cheaper than Henry's net cost last year. Counting what Henry made you only have to move $1/2$ as much dirt per hour to make the same net cost to me.
>
> At the same time you personally will make more than you did. You will have a lot nicer job, fewer worries and have a hell of a lot more time to visit with me and hoist a few beers occasionally.

---

15. From "Items to Consult with Mr. Hearst," a list dated June 21, 1933. Several other lists and memos like this one are filed in the Loorz Papers with the "Recapitulations" Loorz compiled of his meetings with Morgan.

16. There are three such bedrooms, stacked one above the other; along with the Billiard Room itself they form the Billiard Room Wing. But this four-story unit is not so much a wing, properly speaking, as a perpendicular link between the central part of Casa Grande and its Recreation Wing (or New Wing, as that north section was later renamed).

But the hard times were far from over in these first months of the new Roosevelt Administration. On May 5, a man in San Francisco named Oliver Sjoberg told Loorz, "You are quite right in saying that the contracting business is in the doldrums." Sjoberg also remarked, "It goes without saying that jobs are being taken at ridiculous prices and in the main by contractors who just have to take them in order to keep the creditors away."

Hard times had set in closer to home, too. May 6 found Loorz answering a letter from a desperate man—Ernest Baumgartner—whom everyone called "Baum" and who lived in Cayucos, a town midway along the coast road between San Simeon and San Luis Obispo:

> I regret to state that it is positively impossible for me to employ any more workmen at this time. When and if things open up a little later on it may be possible to give you some kind of work.
>
> I was talking over the contents of your letter with some of the boys [in Hearst Camp] and they were very anxious to help you over the tough spot you seem to be in.
>
> I enclose herewith $15 in cash with which we hope you will be able to have your lights hooked up and purchase fuel. We are having a small supply of staple foods set up and are sending them to you by courtesy of Ed Harkins of the Valley & Coast Transit Co.
>
> We will still have on hand a balance in the fund with which we will send another grocery order at a later date. If you are in greater need of something we have not considered kindly let me know at once.

The Loorz Papers contain receipts from Sebastian Bros., the cracker-barrel store still operating in San Simeon today, for the first shipment to Baum and his wife. The grand total came to $6.82, roughly a day's wages for a skilled worker lucky enough to be on Loorz's current payroll.

The money and groceries soon arrived in Cayucos; and thus May 7 found both the Baumgartners writing notes of thanks to Loorz and "the boys." Baum's wife said, "The $15 looked as big to us as $500." She also said that she and her husband had been "without the greatest necessity for 4 days—bread!" Their words were heartfelt, and no doubt tearful.

JULIA MORGAN was at San Simeon on Saturday, May 6, the same day Loorz wrote to Ernest Baumgartner. She left Loorz with a "Probable Summer Program," which included "Fall and Winter possibilities." Her list must have made his head spin. It called for the completion not only of the Billiard Room and the Lower South Duplex but also of Hearst's private Gothic Study—destined to be the innermost sanctum in Casa Grande. In addition, Loorz was to "have all materials on hand to begin [remodeling the] outside pool with fairly large crew on about September 1st and perhaps continue work thru winter to have [the pool] ready for first warm weather of spring following." And he was to "build necessary concrete walls of new extended East Terrace [behind Casa Grande], fill and move oaks from proposed site of Great Hall, to have site ready for actual work on Hall next year." The hard times seemed to be softening for Hearst.

Loorz, with his wife and their two sons along for the ride, had recently driven Hearst's new Cadillac convertible into San Luis Obispo to be worked on. He related the story to his parents on May 8, telling them how he and his family froze going home since the top was down and evidently couldn't be put up:

> However, the history of that car is interesting since it was a personal gift to Mr. Hearst from Arthur Brisbane a few months back. They went back thru the woods here with one of Mr. Hearst's old cars and it got hot and wouldn't pull. After many trials Mr. Hearst said angrily to my chauffeur, "Tell Mr. Loorz to buy some new Fords and Chevrolets that can climb these rough roads without stalling." Brisbane was present and the next day when he went thru L.A. he bought this Cadillac and had it driven here to Mr. Hearst.

Loorz got busy with his latest assignment, backed by Hearst's revolving fund for San Simeon.[17] "Personally would prefer to buy good condition second hand car," he noted on a list he submitted Hearst. "One very fine looking 1929 Buick can be had for $300 cash in San Luis. It is a large seven passenger car and they are willing that we put it to [the] test over the picnic roads."

"*Get it,*" Hearst scrawled in the margin.

---

17. Sometimes called the Sokolow Account or, more often, the Hilltop Fund, it was established in 1932. Its long list of disbursements in 1933 ranged from the Burnett Road project to the covered wagon for Hearst's recent birthday party.

A separate, larger fund was more closely associated with Morgan's work at San Simeon. Known by such names as the Hearst Fund, the Hearst San Simeon Fund, the Hill Construction Fund, and still others, it either supplanted the Regular Fund of recent years (see pp. 28–29, plus their note 17) or was synonymous with it. Specific information on its workings is spotty, but a good deal of circumstantial data exist. Suffice it to say that in this volume, Hearst Construction Fund will be the name it goes by.

Morgan's well-known tallying in the 1940s of the construction costs at San Simeon since 1919 (analyzed much later in these pages) is, for the most part, a tallying of the Hearst Construction Fund. It's much harder to determine Morgan's stake in the Hilltop Fund, which may have supplanted the Special Fund (p. 29, note 17) and whose disbursements fell mostly outside her sphere. On August 1, 1933, for example, Loorz weighed her concerns about Hilltop Fund expenditures for the previous seven months: of $19,334 spent since January 1, she thought that $488 of the outlay might properly belong on her list of expenditures (and that her commission—a nominal $41 in this case—would thus be applicable). But as much as $18,846 for the January-July period was beyond her concern.

FRESH PROSPECTS FOR WYNTOON blossomed abundantly that spring. Loorz briefed Stolte on Monday, May 8—the same day he wrote to his parents about the faulty Cadillac:

> Mr. Hearst is here most of the time and keeps everyone on their toes all the time. Time does not drag on one's hands. They have continued to hash over developments at Wyntoon until they now have sketches, plans and exteriors of quite a large New Castle. He says it is nearly finished and that they can plan on starting the engineering drawings within the week and hopes to get started up there in about a month.
>
> It now looks more like $300,000 than the $20,000 I talked about before. I dont know whether that will eliminate us or not. They may want to do it like here [acting as their own general contractor] but I dont think so. At best I dont believe he would spend more than $30,000 this summer up there. That would be one unit, the dining room, living room & kitchen only. However, as always, no telling how many times it will change before going ahead if at all.

Loorz was paying close attention to the scale of the pending work, what with the original figure having increased more than tenfold; $300,000, with all it implied in personnel, equipment, insurance, and other operating costs could indeed "eliminate" many a prospective builder. As for Hearst and Morgan's consideration of an overall, general contractor (like the F. C. Stolte Co.) for an expanded program at Wyntoon (unlike the independent approach at San Simeon, long-established there), Morgan's recent health problems may have become a factor. San Simeon had always saddled her with excessive responsibility; a bigger program at Wyntoon on the same terms may simply have posed too great a burden, at least for now. Loorz went on to tell Stolte on May 8:

> I understand that his business has picked up quite a little and that may cause his income to increase until he can actually go ahead up there.

With that last sentence, did Loorz have Hearst's newspapers and magazines in mind? Or was he alluding to his land holdings, his mining interests, or some other component of the man's empire?[18] Few if any archives, no matter their origin or the

---

18. The success of the movie *Gabriel Over the White House*, made through Hearst's Cosmopolitan Productions, is one example of how conditions may have improved lately for Loorz's patron. In researching his biography of Hearst, David Nasaw found that *Gabriel* was amply profitable. See *The Chief*, pp. 463–66.

Meanwhile, a distinct tone of optimism appears in correspondence from this part of 1933, from this period of Roosevelt's "Hundred Days"—both in some of Loorz's letters and in certain others. On March 20, soon after the inauguration, Loorz told his parents, "I hope you two are enjoying the actions of the new boss Roosevelt. I hope he only keeps up just as he has started. Everybody around here is hopeful and that alone is half the battle. I look for better times before the close of

subjects they cover, are truly exhaustive. As richly detailed as the Loorz Papers are, they leave plenty of questions unanswered. Even with thousands of such documents at hand, one might hunt till doomsday for a letter or other item that illuminates a given point or validates a certain idea, only to come up empty. Better to let an archives disclose what it will, according to its own logic, than to yearn for what it *ought* to contain.

Loorz wrote to Morgan on May 8 as well. He mentioned her visit of Saturday the sixth. "Hope you arrived home feeling none the worse for a long strenuous day. It certainly kept you at your wits end for a real continued stretch." And then came this passage:

> I do hope the determined fight you are putting up has more advantageous effects than evil regarding your complete recovery. At the same time I hope you are planning in some way to get working drawings out promptly on Wyntoon so that you can at least collect for some of the efforts you are extending. This may sound monetary and cold blooded but there are hundreds of us who do receive compensation for our efforts, so why shouldn't you?

Apart from the distinction between "working drawings" and less remunerative work, Morgan may have had Loorz believing that Hearst wasn't paying her fairly. If so, she was purposefully keeping her young associate in the dark about her finances, just as she had always kept her friends and colleagues guessing. This gentlewoman of the old school would have it no other way. It was quite enough for Lilian Forney, her secretary (who was sworn to secrecy), to know how solvent the Hearst accounts had made Miss Morgan, right into these Depression years; Jim LeFeaver was also trustworthy. (And as for Hearst and *his* trusted secretary, Joseph Willicombe — they would never tell.) But almost no one else was to know. Not even

---

the year." Two months later, Jim LeFeaver sounded upbeat (and a bit tongue-in-cheek, as he often did) in writing to Elizabeth Boyter in New York, a young woman formerly in the Morgan office: "From the newspapers, we understand that things are picking up, so inasmuch as the East is always affected first, we imagine by this time you are beginning to sit pretty." LeFeaver's letter contained some other passages worth mulling over:

> All that are left of the "headquarters force" are Jack [Wagenet] and Dick [Nusbaum] and Mrs. Forney and myself. . . . Furthermore, we have reduced our office space to the status of 1920 [before the Hearst work proliferated] and we still have more space than we need. That's how busy we are.
>
> Miss Morgan is picking up strength gradually, but still does not come to the office. However, she does considerable work at her home [on Divisadero Street], and takes an occasional trip to San Simeon.

From LeFeaver to Boyter, May 22, 1933; Elizabeth M. Boyter Papers, Bancroft Library.

Morgan's sister, Emma, or their two living brothers. Or any other family members, like Emma's son, Morgan North, who later admitted that he and his wife, Flora, knew little about the subject. No, not even Bernard Maybeck or Walter Steilberg or Thaddeus Joy or George Loorz, no matter how esteemed they were in Julia Morgan's eyes. She was simply that private, that circumspect, that firmly disciplined a person. Herein lie antecedents of the Morgan myth: regarding the underpaid architect or even the unpaid architect, especially where the incorrigible Hearst was concerned. The truth is almost always otherwise. Three worn and frayed loose-leaf binders—the Morgan-Forney account ledgers—are finely detailed enough to prove it.[19]

Hearst's burgeoning plans for Wyntoon in 1933 filled Loorz with anticipation. Charlie Badley, a Phi Kappa Tau fraternity brother from Loorz's college days at Berkeley, was one who got an earful from his old friend. "Six weeks with them is usually several months. If he starts the big job up there after these small alterations and we are lucky enough to land it, it will be good for a long time to come, perhaps as long as weather permits, for the next three years."

That was on May 10, a day that found Loorz writing to Harry Thompson as

---

19. Once more in such matters, Walter Steilberg played the inadvertent culprit; similar roles fell to Morgan North and his wife, Flora, along with others who gave interviews in the 1960s and 1970s. (Several of these people were old and forgetful by then.) The stage for this retrospective drama was *The Julia Morgan Architectural History Project*; its two volumes from 1976 are likely to remain biblical for all time. To cast doubts on those books is often to verge on heresy; to leave them unquestioned is to pursue no greater knowledge of Hearst and Morgan. But to cite chapter and verse here— Steilberg said this, Morgan North thought that— could put even a zealous truth-seeker to sleep.

Morgan got paid by Hearst, and she got paid well, albeit tardily in many instances. A full auditing of the Morgan-Forney ledgers lies far beyond the scope of this book on the Loorz Papers. But pending that, some Morgan-Forney data can be cited for the San Simeon job of 1932 and 1933. In 1932, Morgan billed Hearst $20,060 through her Commission Account (reflecting 8.5% of construction costs on that job). She received $18,520—sporadically. Some of those payments stemmed from pre-1932 billings; at any rate, Hearst was at least $1,540 off the current pace when 1932 ended. In 1933 she billed him for $15,891 and received $19,615. The total for the two years combined: $35,951 billed, $38,135 received (see Appendix B on pp. 546–50). Over those twenty-four months San Simeon prompted Morgan's accrual of $30,694 in drafting-room and other operating costs (see Appendix A on pp. 531–45). For her to prosper, her commission earnings had to exceed those expenses. And they did. Hearst's payments during that period kept her $7,441 in the black.

Granted, this is simplistic, incomplete accounting. Other factors need to be reconciled, such as "refunds" (Hearst's reimbursements for out-of-pocket and certain other expenses Morgan had borne). In 1932 she was refunded $1,818 with regard to San Simeon and in 1933 $1,582. That put $3,400 back in her pocket.

In their handling of Wyntoon in 1933, they got off to what for them was a good start. Morgan started billing Hearst in June for her commissions on the new work. Six weeks later he paid 8.5% ($535) on the initial vouchers she submitted (for $6,298 in construction costs to date).

well. Thompson, a Stolte carpenter who had worked at San Simeon in 1932 under Loorz, had just been chosen to be foreman at Wyntoon—namely, on the "small alterations" that Loorz mentioned to Charlie Badley and that the F. C. Stolte Co. had been awarded and was about to begin:

> Harry this little job is not much in itself but I have a lot of hopes for better things. As it now stands they have not told me that we will get the big job that they have recently designed for up there. However, Mr. Hearst seems anxious to get started upon it and has even made motions toward raising the funds. I feel certain that some work will begin on it before the summer is out.
>
> You can help a lot by getting this [small] job done in a hurry. That is what Mr. Hearst wants. He wants to go up there with a party [an entourage] as soon as possible and at present there are not enough accommodations for his guests. Do your best to satisfy.
>
> The people in charge up there, Mr. & Mrs. Boss [E.E. and Fanny], are not particular friends of Miss Morgan, or Mr. LeFeaver but I believe she is some distant relative of Mr. Hearst's,[20] and I hope you will endeavor to make them your friends. Do any little thing you possibly can for them and they will return all favors and will prove to be invaluable help to you. Miss Morgan's office may instruct you to take advantage of anything they have there [that] you can use but please ask the Bosses anyway. Theres nothing they wont do for you if they like you and nothing they wont do to trouble you if they dont. He especially is very wonderful.
>
> You know *Mac* McClure the architect who was here. He is in S.F. now completing the drawings as Mr. Hearst had him sketch them here. He will be up there on the big job and might be sent up on this small one. In any case do whatever he asks and promptly. I believe Mr. Hearst likes him better than anyone in Miss Morgan's office and he knows Mr. Hearst's likes and dislikes best. Of course, you would do this in any case and [also] would if another representative was sent up there. I dont think Mr. Joy is physically able to go up there again.

What rousing words in behalf of Mac McClure. And what sad ones regarding Thad Joy. (Early in 1932 Morgan had told a former employee, "Mr Joy came back with the New Year, but we all see he cannot take hold—It is a serious and very wor-

---

20. The common ancestry between Fanny Boss and W. R. Hearst was, in his case, four generations removed: he had great-great-grandparents on the maternal side named Hill. (The Hills begat Ruth, who begat Drusilla, the mother of Phoebe Apperson Hearst.) Ruth Hill apparently had a brother from whom Fanny (Hill) Boss was descended. In the best tradition of shirttail relatives, Mrs. Boss had a brother named George, a sister named Drusilla, and another sister named Phoebe, who in girlhood was a ward of Phoebe Hearst. The Hill descendants—especially Phoebe Hill, a teacher in adult life—figure in the Hearst Papers. See also *The Hearsts*, by Judith Robinson, pp. 27, 28.

rying problem.")[21] Loorz closed by wishing Harry Thompson the best of luck. As things turned out at Wyntoon in 1933, Thompson would need it.

From San Francisco on May 12, McClure contributed the first of his many letters to the George Loorz Papers. His clear, graceful script is always a thing of beauty; and the insightful, often animated details he conveyed are usually to be savored to the last word:

> We are still "Wyntooning" on a big scale. I have been busy getting the plans into shape and tomorrow there will be a gathering at the site of Miss Morgan, Steilberg, Huber, Rankin, various sub contractors and me. I am going up with Rankin. J.M. goes on the train tonite. . . .
>
> LeF[eaver] told me that it was impossible for the "office" to stand the expense of the various Castle projects' plans without some payment and that he would have to collect for the Arizona [Grand Canyon] house — etc.[22] Also

---

21. Morgan to Elizabeth Boyter, from the same undated letter (postmarked January 18, 1932) as on pp. 18–19, note 4; Boyter Papers, Bancroft Library. On May 29, 1931, Morgan had told another former employee, Bjarne Dahl, that Joy was "in bad shape still"; as quoted in Boutelle, *Julia Morgan*, p. 245, note 6.

22. The key thing here may be Mac's use of "etc." — as in other Hearst projects. (The very next day, May 13, Morgan received a final payment of $4,111 on one of the Beach House accounts; but Hearst still owed her $4,204 on the Marion Davies Clinic, a job finished late in 1932.) Concerning the Arizona work, Morgan billed (and received) $27 for what she called "Prints" (probably blueprints) of the "Grand View Hotel." These scribbles of hers, identified as "June 1933," command no account sheet of their own in the Morgan-Forney ledgers; they appear in an odd place instead: added to a sheet compiled in 1930 for the "San Simeon Poultry Units." A further oddity is that the $27 appears on Morgan's Distribution of Expenses sheet for 1933 as twenty-seven cents. Such discrepancies are rare.

By 1933 Hearst had owned property on the south rim of the Grand Canyon, near Grandview Point, for twenty years. The old Grand View (or Grandview) Hotel had come with the property, as had the Summit Hotel. But he and Morgan had built little of their own nearby except for a cabin in the Craftsman style, as early as 1914. A few items in the Morgan Collection pertain to a "Hopi House" and may be more indicative of what he was planning by the 1930s. Hearst wrote to Morgan in that regard on March 22, 1926 (see Nancy Loe's *Descriptive Guide to the Julia Morgan Collection*, p. 62); two sketches of such a house are also extant (*Descriptive Guide*, p. 82); however, nothing concerning construction appears in the Morgan-Forney data of 1924–40 before 1936 — aside from the $27 (or 27¢) for 1933. In addition, 1933 found Alexander Sokolow writing to a colleague about the Grand Canyon:

> I told Mr. Hearst that I would like him to confirm the expenditure of $1700 for improvements and additions [to existing buildings], as requested by Mr. [R.P.] Gilliland [the caretaker]. Mr. Hearst said he could spend up to $2500, if necessary, for improvements and betterments. He said he did not agree with Mr. Gilliland that he could build a new place for between five and six thousand dollars; that it would probably run into seven, eight or nine thousand, and he did not see the necessity for a new place now.

From Sokolow to [H. W.] Langman, September 12, 1933; Hearst Papers, carton 46 (under "Misc., 1933" [as distinct from "Misc. 1933" in the Loorz Papers]).

one reason for my leaving [San Simeon] was to prevent Mr. H. making further changes. However I'll wager that Mr. H. will continue making plans and changes either with or without me! I can't see what "expense" is entailed except my salary.

That must have been quite a meeting of the minds at Wyntoon—the architect Julia Morgan, the architect-engineer Walter Steilberg, the engineer Walter Leroy Huber, the plumber James Rankin, and the draftsman Warren McClure (for "Mac" was not an architect, despite Loorz's having called him that in his letter of May 10 to Harry Thompson).[23] And whether it was the "small job" or the "big job"—or both jobs—that occasioned that meeting can best be answered by the Loorz Papers. We can turn, for instance, to the letter Mac McClure sent George Loorz from Wyntoon on May 22, 1933:

> There is quite a lot of new sash and frames, a Colonial entrance door, 4 wood mantles, stair rail, and a lot of pilasters and panel mold to dress up the interiors. Miss M. seems to be a trifle afraid it may cost too much and is putting brakes on a little. Mr. H. asked her if it would cost under 5 or 6000 [dollars]. There are 4 new baths as well as a lot of fireplaces etc. Perhaps it can be done.

Mac was describing River House, which dated from the turn of the century. Its remodeling, along with that of some nearby but unnamed buildings, represented the "small job." River House stood on the portion of Wyntoon called the Waterhouse property (named for Clarence P. Waterhouse, whose heirs had sold the parcel to Hearst in 1931). The Waterhouse property was on the McCloud River, just upstream and across the river from The Gables—and from the site of Phoebe Hearst's original Wyntoon Castle of 1902–03.

References to the "big job," meanwhile, can be detected between the lines further on in that same letter Mac wrote to Loorz on Monday, May 22:

> I called on J.M. at her house [in San Francisco] Saturday and heard a lengthy and confused account of [her] San Simeon trip. [She had been there on Thursday, May 18.] Apparently W.R.H. is undecided and vague about building here and apparently left her discouraged. However Steilberg and Wagonet [Jack Wagenet] are to make the drawings and I am to stay here at Wyntoon probably until the job is finished. That is O.K. with me as it is at least a "change" here if not very lively. At least I will have my Sundays—perhaps.

---

23. In writing to Stolte, likewise on May 10, Loorz said, "If the architect 'Mac' McClure goes up on the job as Miss Morgan's representative it will be fine. He knows Harry's work from down [here] and admires the speed and determination with which Harry goes at his work."

Mac got some free time, for he soon told Loorz (in a letter dated June 5) that he had taken "several long trips into Oregon." But he also said, "while I like the country up here, I prefer San Simeon, my first love."

Loorz, meanwhile, answered Mac's letter of May 22 on Saturday the twenty-seventh:

> I believe Mr. Hearst misses you and the Wyntoon sketches for he comes in my office a lot now and of course we have such a little to talk about except figures and facts which soon gets tiresome. . . .[24]
>
> Yes Mr. Hearst did send Miss Morgan away feeling rather discouraged about the [big job at] Wyntoon last week [May 18] but I believe most of his anger was because she told him how tough the excavation etc were [going to be] if they built the building where it was originally located.[25] She suggested moving it forward [closer to the river?] and he seemed peeved about it. After he thot you had worked it out to the best advantage for excavation to have her tell him how much it really amounted to hurt just a little.

The Wyntoon sketches Mac had done for Hearst at San Simeon were for the big job, not for the small one. The latter, in fact, would soon be finished under Harry Thompson, the foreman for the F. C. Stolte Co. And it was the big job that Loorz and Stolte, too, anxiously awaited word on, the partners having prepared a "preliminary estimate" of the "Bedroom Wing." Loorz sent their estimate to Morgan on May 31, right after her visit of May 28. That one wing alone—conceived as a concrete structure four stories high—would need 125 tons of reinforcing steel and would take twenty-two weeks to excavate and pour. The estimate also addressed the 190 windows and the 200 doors the plans called for. But the estimate made no allowance for "plastering as concrete is to be allowed to set for some time before plastering (none this year)." Nor did it allow for "painting, plumbing, electrical, heating, mantels, fixtures, decorating and furniture." The "tentative" costs were left untallied, but we can readily add them up: $64,405, most of which applied purely to rough structural work. The big job was going to be very big indeed.

The projected cost of $64,405 was as competitive as Loorz and Stolte could make it. To put that figure in perspective: the two men had recently been awarded the Walter E. Buck house for $80,000, on which their profit would be minimal (and

---

24. Loorz's office, in the southeast corner of the Recreation Wing (first-floor Theater level), was different from the Architect's Office, a plain wooden structure that adjoined the opposite Service Wing of Casa Grande.

25. Two readings are possible. By "originally located," Loorz meant either the placement of the building on previous blueprints and drawings or the actual site of the old Wyntoon Castle that burned in 1930.

on which their carpenters would have to work for as little as four dollars a day). The Buck house was a mansion in the exclusive Bay Area community of Woodside, near Palo Alto, and the F. C. Stolte Co.'s rock-bottom, Depression-harried figure covered everything from excavation to interior finish.

What exactly *was* this big job at Wyntoon, this job for whose bedroom wing the concrete work alone would cost that much? The Loorz Papers fail to say, probably because Hearst finally had to abandon the big job in favor of more affordable work; and that moment of finality lay close ahead. Yet some version of the job had been in Hearst's mind since at least 1924, when he gained title to Wyntoon and had the engineers Hunter & Hudson prepare measured drawings of his mother's castle. Of course sketches and drawings had also been done by Morgan over the ensuing years (and at times by Maybeck, who by 1933 had dropped from the Wyntoon annals).[26]

Hearst's collecting had been a factor, too. In 1925 he bought a medieval Spanish building—the monastery of Sacramenia—from Arthur Byne, an American architect-antiquarian who, from his base in Madrid, had been dealing with Hearst and Morgan, plus other wealthy Americans and their designers, for several years. Then came Hearst's acquisition of an English tithe barn—the Bradenstoke barn —from sources in Britain. In 1930 he bought another Spanish monastery from Arthur Byne, known as Alcantara; and in 1931 he bought a third medieval building from Byne, the monastery of Santa Maria de Ovila. Walter Steilberg went to Spain in 1931 on Hearst and Morgan's behalf to help Byne export selected portions of Santa Maria, stone by stone, an effort superseding the earlier Alcantara purchase

---

26. The Hunter & Hudson drawings, dated May 1924, are in the Morgan Collection, EDA. This same Morgan Collection contains sketches and drawings of pre-1933 Wyntoon; so does the Bernard Maybeck Collection at EDA; similar items, some in Maybeck's hand, are in the Hearst Castle Archives, San Simeon. However, Maybeck's role in the Wyntoon of 1924 to 1933 is harder to pin down than Morgan's. The Maybeck Collection has much less on this subject (or on the Wyntoon of Phoebe Hearst's era) than it does, for example, on Principia College. In turn, Sara Boutelle's *Julia Morgan* doesn't delve much into this aspect of Maybeck, either; nor does Sally B. Woodbridge's *Bernard Maybeck: Visionary Architect* (New York, 1992). Both authors steered clear of Morgan North's unlikely account in *The Julia Morgan Architectural History Project*, Vol. II, p. 196 (which portrayed Maybeck as having made sketches for Hearst's new Wyntoon Castle as early as the 1910s, and which presented other questionable points).

The Morgan-Forney ledgers throw some light on Maybeck. So do the Hearst Papers (see Morgan to Sokolow, February 14, 1934, plus attachments; carton 57 [under "Julia Morgan"]). The Morgan Collection at EDA contains a single diary sheet, compiled at San Simeon in January 1931 by Julian Mesick (the maker of architectural models for Morgan). Mesick's sheet includes: "Bernard Maybeck, daughter & another guest arrived Sun. noon [probably January 18] for day visit. Mr. M. colored model in mural colors with our assistance." See also p. 527 in this volume for Mac McClure's recounting of a similar visit by Maybeck—in fact, possibly the same visit, whose purpose was for Maybeck to make sketches of a new Wyntoon Castle.

(which the Spanish government had since invalidated but which Hearst hoped he could avail himself of later on).[27]

By 1933 Hearst had proposed various uses and combinations of these English and Spanish elements. The Santa Maria monastery was the centerpiece by then of his dream for a new Wyntoon Castle. The Bradenstoke ceiling timbers may still have been slated for the dining room, but many other rooms also needed ancient material. The monastery components, sent from Spain to San Francisco in eleven shiploads, filled the Wyntoon wish list almost single-handedly. If necessary, the Sacramenia cloister that Hearst bought earlier from Byne (it was stored in New York, where Morgan probably saw it in 1930) could provide plenty of extra stonework; so could the Alcantara material if Hearst could get his hands on it.[28]

At the outset of 1931, mindful of the pending Santa Maria deal, Hearst had told Morgan about plans for Wyntoon that were grandiose beyond all former measure, plans for which the term "big job" in its current 1933 context—as the big job that Loorz and Stolte knew—would have fallen far short:

> I figure $750,000 for concrete work alone. That is, five years at $150,000 a year.
>
> Roughly considering the bulk, it seems to me that if it will take a year to pour the foundations, it will take four additional years to pour the rest of the house.

27. The Morgan and the Steilberg collections at EDA and the more renowned (and much larger) Morgan Collection at Cal Poly have primary material on Santa Maria de Ovila (and, at Cal Poly, on Sacramenia and Alcantara also). The M. H. de Young Memorial Museum, San Francisco (to which city Hearst later gave the Santa Maria monastery), was once a repository of documents on the subject; but those records have since dropped from sight. The Morgan-Forney Collection has the full account of "Mount Olive" (Byne's code name for Santa Maria de Ovila), with its ledger entries extending from February through December 1931.

For a more general but still enticing glimpse (with nearly all eyes on Santa Maria, Hearst's acquisition of the two other Spanish monasteries being dimly known even now), see "Wyntoon—1930" in Alison Sky and Michelle Stone's *Unbuilt America: Forgotten Architecture in the United States from Thomas Jefferson to the Space Age* (New York, 1976), pp. 182–84. See also Robert M. Clements, Jr., "William Randolph Hearst's Monastery," *American Heritage* (April/May 1981), pp. 51–59. Some earlier writers mentioned the monastery (Santa Maria); but Clements, having contributed pp. 182–84 to *Unbuilt America*, was the first to identify Wyntoon as its proposed setting—the first, that is, for a wide audience. Clements was much indebted to Edward Hussey, who was at Wyntoon in 1933 and who kept a diary. Hussey sent Clements a detailed letter in 1975 that included some of the diary entries; the letter was reproduced in *The Julia Morgan Architectural History Project*, Vol. I, pp. 333–36.

28. While eastbound through Wyoming in 1929, Morgan wrote to Julian Mesick, saying that one reason for the trip was to "check up on antique warehousings." She no doubt meant Hearst's warehouse complex in the Bronx, New York, part of which held the Sacramenia crates. From Morgan to Mesick, December 29, 1929; Morgan Collection, EDA.

Three years earlier, in "Hearst Importing a Spanish Cloister," *The New York Times* said the item was destined for Hearst's "estate in California" (December 14, 1926, p. 1:7). Such claims, once dismissible as glib references to San Simeon, are entirely plausible with regard to Wyntoon in the 1920s or even to the concurrent plans Hearst had for the University of California Museum in Berkeley, now

Hearst elaborated on what the plumbing, the roofing, the "pointing up," and several other things would add to the concrete work. "Altogether about $2,000,000" is what he supposed the grand total would be. For sheer size and massiveness, no other architectural fantasy of his—neither Casa Grande at San Simeon nor the Beach House in Santa Monica, neither St. Donat's Castle in Wales nor the building he envisioned for his Grand Canyon property—could quite equal what he had in mind by 1931 for his Spanish monastery elements at Wyntoon.[29]

And thus we needn't assume that Hearst's big job of 1933 represented his imagination gone newly awry. If anything, he was getting back to earth now, having retreated substantially from the heights of what surely ranked as the biggest job of all. Soon there would be further deflating, further moderating of his superheated ideas. He and Morgan, and in turn Loorz and others, would increasingly focus their attention elsewhere in the continuing saga of Wyntoon. Nonetheless, the big job as of 1933—that imposing vestige of an even bigger job—would still have entailed the use of tons of chiseled stone from the monastery of Santa Maria de Ovila. But why all the concrete work that Loorz and Stolte had figured for the proposed bedroom wing and that they would have figured for other portions of the big job had it gone ahead? Because Santa Maria's stonework was to be appliquéd, in effect, to the modern concrete shell. The same thing had been done at San Simeon with old ceilings, mantelpieces, and other building fragments Hearst had bought in the New York art market and from sources overseas. For Wyntoon, though—even at its cooled-down, post-1931 level—the application of crate upon crate of old stonework to the "large New Castle," as Loorz had called it in writing to Stolte on May 8, would have been unprecedented in its scale.

But for now all remained in abeyance. In writing to Morgan on May 31—in the mailing that contained his and Stolte's estimate of the giant Bedroom Wing—Loorz assured her, "We definitely understand that nothing definite has been decided about the above job at Wyntoon."

The matter was soon to change. By Thursday, June 8, Loorz had new infor-

---

that those prospects are better known. See, for example, Morgan to Byne, August 25, 1925; Morgan/ Byne/Hearst Correspondence, Morgan Collection, Cal Poly.

29. All excerpts here: Hearst to Morgan, January 13, 1931; Hearst Papers, carton 12 (under "Morgan, Julia"). Despite his grand projections, Hearst said the "designing and detail work"—or the "modeling and decorative work," as he also called it—would be much less involved and thus less expensive than its counterpart at San Simeon.

In similar letters to Morgan from this part of 1931, Hearst referred to "Mr. Byne's cloister" (January 21) and to "the cloister" (January 23). These are just two examples; Hearst Papers, ibid. He may well have been distinguishing between the Sacramenia material (and its specific components, which included the cloister) and those portions from Santa Maria de Ovila—much as he had between the Bradenstoke barn and the Bradenstoke abbey (as in note 11, above).

mation to share with Mac McClure. Morgan had been at San Simeon three days earlier, on Monday the fifth (and before that on Sunday, May 28). Although Loorz referred to "last week's interview"—indicating, it would seem, her visit in late May—Morgan's more recent visit (June 5) is almost surely what he was speaking of. Either way, his recapitulations for those two dates contain none of the "unofficial" news he divulged to Mac on the eighth:

> Last week's interview with Mr. Hearst netted this *unofficially*. They will clear the site [of old Wyntoon Castle] and excavate for the complete building, build the retaining wall in back [against the hillside], tear down the present kitchen and passage [both of which survived the fire in 1930] and build a temporary kitchen where the court is in back of the Gables. Miss Morgan whispered in my ear that out [our] men could do this work. So if you wish to whisper this *unofficially* in Harry's ear, he'll enjoy knowing, at least, that there is a possibility of work there all summer.

Loorz concluded with this encouraging comment: "Mr. Hearst seemed quite pleased for I believe he can really afford to go ahead with that amount [of work] but was actually worried about the previously arranged & much larger program."[30]

COME THE SUMMER of 1933, San Simeon had its share of activity, even as the small job at Wyntoon gave way to something less than the big job—gave way, that is, to a kind of medium job (though it was never called that). Loorz's tiny hilltop crew was still pushing the Billiard Room and the Lower South Duplex to completion. In addition, Morgan had brought in a man named Martin Charles, who was to fill in for Mac McClure as her on-site representative while Mac was at Wyntoon. "Please take him under your wing," she had said to Loorz back in early May.[31] Among the

---

30. On June 6, two days before writing to Mac, Loorz had similar news for Stolte, though it was less detailed. "Well I went over the Wyntoon job again with Miss Morgan yesterday," said Loorz, referring to her visit of June 5. "Again it has changed." The changes were the same ones he described to Mac on June 8. Had the excerpt of that date not begun with "Last week's interview" (probably a simple error on Loorz's part), the events through this stretch could be more logically aligned.

31. Penciled by Morgan on the Recapitulation sheet that Loorz submitted after her visit of May 6; she returned it to him for his files.

The name "M. A. Charles" appears on one of Morgan's statements for Principia College, showing Charles as her lowest paid of six draftsmen assigned to that job in October 1931 (the work was done in San Francisco); Jack Wagenet was the highest paid. All such monthly statements for "The Principia" are in the Bernard Maybeck Collection, EDA. Charles may have been an itinerant draftsman who moved among the Morgan office and other firms. Although Charles visited San Simeon with Morgan in May 1932, a year before his brief on-site assignment, Jim LeFeaver said nothing of him in writing to Ed Hussey in October 1932 or to Elizabeth Boyter in May 1933; see pp. 39–40 in this volume; also pp. 61–62, note 18. Nor did Thad Joy mention him in 1927, when Morgan's office was at its height; see p. 40, note 30.

duties assigned Charles was a complex puzzle that, with Loorz's help, he was asked to solve: the layout of an old Spanish ceiling for Hearst's Gothic Study. Hearst had bought the "Campos" ceiling in 1930, through the same Arthur Byne who had also procured the Billiard Room's "Barbastro" ceiling for him that year and, far more dramatically, the monasteries of Sacramenia in 1925, Alcantara in 1930, and Santa Maria de Ovila in 1931.

Loorz's crew on the Burnett Road, meanwhile, was inching past the Santa Lucia crest on its way to Jolon. Loorz mentioned the road to Mac McClure on Monday, June 19. He provided a choice glimpse of social history while he was at it:

> Spent a most uncomfortable Saturday afternoon [probably June 17] accompanying the party on a picnic to the end of the new road and thence over a very rough trail on horse-back to the Nacimiento River. They complained so much about the rough road (quite unfinished) and the hazardous, steep, rough, narrow trail, that I felt sick when we reached the other side [of the Santa Lucias]. Did Marion [Davies] kid W.R. about his fine trail. You might know that she was persuaded to take the trip after long and lengthy teasing and coaxing by Mr. Hearst.
>
> Anyway I suggested to Mr. Hearst that they take the Davis Trail back and that I would go back over the trail and have the cars at Davis [Flat] when they got there. He accepted promptly. I know he felt, several times, like telling me a few things about my trail but was very gracious about it and just laughed. He certainly does have to control his temper to put up with some of the things he must have known to be very sarcastic, this referring to many remarks made by the guests about the beauty etc. Was I glad to get back. The worst part for me was that I was in the same car with Eddie Kane and did he rave and criticize the possibilities of any fun on a picnic way back there. The reason being that he always gets very car sick going back, so does Marion and a few of the others.

That was probably one Saturday evening when Loorz *didn't* hoist a beer with King Walters and the rest of the Burnett crew.

Hearst and his party left for Wyntoon right after the following weekend—on Monday, June 26. The next day, Loorz wrote to Martin Charles, the man who had come down from the Morgan office to pinch-hit for Mac McClure; Charles had recently returned to San Francisco:

> Martin, will you pardon me for my frankness, but I must tell you a part of a discussion with Mr. Hearst last evening shortly before he left.[32] It was up in the Gothic [Suite] with him, me in a nice soft chair.

---

32. Hearst and his party probably caught one of the Southern Pacific's northbound sleepers in San Luis Obispo; the group may have paused in the Bay Area or elsewhere before reaching Wyntoon, late on June 27.

Anyway, I told him he could tell Miss Morgan that I had plenty of work outlined ahead, so if she didn't feel very well it would not be necessary for her to
hurry down here. I said, following the above, "Thanks to Mr. Charles the Study
had been worked out very efficiently and carefully, so that barring changes, I had
it all quite clearly outlined." He said, "Is that so—I'm glad to hear it—Miss
Morgan thot and talked very highly of him." He asked, "Is he here?" and I told
him you had left last week end. He said, "What was the matter, didn't he like the
place? Maybe he would have enjoyed it better if we arranged for him to move into
the house [Casa Grande] and be with the guests. We'd be glad to have him.
Maybe he can come back and work with you on getting the Billiard Room finished, we must have that."

Beyond his facetious, satirical tone, Hearst evidently thought well enough of
Martin Charles. But Charles wanted no part of the offer; he told Loorz he didn't
want to return to San Simeon. "How is that for rank ingratitude?" he replied on
June 29. "Mr. Hearst's suggestion about herding me with the guests does not help
matters in the least, as you can imagine. I prefer being with you and remaining a
member of the humble, but honest, construction camp."

Charles was mostly upset about small things, like the Hearst Camp cuisine,
which both he and Loorz ridiculed in these two letters. (Loorz had told Charles, "I
miss you at the table, so do the boys. We have a vacant seat for the next victim."
Charles retorted, "Unfortunately, I was not endowed with that kind of a stomach.
The ten pounds was no exaggeration, and my net loss of weight while on the Hill
was 10³/₄.") All such humor aside, Charles refused to be pacified. He soon dropped
from view, reappearing briefly in Morgan's office annals several weeks later and
then in the Loorz Papers in 1934, but never again.[33] For Morgan his absence meant
that, from here on, whenever Mac McClure was at Wyntoon, the San Simeon job
would have to get by without an on-site person from her staff. Mac was becoming
as hard to replace as Thad Joy had once been.

AFTER HEARST HAD LEFT for Wyntoon on June 26—for what would prove to be
a month-long stay—Loorz's pen pals hastened to tell him about the great man's

---

33. An exchange between Charles and Loorz occurred in May of that year; it began on Friday
the eleventh, when Charles wrote:

Perhaps I had better explain why I am leaving S.F. on Thursday [May 17, 1934]. The fact is, I
am going on a junket this summer, a good fat junket to Europe. You can imagine how badly I
feel about that. Riefstahl, the man with whom I worked in Turkey, has some researches to make
in Italy this summer and has asked me to go along.

Charles evidently meant R. M. Riefstahl, an antiquarian who years before had been prominent in one of the art-market circles—often connected with the Anderson Galleries—that Hearst
had frequented in New York.

arrival. George Wright, an engineer, a wit, and an expert in reinforced concrete (albeit a "Stanford man," as Loorz had warned his fellow Berkeley graduate Julia Morgan on May 31), gave a lively account on June 28:

> We landed in the midst of a whirlwind of excitement that was blown up by the preparations for the arrival of W. R. and his party. Getting everything in ship shape in the allotted time looked like an impossible task but it was done. W.R. was apparently pleased. Poor Miss Morgan was just about a wreck by last night. Truck load after truck load of furniture arrived and every piece had to be placed just so. An ash tray on the wrong table worries her. She deserves the vacation she thinks her trip to San Simeon will be. [She was there three days later, on July 1.]

Fred Stolte, who had gone up to Wyntoon to represent his and Loorz's construction company, gave his partner an equally spirited account, likewise on Wednesday, June 28: [34]

> I have been in McCloud for a few days — since Friday [June 23]. Miss Morgan left last night.
>
> The Hearst party came up last evening and are fully settled in the Gables. Hope they can get some good fishing & hunting.
>
> I believe most of the kinks are ironed out on the jobs and quiet seems to have descended on the Rhine. For a while — everything was hurry — expecting Mr. Hearst. Miss Morgan is getting most details decided and we will have a couple of houses enclosed, very shortly.
>
> As you know we have opened up the old road to [the] old saw mill and have been hauling out the old timber. Miss Morgan wishes to use the natural weathered timber for ½ timber — on the outside [of certain buildings]. She said that I should come down [to San Simeon] and help you with one of those antique ceilings — to get the *uneven feeling*.

Stolte wrote to Loorz again two days later, on Friday the thirtieth. Along with restating some of what he'd said on June 28 (decades later, we can be glad he did), he sounded more the way George Wright had on that same date:

> Well, I guess you know that Mr. Hearst and party arrived at McCloud, Tuesday 10 P.M. [35]

---

34. Stolte's letter is identified as "Wednesday" only, but its text makes it firmly datable as June 28. Among other indicators, the reference to "the Hearst party" pertains to this trip alone — the only trip Hearst made to Wytoon in 1933 with an entourage and, quite possibly, the only one he made there that year in any circumstances.

35. In his diary, Ed Hussey noted 10:30 p.m. as the time of arrival. See *The Julia Morgan Architectural History Project*, Vol. I, p. 334.

Stolte's letters of June 28 and June 30 were handwritten, as were most others he sent Loorz. He

Everything seemed to finish up in good shape—However, I had *many* misgivings, a day or two before.

And I surely take off my hat to Miss Morgan. She was the first one on [the] job and the last one leaving.

Harry Thompson, the foreman for the Stolte Co., told Loorz on June 30 as well, "They have been running Mr. McClure ragged with changes and additions. We are now to build another house about 30 x 60. The Castle [the new Wyntoon Castle] seems to be a minor consideration at present."

Not until July 7 did Mac McClure have a chance to write to Loorz—to unburden his soul, as he put it:

The past month has been the most hectic I have ever endured. As you know we have had J.M. for long visits, one for eight days and one for four, and she just left last night again after a two day stay.[36]

The pressure of work and responsibility is very great. The worst was the three days preceding W.R.'s arrival—house unfinished [probably River House]—3 van loads of furniture all at once—most of it dis-assembled and crated and green hands to do the work. By working at top speed all day long we just barely got things in order for the Chief. I would have had it done sooner but J.M. threw a few monkey wrenches the last day—paint colors must be changed—furniture moved and removed etc. When I finally took Miss M. to town [McCloud] at 10:30 p.m. she very nearly collapsed—never saw her so bad. W.R. arrived and liked what we had done but the next day sent me a very sharp note about broken and marred furniture,[37] and all instances which he mentioned were made before un-

is not known to have made copies of them. Like so many other informal correspondents, he was apt to repeat or rephrase certain details in writing to the same person, as he did on June 30.

36. The "Waterhouse" account, the largest of the Wyntoon accounts in the Morgan-Forney ledgers, extends from October 1932 through June 1939. Nearly all of Morgan's visits from 1933 onward are recorded there. For the period that Mac described, Morgan left for Wyntoon on June 9, June 23, and July 4; but the notations don't tell how long she stayed. However, Ed Hussey's diary (see note 27, above) makes it clear that June 23 preceded what Mac said were four days—or, as the diary has it, five days. (Stolte's letter of June 28 has Morgan leaving late on June 27, thus agreeing more closely with Mac's version.)

For the last of those three visits, Hussey's diary refers to July 5 only; but Mac's words are clear enough to place Morgan at Wyntoon on July 6 as well. This leaves Morgan's eight-day visit as having followed June 9 (logically, since Mac spoke of that one first). The diary is of no help here, for Hussey didn't arrive at Wyntoon until June 16 and didn't mention Morgan until June 24. His diary entries (short, scattered excerpts only) are in *The Morgan Project*, Vol. I, p. 334; see also Vol. II, p. 85b (which differs in citing June 7 as the date Hussey arrived). The Hussey Papers at EDA do not contain the full diary, whose whereabouts are unknown.

37. The original note, which may well have been handwritten, is presumed to be lost. Nor is Hearst known to have kept a copy; and so oblivion would be virtually assured for this and many other communications like it.

packing here—it was unjust and beyond my control entirely but I had to take it. W.R. since has been O.K. but yesterday when J.M. was here he flew into a terrible rage because the laborers cut some underbrush to put in some high stakes for [the] new castle. Again I took the rap although Geo. Wright and Ed Hussey [the new on-site representative from Morgan's office][38] did the dirty work while I was busy elsewhere. However I think things are quiet again and part of W.R.'s bad mood was due to [the] fact that J.M. was trying to sell more castle designs over his own plans.

At any rate we are still alive but things are not as pleasant as could be wished. The program of building is most undecided—W.R. changes his mind from day to day and I would not be surprised if he did very little to main building.[39] Please keep this under your hat.

He is talking about building more cottages and altering present buildings at Waterhouse immediately which I think will go ahead.

Apparently Mr. H. likes it here very much but expects the smooth machinery at San Simeon to be duplicated here at once.

San Simeon's "machinery"—both as a job in progress and as a functioning household with its resident staff—had had a good dozen years to gain its well-oiled status. It posed a hard act for Wyntoon to follow. Besides, the new work at Wyntoon relied on a different brain trust. Whereas by 1933 the San Simeon job ran smoothly with Hearst, Morgan, McClure, and Loorz putting their heads together, Wyntoon took direction from Hearst, Morgan, McClure, and Stolte (in place of Loorz, who

---

38. Hussey, between stints on the Principia College job (under Maybeck), went to Wyntoon (under Morgan) on June 16, 1933, or possibly on June 7; the conflicting dates stem from his diary. See both volumes of *The Morgan Project*, as cited above in note 36. A further reference to Ed Hussey lies in another of Jim LeFeaver's letters to Elizabeth Boyter, dated June 27, 1933. Besides saying that the Morgan office was "doing a little additional work for Mr. Hearst" at Wyntoon, LeFeaver said Hussey had "gone up there as architect's representative." (Boyter Papers, Bancroft Library.) George Wright's letter to Loorz of June 28, 1933 (p. 74 in this chapter) went on to say that "Le Feaver wanted his man, Hussey, to keep time, do ordering, etc."

Mac McClure also had the title of architect's representative. But his and Hussey's job descriptions at Wyntoon were different, officially or not. Hussey acted as a construction-oriented, supervising architect, much as he had for Morgan on her Honolulu YWCA and then for Maybeck on the Principia job in Illinois. McClure was more and more becoming Hearst's personal designer. Hussey probably had few dealings with the great man himself; McClure had them almost every day, just as he and Loorz typically had them at San Simeon. A letter to Hussey from Walter Steilberg (July 3, 1933) epitomizes the difference between Hussey and McClure. "Keep complete records of your [concrete] mixes," Steilberg said in part. "Note quantities and size limits of aggregates; quantity of sand." And so on through similar details that, if anything, were right down the alley of a builder like Loorz but not down McClure's. (Hussey Collection, EDA.)

39. A reference either to the new, monastically oriented Wyntoon Castle or to The Gables, which stood near the site of that proposed development. The area was across the McCloud River and downstream from where the initial "small job" had been done.

nonetheless played an absentee role, more so than Stolte ever did with regard to San Simeon).[40] And now on behalf of Morgan (and LeFeaver) there was Ed Hussey, too—who soon became a kind of fifth wheel in the mechanism.

Mac McClure, in any case, had still more unburdening to do in his letter to Loorz of July 7:

> Here is a little item which you are to keep to yourself or I am to be shot at sunrise.
>
> Two weeks ago when Miss M. was here she told me she was going for a short walk by the flume and not to bother about her. 3 hours later she returned covered with mud, blood, and bruises to such a degree that I had to take her to the hospital. She had fallen off the flume down the wet and rocky bank about 20′—cutting her head open and severely bruising herself. Fortunately and miraculously she was not badly hurt and was out again in two days. Can you beat it?

Loorz heard from the "Wyntoonites" throughout July 1933. On the ninth, for example, Harry Thompson wrote, "I'm glad Miss Morgan is pleased with the work we have done. I couldn't possibly do any more with what I've had to work with and she makes so many changes that it slows up progress." Thompson also said that plans for the big Castle had been altered "two or 3 times" and that there was "nothing definite yet" about them.

On July 9 as well, a different kind of message left Wyntoon. It was a telegram from Hearst to Ella Williams at Cosmopolitan Productions, his film company whose "bungalow" stood on the Metro-Goldwyn-Mayer lot in Culver City:

> Would like to invite a dozen out of the following list to come up to Wyntoon:
> Zasu Pitts, Woodhall, Joan Blondell, George Barnes, Sally Eilers, Hoot Gibson, Mary Carlisle, Joel McRae [McCrea], Joan Bennett, Gene Market, Eileen [Aileen] Pringle, Matt Moore, Paulette Goddard, Charlie Chaplin, Loretta Young, Ralph Graves, Alice Joyce, Clarence Brown, Mary Brian, Maitland Rice, Virginia Cherrill, Cary Grant, June Collier [Collyer] and husband S[tuart] Erwin, Josephine Dunn, Buster Collier, Carmelita Geraghty, Carey Wilson, Julanne Johnston, Randolph Scott, Eileen Percy, Virginia Valli, Charles Farrell, Lois Wilson, Mr. and Mrs. [George] Fitzmaurice.[41]

---

40. Stolte's role at Wyntoon was more limited than Loorz's jack-of-all-trades role at San Simeon. His strong suit was wood construction, much befitting the "small job" and subsequent projects at Wyntoon. Above all, Stolte was there (intermittently at that, often to coincide with Morgan's visits) on behalf of the F. C. Stolte Co., which had been retained as a "cost plus" general contractor. The *cost* part applied to materials and labor, the *plus* part to the company's profit (based on a small percentage of those expenses). Stolte had to make sure, for example, that Harry Thompson and his crew of carpenters were performing as efficiently as they could and that Hearst and Morgan's wishes were being met. In that respect, Stolte was a construction superintendent; but the term has a much broader meaning when applied to Loorz's full-time, year-round responsibilities at San Simeon.

41. Hearst to Williams, July 9, 1933; Hearst Papers, carton 17 (under "1933 Samples").

Would that we knew which third of those thirty-six people comprised the lucky finalists.

Come July 14, it was George Wright's turn to tell Loorz the latest: "We have one large labor crew that does nothing else but go around and pull up stakes as fast as they are placed." Wright also mentioned Fred Stolte and Miss Morgan, each of whom had just returned to the job: "They both seem to think that this time some definite decision will be made regarding the Castle. At any rate W.R. intends to go ahead with a cottage to be erected at the site of the Waterhouse barn. And we have a short road to build."

Thompson wrote again on July 17, saying, "We will have one more new cottage to build at least that is the plan at present."

Loorz got off a letter of his own the next day, July 18, this one to Hearst, whom he needed to keep informed about San Simeon, despite Wyntoon's position in the current limelight. "The [Lower South] Duplex will be ready for furnishing in two or three days, if Miss Morgan doesn't add more decorating when she comes." She was coming right away, actually, that very day; and when Loorz typed up his notes from their meeting, the ones pertaining to the Lower South Duplex filled an entire page.

Morgan had been at Wyntoon as recently as July 14 and would next be there during the first few days of August. In the meantime, Mac McClure wrote to Loorz from that estate on July 28. "We are to have two houses built and furnished by October 1st," he told Loorz, "as well as general revamping of existing buildings. . . . The amount of work to be done is so great that if we get one half accomplished we will fulfill my expectations." Mac also said, "W.R. left [for San Simeon] in a good humor. I made him a new castle sketch (on a new site) which he liked or at least it aroused his interest again, however I do not expect any castle this year, if ever."

The new site, near the confluence of the McCloud River and Angel Creek, was upstream from the original Castle site and across from the setting of the "small job"—across from where River House and other old buildings stood on the former property of Clarence Waterhouse. That meadow-like setting, known as the Waterhouse parcel, was also where the unnamed "medium job" had begun yielding its results. But as Mac indicated, the likelihood that the once-touted "big job" would also take hold nearby, or anywhere else, was becoming more and more remote. Chalk one up to his keen sense of intuition.[42]

---

42. An undated letter of this period from Stolte to Loorz includes this paragraph: "The castle remains undecided. A new location is sought. The two flats across the river from Waterhouse near Angel Creek—seem to be favored at Present. And Mr. Hearst seems quite enthused." Stolte didn't mean, though, that Hearst had expressed his thoughts directly. For in that same letter, Stolte said he had "not met Mr. Hearst, personally," even though he had often had "the opportunity of close contact [with Hearst] in the small cottages that are being remodeled at Waterhouse."

James Rankin was another insider who wrote to Loorz on July 28, relating that Harry Thompson had nearly cracked under the pressure but had managed to pull through. "Perhaps the fact that he was finally able to make a good catch of fish and treat us all to a nice fish dinner helped him over the hump, for in fact I guess it helped us all."[43]

Morgan herself, in an undated letter from San Francisco, told Loorz, "It certainly is beautiful up there, & I am so glad Mr. Hearst could be there & catch all our errors as well as *vacationate*." What a saint she must have been to choose those words over a hundred other possibilities.

ON AUGUST 4, while Morgan was in the midst of a week-long stay at Wyntoon, Loorz answered the letter Mac had sent him from there on July 28. Hearst (who would not return to Wyntoon in 1933, at least not with an entourage in tow) was now back at San Simeon:

> As you know the party are here with us again and all hands are at the wheel. Though very pleasant and full of Pep, Mr. Hearst seems more interested in things up there than here at present. When everything is going O.K. and he doesn't get excited about things it certainly means he isn't particularly interested, doesn't it?
>
> He would like to start work on the outside pool, start a new reservoir etc but told me yesterday, "I want so many things but haven't got the money." Poor fellow, let's take up a collection.

Loorz's letter to Mac also contained this passage:

> They went out to the Grapevine [a separate place from the pergola on Orchard Hill] for a picnic this afternoon. With Marks [Eubanks] and Morris [Maurice McClure][44] on vacation I had to use some new drivers, hope everything works out O.K. It is so easy to displease these people.

Likewise on August 4, Loorz wrote back to James Rankin, the prince of plumbers, greeting him as "Dear Jimmie":

> W.R. seems more interested in the work up there than down here but that makes it easier for us to keep pegging at the same things we are on and get them completed. We are not making a big showing but we are still spending money.

---

43. All such passages in these annals about fishing at Wyntoon almost certainly pertain to the McCloud River. And yet a contemporary article stated, "There is no fishing at Wyntoon because the McCloud River, which winds thirty miles through Hearst property, is gray with volcanic ash"—this from the feature "Hearst" in *Fortune* (October 1935), p. 44. The spirit of the statement lives on in Boutelle's *Julia Morgan*, p. 218 (but see also the photograph of Morgan, with fish in hand, on p. 232).

44. Maurice McClure (who pronounced his first name "Morris") was unrelated to Warren "Mac" McClure, who was seven years older. For the sake of clarity, I'll continue in my usual pattern of identifying Warren McClure as Mac McClure or simply as Mac.

I thot you would be down to put in those two fixtures in the Tennis Court
Dressing Rooms [at the Roman Pool][45] but now I dont know when we will do
much more plumbing. We are concentrating on the Billiard Room and Gothic
Study in which there will be no toilets, thank God.

In writing to Fred Stolte on August 5, Loorz told him—as he had Mac Mc-
Clure the day before—that Hearst wanted to build a new reservoir and that it
would cost "about $30,000." And in telling Stolte—as Loorz similarly had told
McClure—that Hearst had said, "I want so many things and I haven't got the
money," he added that Hearst had laughed in making the statement. "He has been
in splendid humor all week and I've enjoyed chatting with him," Loorz continued.
"Hope we can keep him that way and send him back up there feeling the same
way."

Stolte answered with two letters on August 7, upon returning to Oakland from
Wyntoon. In his first one he reported, "The program is changed somewhat—and
several 8 or 9 room cottages are to be built." In his second one he remarked, "I am
very glad to hear that Mr. Hearst is in a good humor. For a while, I thought things
looked rather bad, he was real peeved, about the castle site." Stolte said of himself
that he'd stayed in the background while Hearst was at Wyntoon and that he'd let
Morgan do the talking. Like the Loorz of 1927–28 at the Beach House in Santa
Monica, Stolte had yet to meet the legendary Hearst.

Stolte's letters moved Loorz to confide in him about Hearst; this was a day
later, on August 8:

> Between you and me Fred I dont think he felt he could afford to start such a large
> building at this time and had to find some fault with the whole scheme. I have felt
> that way about it even before we started up there. About the time each new set of
> plans was about ready to start work he would make major changes.
>
> Anyway Miss Morgan is quite satisfied in spite of everything so that is what re-
> ally counts. As I told you in my last letter [the one dated August 5] I never mention
> Wyntoon to him for a definite reason. When it becomes that last resort I will tell
> him.

What Loorz meant by those final words was that, strange to say, his and
Stolte's partnership was unbeknownst to Hearst. Loorz was employed independently at San Simeon, not on behalf of the F. C. Stolte Co.; and he was afraid a conflict of interest would spoil his rapport with Hearst. His fears proved unfounded.
(In fact, Stolte had also said on August 7, "Miss Morgan mentioned that Mr Hearst
seemed pleased that you were interested in the work at McCloud. So she must have

---

45. San Simeon's two tennis courts occupy the flat roof of the Roman Pool building.

mentioned our association.") Before long Loorz and Stolte learned that their company had been chosen to return to Wyntoon in 1934, apparently with Hearst's full knowledge and approval. The prospect of the big job, however—of the new Wyntoon Castle, with or without the monastery components, and whether on the old site or a new one—remained as much in limbo as ever.

Loorz paused long enough on Thursday, August 10, to portray for his parents the idealized San Simeon—the San Simeon that was already becoming widely known through published accounts and, in Hollywood circles especially, through much-embellished word of mouth:[46]

> Mr. Hearst, the twins (about 18) [Randolph and David Hearst][47] and many guests are here but will leave for L.A. about Sunday. Miss Davies will start another picture [*Going Hollywood*][48] and is diligently training in tap dancing etc. It is not all easy to keep trim for pictures. I think Mr. Hearst personally sees to it that she does keep practicing. The boys [the twins] are very nice and sociable and full of fun.

Five days later—by then it was Tuesday the fifteenth—Loorz had more to tell his parents (who still lived on the family farm in Lovelock, Nevada):

> All of Mr. Hearst's guests and the boys left last night for L.A. Mr. Hearst will leave by aeroplane this morning. Then it will be a little lonesome for a few days for me. Most of the crew like it better while he is away for they can swim in his pools, ride some of his horses and things like that. I like it better while he is here for everybody seems to take his business more seriously.

---

46. Among the published accounts, little appeared before the late 1920s. In 1927 *The New Yorker* ran a five-part "profile" of Hearst by John K. Winkler, foreshadowing the book *William Randolph Hearst: An American Phenomenon* (New York, 1928); the latter described San Simeon and was the first in a long line of Hearst biographies. *The New York Times Magazine* offered a profile of San Simeon itself in "A Renaissance Palace in Our West," by Duncan Aikman—this on July 21, 1929 (Part V of *The New York Times* Sunday edition), pp. 10–11. Two years later an especially detailed feature on San Simeon, "Hearst at Home," appeared in *Fortune* (May 1931), pp. 56–68, 130. Early in George Loorz's tenure *The Atlantic Monthly* followed with "A Tourist in Spite of Himself—At the Hearst Ranch," by the bibliophile A. Edward Newton (October 1932), pp. 461–67. Meanwhile through these first few years of San Simeon's heyday, Arthur Brisbane occasionally described his experiences as a guest; the Hearst newspapers carried Brisbane's front-page column "Today" for millions of loyal readers. Basil Woon, a guest in 1929, devoted a chapter to Hearst and San Simeon in *Incredible Land: A Jaunty Baedeker to Hollywood and the Great Southwest* (New York, 1933), pp. 180–89. In contrast, most of the memoirs and other personal accounts by former guests appeared several years later, even decades later; see pp. 170–71 in this volume, note 27.

47. These youngest of Hearst's five sons would be eighteen later in 1933. Their older brothers were John, who would soon be twenty-four; William, Jr., who was twenty-five; and George, who was twenty-nine.

48. For this and other Davies pictures, see "The Films of Marion Davies," an appendix on pp. 375–404 of *Marion Davies* (New York, 1972), by Fred Lawrence Guiles.

Loorz may have stretched the truth a bit in mentioning the fringe benefits enjoyed by "the crew." In any case, he was alluding more to Hearst's own domestic staff—which looked after Casa Grande and the three outlying houses, such as Casa del Mar—than he was to the carpenters and other tradesmen and workers in Hearst Camp or on the surrounding Hearst Ranch.[49]

STOLTE HAD REFERRED to "several 8 or 9 room cottages" in writing to Loorz on August 7. But a clearer indication of the "Bavarian Village" that was soon to emerge on the Waterhouse parcel at Wyntoon lies in a letter written by Harry Thompson, who told Loorz on August 18, "We have three houses to enclose before winter and they are going to be some shacks." (To make that much progress, he also said, would depend on Mac McClure's getting "the plans out fast enough.")

Thompson's reference to what became Brown Bear, Cinderella House, and Angel House is an important one. Again, though, it was Mac who consistently provided the insider's view. He prefaced a letter to Loorz on Sunday, August 27, by saying, "I suppose you are tired of hearing about the troubles at McCloud":

> When W.R. left here [in late July] he left a pretty definite program with approved designs of proposed houses for us to follow. However since then they have been regularly and completely changed as often as J.M. visited San Simeon. After Miss Morgan's last visit here (a 4 day visit) we were told to proceed without drawings or other data other than some charcoal smudges and other indefinite data.[50]
>
> I might also say that I received daily letters last week requesting so much data and drawings on the other houses that I had no time whatever to do necessary drafting for job progress.[51]
>
> At any rate last Friday morning she called me up and was much incensed because we had not done more "as we had *all* the necessary information." Her anger seems directed somewhat at Harry [Thompson] as well as myself, and has hinted that she might request a change. It is the most difficult position I have yet been in. Harry is trying hard to please, I think, but I imagine the indecision and lack of drawings aggravate him greatly and perhaps he shows it too much in her presence.

---

49. See note 60, below, for further perspective on employee privileges at San Simeon.

50. Morgan had been at San Simeon on July 30, August 9, and August 18; she was also there on the day that Mac wrote to Loorz, August 27. For Wyntoon during this same period, the Morgan-Forney ledgers list the clustered dates August 1–6, August 11–17, and August 30–September 2 (a pattern reminiscent of San Simeon in its early years). Charcoal was not a medium that Morgan worked in, but it was one that Maybeck used; see, for example, *The Morgan Project*, Vol. I, p. 112. The smudgy material may have carried over from his involvement in Wyntoon's development.

51. See note 37, above, regarding the likely fate of such letters (which must have been from Morgan in these later instances rather than from Hearst). If Morgan kept file copies in San Francisco, they didn't survive to become part of the Morgan Collection at Cal Poly or any other archives.

To cap our program, I received a wire from [the] office this morning saying, "Stop all work on houses until Thursday [August 31], when I will be there with new ideas" from J.M. at San Simeon last night. This probably means she will be here over the [Labor Day] holiday week end [September 2–4]—which I have planned to take off. Such is life.

Loorz's reply, dated August 31, showed how pivotal a role he was playing in the Wyntoon pageantry, even from distant San Simeon. He began by telling Mac, "I wrote the telegram for her that you received."[52] Loorz also said, "I asked her to please state what you could go ahead on at least so you'd know what to try to do." He further explained that, concerning Thompson, he knew of no one better for the job, no one who would "fill the bill" to Morgan's satisfaction. "She and I have talked it over frankly and she herself is not in favor of a change right now." But then Loorz added, "She may be [so inclined] after this present visit there with you." And yet Loorz may not have been so attuned as to know already that Mac would, in fact, get part of the weekend off. Just the same, he assured his good friend that he was always happy to hear from him, even if Mac's letters sounded "a little discouraging":

I'll only add that I think Mr. Hearst is personally more responsible for the changes than she is. He just simply keeps her busy all day changing while she is here. She brings down rather completed drawings for his approval. However, it may be that she has already instigated changes which he is not in sympathy with in the face of the fact that you and he had done them up there.

We are plodding along slowly but surely here. She hasn't been down a lot and two times on Sunday and I was away all day.[53] Last Sunday however [August 27], I came up about 7 in the evening and stayed with her until after 11 that night. She

---

52. The collections cited in these annals have no such telegram, whether the original or a copy. Mac, not yet knowing that Loorz had written it for Morgan, indicated it was sent (or perhaps its contents relayed) by her office in San Francisco on Sunday, August 27—an assumption stemming from what Mac thought was her presence at San Simeon on Saturday evening. But Morgan probably wasn't there on August 26, probably wasn't there before the visit she made the next day. Did she phone Loorz from San Luis Obispo and arrange for him to act in her behalf? Similar questions also come to mind, none of them easily answered.

In his diary on Monday, August 28, Ed Hussey wrote, "Stop all work." The entry repeated some of the very words that Mac had been wired the day before. See *The Julia Morgan Architectural History Project*, Vol. I, p. 334.

53. Translation: Loorz had missed two of Morgan's Sunday visits. Before August 27, he had missed her appearance on Sunday, July 30. (He told Mac on August 4, "I had no idea she was coming. . . . She left me some notes and didn't appear to be peeved.") The other Sunday he seems to have missed was as far back as May 28. There's a lesson here: we needn't dwell unduly on every word, every sentence in letters written quickly, naturally, spontaneously—and, in the frequent way of such things, unmethodically—whether by Loorz or anyone else.

was to stay in S.L. [San Luis Obispo] that night so had lots of time. But she was already too tired from her afternoon with W.R. and his drastic changes of Wyntoon that I got little or no information from her. However, she was in a good humor and I enjoyed the hours with her anyway.

The next day—Friday, September 1—brought an event that, perhaps with the holiday weekend so near at hand, left little trace of itself in the Loorz Papers. And thus this brief (and possibly truncated) note from Ed Hussey's diary: "Grade old castle site."[54] The heavy debris from the fire in 1930 had been removed—the crew waited until Hearst left in late July to finish that disruptive job—and the basement of old Wyntoon Castle had been filled. The work that Hussey recorded was nearly the final act. All that remained was to seed the smooth and straightened ground and let the grass take hold, covering the mark of Phoebe Hearst's showplace, as though a grave had been prescribed. Buried deep within it—beneath what became a croquet lawn—were some of her dreams, and some of Maybeck's, too. Some of her son's dreams, and Morgan's, lay entombed there as well. They included the hopes once vested in a medieval English barn and, even more so, those vested in at least one of three Spanish monasteries.

Two weeks later, on September 13, Loorz alerted Stolte that Hearst and Morgan were planning to fly up to Wyntoon in a day or so. Loorz elaborated on the prospect:

> I wish I could let you know more definitely and I will as soon as I find out. He so often cancels a trip like that, like he did yesterday. He was supposed to fly up and meet her here [for her visit of Tuesday, September 12] but didn't feel so hot so didn't come. If he was here I'd ask if it would be O.K. for you to fly up with them.

Loorz added that, under the circumstances, it would probably be better for Stolte to go up to Wyntoon on his own, as he usually did. Loorz also said:

> I think he is just a little hostile toward Miss Morgan for changes she is making to plans that he and Mac produced. When that is going on I find it much better to keep away.

Stolte had recently written to Loorz, "I told Miss Morgan that I would be pleased to go up before and during Mr. Hearst's visit there, (seeing that she has placed this confidence in me)." But as he had also said in that undated letter, "I get the JITTERS when I think of having to go over the job with Mr. Hearst."

Loorz tried to calm his partner in his letter of September 13:

---

54. *Morgan Project*, Vol. I, p. 334.

I know you will enjoy it a lot after the first few times. He is just as shy and bashful as you are and it takes a long time for him to become familiar and sociable. I've always found that it is best to beat [it] as quickly as our business is completed for it is embarrassing when we suddenly run out of something to say.

Never mind that Loorz was almost ten years younger than Stolte. Each of them could be paternal toward the other when circumstances called for it. Loorz and Stolte's exchange may have been premature, however, for Hearst seems not to have made the trip at all. Or if he did, no ready trace remains of it. (As for Morgan's part in this episode, the Morgan-Forney ledgers cite September 17 as her only trip that month to Wyntoon, without specifying the mode of travel; but had she flown, the entry would probably say so.)

While Stolte was taking deep breaths, George Wright, the engineer and wit, was driving to Wyntoon from San Simeon, where he had seen Loorz. The various buildings at the new jobsite would require a revamped power supply; Wright was helping to plan a new system of poles and wires. In recounting his trip north to pursue that work, he provided Loorz with another letter worth saving:[55]

> I thought I should let you know that I am here [at Wyntoon], lest you start worrying that either the car or myself had gone to pieces on the way.
>
> I had my first flat tire this side of Morgan Hill; a rim slipped over the wheel flange, started running at a wild angle in San Jose; I refused to buy a new tube in San Francisco, put on a dainty patch the size of a bed spread.
>
> After cleaning off some of the grime I headed for the Merchants Exchange [the Morgan office on California Street]. My face looked like a boiled lobster from wind burn (the top had blown in two at Cambria) but I put my pride in my pocket and marched up to the office. The door was locked, the place deserted. I phoned LeFeaver, who told me that he knew nothing about any map, knew nothing about the power line, did not know that I was going up. Wasn't that just swell! I phoned Miss Morgan, who was glad I called, who arranged to meet me at her office at noon. She showed me the map, explained what they had in mind. She said that the poles hadn't yet been purchased and that she would remember the information regarding cedar poles. For Mac's peace of mind you might assure him that I put up a good sales talk for cedar.

There was more to Wright's adventures as he limped past the Bay Area en route to McCloud and Wyntoon. North of Richmond, "a valve stem sheared off" and halfway from there to Red Bluff "the head gasket went out." Back on the jobsite itself, he had to contend with the ban on anyone's cutting underbrush for the

---

55. The letter is dated merely "Tuesday night"—probably having been written on September 12.

sake of the new power lines at Wyntoon. Wright figured an act of nature might make the work easier. He concluded his long letter to Loorz by saying, "Can you arrange with God to have Him start a fire up here with a bolt of lightning?"

Loorz knew what Wright was getting at. "I believe the little shrubbery cut this spring caused more discomfort than anything since the Johnstown Flood," he answered on September 16, referring to Wyntoon.

Along with working on new power lines and framing three new houses, the Wyntoon crew had also begun a second remodeling of The Gables, near the swimming pool and tennis courts that Loorz worked on in 1928. (A first remodeling had been done in 1930 and 1931, partly by the F. C. Stolte Co.; come 1933, this second round had awaited the Hearst party's completion of its month-long stay.) The Gables was downstream and across the McCloud River from the Waterhouse parcel, with its remodeled River House and the new houses that would become Brown Bear, Cinderella House, and Angel House — the standouts in the architectural group called the Bavarian Village. The Gables was also near what, until recently, had been the limited remains of the fire-ravaged Wyntoon Castle, designed by Bernard Maybeck for Phoebe Hearst.

Did Maybeck design The Gables as well? He must have. Yet the history of that structure, which began as an overflow guest house for Mrs. Hearst, is obscure.[56] On the one hand, the matter weighs lightly. (Early in 1931, when Hearst's plans for a new Wyntoon Castle were gargantuan, he told Morgan that since it would take "a long time for things to get in shape at Wyntoon," it would be a good idea in the interim to "make some additions to the gables" — on which some new work had already been started in 1930. But then, after saying he didn't want to spend much in the process, he added: "I suppose the gables will be torn down if the big house is ever erected.")[57]

---

56. The Maybeck Collection at EDA contains nothing textual on The Gables; a list of Maybeck's projects refers only to a "Castle on McCloud River" for Phoebe Hearst. (The list was compiled in 1947 for Jean Harris, who hoped to write a book on Maybeck; she and her husband, the renowned architect Harwell Hamilton Harris, were good friends of Walter Steilberg.)

In 1958 an article by W. W. Murray touched on the origin of The Gables; "Wyntoon" appeared in a local-history journal, *The Siskiyou Pioneer* (Yreka, California; pp. 13–20), and included these words on p. 14: "In addition to the Castle another building was constructed for Mrs. [Phoebe] Hearst shortly after. This was known as 'The Gables.' " Despite its brevity, the reference may be the best one we'll ever have. W. W. Murray, more familiar as William Murray, is often mentioned further on in *Building for Hearst and Morgan*. He was a first cousin of Hearst's wife, Millicent, said *The Siskiyou Pioneer*, and had been a frequent guest at Wyntoon in Phoebe Hearst's lifetime. (Years later, though, Mac McClure said Bill Murray might somehow have been more closely related to Millicent Hearst's older sister, Anita Irwin. McClure to Nellie Shewmaker, August 12, 1979; Shewmaker Collection.)

57. Hearst to Morgan, January 20, 1931; Hearst Papers, carton 12 (under "Morgan, Julia"). The Bancroft's version of this letter is the carbon copy (also true of the letters from 1931 cited in note 29, above); the Morgan Collection at Cal Poly lacks the originals.

MORGAN-FORNEY COLLECTION

Wyntoon Castle — before the fire of January 1930.

COURTESY OF SARA HOLMES BOUTELLE

FROM THE PAGES OF STOLTE BLUEPRINT

TOP LEFT:
Julia Morgan.
TOP RIGHT:
Ferdinand C.
Stolte (usually
called Fred Stolte).
BOTTOM: William
Randolph Hearst.
FACING PAGE:
George Loorz.

COURTESY OF J.C. "PETE" SEBASTIAN

LOORZ FAMILY COLLECTION

BISON ARCHIVES

BISON ARCHIVES

Marion Davies' Beach

MARION DAVIES has for many years been queen of Holly-wood's society. And, as befits a queen, she lives in a palace and here friends are royally entertained

BISON ARCHIVES

FACING AND ABOVE: 415 Ocean Front, better known simply as the Beach House.

AUTHOR'S PHOTOGRAPH, 1976

Casa Grande.

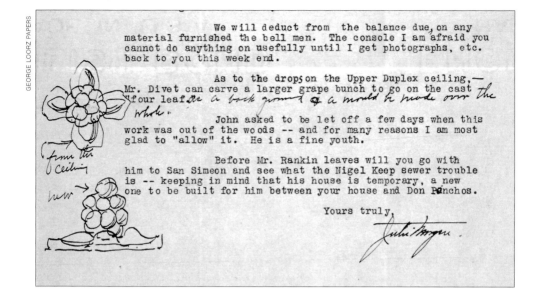

GEORGE LOORZ PAPERS

We will deduct from the balance due on any material furnished the bell men. The console I am afraid you cannot do anything on usefully until I get photographs, etc. back to you this week end.

As to the drops on the Upper Duplex ceiling,— Mr. Divet can carve a larger grape bunch to go on the cast "four leaf" *&c a back ground & a mould be made over the whole.*

John asked to be let off a few days when this work was out of the woods -- and for many reasons I am most glad to "allow" it. He is a fine youth.

Before Mr. Rankin leaves will you go with him to San Simeon and see what the Nigel Keep sewer trouble is -- keeping in mind that his house is temporary, a new one to be built for him between your house and Don Ponchos.

Yours truly,

Julia Morgan.

LOORZ FAMILY COLLECTION

TOP: Excerpt from Morgan to Loorz, March 2, 1932.
BOTTOM: Loorz and the "bell men," sent from Belgium to install the carillon in Casa Grande, 1932.

SAN LUIS OBISPO COUNTY HISTORICAL MUSEUM

ABOVE AND RIGHT:
Tree moving, 1932.

LOORZ FAMILY COLLECTION

AUTHOR'S PHOTOGRAPH, 1974

ABOVE AND RIGHT: Native oaks,
east side of Casa Grande
(site of the proposed Great Hall).

AUTHOR'S PHOTOGRAPH, 1974

AUTHOR'S PHOTOGRAPH, 1975

East approach, town of San Simeon.

AUTHOR'S PHOTOGRAPH, 1988

Estrada-Summers residence, San Simeon.

LOORZ FAMILY COLLECTION

LOORZ FAMILY COLLECTION

TOP: Loorz residence, San Simeon.
LEFT: Grace and George Loorz.

AUTHOR'S PHOTOGRAPH, 1974

LOORZ FAMILY COLLECTION

TOP: The Roman Pool complex, with rooftop tennis courts (Casa Grande behind).
BOTTOM: Roman Pool, main section.

LOORZ FAMILY COLLECTION

LOORZ FAMILY COLLECTION

THIS PAGE: Roman Pool interiors.

AUTHOR'S PHOTOGRAPH, 1975

GEORGE LOORZ PAPERS

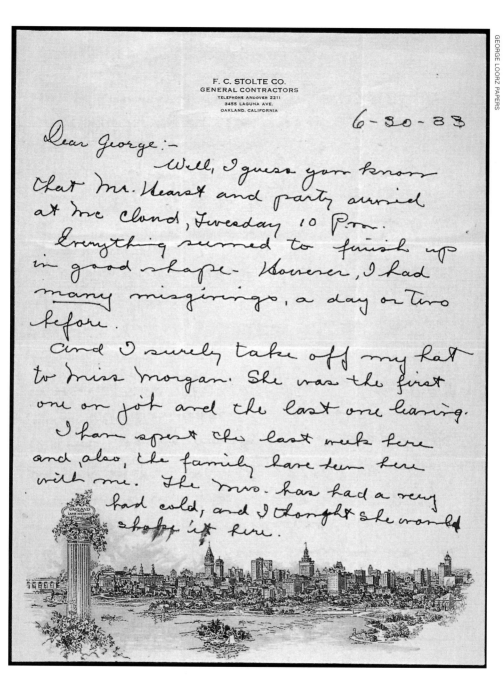

F. C. STOLTE CO.
GENERAL CONTRACTORS
TELEPHONE ANDOVER 2211
3455 LAGUNA AVE.
OAKLAND, CALIFORNIA

6-30-33

Dear George:-

Well, I guess you know
that Mr. Hearst and party arrived
at McCloud, Tuesday 10 P.m.

Everything seemed to finish up
in good shape. However, I had
many misgivings, a day or two
before.

And I surely take off my hat
to Miss Morgan. She was the first
one on job and the last one leaving.

I have spent the last week here
and, also, the family have been here
with me. The mrs. has had a very
bad cold, and I thought she would
shake it here.

Excerpt from Fred Stolte to George Loorz, June 30, 1933.

LOORZ FAMILY COLLECTION

THIS PAGE: Bavarian Village, Wyntoon, summer and fall 1933.

LOORZ FAMILY COLLECTION

LOORZ FAMILY COLLECTION

COURTESY OF JEAN HENRY WILLICOMBE

LOORZ FAMILY COLLECTION

Backcountry scenes
TOP: Hearst and picnicking guests.
LEFT: Hearst and Loorz.
BELOW: Nacimiento River Bridge.
BOTTOM: Burnett Road.

LOORZ FAMILY COLLECTION

AUTHOR'S PHOTOGRAPH, 1990

On the other hand, the matter is one of surpassing importance—not simply because Hearst got up his usual head of steam over that first remodeling of The Gables and never took steps to raze it. No, there was something else. The Gables, with its half-timbered and stucco sides, its quaint dormer windows, its steep roofs whose bottom edges curved gently outward, was right out of the Maybeck playbook, as much so in its woodsier way as the old Castle (built of lava rock) had been. "Maybeckian," his aficionados would have said of The Gables had they also known about that outlying building. More important, its medieval German attributes, retained by Hearst and Morgan in each remodeling, provided a theme, a point of departure, a structural prototype (wood versus stone) for the new houses in the Bavarian Village—that signature component of the Wyntoon fiefdom. Yet the contribution that The Gables made, both on its own and on behalf of the ruined Castle, has long been overlooked.[58]

---

58. The origins of the Bavarian Village beg to be unraveled, along with its themes and prototypes. The first volume of *The Julia Morgan Architectural History Project* is a good place to start. On p. 78, Walter Steilberg went strangely askew while discussing the Spanish monastery once slated for Wyntoon. He told Sally Woodbridge that Maybeck (not Morgan) designed the Bavarian Village after the monastery project had died. "Mr. Maybeck did his worst work on that, I think. I thought it was a caricature of a Bavarian village, even for Mr. Maybeck. From the pictures I've seen of it, it was pretty poor Maybeck, probably because he couldn't go there often enough." But the excerpt is telling, for Steilberg regarded the Bavarian Village as "Maybeckian," never mind his dim view of its merits and his dismissal of what, in reality, was Morgan's work. In many ways the Village *is* more Maybeckian than Morganesque. Not averse to being imitative as well as adaptive, the duo of Hearst and Morgan were consciously (and unconsciously) taking up where Phoebe Hearst and Maybeck left off—and perhaps where the trio of Hearst, Morgan, and Maybeck had more recently left off.

The trend since the 1970s has been to look farther afield for ideas and precedents. In *Eminent Women of the West* (1975), p. 258, Elinor Richey set the course in her chapter on Morgan: "The keening pine forest at Wyntoon reminded Hearst of the Bavarian forest country. Would his architect go abroad and garner ideas for designing a Bavarian village?" Of course she would; and Richey had Morgan making the trip in 1931. Sally Woodbrige followed suit in "Historic Architecture: Wyntoon" (*Architectural Digest*, January 1988), p. 103. Sara Boutelle broadened the date to 1931–32 in *Julia Morgan* (1988), pp. 160, 218, and 245 (this last reference under "The Morgan Atelier," note 3).

Alas, Morgan wasn't in Europe in 1931 (or in 1931–32, the period of her quick trip to Principia College). She hadn't been to Europe since 1902 and wouldn't be there again until the winter of 1934–35. Steilberg said about the timing of the European trip, "I'm not sure, 1929, something like that"; *Morgan Project*, Vol. I, p. 60. Richey, in turn, must have eyed 1931 as a likelier date (she read the Steilberg transcript and others before their publication in 1976). Besides, the old Castle had burned by 1931; and it was the Year of the Monastery, a subject much discussed by Steilberg in Vol I.

Coincidentally, 1931 found Mac McClure telling Julian Mesick about Wyntoon (within a letter cited earlier in this chapter; see p. 52). The letter indicates that Hearst, Morgan, and others were, in fact, looking for additional German themes and ideas. Hearst, for his part, had fresh impressions in mind, having been in central Europe in 1928 and 1930; he went there again later in 1931. (But that year still seems too soon for anyone to be visualizing a Bavarian Village.) Nonetheless, in thanking Mesick for a photograph and "travel folder" she had sent him, Mac said, "The German towers are very helpful and make a valuable addition to our examples of Rhenish castles." He also said, probably with equal pertinence to the new Castle on which Hearst was then focusing, that Wyntoon was

Our command of these details aside, Mac McClure, Harry Thompson, and the rest of the Wyntoon crew had their work cut out for them as the summer of 1933 ended. The medium job, as it were—much beholden to that pine-enshrouded building called The Gables—was getting bigger all the time, even with winter just around the corner.

AT SAN SIMEON, the Billiard Room and the Gothic Study remained at the forefront, as they had all summer. It was also the season of Sekhmet (often spelled *Sechet* at that time); the name, at any rate, denoted an Egyptian fountain ensemble near Casa Grande that featured ancient heads and figures in sculptured granite; their installation lent a uniquely exotic tinge to the hilltop from then on.

The Burnett Road had likewise been at the forefront. In addition, a shorter-term job—the airport hangar, whose prospects had looked doubtful at the first of the year—was about to be finished within its budgeted cost of $5,000. Loorz briefed Hearst on that job on September 22, writing to him at the Beach House in Santa Monica. He also mentioned the continuing Burnett job in San Simeon's backcountry:

> The road is going nicely again. We are able to progress several hundred feet per day which is somewhat of a relief after the [Salmon Creek][59] gorge. Fighting that hard rock certainly caused breakage and delay on our tractors but all are repaired [and] in excellent shape and should cause no further trouble. Unless I am too optimistic, I believe we will be able to get thru nicely without putting on the extra machine and crew from the other [Milpitas] side.

Loorz had more to discuss with his patron: employee use of hilltop amenities in Hearst's absence. Loorz had touched on the subject in writing to his parents a few weeks before. And now the moment was right for a full airing with the Chief himself.[60]

---

still "evolving" and undergoing "various stages of growth and shrinkage." From McClure to Mesic (spelled as in note 5, above), February 5, 1931; Morgan Collection, EDA.

59. A tributary of the Nacimiento River, as distinct from the coastwise Salmon Creek that lies eight miles due west of its interior namesake.

60. The second page in Loorz's letter of September 22 addressed the matter, beginning with "I would greatly appreciate a statement of your preference on the two following subjects":

> A. When the party is away the household help have enjoyed swimming in the pools after work, using their own suits and towels of course as the dressing rooms and lockers are locked.
>
> I find now, which would naturally be expected, that several of my construction crew have assumed the same privileges.
>
> Should I stop, encourage or say nothing about this activity?
>
> B. As above regarding swimming pool use, I find that some of my crew are using the tennis

As for Loorz's optimism about the Burnett job, it proved sound. By October 2 he could tell Hearst, who was still in Santa Monica, "We are up to the point where it is necessary to select the bridge site over the Nacimiento River." Loorz voted for putting the bridge "between the two rocky points just above where the Salmon Creek empties." Hearst knew the spot. He and been there with Loorz during the summer.

Morgan checked up on San Simeon in the meantime, on September 25. Concerning the Billiard Room, she told Loorz that it was "O.K. to send for Joe Giar-[r]itta [and his brother] for setting [the Persian] tile arches."[61] She also told Loorz, likewise for the Billiard Room, to "complete steps, buttresses and mantel hearth border as outlined to Mr. Cardini." For the Gothic Study on Hearst's private third floor in Casa Grande, she said that the same artisan, Cardini, was to "make and antique stone inner jambs and lintel for mantel."[62] There were sixteen other matters for Loorz to oversee, according to his notes of that Monday meeting.

Loorz wrote to Stolte on Wednesday, September 27, right after Morgan's latest visit:

> Miss Morgan reports everything going along nicely up there now [at Wyntoon], with reference to the construction crew at least. She is certainly not happy with the way the Chief and Mac are changing and adding. She went to L.A. [the Beach House] yesterday to see him and was going to tell him that the present budget would not enclose those buildings this winter. Let's hope he is in a position to get more [money]. I am cutting down here as much as possible to leave more for up there. They want so many things though that it is hard to cut down.
>
> The latest reports from the south have it that they are rushing through the

---

courts and at least one was bold enough last night to put on the lights. They use their own racquets and balls as Mrs. Drew [the head housekeeper] has yours put away promptly when the party leaves. The net cost per hour for electricity and bulb replacements is about 80¢.

What do you desire regarding this matter?

Loorz also said, "Though they are careful and tidy in regards to the above, you can be assured that it is the more forward & assuming types that are enjoying the pleasures."

The matter may have had some bearing on Hearst's decision to fire several household employees a few weeks later; see p. 97 and its note 75.

61. The Billiard Room contains three such tile spandrels (arch-shaped door surrounds) from Hearst's art collection, among them a seventeenth-century spandrel depicting Joseph and Potiphar's Wife. The room further contains two wall panels of old Persian tiles, likewise set by the Giarrittas but in the following year.

62. L. Cardini, a marble sculptor based in San Francisco, had played a key role at San Simeon since the 1920s. He not only worked with antique elements, as the Giarrittas did in setting the Persian tiles, but also produced modern elements for the "extension" of objects like the Gothic firemantels in the Billiard Room and in Hearst's private study.

[Marion Davies] picture [*Going Hollywood*][63] and will come here, in force, in about two or three weeks. Whether they will go north at that time will be doubtful but no one knows.

Hearst and Mac had made their most recent changes and additions (on paper) while Hearst was at Santa Monica, Mac having gone down to the Beach House to work with him there.

While Hearst was away, Loorz wrote to his parents on October 5; his words were typically revealing:

> Mr. Hearst has not been here with us for some time and I'm anxious to see him come back. I do enjoy dealing with him even if he is a little difficult to please. I shouldn't really say that for if you are right he always agrees. [What] I should say [is that] he wants so much and I seldom have crew or money enough to give him everything. With him away from here I would soon get tired [of it] and go back to the [contracting] business as it gets lonesome up here and with no one to appreciate the work it get[s] droll.

Julia Morgan or Mac McClure or others may also have found their unwitnessed work droll at times — or rather dull, as the make-haste Loorz probably meant to say.

As for Hearst's plans to return to San Simeon, they could naturally fluctuate as much as his thoughts about design and construction could. On Monday, October 9, Loorz wrote to Millard Hendricks, one of the men working on the Burnett Road. "We expect the party to be with us shortly," he said. "Geo Hearst [Hearst's oldest son] and a few will be here tomorrow unless minds are changed. Perhaps Mr. Hearst will follow over the week end [October 14–15] but that is only a guess."[64]

A few days earlier, on October 5, Mac McClure had written to Loorz from Wyntoon. Mac was back there now after his stint with Hearst in Santa Monica:

> Haven't heard much from J.M. since returning. A letter received yesterday however says we aren't making enough speed getting frames up. Have you seen the designs? The roof framing is, for the most part, very complicated. I have no fear that the houses will be covered before the snow comes,[65] but the Gables remodeling is

---

63. Released on December 23, 1933; see Guiles, *Marion Davies*, p. 400.

64. From "Misc. 1933" (one of the three boxes appended in 1990 to the main body of the Loorz Papers; see p. 26, note 13).

65. McClure was referring here and in the previous sentences to Brown Bear, Cinderella House, and Angel House, as the three largest buildings in the Bavarian Village were eventually named. (But as for the letter mentioned in his second sentence, no such item exists in the three Morgan Collections or any other known archives.)

Concerning nomenclature, Hearst had written to Morgan several weeks earlier about the naming of the new buildings at Wyntoon. See Hearst to Morgan, August 19, 1933; Hearst/Morgan Correspondence, Morgan Collection, Cal Poly.

another big item which is on our hands. The patio, as you probably know, is to be roofed and the downstairs almost entirely revamped. If this is to be done this Fall we will have a full program. If you have any idea how long we will be operating here let me know. Miss Morgan indicated they might try to keep going most of the Winter — Hope not!

October 6 was a Friday, and that evening saw some of the camaraderie for which the Loorz household in San Simeon was justly renowned. The electrician Louis Schallich heard about the gathering in a letter Loorz wrote him on Saturday the seventh:

> Joe Giar[r]itta and his brother left this morning after a few days setting the tile panels in the Billiard Room. Last night they and Cardini were down for a feed and later Arch Parks and his wife dropped in. We had some of the same old thing, you know, wine and song. Anyway a goodly time was enjoyed by all. Wish you had been with us. Joe brought down a gallon and so did Cardini so they furnished their own stuff so to speak.

We can only hope Loorz went easy on the rotgut that Friday evening, for he had to do more the next day than simply write to Louis Schallich; he had to confer with Miss Morgan on the hilltop. Her instructions concerned the Billiard Room. They tended more toward the fine points, now that the Persian tiles had been set by the Giarritta brothers and the other finishing touches were soon to be applied. "Place selected furniture as directed as soon as room is completed," Loorz noted. In addition, "Place one pool table in center and permit Mr. Hearst to approve before having the other two placed." (The room was eventually furnished with two such tables, not three.)

Having conferred with Loorz, the globetrotting Morgan made straight for Wyntoon on Sunday, October 8. Loorz wrote to Mac on Monday the ninth. In the best Hearst tradition of the editorial *we*, Loorz began by saying of himself and unspecified others, "We get out from here so seldom and correspondence seems to keep me connected with the outside world":

> No doubt Miss Morgan is there with you this morning.[66] Hope things are going to her satisfaction. . . .
>
> I left her Saturday night at 10:30 (the rest of the afternoon off) after a rather busy day of furnishing the Billiard Room though it is still full of scaffolding, stone masons, plasterers, decorators etc.

---

66. The main Wyntoon account in the Morgan-Forney ledgers (the "Waterhouse" account) indicates that Morgan left for Wyntoon on October 8 and was there for the three following days, October 9–11.

Morgan, now sixty-one, was seemingly back in full stride. And yet her mastoid condition, although surgically treated a year earlier (and still the subject of follow-up treatments), remained a serious hindrance. Loorz gave Mac an example in that same letter of October 9:

> She was quite strong, that is she lifted heavy chairs etc but Oh the equilibrium. I think she staggered more than ever. While we [were] going thru one of the tapestry boxes in the Vault she just simply fell into it.[67] She said, "I certainly have a jag on tonight." Again she was sketching something leaning on her elbow on a table and went flop down with her face on that. Each time I merely put my arms around her [and] pick her up bodily and set her in the nearest handy spot and go right on with the business. It is really pathetic.

Loorz's letter of the ninth also addressed the questions Mac had raised when writing on October 5:

> As for Wyntoon, I know they will work there as long as weather permits. I am cutting down here as much and as fast as possible to allow more funds for up there. Like yourself she is worried about the Gables alteration starting so late but she says Mr. Hearst wants that to be far enough ahead so they can finish it promptly for an early spring trip up there. She doesn't think he will go up there this fall.[68] He has had a cold and has not felt any too well. I had a long phone conversation with him on Saturday [October 7]. He heartily approved the idea of cutting down here to help out Wyntoon, but not to stop Gothic Study, Billiard Room. He still wants to start the outside pool in November. If you are far enough ahead or shut down because of weather I think he will insist on it.

Hearst obviously hoped to keep the momentum going at San Simeon. The remodeling of the outdoor pool wasn't the only big project he had in mind, and he wasn't getting any younger. In six more months, he would be seventy-one. Loorz, who was then half that age (he was soon to be thirty-five), still saw fit to say of the Chief, "Mr. Hearst looks very well and says he feels fine. I think he looks better than he has for four years."

Those lines appeared in a long letter written on October 10. It went to P. Caredio, described as a "mosaic tile draftsman" (for the Roman Pool job) on a list of workers that Loorz compiled in 1932; Caredio had returned to his native Italy in 1933. In writing to him there, Loorz greeted him as "Dear Friend Caredio." The letter also contained a quick rundown on events to date:

---

67. Possibly the Tapestry Vault, as one of several steel-doored storerooms adjoining the basement of the Theater (on the north side of Casa Grande) was once called.

68. Unless Hearst flew to Wyntoon with Morgan in mid-September (he probably didn't), he was at that northern estate in 1933 from late June through late July only.

Things have been rather quiet on the hilltop compared to last year but we have made quite a little headway at that. Most of the money is being used up at the castle at McCloud, Mt. Shasta, you've heard of the place. We are building five quite large guest houses up there so Mr. Hearst can go there with his guests when he gets tired of staying here.[69]

If only grandeur weren't so fatiguing. Caredio read on, and learned more from Loorz:

The [Roman] pool has never been touched since you left. We had things so well completed that it has not been necessary. Miss Morgan liked it a lot when she saw it and we were glad. The water cleared up [from the salt treatment] in about three months and the bottom is just as plain [as visible] as the walls.

Loorz said the pool had been "the show place of the hilltop to all visitors" ever since its painstaking tile work and other features were completed.

BEFORE MAC MCCLURE got a chance to write again (Loorz told him on October 17, "You owe me a letter"), George Wright checked in on the fourteenth, writing from the Hotel McCloud, where most of the crew lived during that first season at Wyntoon:

I think Miss Morgan has been irritated no end by trivial things that have not suited her fancy. At San Simeon, though you may have foremen who carry out instructions to the letter, the chief reason for the smoothness with which the job operates is your ability to handle Miss Morgan. If you were running this job it would be duck soup. Since his superior happens to lack the knack, Harry's job is difficult. Am I plain enough?

Wright's allusion may have been plain enough for Loorz. But it leaves the rest of us wondering who the "superior" was. Fred Stolte? If so, would Wright have felt this free to impugn him in Loorz's presence? One would think not. Moreover, Ed Hussey, after representing the Morgan office for four months at Wyntoon, had managed to alienate almost everbody. Hussey was ripe, therefore, for some of Wright's devilish word play. Back on June 30, Stolte himself had told Loorz that

---

69. All the structures on the Waterhouse parcel, whether old or new, bore numbers at this time. The Brown Bear, Cinderella, and Angel houses were numbers 5, 6, and 7 (much as the first houses on The Enchanted Hill at San Simeon were A, B, and C). But the five "guest houses" Loorz mentioned probably didn't equate with numbers 1–5, 3–7, or any such combination. He most likely meant the most prominent buildings that the Stolte Co. was working on in 1933: River House, plus Brown Bear and the other two—all four of them being at Waterhouse—and, elsewhere at Wyntoon, The Gables.

Hussey, fresh on the job then, seemed "a likeable fellow." However, through the long, often trying summer at Wyntoon, Hussey made few friends. By September 8, Harry Thompson was in a less allusive mood than George Wright would later be. Known for his bluntness, Thompson had this to tell Loorz:

> Miss Morgan and I get along fine and I realise that her job is a whole lot tougher than mine, so I'm willing and try to help her all I can. The worst part of [the] job is trying to stomach this man Hussey and I can hardly hold [it] in sometimes.

Unbeknownst to Thompson, Loorz had written to Stolte the day before, September 7, telling his partner that he and Morgan agreed Hussey wouldn't qualify as "the man to represent her" at Wyntoon in 1934. But Loorz added, "He has a family and needs the work right now."

The crisis defused itself by mid-October. Hussey learned that Bernard Maybeck was resuming work at Principia College in Elsah, Illinois, after a long shutdown; Hussey's services would once more be welcome. Back to Elsah he went, not to figure again in the Hearst-Morgan saga until long afterward—reminiscently, historically, archivally. And thus Thompson, writing from the Hotel McCloud on October 19, could tell Loorz (who may well have known this already), "Hussey has left to take a job at St. Louis [the main city near Elsah] and things seem to go better."

Thompson had elaborated on some of those "things" earlier in his letter: "Have four good sized jobs under way have roof on one expect to have two more covered in next week and the fourth in about three weeks if the weather holds out." Three of those projects were the eventual Brown Bear and its two similar neighbors, forming the trio that would dominate the Bavarian Village on the Waterhouse parcel. The fourth project was The Gables, half a mile away.

Mac McClure corroborated Thompson's headlong summary when he finally got around to writing Loorz on October 22:

> Our job here has grown to cover a lot of operations. Three new houses [the Bavarian Village] of no mean size and the Gables remodeling which in itself is a "job." Needless to say I have had my hands full and can't give anything the complete attention it merits. The drawings necessary alone would be more than I could turn out if it weren't for the other interruptions and demands on me. However I am doing this [work]; I hope to get the buildings up and covered and let future details be worked out as they may. In any case the probable finish will be different than planned now any way.
>
> Of course we hear much talk about "Getting the feeling" and a lot of time and money consuming antics are indulged in as usual.

Mac also commented on the Hussey situation. "Ed was a sort of hair splitting, exacting, person who sort of rubbed the fur [the] wrong way. Nonetheless Ed was merely forwarding J.M.'s orders." The season had not been without its merits, Mac assured Loorz. "I think my efforts and hard work have been appreciated and I believe J.M. has a higher regard for me than she once had."

An odd thing at this juncture: Morgan, who had been at San Simeon on October 20, was heading toward Wyntoon on the very day of Mac's letter; and yet Mac knew nothing of her recent whereabouts when he wrote it. That's just as well. Otherwise, he might not have included the following lines, which pertain to a little-known episode in Morgan's career:

> I am still uninformed whether or not J.M. went East. I rather think she did as I have heard nothing directly from her for a week. Her trip had to do with a proposed N.R.A. [National Recovery Administration] houseing scheme and not, I think, with her ear.

(No, she hadn't gone east and wouldn't be going. Jim LeFeaver would soon make the trip instead. He left on October 26 and was gone nearly three weeks. He went to Washington, D.C., where he dealt with the federal government on the housing project called Bellshire, slated to be a Morgan design in San Francisco.)[70]

Mac's reference to Morgan's ear — to her mastoid condition — was a more urgent point in his letter of October 22, a point affecting everyone who was close to the woman professionally. The problem had been "eradicated," he told Loorz, but he still feared for her continued well-being. Indeed, as Mac said, "The long sessions of overwork and extreme exhaustion continue as always and she probably will always be so."

Loorz's reply of October 25 contained more on the government project Mac had spoken of and, following that, on the subject that made both of them wince:

---

70. Attempts thus far to learn more about Bellshire (also called Valmonte) have borne little fruit. Sara Boutelle associated the two names not with a government project but with a home for George W. McNear, an old client of Morgan's; see *Julia Morgan*, p. 261, under 1933–34.

LeFeaver's trip to Washington was his longest in 1933, yet he'd been making others for Morgan all year, in part to help her recuperate faster. On February 2 he went to Los Angeles to inspect Hearst's warehouses there (a little-known link in the man's treasure-hoarding chain); then on February 12, LeFeaver went to Asilomar in the Monterey area. He made two more inspection trips to Hearst's warehouses in Los Angeles, one in April, the other in August; those two trips and their precursor appear in Morgan's account for the Los Angeles Examiner Building. Loorz said Morgan went to Los Angeles periodically in 1933 (note 71, below), yet the Morgan-Forney ledgers indicate she made no trips that year to the Beach House or any other job south of San Luis Obispo (where at one point in August she checked on the Monday Club). The sole exception came in late December, when she went to Culver City — as further recounted in the 1934 chapter, p. 104.

She was hoping to hear regarding the proposition you mentioned but there were some objections raised by S.F. residents and it may fall thru. She also feared that they might hesitate to give it to her since she really did not appear [physically] as well and capable as she really is.[71] 'Tis almost too sad but she will not quit, as you say.

Loorz had cheerier words regarding Mac's performance at Wyntoon that season. "I am confident that Miss Morgan has a lot of faith in you and feels that she could not have put a better man on the job. She remarked several times how well you got along up there and how much help you had been."

YET ANOTHER WYNTOONITE wrote to Loorz from the Hotel McCloud—and did he write! Hayes Perkins, a veteran of Hearst Camp (and a prolific diarist) who joined the pilgrimage to Wyntoon in 1933, hammered out three tightly spaced pages of local history and incisive prose on November 1:

McCloud is a one-man town, or rather, a company town,[72] for the Shevlin-Hixon Lumber Co. owns everything here but the dairy, and all the land and timber for a long radius about the place. . . .

Mr. Hearst's present place is about seven miles distant from the town. Most of us stay at the hotel, where charges for rooms are from $9 to $10 per month. The rooms are very good, steam heat, a good lobby, well conducted and as good as anyone could ask for the money. We commute daily to our work, about a half hour in truck or car. . . .

There is no comparison between this place and that at San Simeon. This site is in a deep valley taken up by dense forest. The largest forest trees grow about the houses, and the McCloud River, a flush stream that varies little during the entire year is immediately behind every house. It is very rapid, so there is no possibility of boating whatever. There is a good sized lawn, perhaps an acre and a half, well

---

71. In his letter of October 10 to P. Caredio, Loorz described Morgan's appearance. "Her face that was so twisted about six months ago is straightening up a lot." He also told Caredio, much as he had Mac McClure the day before:

She is stronger but her equilibrium is very bad. She reels and stumbles when she walks. I have to be very careful when with her to keep her from falling. She is just as active as ever mentally and tries to do just as much physically. She comes here then goes up North, [and] often to Los Angeles and told me Saturday [October 7] that she was going East on a Business trip this week. I'm afraid it is "*Ear Business*" but she did not say so. [It would have been for the Bellshire project, the trip LeFeaver later made in her place.] I feel so sorry for her but she seems happy enough. She surely has some fight. Most of us would go jump in the ocean.

A photograph of Morgan, showing her face as Loorz portrayed it, appears in Boutelle's *Julia Morgan*, p. 232 (the same one as the "fishing" photograph cited above in note 43).

72. So much so that James B. Allen gave McCloud several pages in *The Company Town in the American West* (Norman, Oklahoma; 1966); see title spread, plus index listings on p. 202.

cleared and sown to grass at the upper place called locally the Waterhouse, and a smaller area a half mile below at the old [Phoebe Hearst] castle site, now called the Gables. Of course everything is more or less upside down now on account of the construction, but when it is finished, can be easily put into condition again. . . . Personally, I like the Waterhouse site the best. Mr. Hearst seemed to prefer it when here last summer [1933], and stayed at that place all the time.[73] When completed, it will be truly a sylvan retreat, more secluded than is San Simeon and embowered in virgin forest unspoiled.

Perkins concluded his letter many paragraphs later by saying, "This is about all I know, Mr. Loorz." If only everyone who enriched the George Loorz Papers had been as poorly informed!

In writing to Harry Thompson on October 25, Loorz had asked him, "How is old man Perkins? At one time he said he would write but has failed to do so." Yes, Hayes Perkins, who was born twenty years before Loorz, more than redeemed himself (and as Loorz later said of him and his long letter, "He wrote it assuming that I had not been up there and detailed everything").[74]

In Loorz's letter to Thompson, some other matters were touched on as well:

Mr. Hearst is in the air now on his way up here. We have the Billiard Room furnished and ready for his inspection. He has been feeling bum so anything might happen. You heard that he had cleaned house here [fired certain employees] in the household.[75] They have me cut down to just a handful of men so that you can proceed up there.

---

73. As Stolte said of Hearst and his guests after they arrived at Wyntoon on June 27, the party was "fully settled in the Gables" (p. 74 in this chapter). The Gables provided the main housing for the party throughout its month-long stay. (The new, post-1931 remodeling of that building was put off until late summer.) Hearst's use of the Waterhouse parcel must have been confined to buildings worked on during the "small job," such as River House.

74. Loorz to George Wright, November 7, 1933. Hayes Perkins was keeping a diary all the while; in fact, he'd been doing so intermittently since 1897, while in his late teens; the entries relating to San Simeon and, at times, to Wyntoon date from 1928 through 1936, when the diary ends. For the full span beginning in 1897, roughly 2,000 transcribed pages exist as photostats both at Cal Poly, San Luis Obispo (separate from the Julia Morgan Collection), and at the Oregon Historical Society, Portland. A brief excerpt from "Here and There," as Perkins called his grand compilation, appeared in Nancy E. Loe's book *Hearst Castle: An Interpretive History of W. R. Hearst's San Simeon Estate* (Santa Barbara, 1994), p. 29. Further excerpts (but from much earlier than the Hearst portions) appeared as "Here and There: An Itinerant Worker in the Pacific Northwest, 1898" in the *Oregon Historical Quarterly* (Fall 2001), pp. 352–76.

Since then, Louis Pizzitola has opened the Pandora's box that the Perkins material poses with regard to Hearst and his circle. See the diary excerpts in *Hearst Over Hollywood: Power, Passion, and Propaganda in the Movies* (New York, 2002), pp. 262, 267–68, 282.

75. Loorz had told Mac McClure and Fred Stolte about the dismissals on October 17. Mac commented on October 22 that "working for Hearst is very uncertain and one never knows what is around the corner." Ada Drew, the head housekeeper, was among the unknowing ones who got fired.

Then came a passage that minced no words for ears as unprudish as Thompson's; the man Loorz described was part of the Burnett Road construction crew:

> Got to go to San Luis tomorrow to a trial. The little fat mexican Joe Ocon got into some knifing scrape in a dance hall and they called several of us as character witnesses. It will [be] the first trip beyond Cambria for several weeks.

There it was again—that feeling of isolation, of loneliness, of being lost to the larger world. Loorz would never entirely come to grips with it until he left San Simeon at the outset of 1938.

With Hearst having come back, Loorz wrote to Stolte on October 27. The Chief wasn't quite as immortal, it turns out, as Loorz had told P. Caredio recently:

> Mr. Hearst is here. Had a talk with him and he really looks pale. Been [being] cooped up with a cold down there [at the Beach House] for several weeks certainly did tell on him. He seems pleasant enough, however, and this sun may bring him out of it quickly. Boy we dont want fate to change his program for a while yet for his sake as well as our own, How about it?

Morgan was at San Simeon the day after, October 28, and she was there again on November 8. The next time was Friday, November 17. Loorz wrote to Stolte before she arrived on that latest date; he struck some familiar notes in the process:

> Miss Morgan will be here today. Hope she feels stronger than last week [Wednesday the eighth]. She was certainly week [*sic*]. I hope Mr. Hearst doesn't keep her on a long session for that does bother her. With us she can relax a little but not with him. Of course, I've told him she seemed week and he will be very considerate I'm certain.

Likewise familiar was Loorz's allusion to the touch-and-go conditions that the F. C. Stolte Co. often faced in these financially muddled times. He remarked, "It

---

In contrast, Maurice McClure (the unrelated, younger McClure) would be unemployed only "while the party is away," as Loorz specified for Mac on the seventeenth.

"Boy Oh Boy who's next?" Loorz asked Mac that same day. "You knew that several changes had [also] been made on the ranch. Mr. [Arch] Parks now has this ranch only [apart from Milpitas and other outlying acreage] and Barbaree [Bob Barbree] the big job [the Babicora ranch in Mexico], with [Bill] Murray in [Richard] Clark's place in S.F. [at the Piedmont Land & Cattle Company headquarters]."

On October 17 as well, Loorz submitted his "Personal Observations and Recommendations" to Joseph Willicombe for the reorganization of the household staff. One point Loorz emphasized was that "definite rulings should be made to begin with on many items other than the use of amusements," among which were the swimming pools. But he didn't advocate draining the pools to prevent their use in the party's absence, as had been suggested. It would waste too much water, he said, and it would take "weeks and weeks to clear up new water and kill algae etc."

seems that Miss Morgan is continually in as bad shape as we ourselves get, if that is any consolation."

She undoubtedly wasn't as strapped for funds as he thought, yet Morgan may indeed have felt "week." Loorz's recap of her November 17 visit—his notes pertained mostly to the Gothic Study—filled no more than a single page.

An undated letter of Stolte's, sent to Loorz about this time, most likely dates from mid-November. Stolte said he'd been trying to be at Wyntoon whenever Morgan was. (She was last there in 1933 on November 9–11.) Stolte told Loorz, "I feel that I can help in getting some small things cleaned up and off of her mind." And then he added, "She is so *little*. But—'boy' how she can see—and remember."

Loorz soon received another undated letter from Stolte, evidently written on November 18 or 25:

> Miss Morgan arranged a party for the gang—Everyone had a fine time, and Mac was a first class host, in Miss Morgan's absence. Should she be there—thank her on behalf of the boys. [She was next at San Simeon on Monday, November 27.] They and we all, surely appreciated this kind thought.

Mac McClure, who was still at Wyntoon as winter approached, wrote to Loorz on December 1:

> The buildings are all covered and a fair amount of exterior work done on them. More than I expected has been accomplished.
>
> However it is expected that the Gables and one house here [on the Waterhouse parcel] will be finished before W.R. comes up next Summer. This leaves a lot to be done next Spring—as no interior work is done on either the Gables or these houses.

Mac also said of Miss Morgan, "She says she will only come up once again before we close." Morgan, however, made no such trip; but it was too soon for Mac to know that. What he did know was that something else was in the offing—this with regard to Loorz's home turf:

> I am asked, by the way, to take the winter months off—as "I will not be needed at San Simeon." On Miss M's last visit here she intimated that she thought of sending Hatch Lovell back to the ranch (for a while). He was my predecessor [as architect's representative]. Perhaps he is there now.

Personalities, personalities. The 1933 season had had its share of people who had wrung their hands over some clash of wills, some disagreement or conflict— real or imagined. Martin Charles at San Simeon. Ed Hussey at Wyntoon. And others, too, at one of those places or even both: Jim LeFeaver and Harry Thompson and George Wright and Jim Rankin and still more (and, lest we forget, Hearst and Morgan themselves).[76] Now it was Loorz's turn to chafe a bit, the irritant being Hathaway Lovell, Thad Joy's fellow "rep" at San Simeon a few years back. "No Mac," Loorz belatedly said on December 13, "I have heard nothing about the possibility of Lovell coming here and I really hope not." What Loorz was actually hoping was that Morgan would see the light—would see that San Simeon would benefit far more from Mac McClure's presence than from Hatch Lovell's. Loorz offered to intercede for his friend.

In closing, Loorz shared some details with Mac that had yet to become common knowledge (as they eventually would):

> Mr. Hearst has been very pleasant and seemed well pleased with things. Just yesterday, however, he did not feel very well. Neither did he look well. Joe [Joseph Yelinek, Hearst's valet][77] mentions possible heart trouble that bothers from time to time. Lets hope it does not become serious.

Never mind those symptoms. Hearst was all heart and gusto and vibrant enthusiasm in writing to Loorz a few days after, on December 17. Having been at San Simeon through most of the late fall, the Chief had had plenty of time to sharpen his thoughts about the season ahead. He gave Loorz a summary of his plans for the interior of Casa Grande and for other parts of his coastal estate in 1934:

> After the holidays I would like to hurry up the [Gothic] study and get the decorators [the artisans] into it as soon as possible.
>
> I would then like to start on the three bedrooms over the billiard room.
>
> I would also like to alter the ladies' dressing room as planned. And I think while doing this we could tile and finish properly the kitchen and pantry.
>
> Perhaps we can also do the stairs after a model I have given Miss Morgan.
>
> We might put in the north wing [Recreation Wing] elevator and do the bowling alley.
>
> Outside on the grounds I would like to do the outdoor pool beginning February first. I think we can finish the west terrace at the same time.

---

76. Some hand wringing of a different kind was occurring elsewhere. Hearst had spent nearly $136,000 on himself and the party he'd taken with him to Europe in 1928; those staggering expenses had yet to be properly reconciled for income tax and other purposes. See Geoffrey Konta to John Francis Neylan, December 9, 1933; Hearst Papers, carton 17 (under "1933 Samples").

77. Despite the casual, even gossipy nature of many such letters, Loorz almost certainly would not have used *Joe* to mean Joseph Willicombe—any more than he would have used *Will* to mean Hearst himself. Yelinek, like Loorz and McClure, was a generation younger than Willicombe, and younger still than the grandfatherly Hearst. (*Yellinek* and other misspellings appear in the annals at times. But no matter: Joseph Yelinek later changed his Czech surname by spelling it backwards, rendering it *Keniley* or, as some claim it was spelled, an equally uncommon *Kennely.*)

I would like to complete the pergola and the [encircling] road wall [on Orchard Hill] also in time for Autumn planting.

We should enlarge the smaller reservoir to enable us to double our water supply.

Of course we will finish and straighten the road to Jolon when the fine weather comes.

And I think we should make a shorter road from the castle to the creek.[78]

The Great Hall, still a prospect earlier in 1933, wasn't on the list. Other big prospects remained in the running, though, and much of what Hearst outlined came to fruition. Not in a single burst within a single season, but in the usual way, piecemeal over the time remaining to Loorz at San Simeon. Thus were the Gothic Study and the Neptune Pool completed. And so were certain other projects on the list—such as that of reaching the Burnett Road more directly via Orchard Hill, rather than from the former jumping-off point well behind Casa Grande and the Roman Pool.

But some of the things on Hearst's list—like the plastering of the four matching staircases in the main part of Casa Grande—were never completed. As for the latter project and any others on the hilltop itself, those that Hearst left unfinished at his death in 1951 are destined to remain that way—as a tribute to what he and others accomplished at San Simeon in their lifetimes.

As 1933 ended, the aging Hearst and the overworked Morgan were still looking ahead, not behind, just as much as the youthful, energetic Loorz was. Of course it was Hearst's love of earthly splendor that drove them on, that kept this most improbable of enterprises humming.

What else could Loorz do upon reading Hearst's letter but be amazed by the man's enthusiasm, by his boundless optimism, by his firm insistence on defying the odds?

Dream on, Mr. Hearst, he must have marveled. Dream on.

---

78. Hearst's use of *castle* contradicts the oft-heard story that he didn't use the word to mean Casa Grande or, more broadly, San Simeon. The story goes back to 1936 and Mrs. Fremont Older's *William Randolph Hearst*, p. 536: "He says it is not a castle." True, Hearst was more inclined to use *castle* with regard to Wyntoon or to St. Donat's in Wales; but regarding The Enchanted Hill, he sometimes broke character, inadvertently or not. See Victoria Kastner, *Hearst Castle*, p. 163, for another instance of his using the word at San Simeon.

1934

"Certainly Booming Now"

FOUR YEARS HAD PASSED since the Wall Street crash played its notorious part in launching the Depression late in 1929. The crisis had hit bottom in 1933, but conditions were improving now with Franklin Roosevelt firmly at the helm. And yet stability and recovery would elude many parts of the country for the rest of the thirties decade; the trend toward widespread prosperity would have to await the global war that lay still further ahead.

Hearst, seemingly invincible thus far, remained at San Simeon through Christmas of 1933 and into the early days of the new year, accompanied by a big entourage. Loorz wrote to Mac McClure in Los Angeles on January 5, the first Friday of 1934, telling him, "Up here [on the hilltop] as you know they had some 63 in the party. Doubled up in many rooms to make it go around." Loorz also told Mac, "The party is to leave about January 15th. Mr. Hearst said they intended to be away a couple of months returning about April for a short stay and away again." What Loorz didn't say—what everyone certainly understood—was that Hearst's proposed movements were always subject to change, as events over the next several weeks would attest.

With regard to the resumption of work at San Simeon, or at Wyntoon, Loorz made it clear to Mac in that same letter of early January that he was getting mixed signals from Hearst:

> Yesterday forenoon [Thursday the fourth] he seemed to want to get started with a small crew soon. Later in the day while talking to Miss Morgan and I, he said he was in no hurry and we could remain shut down until March or April. No less than two weeks ago he sat down and wrote me a long letter on Sunday [December 17][1] which laid out a large program for this year with the hopes that we go right on and get some of it done right away. So there you have it. He even told Miss Morgan yesterday that she needn't rush Wyntoon Gables and houses for he was comfortably located here and could remain here this summer and she could get it

---

1. See pp. 100–01 in the previous chapter.

ready for the following summer [1935], up there. Now if you know any more about it after all this you are a magician. In spite of all this he looks very well and seems very happy. Except of course that the north wind is causing the East Room Fireplace to smoke too much.

In saying further to Mac, "I am certainly glad to hear that she may send you here again," Loorz indicated that the recent prospect of Hatch Lovell's return to San Simeon was coming to naught. Instead, Mac McClure was likelier to resume the on-site architectural role (as was only fitting), much to Loorz's preference.[2]

Mac knew that Loorz planned to take his vacation as soon as Hearst left in mid-January. "Hope you and the family have a good time and a chance to forget W.R.H.—J.M.—and all the rest of the outfit," went his reply of January 8.

Hearst delayed a week in leaving. But the Loorzes took off just the same for a much-needed eight days at Gilman Hot Springs in southern California, between Riverside and Palm Springs. Upon returning, Loorz found two baseballs awaiting him on his desk. Hearst's secretary, Joseph Willicombe, knew Babe Ruth and had asked him to autograph the balls for Loorz's young sons, Don and Bill.[3]

Loorz resumed his unending correspondence by thanking Colonel Willicombe, as he was often called (the U.S. Army Reserve having given him that title honorarily in 1927).[4] "You certainly must have a drag with the Babe," wrote Loorz on January 30. He went on to tell Willicombe about his recent trip to Gilman Hot Springs. "It may not be a *Carlsbad* but it affords a real place for rest and health improving for those of moderate incomes." He also mentioned having seen the Marion Davies movie *Going Hollywood* (newly released and also starring Bing Crosby), a musical comedy the Loorzes thought would be a big success.[5] "Miss Davies certainly did herself justice," Loorz remarked.

But the young builder had more pressing correspondence to get out on that

---

2. Loorz's letter of January 5 was in reply to one from Mac dated December 29, 1933. Newly arrived in Los Angeles, Mac reported that he had had "a nice talk with J.M." before leaving San Francisco for points south: it seemed likely that he'd be "back at Wyntoon in the spring." Mac further told Loorz, "She also said that after the next picture [*Operator 13*] was done that perhaps I would go to the ranch and work out interiors [for Wyntoon] with W.R."

3. Don Loorz still has his autographed ball; Bill Loorz had his for many years—until his dog laid paws on it.

4. Clarified for me in April 1984 by Bill Hearst, Jr. (the second of Hearst's five sons). Sixty-one in 1934, Willicombe was ten years younger than Hearst and a year younger than Morgan.

5. *Going Hollywood* (1933) brought its director, Raoul Walsh, into the Hearst-Davies fold. A respected journeyman, yet one who could also be farcical, Walsh said Winston Churchill was at San Simeon while the picture was being made (a visit well known to have occurred in 1929—and only then). He also named Douglas MacArthur, Howard Hughes, Somerset Maugham, J. Edgar Hoover, and Ernest Hemingway as concurrent guests. See Walsh's freewheeling memoir, *Each Man in His Time: The Life Story of a Director* (New York, 1974), pp. 254–74.

last Tuesday in January. "As per previous conversations we are starting up construction work with a small crew," began a detailed letter Loorz sent to Hearst at the Beach House in Santa Monica:

> A few men will work on the [Gothic] Study and a few will start about Monday [February 5] on the [enlarging of the] outdoor pool. Perhaps not more than ten men for a few weeks on this work. No doubt I will hear from Miss Morgan with more definite instructions in a day or so.

(As for her being on the job in person, she would next be at San Simeon four days later — on Saturday, February 2. She had last been there on January 13 and, before that, on January 4. She and Loorz had corresponded little in recent weeks, mainly because of the vacation he'd taken; but Ray Van Gorden of Hearst Camp had written to her twice in that period: the flow of letters had continued among the diverse players all along. Morgan, meanwhile, had overcome her ear problems enough to increase her business travel in recent weeks, apart from her visits to San Simeon. On December 27, 1933, she went to the MGM studio lot in Culver City; its Cosmopolitan bungalow, originally designed for Hearst and Miss Davies by Joseph Urban, was now slated for further work under Morgan. More than twenty such trips to Culver City lay ahead for her in 1934 alone, the first being one that she made on January 25. It was a trip that, on her return to San Francisco, found her checking on the nearly completed Monday Club in San Luis Obispo.)[6] Loorz continued with his letter to Hearst of January 30 by telling him:

> There is a lot of miscellaneous odd jobs that have been requested from time to time and which could use quite a crew if we attempted them all very soon.

The "odd jobs" ranged from fence work at the Hearst Ranch poultry unit (also called the Chicken House or Chicken Ranch) to a mechanical upgrading of the elevator in Casa Grande; the jobs also included the building of additional tennis courts on the hilltop. They further included the transplanting of a large Italian cypress tree from the Paso Robles area — a site fifteen or twenty miles east of San Sim-

---

6. On February 26 Morgan would visit that job again in San Luis, where she would also meet with Loorz and thus save herself a side trip to San Simeon; she would not reappear at San Simeon itself until March 4, after a full month's absence. These exact dates typify the precise entries in the Morgan-Forney ledgers, both for drafting-room time and for other costs accrued by the Morgan office.

The first part of 1934 also found Morgan being fully active in another way: in buying a second home in Monterey, a place she would use increasingly in the years ahead. See *Descriptive Guide to the Julia Morgan Collection*, pp. 38–40. (From here on, certain files at Cal Poly — such as those cited in notes 32 and 33, below — will be easier to find through their archival coding in the *Descriptive Guide* than through their series names or page numbers in that compilation.)

eon, though a good deal farther by the roundabout roads of the day. In 1928 an entire row of such cypresses had been hauled in from Paso Robles. Their arrival on the hilltop, along with that of palm trees like the ones Loorz brought from San Luis Obispo in 1932, had quickly imparted an Old World atmosphere to the terraced grounds.

Hearst replied immediately to Loorz. "I think you will have to enlarge your crew," he told him on January 31,[7] "because all the things which you mention in your letter should be done and should be done more or less promptly."[8] He was especially concerned about the Italian cypress:

> Please take great care in moving the cypress tree from Paso Robles. Please take a very liberal amount of dirt with the tree,—more than you think necessary for safety,—more than enough to leave what you consider a sufficient margin of safety and then some more.
>
> We must surely preserve this tree. I do not know where we could get another one of that size. . . .
>
> In fact to get all these things washed up, I would be willing to defer starting work on the [outdoor] pool until the first of March, if necessary; although I would like to begin on the first of February and get all the noisy work of taking out the concrete finished by the middle of March.

Loorz soon had firm orders to begin working on several projects, among them the outdoor pool—which was finally about to be transformed into that quintes-

---

7. Loorz, after writing to Hearst on January 30, went to Los Angeles the next day ("for Hilltop Fund book work in [Alexander] Sokolow's office," as Loorz told George Wright on February 3). Hearst's letter of the thirty-first was therefore hand-delivered, probably in care of Sokolow. An attached note from Joe Willicombe ("Dear George," it warmly began) was also dated January 31; the note exemplified the rapport between Willicombe and Loorz (and between Hearst and Loorz); it also disclosed what may have been a familiar routine for Willicombe:

> After Chief had dictated this attached letter, I learned that you were on your way down, and told him; and he said that if you wanted to see him, he would be glad to talk with you, although he added that he thought the letter covered everything. However, it is up to you. If you want to see him, let me know. I expect to be at the office [in the Examiner Building in downtown Los Angeles] (PROSPECT 9688) between ten and eleven in the morning; but if I am not there when you call, I will surely be at the Beach House (SANTA MONICA 25744) at quarter past twelve; and some time in the afternoon I expect to be at the studio [the Cosmopolitan bungalow] (REPUBLIC 0211 or CULVER CITY 3343).

Willicombe closed by saying, "Hope to see you and Mrs. Loorz before you leave town."

8. Despite Hearst's allusion at the beginning of his letter to extra tennis courts (among other subjects), and despite his lasting hope of having more courts than those atop the Roman Pool, no others were ever built. For the time being, he had in mind a single court in the flat area adjoining the Roman Pool entrance; he was also eyeing the larger area east of there, known by the 1930s as Animal Hill (and before that as Garage Hill).

sential symbol of Hearstian grandeur, the Neptune Pool. Loorz's conference with Morgan on February 3 yielded this note:

> Start work with the approved crew on Monday Feb. 5th. Approx. six laborers.[9] [Frank] Frandolich on swimming pool, Alex Rankin to start removing pipes with labor helper. [Pete] Peterson & one carpenter on Billiard Room doors and forms for present. [Frank] Gyorgy to polish Dining Room [Refectory] tables and stain doors only for present. Plasterer, bricklayer, helper and Glazier to complete present hilltop construction crew. Labor total to be approximately $3000 Mo.

Concerning the outdoor pool, Loorz also noted that the crew was to "move all of group statue[s][10] to safe location from pool and fence [them in]." In addition, his notes from February 3 contained references to an old Roman temple (one of Hearst's architectural gleanings) whose dismantled components had long been piled nearby, earmarked for assemblage next to the remodeled pool:

> Move temple marble, columns and stone, to safe location, perhaps on south side of pool. Layout carefully keeping all pieces in position as at present; Can start removing concrete with compressors as soon as [these] antiques are safely out of the way; Frandolich can chip out the marble ladders [in the existing pool] to make certain they are not damaged.

With the crew's completion of its first full week in the new season, Loorz sent a progress report to Hearst on Tuesday, February 13:

> The cypress tree is safely loaded and enroute this morning. We have a nice tight ball of earth and should have no trouble. Will see that proper guys are placed as you suggest. . . .
>
> The outdoor pool is being wrecked but as you know that concrete is hard and requires considerable handling to get it out to the dump.
>
> We are busy moving the doors to the [Gothic] Study from the [adjoining] Gothic [Suite] Hall.[11] We will proceed promptly with this so the hall should be

---

9. As distinct from artisans and tradesmen like those mentioned further on in Loorz's note: the stone mason and marble setter Frank Frandolich, the plumber Alex Rankin, the carpenter Pete Petersen (the correct spelling), and the painter and gilder Frank Gyorgy.

10. *The Birth of Venus* and other modernistic sculptures by Charles Cassou of Paris. Hearst had commissioned these in recent years, and they had since arrived on the hilltop — there to be placed temporarily by the outdoor pool, pending their use at the full-scale Neptune Pool.

11. The Gothic Hall lies between the Gothic Study and the Gothic Suite, whose cluster of bedrooms, baths, and a sitting room served as Hearst's own living quarters in Casa Grande; the adjoining Hall and Study were also part of his inner sanctum, which comprised the entire third floor in that central part of the main building.

completely finished before the middle of March. This is not a large job but requires everything from brick & concrete work to marble & decorating. . . .

It is a real pleasure to have a crew again and see things real active. Few of the men had a days work since they left the hill [late in 1933]. Some of them had been away five months.

In mid-February, Hearst was at San Simeon briefly for what Loorz called "a little family reunion," the group revolving around Hearst, Marion Davies, and Hearst's two oldest sons, George and Bill:

Mr. Hearst flew up [from Los Angeles] for two days and seemed well pleased with everything. They went back by train last night [February 15] as it was too stormy to fly. He & Marion, Bill and his wife and his personal secretary came in one plane. Their maids came in another. The next day the plane went to S.F. and brought George and his wife.[12]

Hearst wrote to Loorz from his hilltop office on the first day of that visit, February 14:

Regarding the work inside the hacienda [Casa Grande],[13] there are two things I wish we could do and have them over with.

First, and most important, is the fireplace in the East Room. I would like to have this fixed right even if we have to take down all that end of the building. But I do not think we will have to do that.

The fireplace in the East Room (better known as the Morning Room) had smoked badly for years. Hearst suggested some possible remedies. Well that he should have, for the Morning Room was a frequented part of Casa Grande's first floor; it doubled as the Breakfast Room, and it connected the great Refectory dining room with the rear courtyard and the flanking wings of the house.

Hearst also elaborated upon the second problem in that letter of Valentine's

---

12. Loorz to his parents, February 16, 1934. Concerning the trip Hearst made to San Simeon: in flying to or from the Los Angeles area, he often used Clover Field (the precursor of Santa Monica Airport), a facility about three miles from the Beach House.

A letter Hearst wrote to Morgan upon returning to Los Angeles bears the same date. He told her that work was "progressing slowly but sufficiently" at San Simeon and that he had made "a few suggestions" to Loorz. Hearst to Morgan, February 16, 1934; Hearst/Morgan Correspondence, Morgan Collection.

13. More often than not, Hearst referred to Casa Grande simply as "the house," although he occasionally said "the hacienda" or even "the castle." His use of *hacienda* recalled his mother's Hacienda del Pozo de Verona in Pleasanton, California—an estate that Morgan had worked on as early as 1903 and that Hearst himself had begun developing in the 1890s, before his mother took it over. See also p. 296, note 12.

Day, a problem affecting his private Gothic Suite, high up in the front end of Casa Grande:

> The other thing is the stopping of noises in the tower — in fact in both towers.[14] The north tower, however, is much the worse. If I believed in ghosts I would think it was haunted.
>
> Whenever there is any kind of a wind, even a stiff breeze, the moans and groans in the tower are pitiful to hear.
>
> I do not know what the trouble is, although it may be the weather vanes, which are probably old and rusty and creak when the wind moves them.
>
> If it is not that it must be something connected with the bells. . . .
>
> It is a bad trouble, however, and makes sleep almost impossible.
>
> There is a slight moaning in the south tower, but it is only slight in comparison and only noticeable when the wind is particularly strong.
>
> It may be due to some similar cause, but it expresses itself in a much less aggravated and aggravating manner.
>
> If we can get these two things fixed up — the fireplace and the ghosts — the house will be much more habitable.

Loorz replied to Joe Willicombe on February 22; by then the Chief and his companions had been back in Los Angeles for a week.[15] Loorz began by saying, "We have enjoyed reading his *Ghost Letter* several times and use it as an excuse to write the enclosed letter":

> Being favored with a strong appropriate Southerly, I sent out a scout to locate the position of the enemy, the Ghosts of La Cuesta Encantada.
>
> Within a short time the scout returned, reporting that he had located the stronghold of the enemy. He volunteered to go out single-handed and route [*sic*] the ghosts with a hammer and two plugs. This being done promptly all is again quiet on the Gothic Front.

---

14. The matching towers have belfries in their upper portions; their lower portions contain the bedrooms of the Celestial Suite, which forms a fourth floor in this older, central portion of Casa Grande, right above Hearst's suite.

15. In the meantime, Loorz had written to Willicombe on personal business. What he told "the Colonel" on February 19 showed that even an esteemed employee had to be be ever-mindful of protocol:

> My wife's mother and sister will be with us in a few days and will want to see the hilltop. If it is in order, would it be O.K. to bring them up, see the animals and gardens? I would like to just let them glance into the Assembly Room and Dining Room as there is nothing like them. I would see that it was done quickly and safely.

Willicombe was uncommonly slow in answering, but his reply of February 28 filled the bill (provided Loorz's guests remained on hand): "Certainly take your folks up the Hill and show them the place inside and out."

There were two small stubs of pipe projecting about 6 inches thru the roofs of the stair towers, these are the elevator tower [the north tower] and the one on the south. The wind blowing over the tops of these small open pipes made very prominent rumbling noises, much as I imagine Ghosts make. For certain, they would be most disturbing to slumber. In fact, they were so perceptible that they were clearly audible and even disturbing to the noisy workmen in the Gothic Hall.

Loorz assumed a more serious note in explaining that the stormy weather had prevented his working on the East Room fireplace; he also summarized his progress on the odd jobs he and Hearst had discussed. He saved the most serious note for last. Hearst's bull terrier, Buddy, whose recent disappearance had prompted Hearst to offer a fifty-dollar reward, had possibly died on the slope below Hearst Camp (one of the men had spotted some buzzards circling there). Buddy was an old dog who was very dear to his master. Indeed, Buddy had originally lived in New York with Hearst and had been a favorite pet since 1918, the year before work began at San Simeon.

Hearst enjoyed Loorz's account of the "Ghosts of La Cuesta Encantada."[16] He wrote to Loorz from Los Angeles on February 25:

I am very glad the expeditionary forces have completely routed the enemy.

Do you not think decorations of some kind are in order.

Your description of all that is going on at the Hill, not only in the way of work but of weather, makes me feel that it is just as well that we are away during this period.

As for his beloved Buddy, Hearst proved to be straightforward on the question of death, a subject absurdly rumored to be one that frightened him: "I suppose of course Buddy is dead. But if he is, I would like to be sure of it." So would many of us all these years later. We may never know, though, what became of Buddy, for the Loorz Papers contain little else on the matter.[17]

---

16. The Spanish name for Hearst's hilltop appears occasionally in the Loorz Papers; Hearst himself used the name in his letterhead and on other printed forms, such as menus, that were unique to the estate. Nonetheless, for greater ease of syntax, I've used the English version "The Enchanted Hill" throughout my own narration in this book.

17. The notion of Hearst's skittishness about death gained lasting currency two years later with the appearance of *Hearst: Lord of San Simeon*, a scathing biography by Oliver Carlson and Ernest Sutherland Bates (New York, 1936). Pages 310–11 described certain rules that San Simeon's guests supposedly had to obey — "rules not to be violated on pain of instant expulsion." The last of these surpassed all others: "no one shall, under any circumstances, mention in Hearst's presence the subject of death."

Akin to the sentiments Hearst expressed about Buddy, a normal attitude toward death marks an undated note that Loorz received soon after arriving at San Simeon; it began with Hearst's telling him, "I like to get things which are pretty much nearly done sort of washed up and concluded."

THE WINTER of 1933–34 was getting to be a wet one, as Loorz told his parents on February 27:

> Well I hope old Jupiter Pluvius has been as good to you with his rain as he has with us. We really dont want any more for a while. It could wait three or four weeks before we could benefit by more. Everything is knee deep in mud. The fields are so soft that even my caterpillar is stuck out of sight. . . .
>
> Except for rain we would be doing quite a little work. I have quite a few men and things sound good around here again. I like to see things move. That is why I get pretty disgusted during the winter months when we are shut down.

In writing, though, to Fred Stolte the next day, February 28, Loorz disclosed another reason for the slowed pace:

> I have quite a little work going on so life is interesting again. All sorts of equipment from caterpillars to shovels operating but not too many men, in fact, I would like a lot more. However, I am purposely holding down for a good and sufficient reason. You know why, that is so there will be more to clean up Wyntoon debts.
>
> Talking to Miss Morgan, day before yesterday, she said that they would be able to clean Wyntoon up entirely on the next payment. That sounds too good to be true, does it not? However, we cannot kick on that job. It has even helped a little on the others [done by the F. C. Stolte Co.]. . . .[18]
>
> I wish things would hurry up and start on the up and up. I'm getting tired of this confinement. Though I do love to work with Miss Morgan and Mr. Hearst. Both have been wonderful to me. He writes very amusing letters while away and jokes with me while here.

The subject of Wyntoon had come up often in recent weeks and was still coming up. Loorz told Charlie Badley back on February 3, "For this year they merely plan on completing some of the work started this [past] year. The big proposed castle will not be started." Then on March 1 while writing to Harry Thompson, who inquired about the new year's prospects, Loorz said that Morgan did "not plan on starting up at Wyntoon until some time in April at the earliest." He also told Thompson that, for now at least, Hearst himself did "not appear to be in a hurry for

---

Hearst then applied that principle to the Orchard Hill section of the divided driveway: "Therefore I think we should get a wall man to take the place of the poor chap who died and complete the road wall at least on the South side and possibly on the north side too."

18. For the early part of 1934 itself, the Stolte Co.'s other jobs included finishing touches on the Walter Buck residence in Woodside and a remodeling of the Orrick residence in Pebble Beach, near Monterey; Harry Thompson and George Wright were among those who worked on the Orrick job while awaiting a resumption of efforts at Wyntoon. In this same period a member of the Bechtel family (whose late patriarch helped launch the construction of Hoover Dam in 1931) had the Stolte Co. do some follow-up work in a luxury apartment complex on Lake Merritt in Oakland.

anything up there but [that] will no doubt change before summer." Loorz had similar news on March 6 for George Wright, who likewise inquired about Wyntoon.

(On February 3 Loorz had touched on the subject of the new Wyntoon Castle with Wright, much as he had with Charlie Badley the same day—suggesting that prospects for the Santa Maria de Ovila monastery hadn't died entirely in 1933. While speaking of "the proposed pole line and transformer vault" at Wyntoon, Loorz also told Wright that Hearst had recently indicated "a possible location [for the line and vault] which is closer to the proposed new castle site across the river [near the mouth of Angel Creek]."[19] Nonetheless, few other current references to the "Dream Castle," as Loorz would call it on May 11, crop up in these annals, the chances of its realization having all but perished by 1934.)

In his letter of March 6 to Wright, Loorz also gave a good account of the work at San Simeon:

> I have had [Millard] Hendricks here and Roy Barker for two weeks trying to get started on the [Burnett] road. That storm surely fixed it up. It is too wet to tackle it and I want to be certain that the storm is about over. In the meantime I have had them grade the road to San Simeon, to the Chicken ranch, the airport etc. I even used the cat[erpillar] to cut a ramp up to the outside pool so that I can back right in with a truck and [can] shovel direct without wheelbarrows. So it has been real handy to have them [the two Burnett men] here.

Jim Rankin was another standby who asked when his services would be needed, what with work having begun at San Simeon on the full-scale Neptune Pool. In answering him on Thursday, March 8—Rankin had written on March 2 —Loorz got in a moment's fun while approaching the heart of his letter:

> Alex [Rankin] is doing fine. My handy man. However, he and Ray Van [Gorden] went out and played cards with two school-marms last night. They both look O.K. this morning, two long smiles and wide awake, so I guess all was well.

And then on to the business at hand, the business of building for Hearst and Morgan. As Loorz told Rankin:

> The excavation is, as you know, very slow on the pool with the wrecking of that concrete and rock cut, with a short crew and all hand work. So I cannot predict how soon we will have space for you to begin laying pipe. I dont think it will be for about six or eight weeks anyway. In the meantime they may want to start the bathroom [in the first bedroom] over the billiard room.[20] I hope so. . . .

---

19. See p. 78, note 42, for Stolte's description of that site, evidently the same one Loorz mentioned at this juncture.

20. A room formally named Billiard Room Wing Room #1.

> All is well on the Hilltop. Peace and quiet reigns. Miss Morgan has been aw-
> fully nice for many months, not a single real complaint. Maybe that is why pro-
> duction has slowed up? Dont you say yes.

By March 21 Loorz, having talked to Morgan the day before (on her third visit to San Simeon that month), could tell Stolte, "It looks like we can get started [at Wyntoon] before very long." He also told him about the Burnett Road:

> This last week end [March 17–18] I drove around [through San Luis Obispo] to Jolon to start the road crew on that side. I will work from both ends to get the road open. In about 20 minutes the Caterpillar went out of sight and the driver and I shovelled as fast as we could for four hours to get it out. Some Sunday!

But hold the show. On March 25 Joe Willicombe gave Loorz a message from Hearst, who was back at San Simeon from Los Angeles for another brief stay. Hearst had conveyed the message to Willicombe the night before:

> Please tell Miss Morgan and Mr. Loorz that I do not want anything else under-
> taken up here until that fireplace in the East Room is fixed. I have been talking about that for a long time and I do not get anywhere. It is a miserable thing. It smokes all over the house, and when they do not want it to smoke they open the doors and create drafts all through the house. So I wish Miss Morgan or Mr. Loorz would kindly just fix that fireplace whether there is anybody here or not.

Needless to say, the show went on, smoke or no smoke. Loorz's recap of his meeting with Morgan on Tuesday, March 27, contains these entries under "Gothic Study," a subject that had been at the forefront ever since work resumed in 1934:

1. Leave mantles as is at present while Architect looks for appropriate stone mantles [amid Hearst's warehoused antiques].[21] Mr. Hearst not satisfied with present wood lintel mantles.
2. Proceed with plastering and completing West end wall then follow with [plas-
   tering of] girders to be ready for decorators.
3. Mr. [Camille] Solon[22] to be sent down next week or about to put sketches on
   East end girder of main room [the Study proper, as distinct from its adjoining
   alcove at the back of the third floor].

---

21. By 1934 the documenting of Hearst's acquisitions had progressed from quaint, quill-and-ink ledger entries of the early 1920s to methodical, typewritten file cards and other efficient records, among which were hundreds of photographs. Morgan could usually find what she needed by con-sulting these sources—without having to open massive crates. See also note 52, below.

22. Solon's foremost contribution to the hilltop thus far had been his designs for mosaic work at the Roman Pool.

4. Crew can be increased to hasten speed in this room.
5. Arch[itect] to get out detail of bookcase, order grilles from [Ed] Trinkkeller,[23] and sample carving for lower doors from [Jules] Suppo.[24]

Those same notes of March 27 contain five entries under "Outside Pool"— that is, the eventual Neptune Pool, which saw increasing activity with the onset of spring.[25] In fact, by April 9 Loorz could tell the waggish George Wright, "I certainly have a crew of men and I'm right busy and on my toes. It looks like a madhouse around that outside pool. I'm spending the money this month that was expected to be spent at Wyntoon. You birds certainly rob this establishment when you work up there." The letter of April 9 also addressed a minor clash of wills that Wright and Stolte had been having lately. Along with urging Wright to be prudent, Loorz said of Stolte, "Really though he is a good fellow and I'd have to look a long way to get a partner who would cooperate with me as he has besides giving me the name he has in this business."

---

23. An ornamental ironworker based in Los Angeles. His first efforts for San Simeon dated from the early 1920s; before that he had worked for Morgan on Hearst's Los Angeles Examiner Building. In the mid-twenties Trinkkeller went to Spain in behalf of Hearst and Morgan — to steep himself further in the Old World trade he plied for San Simeon and other projects of theirs.

24. Another member of Morgan's inner circle of master craftsmen, based in San Francisco and long associated with San Simeon. Suppo's most compelling work was the exterior wood cornices he carved for the third floor of Casa Grande's central section: for the main west facade of that "Gothic" level, for its opposite east end, and for portions of its north and south sides — and, as of 1934, for the uppermost sections in those side areas.

25. A letter from Loorz to Hearst, dated April 6, reflects another tie-in between the current work on the pool and on the Burnett Road. "Will send compressor for necessary rock work at [Nacimiento River] bridge approach in a few days. We will then be thru with the compressor removing old concrete at the pool."

Regarding the imminent bridge itself, Loorz had this to tell Alexander Sokolow on April 13 (complete with a misspelled "Naciemiento" for good measure):

Mr. Hearst is anxious that I hasten the bridge across the Naciemiento River on Burnett Road. I have been spending approximately $3000 per month on this fund [the Hilltop Fund] in accordance with his orders of last year. If I hasten this bridge along with the other work it would easily mount up to $5000. Will you be able to take care of that amount promptly or shall I speak to him about it?

The familiarity that Loorz enjoyed with Hearst, Morgan, Willicombe, Sokolow, and others was a far cry from anything Camille Rossi could usually have boasted — and Loorz (unbeknownst to himself, of course) still had more than three years of full-time service at San Simeon awaiting him. "Things are running smoothly and pleasantly with construction," he told Sokolow in signing off. "How's things with the legal and financial departments?" From Loorz to Sokolow, April 13, 1934; Hearst Papers, carton 57 (under "Julia Morgan"). The Loorz Papers contain no carbon copy of this letter; there may well have been others like it that Loorz kept in a separate "Sokolow" or kindred file, long since lost or destroyed.

Loorz resorted to capitals in compiling notes from another meeting with Morgan, held on April 19, a Thursday: "LATE ORDERS BY PHONE FROM MR. HEARST TO MISS MORGAN: PROCEED TO COMPLETE ALL ROOMS OF RECREATION WING TEMPORARILY FOR USE FOR LARGE PARTY FOR WEEK END OF April 29th."

Now *that* was a tall order. And by no means a frivolous one. Hearst's birthday was second only to Christmas on his social calendar; April 29, 1934, would find him turning seventy-one—and presiding over another costume extravaganza, this time with a Civil War theme (actually held on Saturday, April 28). Morgan, for her part in the preparations, left her office on April 25 to spend the next three days at San Simeon. She wired Jim LeFeaver from the hilltop soon after she arrived from San Luis Obispo, telling him to secure fifty banquet chairs from the Mark Hopkins Hotel in San Francisco. He arranged their shipment to the big event through Valley & Coast Transit Co., the same carriers Loorz and "the boys" had used in 1933 to help the downtrodden Baumgartners in Cayucos.[26]

But it was not until May 3, nearly a week after the party, that Loorz came up for air long enough to explain those imposing words of April 19; he did so in writing to Stolte:

> Well we are settled down again to a more even program. Perhaps you have heard of the grand rush for his Birthday Party.
>
> One week before his party they called me at 8 P.M. while I was having dinner with the folks at the [Cambria Pines] Lodge. The order was to try to get all of the rooms in the Recreation Wing [of Casa Grande] completed temporarily for occupancy in time for the party.
>
> You remember that dead concrete wing over the Theater with nothing in the openings but tar paper storm covers. Besides that the floors were full of antique stone for later use in the openings of this wing etc. One of the rooms was my paint shop with filled shelves.
>
> Anyway within six days we turned the place over to him furnished with all rooms, closets, bathrooms, including showers, ready for use. That is 11 rooms complete with baths & closets and 2 tower rooms[27] quite comfortable for use but

---

26. See Morgan to LeFeaver, April 26, 1934; Hearst/Morgan Correspondence, Morgan Collection. A further glimpse of the role Morgan and others played in the preparations lies in these words to Stolte, written by Loorz on May 5: "He [Charlie Badley, who was temporarily at San Simeon] was certainly handy while we were rushed through the party arrangements. Miss Morgan used he and Elof [Gustafson] spreading furniture etc and she said they were the two best men I had on the job."

27. Not to be confused with the belfried towers that surmount the Celestial Suite in the main part of Casa Grande: the eventual West Tower and East Tower suites on the top floor of the Recreation Wing (later called the New Wing) have conventional peaked roofs.

no bathrooms. Rankin did wonderful to get as much [plumbing done] as he did. Note that the [concrete] form wires were still in place and had to be cut thruout. The ceilings were painted, the concrete exposed walls were painted and the floors, rough concrete tinted. Hand rails galore up and down steps. In fact, they turned out to be very comfortable [rooms] and the only difference between temporary and permanent was plasterboard instead of plaster & rough floors.

Loorz concluded by saying, "Mr. Hearst is still in splendid condition and seems very happy. Told me yesterday that he would be in Europe for three months and outlined what he wanted complete when he returned . . . oh boy . . . you should read the list."

LOORZ HADN'T HEARD from Mac McClure in quite a while. If Mac spent much time at San Simeon thus far in 1934, as Loorz had hoped he would, he left little trace of himself in the annals; there must have been no impetus for the two men to correspond while they were at arm's reach. In any event, Mac was in San Francisco when he wrote to Loorz on Thursday, May 10, saying he would be returning to Wyntoon that night; he may already have logged some hours there in the past month or so. "Have had a pleasant week and a half in the city," Mac also said, "but I will be glad to be back at McCloud again."

(Concerning the earliest weeks of 1934, Mac's absence from San Simeon— or that of any other on-site draftsman—may have prompted a comment Loorz made to Stolte on February 10: "Though I haven't a real big crew, I am starting up several small structures without plans so you can bet I am real busy." Mac may have been at San Simeon later in February or March; but by April he more likely had gone to Wyntoon for the new season. The first indication of anyone's presence there is a letter from Hayes Perkins to Loorz, sent from the Hotel McCloud on March 31.)

Mac, at any rate, was apparently at San Simeon long enough in that early period to have left some suitcases behind; in his letter of May 10 he asked Loorz to forward them to McCloud. Loorz hastened to reply to his good friend the next day, May 11:[28]

Glad you will be back at McCloud. Hope you will be there when Mr. Hearst arrives. He expects to make an inspection trip of one day on Monday [May 14]. As you well know, that is not a promise. . . .

---

28. May 11 also found Martin Charles (who had filled in briefly for Mac in 1933) writing to Loorz from San Francisco:

I had almost forgotten what a curious place your San Simeon was until I had lunch with Mac one day last week and heard the account of the frantic preparations for the birthday party. . . . Mac tells me that you seem flourishing as usual in spite of having lost a few tonsils [Loorz had

W.R. and Marion flew down to see the preview of Operator 13 last nite.[29] I understand that he is in the plane homeward bound right now (4:30 P.M.). From a hint from Mr. Willicombe the picture was not received well and W.R. is returning with spirits at low ebb. Suggested that it was not the proper time to touch him for an increase in funds.

They plan on leaving about Tuesday or Wednesday [May 15 or 16] for their extended sojourn [in Europe]. The Dame Rumor has it that the party of companions is increasing to be nearly a gang.[30]

Of course, the bunch up there [at Wyntoon] heard the Rumor that he bought the Wheeler place. If he paid the figure that I saw in the correspondence,[31] I commend Wheeler on his excellent salesmanship—W-O-W. Now he will move the proposed site of the Dream Castle.

The Wheeler place was downstream along the McCloud River, below the Waterhouse parcel and the site of Phoebe Hearst's original Wyntoon castle—downstream where the McCloud turned prominently, hence The Bend by name (see map on page xv). The attorney Charles S. Wheeler had owned the property since the late 1800s, not only The Bend itself but also, for many years, the property where Mrs. Hearst's castle had stood till 1930 and on which ground her son had since redeveloped The Gables and its surroundings. Mrs. Hearst had leased that property from Wheeler and had retained Bernard Maybeck as her architect; Wheeler himself had built his own country house at The Bend through the equally renowned architect Willis Polk. And now The Bend was Hearst's, The Bend and all the land Wheeler had kept after Hearst bought the land his mother had used. Indeed, Hearst had now consolidated his holdings along the McCloud River—from above the Waterhouse parcel, with its Bavarian Village; past the site of his mother's castle, now marked by a croquet lawn near The Gables; and on below Wheeler's last stronghold at The Bend. If Wheeler was gloating over the sale, as Loorz suggested, Hearst no doubt was gloating even more over the new prospects of remodeling and developing that lay before him.

---

had a long-delayed tonsilectomy on March 23]. I gather from Mac and Miss Morgan that the Gothic Study is nearly complete and is not turning out too badly.

Another part of this letter from Charles appears in the previous chapter, note 33.

29. Released on June 22, 1934; see Guiles, *Marion Davies*, pp. 400–01.

30. Loorz had given the matter a different twist in writing to Mickey Brennan the previous day, May 10; Brennan, a chauffeur at San Simeon in recent years, had this to read in Loorz's letter: "The Chief and party are preparing for the 3 months voyage to Europe this summer. That means we will have plenty of time to work all day long and get a lot completed."

31. A prime example of Loorz's insider status at San Simeon. Perhaps the documents he mentioned are in the Wheeler Papers or the Hearst Papers in the Bancroft Library (awaiting more digging than could be done for this volume).

At San Simeon, meanwhile, Hearst was still "preparing to leave for a three months tour of Europe," Loorz told King Walters on May 12. "He has had us on our toes expecting a trip thru to Jolon but the time is getting so close for his departure that I'm inclined to doubt it. The boys will be disappointed as they have rushed to get the [Burnett] road cleared and fairly smooth for this picnic." In all likelihood that was one picnic Hearst and his party cancelled. Their last day at San Simeon, until the fall of 1934, was Sunday, May 13.[32]

Hearst's protracted absence meant Loorz and his men could do their work with gusto—no worries of a noisy jackhammer, for instance, disturbing anyone's late-morning slumbers. The Neptune Pool and the Gothic Study were the two main jobs on the hilltop itself. The Burnett Road was the main one elsewhere on the ranch.

Of course a miscellany of other jobs also came under Loorz's superintendence. Some of these were definable as "Miss Morgan's work" through the Hearst Construction Fund; the remainder owed their existence to a separate entity, the Hilltop Fund. From Hearst's standpoint, and that of certain lawyers and accountants, the dollars involved were all part of the same fabric, the grand financial tapestry called San Simeon (comprising not just the buildings and features on the

---

32. The Hearst entourage had last been to Europe in 1931 and, before that, in 1928 and 1930. The latter two trips, and the one in 1934, inspired the sub-chapters "Tourism à la Hearst" in W. A. Swanberg's *Citizen Hearst: A Biography of William Randolph Hearst* (New York, 1961 edition [cited exclusively in these notes]), pp. 406–09, 418–21, 442–44. Despite speaking of these and similar Hearst sojourns as "sultanesque excursions" (*Citizen Hearst*, p. 442), Swanberg later found the travels of Henry Luce to be even more impressive. "The European trips of [newspaper publishers] Adolph Ochs, Roy Howard, Hearst and Colonel Robert McCormick were vacation jaunts by comparison"—this from Swanberg's biography of the man behind *Time* and other renowned magazines (*Luce and His Empire* [New York, 1972], p. 154).

In writing to Morgan during this period in 1934, Joe Willicombe gave exact details on the first leg of the trip. "We leave for the East Sunday night 11:45 [May 20] on the SANTE FE 'CHIEF,' according to present plans. I go as far as New York and hope to return for the summer in California. Chief sails on the REX May 26." From Willicombe to Morgan, May 18, 1934; Morgan Collection (under III/05/08/66).

At this same juncture, Arthur Brisbane traveled cross-country with the Hearst party. He sent word to Morgan from Albuquerque, New Mexico, telling her how pleased he was "to learn from Colonel Willicombe of the great improvement" in her health. Things had been different a year earlier: Brisbane had written a consoling letter to her, knowing she had been "very ill" then. From Brisbane to Morgan, May 21, 1934, and May 4, 1933; Morgan Collection (both items under I/07/02/23). On June 8, 1933, Mitchell Samuels of the New York art dealers French & Company, who'd recently been at San Simeon, had also sent Morgan consoling words—along with highly praiseworthy ones about her work on the hilltop; Morgan Collection (I/07/02/22).

Loorz indicated to Mickey Brennan on May 23, 1934, that Willicombe would indeed be returning to California from New York. "He will come back to his Los Angeles office when the party boards the ship."

hilltop proper but also their counterparts, humble or great, on other parts of the sprawling estate). Someone—somewhere—had a fairly good idea of what all the expenditures amounted to. And yet to identify Morgan's strands within the whole piece of cloth is no easy task: the blends and color shifts and nuances of pattern and design can be as intricate as those in an old Persian rug. To a large extent, though by no means entirely, her work can be associated with the Hearst Construction Fund. Certain other efforts outside her sphere, typified by the Burnett Road, were the province of the Hilltop Fund.[33]

Despite the increased tempo in the spring of 1934, Loorz kept up with his correspondence, as always. On May 23 he answered a letter from Phil Smith, with whom he had served in France during World War I; he hadn't heard from Smith in years:

> My business in Oakland, contracting, is continuing on fairly well, and I could and should go back to it right away. However, this is a very interesting place. I answer to no one but Mr. Hearst personally and his Architect. Both have trusted and shown appreciation of [my] efforts in every way so that I would hate to leave them. They have been wonderful to me and pure business is too often cool.

Many of Loorz's letters continued to have such references—to his feeling of isolation at San Simeon, to his homesickness for Berkeley and the San Francisco Bay Area, to his concern for the welfare of the F. C. Stolte Co. in his absence. But they also refer to the challenging nature of his work, to his deep sense of loyalty to Hearst and Morgan—and, on occasion, to the handsome salary he enjoyed ($5,200 per year) in the midst of the Depression.

In writing to Mac McClure on May 11, Loorz had asked Mac to keep him posted

---

33. The challenge of tracing funds and accounts is exemplified by Loorz and Hearst's exchange of January 30–31, 1934 (partly quoted on pp. 104–05); in further business, Loorz asked if a new greenhouse for Louis Reesing should be "done on Miss Morgan's account" [the Hearst Construction Fund] or on Hearst's "personal Sokolow account" [the Hilltop Fund]. "I do not care how this work is done," Hearst replied (but either way, he wanted Morgan to approve the greenhouse's siting). "I am perfectly willing to have it on my personal account and charged back later to the Piedmont Land & Cattle Company" (a Hearst subsidiary in San Francisco, run by Bill Murray since 1933). Piedmont, as Willicombe had told Loorz on May 15, 1932, would "hereafter . . . pay all bills for construction on the Hilltop"—or at least some of them, as things turned out. Morgan had been notified the same day, though in less detail; Hearst Papers, carton 15 (under "Morgan, Julia").

The new arrangement dated from the same month as the Bills Payable list that Morgan sent John Francis Neylan (pp. 28–29 in the 1932 chapter, plus their note 17); see also the series San Simeon Financial Records in the Morgan Collection (file III/03/07/117), in which a copy of Morgan's covering letter to Neylan of May 31, 1932, is now kept; the same file has a letter from Neylan to Morgan (undated, but probably June 1, 1932) and one from Morgan to Neylan (dated June 2, 1932), both of them pertinent. A reweaving of the tangled web began in that first year of Loorz's tenure, yielding a new mesh, complete with its own knots and snags. The process continued for years to come.

on Wyntoon—therefore Loorz could "look intelligent" when Hearst or Morgan mentioned the subject. Mac, though, was apparently too busy at the moment to correspond. But George Wright came through for Loorz on Saturday, June 2:

> The two new carpenters that arrived today brought the total pay roll up to twenty-three. When [James] Rankin and [George] Addison[34] get here with their crews, we will very nearly be back to last year's strength. There is certainly enough work to be done to keep all hands busy.
>
> As a fire retardent we started whitewashing the Brown Bear [house] today. Can't you imagine the mess? I suggested that we rename it the Polar Bear.
>
> The power line voltage and layout is still undecided. As you suggested, I have refrained from arguing about the merits of the various systems. The various possible plans have been submitted for their consideration, and we are just sitting back and waiting to put in whatever they decide upon. . . .
>
> I wish you were here to go fishing with Harry [Thompson] and me tomorrow.

By keeping in close touch with Morgan, and by being a partner in the company that had the general contract at Wyntoon, Loorz undoubtedly knew more about that job than he had let on to Mac. On June 4, for instance, he wrote to Stolte in that regard:

> Went over Wyntoon work with Miss Morgan and things seem to be satisfactory but she was not real enthusiastic.[35] It was proper for me not to ask any questions as she felt so good about everything here [at San Simeon] that I certainly wasn't going to spoil it. . . .
>
> How are the accounts receivable coming with the Wyntoon work? Remember that when we took the thing [in 1933] at 3% [commission on net cost, adjusted later that year to 3.5%] it was definitely with the idea of cash monthly payments. Now we won't be mean or anything but in a nice way I will mention it sometime if they are falling behind.

On June 4 as well, Loorz wrote to his old friend Jack Hall; he elaborated in essence on certain details in the same day's letter to Stolte:

> Yes we [the F. C. Stolte Co.] have quite a little work Jack. It has held up for us thru the depression quite well. Needless to say Jack that we are working on close margins and though we are able to pay all the overhead including Mr. Stolte's salary of $75.00 per week there has been little left to split with Geo. C. [Loorz].

---

34. Addison was a sub-contractor from Oakland who specialized in brick and hollow-tile work (such as in fireplaces and flues). Like Rankin, he also had San Simeon credits to his name.

35. Loorz may have seen Morgan when he passed through San Francisco on the weekend of June 2–3. Or he may have conferred with her about Wyntoon when she was at San Simeon on May 31. Or he may have done so in the meantime by phone. His papers through this stretch leave these

Loorz was making $25 more per week at San Simeon than Stolte was being paid; thus did Loorz put a fourth of his hundred-dollar salary "in the company" every week, as Morgan learned long afterward.[36] Three days later, June 7, Loorz again wrote to Stolte about Wyntoon:

> No Fred, I dont think Miss Morgan is displeased with our work. I think she would have grumbled about it a bit if she felt that way. What I think is, that she resents the many many changes that she has to make that Mr. Hearst and Mac made without consulting her. Also she resents the excessive cost of the finish etc when he is not providing funds accordingly. I did not mean to worry you.

Here as elsewhere in the George Loorz Papers, Loorz demonstrated a solid grasp of events at Wyntooon—even though he had yet to see the abundant new work that had been done there in the past year.

EARLY IN JUNE 1934 the Loorzes sent their two boys, Don and Bill, to stay for several weeks with Loorz's parents in Lovelock, Nevada. After they arrived in Lovelock, Loorz wrote to his boys, who were now six and eight, and also to his parents in the same letter, dated June 11: "We wanted so to get into San Luis [Obispo] on Saturday to see the Fiesta Parade with Don Poncho [Pancho Estrada][37] leading it but we could not, I had to pour concrete."

The pouring Loorz spoke of took place on June 9 and may well have been at the outdoor pool—the Neptune Pool—whose new concrete walls had begun rising three days before. Loorz's "Recapitulation" from a meeting he had with Morgan on June 14[38] began by saying, "Make certain to strip forms carefully & com-

---

distinctions unclear. Morgan had made her first trip to Wyntoon in 1934 on May 22–24. She was about to head that way again on June 6, returning to San Francisco on June 9. See also note 53, below.

36. Loorz to Morgan, July 25, 1936 (pp. 266–67 in this volume). Regarding Loorz's current stake in the company, the Oakland legal firm representing the Stolte-Loorz partnership confirmed on June 8, 1934, that Loorz still held the full half-interest he had begun with when the company was incorporated in April 1932: 250 of 500 shares. Stolte, meanwhile, had pledged 248 of his 249 shares to a private party as security for a loan. The remaining one share was held in escrow. See also note 90 in this chapter.

37. Francisco "Pancho" Estrada, a wrangler and honorary "mayordomo" on the Hearst Ranch, evoked the romanticized Hispanic past of the Cambria-San Simeon area. His father, Julian Estrada, was the grantee in 1841—during the Mexican regime—of Rancho Santa Rosa, part of whose acreage had been among the Hearst family's coastal holdings since the 1860s and 1870s.

38. Despite some fifteen trips to San Simeon that Morgan had made thus far in 1934 (many of them combined with trips to the Cosmopolitan bungalow and other Hearst jobs in Los Angeles), she could still be excessively modest about her attainments—and excessively critical of herself. Three days before she saw Loorz on June 14, she wrote to the architect-antiquarian Arthur Byne in Madrid, who remembered San Simeon vividly from his visit there in 1930:

pletely." The need for precision may have been obvious, yet it was surely worth spelling out.

More of Loorz's recap notes from that meeting pertained to the Gothic Study and the work of Camille Solon and other artisans in that room. "Mr. Solon's figures to[o] 'wispy' and grouping should be more in panels than to appear continuous up and down girder," went his final entry; the reference was to Solon's paintings of Biblical scenes and other ancient stories on the arches in the Study. "Instruction given direct to Mr. Solon with other suggestions." The meeting with Morgan prompted Loorz to set down the following words also, as a note to himself:

> Mr. Solon came down from scaffold next morning [June 15] after working an hour, quite a nervous wreck bound for S.F. and a few days rest. After 15 minutes of my most sympathetic conversation, he laughed, threw his shoulders back and climbed back up the scaffold. I hope it was a cure.

In the wake of Morgan's visit on Thursday the fourteenth, Loorz wrote to Fred Stolte:

> Miss Morgan was here yesterday and told me about progress and changes at Wyntoon. She still grieves over the many changes and says that with them all they have not improved the houses. So it is not our work that makes Wyntoon a bit of a "Black Eye" or tooth ache for her.
>
> I am going out the [Burnett] road this morning to make my weekly visit and I'm taking the Mrs. with me. She has a cart load of books to read while I am arguing with the foreman. She apparently knows just what to expect. It is seldom that she gets to go with me on this job. Taking advantage of the kiddies being away. . . .
>
> . . . I have a lot of detailing and designing to do on this job all the time. I have just designed a 100 ft. bridge and will have time [over the July 4 holiday] to detail all joints.

Loorz's bridge was a wood-trusswork span over the Nacimiento River—a crucial link in connecting San Simeon with Jolon at long last.

> On account of conditions, work has gone along very slowly on the Hill, which has paralleled an inactive two years on my own part. I hope a "pick-up" is really coming and that next year will let us make some appearance of finish to at least parts long years under way.

True, San Simeon had its usual share of unfinished rooms and other features as 1934 reached its mid-point. But two *years* of inactivity for Morgan? Come now! How unworthy could one architect feel? (Perhaps deeply so on a late-spring Monday in the often chilly, fogbound San Francisco of that season.) Byne, though, would surely have been dazzled by the Billiard Room, the Duplexes, the Celestial Suite, the Roman Pool, and still other projects that had come to fruition since 1932—never mind the headway made in the Gothic Study and on the Neptune Pool. From Morgan to Byne, June 11, 1934; Morgan/Byne/Hearst Correspondence, Morgan Collection.

In writing to Loorz on June 16, Stolte touched on the fortunes of the construction firm he and Loorz jointly owned, and not just with respect to Wyntoon. "I am becoming a little more optimistic as to the future," said the elder partner. "Conditions seem to be better or we have found a way to live in the worst possible situation—1933—and get by." He mentioned having landed another General Petroleum gas station job—a standby for the F. C. Stolte Co. in those days—this time in Stockton. The company had also landed a private job in San Francisco for which Morgan was the architect; the client was a friend of hers named Else Schilling. Loorz and Stolte's connection with Miss Morgan was beginning to pay off apart from the Hearst work.[39] Stolte further mentioned that the company had made a profit of roughly $4,000 thus far in 1934, a marked improvement over its performance in 1932 and 1933.

As for Wyntoon, where Stolte intermittently went on behalf of his and Loorz's company (as he'd begun doing in 1933), he had some words to say about Jim LeFeaver, Morgan's office manager and in-house engineer: "Mr. LeFeaver seems to have *loosened up* toward me just a little and chats a little more. I have attempted to consult him in most of engineering items."

LeFeaver could seem formidable to those who didn't know him well, much as Joe Willicombe could to the uninitiated. Loorz had reassuring words for Stolte with regard to LeFeaver. "He is really a fine fellow when you know him. He is slow to make friends but when he does I think he will stand by them."

Morgan's visit to San Simeon on June 26 yielded just one page of recap notes, devoted once more to the Gothic Study and the Neptune Pool. For the Study, Loorz recorded that a new man named Ted Linforth was "to receive $7.00 per day" for helping Camille Solon with the arches in that room. Linforth was to "look up costume[s] and figures in character with period of painting for suggestions for Mr. Solon." Morgan herself, whose architectural library was substantial, supplied some or even all of the books, portfolios, and old photographs that were needed. (Two months later the same was true. Loorz's notes for her visit on August 25 included "Architect to send down large book for Mr. Solon to use in selecting new subjects.")

On June 29 Morgan spoke of herself in telling Loorz, "[I] don't expect to come again until the 10th or 11th of July, holidays, Wyntoon, and Los Angeles to be fitted in between." A simple enough statement, yet one that might be misconstrued

---

39. The Schilling job was one of three in San Francisco that the Stolte Co. worked on for Morgan in 1934 (the two other clients being Johanna Volkmann and the Century Club). In the same year, the company also worked on two of Morgan's jobs in Berkeley, the A. F. Hockenbeamer and Selden Williams residences. All five jobs are minutely detailed in the Morgan-Forney ledgers; four of the jobs are sketchily detailed in the "Trial Balance" (accounts payable and receivable) sheets compiled by the Stolte Co. for 1934 and preserved in the Loorz Papers.

years later as fuel for the Morgan myth—that often overwrought image of Morgan's varied workload for a string of clients. In reality, everything she alluded to in that sentence would be for the greater good of the Hearst accounts. Her first stop was at Wyntoon, where she appeared on July 6–7. After briefly returning to San Francisco, she went south. July 10 found her checking on the Cosmopolitan bungalow in Culver City (mostly with regard to its new projection room, a job she'd been pursuing all year). It also found her checking on a house a few miles away in Holmby Hills for George Hearst (who was in Europe now with his father); this was a smaller remodeling job compared with her work since 1929 on young George's house in Hillsborough, near San Francisco. And then she looped back from the Los Angeles area to San Simeon, appearing there on the second date she'd projected for Loorz, July 11. There was method to her roundabout madness, to be sure, as her job ledgers of the period closely attest.

At the outset of this stretch—on Friday, July 6, while Morgan had her sights on Wyntoon—Loorz wrote to her in a new vein; she had written to him on July 4, asking how his recent medical appointment in San Luis Obispo had gone.[40] Loorz gave her the full details:

> While examining me he [Dr. James Marshall] noticed that my back was very sunburned and asked me how come. I told him I had worked the whole of Sunday [July 1] in our back yard with my back exposed. The day being slightly overcast and the sun not very hot I had not expected to burn much and was still at that moment not particularly painful. He leaned back smiling quietly at me and said, "It takes a college education to make a man do *smart tricks* like that, you are going to blister plenty."

Loorz continued by telling Morgan he had been immobilized for the past few days, thanks to his huge blisters:

> So you can see that I had to abandon some carefully made plans of things I had hoped to accomplish in the office while the boys [Don and Bill Loorz] were away on vacation. It is very difficult to do any office work when the crew is working. I wanted to list my steel and material for the Pavillion [the Neptune Pool pavilion]

---

40. Morgan naturally had had more to touch on in her letter of July 4, which was handwritten. Concerning the colonnaded structures slated for the far ends of the Neptune Pool:

> The marble columns of the pavillons [pavilions, or colonnades] are set, not by the step line, but by the centers established on the floor plans. Of course there is a relationship, & a drawing was mailed Tuesday [July 3] showing the *probable* step relationships.

But then she added, "Mr Hearst is against the marble for the steps, so I am in the midst of a problem."

and order [those items]. I wanted to sketch up those partitions for the bear pits [in the Orchard Hill section of the zoo] which I hope we'll be able to get before Mr. Hearst returns. . . .

You wouldn't think at my age and experience, it would be possible *TO BE QUITE SO DUMB AND YET SO HAPPY,* in reference to much of the above letter.

Loorz had more to say about his sunburned back in writing to Fred Stolte on July 10—and about the reason for his "own darn foolishness" in the first place:

The wife and I are very busy all evenings, mornings, Saturday afternoons and Sundays trying to get a small swimming pool ready for the boys when they return [from Nevada]. We hope to surprise them and hope they will like it. . . .

We dug the pool by means of horse and slip scraper and car and slip and by main strength with shovel. There is a lot of clay [in the soil] so I worked the clay up and plastered the pool to exact shape. Now I am running a skin coat of plaster over it hoping that it will hang together while I'm working [on the hill]. When I get the water in I'm sure it will be O.K. It is 30 feet long, 16 feet wide, sloping from 2–6 to 4–0 in depth. So far it has cost me about $35.00 for the cement, drain pipe and valve and a little help on labor. When a bum comes and wants something to eat we give him a few hours digging at 35 or 50 cents per hour.

He urged Stolte to bring his family down for a week's vacation at San Simeon. "Better come and help us initiate the pool," he said, referring to his homemade, backyard pool[41]—not the spectacular Neptune Pool on Hearst's Enchanted Hill.

On July 14 Loorz wrote again to his sons and parents in Lovelock, making sure not to mention the pool:

Since I've been able to get out with a shirt on my back Mamma and I have been working in the back yard a lot. Our flowers look fine. The tomato vine you two planted has lots of tomatoes on it. The squash is now bearing heavily. The squash grow quickly and we will have a lot more than we can use. The corn is also doing nicely. . . .

The strike is certainly affecting us here. We will be unable to get supplies and I may have to shut down if it holds out very long. Thank goodness we have the ocean handy with plenty of fish and some vegetables in the back yard.

The strike Loorz mentioned on July 14 was no doubt the one that had gripped San Francisco Bay for the past two months. Remote San Simeon had relied on shipping from Oakland and San Francisco ever since the first buildings were staked out on the hilltop back in 1919. But those ports weren't the only ones affected in the

---

41. The Loorz family's former home in San Simeon remains in use, but its pool has long since been filled in. Theirs was the middle of three such tile-roofed houses on the ocean side of the street.

late spring and early summer of 1934; Depression-weary longshoremen had been staging walkouts up and down the West Coast. At any rate, it was San Francisco itself that had just witnessed "Bloody Thursday" along its waterfront on July 5. And it was San Francisco that was about to be throttled by the historic general strike of July 16–19.

Midway through his European sojourn—from St. Donat's Castle in Wales—William Randolph Hearst pulled strings long enough and powerful enough to help choke that long-festering strike from six thousand miles away. (Meanwhile, Hearst's guests at St. Donat's in July 1934 included Arthur Byne, the antiquarian from Madrid whose purveyings to Hearst still influenced the work at San Simeon.)[42] In wielding his clout in the general strike, Hearst also helped to promote a growing image of himself as a worried reactionary, a discredited "old progressive" who was now dead set against labor and the common man. His interview later that summer with Adolf Hitler only worsened matters.[43] Perhaps to George Loorz, Julia Morgan, and others who knew him closely, Hearst was a virtual saint in his best moments. But to many who knew nothing of his benevolent, altruistic side, who knew nothing of his disarming humanism, the man had become by 1934 the devil incarnate. Some, in fact, with memories reaching back to the Spanish-American War and other complex episodes in Hearst's life, thought he always had been.[44]

---

42. From the Savoy Hotel in London, Byne wrote to Willicombe in Los Angeles regarding a Spanish ceiling he had procured for Hearst. Byne said, "While staying with Mr. Hearst at St. Donat's Castle, he cabled you, at my suggestion" about the ceiling and its status with "the Customs officials." Byne to Willicombe, July 26, 1934; Morgan/Byne/Hearst Correspondence, Morgan Collection.

43. In the early 1940s Hearst recounted the infamous Hitler episode while writing his front-page column, "In the News," for his chain of papers; the account, plus several others from that column, also appeared posthumously in Edmond D. Coblentz's compilation of 1952, *William Randolph Hearst: A Portrait in His Own Words*; see pp. 103–05 in regard to Hitler. W. A. Swanberg provides a good summary of the interview with Hitler and its fallout—along with some recounting of San Francisco's general strike—in *Citizen Hearst*, pp. 442–49. The strike itself and the role Hearst (and especially his attorney John Francis Neylan) played in breaking it are more fully discussed in Kevin Starr's *Endangered Dreams: The Great Depression in California* (New York, 1996), pp. 84–120.

44. With regard to the Spanish-American War of 1898, Hearst's reputation seesawed through the twentieth century. At the quarter-century mark, Oswald Garrison Villard lamented the public's short memory of the episode. He asked, "Who remembers today the wicked and dastardly part which Hearst played in bringing on the war with Spain? Who remembers his strident appeals then to the basest of passions? Who remembers the bitter outcry against him?" Villard's answer: none but a few. From *Some Newspapers and Newspaper-Men* (New York, 1923), p. 15.

On May 3, 1935, *The New York Times*—though no friend of Hearst's—offered a calmer perspective; the following words, from p. 18, were part of an editorial on the nature of war (under "Topics of The Times: War With Spain"):

Cuba fought an unsuccessful ten years' war for independence in 1868–78 while Mr. Hearst was in pinafores and knee pants. When we went to war in 1898 after the destruction of the [bat-

SAN FRANCISCO'S GENERAL STRIKE was in its second day—July 17—when Loorz wrote to Mac McClure at Wyntoon. He said at the outset, "I have that fault of answering all correspondence so promptly that people nearly always owe me a letter. . . . I am now one-up on you again." (But if Loorz was replying to something Mac had written since their exchange of May 10 and 11, the letter is missing.) On July 17, in any case, Loorz had these words about Wyntoon for his friend:

> I hope things are going real well there with the gang. Hope you like to work with F. C. [Stolte]. He likes the place a lot and though we make very little on the job and in fact I will not make anything personally, it has certainly been a fine thing to have that job.

And then Loorz turned his attention to San Simeon and a scene that Mac could easily visualize:

> The marble men are very busy with a large crew in the [Neptune] Pool. [Frank] Frandolich is setting up those marble columns for the Colonnades or Pavilions at either end of the pool. We are making good headway but as you know it is very expensive work and I've had to keep quite a crew busy. We are making good headway in the [Gothic] Study but that too is so detailed with carved stone and carved wood and expensive ornamental and figure decorating that it is necessarily slow.
>
> Certainly Mack [sic] I will let you know as soon as I hear about when the party will be back. I just heard that the Twins [Randolph and David Hearst] have been given permission to go up there but are not to come to the hill here. So if you have not heard the rumor [now] you have it. I dont even know that they want to go there but Mr. Willicombe himself said they had that permission.

---

tleship] Maine it was the fourth year of another Cuban insurrection. If Mr. Hearst took us into the war it was not out of a clear sky.

Hearst's role was naturally applauded in the "pro" biography of the mid-1930s (*William Randolph Hearst: American*, by Mrs. Fremont Older) but stiffly decried in the two "anti" biographies of the same period (*Hearst: Lord of San Simeon*, by Oliver Carlson and Ernest Sutherland Bates; and *Imperial Hearst: A Social Biography*, by Ferdinand Lundberg; all three titles New York, 1936). In any case, the question of his role soon entered a long decline; few noticed that in 1949, just after the half-century mark, the elderly Hearst received Cuba's highest foreign decoration—the Grand Cross of Cespedes—for his part in ending Spanish rule in that country.

Nearly forty years later, John Tebbel (whose *Life and Good Times of William Randolph Hearst* had appeared in 1952) wrote *The Press and The Presidency: From George Washington to Ronald Reagan* (New York, 1985; co-written with Sara Miles Watts). Tebbel and Watts observed on pp. 303–04 that Hearst and his rival Joseph Pulitzer (of the New York newspaper *The World*) had long been neglected "in general histories of the United States" and that "in specific studies of the [Spanish-American] war they usually appear as no more than footnotes, when they are mentioned at all." The tide began turning, though not dramatically, through a spate of books in the late 1990s—spawned by the centenary of 1898 and the dawn of a new millennium.

The subject of permission also cropped up in another letter Loorz wrote on July 17. "Dear Mamma, Dad and Boys," it began, its recipients being Loorz's parents and their houseguests, young Don and Bill Loorz, in Lovelock, Nevada. Since that foursome would soon be heading to San Simeon, Loorz had some important news to convey:

> Now I [dont] want to disappoint you a bit because they issued a new order to the Gateman yesterday by phone from Los Angeles. Yesterday morning on the road up he stopped me and told me that he had orders not to admit anyone but my workmen. That he couldn't admit workmen's families or even salesman [*sic*]. They gave the same orders to the Ranch Superintendent [Randolph Apperson, a first cousin of Hearst's].[45] Therefore, I fear that while Mr. Hearst is in Europe where I cannot reach him that it will be impossible for me to get you into the grounds or the building [Casa Grande]. I am real sorry for that I know is the main reason for you taking the long trip down here, but I honestly cannot help it.

So much for the hilltop staff and other employees having the run of things in Hearst's absence. The restrictions Loorz described may have been less stringent at other times; but in large measure The Enchanted Hill would remain a secret, inpenetrable compound for years to come.

Morgan put in a long weekend session on the hill at this juncture, from July 20 through July 22. Loorz's notes for the Gothic Study and the Neptune Pool included a detailed one on the latter project, updating the status of its enlarged, 104-foot basin. "Mr. LeFeaver to phone Vermont Marble Company [in San Francisco] asking them to put on more setters if convenient. Their carload of marble is here and there is lots of room for men to work."[46]

Camille Solon, the decorator of the Gothic Study and the beneficiary of Loorz's pep talk back in mid-June, must have taken a temporary leave after all. Loorz wrote him a consoling letter on July 30; he told Solon he hoped the following words would not bring to mind "the Discomforts of the Hilltop":

> We have made you the *cutest* scaffold that you can move around like a wheelbarrow, all over the Study Floor. However, greater complications turned up. After taking down your scaffolding and erecting the portable [one] the floor was still so jammed that you couldn't have moved ten feet. Consequently I have three men

---

45. The son of Elbert Clark Apperson, who was both the brother of Phoebe Apperson Hearst and, years before, a superintendent of the San Simeon ranch (for the original George Hearst). Randy Apperson had a much older sister named Anne Apperson Flint.

46. On August 2, Loorz told King Walters, formerly of the Burnett Road crew, "We are spending all available funds on the outside swimming pool. We have a real crew working at present and it seems like old times. They are now setting the marble with about 15 men."

lowering plaster materials, work benches etc. We really need these articles but will have to take them up as we actually use them or you couldn't get anywhere. So Camille, in case there is still some few obstructions will you please bear with me as I'm really doing my best.

Both Loorz and Morgan were concerned that the Gothic Study be finished before Hearst returned from Europe; Solon was worth coddling if need be. Loorz closed his letter of July 30 by telling Solon how refreshing his backyard pool was in the recent hot weather. "You'll certainly have to join us some evening after work."

The ploy was successful. As Loorz told Morgan on August 2, "I expect Mr. Solon to be on deck for Monday [August 6] quite fresh and ready to cooperate. I had a card from him which stated that 'He was happily recuperating from his *Grouch*.'"

Morgan herself could show a temperamental streak at times. Dell Clausen, a plasterer working at San Simeon, could vouch for that, as Loorz told Stolte on August 3:

> The type that can please Miss Morgan are few and far between Fred. It took Dell several months to really win her over although she knew from the beginning that he was exceptionally good. In fact, she has since gone back and is using his own textures that he started with and has almost entirely abandoned the textures she used to use.[47]

----

47. The matter of plasterers — and of their textures — appears at other times in the Loorz Papers, summer of 1934. Back on June 20, George Wright told Loorz in reference to the Bavarian Village at Wyntoon:

> F. C. [Stolte] has already sent up [Henry] Koenig, who is well along with the first coat on the Brown Bear [house]. Because of the many changes to the Turrets [the eventual Cinderella House], I don't see how that building can be ready for plaster as soon as Koenig is done with the Bear. If another plasterer [namely, Dell Clausen] were here too, they would both work themselves out of jobs in a short time.

In an undated letter from late July-early August, Stolte told Loorz of Wyntoon, "The job seems to be progressing O.K. — with exception of plaster, we can't seem to get the right texture." And thus Loorz's letter of August 3 to Stolte, partly quoted in the main text above, began with more on Clausen, Morgan, and Koenig:

> I hope you have things straightened out with the plaster texture. I feel certain that Dell could please her. So if you think it really necessary I will let you have him for a short time until he has Koenig straightened out. If she wants very many different textures on the various jobs [at Wyntoon] I think we will do better with someone more experienced and mechanical than Koenig.

Loorz got minutely specific for Stolte on August 11, once more with regard to Wyntoon. "My guess would be [that] a carpet float finish," he said, "with a close gentle roll, very sandy looking, would please her most on the exterior of that type of building." He also said, "By gentle roll I mean I mean [*sic*] that when he spreads his finish coat in bumps to get the unevenness he must work them down a lot to prevent the look of actual bumps."

Stolte had had some misgivings about the plumber Jim Rankin—about the rates he was charging as a sub-contractor at Wyntoon. Loorz addressed the matter in that same letter of August 3; he brought up some other points as well:

> [Rankin] is our booster and very worth while especially on Hearst Jobs. Please give him whatever you can and I know we'll be ahead of the game. They [the Morgan office] have always been willing to give him his 10% commission so I dont think we should do anything to cut him out of it. I also know that Miss Morgan does not feel that he should get everything but when he complains she regrets [it] and goes right back to him. Do you think I'm correct in my assumptions?
>
> According to Miss Morgan things are going quite O.K. up there [at Wyntoon]. She is just now beginning to feel that you really are getting somewhere and is really satisfied with the altered buildings. Says they look real fine. Keep up the good work.

The calculating Loorz also said, "From now on I'm going to keep an eye open for prospects of the Hearst type when they visit up here," meaning Hearst's guests. "The trouble is that most of them are from Los Angeles. Maybe we can open up an office down there someday." Always thinking, always looking ahead—that was Loorz at his most typical. (He was always inclined to be flexible, too, a trait that spared him any misgivings about southern California, despite his ties to the Bay Area. Hearst himself was already pointing the way: here was a San Francisco blueblood who had spent his middle years in New York and who now lived in Los Angeles much of the time; for him, the cultural rivalry between California's premier cities was absurd. Morgan probably concurred, having done ample work over the years in cities like Long Beach, Pasadena, Hollywood, and others around "the Southland.")[48]

The Burnett Road had recently been completed, a job Loorz was proud of. Stolte was planning a trip to San Simeon. In a letter dated August 11, Loorz encouraged him to try the new route:

> I just wanted to tell you that it would be a lot closer for you to come down by way of our new road thru to Jolon. It is rough and very dusty and will be until the first

---

48. Aside from her work in the greater area for Hearst—and also for Marion Davies and, most recently, for Hearst's oldest son, George—Morgan's efforts for such clients as the YWCA included buildings as far afield as Riverside; see Appendix A on pp. 531–45.

Beyond the Hearst connection, Morgan had also done at least one Southland job that exemplified the tie-in Loorz was contemplating. In April 1926 she began designing an atrium and other features for Mrs. Cecil B. De Mille—as additions to the home in the Los Feliz area of Hollywood that Mrs. De Mille and her famous husband occupied. The job ran through December 1926, generating $786 in operating costs for the Morgan firm. (The Minerva Club in Santa Maria and the De Mille project were tied for ninth place among Morgan's non-Hearst jobs that year, a field led by the YWCA

rain when we can grade it properly. However, it is an interesting ride and I would drive thru to Jolon and meet you with my keys. It saves 80 miles [over the prevailing 125-mile loop through Paso Robles, San Luis Obispo, and Morro Bay] but not a lot of time as it is a slow road. You turn right [from Highway 101] just as you approach the bridge going into King City and drive 20 miles over perfect highway to Jolon. If you would phone me the night you leave Oakland and tell me about when you will reach Jolon, I'll be there. At the same time I'd take you thru the big place there at Milpitas.

That trip would be impossible today unless one had unlimited access to the Hearst Ranch and the adjoining lands of Fort Hunter Liggett. Hearst sold his Milpitas property, surrounding Jolon and Mission San Antonio, to the government in 1940 (a time when several other land owners in the area did the same). The "big place there" that Loorz mentioned was the Milpitas Hacienda, which Morgan had built for Hearst through W. J. Smith ten years before the sale and which became the headquarters at Hunter Liggett once the government took over.

Loorz ended his letter of August 11 by telling Stolte, "I am certainly booming now with over a hundred men and all [the] small jobs necessitating changing every few hours."

The Gothic Study and the Neptune Pool continued to dominate the work at San Simeon. Jules Suppo, having done fine woodwork for the project since the early 1920s, had been retained to inlay the bookcases for the Gothic Study. (He was likewise busy in 1934 with complements to the massive cornice he had carved for Casa Grande's third-floor facade in the 1920s: matching work was now required for the uppermost side areas of that central "Gothic" part of the building.) Suppo's studio was on Polk Street in San Francisco.[49] With regard to the interior portion of his current work—the bookcases for the Study—Loorz told him encouragingly on August 14, "Everything seems to fit nicely." Everything, that is, that Suppo had completed thus far and forwarded to the job. By September 5, with

---

building in Honolulu and the Margaret Baylor Inn in Santa Barbara.) The De Milles were friends of Hearst and Davies; but they were better known to Morgan through the YWCA Hollywood Studio Club, which Morgan had begun working on in 1922 and whose building committee included Mrs. De Mille.

49. The exact address was 2423 Polk Street, near Russian Hill. Suppo had been prosperous enough in the mid-1920s to have Morgan design a new studio for him (1924–26) at 718 Natoma Street, a flourishing artisans' neighborhood in the South of Market commercial district; the studio on Natoma Street superseded a former studio of Suppo's on Eighth Street. His later place on Polk Street was a residence-studio, which Morgan first worked on after he had been there a while—in fact, a full decade after the Natoma project, mostly in 1936. See Boutelle's *Julia Morgan*, pp. 142–43 (whose date of 1925 for Polk Street applies more properly to the work on Natoma Street).

Hearst's return from Europe drawing closer, Loorz adopted a more urgent tone with Suppo. "We are anxious to get the inlay work as soon as possible. We have all of the cases nearly roughed in and can complete them as quickly as we receive your work."[50]

When Morgan was at San Simeon in early August, she referred to Suppo's recent efforts. Loorz noted under "Gothic Study" in his summary, "Work on bookcases and [Neptune] pool to take precedence over all other work. This means slowing up on outside cornice for a while." His dates on his recap notes normally cite the day of her visit—in this case August 7, a Tuesday. Yet both the Morgan-Forney ledgers and the Morgan Collection at Cal Poly indicate she appeared sometime on the weekend of August 4–5. (She was heading north then after still another trip to the Cosmopolitan bungalow in Culver City—her sixteenth in 1934—along with another stop at the George Hearst house in Holmby Hills.) However, the letter she wrote Loorz from San Francisco on Wednesday, August 8, sounded as if she'd been at San Simeon the previous day. Loorz had to provide some mental bracketing in reading her first sentence: "Thinking it over coming down Hill, I thought best to see that bookcase drawing again before sending, for I realized the lower case was not made at girder ends just as I'd described it to you." She also discussed the Neptune Pool colonnades—the "pavillions," as she and Loorz sometimes spelled it.

That sumptuous outdoor setting was far enough along for Loorz's notes from her visit on August 16 to contain this entry: "Try to get temple started [assembled] to indicate proper balance from approach on roads [leading] up [to] hill." The ancient Roman temple, comprising six huge columns and a massive top section, had been acquired by Hearst in 1922 and had awaited its moment on the hilltop ever since. Its ultimate role as the centerpiece of the new Neptune Pool complex would soon be realized.

MAC MCCLURE WAS OVERDUE in writing his memorable letters to Loorz. He came through with a good one from Wyntoon on September 6, datelined "Mc-Cloud":

It has been an eventful summer on the whole. The houses have moved along steadily toward completion (externally) and now the place has quite a finished ap-

---

50. Both letters from Loorz to Suppo are among twelve such letters, dating from April 4, 1933, through November 1, 1934. The longtime Hearst aficionado Winton Frey obtained photocopies of all twelve in 1973 from Andre Suppo, Jules Suppo's son, and sent them to Loorz, by then a man in his seventies. Despite the range of the Loorz Papers, the collection doesn't contain Loorz's carbon copies from the 1930s of the twelve outgoing letters.

pearance, with much of the half timber and plaster on and the grounds and pathways neat and shining. I think Miss M is more or less satisfied and I hope W.R. is likewise but who can say?

We have an artist lady here [Doris Day][51] painting shutters and decorations. She came about a month ago with a carload of baggage and a large parrot in a cage. I met her at [the town of] Mt Shasta and hauled as much as possible in the coupe and Geo W[right] went over later for the rest and "Nicky," the parrot.

Nicky is the apple of her eye and although she has been told to keep him out of the McCloud Hotel she hates to leave him out on the job and occasionally spirits him into the hotel via the back stairs. It is more fun than trouble, however, and is O.K. by me.

I think the shutter decorations will prove expensive however and doubt if $50 each will cover them—(there are only about 60 of them).

Very little changes have been made by Miss M. She has a few suggestions, chiefly about the garden, but spends much of her time, when here, working on the cataloging of the San Simeon "treasures."[52]

She left here last Sat. night [September 1] (midnight when I put her on the train) so I had a late start on my week end trip, which was to Crescent City on the coast (via Grant's Pass Oregon). It is a nice change from this dried up place and I thoroughly enjoyed seeing the ocean again. . . .[53]

The new plasterer "got the feeling," at least partly and our plaster is no longer "nervous" but is "happy" or at least so we are told. By the way, Geo. you may be interested to know that Miss M thinks Dell Clauson [sic] is a relative of yours or so she inferred at least—Don't know how she got that! She thinks Dell is pretty good, too. . . .

---

51. See Boutelle's *Julia Morgan*, pp. 85, 219, plus 247 (this last reference under "Wyntoon and Other Hearst Projects," note 3).

52. Morgan and her office staff in San Francisco had been keeping track of Hearst's acquisitions for San Simeon since 1919. But many ledgers and other files of those early years were primitive. Not until 1927, when W. R. Williams took charge of the San Simeon warehouses, did adequate record keeping arise. Meanwhile, the best efforts in Hearst's behalf were being made in New York from the late twenties onward, with the documenting of myriad items that entered his Bronx warehouse (some of which went on to California). These methods influenced Morgan and Williams; and yet even through the 1930s a certain provincialism still colored much of their work. However, in 1934 and 1935, Morgan and H. C. "Jim" Forney (the husband of her secretary, Lilian Forney) began compiling a noteworthy set of volumes—"pictorial inventories" of the silver, sculpture, paintings, and metalwork that Hearst had at San Simeon and Wyntoon. Morgan's role in this project or a similar one is quite likely what Mac was referring to.

53. As to Morgan's northern travels, she had gone to Wyntoon on August 30, according to the Wyntoon Waterhouse account in the Morgan-Forney ledgers; the dates August 11–12 and 21–22 are also recorded. For the earlier part of the summer, the dates recorded are June 22–23, followed by July 6–7, 16–17, and 27–28. See also note 35, above.

The days are getting much cooler here—or the nights I should say. I hope W.R. does not wait too long or he will freeze in his unheated houses—Waterhouse & Wheelers.[54]

Loorz answered Mac on September 11, beginning with "Boy I was pleased to get your letter":

It was real newsy and I enjoyed it. I really feel ashamed of writing so promptly and keeping you always on the spot so to speak, owing me an answer. I do it chiefly so that I will not lay the letter aside and finally forget to answer it at all.

Yes I know that Miss Morgan is quite pleased with Wyntoon. She admits that it turned out much better than she anticipated and much better than originally planned.

I know the artist lady Miss Day. At the beginning of the decorating in the [Gothic] Study Miss M. talked to me about the advisability of having her come and work with Solon. I only shrugged my shoulders and she knew how I felt about it. She brought her out here and she [Doris Day] went over everything and raved about most everything. It was the proper thing to do for she is now working isn't she.

Anyway it was decided to bring a young decorator Ted Linforth, a son of one of Miss M.'s clients and very personal friend.[55] Young and inexperienced but very talented and a smart boy. But—it is too long a story to go into detail—try as the boy might he could not please the master and he was reduced to slinging paint with [Frank] Gyorgy and Mr. Solon has done the big job almost single handed. The space [on the Gothic Study arches] is covered with typical Solon sketches

---

54. Mac's letter included this paragraph:

I hear a little about San Simeon but not a great deal. Martin ([Jim] Rankin's man) says he heard Mrs OB [Frances O'Brien] is dead but Rankin does not know about it. Is it so? and if so I am very sorry to hear it. Too bad she couldn't have remained on the job [as head of the Household Department] as they certainly have never found a better.

The allusion was to O'Brien's replacement in 1932 by Ada Drew, who had clashed with W. R. Williams and who had since been fired (as part of the "house cleaning" Loorz described in October 1933; see p. 97, plus its note 75). Albert Redelsperger and his wife, Augusta, succeeded Drew.

In answering Mac on September 11, 1934, Loorz said he knew nothing of Frances O'Brien's death. He also said, "Things are really running smoothly about the household and [in] all departments on the hilltop. Albert was a good selection. . . . I have no complaints."

55. Regarding the Linforths, see Boutelle, *Julia Morgan*, pp. 134–35. Another young man from Berkeley, Phillip Joy (the son of Thad Joy, who remained too infirm to work), was also at San Simeon for part of the 1934 season, as he had been during some previous seasons. Loorz's recap notes from Morgan's visit of May 31 had included this entry: "When school is out Phillip Joy will come down to waterproof statues and work with Mr. [Frank] Gyorgy in touching up C. House [Casa del Sol] Ironwork."

and dull tones. According to Miss M. he must go over all of it again and really do the job. That is put more color in the costumes and improve figures above the sketchy layout. You know as well as I do that they are just as Solon planned them and [are] the best he can do and perhaps alright to some. For myself I think she is right but I told her she could never get it out of Solon. We have one real good one rich in color and not too bright but that was done by Ted. That was his Waterloo for too many admired it and Mr. Solon heard. Besides that Ted made the mistake of talking to Miss M. when she came down. It is Solon's drawing and story but Ted's hand and coloring.

Just as we are about to complete the Study we are obliged to make such changes as tear out two cast Stone Doorways, replacing one with an Antique and the other with a carved stone imitation. We must tear down an end wall [at the east end of the main Study area] to build supports for a heavy Antique Stone Panel etc.[56] Boy you know the story too well. We have gone all too nicely until now. If we get the room completed by the return of Mr. Hearst I miss my guess. By the way talking to Mr. Willicombe over the phone yesterday he said he expected him back in about two weeks. That meant N.Y. of course.

Loorz wrote to the electrician Louis Schallich the next day, September 12, about the Neptune Pool:

The marble men [from the Vermont Marble Company] are thru in the large pool [the main basin] and soon will be in the upper [alcove]. Dell [Clausen] is plastering the walls above the marble and Mac[57] is setting the main Venus statue. We hope to put water in the pool sometime next week. I dont know how we can do it without Jimmie [Rankin] so I suppose he will be down to show us how. I hear that he raved when he got to Wyntoon because of the amount of work they had done without him. Says it is all wrong. Poor Jimmie and he is so nice to kid and dig into.

Morgan was back on the job on Saturday, September 15. Her visit yielded the usual spate of notes by Loorz on the Gothic Study and the Neptune Pool. Regarding the latter subject, he made this entry:

Vermont marble Co. can send down coping of white marble for top of Rear wall of main pool. Send in to the [Morgan] office the dimensions of the steps in the upper pool wall so that Arch[itect] can have details of consoles made for each step. Marble Co cannot plan on completing this part of contract at this time.

---

56. A French Gothic heraldic sculpture, which Hearst bought late in 1933 through the Thomas Fortune Ryan sale in New York. Here was a prime example of how a recent acquisition could influence the work at San Simeon as much as one that had long been stockpiled.

57. Not the same person as Mac McClure: Loorz may have meant John McFadden (mentioned later in this book) or possibly a sculptor from San Francisco named Max Mindner.

In addition, Loorz's entries under "Miscellaneous" included this item:

[Italian] Cypress tree ordered from West Coast Nursery [in Palo Alto] to replace dead one on upper terrace. [This tree is the] Only established one available. Cost $875.00 planted in hole and guaranteed. Notified [the nursery] that payment would be slow giving [us] time to check up on its progress.

A few days later—September 19—San Simeon experienced a late-summer, subtropical rain.[58] Saturday the twenty-second found Loorz describing the event to George Wright, who had been at Wyntoon since April and who was still there:

We had a great electric storm Wednesday and lightning struck all over the place. Burned the upper log barn in the animal field [the main zoo compound, below The Enchanted Hill]. Started fires near Chelano [Chileno] Camp and several around Pine Mt.[59] Actually struck and shattered a pine tree on China hill, you know the one just across the road from the approach to the Castle. Many eye witnesses swear they saw a bolt strike the North tower [of Casa Grande] and sparks fly in all directions. It sounded like it in the office where I was hiding as it was pouring down at the same time. . . .

It is still very foggy actually dripping but not quite enough to be called a rain. We needed it as we will soon need a lot of water for the pool. The pool is already for water except for the placing of the heavy statues [by Charles Cassou] where Miss M. wants them.[60] The light 7 ton bases of brick are now on rollers so that we can put them about promptly. Sounds bad but really she has ordered them moved but once so far and they are awaiting a second inspection.

We are just starting the short road down the hill. Thursday [Millard] Hendricks and I walked over your line of stakes prepared to find all the faults imaginable. Several times where you flattened out a bit we were tempted to make

---

58. The day before the storm, Morgan wrote to Arthur Byne, the antiquarian in Madrid who had seen Hearst at St. Donat's Castle in July. "Am gradually coming back to a normal existence," she said in part, "enough so to have had a busy summer shuttling up and down from one end of California to the other on [the] most varied projects." Busy indeed. And varied indeed, thanks almost entirely to her greater Hearst pursuits. Having been at Wyntoon as recently as September 11–12, and having gone straight from there to Los Angeles to check once more on the Cosmopolitan bungalow and the George Hearst house (the Beach House, last visited in mid-August, required no further attention in 1934), Morgan was as much in the throes of her "normal existence" as she had ever been. Her other travels in 1934 pertained mostly to jobs around the Bay Area, like the Selden Williams and the A. F. Hockenbeamer houses in Berkeley. For the quoted portions here, see Morgan to Byne, September 18, 1934; Morgan/Byne/Hearst Correspondence, Morgan Collection.

59. Both areas are within a few miles of The Enchanted Hill, the former to the west, the latter to the east.

60. These were some of the marble sculptures that Morgan had told Loorz on February 3 to remove from the immediate building site; see note 10, above.

changes but soon found your very good reasons as we went along. It will make a much better road than I imagined even after talking to you about it. We could not conscientiously make a single change. Do you happen to remember or is there a record of the length of the new road in some book here in the office?

This was the road that Hearst had spoken of in December 1933—"the shorter road from the castle to the creek."[61] Upon its completion, it would veer downward from the saddle between China Hill and Orchard Hill—the two outlying, westerly summits of the overall Enchanted Hill—and make its way to a major watercourse, Arroyo de la Cruz, by local standards a river more than a creek. Hearst, however, may have meant Burnett Creek, the tributary along which the Burnett Road began its journey through the Santa Lucia Range.

Loorz also wrote to Morgan on September 22 and recounted for her, as he had for Wright, the "electric storm and fires," which had been "very exciting."[62] He gave her a more detailed update on the Gothic Study, along with a few words about the Neptune Pool:

> Mr. Solon is working on the girders [in the Study] somewhat as you suggested and has vastly improved those he has gone over. That is, according to my own judgment. He has introduced some bright yellows etc that have lightened up the brownich [sic] tint. He has outlined and drawn the figures more carefully. I dont think he has put in more bright reds and greens however. Maybe that can be added in spots later if wanted.
>
> The rain has caused us to lay off work on the pool. Work is rapidly shaping up in the Study with the doorway and stone panel soon completed.[63] We have received no more work from Mr. Suppo but hope to by Monday [September 24]. I had to take all carpenters off that work as we had no more material to work with. We did put up the mouldings around the stairway doors of the hallway [the Gothic Hall].

Fred Stolte, who along with Jim LeFeaver of Miss Morgan's office had been at Wyntoon over the weekend of September 22–23, had surprising news for Loorz

---

61. See p. 101 in this volume. The subject of the proposed, more direct road had come up at least a year before Hearst's reference to it in 1933 (Loorz to Dick Boyd, November 23, 1932). See also p. 140, below (Willicombe to Loorz, October 12, 1934), regarding an apparent delay in the building of this new road.

62. If Loorz posted his letter on the day he wrote it (a Saturday), it would have reached Morgan after she returned to San Francisco (she had left there on Sunday, September 23, to be at San Simeon on Monday the twenty-fourth). Meanwhile, LeFeaver had gone to Wyntoon in her place on Friday the twenty-first and had stayed there through Sunday the twenty-third (Morgan-Forney ledgers). Morgan was next at Wyntoon a week later, on September 28–29.

63. The same architectural elements that Loorz mentioned to Mac McClure in his long letter of September 11.

upon returning to Oakland. In a letter dated September 24, Stolte said that E. E. Boss and his wife had been relieved of their duties as caretakers. On a cheerier note, Loorz learned that Stolte and LeFeaver had gone fishing together. "He, Bob Lang, Harry [Thompson] & myself went down the river yesterday (Sunday)," said the elder partner. "Caught a nice mess." Stolte also commented, "The job seems to be progressing satisfactorily. Landscaping & roads are complete and plaster & outside trim is progressing nicely and almost finished."

About a week later George Wright answered Loorz's "newsy letter" of September 22.[64] He referred, as Stolte had, to the Bosses' dismissal and then gave other details of life at Wyntoon during the 1934 season:

> The hotel is bulging with a construction crew that is about the same strength as that on the job last year. The so-called permanent guests may resent the intrusion of such a large foreign element, but that is there [their] hard luck. When I first came up here and found out how little work was definitely planned, I didn't think that the architectural office would be able to keep up with decisions fast enough to keep as large a crew going as we have had here for some time.
>
> At the first of the season it seemed as if there would be little need for laborers outside of a few to keep the carpenters supplied. But there has been many a time when Harry would [have] liked to have supplemented the crew of fourteen that have been steadily employed ever since the job has been well under way. . . .
>
> Two of the buildings [in the Bavarian Village on the Waterhouse parcel] are completely plastered, the third nearly so. Tile is going on the roofs, and of course exterior carpenter work is done. Within a short time all scaffolds will be down. Mrs. Day is just about finished painting pictures on the Brown Bear [house]. So you can send the chief up here to give the place the once over when ever you are through with him down there.
>
> We, who have seen both [decorators], feel very thankful for Miss Morgan's choice of Mrs. Day for the decorator rather than another we could name.

The temperamental Camille Solon was evidently the person Wright alluded to. As for E. E. Boss and his wife, Fanny (a distant cousin of Hearst's), they had somehow run afoul of Julia Morgan. "It doesn't pay to cross Miss Morgan," Loorz told Louis Schallich on October 1.[65] He also told Schallich, "Now we are expecting

---

64. Wright's letter is dated "Monday night," most likely having been written on October 1.

65. Mr. Boss, who had been at Wyntoon since Hearst began acquiring property there in 1924, took the dismissal in surprisingly good spirit. He told Joe Willicombe a few days after the episode:

> We expect to leave here Oct. 5 if Mr Kower [Eugene Kower, the new caretaker] is through with us. We find them delightful people and it has been a pleasure to show them all we can, and tell them as far as possible how to meet emergencies. . . .

the party home any day and all work on the pool has stopped. We are to concentrate on the [Gothic] study only and greatly reduce my crew as soon as possible."

The shadow of Hearst was falling upon the land, the presence of the great man could almost be felt. Loorz relayed the latest news to Stolte on Saturday, October 6:

> Mr. Willicombe phoned me that it looked like Mr. Hearst would leave N.Y. on Tuesday and be in L.A. on Thursday. That means we can expect him here or in Wyntoon any time. *RUMOR* has it that he intends to fly to Wyntoon before coming here. He has written Miss Morgan that he has a lot of new ideas to try out at Wyntoon, so make up your mind that you'll make lots of changes. Ho Ho. I'm glad he didn't say he'd try that here.[66]
>
> Mr. Hearst sent a special maid to accompany 11 small blooded [pedigreed] dogs of various types back from N.Y. and Europe. I have to rush up kennels with large runs within a very few days to accommodate them. I started yesterday to move the garages [near the indoor Roman Pool] to make room. One section is moved and the kennels are started this morning. Can you beat it?[67]

In replying on October 8, Stolte said with regard to Wyntoon: "We have been expecting the tour of inspection momentarily, and I carry my nite-shirt in my pocket in case of an emergency call." Stolte's humorous words aside, he'd been doing his homework all the while — by keeping up with the foreign dispatches Hearst sent to his mighty chain of newspapers around the country. "In reading several of Mr. Hearst's European articles," Stolte said, "I felt that we may expect some new

---

Mrs. Boss joins me in thanking you for what you have done for us, and wishing you health and happiness.

From Boss to Willicombe, October 4, 1934; Hearst Papers, carton 57 (under "Bi-Brn"). Small world: a radio station where Boss later did menial work was taken over by the Hearst Radio Corporation; this resulted in a "clean sweep" dismissal that included Boss. His sister-in-law Phoebe Hill appealed to Hearst, who took the cue: "Col W [Colonel Willicombe] — Please ask Radio Corporation to restore Mr. Boss. Why was he dismissed. He is a good man." See Hill to Hearst, May 8, 1937, plus attached items, two of them dated June 19, 1937; Hearst Papers, carton 23 (under "1937 Samples — Requests").

66. The Morgan Collection at Cal Poly contains no such letter from Hearst; in fact, for 1934 it contains no Hearst-Morgan correspondence of any kind from late June to late October (but see note 71, below). Nor has any such letter surfaced thus far in the Hearst Papers at the Bancroft Library. Because Morgan had not been in Europe for more than thirty years, and because Hearst had been there during several recent summers (1928, 1930, 1931, 1934), he surely was more apt than she was to have "a lot of new ideas to try out at Wyntoon." See p. 87, note 58, for the influential claim that it was Morgan who was so inclined, thanks to the trip she purportedly made in 1931 (set forth by Elinor Richey in *Eminent Women of the West*).

67. See note 81, below, for another portion of this letter of October 6 — and for another portion of its reply of October 8.

or rather very old ideas—incorporated—in the plans for Wyntoon. Did you read the last article on Germany and the walled towns?"[68] Stolte also told Loorz that he'd signed up two more General Petroleum stations, one in Santa Cruz and the other in San Francisco, and that he'd "started the Berkeley job for Miss Morgan"—a small addition to the house she originally built in 1928 for Selden Williams on Claremont Avenue.[69]

In writing to Louis Schallich again, this time on October 11, Loorz repeated part of what he'd told Stolte a few days earlier—that Hearst had purchased "a bunch more blooded dogs" on his trip and that Loorz was having to build new kennels for them. He also told Schallich how good the Gothic Study looked, all its features being "nearly completed." He said that Camille Solon's painting didn't "look so bad now that it all is toned together with walls and furniture." Regarding the work outside, Loorz said he would avoid filling the newly marble-lined Neptune Pool since it had become "almost too cold to swim." Besides, with construction continuing on the two colonnades and the old Roman temple, "the pool would be dirty all the time."

Loorz's pulse must surely have quickened as he read a letter from Joe Willicombe, dated October 12 in Los Angeles and prompted by a long report Loorz had sent him a month earlier. Willicombe had relayed the details to Hearst in New York, the Chief and his party having returned there from Europe in late September;[70] Loorz's report comprised a "summary of the work accomplished" during the four months Hearst had been abroad; it included the welcome news that the vexatious East Room mantel had been "deepened and proper louvered vents installed."

---

68. This and similar dispatches were undoubtedly newspaper articles, since Hearst seldom contributed a byline to his magazines; Stolte probably followed them in the *San Francisco Examiner.* Whereas editorials by Hearst and signed letters by him to his editors often commanded a front page, his travel articles must have appeared inside—where they still await discovery by determined eyes.

69. Boutelle makes no reference to any work after 1928 on the Williams house; see *Julia Morgan*, p. 166. The surviving Trial Balances (accounts payable and receivable) of the F. C. Stolte Co. contain a misspelled "Seldon Williams" among many other listings for 1934. The Morgan-Forney ledgers, which cite the F. C. Stolte Co. for this job (done for Mrs. Selden Williams, now widowed), provide the best evidence.

70. Eight years later the Hearst insider Harry Crocker recounted the Chief's visit with President Roosevelt on October 8, 1934, an episode that occurred just before the Hearst party went home to California. "If you will remember," Crocker wrote Hearst, "we returned to New York the next morning. On the train you told Marion and me of your concern over the fact that the President regarded as heaven-sent certain of his inspirations." And so on with Roosevelt's "interest in the occult," which ultimately bore on his prescience in 1934 of the world conflict that lay ahead—a "rather remarkable" outlook, Crocker noted, thinking it "might be material for a future column" by Hearst. See Crocker to Hearst, May 18, 1942 (written a week before Hearst's final installment of "In the News"); Hearst Papers, carton 35 (under "1942 Samples").

Ever the emphatic secretary, Colonel Willicombe got right to the point in address-ing the young builder. "Confirming telephone message," he told Loorz, "I have fol-lowing memoranda from Chief regarding your report of September 14th on con-struction at San Simeon":[71]

> Referring to paragraph six of BURNETT ROAD item, in which you discussed running new and better road from hilltop to first bridge at bottom of canyon, Chief said he would like to discuss this with you. Therefore advise delay until he returns.
>
> Have made memorandum to get you on telephone to discuss this with Chief at first opportunity.
>
> Chief says he would much prefer cattle guards between hilltop and Milpitas in-stead of the nine gates you mentioned [scattered along the Burnett Road, Loorz having called them a "beastly nuisance"].
>
> Referring to your suggestion in paragraph three of PIPE LINE BEARTRAP SPRING TO BURNETT item in which you state that you could construct the reservoir at the Beartrap Flat [on the Burnett Road], etcetera, Chief says:
>
> "This would make grand fishing hole. We can make it extra large."[72]
>
> You stated regarding the STUDY that Solon hopes to have very presentable

---

71. The four-page report was conveyed as a letter to Willicombe on September 13, 1934; the last page has a notation in Loorz's hand regarding some follow-up details he telephoned on Septem-ber 14 to Jean Henry, an assistant of Willicombe's (and one whom Willicombe later married).

The "memoranda" Willicombe mentioned on October 12 (actually a single item) was enclosed with the letter Loorz received. In a postscript, Willicombe said: "To avoid possibility of misunder-standing, I am sending Chief's memorandum, which kindly return in attached envelope registered." Loorz undoubtedly did so; however, no such item has surfaced yet in the Hearst Papers.

The Morgan Collection at Cal Poly has a transcription of the body of Loorz's letter (the report proper), dated September 14, 1934, and filed with the Hearst/Morgan Correspondence.

72. A letter from Loorz to King Walters on August 2, 1934, puts the pipe line and reservoir in more understandable perspective:

Just Monday [July 30] we brought the [Burnett Road] equipment back to this side of the [Nacimiento] river and we're taking out some of the worst curves and reverses. We will try to improve it a lot especially the part of the Tieslau road [of 1932] down Salmon Creek. Then we plan on digging a reservoir at the Bear Trap where your [road crew's] camp was. You see we piped the spring from above to Burnett House where we will soon plant a grove of redwoods [actually, giant sequoias]. This reservoir will serve for fish mainly and for storage [of water for the cattle operation] as well.

In his report to Willicombe of September 13, Loorz said the pipe line was among the jobs "done on the Hilltop Fund account and charged back to Piedmont Land and Cattle Co. as in-structed"—versus "construction under Miss Morgan." The distinction is clearer in this instance than in many others. (A good example of a muddled instance lies in the airport work of 1935; see pp. 200 and 218 in the next chapter, plus their notes 95 and 129.)

job by October 4th. Chief says in that connection that he will be home about October 20th.

As telephoned, Chief hopes that the Breakfast Room [East Room] fireplace "works well." When you talk with him on the telephone I suggest that you discuss this also.

Chief says finally:

"A lot more has been done than I had hoped. I will be coming home to a different ranch. Please thank Mr. Loorz."

He also is glad that you are enlarging the kennels.

Chief indicated in his letter that he may go to Wyntoon about November first, from which you may infer that he is likely to be at the ranch between the date of his arrival, October 20th, and the end of the month.

Hooray, Loorz must have thought: the Chief is in a chipper mood!

MORGAN WAS AT SAN SIMEON on October 20 for Hearst's arrival. What better indication of the vital, indispensable role the Hearst projects had long played in her life — and, as a result, of her sheer devotion to Hearst himself? It turns out that a Tyrolean costume party at the Beach House on Sunday the twenty-first is what kept him from showing up until Tuesday. Loorz gave Stolte the latest news that evening:

> Well it is now 7 P.M. and the chief just arrived a few minutes ago. We have been expecting the plane to land all day and Miss Morgan has been waiting for him since Saturday. She is very tired but really had not much to do to make ready this trip. She has walked around looking over things in general and going over winter programs etc with me.
>
> We had company for dinner tonight [at home] but she felt a bit weak and really wanted me to stick around [on the hilltop] to help in case of necessity. . . . If she is with him for many hours I'll certainly enjoy the wait till she leaves. I have enjoyed her visit a lot. It is about the first time she has remained over night since I've been down here. That is excepting the rush when we fitted up for the xmas party.

(Morgan had been at San Simeon for one day in early December 1933; she hadn't been there at all in December 1932. Loorz's quick-typing reference was more likely to the days she'd spent on the hill in April 1934, preparing for Hearst's birthday party. In addition, though, Loorz told Camille Solon on April 15, 1933, of three consecutive days during which she had recently been on site.)[73]

---

73. If Morgan had, in fact, stayed over infrequently in recent years, clustered dates like July 20–22 (see p. 127 in this chapter) suggest she had spent late evenings and the wee hours in San Luis Obispo.

More details awaited Stolte in Loorz's letter to him of October 23:

> She feels that things are in good shape at Wyntoon and thinks the new manager or caretaker [Eugene Kower] will be O.K.[74] About all she has to worry about, I think is that as always at this time of year she finds herself deeply indebted to everyone. I hope this time that she will be able to get a bit more from the chief. It would make things much easier for all concerned. . . .
>
> The wind is blowing and it is quite cold. It means all fireplaces must be booming and that always means trouble for sooner or later one will flare up and smoke. If I can only keep those I've constructed behaving properly.[75]
>
> Well all I hope is that we can get Mr. Hearst to loosen up a bit with funds for Miss Morgan and permit at least a small crew on Wyntoon over the winter months. She cannot do it at the present rates.
>
> I'm beginning to realize how impossible it will be for me to get away from here. She would be disappointed and that would take all her other work away from us. Boy we [the F. C. Stolte Co.] would certainly miss her work, wouldn't we?

Loorz touched on the same point the next day, October 24, in writing to Jack Hall, an old friend from his days in Phi Kappa Tau at Berkeley:

> I dont see how I can possibly plan on getting away from here as I'm afraid Miss Morgan would be too disappointed. That would mean a lot to us just now as we have the big job up north [Wyntoon][76] and several smaller alterations from her in the bay district. She has been awfully good to me Jack. I owe her a lot.

---

74. Loorz may well have received Stolte's most recent letter by this time, dated October 19 and evidently sent from Wyntoon, with words about that northern project:

> Undoubtedly you are now in the midst of a tremendous rush. Hope that you may survive the present one and prepare for the next.
>
> We are pepping up & cleaning up here, expecting a visit, also. The tile is about ½ completed on the roofs, and landscaping is almost complete. The jobs are really *looking up* from outside.

Stolte also said he'd lined up some new commercial work in the Bay Area. "House building," though, was a "*minus*-quantity," thanks to "our Mr. Sinclair." Stolte meant Upton Sinclair, the Democratic (EPIC) candidate for Governor whose current role in state politics had "stopped many possible prospects."

75. The structural portions of the two fireplaces in the Gothic Study (one in the Study proper, the other in the adjoining east alcove) dated from 1931—the period of the "roof raising" that was done in this mid-section of Casa Grande under Camille Rossi. But it can often be hard in these matters to say exactly where Rossi's work gave way to Loorz's (just as it's well nigh impossible to separate certain efforts made through the Hilltop Fund from those beholden to the Hearst Construction Fund). In any case, the recap Loorz provided of Morgan's visit on October 15, 1934, included a discouraging note: "Tried both fireplaces in Study and regret to state that they do smoke."

76. Although the much-touted "big job" (the Spanish monastery) had fizzled in 1933 and was barely warranting further mention in 1934, Loorz had good reason to be using the same term in a new context: the Bavarian Village and other projects at Wyntoon were big by any standard.

Of those lesser jobs in the Bay Area, there were five all told. Along with the Williams and the Hockenbeamer houses in Berkeley, there were Else Schilling's house in San Francisco and, in the same city, Johanna Volkmann's house. The fifth job was also in San Francisco: the Century Club, a women's building that Morgan had originally worked on some twenty years before.

Morgan had bigger fish to fry, though, as October 1934 entered its final week. Soon after her layover at San Simeon, she went to Wyntoon for a longer period that began on Saturday the twenty-seventh. October 27 also saw Loorz writing to his father in Lovelock, Nevada:

> Mr. Hearst is back here and we are enjoying his visit. He seems well and happy and is quite pleased with everything we did while he was away [in Europe]. So I guess I'll be able to stay on the job for a while longer. He is going to fly up to Wyntoon, McCloud, on Monday [October 29] if the weather is good. He is going up to look at the work we have been doing up there. I do hope he likes it just as well.

This was the same trip that Colonel Willicombe had predicted on October 12 would be taking place "about November first." Hearst spent five days at Wyntoon.[77] Then he flew back to San Simeon on Saturday, November 3. Morgan was on the plane with him, a full seven days at Wyntoon behind her. At San Simeon she had a brief session with Loorz, one yielding an unusually short list of recap notes, mostly on the Neptune Pool. Then she left for San Luis Obispo to catch a train home to San Francisco. It was her last visit to the ranch in 1934.[78]

In the meantime, through a letter dated November 1, Loorz heard from Frank

---

77. The five-day span is somewhat conjectural: Hearst may not have been solely at Wyntoon as of Monday, October 29. On Thursday, November 1, "Story Favoritism Blamed For Hearst-Metro Break, Sending Davies to WB" appeared in the Hollywood trade journal *Daily Variety*, pp. 1, 3. "Deal between Hearst and Warners [Warner Bros.] was consummated in less than 72 hours," went the report. "Publisher-producer [Hearst] and Jack Warner got together Monday [October 29], and by Tuesday night the new combination was set, with signing of binding papers accomplished yesterday [October 31]." (One of Hearst's film executives, Edgar Hatrick, did the actual signing, allowing Hearst to be elsewhere, perhaps for most of the week.)

Jack Warner's version of what happened that Monday appears in *My First Hundred Years in Hollywood* (New York, 1965), p. 236: "I met him [Hearst] and Marion at their Santa Monica beach house, and a multimillion-dollar proposition was settled in five minutes flat." See also pp. 148–49 in the present volume.

78. Morgan's travels in this stretch can be pieced together through the Morgan-Forney ledgers. The main Wyntoon account (the Waterhouse account) contains this entry under October 27: "Miss Morgan to Wyntoon," followed by "to S. S. by plane with Mr. Hearst." The main San Simeon account, under "Travel Miss Morgan" for November 3, contains a further detail: "to SS by plane, return on train." The Wyntoon entry was assigned a cost of $17.50, as was the San Simeon entry. The two figures equal the $35 normally assigned a separate, round-trip visit to either place. This time, since Hearst provided part of the transportation, Morgan's entire week in the field counted as a single, encompassing trip that began and ended in San Francisco.

Hellenthal, his counterpart at the Beach House in Santa Monica and on other Hearst-Morgan jobs in the surrounding area. Hellenthal sought the name of the man who had made the "silvered wire screens" for the bookcases in the Beach House several years earlier.

Loorz's answer was enough to tantalize any archivist or historian. "Frank," he said on November 2, "I have some old Beach House records in the attic of my Berkeley home, now rented. This man's name will be in those records. My tenant might gladly send the files to me." Whether Loorz got hold of those files from 1927–28 is unknown. The Loorzes, in any event, sold their house in Berkeley in 1936. Perhaps the Beach House records still exist somewhere; alas, they can't be counted among today's George Loorz Papers, which for all their diversity contain no such files. (A trove of Frank Hellenthal Papers—if such should ever surface—could easily throw more light on the matter of Loorz's early records.)[79]

On November 3—the same Saturday that Hearst and Morgan flew in from Wyntoon—Loorz wrote to Stolte:

> Well I guess your rush is over for this year. Hope you made personal contact with Mr. Hearst and that you enjoyed it. He has been very pleasant to me and I look forward to an enjoyable winter working with him here on the hilltop. This in spite of the fact that we get some very unreasonable calls when we least expect them.
>
> The day before he left [for Wyntoon], Willicombe called me at about 9 P.M. and said that Mr. Hearst had just told him to consult me about getting the zoo off the hilltop as soon as possible. Willicombe said, "If you meet a few tigers and bears and lions etc on your way up the hill in the morning you will know what it is all about, just get busy and house them someway."

---

79. Concerning Hellenthal himself, he was a native of Seattle who hailed from "a family of builders and engineers"; he was three years older than Loorz and was likewise a veteran of World War I:

> After resigning from the Army in 1920, Mr. Hellenthal came to Santa Monica, where he has since specialized in the construction of high class residences. Few builders in Southern California have erected so many large and expensive homes as he has. During the last few year[s] he has erected about two and a half million dollars worth of large mansions in the [Santa Monica] Bay District, including the homes of Marion Davies, Louis B. Mayer, Irving Thalberg, Cedric Gibbons, Jack Gilbert and others. He also erected the Marion Davies Hospital [the Davies Clinic in West Los Angeles]. In addition to his operations in Santa Monica, Mr. Hellenthal does practically all the building for William Randolph Hearst in Southern California.

From Charles S. Warren, *History of the Santa Monica Bay Region* (Santa Monica, 1934), pp. 116–19. A further reference to some documents concerning the Beach House—though perhaps not the same ones Loorz mentioned on November 2—appears in a letter from Loorz to Hellenthal on January 2, 1935.

More than a decade had passed since the Camp Hill of Hearst's former years began evolving into The Enchanted Hill. Through much of that stretch, the animal-loving Hearst had been stocking his ranch with herds of zebra, buffalo, and other grazing species, most of which roamed freely over acreage bordering his lofty retreat. On the main hilltop itself, he assembled a more conventional zoo, comprising species like those that prompted Willicombe's phone call. And yet as late as 1934, some animals of the lion-and-tiger kind still awaited better housing in compounds like the bear grotto on adjoining Orchard Hill (a structure Loorz mentioned to Morgan in his "sunburn" letter of July 6). Confined to a small area near the garages and the Roman Pool, the hilltop animals had long proved to be too close for comfort. Their shrieks and howls could pierce the air at the oddest times, startling Hearst's less-seasoned guests.

As for the first part of Loorz's letter to his partner on November 3, Stolte wrote back that, yes, the rush at Wyntoon was over "for a while"—this in a letter headed "Wednesday" only (probably written on November 7 rather than October 31):[80]

> Despite the rainy weather, I believe Mr. Hearst enjoyed the visit; he surely didn't mind walking around in it.
>
> I met him the second day for a few seconds only—I thought that Miss Morgan could answer any embarrassing questions.
>
> The first eve, on their arrival, I fell into the job of showing them around the houses. So if he should ask you who the tough guy with the spotlight was—why you are prepared.

The brevity of Loorz's recap notes from November 3 aside—the Gothic Study, for example, went unmentioned—Morgan may have checked on that project once more before she left San Simeon. Loorz, at any rate, armed with detailed notes from her long visit of October 20–24, had much to tell Ted Linforth about the Study on Tuesday, November 6. Linforth was the young man who, along with Thad Joy's son, Phillip, had helped Camille Solon in recent months:

> Solon has not yet returned and I presume that he has contacted Miss Morgan there in S.F. You know of course that she intends to sail [to Europe] tomorrow November 7th. So far the programs [*sic*] still stands as I told you, that is, Solon is to return and re-do the two repeats in story and design [on the Gothic Study arches]. Mr. Hearst has definitely decided that it is not only too brown but must not be brown at all but the whole background must be made to indicate that the painting is on stone instead of wood. That means that gray will predominate.

---

80. Stolte may even have written the letter as late as Wednesday, November 14. If so, it further complicates a stretch in which two undated (but partly datable) letters of his lie in close proximity. Excerpts from the other letter appear on p. 148 of this chapter.

This last for your enlightenment in case you may be called to change the back-grounds. Mr. Hearst really likes the figures both in design and color and unless prompted I dont think he will ask for brighter colors.

Loorz also mentioned to Linforth the new cornice work on the long sides of Casa Grande's Gothic level—the wooden components that Jules Suppo had been carving in 1934 (and to which Linforth may have helped apply a finish stain):

Miss Morgan liked the [new upper] cornice very much since it did tone in with the [older] lower cornice as it never has done before. I didn't bother to mention that some color was put in to darken it. As long as she liked it nothing more was necessary and I dont think that is deceiving [her] either for she is smart enough to know her-self I think.

Hearst's recent trip to Wyntoon had borne the usual fruit, as Loorz explained to Stolte on November 15:

Mr. Hearst is very active, comes out everyday and talks over this and that with the vim and vigor that he had 7 years ago when I first knew him [on the Beach House job in Santa Monica]. You know he has Mac back making alterations and inte-riors of the Wyntoon houses. Oh boy, if he doesn't change his mind again Harry [Thompson] will have a headache when he hears about some of the changes. The nice tile roof just completed may have to be altered quite a little. Ho Ho, Let's hope he lives a long time doing just the same things that he has in the past.

It is good to have Mac back. Between the two of us we manage to entertain Mr. Hearst several hours each afternoon. Mac of course is with him most of the time. He has been very pleasant and very interesting so it really makes things on the hill worth while.

In that same letter to Stolte of November 15, Loorz delved into the business side of the "Wyntoon proposition" that had been concerning the two partners, es-pecially Loorz himself:[81]

---

81. Loorz addressed the matter in writing both to Stolte and to Jack Hall on June 4; see p. 119 in this chapter. Then in a longer letter on September 6, Loorz told Stolte:

Now I had a nice long talk with Miss Morgan yesterday [when she was at San Simeon] regard-ing Wyntoon. Some of it you will get direct from her or hear of it at the job so I will not go into detail except [about] the part that really concerns ourselves.

1.st She is perfectly satisfied with Harry and our present set up.

2.nd She talked frankly about our commission up there being very reasonable and she appreci-ated it but wanted to know if we were perfectly satisfied. If not she would have been willing to increase the percentage.

I went into detail about it again so that there would be no misunderstanding. I said that I thot you were billing for your expenses on the trips up and [that you] should. I told her that we

I now feel that both Miss Morgan and Mr. Hearst are satisfied that you are handling the job just as well or better than anyone else [could]. I believe we could get
more for the work without them taking some of the sub-contractors away from us
and without fear that they will attempt to do the job with there [their] own superintendent as LeFeaver wanted in the beginning [in 1933, an approach that would
have resembled the prevailing one at San Simeon]. I had in mind that we would
begin the new year [1935] by asking for 5% [formerly 3% and then 3.5%]. She
told me we could have it. What do you think? Hellenthal in L.A. gets 10% [on the
Hearst-Morgan work there] but he certainly carries a big balance all the time. I
like the idea of checks coming in regularly [instead].

---

were getting equipment rental [fees] on equipment that might otherwise be rusting in the yard
and that we were charging considerably less than N.R.A. [National Recovery Administration]
prices. I told her that we were getting everything [due us] on the job, that is all sub-contractors
were coming thru us and we were [omitted word or words] and expected our commission on
their work. And most important of all that we could not carry the job financially on our low
percentage[,] that that was up to them [Hearst and Morgan]. In short they would have to continue paying promptly. She understands that we would have to have 10 percent and more if we
had to carry the job like we did once before [in the 1929–31 period].

We decided to leave it as it is at present and if You and I find that we need more that we shall
feel free to take it up with her at anytime.

3.rd I explained and she O.K.'d 10% on all the smaller alterations [apart from larger jobs like
the Bavarian Village houses or The Gables].

I expressed our appreciation of the work she had given us and she said we had good foremen
and that she was pleased with your work.

By the way when we were deciding on the percentage at Wyntoon [in 1933, originally 3%
versus 3.5%] she assured me that she thot Mr. Hearst planned a larger development further up
the river and that we would surely get it. . . .

Let me repeat that my idea is that at 3½% on the net total cost plus equipment rental and
traveling expenses[,] *almost net cash* is a good deal more than 10% on part of the cost and *payments coming sometime*. Besides that we have them feeling indebted to us rather than that we are
indebted to them.

Amid these last paragraphs, Loorz also said, "I hope I expressed your thots as well as my own
and if I did not will you please sit down and tell me so." Stolte's next known letter to Loorz, dated
September 24, had no bearing on the subject. In writing to Stolte on October 6, Loorz persevered:

I wish you had at least mentioned what I talked about in my last letter when you wrote. Are
they meeting your bills cash monthly? If not, then we should ask for an increase in percentage,
because that is, without doubt, the only reason we have been accepting such a low percentage.

I did not want to take this question up further with Miss Morgan without first consulting
you.

Stolte replied on October 8. "Sorry to have missed your *main question* in a past letter," he began.
"However the letter is read at one time [previously] and answered at another [now], mostly aboard
S.P. [the Southern Pacific train]." After telling Loorz, "The payments for Wyntoon have been
O.K.," Stolte spoke well of the job, but he offered few other details of the kind Loorz was seeking.

Loorz went with the more general flow for the moment, telling Harry Thompson on Novem-

Loorz's letter of November 15 was in part a reply to another undated one from Stolte. (The elder partner had reported, "We should be ahead of things this year financially. Net profit should be in neighborhood of $10,000 for year—not considering equipment rental.") Loorz therefore had these further words for Stolte in regard to their jointly owned company:

> It is a pleasure to think that we will be in the clear next year for a change. Besides that we can raise more cash if we should have to have it. We certainly cant talk depression Fred. We must be very grateful.

As for Loorz's thoughts about Wyntoon—and with regard to percentages—Stolte wrote the following on November 17, using stationery headed "PARK HOTEL, Mount Shasta City, Siskiyou County, California, Elevation 3555":

> It is also a big help to hear that you feel both Miss Morgan and Mr. Hearst feel satisfied with our carrying out of their work. I surely have tried to handle the job efficiently.
>   About the %—why I shall leave that to you. It is undoubtedly worth the extra [amount], however, I would not [want to] jeopardize their feeling toward us.

Stolte also said, "I am greatly pleased to hear that Mr. Hearst feels, so full of pep, hope it may continue for about 50 years more." Then he had this to tell Loorz:

> We have just about completed the various jobs for Miss Morgan; the owners seem to be quite happy and satisfied and I hope Miss Morgan is—also.

The partners' recent correspondence had touched again (as it first had on August 3) on the prospect of their working in the Los Angeles area. In the same undated letter that projected a profit of $10,000 in 1934, Stolte told Loorz about a colleague, Claude Barton, who had "returned from L.A., where he was building a house for a relative":

> He seems to feel that there is quite an opportunity there; in larger homes and movie work. At one time you mentioned the possibility of connections there.
>   I thought perhaps you might bear it in mind as I believe I could help you handle any work that may develop. I was thinking of the changes necessary to Miss Davies cottage [the Cosmopolitan bungalow], etc; at the studio [Metro-Goldwyn-Mayer in Culver City].

The bungalow had housed Hearst's film enterprises, Cosmopolitan Productions, since the mid-1920s. Although it provided much more than a posh apartment

---

ber 7, "Good reports come back to San Simeon regarding your work and in fact all of the work there at Wyntoon. This should suffice to make you content without any further comment from me."

and dressing room for Marion Davies on the Metro lot, that image was destined to be the bungalow's most enduring one.[82] All the same, at this juncture in 1934 the Hearst-Davies association with Louis B. Mayer and MGM had recently ended. Loorz had little to say about that transition in answering Stolte on November 17 (the letter crossed with Stolte's of the same date from the Park Hotel). In his usual way, though, Loorz kept the historical dialogue flowing as richly as ever:

> I had thot about the job moving the [Cosmopolitan] cottage and theater from the Metro Goldwyn Mayer Studio to Warner Bros. [in Burbank]. However, Fred, Frank Hellenthal has been doing all of Miss Morgan's work in Los Angeles for the past ten years and more.[83] After I left Santa Monica [in 1928] he got in on the Hearst work and has done every bit of it since. Mr. Hearst knows him personally and likes him very much. He just finished the theater, in fact, Mr. Hearst never even went to look at it,[84] so naturally he is already doing the moving job. I thot it best not to say anything about it. Besides all this LeFeaver and Hellenthal are graduates of the same University and are very friendly. In fact, Frank is a very fine fellow.[85]

---

82. The term *bungalow* was being used for the Cosmopolitan unit at least by the late 1930s and perhaps long before. "Cosmopolitan Bungalow" appeared in the second of Morgan's two accounts for that building, the one involving her partial re-erection of it in Beverly Hills after its days in Culver City and Burbank had passed; see Appendix A, p. 544.

In *The Lion's Share: The Story of an Entertainment Empire* (New York, 1957), p. 106, Bosley Crowther gave this account of the Cosmopolitan headquarters during the MGM period: "A fourteen-room bungalow was built for her [Miss Davies] near the front of the studio lot, and there, in this elaborate pavilion, she and Hearst held frequent court." Then in *Hollywood Rajah: The Life and Times of Louis B. Mayer* (New York, 1960), p. 123, the same author—Bosley Crowther—spoke more facetiously of "a fourteen-room 'bungalow' that had something of the elegant simplicity of the 'dairy' of Marie Antoinette." Through Swanberg's reliance on *Hollywood Rajah* a year later in *Citizen Hearst*, p. 387, Crowther's second account of the bungalow gained enduring fame.

83. At least one project of Morgan's in the area had not been done through Hellenthal. Louis V. Bechtel, a builder in Hollywood (evidently no relation of the more renowned Bechtels), is named in the Morgan-Forney account of the job for Mrs. Cecil B. De Mille; see note 48, above.

84. Boutelle's *Julia Morgan*, p. 236, misidentifies a photograph of the bungalow in its MGM phase as "Projection room, Cosmopolitan Headquarters, Hollywood, 1925." The original printing of Ginger Wadsworth's *Julia Morgan: Architect of Dreams* (Minneapolis, 1990) depicts the theater on p. 90, identifying it as the theater at San Simeon; the errant but fascinating (and rarely seen) photograph was replaced in later printings.

85. LeFeaver, born in Ohio in 1885 or 1886, was roughly the same age as Walter Steilberg and three years older than Fred Stolte. LeFeaver graduated from Ohio State University in 1911 with a degree in engineering. Hellenthal, born in 1895, attended the University of Washington for three years (starting about 1913) and studied engineering; but he seems not to have graduated before joining the Army. One thing LeFeaver and Hellenthal *did* have more closely in common was that they each had a namesake son: James, Jr., and Frank, Jr.

In a negative vein, Bert Johnson, an employee of Loorz's in Santa Monica in 1927–28, had made some unflattering claims about Hellenthal on April 12, 1932. "All he has been doing down here

However, Fred, Mr. Hearst has been very friendly and frank with me and I will spring the question of work in L.A. one of these days. I dont want to scare him so I'll work up to it gradually. He's getting familiar enough so that he kids me now, tells jokes and laughs lustily.

Harry Thompson, the foreman on the Wyntoon job, wrote to Loorz that same day, November 17, replying to a recent letter.[86] Thompson said to Loorz, "It is also a big help to hear that you feel both Miss Morgan and Mr. Hearst feel satisfied with our carrying out of their work."

Loorz assured Thompson on November 23 that there was nothing to worry about:

Mac and Mr. Hearst are spending hours per day making nice pictures for you up there. It looks like you'll be there a long time if it all goes ahead as he plans it and then is changed a couple of times. He selects the fanciest trim he can find in all available books and Mac draws them up.[87]

After Hearst and Morgan were at Wyntoon three weeks earlier, Morgan embarked on a long trip to Europe (the one Loorz mentioned to Ted Linforth on November 6). Except for some trips she made to Honolulu in the 1920s (mostly because of her YWCA projects), she had last been abroad during her student days in Paris, right after the turn of the century. The launching of her career, followed by World War I and then especially by her immersion in the endless work for Hearst, had kept her in California almost entirely. Now she would be away from San Simeon, from Wyntoon, and from her other work in California for nearly five months, until the spring of 1935; in turn, the trip would stand first in a series of foreign travels and other journeys for Morgan over the next fifteen years, the last recorded one occurring in 1950. Her earnings through the Hearst commissions, above all, made this first trip and its successors possible. Hearst took it upon himself to make sure her trip in 1934–35 would be a rousing success. Several days before she left, he told her that one of his own cars—sent from England for the occasion—would be

---

is knocking the work at the beach house," Johnson told Loorz, "even doing outright lying to gain his point." Johnson also divulged, "There is plenty of his work that falls plenty short of the kind of work done when you were there."

86. Loorz to Thompson, November 7, 1934 (quoted in part at the end of note 81, above).

87. Hearst was a book collector of long standing, one who had hundreds of portfolios and other architectural volumes ready at hand; he and Morgan had often consulted such works in choosing Spanish and Italian motifs for San Simeon. For the Teutonic realm of Wyntoon, Hearst delved into translated works like *Old Nuremberg* (Nurnberg, 1928); meanwhile, he had been familiar enough with German since boyhood to tackle the real thing—works like *Danziger Barock* (Stuttgart, n.d.) and *Die Zimmergotik in Deutsch-Tirol* (Leipzig, 1897).

awaiting her in Naples, ready to take her to Pompeii and other places in Italy before she headed north into the heart of Europe.[88]

At this juncture in 1934 Morgan left Jim LeFeaver in charge. (In charge, that is, of her overall practice, whose headquarters remained in the Merchants Exchange in San Francisco. Mac McClure, meanwhile, would serve as her on-site representative at San Simeon during her sojourn. As Hearst said in writing to her from that estate on October 26—with a rare omission of "Mr." in Mac's case— "Since you are going to leave McClure here, I am sure you need not worry about affairs at home.")[89] Loorz wrote to LeFeaver in San Francisco on November 8, the day after Morgan and her sister, Emma North, sailed from there. Regarding the Neptune Pool, Loorz told LeFeaver: "You will note by the enclosed notes [Loorz's recap from Morgan's visit of November 3] that Miss Morgan and Mr. Hearst have decided that the concrete of the colonnades must be white. In fact, they want it just like the plaster we placed around the pool [as a temporary finish coat on certain items for the winter months]." Morgan's underlings were well prepared to keep things going in her absence without missing a beat.

Loorz took up additional matters concerning the Neptune Pool on November 27, writing once more to LeFeaver:

> Well I talked to Mr. Hearst after talking with you yesterday and he says we can do as we please. I started off with a laugh, saying that I wanted to ask him a question and thot I knew his answer but would ask anyway. He laughed heartily and said, "Alright, what can I do for you?"
>
> I put my question this way, "We can pour the second pavilion [colonnade] by xmas by concentrating definitely upon it but not if rain delays us anything like on

---

88. See Hearst to Morgan, October 26, 1934; Hearst/Morgan Correspondence, Morgan Collection. The same archives contains a related letter from Willicombe to Morgan, dated November 1 (sent by him from San Simeon while Hearst and Morgan were at Wyntoon). "Mr. Hearst has instructed me to take care of the details of your trip abroad. If there are any that I have not mentioned to you [further on in the letter], please let me know."

This historic trip of Morgan's is the same one that others have assigned to 1931 and 1932 (or even to 1929); see p. 87, note 58. Aside from these errant references, one that appears in *Julia Morgan* (p. 245, under "The Morgan Atelier," note 3) is partly right in Boutelle's citing of 1935—this in an entry following her reference to the non-existent trip of 1931–32.

In his personal collection, Don Loorz has three postcards from Morgan that help trace her whereabouts early in the trip. The first one, dated December 5, is from the Canary Islands. The second, dated December 17, is from Naples. The third, dated December 26, is from Rome.

89. From the same letter cited at the outset of note 88. More than eighty-five percent of Morgan's work in 1934 stemmed from the greater Hearst accounts; she would indeed have little else to preoccupy her while she was gone. Her office's two largest non-Hearst jobs through late 1934–early 1935 were follow-up work on the California Crematorium, Oakland, and a new project, the Homelani Columbarium in Hilo, Hawaii. See Appendix A, pp. 535 and 542.

the present one." He said, "It is almost certain to rain and it really doesn't matter, you do just what you think best."

With the weather even threatening right now and with your permission I will begin reducing the crew after we pour next week. It is certainly not worth the chance to risk leaving the plaster forms over the winter. There is also the possibility of saving many or most of the coffers when we strip them from the present pavilion. This will save a good deal of labor and material in castings.

The year before, on October 14, George Wright had spoken of how Loorz's "ability to handle Miss Morgan" made all the difference in the work at San Simeon. Loorz's knack for handling the often serious James LeFeaver — "Jim" to a few trusted friends like Loorz, who was a good twelve years younger — was also a boon.

LOORZ FOUND TIME for a family outing on November 25. He told his brother, Claude, about it three days later.[90] "Last Sunday I took the whole gang duck hunting on Morrow Bay," he wrote (misspelling *Morro* in the process). "We rowed out on the bay at daylight and rowed and rowed until noon. We had very little shooting but lots of excitement especially when Bill fell overboard in shallow water."

Loorz continued by saying, "It seems funny but little boys really do more thinking than we give them credit for. They still get into lots of mischief but are not bad":

Day before yesterday they came in very late for supper and we didn't know where they were. Here they come and Oh Boy you should have seen them, smell WOW. After dark they were near the [Hearst Ranch] corrals looking for mushrooms. They walked into what they thot was plowed ground and it was wet manure

---

90. Wednesday, November 28, was the day before Thanksgiving, which in 1934 fell on the last (or fifth) Thursday of the month, rather than on the fourth one, as it would now. And so when Loorz told his brother (and his sister-in-law) in this same letter, "Mr. Stolte and his family will be with us over Thanksgiving," he meant for the period beginning the next day, November 29. Loorz spoke of that event while writing to Olin Weatherford of the F. C. Stolte Co. on December 7:

Fred and I had a lovely visit together this last Thanksgiving. We did a lot of business and arranged to make various changes and adjustments and both [of us] agreed quite splendidly. Between you and I, I had the pleasure of raising his weekly salary [$75] to equal that of mine here [$100]. Thanks to you and the general stations [the General Petroleum gas stations] and to Miss Morgan's various jobs the Company showed a profit for the first time since I've been here. I really appreciate you and all the boys [based in Oakland] and hope it can continue.

Loorz also spoke of a new direction that he and Stolte had discussed during their holiday visit: the prospect that their company might compete for jobs in the local area, beyond the Hearst-Morgan pale. This was a logical — and more focused — outgrowth of the partners' recent thoughts about seeking work in Los Angeles.

freshly scraped from a very sloppy cattle corral. Well Bill went in first and got absolutely stuck. Don said, "I couldn't come home and leave him there so I had to wade in and get him." He managed to get Bill out and then got stuck himself. While walking home a friend stopped and asked them if they wanted to ride in his car. They declined stating the facts and of course they were not begged to enter. Fortunately I [had] built a shower in the garage and we herded them in there for a general cleaning.

The Loorz boys enjoyed an idyllic childhood in the bayside town of San Simeon. They rode their plowhorse, Pat, launched their driftwood raft on the nearby lagoon, swam in their backyard pool overlooking the beach, romped through the poison oak in the ravines, climbed about the ruins of the old whaling station on San Simeon Point — and slipped in more cowpies than they cared to recall. Don was in the third grade that fall of 1934 at the one-room Pacific School, across the street from the Loorzes' house; Bill was in the first grade. Mrs. Loorz, meanwhile, was pregnant with her third son, Bob, born the following March.

One of the Loorzes' good friends, Arch Parks, had been replaced as Hearst Ranch superintendent earlier that year by Randolph Apperson, Hearst's cousin, leaving Parks to pursue ranching in Gilroy, south of San Jose. Parks and Loorz kept in touch for a few years afterwards; he had ample praise for Loorz in writing to him on December 1.[91] "And George I want to tell you," he said in part, "that after you got on that job, it was a different out fit all to gether, both on the hill, and down at the ranch." And then an unexpected, revealing barb concerning Loorz's predecessor: "Rossi was a queer make up. Seemed to glory in human misery."

His shortcomings aside, Camille Rossi had laid a solid foundation for Loorz to build upon — literally so in the massive concrete work that characterized the former "outside pool" no less so than its recent successor, the Neptune Pool. On Tuesday, December 11, Loorz wrote to Jim Rankin in Oakland concerning that majestic job:

---

91. Parks was replying to a letter dated November 16, in which Loorz had told him and his wife:

> The ranch has spent many many thousands of dollars since you left and let's all hope it is for the benefit of the ranch. I reserve my opinions. I do know that it certainly is not in keeping with the economy program they demanded of you. Apperson [Randolph Apperson, successor to Parks] says it is almost entirely [Bill] Murray's idea and I dont think he agrees with much of it. Anyway he is a nice fellow to work with but not the warm friend we were Arch and you Phil [Phyllis?]. I shall always consider you very close friends and I only hope you sincerely feel the same way about us.

> Nonetheless, Loorz and Randy Apperson proved compatible over the next several years, both as friends and as fellow employees.

Jimmie, I know you are anxious to come down and play with those pipes and fittings on that gorgeous pool. Well I'll try to have my forms stripped and cleaned up by next Wednesday [December 19] so that you can be here at that time and start filling the pool. Dont start telling me that you need more time than that for it will be impossible to give it to you before that. My concrete will then still be too green to do it wisely but I'll take that chance. Now Jimmie, put your hands together, throw your shoulders back, get that ghastly twinkle in your eye and *quietly* have the water in the pool and partly filtered by *Xmas*.

Then on December 12, Loorz wrote to LeFeaver in San Francisco, likewise concerning the Neptune Pool:

It looks now that it would be unwise for us to shut down next Saturday [December 15]. Mr. Hearst wants water in the pool for xmas and we should completely strip and cleanup around the pool so they could really use and get the benefit of that portion that is completed.

Along with that subject, Loorz had this one to discuss in the same letter:

Mac has told you that we poured the tree boxes on the West Terrace. This was one of Miss Morgan's last day instructions [before heading to Europe] & later requested by Mr. Hearst. I can now take down the concrete tower that has been left there since the terrace pour last year.[92]

Loorz went on to tell LeFeaver, "Perhaps it is not too soon to discuss our winter program"—whereupon he hammered out two paragraphs of details. And then he added:

My idea is, if we can continue to show Mr. Hearst some progress around the pool he may not request that we start any new rooms in the Castle. This is what Miss Morgan hoped. Of course she outlined some rooms but hopes we will not have to do more than [the two] small [book] vault towers off the [Gothic] Study.[93]

---

92. Loorz may have meant a subsequent "terrace pour": the main one on his watch had been done a full two years earlier. As for the request by Hearst (who had sent word to Mac McClure and to Louis Reesing, the head gardener, on November 29, 1934), Hearst told Reesing:

Miss Morgan has designed concrete boxes for the palms on the West terrace.
    I think you should have those boxes poured according to her designs before putting in the palms. Otherwise you may have to make other transplantations later.
    It will not take Mr. Loorz long to do this and we can proceed to finish up the terrace.

93. Tower-like only in their being perched above the two large stairwells at the back of Casa Grande's mid-section.

    The subject dominated a letter Loorz wrote on December 14; it went to Jack Wagenet, Morgan's head draftsman in San Francisco. "I am enclosing your sketch with dimensions of the doorway as at present to Study Tower vaults." Besides giving Wagenet other information, Loorz told him that Mac McClure had helped in the matter.

LeFeaver visited San Simeon on Monday, December 17, much as Morgan would have if she had not been in Europe then. (That very day, LeFeaver's wife probably received a letter Loorz had written her on the fifteenth. Mrs. LeFeaver was likely to be receiving a bull terrier from Hearst, whom Loorz had caught in a "particularly happy and informal" mood the day before. Loorz told her, "It would be real nice if he gave you one of the new litter since they are grand-puppies of *Buddy*, his only house pet he had for sixteen years." Buddy, of course, had disappeared earlier in the year.)[94] Loorz wrote to Stolte on December 18 about his meeting with Jim LeFeaver the previous day:

> Things turned out just as I wished and I will continue thru the winter with a very small crew to complete the things that Mr. Hearst wants right away.
>
> We did a little talking about Wyntoon but only in general and about the plans and changes. Mac is going up to his office now [next to the Service Wing of Casa Grande][95] to do some detailing on the Gables so that we can get some millwork ready for a rush start [next season].

Loorz wrote again to his friend Jack Hall on December 20. He admitted having supported the crusading novelist Upton Sinclair for governor over the mainstream politico Frank Merriam in the November election, saying it was "a choice of accepting the lesser of two evils." That was one bit of news that Loorz undoubtedly declined to share with Hearst. Along with Hearst's fellow movie mogul Louis B. Mayer and even his arch-rival Harry Chandler of the *Los Angeles Times*, the Chief had helped derail Sinclair's EPIC campaign—the doomed, utopian quest to "End Poverty in California."[96]

But Loorz had more than politics to discuss in his letter to Hall:

---

94. See p. 109 in this chapter.

95. Formally called the Architect's Office, this small wooden building was used more by Mac McClure during the 1930s than by Julia Morgan. But in general accounts "the Shack" has long been identified with Morgan alone, to the exclusion of the less-renowned McClure or other associates. See for example *Fabulous San Simeon: A History of the Hearst Castle*, by Oscar Lewis (San Francisco, 1958), pp. 56–57. In the first week of Loorz's tenure, the little building figured as "Mr. McClure's office" in some notes Morgan sent Loorz (February 9, 1932).

96. The subject is covered extensively by Kevin Starr in *Endangered Dreams*, pp. 121–55, and exhaustively by Greg Mitchell in *The Campaign of the Century: Upton Sinclair's Race for Governor of California and the Birth of Media Politics* (New York, 1992).

Right before the election, Loorz told his parents on November 5, "We are very much interested in the present Governorship race and you may be surprised but I think I'll vote for Sinclair. I'm positively disgusted with the way the Republicans are knocking and defaming his character."

Immediately after the election the prolific Sinclair began recounting the campaign and his defeat. He had choice words for certain adversaries whose actions he had long "observed." Although Hearst wasn't mentioned by name, Sinclair left little question about whom he was portraying in an early passage:

I'll be laying nearly all of the crew off tomorrow [December 21] and it will be quiet around here. I will have plenty to do personally but there wont be a lot of planning and worrying about it. There'll be no rush except getting xmas trees put up and placing packages and sending. It becomes quite a mad-house.[97]

A madhouse indeed. In the midst of the activity, Hearst decided that Sunday, December 23, would be a fine day for a trip to Jolon and the Milpitas Hacienda over the new Burnett Road. Not a farfetched idea, really; for despite their shortness and their crisp evenings, many December days are euphorically mild in this part of California. (Loorz had told some relatives on December 11, "It was really hot here yesterday, as high as 85 I think.") Colonel Willicombe wrote to Loorz about Hearst's thoughts on Saturday the twenty-second:

> Chief was very much surprised when I told him the road to Jolon was not an all-year road, that it was not passable in winter.
>
> He asked that you proceed to make it an all-year road, building bridges where necessary and fixing the surface so that cars can pass over it at all times of the year.
>
> Chief says there is rock enough along the route to take care of the surfacing, and he surely wants it navigable for twelve months.
>
> Best wishes to you and yours for the holidays.
>
> P-S The trip to Jolon Sunday has therefore been abandoned.

Was there never to be any rest? Willicombe wrote to Loorz again, this time on Christmas Day. "Discussing the all-year road again today Chief says where the road goes through that canyon there is enough rock,[98] if you widen the road a little, to pave all the road. You might have this in mind when you talk about it."

I saw our richest newspaper publisher keeping his movie mistress in a private city of palaces and cathedrals, furnished with shiploads of junk imported from Europe, and surrounded by vast acres reserved for the use of zebras and giraffes; telling it as a jest that he had spent six million dollars to make this lady's reputation, and using his newspapers to celebrate her changes of hats.

From *I, Candidate for Governor: And How I Got Licked*, by Upton Sinclair (Berkeley, 1994; originally Pasadena, 1935), pp. 4–5.

97. The previous year, almost to the day (December 21, 1933), Loorz described a similar scene, which must have been an annual commonplace at San Simeon. He told his parents, "Packages are coming in by the carload and you should read the price tags. The store in L.A. send[s] up thousands of dollars worth of stuff and Mr. Hearst selects just what he wants [for family members and friends] and the rest is sent back. Talk about toys for the little twins of George's." (He was referring to Hearst's son George, whose son and daughter — George, Jr., and Phoebe, born in 1927 — were the oldest grandchildren of Hearst and his wife, Millicent.)

98. In the Salmon Creek gorge, on the back side of the Santa Lucia Range. During these last days of the month, now that mild weather had led to rain, Hearst was also thinking about another type of rock. "The plane could not get off the field today," Willicombe told Loorz on December 28.

Loorz had other things in mind, though, when he wrote to Hearst on December 26:

> Words cannot express my appreciation of the finest gift I have ever received. The *one* thing I really wanted was a good wrist watch. . . . I accept it as an expression of your personal regard rather than because I happen to be one of your many fortunate employees. I only hope that my activity in your interests have merited such a fine gift.

Loorz also owed LeFeaver a word of thanks — "for the many boxes of candied fruit." He used the occasion to bring Morgan's stand-in up to date,[99] now that the Christmas rush had passed and the New Year's holiday was at hand:

> As you know things are real quiet on the hill, that is in the construction department. Even if we had men it would be too wet to do anything. In the household, however, tonight and tomorrow bid fair to be the first and largest day in the year. They have one of their largest crowds here with every room filled. Oh boy, the headaches there will be around here on Tuesday & Wednesday [January 1 and 2].
>
> Mr. Hearst writes notes and calls me on the phone almost daily to request some little things immediately and ask for some larger things to be done as soon as he leaves [for an extended period]. In a way it seems that it is a waste of time to be here when the crew is gone but it just works out that you'll have to keep a man here when Mr. Hearst is here. They want such things as heaters, phones, felt strips, doorclosers, rattles stopped etc. I manage to take care of a few of these each day. The pool looks wonderful & a *few* have used it.

Those words to LeFeaver closed out the year, a year that for the most part had withstood the Depression's withering presence, as though the twenties had never died. Loorz dated the letter "December last, 1934."

"It sunk to the hubs in mud when Ray [Crawford] tried to hop off. Chief would like you kindly to get busy immediately spreading gravel on the field to make it more serviceable."

99. He brought his labor foreman, Frank Souza, up to date in this same period. On December 28 he told Souza and his wife, Mabel, "We had a very jolly xmas and you will be surprised to know that we had two china boys with us for dinner. They were our cook and waiter from camp. Did they enjoy it?":

> They had come down to see the boys presents and to see our tree and stayed until we were ready to eat so I invited them to stay and they excepted [accepted]. I'm really glad for they enjoyed it so much and our boys enjoyed them. Our boys sort of feared chinamen and they now know that there are good chinese as well as any others.

Loorz's final comment was just as blithe, just as emblematic of the times: "It did seem queer, however, at first but they are perfect gentlemen, clean and well dressed." (A week later — January 3, 1935 — he told his parents, "My chinese cooks gave the boys each a small silver boat complete with sails, oars, guns etc, mounted on a carved wood teak block and all encased in glass.")

1935

Casting a Wider Net

IN GOING BEHIND THE SCENES at San Simeon, the Loorz Papers naturally challenge some myths—in fact, a good many of them—about Hearst and his storied estate. Consider the man's alleged fear of death: he was said to be so phobic about the subject that he forbade its mention in his presence (a symptom, supposedly, of his chronic delusion of immortality—or perhaps of his frustration in knowing that he could never attain it). Of course the episode in 1934 involving his dog Buddy is enough to dispel that notion. Yet there are plenty of other notions to contend with, from those that give up the ghost willingly when tested to those that cling to life tightly, determined to mock reason, logic, plausibility. Among the latter: Hearst was a wet blanket about drinking. After all, Marion Davies overindulged, and so did many of her Hollywood friends. A cocktail or two before dinner and a bit of wine with the meal—that was about all the stodgy old man would allow.

George Loorz was an insider who knew otherwise, at least where holidays and other special times were concerned. In writing to Jim LeFeaver on the last day of 1934, he had predicted—with good reason—a lively New Year's celebration for San Simeon. And early in January 1935 he wrote to Mac McClure in Michigan (leaving the letter undated, a rarity for Loorz); he recounted for Mac, who was visiting his home town of Royal Oak, that San Simeon's Christmas celebration had been just as lively:

> For the Party, you will know that all got gloriously drunk and were dumb with headaches and hangovers the next day.

Those twenty-one words are as bold, as potentially revealing as any to be found in accounts of San Simeon, whether oral or written. (Years later, though, an elderly but still incisive Mac spoke of people—"outsiders" in this case—who "like to insist that a lot of hell raising went on in San Simeon." He said, "Actually it was tame and quiet by today's standards," and he applauded Adela Rogers St. Johns for

her deft handling of the subject.)[1] Be that as it may, Loorz didn't elaborate in his
letter to Mac; he probably figured he had tattled enough. But he did go on to share
other details with his good friend about the recent Christmas interlude:

> The 10 trees [on the ground floor of Casa Grande] were and [an] ugly display of
> wealth and superfluous tensil & ornaments. Really very beautiful except that you
> could see no tree. As promised, Mr. Williams [the warehouse manager] did not
> complete decorations until 8 A.M. xmas morning. As he planned, he was present
> to receive his [bonus] envelopes from Mr. Hearst & Miss Davies on that tired
> xmas day. I dont mean to be unkind Mac [about the unpopular Williams],[2] just
> talking our usual line.

In a completely different vein, Loorz also said that Julia Morgan (who had
now been abroad for nearly two months) had sent each of his sons a postcard from
the Canary Islands. "She made a few wise-cracks in her own inimitable manner
and they were interesting." Her card to Don Loorz survives; the one she sent Bill
Loorz does not. The former one says, "This may reach you by Christmas time —
in which case, 'Merry Christmas' to you — We have had a fine sea voyage & a few
hours ashore here!"[3]

A letter dated January 5, 1935, found Loorz assuming his more workaday tone,
this while writing to Fred Stolte at his home base in Oakland:

> You knew that Mac went East for the holidays, did you not? Well he is to go back
> up to the [Morgan] office to start detailing [for Wyntoon] as soon as he returns.
> As soon as they get out any details we should get the mill started running the stuff.

---

1. McClure to Nellie Shewmaker, August 12, 1979; Shewmaker Collection, courtesy of Shirley
Shewmaker Wahl. Mac was referring to *The Honeycomb* (New York, 1969), a book by St. Johns that
he'd previously sent to Mrs. Shewmaker. "If you already read it," he told her, "go over it again."

2. Williams, who had managed the San Simeon warehouses since 1927 and who also performed caretaking duties on the hilltop, could be a stubborn, cantankerous man (as recalled for me
in the 1980s by J. C. "Pete" Sebastian, Eddie Shaug, and William Reich).

Part of what Loorz told Mac recalls the letter he wrote his parents during the previous holiday
season (December 21, 1933; see p. 156, note 97). Loorz told them, "We are splicing a tall xmas tree to
raise and decorate outside on the terrace [facing Casa Grande]." He exaggerated in saying that "one
about 40 foot high" would go in the Assembly Room but then said, more plausibly, that "four 20 foot
ones" would go in the adjoining Refectory. Either way, it was "quite a job" that kept "several men
busy early and late."

3. The surviving card and three others from the trip were lent to me by Don Loorz on September 29, 1999; copies of all four have since been added to the George Loorz Papers at the San Luis
Obispo County Historical Museum.

In traveling to Europe late in 1934, Morgan began by sailing to Acapulco and then going
through the Panama Canal; see Boutelle, *Julia Morgan*, p. 245 (both the errant 1931–32 entry and the
more accurate 1935 entry in note 3 under "The Morgan Atelier"). After Morgan crossed the Atlantic, the Canary Islands may well have been her first landfall.

Mr. Hearst wanted the Gables and one of the houses [in the Bavarian Village] by July if possible but of course he does not insist when they tell him they will need additional funds. Let's wait till Mac gets back and then I'll inquire again. I could have Mr. Hearst write LeFeaver asking him to get going but I rather hesitate to do that. I feel certain that he [Hearst] would if I suggested it. He has told Mac but Mr. LeFeaver doesn't take orders thru Mac very seriously.

Loorz, in the same letter, had Willicombe's message of December 28 in mind when he told Stolte, "I am going to rush the grading and surfacing of the airport. It got so wet that the large plane got stuck so they want it gravelled and oiled."[4]

Back from Michigan via Los Angeles, Mac was at his drafting board in San Francisco by Monday, January 7. "The office work is much the same as ever," he told Loorz the next day. "LeFeaver is leaving a lot to my own discretion and direction. Miss Morgan wrote a letter [from Europe] to the office family—apparently all is O.K."[5]

The winter of 1934–35 was a rainy one—in mid-January Loorz told his labor foreman, Frank Souza, that the hilltop had had nearly thirty inches already—and the rains would last well into the spring that season. Loorz gave LeFeaver a briefing on January 11:

Mr. Hearst says it will not be necessary to hurry back on construction as long as it is raining and as wet as it is at present. That means that it might be better not to figure on starting on the [Neptune Pool] colonnade work around the first of February.

John [Vanderloo][6] is back with his one moulder and helper. Pete [Petersen] is doing some necessary repair work and between rains is working with one more carpenter and helper trying to get the third log barn constructed [for the animals in the main zoo area].[7]

Val Georges [the resident ironworker] is back working on the fire screens as we planned. Mr. Hearst likes his screen [in the Gothic Suite] very much and cancelled his order for some of them from Los Angeles.

---

4. See pp. 156–57 in the previous chapter, note 98.

5. The obvious question here is whether LeFeaver or someone else in Morgan's office kept the letter. In any event, the Morgan Collection at Cal Poly does not have it.

6. Vanderloo specialized in cast-stone decoration and ornamental plasterwork. His father, Theodore Van der Loo (who used an older spelling of the family name), preceded him out of Oakland in doing similar work at San Simeon as early as 1920 and for several years to follow.

7. The "main zoo area" denotes the elevated rangeland lying between the coastal plain and The Enchanted Hill—an area comprising some 2,000 acres and crossed by the long, winding driveway from the town of San Simeon and the Hearst Ranch headquarters to the hilltop itself.

How soon will we receive those shades for the standards in the [Gothic] Study? Those with the old parchment shades.

Mr. Hearst keeps wanting more and more lights and I think Miss Morgan keeps wanting dim. Oh boy when she sees all the lights he now has in the Study.

January 12 found Loorz telling Henry Tieslau, formerly of the Burnett Road, "I'm still here with my ball and chain." Indeed, Loorz was embarking on his fourth year at San Simeon. Yet he wasn't about to rest on his well-paid laurels, wasn't about to assume complacently that he had a bright future working for Hearst and Morgan. Cabin fever — or maybe castle fever — flushed his cheeks again, just as it had during the past two years when the crew was small and the days were short. "Its a good place," he admitted to Tieslau, "but I really would like to get back to civilization for a while."

(Never mind that Loorz was singing the blues. Hearst was about to wax poetic — having just heard from Morgan in Italy. Hearst's reply is among the more engaging letters at Cal Poly, drawn from his many episodes of travel abroad. Fortunately, Morgan brought the letter back from Europe and filed it.)[8]

Loorz struck a pent-up note again on January 15, this time in writing to Olin Weatherford, a key man in the F. C. Stolte Co. who superintended many of its "General Pete" gas station jobs in the Bay Area and elsewhere in northern California:

Well it looks like Fred manages to keep a few of you fellows busy anyway. Hope it continues that way. I'd really like to get back into the old office [in Oakland] for a change, especially during the winter here when I have few men. I have plenty to do but I dont seem to be able to get the pep to do it for it lacks interest. We like it when we really produce something, patching leaks, handling cook house and ordering chauffeurs & mechanics around is a job but there is little real production to it. . . .

Maybe Olin, if we get this alteration job in San Luis, you will be able to come down on it.

Here was a prospect that could prove to be just what the doctor ordered, not only for Loorz but for other "Stolteans" as well. The job in question was the W. T. Reid Company's Ford showroom and service station in San Luis Obispo.[9] Soon af-

8. See Hearst to Morgan, January 14, 1935; Hearst/Morgan Correspondence, Morgan Collection.

9. A Shell gas station has since replaced the Reid facility, which occupied the southeast corner of Monterey and Santa Rosa streets. Early in December 1934, before he went to Michigan on vacation, Mac McClure contributed some helpful sketches on the Reid job; later on, Loorz had to insist that Mac accept twenty-five dollars for his efforts. In 1935, Mac also pitched in on some remodeling

ter Loorz went to San Simeon in 1932, he'd begun to figure some jobs in his spare time for the F. C. Stolte Co., most of them around the San Francisco Bay Area; however, the Reid job was the first one in far-removed San Luis Obispo County. Better yet, it was one that he and Fred Stolte shared equally in landing through a sub-contractor they both knew, Bob Hoyt, who lobbied in their behalf. Thus did Loorz and Stolte start making good on their recent hopes of extending themselves farther south (although Los Angeles, which headed their original wish list, re-mained too distant). And thus also did the two partners, spurred by this job in San Luis Obispo, start putting their heads more closely together than ever before — even more than they had for Wyntoon or for Morgan's jobs in the Bay Area. The Reid job was the harbinger of the Stolte Co.'s solid presence in the greater San Luis area. Obviously, it was a presence that thrived through Loorz's proximity in San Simeon; yet it was likewise one that made quick headway through Stolte's input and helpfulness. This befitted the partners, surely, where *all* their work was con-cerned, whether for Hearst or Morgan or anyone else.

Loorz, in particular, was conversant with local conditions through his three years at San Simeon. He saw San Luis Obispo County and its adjoining areas as a virgin middle ground between San Francisco and Los Angeles — as a territory whose jobs were often too small for the metropolitan contractors and, just as often, too big for the contractors based in San Luis, Paso Robles, Santa Maria, and other rural or isolated towns. Stolte, for his part, knew by now that he could trust his young partner implicitly. Besides, the worst of the Depression was over. Good rid-dance, they both thought: opportunity was knocking, and they'd better be ready to answer. Old man Hearst wouldn't last forever. And sad to say, neither would Miss Morgan.

But as much as Loorz was itching to get back into the contracting game (Stolte, of course, had never left it), the young builder's prime responsibility was still San Simeon, despite Hearst's off-season budget and the persistent rain.

LOORZ HAD AMPLE TIME for his correspondence that January. He wrote to George Wright the same day he did to Olin Weatherford about the Reid job, on Tuesday the fifteenth:

> Right now things are quiet as you know but with his Highness here and calling every day or so and wanting to discuss work for the coming summer it is necessary

---

by the Stolte Co. for Loorz's brother and sister-in-law in San Francisco, Claude and Freda Loorz. As George, the elder brother, told those relatives on February 21, "I drew it all up [the requisite plans] and it just happened that Mac came down to do some work for Mr. Hearst so I had him doll it up a bit for me."

that I be here. So when he leaves they tell me to get [depart] and take a couple of weeks right away before work starts up again in Spring. What a hot time to take a vacation, especially with my family expecting the stork about the first of April. Maybe now would be the time to go to the big city and step out a bit.

I enjoyed having Mac here for the few weeks [in November and December]. He certainly has a sense of humor and we collaborated at length on every detail. My spare time did not hang heavily. Right now I miss him. . . .[10]

. . . It has stopped raining but for how long? If it stops I'll be rushing the airport surfacing. That will be an interesting job with a lot of equipment.

I will shoot [dynamite] the devil out of a red-rock hilltop in the field near the old Dobie [the Castro adobe on Oak Knoll Creek, near San Simeon Bay]. Then I will move the shovel in with as many trucks as it will handle.

For a real surface I feel that I will have to set up a crusher and bunkers. A fine red rock[11] well rolled and tamped should make a very fine surface, if placed on top of a well rolled coarse sub-grade.

On the field I will have both cats [Caterpillar tractors] spreading and moving dirt as we intend to do some grading. Then there will be the rolling and blading. I could really use you on that job and think you would like to take a good share of the layout and responsibility. . . .

By the way they rented a Ford tri-motor [airplane] for the past two months, while they are overhauling the big one [the Douglas]. Well our hangar was about 6 inches too short for it. It got too wet to take off so it has stood there in the rain for weeks. However, as it is aluminum it does not seem to suffer even in the slightest.

Perhaps you heard that the chief had ordered a new Volti [Vultee] single motor job, six or eight passenger & pilots. I never heard of one but they say they are quite some plane. I hope it has the proper wing spread to fit our hangar, if not, then we get another job right soon.

. . . Wouldn't I love to take a trip to Jolon over our new [Burnett] road. I'll bet I couldn't get to the first creek without walking.

Three days later—January 18—Loorz told Jim LeFeaver that, in talking to Hearst, he had learned the party didn't intend to leave San Simeon for at least a month. He also had this to tell LeFeaver:

He asked me when we were going to start on the outside [Neptune] pool, about the first of February? I mentioned that I thot it was his own choice to delay it a while as long as it is raining as it has been. He said, that would be O.K. as he was really in no hurry and would see me later about it.

---

10. Mac shared Loorz's sentiments—up to a point. From San Francisco, where he was still focusing on Wyntoon, he wrote Loorz on January 16: "I miss your company but otherwise do not wish to return to La Cuesta [Encantada]."

11. A local term for decomposed basalt, common to the Franciscan geological complex in this part of California; red rock is still widely used in the Cambria-San Simeon area as a paving gravel.

In addition, Loorz gave LeFeaver some variations and further details on what he'd recently told George Wright and others about Hearst:

> Because the aeroplane has been grounded since the beginning of the rain he has asked me to bring the road equipment in as soon as it dries at all and begin surfacing the complete airport [both runways, etc.]. I have the compressor and equipment ready to begin drilling and preparing a red rock quarry so that we can shovel and load trucks promptly when it dries up. Some grading will be necessary. Then before the summer is over we are to erect another hangar for the new plane. He intends to keep the old one as well.
>
> For the above grading & gravelling the cost will be at least $6000. Do you prefer that I put this on the construction payroll [the Hearst Construction Fund] or leave it on the road account, Hilltop Fund?[12]

Loorz let LeFeaver reflect for a moment, providing him with an easygoing passage:

> Mr. Hearst said he had received a very pleasant letter from Miss Morgan. Said she appeared to be having a very fine time. Said she should be in Southern Germany by this time.[13]

And then it was back to business—two paragraphs' worth—in this same letter of January 18 to LeFeaver:

> At present he feels that we should plan on doing the women's dressing room over and finishing up the pantry this summer. This was not in the program when Miss Morgan and I last talked about it. He may let it go but if he should ask for it we should plan on starting it shortly after he leaves as it will be a slow job at best.[14] Of course, if Miss Morgan didn't leave sufficient information we might have to wait. She has told me the general layout of every thing but [in] no detail unless she intends to repeat the present finish.

---

12. The "road account" alluded to the Burnett Road, which relied on the Hilltop Fund but was not synonymous with it. In 1935 no more than ten percent of that revolving fund was spent on Burnett activities of varying kinds: culverts, surfacing, further bridge work, and so on.

13. See p. 161 and its note 8. Hearst's reply to Morgan of January 14 began with "I got your letter"—most likely the only one she sent him during this part of her trip.

14. Both the Ladies' Dressing Room (off the East Room or Morning Room) and the Pantry (adjoining the Kitchen) appear in these annals in 1933; see p. 100. The Ladies' Room, originally completed under Camille Rossi, seems not to have been altered under Loorz; and except for minor efforts by Loorz's crew within the Pantry-Kitchen area in 1937, that section is still unfinished. As for the urge to launch those projects in 1935, Hearst must indeed have "let it go," as Loorz thought (and probably hoped) he might. However, the corresponding Men's Dressing Room *was* altered under Loorz; that area between the Morning Room and the Billiard Room had formerly (with a different floor plan) been Rossi's office.

The boys taking care of the outside pool report some leakage now that was not noticeable at first. It has been so wet I haven't attempted to locate the trouble. We stopped heating the pool about two weeks ago and that is about the time it started leaking. I have an idea it may be where the [concrete] slabs join, the old and new. It may need some pointing [re-grouting] of the marble [veneer].

It was Stolte's turn on January 21 to get an update from Loorz—on a variety of subjects:

Well it has been raining so much that things are still dripping wet even though the sun is out and we have a drying wind. It is too wet to start anything. . . .

Mac writes that they have a carver working on Wyntoon trim. Perhaps you knew about it. No further word has come about work up there. I suppose it would be nearly impossible to work up there anyway. . . .

Mr. Hearst is here and as you have read [in his newspapers], is very busy writing and dictating [editorials and the like].[15] Boy he is working as hard as he ever did in his life. He seems to enjoy it for he is still very pleasant.

Did I thank you for the balance sheets? I'm glad to receive them. However, I note the usual size of accounts payable [on the Wyntoon job]. I was hoping that would be lower. I think LeFeaver will be able to make a more generous payment this next week. . . .

If we [the F. C. Stolte Co.] can slide along this year as well as last we should be able to hold our heads up next year.[16]

In writing to Loorz on January 22, LeFeaver addressed the very matter Loorz was concerned about, namely, accounts payable from the 1934 season at Wyntoon (albeit with reference to work that had recently been done at San Simeon):

Am glad Mr. Hearst is not pressing to start at San Simeon because we really need the breathing spell for allowing our budget to recuperate. The marble and plumbing bills for the [Neptune] pool were very heavy, and besides Cardini's [sculptural] work amounted to considerable.

We would like to get these all well reduced before we start up again.

---

15. After Hearst returned from Europe late in 1934, he started denouncing Communism with renewed fury; he was also gearing up for his break with the Roosevelt Administration. For the immediate moment, he was especially keen on stopping American entry into the World Court; Swanberg's *Citizen Hearst*, pp. 468–75, gives a summary. Hearst's fellow opponents to the World Court ranged from the humorist Will Rogers to the "Radio Priest" of Detroit, Father Charles E. Coughlin (whom Swanberg, in an unattributed passage on p. 445, said was a guest at San Simeon in 1932).

16. Loorz also discussed the Reid job in San Luis Obispo—the one he and Stolte hoped to land through Bob Hoyt:

If we get the job Fred, let's assume the responsibility of everything. What I mean [is] lets hire the brickmen, plasterers, etc and do it ourselves. If we select the right men I think we can make

LeFeaver's letter also addressed the airport job that Loorz mentioned on January 18. Hilltop Fund or Hearst Construction Fund? That had been Loorz's question, however loosely phrased. LeFeaver advised doing the job through the "regular account" (the same in this case as the Hearst Construction Fund),[17] since the Morgan office wanted "to keep all of the work under the one heading as much as possible." As he explained, "There are a number of pertinent reasons why the work should not be split up into various different accounts." Fair enough. But the exact meaning, the exact details are so often elusive in these situations. Suffice it to say that the Morgan office and Hearst's controllers and Loorz himself were three pencil-wielding powerhouses that enjoyed working with numbers and churning out reams of tally sheets and similar records. Some of these papers survive; others don't. Suffice it also to say that to build for Hearst and Morgan cost money, regardless of what a given fund or account was called or which of them was used. As LeFeaver put it, "If Mr. Hearst could appropriate a little extra for this [airport] work . . . we could take care of it very easily." Perhaps he thought that at some opportune moment Loorz could nudge Hearst toward relaxing his grip. (If so, he was wrong, at least for now. For as Loorz replied the next day, "I'll be honest Mr. LeFeaver, I dont just know how to approach Mr. Hearst regarding a little extra appropriation. It is really surprising just how much he expects to get from the monthly allotment [he provides]"—by which, in this instance, Loorz meant the Hilltop Fund.)

In closing on the twenty-second, LeFeaver shared some kind thoughts with Loorz about Morgan, much as Loorz had done a few days before:

> We have had one letter from Miss Morgan and she said that at that time she already felt well repaid for the trip [to Europe].[18] We could not gather definitely as to the state of her health, but she does say that she is becoming enthusiastic about doing things, and to us that is a very good sign.

Likewise on the twenty-second, Stolte wrote to Loorz—in quick reply to his partner's letter of the day before:

> Mr. LeFeaver has requested us to dig up some soft pine for carving [for Wyntoon]. The local market seems to be entirely out of this wood. So we shall send [our] truck to McCloud, and if possible, get some of our stock at our shop. If this is possible in 6 feet of snow.

---

money by it. I'd like to try it anyway. That brick job would scare anyone [else] to death if they went to figure it.

17. LeFeaver's phrasing was also loose. See the 1932 and 1933 chapters, note 17 in each, for more perspective on *regular* in the sense of an account or fund.

18. Probably the same letter that Mac McClure told Loorz about on January 8; see p. 160, plus its note 5.

Loorz himself was at the typewriter on January 22 as well, writing to Mac Mc-Clure in San Francisco:

I knew you would be treated properly in the office. Mr. LeFeaver is quite aware that you are on the "in" with reference to Wyntoon so I'm certain he'll make it comfortable for you.

Talked to Mr. Hearst yesterday and he is still quite good natured and happy. Carey [Baldwin, the zookeeper] wants another room added to the giraffe barn because it's too crowded for three especially since they are hoping that one will have a calf in April. She doesn't look it however. Anyway the possibility makes it interesting to W.R. and the addition will be forthcoming immediately.

A week later, on January 29, Loorz wrote to his "cat skinner," the heavy-equipment man Bud Sweeters:

The airport job which was in such a hurry has been postponed again for a while so you will have time to recuperate before swinging on to the shovel. In the meantime I am developing the quarry and shooting it up good so that you should have fun loading trucks.

We have enjoyed a couple of weeks of delightful weather. Just like spring. So much like it that I have felt like laying down and sleeping instead of working. They really have kept me quite busy sketching and figuring small jobs, like giraffe barn addition, poultry plant pens & shed, barn, corral and house alterations at Pico [Creek Stables] etc.[19] However, I have everything under control this morning. Finished the last sketches a few minutes ago.

The type of balmy weather Loorz mentioned typically graces the San Simeon area at intervals in January and February — especially in January — even during the rainiest winters. Days on end pass with scarcely a chilling breeze or a cloud in the sky. These entrancing lulls had a great bearing on Hearst's having come to regard San Simeon as a winter home. In that vein, his more frequent use of the estate in the fall through spring months of the 1930s — the golden heyday period when movie stars and other celebrities filled his guest lists — came as close to reflecting a steady pattern as anything he ever did in his mercurial life.

January 29 was a day on which Loorz also wrote to Frank Souza, beginning with "Enclosed find check — the three sweetest words in the English Language":

It certainly has been nice weather for work but the Chief says to wait until about March 1st. That pleases LeFeaver for they ran behind quite a little last fall. When

---

19. Loorz was speaking of three localities: the main zoo area ("giraffe barn addition"); the Chicken House and its poultry plant, near the Hearst Ranch headquarters ("pens & shed"); and Pico Creek Stables, nearly three miles down the coast toward Cambria ("barn, corral and house alterations").

they got Cardini's bill and Rankin's [for plumbing] they were surprised at the amount it had grown.

Pete [Petersen], Elof [Gustafson] and [C. J.] Bobst[20] have a few days work adding a room on the giraffe barn. They hope to have a baby giraffe and want a private stall for the mother. George Gillespie went to work Monday [January 28] with two men. He will start a fence around the ridge below the reservoir [opposite the main hilltop] where [Nigel] Keep is now planting pines. Val [Georges] is making fire-screens and that is about all there is doing.

Hearst himself entered the lists on February 2, writing in pragmatic detail to Loorz about the work at San Simeon:

I would like the things done first which we are going to need first.

There is now no use grading and surfacing the landing field until fall. We will not need the surfaced field until the rains come on, towards winter.

Of course there may be an opportunity to do the work before fall, and I do not object to that; but I do not want the work to interfere with the more pressing things.

2. The road to the other ranch [at Jolon] we are going to need during the summer,—in fact from the spring on.

If you could work on that so as to get it ready for actual use by May first at the latest, that would be a useful thing to do.[21]

The [Neptune] pool we are going to need in the summer.

If you could get that completed by May first, I would be very delighted.

I am merely using these as examples. Whatever we have to do let us do immediately if we can use it during the summer, and let us postpone until later the things which will not be needed until winter.

3. Before anything is done in the [Gothic] study I would like to talk with Mr. Solon. I want to discuss with him the desirability of leaving the arches as they are or modify them slightly to make them look more as if they were painted on stone than on wood.

I really do not know which I want to do, although I am inclined to the latter.

I do not know that we will do any other interior decoration until Miss Morgan gets back, but if we should attempt any, I would like it to be the three rooms over the billiard room.[22]

Hearst closed by saying he didn't think Morgan would be getting back "before the middle of April."

---

20. Gustafson, like Petersen, was a skilled carpenter; he remained associated with Loorz and Stolte for many years. Bobst was a laborer.

21. In a short message to Loorz dated January 24, Colonel Willicombe had aired the same topic: "Chief also said to-day to tell you that when you get to work again, and the weather is sufficiently good, one of the first things you might do is fix up the road to Jolon."

22. All three are bedrooms; together with the Billiard Room itself on the ground floor of Casa Grande, they form the Billiard Room Wing.

LOORZ AND HIS WIFE finally got away for a few days in early February, though more on a business trip than on a vacation. They went to the Bay Area, where Loorz bought a rock crusher for the proposed paving of the airstrip and the Burnett Road. With the stork about to appear, as he had told George Wright on January 15, and with Hearst and his party staying on at San Simeon, those few days were as close as Loorz himself came to vacationing in 1935. (The rest of the family, however, went to Nevada that summer for a few weeks.)

By Monday, February 11, Loorz was back on the job and had the following news for LeFeaver:[23]

> I haven't seen Mr. Hearst about the plant for he has a very big party, including some Vanderbilts I am told. They landed in the bay in a very large Amphibian and taxied right up on the sand thru quite heavy breakers just as simply as you please. Did San Simeon have a thrill that Saturday afternoon and turn out to see the sight?[24]
>
> On my way out [of the Bay Area] Friday morning [February 8] I stopped to see about some fine large timbers that had been taken from the Berkeley High School. I bought about 16M. ft. at $15.00 [per thousand board feet]. I will use nearly all of it for small bridges on the Burnett Road and will use the cuttings for blocking. We are nearly out of timbers for rigging, moving trees etc since we have purchased noon [none] since I've been here. This buy alone would more than pay for my trip.

There was more to Loorz's trip, more for him to tell LeFeaver. Loorz had stopped at Jules Suppo's studio in San Francisco and had gone over that artisan's remaining woodwork for the Gothic Study — specifically, for the little tower-room book vaults. Suppo was "certainly making those rooms very rich and expensive," said Loorz. In doing so, Suppo was "acting on a general direction from Miss Morgan":

> Let me be frank and say that I dont think even Mr. Hearst would want us to go to that expense in those rooms that will perhaps rarely be open. It is really beautiful [work] but I dont think a lot of the detail will count in the room [the adjoining study itself] when assembled.

---

23. Loorz also wrote to Stolte that day, touching on a key point they had discussed in November (pp. 146–48). "Mr. LeFeaver, as I said [Loorz had just seen Stolte in Oakland], agreed to the five per cent [for Wyntoon] and I think all you have to do is apply that amount when you bill. If you wish you can call him at the time, he might wish to wait for Miss Morgan but I'm quite certain not."

24. Inasmuch as Gloria Morgan Vanderbilt had visited San Simeon in 1931 (a trip she recounted in *Without Prejudice* [New York, 1936], pp. 199–204), the main celebrity in question was more likely William K. Vanderbilt, Jr., another member of that famous family. His seaplane — actually, a Douglas flying boat called the Dolphin — could be transported on the afterdeck of his yacht.

As things stood, Suppo would need much more time, despite having three helpers in his studio. Loorz signed off by telling LeFeaver, "If you are going to put his crew on Wyntoon he should put extra men on this job [for San Simeon]." Loorz wrote to LeFeaver again three days later, on February 14:

> Mr. Hearst has hardly left his rooms before 4:30 P.M. except one afternoon to ride down to see his new Vultee plane. It was on his way back that Mac [who was temporarily at San Simeon][25] got to see him for a very few minutes. Though I have several things to take up with him, even things that he asked me to get in touch with him about, I have not bothered him for he may not feel very well. Also the boys [Hearst's sons] are still here. Therefore, I can report nothing new to date.
>
> Pete [Petersen] & [Otto] Olson[26] & [Dell] Clausen are back on the [Neptune Pool] colonnades. [Frank] Frandolich & his helper are setting more marble on the [roof of the nearby Roman] temple. It actually rained last night and is still threatening so I will not rush the work for a while yet.
>
> Ray [Van Gorden] & mechanics have been plenty busy driving guests up and down the hill etc. We keep no regular drivers so we have to scramble when they ask for about six cars within 20 minutes.

It was in writing once more to LeFeaver, this time on Friday, February 22, that Loorz provided us with further glimpses of San Simeon's social history—firsthand, revealing glimpses that rank among the choicest to be found, from the obscurely archival to the widely published:[27]

Vanderbilt had a summer home on Long Island known as Eagle's Nest, whose Spanish overtones were akin to those on Hearst's Enchanted Hill.

25. Mac had been away from San Francisco long enough to write to the Morgan office from San Simeon, with an update on Wyntoon (Stolte to Loorz, February 13). Next, "Mac came down to do some work for Mr. Hearst" (Loorz to Claude and Freda Loorz, February 21). And then, "[I] was surprised to find Mac gone this morning" (Loorz to LeFeaver, February 22).

26. A master woodworker and also a carpenter, as later passages in this book will make clear. Olson was misidentified as an ironworker by Sara Boutelle, who got little more than a glance at the Loorz Papers before their processing and cataloguing began in 1988; see *Julia Morgan*, pp. 219, 220. Had the Papers been at her disposal, Boutelle might have seen a letter from Loorz to Stolte dated August 5, 1935. It began in jest, "This will introduce OTTO OLSON, the bearer, a Damn Good Irish Carpenter."

27. Precious few guests or others outside Loorz's circle must have kept diaries or written letters about life at San Simeon (but see p. 97, note 74, regarding a diarist *inside* his circle); in any event, few such primary documents (among them Hugh Walpole's journal, quoted in note 152, below) have ever surfaced. But secondary glimpses abound in latter-day books and articles. Whereas the first published writings—mainly descriptive accounts—appeared in the late 1920s (see p. 81 in this volume, note 46), the typically breezy yet sometimes eloquent memoirs—the Old Testament of San Simeon's social history—remained scarce for another decade or more. One of the earliest was Gloria Morgan Vanderbilt's book of 1936, *Without Prejudice* (cited above in note 24). Another early book was *Of All Places!* (New York, 1937), written by the Abbe children, Patience, Richard, and Johnny. "You

I have three cars waiting to take the remainder of the party to the airport where they will fly to L.A. Supposedly to see the Santa Anita Handicap. They expect to be back about Monday [the twenty-fifth]. This has been the longest continuous stay since I've been here.

Loorz also told LeFeaver, "I'd like to hop in and complete the [Gothic] Study as soon as he departs for a while. I'd hate to have Miss Morgan come back and see it just as she left it."

As for the trip to Santa Anita Park, a new racetrack that had just opened near Pasadena, Loorz told his parents on February 25, "Mr. Hearst and party went down to L.A. Friday to attend the [horse] races. They are expected to land in a few minutes, three or four airplanes."

Morgan, meanwhile, had a few more weeks to go on her European sojourn. She sent Loorz a postcard dated February 26, its stamp having been cancelled in Paris. With the carillon in Casa Grande's twin towers in mind, she had chosen a picture of an enormous bell at the Cathedral of Chartres in northern France.[28] "I have investigated dozens of bellfrys & their contents," her message said. "This sample illustrates the fact that the hanging generally is not a *delicate* matter." She also said, "The car ate up the German chains in a jiffy,—(on the car) but otherwise it is a wonderful car—& the trip in character."[29]

---

could enjoy yourself with all there was there," they naively said on p. 230. "You could go jump in the outdoor pool, the most beautiful one we ever saw, with statues."

The 1940s yielded more books; they included Irvin S. Cobb's *Exit Laughing* (Indianapolis, 1941) and Ilka Chase's *Past Imperfect* (New York, 1942). The 1950s—to continue citing books only—yielded Ludwig Bemelman's *To the One I Love the Best* (New York, 1955) and Irene Castle's namesake, *Castles in the Air* (New York, 1958). The 1960s and 1970s saw memoirs by celebrities like Charlie Chaplin, Colleen Moore, David Niven, and Adela Rogers St. Johns. Even Marion Davies had her say—posthumously, for she died in 1961—with *The Times We Had: Life with William Randolph Hearst* (Indianapolis, 1975).

The heyday of such books has passed. Too few old journalists or faded movie stars remain alive to write them. Fortunately, the Hearst Castle staff began an oral-history collection in the 1970s: some surviving legends, all of them gone now—King Vidor, Frances Marion, and Eleanor Boardman, among others—gave taped interviews before it was too late.

28. As early as 1919, Casa Grande's towers had taken their cue (on paper) from a cathedral in Spain rather than from one in France—namely, from the single-towered Santa Maria de la Mayor in the city of Ronda.

29. In puzzling over this typically Morganesque passage, one should bear in mind the woman's knack for the comical. Morgan may have thought "German chains" could be construed as a chain of newspapers or a group of chain stores. Her humor also animates the postcard she sent Don Loorz from Paris on February 22, with its reproduction of Jacques Louis David's famous painting of the red-caped Napoleon, crossing the Alps into Italy on his rearing mount. "This horse looks a bit more active than your steed," she told young Don, "but in cowboy costume you can run competition with the rider!" The card is the fourth to Don Loorz from Morgan's trip in 1934–35; all four were lent to me in 1999; copies have since been added to the George Loorz Papers.

(Three days before Morgan's postcard left Paris, her secretary received a card in San Francisco, sent from Germany by Morgan, who then went to Holland. Lilian Forney recounted things for Elizabeth Boyter, a former employee of Morgan's who was living in New York. Mrs. Forney told Miss Boyter, "Everyone is fine—Jack Wagenet and Dick Nusbaum are still in the drafting room, well and happy, and Mr. LeFeaver is still 'dictating.'" She also mentioned Ray Carlson, but not the itinerant Mac McClure. "When you come back home again," Mrs. Forney added, "you're going to see two grand new bridges" that were being built then—the Bay Bridge and the Golden Gate.)[30]

Morgan's postcard to Loorz was enroute from Europe when he wrote to the painter Earl Caulkins; that was on February 27. Caulkins was waiting out the off season in Paso Robles (a town right across the Santa Lucia Range from San Simeon yet dozens of miles away by existing roads):

> I've just started up on this past Monday [February 25]. I brought Frank [Gyorgy] back on the job to do a little gilding and patching and I'm having to scratch my head to keep him busy. What is worse it looks like it is going to be a kind of skinny season for painters and decorators around here this summer.[31]
>
> Solon has a little more changing to make in the Study ceiling to satisfy Mr. Hearst and if he would want you it would certainly be O.K. with me. However, you know that man, he thinks no one but Solon can do anything correctly, so that's that.
>
> . . . As far as Wyntoon (McCloud) is concerned there are no painters working. When they do I'll ask my partner to see that you get on. Of course, Miss Morgan has some old man in charge of painting and so far he's handled it alone.

The hilltop crew—the Hearst Camp crew—that Loorz put together during that last week of February consisted of twenty-three men, eighteen of whom were craftsmen, tradesmen, or laborers. The remaining five were a cook, a waiter, a janitor, a timekeeper, and Loorz himself.

The Burnett Road crew, however, was its own entity, just as it had been during the three previous seasons. King Walters had worked in Los Angeles instead in

---

30. From Forney to Boyter, February 23, 1935; Elizabeth M. Boyter Papers, Bancroft Library.

31. Loorz spoke highly of Caulkins later in 1935, while writing to Fred Stolte. "He is the best all around painter I have ever had work for me." It was October 23 by then: Caulkins was going to San Francisco to paint the house that the Stolte Co. had been remodeling for Claude and Freda Loorz—"the kidlets," as George Loorz usually called them.

Back on February 27 Loorz also wrote to Phillip Joy, telling him he could return to work at San Simeon "right away" if he wanted to. "Just now we're *daubbing* in simple painting but you should do better when we come to the decorating." Loorz closed by mentioning Phillip's father, Thaddeus, who remained weak after the episode in 1929 (see pp. 44–45, plus their note 38). "Give my best to your Dad and folks. It's about time they paid us a visit on the hilltop."

1934, but he and Loorz still kept in touch. Walters, like Earl Caulkins, was among those whom Loorz wrote to on Wednesday, February 27 (besides, a letter from Walters had just arrived):

> We started cleaning out the road on Monday and the boys will be way beyond the summit by tonight. I drove to the summit before they started and I dont know how much further I could have gone. We are only guessing that we have bad slides at the [Salmon Creek] gorge for no one has been out [that far]. With good clean gutters like we had on this side we may not have as much trouble as we expect.

In telling Walters that all such work had gone "economically & promptly right thru to completion last year," Loorz meant more than just the Burnett Road. He also meant the road "from the castle to the creek" (as Hearst had phrased it late in 1933).[32]

The Wyntoon job also resumed during that last week of February, a month earlier than in the previous year. Stolte told Loorz on March 2 that Harry Thompson had gone up to McCloud and that Mac McClure had, too.

Except for their recent trip to the horse races at Santa Anita, Hearst and his party remained at San Simeon, the host himself having been on hand almost constantly ever since he returned from Europe in the fall. (Over this and other protracted stretches, the "party" fluctuated. Many guests stayed only a day or two; some stayed much longer.) On March 4 Hearst sent Loorz a memo through Colonel Willicombe, addressing a matter that had cropped up a few months earlier but that still awaited resolution:[33]

> I must get the wild animals away from the immediate vicinity of the house. Therefore I would like to build the cat pits and the bear pits, etc., this summer. The cat pits we will re- do as planned [with partitions] making six [pits] in all.
>   The [new] bear pits can be made at the next bend [in the driveway going down, alongside Orchard Hill] and can also be six in number.[34] The cost of these

32. See pp. 101, 136, and 140. In addition, a letter from Loorz to Hearst (undated: probably written late in 1934) acknowledged that Hearst was "grievously disappointed" with the new road—a scarred hillside being mostly to blame. Yet Loorz assured him that they had chosen "the most direct route down the hill and decidedly the most economical."

33. See p. 144: Loorz to Stolte, November 3, 1934.

34. Two bear grottos had been built in 1931 on the north side of Orchard Hill; the partitioning of them—to house species besides the polar bears that were already there—began later in 1935. The newer "pits" Hearst envisioned at the "next bend" in the driveway (immediately west of the grottoes) were never built; they may equate with the "proposed excavation below [down the road from] the Grotto," which Loorz mentioned to Hearst on January 7, 1936, and the "excavation" Loorz mentioned to Willicombe on June 9, 1937 (pp. 232 and 328).

As for removing the lions and kindred species from Animal Hill (near the Roman Pool), Hearst may not have done so before that part of the zoo was disbanded, a process that took place in 1937;

latter need not be great. They need not be deep. Bears do not jump. Moreover people like to get reasonably close to them and feed them.

Suppose we plan this construction in detail and get an accurate idea of costs.

That same winter day, March 4, found Loorz giving Fred Stolte a glimpse of San Simeon in full swing:

> Mr. Hearst is still here and feeling fine. Expect them to leave in a couple of weeks but who knows. Four of the [Hearst] boys have been here quite a bit lately. One left for S.F. today with our new Chrysler. Just when I get enough cars to handle the guests they come and take some away. Then I have to talk for another.[35]

With a little imagination, Stolte could easily have read between his partner's lines. The allure and mystique—plus the strain and frustration—of dealing with Hearst and his entourage were things that Stolte himself knew firsthand from the past two seasons at Wyntoon.

THE UNUSUAL, THE UNFORESEEN, the unexpected were forever cropping up in the lives of Hearst and those around him. On March 5 Loorz addressed just such a matter. Roy Grady, an old friend of his in Oakland, had got wind of Hearst's wanting to buy "all the Cast Models now in storage at the Palace of Fine Arts," a group of objects "left from the old Fair." Grady was referring to the Panama-Pacific International Exposition, which had been held in San Francisco in 1915 and in which Hearst and his mother had been involved, as had Morgan. Nonetheless, Loorz knew nothing of the prospect mentioned by Grady on March 1:[36]

> In this case, you are one-up on me for I have never heard about the Cast Models from the Palace of Fine Arts. No doubt, Mr. Hearst will be interested and may even buy them as he does nearly everything he hears about but I wouldn't even hear about it until they gave me instructions to start hauling them.

---

for that matter, he may not have removed "the beast" and other bears from Animal Hill before the disbandment occurred (p. 235: Loorz to Morgan, January 16, 1936). Loorz's letter to LeFeaver of October 9, 1935, refers briefly to the "cats" and their quarters (p. 219). In this volume, though, all the other quoted references to "the grotto" and the like seem directed toward the existing bear grottos.

35. Loorz signed off on March 4 by describing something that, along with his homemade swimming pool, he took great pride in sharing with Stolte and others. "Boy you ought to see my garden. I have it trim and neat clear back to the ocean now, at last."

36. March 1 is also the date on a letter Loorz received from Charles Kelly, District Manager of the Midland Counties Public Service Corporation, based in Fresno. "Enclosed find complete file on Hearst electric line construction," wrote Kelly. The file comprised sixteen pages, mostly copies of letters dating from 1924, some written by Morgan. The Loorz Papers include several outlying items like the Midland file—items often hard to find anywhere else. Another prime example is a group of doc-

Grady's information proved accurate. Hearst bought the plaster models—
or at least some of them—and shipped the items to San Simeon: more crates for
W. R. Williams to jostle in his beachfront warehouses. The models, though, did not
see the light of day again until they were dispersed from those warehouses after
Hearst's death in 1951.[37]

Loorz had recently heard (through an undated letter) from another old friend
of his, a college chum from his Berkeley days named Armand Brady, who was as
much a wag as George Wright:

> I see by the papers where Hearst is building several Tyrolean Castles up at
> McCloud. I want the one with the southern exposure for mine. So kid fix it up
> with Bill so I can take my one clean shirt and the old socks and go up there for
> the summer.[38]

Few could match wits with the likes of Armand Brady. Nonetheless, Loorz
gave it his Boy Scout best in answering his friend on March 8. He divulged some
key information in the process:

> Yes *we* are building several German style houses for Mr. Hearst at McCloud.
> They could be called castles since they are quite large compared to most homes.
> They are small compared to this institution. One of them has 13 bedrooms with

---

uments that LeFeaver sent Loorz on February 25, 1932, pertaining to the Belgian carillon for Casa
Grande's towers.

37. See Robert C. Pavlik's article " 'Something a Little Different': La Cuesta Encantada's Architectural Precedents and Cultural Prototypes," *California History* (Winter 1992/93), pp. 463–77,
548–49. It delves into the importance for San Simeon of the Panama-Pacific Exposition—and
into Hearst's efforts to acquire the kinds of items that Loorz and Grady were talking about. Pavlik,
however, thought Hearst came away empty; others have concurred. (In some later correspondence
Hearst seemed to be vacillating, seemed to be lacking any Exposition models at all; see Hearst to
Morgan, March 9 and 14, 1937; Hearst/Morgan Correspondence, Morgan Collection. But see also
p. 258 in this volume: Loorz to Morgan, June 12, 1936.)

Hearst had wanted the models since at least 1925. A letter of his at Cal Poly alludes to San Simeon as a future museum—a place where some of the "models and art works" would be "largely open
to public inspection," much as Hearst would also make some of them accessible through "various
plans" he had "for memorial buildings in the University of California." See Morgan's file copy of
Hearst to Hale, April 11, 1925; ibid. Hearst's allusion came two years before his oft-quoted letter to
Morgan of February 19, 1927—in which he spoke unmistakably of San Simeon as a museum.

38. Regarding the "papers" he'd seen: Brady, an attorney for a title company in Sacramento
(and later employed by Loorz and Stolte), may have been referring to the *Sacramento Bee* or other
newspapers in northern California.

A few months earlier (September 26, 1934) Loorz had described San Simeon's remoteness for
Brady and his wife. "We are just fifty miles from San Luis Obispo which is in itself just a second rate
town. We get in there very seldom. In fact, we do most of our buying from Monkey Wards." Loorz
had added, "Though there is a one horse store here [in the bayside town] that has *1* copy of everything from a can of corn to a Blue-Jay corn plaster. That is everything but what you want."

bathrooms and Living Rooms. Note that I said we. That is the F. C. Stolte Co. is building them. You know, I hold just 50 shares of the company, Mr. Stolte 48 & our lawyer 2, a corporation.[39] You see, by being the nice boy you taught me to be, I keep my fingers crossed and have managed to keep my partner & crew going quite well even from here. If Julia Morgan, Arch[itect] & Mr. Hearst live a few years more I should be well on the way. Do a little praying for me Armand or better still do a little *holding* for me for I have more faith in it. Isn't it terrible?

Hearst and his party finally pulled up stakes at San Simeon in late March, as Loorz explained to Jim LeFeaver on the twentieth of that month:

Mr. Hearst is leaving today unless he changes his mind before this afternoon.

In a general conversation regarding present work he asked for another metal warehouse [in the town of San Simeon] right away. He really wants the [proposed] concrete warehouse but the present plans call for wrecking the old one and we would have little extra space. We wouldn't have it right away and it would cost a lot more money.

He wants to erect two [warehouses: the metal and the concrete units] but has agreed to one at a time and wait a little on the next one.[40]

I am practically ready for the steel in the [Neptune] colonnades. John [Vanderloo] has a few more panels to cast [for their ceiling coffers]. I can hardly understand why they are not all ready since he started on January 7th. . . .

He [Hearst] wants us to start a small crew and pour a few more beams at the Pergola [on Orchard Hill]. Fortunately we have 100 bird heads cast [for the ends of the beams] and three men will make a big showing. He suggests we order at least 200 columns for the summer but I think he'll be pleased with 100. It would cost quite a little to get footings for the 200 in addition to the beams.

He hopes we can have the [Gothic] Study completed by his return. We should do it complete with painting with proper crew. He does not want to

---

39. When the F. C. Stolte Co. was incorporated in 1932, the new entity comprised 500 shares of common stock, not the 100 shares Loorz indicated to Brady; no preferred stock existed. See also p. 120, note 36.

40. The town of San Simeon had four warehouses at this time. Warehouse #1—the "old one" in Loorz's preceding paragraph—was the wooden freight shed of 1878, built by Hearst's father, George Hearst. Warehouses #2 and #3 were plain, corrugated steel structures of the 1920s. In distinct contrast, Warehouse #4 (likewise a Hearst-Morgan structure) was built of concrete in a missionesque, Spanish Colonial style; had the new "concrete warehouse" Loorz referred to been built, two such structures would have distinguished the setting. Instead, Hearst put up only the additional "metal warehouse" that Loorz mentioned (Warehouse #5), leaving the potential Warehouse #6 to languish on paper forever more; see also note 44, below.

The "old one" of 1878 (Warehouse #1) still stands, as do Warehouses #4 and #5. One of the earlier steel structures (Warehouse #2) was razed in the 1980s. In the 1990s, most of Warehouse #3 was also razed (but has since been rebuilt).

change the beams now [Solon's painted arches]. He bought new rugs[41] that just
match the ceiling and so we may not have to touch them — ho — ho. . . .

. . . I intend to put all carpenters (four) in the Study in the morning. Pete [Pe-
tersen] is getting ready this afternoon. The thing I dislike most is to move furniture and cover it up.

Two days later, on March 22, Loorz provided his parents with further glimpses
of life at San Simeon, courtesy of the Chief himself and his innermost circle:

Mr. Hearst and party left us yesterday. The first time they have been away in five
months. They will be back again in about five weeks. I think they will surely be
back for his birthday April 29th. He always tries to be here xmas and his birthday
and has ever since I've been here.

The day before he left I enjoyed an hour with him in the large Assembly Room
[in Casa Grande]. Marion Davies, young John [Hearst] and wife & Arthur Brisbane were in the room at the time. The day before that I sat in conference with
Mr. Hearst, Young William [Hearst], & Arthur Brisbane. It was interesting to say
the least. He usually comes to my office but not feeling well he asked [me] to come
in there. He has been awfully considerate of me and I like him for it.

Loorz pounded out two pages of tightly packed details for his good friend
Arch Parks (the former Hearst Ranch superintendent) on Saturday, March 23. As
he often did, Loorz touched on certain details conveyed in other letters — but not
without finding new ways to be informative:

We just finished building two large covered pens 100 x 150 for [W. H.] Henry at
the chicken ranch.[42] He has bought a lot of prairie chicken[s] from Canada. Now
when this rain is over we will start building a large wild duck pond and pen. The
Chief is determined he will raise some of the wild game for his table.[43] I dont
blame him, I'd do it to[o] if I could afford it.

---

41. A set of three Persian (Bakhtiari) carpets, acquired from the dealer H. P. Philibosian in
Los Angeles.

Another kind of textile art (a kind dearer to Hearst) had recently drawn attention. In this case
a dealer far more renowned than Philibosian wired Hearst at San Simeon. "BELGIAN AMBAS-
SADOR HAS WRITTEN THAT BRUSSELS EXHIBITION OF BELGIAN ART IS MOST
ANXIOUS TO HAVE LOAN OF YOUR TAPESTRY CREDO." The dealer meant *The Credo*,
a Gothic tapestry owned by Hearst since 1923 and warehoused in New York. "I DO HOPE YOU
WILL GIVE THIS FAVORABLE CONSIDERATION AND AGREE TO LEND IT." Hearst
scrawled on the telegram: "Certainly will do as you wish about Credo tapestry." From Joe [Joseph
Duveen] to Hearst, March 14, 1935; Hearst Papers, carton 19 (under "1935 Samples").

42. Henry and his wife were the parents of Jean Henry, who married Joseph Willicombe in
1939.

43. Hearst wrote a long letter on the subject two years later. The gist of it: "When I started the
poultry farm it was with the idea of supplying the Hacienda on the Hilltop and Santa Monica [the

This week we will start erecting another tin warehouse for [W. R.] Williams. It will go across the track from Sebastians store.[44] In fact, we will erect two before we finish. It will be wonderful for the men to get work again, the rain & winter shut down have them all back on short rations.

At this juncture—still on Saturday the twenty-third—Loorz said to Parks, "I might just as well tell you a lot more about myself while I'm at it." He assured his friend, "If you get bored reading just turn out the light and go to sleep":

I drew up plans for an alteration of the Ford Building, W. T. Reid Co., in San Luis. My plans and bid were excepted [accepted] and we will start work there in a short time. I sent all [the] dope to my partner and he will handle it. I dont want them to get anything on me here, that is regarding doing my own work on their time. I use plenty of their time writing and that doesn't seem to make so much differ-ence. It seems that the most essential thing here is to be on the job, day and night, whether you actually produce or not.

Then I'm right now drawing up plans for a nice pent house apartment for my brother in S.F. . . . When I get it all planned and figured my partner will handle it. Though he's my brother [Claude Loorz, not Stolte] we'll still take a little profit for we had to beat competition. That's what he wanted. . . .

You see Arch I dont want all my eggs in one basket and suffer when they decide against me here. I'm prepared for it right now, though they are still awfully good to me.

Mr. Hearst was quite sick for two weeks. For about a week he didn't see anyone but Willicombe and took no phone calls. He had quite a fever but recovered rap-idly. They left for L.A. last Tuesday[45] after the longest continuous stay on the hill

---

Beach House] primarily—and secondly supplying the ranch with excess production." From Hearst to W. W. Murray, February 27, 1937; Hearst Papers, carton 23 (under "1937 Samples").

44. Loorz clarified the matter on April 19, once more in writing to Arch Parks. By then, the plan for a new concrete warehouse (the prospective Warehouse #6, as in note 40, above) had given way to corrugated steel:

I suppose I mentioned that we were going to put up another two metal warehouses in San Sim-eon for [the] Antiques [Department]. I took up all those [additional narrow-gauge railroad] tracks [beyond where they connect the wharf with Warehouses #1, #2, and #3] and will move the scales as the [new] warehouses will go right across the road from Sebastians and in line with the other metal warehouses [#2 and #3]. The whole thing looks cleaner with just the grading done so far. It will improve the looks of the town and I hope will stop a lot of that wind that whisks around the Sebastians corner and down the main drag to our house.

This equally long, varied letter also found Loorz telling Parks, "Boy you sure have one loyal supporter in Mr. Henry [of the Chicken Ranch]. He certainly wishes the old times could return."

45. Loorz had told LeFeaver on March 20, a Wednesday, that Hearst might be leaving that day; but the suspected delay must have occurred, for Loorz told his parents on March 22 that Hearst

since it started [in 1919–20]. Five months all told in one stay. Talk about a happy household when they left. I thot the place was going to blow up the way those housekeepers were getting on each other's nerves. I saw smiles yesterday and day before that I haven't seen in weeks.

Carey Baldwin and Van Dormen[46] are planning on a trip to Africa to observe animals in their native haunts, this summer. He asked for a leave of absence and they said O.K. Says he wants to take at least one real trip before he gets married. Of course, he hasn't found the girl or like the rest of us Arch, he couldn't wait.

Loorz's line about using "plenty of their time writing" may be the most telling one of all. If certain conditions—unique conditions—hadn't prevailed at San Simeon, the Loorz Papers would surely have suffered.

Morgan got back from Europe a little sooner than Hearst had predicted, about the end of March.[47] In the meantime, the stork arrived as anticipated at the Loorzes' household; their third son, Bob, was born on March 26. Through his endless letters and phone calls, Loorz spread the happy news far and wide.

The responses piled up. One of them, dated April 4, came from Mac McClure at Wyntoon:

Greetings to Robert Carl!—and congratulations to his parents. . . .

Our first month up here is ended and has shown considerable progress too. So much remains to be done, however, that we will hardly do more than get the inside work done by June. I understand that no extra money was *asked* for and an endeavor is being made to keep within scheduled expenditures—am I right? In

---

had left the previous day, a Thursday. The "Tuesday" Loorz mentioned to Parks is a transposition or typographical error.

Like the letter to Parks, the one to LeFeaver on March 20 also elaborated on Hearst's recent sickness. "It started from a cold and confined him to his room for two weeks. In fact, to his bed for more than three days with quite a fever." Loorz added, "Many of the people here were quite sick during this period. Louis Reesing [the head gardener] was very bad and lost two weeks." Extremes of weather, well known on The Enchanted Hill in late winter, may have been the cause. As Loorz told his sister, Iva, on March 22, "We have had rain, hail, ice, wind and heat, all within the past two weeks so there are a lot of colds and even influenza."

46. In writing to Loorz from Los Angeles on December 27, 1933, Ray Van Gorden mentioned Van *Durman* as well as Otto Olson; four days later he said he hadn't seen "Otto or Van as expected" in that city.

47. So much sooner, in fact, that weeks later a friend of hers in Missouri was still hoping she would stop there on her way home. "I understand that Miss Morgan is abroad," wrote Frederic Morgan, Director of Principia College; his recipient was Bernard Maybeck's wife. "I will appreciate anything you can do to help me reach her, so that we might urge her to pause in St. Louis upon her return. I should be so grateful to have her see the beautiful work which has been accomplished [in nearby Elsah, Illinois]." Director Morgan also referred to Ed Hussey ("that Master Mind of all Detail"), who'd devoted himself to the Principia job since leaving Wyntoon in 1933. From Frederic Morgan to Annie Maybeck, May 14, 1935; Bernard Maybeck Collection, EDA.

any case we will be able to house a party by midsummer, and as I always expected we will probably rush up some temporary work [at] the last minute. Our interiors are coming fine. Much of the carving is already done and we have most of the paneling etc in place already. As you probably know, the moldings were run at Chico [midway between Wyntoon and Sacramento].

My trip to the city was to see J.M. and to go over all the changes with her. (The "office" had told her nothing but left all of the "pleasure" for me.) Of course she was a little surprised at some of the developments but took it all well enough, but had a lot of suggestions and criticisms, none of which will exactly speed up the work. She left last nite for L.A. and will probably be with you before you read this.

I think she looks very much better and am sure the trip helped her. However her improvement will prompt her to become very active again, I'm afraid, and will undo a lot of the good the trip may have done.[48]

Mac was right about Morgan's imminent arrival at San Simeon: she was there to confer with Loorz on Saturday, April 6.[49] Loorz's recap notes contained twenty-six entries, most of them concerning the Neptune Pool and the Gothic Study. One entry said, "Arch[itect] to bring Mr. Solon down on next trip to start him on touching up and finishing Study paintings." A few other entries pertained to the indoor Roman Pool, where Loorz was to "set up trial floods." Hearst was hoping they could provide that building with more dramatic lighting, not only in the surrounding room but also in the pool itself—under the water.

Soon after his conference with Morgan, Loorz heard from Stolte, who wrote to him on April 10:

Well, we are going full blast at Wyntoon and the budget is shot plenty.

Asbestos roofing, power line equipment and high priced millwork all come at once. We send in two weeks of future costs so the [Morgan] office is quite well informed on the costs there.

On the last trip north Miss Morgan said that she had received a rather anxious letter from Mr. LeFeaver, regarding the added costs.[50] However, I fail to see where

---

48. Stolte stuck to the positive in mentioning the same subject. He told Loorz on April 4, "Met Miss Morgan in [her] Office last Monday [April 1], she surely seems and appears much better. I believe her trip has done her a lot of good."

49. Mac was also right in saying Morgan had left for Los Angeles late on April 3. The Morgan-Forney ledgers cite April 4 as her earliest travel date in 1935. She was at the Beach House that day— for "Service Wing additions and alterations," a job involving a separate, freestanding structure (321 Ocean Front versus 415 Ocean Front), whose progress she would check on intermittently through August.

50. No such letter exists in the Morgan Collection. Stolte's reference to "the last trip north" is puzzling. LeFeaver had gone to Wyntoon on March 25, his only trip there in 1935. But Morgan (likewise according to the Morgan-Forney ledgers) didn't go there for the first time that year until April 16–17.

it can be cut, and continue to do the work as laid out. She mentioned that some material bills could be postponed. Perhaps we are accustomed to this?????

Labor and material will average about $6000 per week for several weeks to come.

Stolte wrote again the next day, April 11, saying he had talked to Miss Morgan on the ninth: "It seems the program remains the same, Gables & Brown Bear by June 1 or earlier." Therefore, he added, he was "going up to McCloud for a few days to help the job along."[51]

Loorz wrote back to his partner immediately. First he said he'd be checking up on their W. T. Reid job in San Luis Obispo the following day, April 13.[52] The refrain was all too familiar: "Boy it's the bunk the way they want things when they have no money," a reference this time not to Hearst but to the Stolte Co.'s new client in San Luis. And then Loorz told Stolte about his daily work, his more pressing work: "I've got things going like wildfire here on the hilltop as well so you can bet I have plenty to think about. So many things I'm doing in a rush and I've had the rain [and] mud to contend with."

The weather remained a factor at San Simeon well into April, as a letter Loorz wrote to Morgan on the sixteenth indicated:[53]

Well the rain is still falling and everything is wet. We have been unable to work on the Colonnade for several days. There is just a couple of more days on steel work and it will be ready to pour. However, because of the rain it has not been practical to haul the sand from Monterey.[54] The gravel I have on hand for the job has been so wet that we cannot put it through our screens for grading. I hate to delay but———.

While it has been raining we have been able to make quite a little headway in the [Gothic] Study Towers, with all hands on that work.

51. A second letter that Stolte wrote Loorz on Thursday, April 11, contains these lines: "Miss Morgan is going up north, Tuesday [April 16]. So, I shall stay until she gets there. Send any messages to me there."

52. Despite Loorz's proximity to San Luis, his role may have been viewed differently by certain associates; and yet Olin Weatherford's words of April 3 may have been partly in jest: "Mr Stolte said he was glad you could help him out on the job down there, dont guess I will get to go down after all." (Loorz had once thought it possible; see p. 161 for his letter to Weatherford on January 15.)

53. Another letter — heading Loorz's way — also bore the date April 16. Frances O'Brien, who preceded both Ada Drew and Albert Redelsperger in running the household at San Simeon (and whom Mac McClure had once heard was dead), asked Loorz to help some relatives of hers "see the ranch." O'Brien assured him that the party would "only stay a short time" and that she would "try to reciprocate" someday. Loorz told Arch Parks on April 19 that he was "thrilled to receive" Mrs. O'Brien's letter but was "very much disappointed" in its lack of news.

54. The Salinian granite along the northern part of the Big Sur coast and on the Monterey Peninsula yields a distinctive white sand — ideal for the cast concrete work that surmounts the white marble columns of the Neptune Pool colonnades.

In contrast to the massive bell towers of Casa Grande, the "Study Towers" were small, intimate spaces—storage vaults for rare books and manuscripts—that flanked the main section of the Gothic Study (also called the Gothic Library, because of its extensive shelves and thousands of books). The two book vaults were the ones Loorz mentioned to LeFeaver in December and, more recently, in February; their completion, Miss Morgan had hoped, would be the extent of any new work done inside Casa Grande during her recent trip abroad.

THE SANTA MARIA ARCHITECT Louis Crawford wrote to Loorz on April 18. Crawford was best known for his recent Santa Maria City Hall, a tile-roofed, Mediterranean structure built through the PWA (the Public Works Administration); he had since begun designing schools in the "Central Coast" area as PWA jobs. In Arroyo Grande, midway between San Luis Obispo and Santa Maria, a new grammar school was ready to be figured.

Crawford wondered if Loorz was interested. Loorz quickly replied that he was.[55]

The successful collaboration between Lou Crawford and the F. C. Stolte Co. included the Arroyo Grande job and, soon afterward, the grammar schools Crawford designed for the small towns of Cambria and Morro Bay, both of them close to Loorz's home base in San Simeon.

The Reid job in San Luis and the Arroyo Grande School weren't the extent of Loorz's current moonlighting on behalf of the Stolte Co. The very day Crawford wrote to Loorz also saw Loorz writing to Stolte about a house that Frank Souza, the

---

55. Crawford's letter of the eighteenth and Loorz's of the next day may have been mere formalities. A sub-contractor in San Luis Obispo, James Quaglino of the County Roof Service, gave Loorz "confidential" information about the Arroyo Grande job as early as April 5—Crawford having told Quaglino the week before that he hoped to get "some reliable [general] contractors to bid on this work." Loorz brought Stolte on board on April 10:

I am going to take out plans on a small frame school in Arroyo Grande, just below San Luis. It is a simple, straight, 10 class room job. . . .

The architect [Crawford] will back us because of an angle thru a close friend [Quaglino]. The fact is that the local contractor is not big enough to do the job and the architect wants his foreman to run the job and to use as much local labor and subs as possible. This foreman will run it for us and the Arch[itect] will help him out. We'll put a good time-keeper and wide awake young fellow to follow up. The job is expected to run around $40,000.

Because of my connections here, the local contractors (subs) and material men are frankly behind us. They are afraid some contractor from L.A. or Santa Barbara will take the job and they'll lose out. All will give us the low down I'm certain.

Stolte's second letter of April 11 (see note 51, above) included a quick, supportive reply. "I can see no reason for not figuring your school job there. After this trip north [to Wyntoon] I can come down and help you with the figure."

labor foreman on The Enchanted Hill, was building for himself in nearby Cambria. Loorz told his partner he was "handling the job" in Souza's behalf through the F. C. Stolte Co., largely to help Souza (who was recovering from a back injury and couldn't work) with such details as payroll and insurance.[56]

Loorz's reference to the Souza job appeared as a postscript on April 18. The heart of his letter to Stolte, written on a Thursday, included the following:

> I certainly am busy with Mr. Hearst expected this afternoon for the Easter week end. He phoned and sent a registered letter to inform me that he would be here so I suppose he will want me to be here personally on Saturday and Sunday for a while at least.[57] Ho Ho, such is life out west.

Yet Hearst may have changed his plans somewhat: on Friday the nineteenth Loorz told his parents, "Mr. Hearst and party are expected back tonight for the Easter week end. They are in L.A. at present working on another picture at Warner Brothers [*Page Miss Glory*, starring Marion Davies].[58] We'll be glad to have them back for a few days to get some definite decisions on several things."

MORGAN WAS AT SAN SIMEON to confer with Hearst on that Easter Sunday, April 21; she was also there the next day (probably having laid over in San Luis).[59] Loorz's notes contain relatively few entries, but they pertain to conferences held on both

---

56. Situated on the southwest corner of Center Street and Burton Drive in downtown Cambria, the house later became a restaurant (at first the Grey Fox Inn and then Robin's).

Frank and Mabel Souza's daughter, Frances, grew up in the house in the 1930s and 1940s. In 1984 she invited me to her home in Harmony, just south of Cambria, to meet a man who had worked on her father's labor crew at San Simeon in the 1920s. The old-timer—a notable player further on in this book—was Maurice McClure, who later mentioned me to George Loorz's sons. Thence came the call I received from Bill Loorz in 1988 (as described in my older preface; see p. xiii).

57. The Loorz Papers contain no such letter from Hearst. But a brief one that Willicombe sent Loorz from Los Angeles on April 15 bears this postscript: "Chief will be at San Simeon next Saturday and Sunday [April 20–21]. Will you kindly get this word to [W.R.] Williams and [Louis] Reesing and [Nigel] Keep and oblige."

58. Released on August 29, 1935; see Guiles, *Marion Davies*, pp. 401–02. (As for Loorz's reference to "another picture at Warner Brothers," the film was the first Davies vehicle made through that company; see p. 190 in this chapter, plus its note 74.)

59. The main San Simeon account in the Morgan-Forney ledgers cites April 20 for this visit, suggesting that Morgan left San Francisco that Saturday to see Hearst on Sunday. Meanwhile, the one Santa Monica account for 1935 (it regards the Service Wing at the Beach House) puts Morgan there on April 21 or, more plausibly, the day after. Her visit must have been a partial one (entered as $22, whereas some other check-ups she made on the Beach House in 1935 ran as high as $55). Perhaps she went south on April 22 for a late visit—after concluding a shorter second session with Hearst and Loorz. Indeed, her first session at San Simeon was the lively one. As Loorz told Stolte on Thursday, April 25 (Hearst had also left by then), "I have things running smoothly and consistently here again after the Sunday brainstorm of rush."

Sunday and Monday. "Work to begin on Billiard Room wing at early date," goes one of his entries. "Floods thru diffused glass to be tried over Roman Pool; Mr. Hearst still desirous of underwater lighting," goes another one.[60] Loorz wrote to Stolte on the second of those two days, Monday, April 22:

> Well they certainly have me busy on this hill. They told me to speed up and spend more money this month. I dont know where it is coming from for he did not give her any more and she doesn't realize that I have spent our share of the allotment.
>
> I think he just asked for a few more things and she is going to give him them even if she goes in the hole. Between you and me I'm not going to splurge too much. The pay checks are already getting behind.
>
> . . . I was up there Saturday afternoon waiting around for Mr. Hearst. Then I spent a most wonderful Sunday (Easter) with Miss Morgan here and the chief just a bit unreasonable but kind. I got home at 10 P.M.[61]

Stolte answered on April 24, with an update for his partner about the big job up north:

> I have been trying to get all the loose ends going, for Wyntoon. Carvers, tile setters, roofers, power line and etc. And their materials yet to come from [the] East. The big spring drive is on it seems. What do you know about June 1. The Gables and Brown Bear are to be finished.

He also asked Loorz if he should "go slow on expenses at McCloud." Loorz's reply was all business: "I know how rushed you are at Wyntoon and I know it will take a lot more of your time. You'll have to speed up a lot to do what he wants by June but do it whatever you do. Our very existence on the job depends on it."

The next day, Loorz had more to tell Stolte about Wyntoon. "I would frankly ask Miss Morgan about how many grand she wants you to spend per month and I'd do it. She will surely spend too much but keep checking [with her] and keep them [Morgan and LeFeaver] advised."

The first of those letters to Stolte, dated April 25, coincided with one that Loorz sent Joe Willicombe in Los Angeles. The subject required Hearst's judg-

---

60. On May 10 Loorz told Louis Schallich, "Miss Morgan tried a couple of flood lights on the ceiling of the Pool but it did not satisfy Mr. Hearst. I think he will insist on the underwater lighting sooner or later. Oh boy, how I do dread that job." Schallich, in turn, sent Loorz a sketch on May 31. It showed how a light could be placed near the diving board the pool had at each end. The lights would rest at the bottom of new features: vented columns (through which wiring could run and pool water move). The columns would be attached to the vertical walls beneath the diving boards.

61. Another indication (as in note 59) that Sunday was the more eventful day—almost as though nothing happened on Monday itself. However, Loorz identified his recap notes from Morgan's visit as "Sunday April 21st & Mon. April 22."

ment, and Loorz knew the Colonel would convey the main details to the Chief (Willicombe being a past master at summarizing countless messages for Hearst's perusal). For our part, we can try to visualize something that Loorz and Willicombe — and of course Hearst and Morgan — knew intimately from firsthand experience:

> The [construction] tower and scaffolding near the East Room [or Morning Room] is being used daily. We have a gin-pole on the tower used to hoist everything for the [Gothic] Study and for all work on the roof. It has been used every day this week.
>
> In about two weeks we will have the most of the hoisting completed for the Study Towers and could dismantle the [construction] tower. This would mean that I would have to rig up another hoist for the roof tile which Miss Morgan hopes to get on this summer. However, I could erect a simple one hanging out from the roof for roof tile and the remainder of the cornice [by Jules Suppo: for the uppermost side walls of the Gothic level].
>
> If they contemplate raising the service wing [on the south side of Casa Grande] as has been continually mentioned to me the tower of course would be used for the concrete. Except for this need I would be pleased to take it down at once.

Had Hearst gotten word to Morgan on this, and had she passed the message along, Loorz's notes of Monday, April 29, would have been the perfect vehicle for recording it. Yet nothing appears there about the construction tower. Enough was said, though, about other matters, some of them painstaking and intricate, to befit Morgan's high standards:

> Worming of lower doors of Study bookcases overdone. Putty up some holes. (Mr. [Frank] Gyorgy attempted to match middle doors of each case which are very wormy antique wood. Even these stand out too much because of the light color in the worm holes, perhaps a darker stain in the holes would help a lot.)

Loorz's recap also mentioned an engineering matter — a reminder for us that Morgan was an *architect*. Calculations, such as Jim LeFeaver or Loorz himself provided at times, weren't her strong suit, much less her passion. And when a job required full-fledged engineering, specialists like Walter Steilberg or, more often, Walter Huber (non-staff members, both of them) were the people she relied on. "Send sketch of Garden Wall layout below West Terrace so that Mr. Huber can design wall sections," Loorz noted on April 29.[62]

---

62. The task proved to be minor. Under June 26, the main San Simeon account (Morgan-Forney ledgers) has this entry pertaining to May: "W. L. Huber engr. serv. West Terr. 1250 [$12.50]." Minor or not, Loorz's recap notes from Morgan's visit on May 11 included an eye-catching reference to the same project: "Make footings heavy enough to receive future tower at South end."

But wait a minute. April 29 was Hearst's birthday. The Chief was seventy-two now. Had the man broken the pattern Loorz had grown accustomed to—that of spending Christmas and his birthday at the ranch? He had indeed. He'd marked the occasion at the Beach House, where he and Marion Davies had planned to regale a big crowd on the weekend of April 27–28; but when Marion's father, Bernard Douras, died on April 26, the festivities had been cancelled.

Morgan, who early in 1935 had heard from Hearst about his forthcoming birthday,[63] had been in San Francisco most of that sad April weekend, pending her late-Sunday trip to San Luis and her visit with Loorz on Monday. (Naturally, she hadn't forgotten Hearst. "Nothing could have given me so much pleasure as the beautiful bronzes of my Mother you sent me as a birthday gift." So went the note Hearst wrote her on Tuesday, April 30.[64] Perhaps Willicombe laid it aside for hand-delivery, knowing that Morgan would be at the Beach House on Wednesday or Thursday.) Her trip to Santa Monica was for another go-round on its Service Wing —as distinct from the proposed and ultimately long-delayed work on Casa Grande's Service Wing.[65]

And then it was back to San Francisco—and then on to Wyntoon, where Morgan put in a Monday-Tuesday stint, May 6–7. Stolte, who'd been at Wyntoon the previous week but who'd since returned to Oakland, went north again for Morgan's visit. He wrote Loorz on Sunday the fifth, before leaving home; he told

---

63. In writing to Morgan in Europe (p. 161 in this chapter, plus its note 8, and p. 164, note 13), Hearst had said, "You and Miss [Alice] Head [of Hearst's National Magazine Company, London] can probably come over [to America] together. She is going to come over for my birthday party, and I would like to have you both there." From Hearst to Morgan, January 14, 1935; Hearst/Morgan Correspondence, Morgan Collection. The most recent costume bash at the Beach House—the Tyrolean party of October 21, 1934 (p. 141)—is sometimes assumed to have been a *birthday* party and, in turn, to have taken place in April 1935.

64. Hearst's letter of April 30, 1935, is from a file in the Morgan Collection that pertains to portrait plaques of Phoebe Apperson Hearst; see *Descriptive Guide to the Julia Morgan Collection*, p. 62 (under III/05/08/66). One could easily assume that Hearst was writing from San Simeon, for his letter bears a plainly designed heading: "La Cuesta Encantada," stacked above an equally plain "San Simeon, Cal." But in this instance he was using (or perhaps using up) old stationery. By 1935 his San Simeon letterhead had, for some time, been larger and bolder:

Office of
WILLIAM RANDOLPH HEARST
La Cuesta Encantada
San Simeon, California

65. See notes 49 and 59, above, regarding the Service Wing in Santa Monica. In contrast (but with minor exceptions), at least ten years passed before the Service Wing at San Simeon was enlarged. See pp. 510, 514, and 518 in this volume.

his partner, "We have about 60 men at McCloud, on various parts of the work."[66] (He also said the Reid job in San Luis sounded as if it were "going good," joshing with Loorz in the process. "How do you like contracting? Can you still TAKE IT.")

If Morgan and Stolte had stayed longer at Wyntoon (they both returned there a week later), they would have been on hand when a letter from Loorz arrived for Mac McClure, dated May 7 (in belated reply to Mac's letter of April 4):

> Well here we are in the center of another of the yearly rushes just like you are. Only yours is a lot bigger right now I guess. However, I am rushing the [Gothic Study] tower rooms with walnut [book] cases etc. Also there is a great rush down the hillside where they are making a 40 foot wide terrace. Another retaining wall that nears 20 feet at the highest point.[67] There wasn't enough unfinished area on the hilltop so we take in some more. However it will make the place look like a real entrance and they may yet use it for that. At present it is intended to be a pedestrian and equestrian entrance and walkway between tight rows of orange trees.

Loorz also said he'd "enjoyed working with Jud" — a reference to Jud Smelser, a man whom Mac knew well and whose letter-writing skills approached Mac's and George Wright's:

> I haven't had much chance to visit and get really acquainted with him but he really has been a lot of help handling the car situation [the chauffeuring]. He took a lot of the responsibility off my hands and did it to satisfaction. I suppose he has told you that I am now trying him out as a foreman on the road crew. I dont know

---

66. On May 1, Olin Weatherford of the Stolte Co. had written similar words for Loorz: "As you know we are going strong up at McCloud and Mr Stolte is putting practically all of his time to that job now." Weatherford also said, "But we still build Service Stations. There is four G.P. [General Petroleum] Stations coming out [for bid] in the next three weeks. We should take at least four of them."

67. This equates with the "Garden Wall" in Loorz's recap of April 29; see p. 185, plus its note 62. An irregular series of such walls demarcates most of the hilltop proper — an area recalled by old Hearst employees as having been "inside the wall." Adjacent areas like China Hill and Orchard Hill fell "outside the wall." The distinction, explained to me in the 1980s by the former gardener Pete Sebastian, was more than merely descriptive, more than evocative of San Simeon's likeness to an Old World hill town or walled city; the distinction stemmed mainly from the existence in Hearst's day of such entities as the Garden Department, the Household Department, the Construction Department, and so on. These in turn paralleled the existence of the Hilltop Fund and other building funds, mentioned at times in this volume.

When speaking of these "inside" or "outside" areas, Hearst himself used *walls* in the plural; that, in fact, may have been the more logical, more idiomatic form in the local tongue. See, for example, Hearst to Morgan, April 15, 1935; Hearst/Morgan Correspondence, Morgan Collection.

how he will work out or whether he will like it but he certainly seems to have the interest of the job at heart and is anxious to see things go, so I expect him to turn out O.K.[68]

On May 7 as well, Loorz wrote to Morgan, telling her about the Gothic Study and also about progress at the Neptune Pool. His letter clarified that the new terrace and retaining wall he described to Mac were going in just below the big West Terrace, which adjoins the pool area.

(The surface of the new "terrace" was merely hard-packed dirt, not concrete-and-tile work like that on the more formal terraces closer to Casa Grande and the three outlying houses. And yet Hearst didn't view the new terrace as a trifling feature. Back on April 11, before it was built, he had asked Loorz: "Could that terrace be carried around the northwest corner [partly encircling the Neptune Pool, like the brim of a hat] so as to join the north terrace?" Hearst probably didn't mean the huge North Terrace itself; he more likely meant the smaller terrace between there and the driveway. If laid out in staggered levels, in response to a rising slope, the new terrace could indeed have been extended—past the Neptune Pool and around to the north side of the hill. The job never gelled. True, a lean stretch of driveway, near the deep end of the Neptune Pool, could have proved daunting; but Morgan and others had overcome greater obstacles posed by Hearst. All it would take for the design, engineering, concrete work, and decorative touches was money.)[69]

Mac McClure had Loorz's letter of May 7 in hand by May 9, and he answered it from Wyntoon that same day, kidding Loorz for having been so mum:

---

68. Jud Smelser's name first appears in the Loorz Papers in 1934 (Mac McClure to Loorz, January 8; followed by George Wright to Loorz, October 1). In the earlier letter, Mac said Smelser was "an old acquaintance" of his "through a previous association in Los Angeles." (In fact, Smelser would tell Loorz on December 19, 1936, that by then he'd known Mac for a dozen years.) After starting as a laborer at Wyntoon in 1933, Smelser began helping Ed Hussey in September of that season; and then, as Mac explained early in 1934, "when Ed was sent away he fell into the book-keeping job." In other words, Hussey's return to Principia in October 1933 allowed Smelser to assume a new role at Wyntoon, a step hinting at the flexibility he would later provide under Loorz at San Simeon.

69. In writing to Morgan in 1936 (pp. 239–40 in this volume), Loorz called the new terrace "the West entrance." Thus its use as a prominent access might seem to have begun. But the cul-de-sac in the hilltop driveway (on the south side of the estate, just below Casa Grande) remained the preferred arrival and departure point for Hearst and his guests right through the 1940s. Indeed, Hearst's letter to Morgan (the one from 1935 cited in note 67) said the west staircase needn't be approachable by car but merely on foot and horseback.

All the while Hearst envisioned an imposing feature, sometimes called the Grand Entrance, with fountains and divided stairways on the north side of the hill (between the Neptune Pool and the Roman Pool: adjoining the North Terrace, with its axis crossing the smaller terrace that he was probably asking Loorz about on April 11, 1935). In fact, "grand entrance" appears in a letter Loorz wrote Morgan on August 29 that year—Hearst having used the term recently. But in that case Hearst was speaking more of the Neptune Pool area. In any event, little besides rough concrete work

The tables are turned! You take a long time in answering your correspondence while I do mine while they are still hot.

I am glad to know you are busy too. Miss Morgan usually drops a few hints about what is being done at the ranch and Santa Monica but the picture is still a trifle hazy. Yes—we are in it right up to our chins or rather over our eyes. I anticipate that from now until the arrival of W. R. there will be "no rest for the wicked." However I do see how we can, at least, have enough of the building done to accommodate them and that is really more than I sometimes hoped. The carved interiors are nearing something like completion and are fine, if I do say so.

J.M. has just left us after a typical visit. I have a list of notes,[70] mostly very small things, which we will have to get done "before Mr. H. thinks we are idiots,"—but all in all she is not too hard on us. If we could only do the essentials first and then do the "fiddling around later" it would be all right. However I suppose we will fiddle right up to the last week and then throw any thing together in any way, shape, or manner.

I am glad to know the "family" is well. I am also glad to hear (from J.M.) that you may come up later to build a bridge—we need the bridge and your moral support too.[71]

At San Simeon, the wet weather continued to hold sway. "We had another 4.83 inches of rain this last week and it certainly delays construction," Loorz told Hearst on May 10. "It is too wet to even start yet on the road.[72] We cannot get into

---

was ever completed in the North Terrace-Grand Entrance area (although most of the flanking smaller terrace, that narrow section closer to the driveway, was completed).

When the estate opened to the public in 1958, "the West entrance" that Loorz mentioned in 1936—and that Hearst referred to in 1935—finally came into its own. It figured as a starting point for tours of the grounds and buildings, a function it still has today. Then in the 1960s, with tours on the increase, the smaller terrace on the north side assumed a similar function.

70. As I suggested earlier (on p. 75, note 37), these memos to Mac were probably handwritten, unduplicated, and, for the most part, unsaved. For its part, the Morgan Collection at Cal Poly contains almost nothing of the kind.

71. Loorz's reply of May 29 (pp. 191–92) stated a position on Wyntoon that didn't change for him until 1938—that is, not until his six-year stay at San Simeon ended. Sara Boutelle, though, said he went to Wyntoon "to supervise whenever San Simeon work slowed down"; she did so in a context predating 1938 (see *Julia Morgan*, p. 219). Whence came the discrepancy? Probably from Loorz himself, who wrote to Mrs. Boutelle in 1975, when he was seventy-seven, summarizing (incorrectly in places) his work under Morgan from 1925 on. In referring to the Wyntoon of the mid-1930s, he accurately said that Fred Stolte "directed the construction" from Oakland. But in that same context he also said of Wyntoon: "I visited the job very often." From Loorz's pencil draft of the letter; courtesy of Don Loorz, May 29, 1990.

72. Loorz had told King Walters on February 27 that the crew had begun "cleaning out" the Burnett Road. But the late winter and spring rains could have drowned their efforts, even into May. Another possibility: Loorz was telling Hearst about a different road.

the beaches with our trucks to haul necessary gravel & sand for the warehouse foundation, pergola, wild duck pool [at the Chicken Ranch] or colonnades."

Loorz also told Hearst (who was briefly at San Simeon to meet Morgan on Saturday, May 11),[73] "In the meantime we are making fine headway with the tower rooms in the Study. They have been simplified as per your request and a few weeks should complete them." In addition, "We finished the small shelves for your midget books."

But rain or shine the show went on—or at least the correspondence did. Loorz wrote to Stolte right after Morgan's visit of the eleventh, a visit falling midway between her trips to Wyntoon in that first half of May:

> Miss Morgan was here yesterday and we had a very fine day. She was very happy even with Wyntoon. Mr. Hearst was just wonderful and I enjoyed talking to him in his room in his bathrobe at 9 P.M. last night after she left. He looks fine and is in [a] splendid mood. Very happy about their new connection [that he and Marion Davies have] with Warner Brothers Studio.[74] They are really enjoying making this picture [*Page Miss Glory*].
>
> Miss Morgan told me how they were getting behind in payments up there. I hope it has not become too much of a handicap. Down here with me I've already made them holler. Last week they asked me to rush a bit when I knew they could not afford to do it. They both knew I was right and I'm to go on as I see best.

The rapport Loorz had developed with Hearst and Morgan was almost uncanny. Few others in their employ had as deft a touch. With regard to Hearst himself and the work he wanted done at San Simeon, Loorz quoted him for Stolte in this same letter of Sunday, May 12: "He said, 'You just use your own judgment and give it to me when you think best.'"

HEARST WAS BACK AT SAN SIMEON for a much longer stay as of the next weekend, May 18–19. In turn, letters and memoranda began flowing Loorz's way through Colonel Willicombe. May 21 brought the following:

---

73. Hearst may have appeared on short notice, without many others in tow. Loorz's letter to him of May 10 was enclosed with another one dated May 10, addressed (and quite possibly sent) to Willicombe in Los Angeles.

74. Though less royal an arrangement than Hearst and Davies had had with MGM through 1934, their liaison with Warner Bros. was similar: the studio underwrote the Davies pictures (and other Cosmopolitan Productions of Hearst's); Hearst, for his part, provided the studio with story material and ample publicity through his media empire. The arrangement lasted till the beginning of 1939, briefly outliving the final four performances by Miss Davies, who retired in 1937 after a career that began twenty years earlier and comprised more than forty films.

Chief told me to-day to ask you to hurry the enlarging of the hangar, as the new plane will be here not later than the middle of June. . . .[75]

Chief asks if there was any way of lengthening the field. I said I understood that was unlikely on account of the drop at one end. He said he thought that could be filled in, also that you could "put in a great big sewer pipe—say six feet in diameter which would carry off the water," and work it out that way.

May 24 brought further word from on high:

I told Chief you were hot after the mosquitoes and in fact had been after them for ten days and would give them the final sock in [a] day or so. He said okey, never mind the expert [the exterminator]; but he suggested that we ought to start after them every year as soon as they start breeding, in fact before they have a chance to breed, and clean up and oil up to head them off. I suggest that you put them on your schedule for regular attention whether Chief is coming to ranch or not.[76]

Willicombe had a chance to catch up on other business when Hearst and Loorz inspected the Burnett Road on May 28; the next day, Loorz told Mac McClure about the trip:

I spent a good part of the afternoon yesterday with W.R. on a little drive to the Nacimiento [River]. Just the two of us and we became quite chummy before we got back. He hopes to fly up there [to Wyntoon] with Miss Morgan tomorrow.[77] If so, he'll be there before this reaches you. He is in a very good humor and may be so happy with the place that he will not change quite as much as you expect him to.

I think I can talk him out of the bridge trip as much as I would like to come up. I dont think the [Morgan] office would enjoy me making the trip for that pur-

---

75. In writing to Morgan on May 14, Loorz had posed a question. "Mr. Hearst, in view of the cost and shortage of funds, said that I should go ahead and lengthen the present hangar to receive the two large trimotors. This would cost about $2000. Shall I order the trusses & proceed right away?" His recap of Morgan's next visit, May 21 (coinciding with Willicombe's letter), gave the answer. "O.K. to order trusses & proceed with addition to Hangar."

76. Two years before (June 9, 1933), Willicombe had told Loorz, "There are mosquitoes on the hill for the first time in my recollection and Chief would like to stamp them out." Willicombe had also mentioned Frank Whitcomb, a man who knew the mosquito situation well: "He showed me one the other night as big as a hummingbird."

77. Morgan had just been to Wyntoon; the main Wyntoon (Waterhouse) account in Morgan-Forney cites her visit as "May 25–6–7." The sole mention of a flight in this period appears in the main San Simeon account, under May: "20th by plane," evidently stemming from her visit with Hearst and Loorz on May 21 (a visit otherwise unrecorded, both in the Morgan-Forney ledgers and in the similar series at Cal Poly: San Simeon Financial Records [III/03/07/111]).

pose.[78] Anyway, my [Nacimiento River] bridge stood over the winter and he thot it was O.K. when he saw it for the first time yesterday. I have built another the past week and will build a few more as we can afford it. Now that I have the cob-webs brushed away on my designing it goes pretty fast. With all the men I am working on the various units I have really very little time for figuring and designing, however.

The two small tower rooms [off the Gothic Study] look very well and are of course, quite similar to the Study [proper]. However, since Miss M. has not been here often and then only for a few minutes for me to consult with her I have done most of it according to an old sketch and my own guesses.[79] I suppose there will be a lot of "Idiots" around here when she sees them [the tower rooms] but I'm quite certain that Mr. Hearst likes them so we may not have to change them.

Energetic and verbose, Loorz had most of a second page to fill yet; part of his further outpouring on May 29 went like this:

Mac business on the outside looks a lot better. I'm going to try the Arroyo Grande School [through Louis Crawford], a P.W.A. job. If I come out O.K. I'll open an office right here and take on anything I can get within the surrounding country. I can employ a couple of good responsible men without shirking on this job. Now is the time to get started for there will be lots of money spent in the next few years and why should I wait. Maybe I'm ambitious and foolish for I really would like to take it easier. However, I feel that I can do it and make good so why not try. Then maybe I can quit this answering the whistle daily etc. . . .

I found Judd [Jud Smelser] to be almost indispensible to me in the capacity of head chauffeur or transportation manager so he's back on the job [instead of overseeing road work] and in the center of all scandal. No doubt he has told you about the latest — one of the kind that you can [imagine having] happen[ed].

Loorz's letter was enroute to Mac when Stolte sat down to peck out a few lines from Wyntoon on the evening of Thursday, May 30:

Just to let you know that we are still on the job here. We are laying floor in the Gables at 8:30 P.M. Also the painters are staining woodwork, so that we may be a little further completed for tomorrow. A rumor is around that Mr. Hearst is visiting tomorrow.

The power line is in good shape to finish. We are stringing wire, about 3 miles complete. Logs are being hauled to the mill, and [the] trench is being dug for the under ground cable. About a week should see juice on the line.

---

78. Instead, the job became Walter Huber's a year later (and, at $500, much more expensively so than his recent work for the "Garden Wall" at San Simeon; see note 62, above).

79. So far in 1935 Morgan had been at San Simeon on April 6, April 21–22, and April 29, followed by visits on May 11 and May 21.

George [Wright] and Harry [Thompson] have been working like Trojans in fact all the gang are going places.

Mac seems quite happy this year and is mixing some with the boys.

I have been here almost a week and still lots to do, however I surely enjoy the work. Always enough trouble to keep from getting lonesome????[80]

Stolte said more about Wyntoon on June 2. He told Loorz that the job up north was "running into quite an expenditure"—$40,000 or so having become the amount since late April. At this point the Reid job, recently completed in Loorz's territory, was easier to assess. As Stolte put it, "The job at San Luis has been quite a pleasant surprise in more ways than one. First, the profit and last but not least, that the Big Boy [Loorz] is still pretty good at [lump sum] contracting, and hasnt become a T & M [time and materials] contractor. Ha. Ha."

Apart from the challenge Loorz had enjoyed in tackling the Reid job, he and Stolte knew they needed to diversify more. Their Hearst-Morgan prospects had an uncertain aspect about them, at times an unnerving one. The partners recognized that they'd better push themselves hard for the sake of new ideas, new chances, new directions. Never mind the five- or six-hour drive that separated them; they could always rendezvous somewhere between their home bases. As Loorz told Stolte on June 4:

Miss Morgan will be down Thursday night [June 6, for a Friday visit][81] according to present plans so I wont be able to get away Friday but if it is more convenient and you cant make the trip down here I'll meet you in Salinas as stated, Saturday night. I've always stayed at the Franciscan Hotel there.

But make no mistake. Loorz's day job remained in a category all its own, and he still loved to share some of his unusual experiences with friends, colleagues, and loved ones. In writing to his parents on June 5, he gave them a further glimpse of the idolized San Simeon, that playground for Hollywood film stars and other notables who paid court to Mr. Hearst and his young chatelaine, Marion Davies:

Just a little interesting was the fact that I had to drive some guests yesterday in a hurry in my own car. They were George Hearst, Jean Harlow and Bill Powell.

---

80. Stolte had sent Loorz similar news on May 21. He mentioned having "75 men on the various jobs there." In particular, George Wright was "doing nicely on the power line" and Harry Thompson seemed to be enjoying "the rush." Stolte also reported, "We have gotten together a first class bunch of carpenters"—something "rather unusual for a quick selection." All of them seemed "to want to go places."

81. Entries for June 7–8 and June 22 appear in Morgan-Forney. But the Loorz Papers contain no recap notes from either of those visits. This same period saw Morgan at the Beach House on (or the day after) May 31, followed by two visits to Wyntoon, cited as June 4–5 and June 12–14.

They were very pleasant and full of fun. They had just returned from an aero-
plane flight. It happened to be Bill Powell's first plane ride. Miss Harlow said,
"That is a surprise." George said, "I'll tell you a surprise for you. The pilot on that
plane was the one that flew you to Arizona when you married your last husband."
She said, "He was? I thot he was familiar but I really didn't recognize him. What's
more he stood up with us." "Of course," she said, "he had on dark glasses but I
should have recognized the mustache."

Armed with his manual typewriter, Loorz wrote quickly, spontaneously, seldom tinkering with his letters before mailing them off. His recipients would know
well enough what he meant to say. And thus his recounting of George Hearst's and
Jean Harlow's words was sufficiently clear. Loorz concluded that passage by telling
his parents that Miss Harlow and William Powell seemed to be "very close friends."
Indeed they were. In fact, 1935 found them planning to marry. They remained engaged right up until Harlow died two years later at the tender age of twenty-six.

ON JUNE 12 Loorz informed Stolte that he hoped to make San Simeon—mostly
the Loorzes' house, that is—a branch office of the F. C. Stolte Co. "I actually feel
that we may do more business here than you will up there," said Loorz, "not counting the Hearst jobs, of course." He sought his partner's opinion.

Stolte replied from Wyntoon on June 14: things were "entirely satisfactory" in
his view. "I believe your chance[s] of profit are much better there than in Oakland.
So here's good luck to the branch office."[82] For a construction company that,
within ten or twelve years, would have several offices in the northern half of the
state, this was a strategic step. Innocent and hopeful on the one hand, bold and confident on the other.

What more impressive way for Loorz to operate that branch than to treat his
local associates to a tour of the Hearst place? "Why not make your first visit to the
hilltop here right soon?" he asked the Santa Maria architect Louis Crawford on
June 19:

> Any day would do and the earlier in the morning the better. We can see so much
> more before the guests start wandering about, about 11 A.M. Just let me know. I feel
> sure that you will want to see the place several times for there is a lot to it.

---

82. Since Stolte was at Wyntoon on June 14, his letter naturally contained the latest details.
"The job here at McCloud is still In Progress. Yesterday noon Miss Morgan said Mr. Hearst [who was
still at San Simeon] wanted the power line run to the wheeler place [The Bend, downstream from
The Gables] also some remodeling. We have about 95 men on the payroll and it sure keeps a fellow
out of mischief."

Stolte also had some troubling news. "We have been keeping the payroll up to date but the bills
are piling up. I have not bothered Miss Morgan for I know she feels or rather knows the financial
situation. They are about 5 weeks behind."

Crawford's jaw must have dropped when he read that. And surely he must have jumped at the chance, although the Loorz Papers contain no evidence that he did.

The Public Works Administration that Loorz, Crawford, and others in the building industry were tapping into was of course a brainchild of the Roosevelt Administration—the very administration Hearst had helped put in the White House in 1932 but had since begun to decry. Ironically, the same day Loorz invited Crawford to San Simeon, June 19, President Roosevelt took Congressional action that soon led to the Federal Revenue Act of 1935, or the "wealth tax." He thus added insult to injury for the lordly Hearst, California's new Personal Income Tax having been approved by Governor Merriam on June 13. Roosevelt was, in effect, pointing a finger at Hearst, who was already passing through one of the most heated stretches in his picturesque, often stormy life. (Hearst's interview with Adolf Hitler in August 1934 had backfired badly on the old newspaperman, with lasting repercussions; his dread of Communism was also backfiring. Skeptics would long scoff at Hearst's die-hard "Americanism," saying it was merely a cynical, elitist subterfuge, a synonym for fascism, anti-intellectualism, and other unsavory *isms* of a troubled era.)[83] The gradual rift between Roosevelt and Hearst, many months now in appearing, quickly deepened once the Revenue Act was passed. The Hearst press railed against the Roosevelt Administration and the New Deal as never before.[84]

---

83. An early example of that criticism can be found in Raymond Gram Swing's *Forerunners of American Fascism* (New York, 1935). And yet its chapter denouncing Hearst (pp. 134–52) was civil compared with Ferdinand Lundberg's foreboding words of 1936 throughout *Imperial Hearst: A Social Biography*. Lundberg's final sentence (p. 381) echoed down the years, providing a sacred hymn for many a nay-sayer: "The truth can make us free, and the truth about Hearst can expose, deflate and destroy a man who would doom this country to the death that inheres in political reaction, whether manifested as outright fascism, or concealed in the guise of Americanism, rugged individualism, or other demagogic appeals."

84. June 19 found Hearst preparing for battle in another way: by clamping down on local predators—unpolitical ones in this case. Willicombe explained the matter to Loorz:

Chief says he knows this is not the time when coyote skins are good; but he will give any of the boys [ranch hands, workmen, etc.] that want to shoot coyotes or trap them or poison them, five dollars per coyote, and they can keep the skins.

Of course Chief does not want to let anybody and everybody go trapping and shooting and poisoning around the ranch.

He would want you to pass on the ability and reliability of applications for permits to shoot or trap or poison the varmints.

But mainly, he would like to encourage the boys to get out and slay all of the coyotes they can; and if you do not think five dollars a head is enough, please make a suggestion as to the right reward, as Chief will even pay ten dollars if necessary.

Willicombe asked Loorz to talk with him about it the next day — or, if he got the chance, with Hearst himself. Loorz went on to recruit two trustworthy men who thought the five-dollar bounty

Loorz, meanwhile, may have supported Upton Sinclair's recent bid for California's highest office, yet he seemed as inclined as Hearst was to lampoon the powers in Washington. On June 27 Loorz heard from Colonel Willicombe. "I am returning the New Deal statistics," said Hearst's secretary, "which are very funny. Thanks for giving me a look at them":

Population of U.S.	124,000,000
Eligible for Townsend Pension	50,000,000
Balance	74,000,000
Prohibited from working under Child Act and Working for the Government	60,000,000
Balance	14,000,000
Unemployed	13,999,998
Leaving to produce all the Nation's Goods	2

YOU and ME—and I'M ALL TIRED OUT.

Loorz and Willicombe's chuckle came a few days before Hearst began his long-anticipated stay at Wyntoon—the "big long party at Wyntoon" that Fred Stolte, Mac McClure, George Wright, Harry Thompson, and the rest of the crew had been scrambling to get ready for all season.[85]

"Am taking a few minutes off for a breathing spell and in order to get my mind off this hectic whirl I will drop you a few lines." Those were Mac's opening words when he wrote Loorz a letter marked "Wyntoon—Sat eve" (most likely indicating June 29):[86]

F. C. [Stolte] is here and doing his darnedest to get things ready for the visit. As far as we know the chief arrives tomorrow but I feel that he will not for another day or two.

This last week has been one of the worst I have ever put in. Personally I do not

---

was fine; they were also given room and board in Hearst Camp. Pity the poor coyotes. By the end of 1935, "Trapping & Furs" in Loorz's breakdown of the Hilltop Fund stood at $2,471. In the meantime, Willicombe wired Loorz an update, from Wyntoon no less, on August 17: "Chief instructs remove traps off road and sides of road [at San Simeon] or somebody will get injured and sue Chief and you too. Chief asked you give this your prompt attention."

85. The quoted words come from a longer passage: "The chief plans on a big long party at Wyntoon this summer and I dont know whether or not I will have anything to do with it." From Loorz to Mickey Brennan, April 5, 1935 (misdated March 5, along with another letter in that stretch).

86. Morgan was now halfway through her longest visit to Wyntoon in 1935 (June 25–July 3 in Morgan-Forney), a factor that, along with other evidence, virtually confirms June 29 as the missing date on Mac's letter.

think it worth such an effort. We have worked until midnight for five nights running—and now as I write this I can see J.M. tugging and lugging porch and lawn
chairs herself, but I am too tired and calloused to go out and either stop her or
help her. All of the rooms have been furnished and refurnished about four
times—curtains changed and rugs rolled out and rolled up again until we were
cock-eyed—So let the Chief come soon, says I—at least it will put a stop to this,
whatever else may be in store for us. We had a full car load of antiques arrive today [by train] and J.M. and I spent the entire day at the depot at McCloud personally investigating the subtle colors of rugs etc[87]—while our furniture movers
sat on their fannys at the job because there was no one to direct them—Of course
when she came out at four o'clock she was wrathy because so little had been done.

For two or three days I have been biting my lips and counting [to] ten to keep
from expressing myself but have managed to keep silent so far. Perhaps if we can
get through this the next [time] will not be so bad.—If she would only allow us to
do our stuff and plan our own work and program.

Well Geo—don't think this is "getting me down" because after all we may
only work until midnight again and then we can have the rest of Saturday off—
Whee!

Mac was indeed weary—he wasn't exaggerating when he described the long
hours the crew had been working. The electrician Louis Schallich told a similar
tale in writing to Loorz on July 8, a few days after Hearst and his party arrived:

Should have written you a letter from here before but in the past month this place
has been a mad house. We have been working day and night and everyday. . . .

As usual the most important work on the project has been the plumbing and
steam work. Same old Rankin still talks with his hands. He is the most kidded
man on the job and has to like it. "Society Jim" is his new nick name.

The guests are about the same as at San Simeon and act about the same also.

Saturday evening [July 6] Miss Davies had a theater party showing her latest
picture at Dunsmuir.[88] All the guests Mr. Hearst etc. were there. The whole town
was lined up before the theater to get an eye full of the movies people. This was a
treat to the home folks but to us it was just another picture. . . .

---

87. Since 1920, Hearst's shipments of antiques and furnishings to California from New York
(the center of his collecting) had primarily been by train. The freight cars bearing these goods—
mostly for San Simeon—were called the 1st Carload, the 2nd Carload, and so on through the 1920s,
during which nearly sixty carloads arrived in California; in 1935, from May onward, the 86th
through the 90th carloads headed west—mostly in behalf of Wyntoon. They contained many Germanic items, a staple at that estate, and also Early American items, in keeping with a secondary
theme. One of these shipments, the 88th Carload, included Persian rugs and carpets, probably the
very ones Mac mentioned in his letter.

88. Evidently a private preview of *Page Miss Glory.*

No doubt, with the big pay roll up here, it has cut your force down at San Simeon. . . .

. . . Fishing is good but only about two guests enjoy it. The rest lay around sun bathing at the pool.

We are working now from 10 AM. until 630 P. which are nice hours after a month of from 7 AM. until midnight.

Things *had* slowed down at San Simeon, enough for the sculptor L. Cardini, for instance, to relax at Adams Springs in Lake County, north of San Francisco. "I have good time here in the mountain," he wrote on a postcard Loorz received in early July.

Loorz nonetheless had plenty of things to do.[89] There were always letters to write and outside jobs to figure in addition to supervising the work that crept along at San Simeon.[90] One of his letters went out to Stolte on July 11:

After talking with you about the Wyntoon accounts and going over the books I found it hard to sleep. Especially when I hadn't even paid my men for five weeks down here. Therefore, I told Miss Morgan with tears in my eyes that we couldn't do it.[91] We'd either have to have cash right away or shut down. There was no use waiting as much as I dislike saying it. But since the most they can give you is $15,000 per month, it would take 4 months for them to pay up if you didn't do 1¢ of work during that period.

She agreed with me and shook my hand sympathetically. She said, she didn't dream it was that much behind or she wouldn't have allowed it. So she wrote to

89. At 4:00 P.M. on July 8, Hearst's valet, Joseph Yelinek, wired Loorz from Wyntoon. "Please look around and also ask Mrs. Albert [Augusta Redelsperger, the head housekeeper] to look in [Gothic?] Sitting Room, Mr. Hearst's [South Gothic] Bedroom or in the Studio [the Architect's Office?] for Drawings of Wyntoon. You better go with her to identify them."

90. The Stolte regular Olin Weatherford joshed with Loorz in late June. "Say whats the matter with you? Havent you enough work to do at the Ranch, without going out and contracting on the side? Will have to report you to Mr H."

91. Loorz had given his men four days off, Thursday through Sunday, July 4–7, partly to reduce his backlogged payroll. He was in the Bay Area over that long weekend, and he stayed till Tuesday the ninth. He saw Morgan in San Francisco—sometime after a trip she made to the Beach House (July 6 in Morgan-Forney, a week before she returned to Wyntoon for the July 12–14 period).

Morgan had been back from Europe for more than three months now. Meanwhile, she'd left the Bay Area for the sake of her Hearst accounts only, a pattern she maintained till the end of the year. She pursued her largest non-Hearst account in 1935—the Homelani Columbarium in Hilo, Hawaii—*in absentia*, and she continued to into 1936. Early that year she enlisted Bjarne Dahl (who had remained in Honolulu after working on her YWCA building in the 1920s) to inspect the job in Hilo.

see what Mr. Hearst wished to do about it without quoting us at all.[92] There is
no reason why he cannot give her a lump sum as has been promised for some
time.

Loorz next mentioned a job that the Stolte Co. would be doing for Morgan—
their first for her in 1935 aside from the work at Wyntoon. (To some degree, the
company's recent efforts around San Luis Obispo may have stemmed from her
long absence in Europe.) The job coming up was on Morgan's home turf: her alteration of the Edward C. Bull residence on Union Street in San Francisco.[93]

These smaller, more workaday jobs prompted Loorz to tell Stolte (in that same
letter of July 11):

> Fred I think the depression is over. I think we should go back on [union] scale. I
> think we ought to try to work in some young carpenters for foremen. I think we
> ought to try to get both the Corlett job and the Clark job which are close together.
> I looked at the sites and buildings and though they are alterations I'm not afraid
> of them and I think we can make a little as we always have. . . .
>
> I think it would be better to chuck Wyntoon unless one or both of us are there
> [in Oakland] to give personal attention to all of our clients. . . . I know local Ar-
> chitects think we have too much business to give proper attention or service and
> maybe they are right. Wyntoon might die tomorrow but the building business is
> going to be bigger and better right now and for some time to come. Maybe I'm
> too enthusiastic but in that case it is fun to be wrong.

The "Corlett job and the Clark job" referred to Will Corlett and to Birge
Clark, both of whom were Bay Area architects. Corlett's Theta Chi Chapter House
at Stanford University in Palo Alto was out for bid and so was Clark's Phi Delta
Gamma House, likewise at Stanford. The F. C. Stolte Co. was the low bidder on the
Corlett job and may also have been on the Clark job.[94]

Stolte wrote to Loorz on Tuesday, July 16, the same day the bids were opened
on the Corlett job: "Harry phoned last eve and said Mr. Hearst wanted a 13 room
addition to [The] Gables to start [next] Monday." He assured Loorz he would see
to it that Hearst came forward "with a substantial payment" before any such work
was undertaken.

Loorz was also at the typewriter on July 16, corresponding with Jud Smelser

92. Typical of its thinness through the mid- and late thirties, the Hearst/Morgan Correspondence in the Morgan Collection skips from July 9 to August 12, 1935.

93. See Boutelle, p. 262 (cited under 1935 in the appendix "Buildings by Julia Morgan").

94. Birge Clark had designed part of the Menlo School and Junior College (now called Menlo
College); it was built in Atherton, next to Menlo Park, by the Stolte Co. in 1931—a job Loorz likened
to the one coming up in Arroyo Grande through Lou Crawford.

at Wyntoon. Smelser, who'd recently mastered the fine art of chauffeuring at San Simeon, had gone north with the Hearst party to ply his trade. Loorz was predictably himself in telling his new friend, "It really is lonesome here with the gang all gone and, oh boy, hotter than hell." Yet Smelser was down-home enough, and rakish enough, to deserve more. Loorz rose to the occasion:

> Would love to sit in [on] a good bull fest with you and Mac. When we got down to real dirt I'd have to listen which is not my natural habit. I've been too busy to hear any dirt since the night the queen went down the hill hoping to wet her whistle at Sebastian's.

Surely he didn't mean *Miss Davies*. No — surely he *did*. Not quite thirty-seven, Loorz was still cocksure enough to tell a ribald tale out of school. And so was the outwardly cautious Mac McClure, soon to be thirty-eight (the same age as the queen herself). And so, too, were Jud Smelser and several others in this rarest of circles. If only the houses by San Simeon Bay had walls that could talk! The Loorzes' old home could easily be the spiciest one of all.

On July 20, Loorz hammered out another one of his richly detailed letters to Arch Parks in Gilroy:

> Wyntoon has proved quite a nice job but — as usual — we let them get into us for many many thousand and now we are holding the sack. They just rushed the place like mad for two months getting ready for the chief without regard for the amount being spent. So it was just close to 60 grand ten days ago when I went up to the city [Oakland] and checked over our books. . . .
>
> We are leveling the airport [at San Simeon]. You remember the two bumps at each end of the main runway, well we are making the whole field nearly level. We intend to move about 50,000 yards of earth before we finish. We bought a 50 diesel caterpillar and an 8 yard carryall and does it move dirt. I have just three men working. One skinner works from 4 A.M. until noon and then one works until 8 P.M. The foreman works during the 8 hrs of the day, sets all stakes and directs and uses the road cat to rip up the surface for the carryall.[95]

---

95. The airport project shows how closely linked "Miss Morgan's work" and the non-Morgan type could be. As Loorz told Willicombe on July 29:

> This will advise you that both the original Hangar and the recent addition to it were paid, or will be, from Miss Morgan's Funds [the Hearst Construction Fund]. This was definitely agreed upon by both Miss Morgan and Mr. Hearst.
>
> For your information, all of the lighting, grading and the present grading & surfacing have been handled [in contrast] thru the revolving fund [the Hilltop Fund]. Miss Morgan had no objection to the grading etc being handled this way but did want the building part [the hangar] to come thru her office.

In this instance the hangar was properly an architectural matter, which warranted her involvement (and thus affected her commission).

Loorz wrote that same day, July 20, to Louis Schallich, who was back in San Francisco after his stint at Wyntoon:

> By golly Louis we are certainly cut down to rock bottom at this place. Pete [Petersen] is the only carpenter on the hill. Gyorgy has been off for a month or more. Val George[s] is gone and only about half the labor crew [is still here].
>
> . . . If there was anything doing I certainly would send for you and will do so if they go ahead with the [Roman] pool lighting.[96] They seem to have spent all of the money at Wyntoon. . . .
>
> This place is certainly lonesome, nothing going on in the Castle at all. Just working on retaining walls below [the] west terrace and finishing up the colonnade balustrade and paving [at the Neptune Pool]. With a small crew it certainly goes slowly. . . .
>
> Oh yes, since they kicked Jimmie out at Wyntoon he says he will be down here Monday [July 22] to install the new burner in the donkey boiler. So I'll hear all about the dope at Wyntoon and find out whether you really behaved or not. I'll know all about it first hand. I'm greasing up my arms so that I can talk his language.

Loorz wrote to Mac McClure on July 22, telling him that "Smiling Jimmie" Rankin had indeed arrived at San Simeon that morning. "Now that we have someone to kid we are O.K.," said Loorz. "Ought to be lots of fun after the quietude that has prevailed around here for the past two weeks. Honest it seems like a morgue. Even worse for the stiffs in a morgue don't complain of heat,[97] work, slow pay etc."

In signing off, Loorz stated his position on his outside work in the local area, after which he closed with some words about Wyntoon—and about Hearst:

> The net result is that I'll be away from here once in a while and they might tire of that, if so, I'll be numbered among the missing. I cannot lose the opportunity when it presents itself, especially when this job [at San Simeon] as you know is from month to month. No telling when the axe will fall, deserving or not. It has done so before and may repeat anytime.
>
> Mac, say hello to Jud, Harry and all the boys for me and keep me posted about the temperature of our chief. Let me know when the plane leaves the ground with him in it and I'll then expect him.

WHEN LOORZ'S WIFE and three sons went to Nevada that July, Loorz invited Carl Daniels to stay with him. Daniels had supervised the Reid job in San Luis Obispo

---

96. Was Schallich's scheme of May 31 in the offing? It may have been; see note 60, above.

97. Hot weather, mentioned in the Loorz Papers in several places, descends on The Enchanted Hill at times from late spring through early fall—as it does on similar elevations in California's southern Coast Ranges—with temperatures often measuring twenty or more degrees higher than those along the coastal plain.

for the F. C. Stolte Co. and was about to start the Arroyo Grande Grammar School. Loorz mentioned Carl Daniels in writing to his family on August 1 — and he mentioned a good deal more in the same letter:

> Carl came in shortly after I got home last night and I suggested we go to the pines [The Pines Cafe, at the Cambria Pines Lodge]. We did and found it to be the yearly banquet of the Chamber of Commerce that we attended last year. They insisted that we eat with them and worse, they called upon me as Mr. Hearst's Superintendent to say something about Mr. Hearst or his place. Oh boy, it was the wrong time to ask me to say anything for it was the most remote thing from my mind. Then too I had overheard Mr. [L. O.] Fox and others talking in undertones about how Mr. Hearst didn't pay much taxes etc and I was really peevish.[98]
>
> I merely got up and thanked them for the compliment and said that "Being connected to Mr. Hearst's organization as I am, I hear so much about him and even overheard remarks this evening that [would] concern him. I'm not going to take time to tell you of his many fine qualities for it [is] too serious for [an] evening such as this. I will only say that I wish you could know him as I know him and I'm certain you would feel the same as I do. Not because I look to him for my support and livelihood for my own business nets me more but in several years of association I have always known him to be a perfect gentleman."
>
> The second I started I knew I had hit an unusually serious key as their faces registered it plainly. When I sat down I almost regretted that I had mentioned it for there was none of the laughter that had been prevalent. 'Twas only for a moment and Doc Lowell [Dr. Frank Lowell], chairman, said "Mr. Loorz is perfectly right. I too know him well and I cannot say too much for Mr. Hearst as a man and as a real value to this community." He said it beautifully and it was impressive. . . .
>
> At the conclusion of the banquet several strangers came to me and even shook my hand and said they were glad to hear me say what I did.

Loorz and Daniels were asked to dinner by several of their neighbors in San Simeon that August, as Loorz told his wife early on Tuesday the sixth:

---

98. Fox and other Cambrians had no doubt read news dispatches like the Associated Press item from Sacramento dated April 19, 1935 (here as printed by *The New York Times* on April 20, p. 17): "THREAT TO CALL HEARST. California Income Tax Bill Author Assails Publisher." The assailant was Ford A. Chatters, whose proposed tax measure had recently gained the state assembly's resounding support. (It was the same measure that Governor Merriam approved on June 13; see p. 195 in this chapter.) Predictably, the measure had been opposed by Hearst and certain other Californians, among them the novelist Kathleen Norris and her husband (both were longtime Hearst loyalists).

The dispatch quoted Assemblyman Chatters as having told his fellow lawmakers about the "deliberate and persistent campaign conducted by the Hearst papers against the income tax measure." Chatters also told them, "There has been the grossest kind of misrepresentation and if these

Well the entertainment still goes on. Last night Bud [Sweeters] invited us over to a venison barbecue out on the point [at San Simeon Bay]. We didn't go out until 7 PM and they were just ready to eat. Lots of good meat, salad, chili beans and pie. It was very good and Carl and I ate ravenously. Then we sat around the fire and talked aeroplanes and hunting, then John Reilly[99] got his mouth organ and Bud the guitar and they entertained us for an hour and we went home.

I expect Miss Morgan today. Wish I had more completed to show her but I just can't do it with the number of men I have at present. She wants as much as possible to show Mr. Hearst when he returns [from Wyntoon] which may be very soon.

At a glance, it seems odd that Loorz thought Morgan would be at San Simeon on August 6. He'd written to her on August 1, following her visit of July 30. (Before that, she'd last been at San Simeon on July 17; in between those visits, she'd gone to Wyntoon and, a few days later, to the Beach House.) But her reply to Loorz of August 3—identified only as "Sat. P.M."—may not have reached him yet. Part of Morgan's handwritten letter said, "Mr Hearst writes he expects to come down for a picture and then return to Wyntoon. We are not completed at Santa Monica, but the kitchens etc can be *usable* on short order—I will be up there Monday." Up at Wyntoon, that is, for two days starting on August 5, as the Morgan-Forney records show.[100] As for the more elusive details (go *where* exactly for *which* picture under *what* circumstances?), we should be glad that vagueness is the exception in the Loorz Papers, not the rule.

With that latest trip to Wyntoon behind her, Morgan wrote to Loorz from San Francisco on August 7 (her letter was handwritten once more, but this time it was a good deal easier to follow): "Mr Hearst says he would *very much* like to see 'something different' on the Hill when he gets back—I told him I did not see how he could expect anything *excitingly different*, given our program, but that we were steadily pushing the [Neptune] pool area."

Hearst's version of what Morgan told Loorz was contained in a memo from Colonel Willicombe, sent from Wyntoon on August 8: "Chief instructed me to-day to send you a reminder that when you finish the airport, he does not want any more road building or fence making or other added expense incurred, but to confine op-

---

tactics are continued I propose that we bring Hearst here [by subpoena to Sacramento], as well as the Norrises, and let them advise us as to those statements."

99. A waiter in the Hearst Camp dining room and the brother of Joe Reilly, a night watchman on the hilltop.

100. Morgan's letter is datable not only as August 3 but also as August 24; if the twenty-fourth applies, then her trip to Wyntoon would equate with the "Aug 26" in Morgan-Forney (her second appearance there that month). However, August 3 for the letter (followed by August 5–6 for the Wyntoon visit) seems likelier. Uncertainty haunts the Loorz Papers through much of August 1935.

erations to the regular program, including the pergola as part of that program."
Another instance of mixed signals? Perhaps it was. If so, Loorz wasn't unduly surprised.[101]

Loorz concluded a birthday letter to his mother on Monday, August 12, with
these words:

> It is very hot here on the hilltop but not like it is there [in Nevada] I suppose. You
> feel it just as much though since it is so damp. But it is always nice when I drive
> down home to San Simeon. It was just simply a perfect day yesterday. Hundreds
> of people were out on the beach and pier and in boats.[102] We seldom have very
> many way up here on this coast. I can expect a lot of company when that road fi-
> nally gets thru.

The road Loorz meant was the coast highway from San Simeon to Carmel,
perched along the steep slopes of the Santa Lucia Range through the Big Sur country. Its construction had been continual since the early 1920s (echoing Hearst's protracted efforts at San Simeon); and though the bridging of a last few canyons remained to be done, the road was open by 1935 to local traffic as far north as Big
Creek, halfway to Carmel. Loorz and Carl Daniels had a harrowing experience
while driving on that twisting route one evening — near Pacific Valley on August
7 — as Loorz recounted for Stolte and others over the next couple of days. He told
Stolte on August 9:

> Now for the thriller, night before last we went up the coast (50 miles) to do a gratis
> job. The Women's Club of Cambria are going to erect a memorial to the senator

---

101. He was quite surprised, though, by an earlier memo from Willicombe, dated August 5, in
which the Colonel said:

> I got hell for those notes issued in the purchase of some of your equipment. But it is all right
> now. The main thing is NEVER USE THE CHIEF'S NAME FOR NOTES, IN FACT
> FOR ANYTHING, without checking back and getting an okey.
>   What might seem harmless to you or someone else still might have great significance. How-
> ever, in this case, ALL'S WELL THAT ENDS WELL.

Willicombe also showed Loorz a memo he had sent that same day to "Jack" (John Francis
Neylan), the attorney who once doubled as Hearst's iron-fisted controller in San Francisco. The
"misunderstanding," Willicombe assured Neylan, would "not occur again."
    Loorz had a different version, which he sent to Mac McClure at Wyntoon on August 22: "I
have received several polite little bawl-outs via Willicombe since he has been up there but I haven't
even answered one of them" — like the one about "signing a note" that had "definitely" been approved by the high command before Neylan blew the whistle. Loorz spoke of himself as faring poorly
in these situations: "George becomes the goat."
    102. The pier was distinct from the one at the far leeward end of San Simeon Bay, built in the
1950s and still in use. The old pier dated from the 1870s and stood next to Hearst's warehouses, closer

responsible for getting this coast road started and asked me if I would visit the site and make a working drawing out of their sketches.

Well coming back about 8:30 at about 40 miles per hour in low ratio, as we rounded a slight curve a couple of horses loose on the road, were startled by our headlights & one jumped right out in front of the machine. Carl was driving. He put on the brakes & veered to the left to try to miss him, which he did but we were then headed for and only a few feet from an embankment. So he jerked the wheel to the right as hard as he could to pull back, it came back alright but it was too sharp and with new tires on the rear that wouldn't slide, over we went.

Now, here's one for the records. We turned completely over until we were right side up. We got out kicked the glass off the road turned around and were on our way home in less than three minutes.

Needless to say, they weren't wearing seatbelts. In any event, the Rigdon Memorial Park that Loorz designed was established in honor of State Senator Elmer Rigdon of Cambria, the "Father of the Roosevelt Highway." (The Roosevelt Highway has since become the Cabrillo Highway or, more simply, State Highway 1.) The Rigdon Memorial is a mile south of Big Creek, alongside a rivulet the Women's Club named "El Senator Creek." A drinking fountain and a small grove of trees mark the spot today.

Miss Morgan was among those that Loorz told about the episode in Pacific Valley. She hastened to reply with another of her handwritten "Sat. P.M." letters, this one datable as August 10:

> That accident makes ones hair rise up! Am most thankful no harm was done — It just was not your hour.

She went on to mention a new phase of work, a long-awaited phase — the surfacing of the big West Terrace, a job also pending for the contiguous levels closer to the Neptune Pool:

> A terrace general pavement layout is about ready, but would like to see it rough sketched in place. Jack [Wagenet] will mail a copy down Monday [August 12] as I just find no print has been made yet.
>
> Will get the figures on [green serpentine] "stars" first of week from the Vermont Marble Co.
>
> Will try to work out some less expensive finish for [the flooring of?] the [Roman] Temple — to discuss at least.
>
> The sum total of effort *ought* to look like a change to Mr Hearst on his return.

---

to San Simeon Point; although long dismantled, the old pier left traces of its pilings, visible at low tide on winter afternoons.

Morgan closed by saying, "I am going to make L.A. [Santa Monica] Wednesday [August 14] & Ranch Thursday."[103]

In the realm of "outside" jobs, another prospect had recently come to Loorz's attention: the Santa Ynez Valley Union High School, designed by E. Keith Lockard of Santa Barbara. Loorz heard about the job from a hardware supplier but too late to submit a bid. "We are now operating from Mr. Hearst's place at McCloud," he told the hardware man on August 13,[104] "to Arroyo Grande. Now that we have opened an office here [in San Luis Obispo County] we might figure as far south as Santa Maria but not further, I believe." Lockard was also the designer of Santa Maria Junior College, a job Loorz would land in 1936. And by then Santa Maria would no longer mark the southernmost range of the new San Simeon branch. Instead, the distinction would fall to Lompoc, a town nearly as far into neighboring Santa Barbara County as Santa Ynez—roughly a hundred miles from Loorz's home base.[105]

HEARST AND HIS PARTY remained at Wyntoon throughout July and well into August. Mac McClure gave Loorz another inside glimpse from that estate on August 15 (complete with more misspellings than he normally made):

No doubt you are pretty well informed on "news from the firing line" however here is my contribution, for what it may be worth.[106]

This has been a very tough session and apparently it isn't getting much better. My duties are so numerous and involves so many angles that I am about swamped

---

103. The entries for "Travel" in the Morgan-Forney ledgers indicate either the day (or days) spent on a given job or the day spent en route. No hard and fast rule exists. The Beach House visit Morgan spoke of yielded an "Aug 13" (the day before she appeared); the San Simeon visit yielded an "Aug 15" (the day she was actually on hand).

104. Loorz also wrote that day to the architect Lockard, who was seeking bids for another job—a "Paso Robles Ranch House." Loorz told him, "We will be pleased to figure your job and assure you that homes are our specialty. We took the school [Arroyo Grande] only because there are not a lot of fine residences being built just now."

105. But only on paper would Loorz gain a brief toehold in Lompoc. The Veterans Memorial Building in that town—"a fairly plain reinforced concrete job," as Loorz told Stolte on January 16, 1936—was soon awarded to another builder. From "F.C.S. [F. C. Stolte Co.] 1936"—one of three boxes appended in 1990 to the main body of the Loorz Papers; see p. 26, note 13, and p. 233, note 2.

Loorz ranged almost that far in working on—not just in bidding on—the Los Alamos School, one valley north of Lompoc. Otherwise, he confined his southernmost efforts to the Santa Maria area. (Los Alamos figures in Hearstiana as well: in the mid-twenties, while driving to San Simeon, Hearst and Adela Rogers St. Johns stopped at a roadside diner in that little town, an episode recalled long afterward by St. Johns in *The Honeycomb*, p. 127.)

106. If a letter that Jud Smelser wrote Loorz on August 14 went out promptly, Loorz was indeed up to date—at least on gossip: "Mama & Papa [Marion Davies and Hearst] quarreled all night last night and this A.M. we had orders to pack but they have since been cancelled."

trying to keep up with them. The ware-housing is assuming large proportions, and I wonder very much how I am going to keep the cataloging, etc ahead of the arrivals. (Our fourth carload is on its way I understand.)[107]

Our main activity, at present, is planning future work. As usual, all sorts of pretentious schemes are being worked out, and before I am half through with one, a new idea is sprung.

The worst condition to face is the necessity of doing practically nothing in the face of constant orders [from Hearst] to start this or that project "immediately." These orders are usually followed up by petulant enquirys as to "why we didn't get some men and get things moving." I have resolved to make no mention of finance to him and apparently whatever anyone else may have said has had little effect. I hate to have him think I am ineffectual and stalling when the real reason for non-action is something else, however.

Just now we are starting a large terrace development at The Gables. It is a large project and will take time and money (perhaps $20,000). Mr. H. insisted we start now and at Miss M.'s suggestion we are using [caretaker Eugene] Kower's road crew and funds for part of the work. I am not too sure this will be a successful arrangement.

In general, however, we are worrying through in some way or another and I imagine everything will work out without too much trouble. There is no sign of a break yet as far as the party leaving is concerned.

Last night Hans & Fritz (the dogs Jud [Smelser] brought up) got badly stuck with porcupine quills which caused more furore and "noise" than when Gandi [Gandhi, a dachsund belonging to Marion Davies] got caught in the trap last winter.

Speaking of Jud, it surely was a surprise to see him back again. Perhaps it would have been just as well if things had been allowed to cool down naturally. Mrs K[ower] is a very nervous and irrational woman (when arroused) and I am a little afraid of her.[108]

It's a great life and as J.M. says a sense of humor is a valuable asset. Sometimes I think she is very much fed up with the out fit too.

---

107. What Mac called the fourth carload may well have equated (in the larger scheme of things) with the 89th Carload out of New York, a potpourri of roughly one hundred examples of Early American furniture and about twenty examples of German decorative arts. A warehouse in Mount Shasta, a town on the main highway between Dunsmuir and McCloud, held surplus items from this shipment and others like it.

108. Smelser and Mrs. Kower had come to blows soon after the Hearst party arrived at Wyntoon in July. Besides, as Smelser had said of her, "She doesn't like Mac"—this from an undated letter to Loorz that month. "Says he is a red & communist etc. So that's the reason I know she was laying for me." Loorz sympathized. On July 25 he told Smelser that Morgan had indicated she was "not too proud of her appointment" of the Kowers.

Smelser had avoided dismissal through the good offices of Willicombe and, ultimately, Hearst—as Loorz learned in a letter Smelser wrote on August 9. Smelser's next letter to Loorz

It was during that summer of 1935, while Hearst and his party were in residence, that *Fortune* magazine prepared a feature that remains one of the most detailed portrayals of Wyntoon in printed form. Entitled simply "Hearst," the feature appeared in October 1935, replete with photographs and text—and, plausibly at first glance, with claims that the Hearst empire was financially as sound as could be.[109] (Critics said the feature had been concocted to keep investors bullish on Hearst stock, lest the man's Depression-weary finances decline even further.) One photograph showed Hearst lounging in a garden chair, the very kind of chair Mac had watched Morgan lug about while writing his late-evening letter to Loorz on June 29. Contrived or otherwise, the *Fortune* feature remains an invaluable fund of information on Wyntoon, surpassed only by the George Loorz Papers and, along with them, the Morgan-Forney Collection.

Loorz answered Mac's letter of August 15 a week later. By then he'd heard from Willicombe that the party would be leaving Wyntoon on the twenty-eighth, bound for San Simeon or Los Angeles. As usual, he had much else to tell Mac:

> The work we are doing in marble and cement around the [Neptune] pool area is so expensive that you make little showing with quite a little money.[110] You know there is a lot of cast stone [work] and you also know what that means. . . .

(August 14; see note 106, above) prefigured some key passages in Mac's outpouring of August 15. Smelser said Mac seemed "fairly happy," as much as it was "ever possible for him to be." But then Smelser also said, "Life is so difficult for him. He seems to be in a turmoil right now as to how to get work started [that] W R wants. [Through] Kower or the Stolte Co. that is the question."

109. The feature (pp. 42–55; 123–62 *passim*) begins with a sidebar, "The Story of Wyntoon." It relates how Hearst launched his version of Wyntoon after his mother's "Castle" burned in 1930, leaving all his efforts in the late 1920s unmentioned (along with his ideas for things like the Bradenstoke barn). Elsewhere in the feature, Wyntoon's main components are well enough described—the Bavarian Village, The Gables, The Bend. But Santa Maria de Ovila, the Spanish monastery that figured so prominently in 1933, goes entirely unmentioned—as it does in most other published references to Wyntoon. Thus the methodical W. A. Swanberg, who left few stones unturned in mining printed sources, had only this to say: "Possibly Hearst envisioned erecting the monastery, or part of it, at San Simeon. If so, the plan was discarded" (*Citizen Hearst*, p. 468). Had Swanberg said Wyntoon instead, he would have hit pay dirt; 1961, though, was too soon for that.

Fifteen to twenty years passed before Wyntoon became more decipherable. The book *Unbuilt America* appeared in 1976, followed by the article "William Randolph Hearst's Monastery" in 1981 (see p. 69 in this volume, note 27). Meanwhile, Cal Poly received the Julia Morgan Collection in 1980; and then 1988 brought Sara Boutelle's long-awaited book, *Julia Morgan*. But it has remained for the Loorz Papers—backed by the Morgan-Forney Collection and further supplemented by Cal Poly's holdings and others cited in this volume—to offer the most balanced account of events at Wyntoon. Even so, many details, many signal facts, still await discovery.

110. Loorz's notes from Morgan's visit of August 15 included this entry: "New cement steps too uneven and amateurish, make sharper edges, too [much] rounding. Try to true up bottom line of nosing on steps already placed."

You are quite right about Miss Morgan, she is decidedly fed up. Things have gone quite smoothly here and she uses the day of her visits here mostly for leisurely wandering around moving a lamp here and a nic-nac there discussing Wyntoon, Beach House and personalities. Her visits have really been enjoyable and have helped to break the monotony of things around here. If something doesn't break before long to excite us a little bit I'll have to shut down for a week. Not one but many of my boys show the signs of it. It is always more exciting and interesting to my crews when the party is around. They seem to have more of a goal to work for. An occasional glimpse of the chief or some other celebrity helps them to forget their enforced isolation.[111]

Morgan was at San Simeon, in fact, on August 22, the very day Loorz wrote to Mac. Loorz's recap notes amounted to a modest eleven entries, which pertained mostly to those old standbys, the Gothic Study and the Neptune Pool. "Mr. Solon to arrange to be completed by [next] Thursday [August 29]," he noted on the Study. "Mr. Hearst's unexpected call Tuesday [August 20] found the room clean but not furnished but he appeared to be pleased with Mr. Solon's work."[112] On the outdoor pool, Loorz's notes pertained to the work that the marble sculptor L. Cardini and a few helpers from San Francisco were doing on the reassembled Roman temple; the notes also pertained to the flanking colonnades (which, in pronounced contrast to the temple, were new structures created expressly for San Simeon).

The work on the ancient Roman temple would soon include the incorporation of a Renaissance sculpture group in the upper part of the temple. The group was of Neptune and the Nereids and, like the old temple, had entered the Hearst Collection in 1922.

Since Hearst and company might soon be descending on San Simeon, Loorz had these words for Stolte on Friday, August 23:

---

111. Some further details that Loorz conveyed on August 22 included these comments on his extra-vocational work: "Truthfully, Mac there was never a time in my ten years in business when it was apparently so easy to step out and get contracts." The optimistic Loorz had thus "decided to forget there was a depression."

112. Had Hearst been there in person? Would Loorz have written this line if he hadn't been? The simplest answer is to say that Hearst flew down to San Simeon from Wyntoon. If he did, though, a letter from Willicombe (not a telegram), bearing the same date as the "unexpected call"—August 20—must be explained. "Presume the landing field is all finished so that planes can land safely," he told Loorz. "Better telegraph me confirmation so that there will be no doubt." Then on Friday (August 23), Willicombe wired Loorz from Wyntoon, "Please have landing field so that plane can land safely Thursday [August 29] at latest."

Meanwhile, Morgan's visit (Loorz identified it as "Thursday—August 22, 1935") appears as "Aug 23" in Morgan-Forney, an entry suggesting that Saturday, August 24, may have been the day she appeared; but Morgan-Forney also cites August 21 as the day of (or the day before) a visit she made to the Beach House, her last in 1935.

Everything is taking on more of a hustle in preparation and it sort of cheers things up. I hope Miss Morgan doesn't come down with a lot of hurry up ideas that we haven't money for.[113] What we can do will not count a lot to change the appearance of things.

In part, or perhaps to a great degree, Loorz was alluding to the Neptune Pool area, that infamous devourer of construction funds. On a more prosaic level, he could at least tell his partner that he was making good progress on the airport surfacing.

Stolte replied on August 25 from Oakland. "If Miss Morgan goes to McCloud this eve," he wrote that Sunday, "I shall go up for a day or two. This will probably be [the] last trip before Mr. Hearst leaves, and some estimates may be required." Morgan did, in fact, leave on Sunday. For as she told Loorz two days later, "I saw Mr. Hearst at Wyntoon Monday before he left for the south. He is keenly interested in seeing San Simeon's developments."

Leave it to Jud Smelser, though, to provide the *real* news on August 25 — direct from Wyntoon itself ("no news except bad news," as he told Loorz):

> It has now developed that Mamma & Papa [Davies and Hearst] are coming back Sat [August 31]. Nothing official has been announced at all yet but I heard them say this themselves. However that may be some of her chicanery (spelling?). That may be changed today too for she went home early last night [to Brown Bear, probably from The Gables][114] in a huff & he followed later in bad humor too. Soooooooooooo.

Some kind words were included — bestowed on none other than Willicombe, who'd already saved Smelser's neck and who'd been instrumental all summer in maintaining peace amid the towering pines. "I can get some good snickers out of him," Smelser chuckled. "He's much more grandma ish than one suspects at first glance."

Hearst headed to Los Angeles by way of San Simeon, and he did so in a most atypical way. He flew to Jolon, to his landing field near the Milpitas Hacienda: the revamped airport at San Simeon wasn't quite ready yet, despite Loorz's recent efforts and those of his paving crew. This "back forty" approach to The Enchanted Hill gave Hearst a chance to traverse the entire Burnett Road. Loorz gave Morgan some details on August 29:

---

113. On the one hand, Loorz sounded as if he expected to see Morgan soon — perhaps the next day; see note 112. On the other hand (if she had, in fact, appeared on August 22), he may already have known that her next visit lay more than a week ahead.

114. Much like Casa del Mar and its fellow houses on The Enchanted Hill, Brown Bear and its fellows at Wyntoon provided sleeping quarters mostly. The Gables, though a far cry from Casa Grande at San Simeon, was similar in having the sole dining room and other rooms for group use.

I did not see Mr. Hearst to talk to, he left [the hilltop] hurriedly as soon as he got up yesterday morning.

I met him when we went after him at Milpitas where he landed but only to say hello since he rode in another car. They said he went to the [Neptune] pool section as soon as he arrived on the hill but apparently passed no remarks to anyone but Mr. Keep and that hurriedly, which was to the effect that it was now a grand entrance.[115]

He did go in and talk to Mr. Solon [in the east alcove of the Gothic Study] and said that he liked the work very much. The stone doorways were quite clean when he went in and the room in general [was also clean] though not furnished.[116]

Up at Wyntoon, in the party's absence, silence had fallen. So had some early snow in the nearby mountains. George Wright, long voiceless in these annals, described the ensuing mud when he wrote to Loorz on August 29. "Today the McCloud is like the Colorado: too thin to plow, too thick to drink."

Wright also said, "We march to work up here to the tune of the Funeral March—things are that dead."[117]

LOORZ TO STOLTE, Wednesday, September 4: "Well the chief is still here with his girl friend. I think the present intention is to be here over the week end and then return North but who knows." Once more, though, Loorz's well-meaning but quickly chosen words can be misleading. Had Hearst been at San Simeon for sev-

---

115. See note 69, above.

116. On August 26, while Morgan was at Wyntoon, her office sent Loorz precise instructions, which included photographs, on the furnishing of the Study's east alcove. With the help of the warehouse manager, W. R. Williams, he was to locate the following items—identified by inventory numbers—for Morgan's inspection and potential use:

Photograph	4016	Florentine Renaissance Octagonal C[enter] Table
"	1845	Carved Walnut Centre Table
SSW #8288	3004	Vargueno
Photograph	1164	Walnut Spanish Vargueno
SSW #8277	3332	Vargueno
SSW 8275	4122	Walnut Vargueno
SSW 8274	4151	Vargueno
Photograph	6291	Stone Statue Representing St. Barbara

"*The photographs* come back here," Loorz was told, "needless to say." He probably also knew that the SSW (San Simeon Warehouse) numbers were the ones used locally by Williams, whereas Morgan used other inventory numbers. Her own PC (Pacific Coast) system, for example, differed greatly from the Williams system, thus requiring—to this day—frequent cross-referencing and conversion.

117. Wyntoon livened up no doubt when Morgan appeared on Labor Day Weekend (Saturday, August 31, and the following day, according to the Morgan-Forney ledgers).

eral days already? It sounds as if he had. And yet he'd probably been there only a day or two now, having returned from Los Angeles after his brief appearance of the week before.

The timing was good, at any rate, for Morgan—fresh off her latest trip to Wyntoon—to see about the job. She met with Hearst on Thursday the fifth and then with Loorz. Afterwards, Loorz and Camille Solon, recruited from the Gothic Study, prepared cardboard mock-ups of the Neptune and Nereid figures for the Roman temple at the Neptune Pool. As specified in Loorz's recap of the meeting, the mock-ups were placed in "the Temple Pediment for inspection"—in this case by Hearst himself. "Mr. Hearst saw them and liked them," said a follow-up note that Loorz made on his list. But as Loorz also noted, knowing that Morgan already expected as much, some fine-tuning of the proposed placement would be needed before the statuary itself could be installed.

Another of Loorz's notes from September 5 also concerned the Neptune Pool: "Place the two trial columns in the new locations after extending them three feet." The entry was likewise accompanied by a follow-up note: "Mr. Hearst seemed to be pleased with these also." Had two such columns been permanently installed, the outdoor pool would have looked distinctly different. The columns, surmounted by sculptures, would have flanked the Roman temple—would have occupied the open spaces between the temple and the north and south colonnades. These free-standing objects would have been nearly four feet wide at their bases and more than twenty-five feet in height. The effect would have been pure World's Fair—a dreamy throwback to the San Francisco of 1915 or even the Chicago of 1893.

That first week of September 1935 was one that Loorz's second son, Bill (who was seven), spent in San Luis Obispo General Hospital. "Bill has been sort of sick at his stomach for the past three days," Loorz had told his parents on Tuesday, August 27. "Too much party Saturday night and picnic Sunday. He eats so much watermelon and drinks too much lemonade."

But young Bill had appendicitis, not just a stomach ache; and he underwent surgery on September 1. Miss Morgan wrote to him on September 6, as soon as she got back to San Francisco from her visit of the previous day at San Simeon. "Dear Bill," she began:

> I have looked around just now desperately to see if I could find something here [in the Morgan office] you would like, as there have been so many people calling today I could not get out to find you a surprise—I found a case of books—& will send you another tomorrow as more than one will make the envelope too thick to go in the mail chute here.
>
> I hope they will roll you out on the porch so you can see the sky and hills—and when you see little stray clouds, just think they are my thoughts and good wishes out trying to find you and doing it—.

She closed with "affectionate best wishes." As though a loving grandmother or a doting aunt, she wrote to Bill in a similar vein several times that month.[118]

GEORGE WRIGHT wrote to Loorz from Wyntoon on September 10, two weeks after Hearst and his party had left that sylvan retreat on the McCloud River:

> Our crew is cut down to the bone, and even yet we can't get used to it after the rush and push of a short time ago. We have been finishing up the "left-overs," but that is nearly caught up now. I presume that the interior of the Turrets [the eventual Cinderella House in the Bavarian Village] or [the adjacent] Angel House will be next on the program, but as yet no details are out.[119]

September 10 also saw other letters going out. Loorz himself wrote one to the carpenter Elof Gustafson in San Francisco, where the Stolte Co. was completing a residential job for Loorz's brother and sister-in-law, Claude and Freda. Loorz told Gustafson, "Mr. Hearst has come and gone and all is again quiet and serene here on the hill." Moreover, "He didn't bother us in [the] construction [department] but did change a few more things about the household and the garden [departments].[120] We will look for him back in about three weeks."

Loorz wrote to Stolte on the tenth as well, saying he supposed his partner would "be at Wyntoon for a few days with the chief returning [there from San Simeon]." He could also have said, but didn't, that he supposed Miss Morgan's plans to visit Wyntoon would prompt Stolte to head north. That was still the pattern—for Stolte to drop whatever he was doing in Oakland or elsewhere and make a beeline for Wyntoon whenever Morgan was about to show up. (This time she left San Francisco on Saturday the fourteenth; after spending three days at Wyntoon, she flew home in one of Hearst's planes.)

---

118. Morgan's letter of September 6 and the others mentioned here are privately held by Bill Loorz, who gave me copies on November 27, 1989.

Before returning to San Francisco on September 6, Morgan sent two postcards to young Bill early that morning from San Luis Obispo, where she probably had spent the night after being at San Simeon on the fifth. One card showed Mt. San Antonio (Old Baldy) as seen from Mt. Wilson, above Pasadena. Her message to Bill said in part, "This looks a bit foggy, but it is way up in the mountains and pretty—I saw it last week—." (She had gone south for the Beach House job about August 21 but evidently not since then; perhaps she had glimpsed Old Baldy through smog-free skies, from forty or fifty miles away.) The card to Bill also bore a "good luck" horseshoe drawn by Morgan, as did its companion card. These two postcards plus another from 1935 (cited below in note 128) were lent to me by Bill Loorz on April 3, 1998; copies of all three have since been added to the George Loorz Papers at the San Luis Obispo County Historical Museum.

119. Wright said nothing about Hearst or his guests, but others at Wyntoon had them in mind on September 10. Smelser, who also wrote to Loorz that day, reported "no word of the parties arrival yet at 2:30 PM."

120. The bracketed insertions are in keeping with the terminology described in note 67, this chapter.

In the interim, Loorz wrote Charlie Badley and his family on September 11. Things were "going nicely" on the Neptune Pool: "a grand rush with marble setters and cement workmen." Loorz said everything else was "quiet on the front," now that Hearst was "back in Wyntoon with his lady friend."

Then on September 13 Loorz wrote to San Simeon's longtime orchard man, Nigel Keep, who had just reached port in Long Beach after a brief vacation cruise. The head gardener on the hilltop—Keep's counterpart "inside the wall"—was the subject of the hour:

> Please, Nigel, in confidence, Louis Reesing turned in his resignation last week to take effect not later than October 1st. He hasn't received an answer but he talked tough answering some complaints so I dont think they'll try to talk him into staying. I knew this would be very interesting news, so I couldn't help saying so.

How fortunate (at least for us) that Loorz seldom kept things to himself—in this situation and in so many others, some of them downright touchy. The Reesing matter had been smoldering for weeks, resulting in one of the more poignant letters in the Loorz Papers: in fact, an unsettling letter in many ways. Who better to write it than George Loorz? And who better to receive it than someone as humane, as firmly sympathetic as Julia Morgan?[121] Their kind thoughts aside, though, Reesing was through.

---

121. Loorz had written his letter to Morgan on August 9, 1935. He began by addressing the fate of "the Heaton boys," formerly in the Garden Department:

> I know nothing except what I have heard since they were dismissed as to why they were dismissed.
>
> The only possible clue that I have heard of is that about two months ago and several times previous money was apparently taken from guests in the houses [Casa del Mar, etc.]. The last time the figure $500 was mentioned & the Heaton boys being located in that section of the garden were called in and questioned, as was every other party working at or near these houses. This was all done quietly by Mr. Willicombe without notifying anyone.
>
> Shortly after this the garden [operation] was transferred to the ranch payroll. Then two weeks ago when Louis Reesing was away on his vacation, Mr. Willicombe called Mr. Apperson here and Louis in Menlo Park telling them to let the boys goes [sic] with two weeks advance pay at the end of the month. He gave no reason only stating that Mr. Hearst wished it so.
>
> I feel confident that Louis Reesing had nothing to do with it. He resented very much when his men were questioned for he says they never go into the houses and there [their] jobs were too dear to them to take a chance. Though he and Cliff [Heaton] differed on many small methods two of three years ago, he has come to know how valuable Cliff really was and used him a lot.
>
> Personally Miss Morgan it hurts me. I felt that Cliff was the most loyal & efficient man in the garden without exception. He possessed the sweetest disposition which so helped him in that position. He was on our side, that means yours, 100% first last and always.
>
> I felt very much like sending this wire to Mr. Willicombe [at Wyntoon]:
>
> "I AM FULLY AWARE THAT THE GARDEN DEPARTMENT IS NONE OF MY

COURTESY OF JEAN HENRY WILLICOMBE

LEFT: Joseph Willicombe, the "Colonel."
BELOW: *Mr. Hearst and Buddy*
(photograph by Martin Munkácsi, 1933).

© HEARST CASTLE ®/CALIFORNIA STATE PARKS

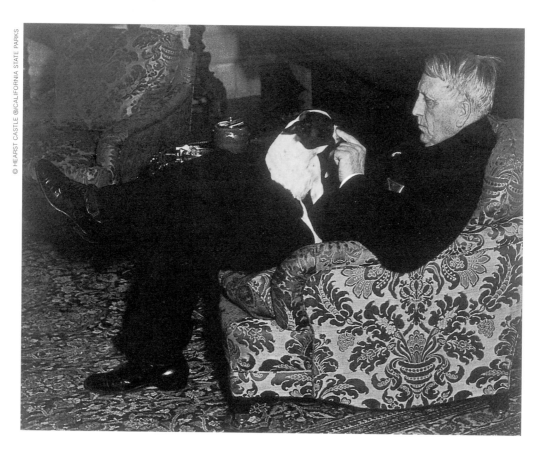

LOORZ FAMILY COLLECTION

LOORZ FAMILY COLLECTION

ABOVE: The Appendicitis Kid.
LEFT: Homemade swimming pool,
(Bill Loorz, second from left, back row);
Arroyo del Puerto behind.
BELOW: School play, San Simeon
Community Center (Charley Villa,
Georgianna Brunner, and Don Loorz,
far left; Danny Lanini, far right; other
children unknown).

LOORZ FAMILY COLLECTION

LOORZ FAMILY COLLECTION

AUTHOR'S PHOTOGRAPH, 1975

TOP: Local citizens and William K. Vanderbilt's flying boat, February 1935.
BOTTOM: San Simeon warehouses #2 and #3.

COURTESY OF JEAN HENRY WILLICOMBE

TOP: Hearst as greeter,
Casa Grande.
BOTTOM: The East Room
(or Morning Room).

LOORZ FAMILY COLLECTION

VANDERLOO COLLECTION

BISON ARCHIVES

THIS PAGE: A social hub: the East Room (Marion Davies and Charlie Chaplin readily identifiable in the bottom photograph, which is by Munkácsi, 1933).

LOORZ FAMILY COLLECTION

Christmas in Casa Grande
RIGHT: The Assembly Room.
BELOW: The Refectory.

LOORZ FAMILY COLLECTION

LOORZ FAMILY COLLECTION

106 Las Palmas_Gran Canaria. La Atalaya

LOORZ FAMILY COLLECTION

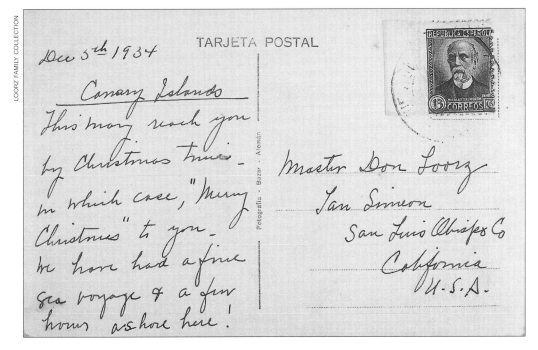

TARJETA POSTAL

Dec 5th 1934

Canary Islands
This may reach you
by Christmas time —
in which case, "Merry
Christmas" to you —
We have had a fine
sea voyage & a few
hours ashore here!

Fotografía · Bazar · Alemán

Master Don Loorz
San Simeon
San Luis Obispo Co
California
U.S.A.

Julia Morgan in Europe, fall 1934–winter 1935.

GEORGE LOORZ PAPERS

257 — CATHEDRALE DE CHARTRES — Le Bourdon — ND

RIGHT AND BELOW:
Morgan to Loorz,
February 26, 1935.

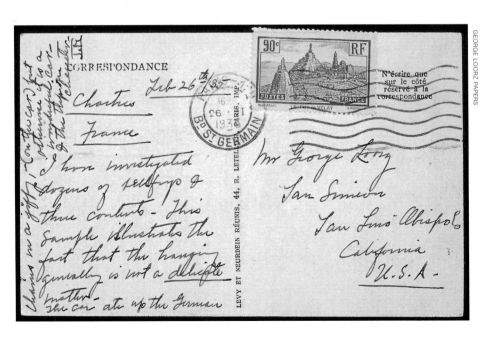

GEORGE LOORZ PAPERS

CORRESPONDANCE

Feb 26th/35

Chartres

France

I have investigated
dozens of bellfrys &
their contents. This
sample illustrates the
fact that the hanging
generally is not a _delicate_
matter. the car ate up the German

Mr George Loorz
San Simeon
San Luis Obispo
California
U.S.A.

COURTESY OF JEAN HENRY WILLICOMBE

Hearst and Helen at Wyntoon, summer 1935 (photograph by Peter Stackpole).

COURTESY OF JEAN HENRY WILLICOMBE

COURTESY OF JEAN HENRY WILLICOMBE

TOP AND BOTTOM: The Hearst-Davies croquet team, Wyntoon 1935 (photographs by Stackpole).

LOORZ FAMILY COLLECTION

LOORZ FAMILY COLLECTION

TOP AND BOTTOM: The Gables, before and after — or possibly after and before.

SAN LUIS OBISPO COUNTY HISTORICAL MUSEUM

RIGHT: The outside pool, yet to become the full-fledged Neptune Pool.
BELOW RIGHT: Excerpt from Morgan to Loorz, undated (summer 1934?).
BELOW LEFT: North colonnade, deep end of Neptune Pool.

AUTHOR'S PHOTOGRAPH, 1974

GEORGE LOORZ PAPERS

GEORGE LOORZ PAPERS

LOORZ FAMILY COLLECTION

The Neptune Pool
LEFT: Sketch by Morgan for one
of two great columns, meant to flank
the Roman temple but never erected.
ABOVE: Roman temple facade.
BELOW: View uphill from the shallow end.

AUTHOR'S PHOTOGRAPH, 1974

LOORZ FAMILY COLLECTION

LOORZ FAMILY COLLECTION

LOORZ FAMILY COLLECTION

TOP LEFT: Loorz and Ray Van Gorden. TOP RIGHT: Despite his "outside" efforts that began in 1935, Loorz's main work through 1937 was still for Hearst and Morgan. ABOVE: Mess Hall, Hearst Camp.

AUTHOR'S PHOTOGRAPH, 1990

AUTHOR'S PHOTOGRAPH, 1990

Two schools designed by Louis Crawford, Santa Maria, and built by the F. C. Stolte Co., San Simeon branch, 1936 TOP: Cambria. BOTTOM: Morro Bay.

GRAND CANYON NATIONAL PARK #6255

GRAND CANYON NATIONAL PARK #1222

TOP LEFT: Hearst's Grand Canyon holdings originally included the old Grandview Hotel, razed in 1929.
TOP RIGHT: In the late 1930s his holdings still included the cabin that he and Morgan built in 1914.
RIGHT: Hearst and friends soon after he bought his South Rim property in 1913 (Will Rogers in the lead).

GRAND CANYON NATIONAL PARK #10892

All the while Hearst's plans, Hearst's itinerary remained a prime subject of rumor, of anticipation and second-guessing. "I just got word that the party might leave for here this afternoon"—a typical line (in this case from Loorz to Stolte, September 19), and one of dozens of such passages in the Loorz Papers. Yet even if that date actually marked Hearst's latest departure from Wyntoon, the Chief still took his sweet time, probably by going to the Beach House first, in getting to San Simeon. Either way, wherever he went, Morgan quite often followed.

Her visit to the hill during these last days of September—she hadn't been there in three weeks—fell on Wednesday the twenty-fifth. First she met with Hearst, then with Loorz, the usual sequence when the lord of the manor was home. ("Well here I am in my office waiting," Loorz told Stolte that day, "waiting for Miss Morgan and the chief to finish their session so that we [Loorz and Morgan] can complete ours. Waiting makes me nervous so I thot I'd sit down and talk a bit.")[122] Another trait to applaud: the young builder's restlessness.

Once Loorz got his turn, Morgan kept him busy making notes on the Neptune Pool and its ancient Roman temple, among other projects. "Cardini to carve shell background and portion to drape around Neptune figure as outlined in chalk," he noted for the temple pediment. He also noted that their specialist in cast stone and plaster of Paris work, John Vanderloo, should "proceed with casting of Temple back wall as per approved sample." In a typical instance of Morgan's keen attention to detail, Loorz recorded that Vanderloo should "try to get a little more yellow tone to black sand background, similar to [antique granite] columns"—all six of which, along with the modern back wall Vanderloo was working on, would support the massive pediment and its Neptune sculpture group. For Vanderloo to achieve the desired effect on the new wall, Morgan advised that he "not rub down [its surface] quite as much as [in] sample."

The letter to Stolte on September 25 did more than simply calm its writer's nerves. Loorz delved into his and Stolte's work for Morgan, both the Hearst and the non-Hearst variety:

> Well here is some dope I got from Miss Morgan. The [Edward] Bull job [in San Francisco] must be ready on the 11th [of October] for the owners to move in. . . .

> BUSINESS BUT IN THE INTEREST OF THE GOOD OF THE HILLTOP I FEEL THAT A TERRIBLE MISTAKE HAS BEEN MADE IN DISCHARGING CLIFFORD HEATON WHOM I CONSIDER TO BE THE MOST LOYAL AND EFFICIENT AND HONEST MAN IN THAT DEPARTMENT."
> I didn't! The mail is leaving.

By then Loorz had reached the bottom of the page. He rested his case and signed off, "As ever."

122. Loorz misdated his letter September 24. His recap notes from that Wednesday are correctly dated September 25.

Do all you can to make it. She admitted that she delayed it some by holding up the painting specifications.

Then she has two [Hearst] radio stations coming out for figures right away. One in Redwood city on the mud flats like that filtration and sewerage plant you figured. I'm certain they would prefer [King] Parker on the job thinking that he could handle it more promptly etc but she wants to give us a chance to figure it. . . . She thot maybe we were too busy to give it the personal attention that it would need. . . .

Miss Morgan has another job coming out at the King's Daughters home [in Oakland] before long and I hope it has no bond requirements and that we will have a good chance for it. She has still another job and [it's a] small Physician's & Surgeon's building in Berkeley [for F. C. Turner][123] that will very likely go ahead. That she told me would go to the owner's builder Mr. [H. K.] Henderson since he got the doctors together etc and made the job possible for the owner. So we mustn't feel hurt if we dont get a chance at it. . . .

No, Loorz and Stolte need not have felt hurt, even though the Hearst radio work was awarded to other bidders.[124] King Parker also missed out, despite having built the Berkeley Women's City Club for Morgan and, previously, the Phoebe Hearst Memorial Gym. Instead, it was the Kings Daughters job in Oakland that went to Loorz and Stolte.[125] And it was none too soon. Nineteen thirty-five suddenly stopped looking as if it would be a laggard year in the Stolte Co.'s work for Morgan — except, of course, at Wyntoon.

The change naturally didn't take hold overnight. Hence Stolte's reply of September 27, an understandable reply, in which he remarked to Loorz, "I would like to do a real job for Miss Morgan one that was completely planned, and could be pushed through. Cant seem to make much of a reputation on repair jobs." The Edward Bull job in San Francisco (Stolte was now "crowding" it) prompted that last comment.

---

123. In the Morgan-Forney ledgers, the account for the "F. C. Turner Medical Bldg." is also identified as the Elsie Lee Turner job. Similarly, an account for an adjacent project in Berkeley, the "F. C. Turner Office Bldg." of 1936, is also identified as the Mrs. Gertrude Turner Huberty job. (The two women were daughters of F. C. Turner.) H. K. Henderson was the contractor on both jobs.

124. A builder named McLaughlin landed part of the Hearst Radio KUP project; G. H. Meese got the other part. The two portions — the "two radio stations" Loorz mentioned — are listed as a combined KUP facility in Appendix A, pp. 535, 542, and 543. A year later the F. C. Stolte Co. secured the similar Hearst Radio KYA project (also designed by Morgan).

125. The Morgan-Forney ledgers contain four accounts for Kings Daughters jobs (1924, 1935–36, 1936–38, and 1941), all postdating the full-scale work done by Morgan for that institution about 1913. The second of these latter-day jobs, the "Building for Male Attendants" in Morgan-Forney, was the one secured by the F. C. Stolte Co. in 1935. (The third job of the four would go to the Stolte Co. a year later.)

In writing to his parents on October 2, Loorz provided them with details about his increasingly important work for the Stolte Co.—as well as his more accustomed pursuits:

This government school job [Arroyo Grande] has a lot of red-tape connected with it. It is a good thing I can type and can make out reports. It would keep an unexperienced person busy continually getting reports out for them that dont mean a thing. . . . Anyway, we hope it comes out as we plan with a nice profit otherwise it will just be a lot of grief for some more education.

Our other work around the bay district is going nicely. Some complaints now and then but in the main all is well. We have lots of work and I think we could get a lot more if we could afford it and tried. Everything we have and can borrow is tied up in the work now so we cant do any more. . . .[126]

Mr. Hearst and party were here for a couple of weeks but have departed again.[127] Suppose they will be back over the week end [October 5–6]. He still seems satisfied with my work. Hope so, another year or two here wouldn't hurt but I feel certain I could make more if I left right now. However, the outdoor life here is splendid for my health and that is something.

Loorz wrote in equal detail to Morgan two days later—on Friday, October 4:[128]

Mr. Cardini is getting along nicely with the statues [for the pediment in the Roman temple]. He has [all] three of them cut down and two of them raised to position to fit. I believe they will work out alright. Neptune's head might be a little close to the cornice above but that can be judged better when all three are in position and the shell modelling [is installed] in back. If necessary it can be brought

---

126. Loorz had told his parents on August 27, "I will make twice as much in the business this year as I will here on this job [at San Simeon]. So you see how well it paid me to invest all my savings in that little business." Insofar as he meant his savings from late in 1928 through early in 1932, Loorz was speaking of the $3,273 he had put in the company at its incorporation in April 1932 (pp. 20–21, note 6)—the equivalent of more than a year's wages for him before Hearst waved the magic wand. It's unclear whether Loorz had banked as much as $3,273—an impressive amount in the early thirties—or whether he'd been leaving part of his wages "in the company," where they accrued to his credit.

127. After spending five or six days at San Simeon in early September, Hearst had returned in late September, likewise for five or six days.

128. Morgan had returned to San Francisco by then after her latest trip to Wyntoon (October 2–3 in Morgan-Forney). A postcard of a spotted fawn, sent to Don and Bill Loorz early on Wednesday the second, was postmarked in the Siskiyou County town of Dunsmuir. "I chose a fine wet day to come to [the] mountains," she told the boys; "even the little animals know better & are just *scuttling* to get under cover." She closed by saying, "My bestest to you all." This postcard and two others from 1935 (cited above in note 118) were lent to me by Bill Loorz in April 1998; copies of all three have since been added to the George Loorz Papers.

out just a little and the plaster brought out to it. It is only a matter of an inch or so and I dont feel it would make much difference.

We are setting the Temple [entablature] stone and it looks very good to me. It varies a little from the samples but the variation is not far either way and should be an advantage and can be brought together [harmonized] if necessary. He [John Vanderloo] is making good headway on that and the [adjoining] balustrade casting. . . .

Now here's something that I am sorry came up but I dont know what is best to do about it. Just before Mr. Hearst left he called me and asked how much longer it would take to complete the airport and I said approximately two weeks. He said, he wanted to bring that crew up [the hill] and get right to work on the Pergola. Said he wanted to keep right at it until it was finished because it has been dragging so long. He asked how many more columns we needed [for the arbor] and asked me to order them so that we would have them when the bases were ready. I know this [air]port work is unfairly on another account and that your present budget could not stand the suggested work on the Pergola.[129] Please tell me what to do.

Wednesday, October 9, a day that found Morgan leaving San Francisco for a Thursday visit to San Simeon, also found Loorz writing to her right-hand man, Jim LeFeaver.[130] First, the nuts-and-bolts details: some serpentine "stars and circles," designed to accentuate the decks by the Neptune Pool, had recently arrived; Loorz hoped the similar midnight-green accents for the West Terrace (for which red tile was no longer planned) would also be arriving soon; his crew was ready to insert them. Next, the more alluring, pie-in-the-sky details:

Mr. Hearst walked into the office in splendid spirits about five last night [October 8][131] and we spent an hour of building and creating new projects. An airport on a

---

129. The "account" Loorz alluded to was the Hilltop Fund, rather than the Hearst Construction Fund. His reference to unfairness may have meant that little or no profit awaited Morgan in this phase of the airport work.

130. This date and the previous one, October 8, also apply to a visit made by one of Morgan's draftsmen, Dick Nusbaum, to Wyntoon. Morgan herself was next there on October 20.

131. On Saturday, October 5, Morgan answered Loorz's letter of the day before by saying she'd be "up on Tuesday, so far as seen now." (She also said, "Am glad the Temple is working out well.") But by Tuesday her plans had changed, no doubt because Hearst's had. He hadn't appeared on the weekend of October 5–6, as Loorz had thought he might. Instead, he stayed in Los Angeles until the eighth; he flew up to San Simeon that Tuesday afternoon — right before he saw Loorz.

Together, the Loorz Papers and the Morgan-Forney Collection converge upon and align these details, as they do in many instances. In addition, the Morgan-Forney files contain a letter that H. C. "Jim" Forney (Lilian Forney's husband) wrote to his mother on October 14; it told of his recent visit to San Simeon, where he worked on the inventorying of Hearst's art collection (a job he also pursued there in September). Forney witnessed Hearst's arrival on October 8, an event memorably described in the letter. But Forney also said, in regard to Morgan's visit on Thursday the tenth, "Miss Morgan

hilltop above the fog was one. Oh boy, it would be an expensive project if it goes ahead. Sooner or later he will do something.

In thirty minutes he moved the [hilltop] zoo, constructed new bear grottos and divided the present ones for cats. He levelled animal hill out here [behind the indoor Roman Pool and the garages]. We tore down the shop [in that area] and lowered a dozen oaktrees in groups of five making tremendous concrete boxes, excavating under them and letting the trees right down into position. Moving one tree at a time is a big job [but to] move a close group of about five is still bigger. Anyway he laughed a lot and seemed happy so we will put it down as a successful interview.[132]

Loorz gave Stolte a variation of the same story when he wrote to him early the next day, October 10, before Morgan arrived from San Luis Obispo:

Mr. Hearst came in the office night before last about 5 o'clock and we talked for an hour and a half. We went over the political situation, taxation, War[133] and things in general besides tearing down arenas, constructing bear pits, airports etc. Boy he was in a good humor and laughed heartily and even told simple jokes.

Loorz also told Stolte that, with Morgan on hand, he'd be having "a filled day." His notes from that Thursday meeting—he still called such notes a Recapitulation—were confined to a single page.[134] The first entry, under "Neptune Pool Area," went as follows:

Cardini to proceed with new shell and drapery arrangement at Temple gable [pediment] if Mr. Hearst approves. (Mr. Hearst saw the layout and came in to say that he did not want it. Said it was O.K. to leave the low shell [backdrop] but no more [than that] as he preferred just the plain statues [Neptune and the Nereids].)

Morgan subsequently corrected Loorz's entry, having received his typewritten minutes in San Francisco after she returned. "O.K.," she noted. "But this means working the plain back filler off the even face [of the temple]."

---

came down on Wednesday." Did he mean that she appeared at San Simeon the evening before her visit? Or merely that she had reached San Luis Obispo by then? The latter is more plausible.

132. A variant transcription of this excerpt, conveyed as a single paragraph, appears in Boutelle, *Julia Morgan*, p. 213.

133. Quite possibly that perennial subject of the era, the Great War of 1914–18. Or perhaps the more recent Italo-Abyssinian War, as Hearst was calling it in his newspapers, Italy having launched its invasion of Ethiopia just the previous week.

134. On October 10 Loorz wrote to Harry Thompson as well, responding to a letter of September 23 (Thompson had said in part, "Went fishing yesterday [at Wyntoon], caught a mess of beauties 12 inches and better, just getting good again"). Loorz put his "Recapitulation" duties in clearer perspective when he told Thompson, "Miss Morgan is due today so I will have a continuous session from now until then. I'll get a break during the afternoon while she is with Mr. Hearst."

LOORZ KEPT PROCEEDING CAUTIOUSLY, but steadily, with his "outside" work for the F. C. Stolte Co., lest some spoilsport cry foul. His caution, his sense of timing, his undeniable competence proved a winning combination. On October 14 he told Carl Daniels that the Hearst Ranch management in San Francisco was about to engage the Stolte Co. for a job at Pico Creek Stables, a portion of the ranch lying between San Simeon and Cambria.

But more success meant more work for Loorz, who had just turned thirty-seven. "It looks like the ranch is going to give us a contract on some barns and paddocks at the horse ranch," he told Stolte on October 22,[135] referring to the improvements at Pico Creek:

> I had the plans all drawn and gave them a figure and all was acceptable but they decided to add more to it, make the rooms on the end of it [the main stables compound] two stories high etc. All of which means I have to draw it over again and get out new figures. You said it when I took on drawing plans and specifications as well as contracting and superintending I took a big bite.

All the while over the past few weeks, the efforts of L. Cardini, John Vanderloo, and other artisans to finish the Neptune Pool remained at the fore. Loorz's notes from his meeting with Morgan on October 28 began with another reference to the use of cardboard mock-ups, this time to help complete the back support wall for the fragmentary Roman temple (whose six ancient columns supported the front of the assemblage). The back wall, built of modern concrete, was to have a decorative frieze along its upper edge, beneath the ancient entablature and pediment sections of the temple; the frieze was a takeoff on some of the sculptures done for the Parthenon in Athens. Upon using the cardboard, Loorz gained Hearst's approval of the scheme and quickly put Vanderloo to work on casting the frieze.

Morgan's comments on October 28 also addressed the matter of the surmounting statue in the temple ensemble. As another of Loorz's entries indicated, "Make a long straight handle for the trident of Neptune and make an offset hand holder to fit in the present hand."[136]

The rains that hampered work throughout the early months of 1935 returned to San Simeon that fall. Concerning the landscape architecture on Orchard Hill, Loorz had this to tell Morgan on November 5:

---

135. In turn, Stolte projected for Loorz on October 28 a net profit to the F. C. Stolte Co. of $15,000 in 1935. The amount was half again the $10,000 that, roughly a year before, the elder partner had projected would be their profit in 1934; see p. 148.

136. Contemporary photographs show that, soon after its installation, the Neptune figure held a three-pronged spear in its left hand; it no longer does.

If the rain does not bother us further we will be able to have the present set of 100 columns in place by November 27th. That is on the Pergola.

We will be able to place about 25 columns per week thereafter *if* it doesn't rain. We will need 122 more columns to complete the work.

As for completing the Neptune Pool, a good deal more remained to be done, as Loorz indicated in that same letter: "I have both compressors going steadily at the pool, mainly taking down the statue pool walls [opposite the temple] preparatory to changing them to the new details."

That wasn't the only change pending at San Simeon or on the greater Hearst Ranch, as Morgan's letter to Loorz of November 6 indicated:

If you can arrange to take me over to Jolon Friday [November 8], please do so. In any case I will be down then, and will be over [from San Luis Obispo] earlier than my usual time—to make the usable day longer.

We have plans for the work there, but find changes have been made that may not be worth keeping,—apparently not.

Loorz's notes from that meeting in early November contained a simple entry concerning Morgan's letter: "Hold work at Jolon until new studys are submitted to Mr. Hearst for approval."

Hearst's approval of those studies—or his rejection of them—may have had to wait a while, for he had gone to New York, where he stayed at his own Ritz Tower, a hotel and apartment complex on the corner of Park Avenue and East 57th Street. Hearst had more pressing things on his mind that November—Roosevelt's federal "wealth tax" and California's new income tax, among others[137]—but he didn't forget about San Simeon entirely. Loorz got two telegrams from him on November 16, both of them brief and pointed. "Please proceed with [the partitioning of] one [bear] grotto—then with the other," went the first message. "Please proceed promptly as soon as possible with new Kennels," went the second message.

---

137. Back on September 30, "Hearst Quitting California" had appeared in *Daily Variety* (pp. 1, 3). Hearst had responded with a letter to the editor, dated October 16, 1935, and published in that trade journal on October 23 as "Why I Am Leaving California, by W. R. Hearst" (pp. 1, 4). His letter said he intended to live mainly in New York because of the new California state income tax. Adding that levy—fifteen percent in Hearst's case—to his other tax obligations was the final straw: nearly ninety percent of his income would be lost to taxes. The fireworks set off by his pronouncement (some of them duds) are summarized in Swanberg's *Citizen Hearst*, pp. 474–75. See also the front page of the *San Luis Obispo Daily Telegram* (October 23, 1935), as partly illustrated in Nancy Loe's *Hearst Castle: An Interpretive History of W. R. Hearst's San Simeon Estate*, p. 93.

Loorz wrote to Stolte on November 22, telling him about his outside work as well as the work at San Simeon. In the former regard, a prosaic but important job was in the offing—the Santa Maria Sewage Plant:

> It looks like there is money to be made in that kind of thing, here in the middle of the state where the jobs are a little too small to interest real builders. Maybe a couple of low bids from us will scare them out of here entirely.
>
> Things certainly look good here [at San Simeon] and I guess I might just as well throw my shoulders back, my chin out and fight it out for about six months.
>
> Fred I'm certainly glad George Wright is with me. He is detailing all the steel for the [bear] Grotto additions and is doing a good job of it. He has taken over the responsibility of the Pergola layout. I also had to use him to help me with this [Santa Maria] estimate.
>
> I would rather have him than anyone I've worked with because he does just what you tell him, just how you want it, quickly and neatly.

Loorz closed by saying of himself and Stolte, "Sometimes I think both of us were very lucky we met up, what do you think?"

Stolte replied the next day, November 23. "Yes the dutch combination still seems to be working O.K.[138] I have often thought of our first job together, at 12th & Franklin [in Oakland][139] and whether Mr Fate had anything to do with it all."

Loorz wrote to Hearst at the Ritz Tower in New York early the next month, December 2:

> According to instructions from Miss Morgan we are planning on stopping the work on the hilltop on December 15th.
>
> By that time we will have the new kennels completed and be well along on the divisions of the Grotto but cannot be completed. Shall I keep that crew which is working on the Hilltop Fund on until the Grotto can be used again?
>
> In the rush on these two units I have slowed up the work on the Pergola. Will proceed with this work as men are released from the two units mentioned. Shall we stop this work on December 15th?

---

138. The Loorz Papers contain several references by Stolte and Loorz to the heritage they shared. In these instances the partners often used *Dutch* in its archaic sense—meaning "Germanic."

In 1951, while addressing a Rotary Club in the Bay Area, Loorz spoke of his family: "My father was born in Germany; my mother, also foreign, [was] Missourian of Scotch-Welch parentage. That makes me HASH. I married an all Irish gal—Sullivan-Hurley. We have three boys, that makes them Hash with Onions." From "Self Introduction—Rotary," a typescript privately held by the Loorz family; courtesy of Don Loorz, May 29, 1990.

139. A parking garage (to the best of Don Loorz's memory). Frank Clinton Merritt's book, published in 1928, mentions a garage for Lloyd Brothers (pp. 8–9 in this volume)—too early a job, perhaps, to have included George Loorz. In any case, another building occupies that corner in Oakland today.

There is such a demand for mechanics [artisans] on the outside that I hesitate to lay off about five of our best men. I'm certain they will receive employment immediately and may not be available when we need them in the spring. I refer in particular to such very skilled men as our ironworker, ornamental plasterer, marble mason & mantel expert.[140]

I assure you this is not a dream for I have had a good deal of difficulty to get carpenters for our grotto work and I had to raise from $7.20 per day to $8.

Prices have advanced from 10 to 20% on nearly all supplies within the past two months.

Colonel Willicombe answered Loorz on Hearst's behalf. "Replying your letter second," he wired, "Chief says yes finish grotto, also keep on with pergola until finished, and keep skilled workmen you mention and keep them busy."

That was on December 6. In the meantime, Morgan conferred with Loorz at San Simeon on Monday, December 2.[141] Regarding the outdoor pool, he noted, "In general all new concrete work in the Neptune area that cannot be completed [now] with marble coverings, plaster, cast cement etc will be covered with white plaster scratch coats for the winter. All to look tidy and white."

LOORZ WAS TOO CONSCIENTIOUS to be unconcerned about the potential conflict his local work for the Stolte Co. posed. He must have been losing sleep as a result, for he poured his heart out in a long letter to Morgan on December 4:

Before I discuss the following Miss Morgan, you must know that my feelings and regards for you and Mr. Hearst is far more than just business associations. I both admire you and feel that you are one of my closest personal friends and as dear to me as my own family. I enjoy the trust and confidence that you both have expressed in your dealings with me.

As I have mentioned before I am well aware that besides being generously compensated for my work here I have learned a lot that will be of extreme value you [sic] to me. In addition I have developed an appreciation of some of the finer things in art that will give me much happiness.[142]

Now, Miss Morgan, it is unfortunate that Mr. Stolte cannot operate efficiently

---

140. The ironworker was Val Georges, the plasterer was John Vanderloo, the mason was Frank Frandolich, and the "mantel expert" was John McFadden (who was also an electrician).

141. Over the past four weeks, following her visit of November 8, Morgan had been to San Simeon twice, on November 19 and 25. (And on November 12 or 13 she had been to Wyntoon for the last time in 1935.) Loorz's recap notes from her two late-November visits are missing; so are those from her visits of December 10 and 16.

142. Since 1958, tour guides, housekeepers, and many other employees at Hearst Castle have had precisely the experience that Loorz described in this sentence.

or satisfactorily, construction for my clients this far South. I must always take the responsibility of figuring work of any consequence either here or up there. Otherwise we either do not do the work in open competition or the gamble is too great. . . .

I have handled three jobs in this district during the past six months.[143] The net profit to us when those jobs are completed should be at least $6,000. Fortunately I have a very good man [Carl Daniels] who runs the largest job [Arroyo Grande] and does all the contact work. However, I let the sub-contracts and sign all the checks, almost 100% by mail. My average time away from the hilltop during a whole month is two afternoons. I have actually been on the Arroyo Grande School but twice and it is nearing completion. There would have been a good deal more profit in the jobs if I had been free to follow them up more closely. You know how things go ahead much more promptly and smoothly when you can keep continuous and close contact on your jobs.

I have felt that it has been absolutely necessary for me to be on this job [at San Simeon] 44 hours per week. With the responsibilities that take a good deal of my attention on Saturday afternoons and Sundays, I have averaged more than that. You know that phone calls and requests come as frequently on Sundays as on week days either from Mr. Willicombe or Mr. Hearst. . . .

As you well know my responsibilities include the following in addition to construction: chauffeuring and private cars, trucking & transportation, trapping and furs [coyotes, etc.], water supply and maintenance, new roads and upkeep, gate repairs (a broken gate on Sunday means a call and getting a man somewhere to repair [it] as they cannot be left open), household repairs and upkeep (often calls for men on holidays). Chauffeurs in any number are called at any time and since I keep and pay no regular chauffeurs who loaf while waiting it takes a little quick thinking at times to meet the demand. . . .

Miss Morgan I am confident that with times as they are I can do a lot better by taking contracts by several times than I can earn here. However, I do love my work on this hilltop with you and Mr. Hearst. . . .

On the other hand the opportunity right here in this County [San Luis Obispo] is such that I feel I can make as much as $20,000 in the coming year on P.W.A. contracts. I know well that you would not ask me to give up that opportunity. If you feel that you would not care to break in a new man I feel certain that I could arrange someway to carry on somewhat as I have during the past few months. If it could be understood that I could be away a little more than

---

143. Two of these were the W. T. Reid job in San Luis Obispo and the Arroyo Grande Grammar School. A third one, which Loorz mostly just "handled," as he said to Morgan (rather than profited by), was the Souza house in Cambria; however, he may have meant the more recent work at Pico Creek Stables for the Piedmont Land & Cattle Company.

I have [been] I could open an office in one of the neighboring towns, put this man of mine there and handle it. That would keep the name San Simeon out of it.[144]

The Loorz Papers contain no reply from Morgan. In fact, not until Loorz and Stolte corresponded on the subject more than two weeks later did it resurface.

For the moment it was more newsworthy, albeit sadly, that Loorz fired George Wright on Monday, December 9. Wright, whose drinking had always worried the teetotaling Stolte and sometimes even the affable Loorz, had overindulged on the weekend and missed work Monday morning. He wrote to Loorz that evening from the Anderson Hotel in San Luis Obispo, rankled that Loorz had dismissed him in writing rather than in person:

> But don't expect a list of alibis. There will be none. I only repeat that I explained why I wasn't able to be on deck this morning. Had I known at the time what was coming, I would certainly never have mentioned it. . . .
>
> Naturally, my pride was hurt, but I'll get over that. I lived rather well before I knew the F.C.S. Co. existed, and I'll not go into a decline now. But I was disappointed in your method. Everybody has unpleasant duties to perform at times. When I am put to it, I dread it of course, but I never fail to look my man in the eye when I tell him. It is so disappointing to see some one you have always respected loose [lose] stature. So you inadvertently put us both on the same plane. And that's a laugh to end it all with.

Maybe Loorz *had* acted hastily — maybe the pressure *was* getting to him. He had to go on, though; the Chief would be returning soon from New York. Loorz wrote to Morgan on Friday, December 13, in that very regard:

> Mr. Hearst arrived early yesterday and went straight to the [Neptune] pool area. He seemed to be well pleased with it. Especially mentioned the treatment at the upper [statuary] pool.
>
> He then walked over by the back of C house [Casa del Sol]. He noticed the [marble] lions and beckoned me and said, "Of course these won't stay here." Ap-

---

144. Amid these paragraphs is another telling line, one referring to some conflicts of interest that, nearly ten years before, had undermined a job that Morgan, with Loorz's help, was able to put on sound footing — the Beach House. As Loorz said, "Remembering the difficulties that beset the Carpenter Bros [the builders] when we took over Santa Monica, I have carefully guarded [against] that."

parently he will want them back in the East room [the Morning Room in Casa Grande].[145]

He then walked all thru the house [Casa Grande] with Mr. Williams [the warehouse man]. He was more than delighted with the Doges [Suite] and the Library. He certainly remarked about all the nice new things you had there. Little, if any, missed his eye. Seemed real thrilled about everything. That should be some compensation for your late work the other night [December 10].

By now, Casa Grande and the three smaller houses were already realizing the museum status that Hearst had alluded to in 1925 and that, in a much better-known passage two years later, he had clearly projected for them.[146] Both the Doges Suite and the Library hailed from Camille Rossi's era; they underwent little or no re-modeling under Loorz. Yet the enhancement of their interiors typified what was taking place now in several rooms of an earlier day. The Doges Suite, a lavish group of guest rooms on the mezzanine level at the back of Casa Grande, was being en-riched mostly with Renaissance and Baroque objects. The Library, sprawling be-tween the Assembly Room on the ground floor and Hearst's own Gothic Suite on the third floor, was becoming a repository of ancient works—epitomized by the Greek pottery collection that would eventually comprise more than two hundred examples (but whose numbers were reduced after Hearst's death).[147] There was more for Morgan to read in Loorz's letter of Friday the thirteenth:

The water is going back in the [Neptune] pool. It was nearly cleaned when he came out and I asked him if he wanted the water back in. I said it was already [all ready to be filled]. They, Miss Davies and he discussed it, and decided that it would look better with the water in it even if they didn't use it.

---

145. Loorz's recap of Morgan's visit on December 2 had included this entry:

Take the two kneeling lions from the [vestibule of the] breakfast room [the East Room or Morning Room] and place them on the altered buttresses [at] lower C. house [Casa del Sol]. Replace with smaller figures [two similar lion plinths] brought up by Mr. Williams. Arch[itect] to select proper columns to be installed later on the [backs of the] new figures in the breakfast room.

After the two pairs of sculptures and perhaps even other pairs were shifted about, a single pair of such "crouching lions" remained in the vestibule of the Morning Room. (Some of these medieval lions were the kind that originally, with columns in place, helped support a pulpit). A second pair of lions, possibly from the 1935 episode, was added to that vestibule setting in 1937. The late-arriving pair is still on display; the earlier pair was dispersed after Hearst's death.

146. See note 37 in this chapter; see also Hearst to Morgan, February 19, 1927; Hearst/Mor-gan Correspondence, Morgan Collection.

147. Morgan's efforts in the Doges Suite, for example, had not been confined to the session on December 10 that Loorz mentioned three days later. She had written to Hearst in New York nearly a month earlier, telling him about the decorative items recently added to those mezzanine rooms. See Morgan to Hearst, November 19, 1935; Hearst/Morgan correspondence, Morgan Collection.

He was tired in the afternoon from having gotten up so early and the long ride [out from New York?][148] and Albert [Redelsperger, the butler] said in not too pleasant spirits by supper time. That is quite natural being so tired.

I will let a few men off this Saturday [December 14] and will be able to make considerable more showing by keeping the Pool crew for a few days next week.

Hearst was undoubtedly feeling better when he wrote to Loorz on Sunday the fifteenth, but his letter wasn't about what he'd seen on his homecoming tour the previous Thursday. It was about conditions in Hearst Camp:

I think the little cabins that the working people occupy can stand a good deal of improvement.

First, suppose you take a force of men and put the cabins themselves in first-class shape.

Put heavier floors on so there will not be so much leakage of air; fix the roofs if they need it; and make the place as comfortable and as agreeable as possible.

Then please get new beds—iron or brass—and please get new sheets and blankets throughout of a good kind.

The blankets can still be gray blankets, if those are preferred; but they should be heavy, warm, woolen ones of the best class.

Get rugs for the floor—carpet rugs of course—and make the places as nice as possible.

How about baths and showers? Would it not be well to put a toilet, basin and shower between each two cabins, so that the men can have access to these bathrooms without going into the outer air?

I feel that we ought to do these things and I would rather do this before we resume our own construction.

If we started a crew the first of January, we could have things pretty well done by the time the men get back.

This type of grand gesture, this elaborate paternalism, seems an instance of the kingly Hearst at his most benevolent, his most humane, his most enlightened. Taken at face value from a vantage point several decades removed, his proposal seems wholly practical—straightforward and in no way patronizing. And yet many a critic or appraiser of Hearst's life could easily think otherwise. For that matter, Loorz himself looked askance at what had been, in reality, a long-festering problem.

---

148. On December 10, while westbound to California, Hearst had stopped in Topeka, Kansas, to meet Governor Alfred M. Landon, a Republican that Hearst and others hoped could dethrone Franklin Roosevelt in the 1936 election. See Swanberg, *Citizen Hearst*, p. 476. See also David Nasaw, *The Chief: The Life of William Randolph Hearst*, p. 516.

But back to the moment as 1935 drew to a close. On December 17, Loorz gave Morgan an update that summarized Hearst's thoughts about sprucing up Hearst Camp; he also mentioned some heftier work:

> Mr. Hearst stepped in [to my office] and asked me to keep right on the bear pits until they were completed so they could let the bears out [from Animal Hill]. Besides he added new pools to each division. Not big but [had we known] they could have been in with the rest which are being poured today.

Likewise on December 17, George Wright (sounding more like his old self) wrote again to Loorz, this time from the San Carlos Hotel in downtown Los Angeles, next to Pershing Square:

> I was a little bitter when I left; so I was bent on heading as far south as possible. I have always had a yen to go to Mexico City and I thought that would put as many miles as possible between us.
>
> But I stopped here in Los Angeles, had some good laughs, and regained my sense of humor. I think this is a good place to hang my hat; so I'll stay, if I can get located.
>
> Now the request. In seeking the position of chief engineer and general manager of several firms it is necessary to give the names of your employers for the past forty odd years — and the reason for leaving. Should they write you regarding me, may I ask that you do not overstress the point that I was dismissed for degeneracy, drunkenness, disrespect, moral turpitude, and the various other charges you have booked against me? . . .
>
> No I wasn't with Thelma Todd at the time.[149]

In answering Wright on December 20, Loorz admitted that the only time he'd seen him drunk was "that Saturday night" (December 7, before Wright's dismissal on the ninth). And even though Loorz couldn't excuse Wright's weakness for "John Barleycorn," he also admitted that he missed his former employee:

> We have had to raise the bottoms of the moats and put in elevated pools in each division of our new Grotto. It means a lot of pencil work for me. There has been a lot of changes and correspondence on the Santa Maria [sewer] job [also], all of which you could have handled just fine.

With Christmas about to descend, Loorz had entirely different words for Morgan, whom he also wrote to on December 20. "Mr. Hearst left yesterday for a quick

---

149. Todd was an actress (though not part of the Hearst-Davies circle) who had been found dead early on December 16, as much of the world knew when Wright wrote to Loorz the next day. See *Hot Toddy: The True Story of Hollywood's Most Sensational Murder*, by Andy Edmonds (New York, 1989).

buying trip in L.A." He also told her that a task mentioned several times in the past had finally been accomplished. "The minute he left we put up the scaffolding in the dining room [the Refectory] and hope to have all the additional lanterns in place and all ship shape when he returns, today or tomorrow."[150]

As for the situation Loorz aired in his long letter to Morgan on December 4, it finally cropped up again in a letter he wrote his business partner on the twenty-first:

> Fred you will be surprised to hear that I have asked Miss Morgan [to] relieve me on this job when convenient, no rush. I made her a proposition, if she wished me to run it and be here always when she or Mr. Hearst are here with an assistant on the job at all times O.K. However, I said, if she thot she had to have someone here steady I'd stay and work with him and show him all I know about the job. She didn't have the heart to speak to Mr. Hearst about it her last visit. We shall see. It would be nice if I could get it like [the situation you have at] Wyntoon but as it is it is like being in the army.

Stolte answered Loorz's letter promptly, on December 23:

> Your decision to arrange for a discharge from a steady diet comes not entirely unexpected. I had been wanting to talk to you of this as I felt you were loading up yourself with a lot of work, with all the outside jobs, and I have been of very little help there.
>
> It had been on my mind to suggest a trade of jobs, to give you a change of climate etc., if no other arrangement could be made.
>
> There seems to be a lot of work coming out for figures in the new year. So we should be able to do as much work in 1936 as in this year. The jobs from $50,000 up have very little competition.

Happy news came Loorz's way from George Wright, who wrote from Los Angeles on Christmas Day that he had found work with an engineering company the previous week. "I think that when you discharged me, you actually kicked me upstairs. So I am well pleased with the whole business."

Wright's letter, of course, would be a while in arriving. In the meantime, the Loorzes spent the holiday at home with their three sons. Alex Rankin (Jim Ran-

---

150. Back on June 27, right before Hearst went to Wyntoon, Loorz had told LeFeaver, "We could really do without the ironworker [Val Georges] for a while, except that he does all our blacksmith work":

> Also Mr. Hearst keeps sending pictures of [antique] ironwork down [from his office] for me to have our iron worker duplicate [mainly for Wyntoon]. I have enough of them to keep him busy for three months. He [Hearst] has repeatedly asked for two more lighting fixtures in the Dining Room. Wants this man to make them like the present ones. So I really haven't had the courage to let him go.

kin's son), Jud Smelser (the Wyntoon watchdog), and Ed March (the new head gardener) joined them for "eating, drinking, singing and jabbering," as Loorz told
Charlie Badley two days later. The group was entertained by the toys Miss Morgan
had sent, as that same writer — the ceaseless Loorz — recalled for her a day sooner,
December 26:

> The little electric Questions and Answers you sent to Don proved to be the high
> spot of the well filled toy room.
>   We all stretched our imaginations and recalled our schooling trying to answer
> questions all the way from Jokes to Chemistry. Don plying the questions con-
> tinually. . . .
>   We thank you also for the other toys and the ginger bread men and the nick-
> nacks. Things you can obtain in few places and that always catch the eye. Though
> Bobby is a bit too young to know what it is all about, he has certainly been inter-
> ested in the xmas tree and the numerous pieces of paper. So much so that we have
> had to halt his traffic on the kitty-car until things are removed. He rolls right up
> to the tree and starts dismantling. His mother caught him with two broken [orna-
> ments] and a bit of stain on his lips. We found nothing inside his mouth so appar-
> ently she just reached him in time. She had placed chairs around the tree laying
> down but he forcefully shoved the chairs back into the branches until he could
> reach the colorful ornaments.

In closing, Loorz said a few words about The Enchanted Hill:

> The pool area looks fine with the statue bases all covered with marble, the [Birth
> of Venus statuary] niche completed and the two portions of [cast stone] railing up
> either side at the lower end of the Neptune stairs. The weather has been fine and
> I think they used the pool for Mr. Hearst insisted that they bring it up to 75 de-
> grees which meant two all night runs [of the boilers].

Except for a light rain on December 26, the mild weather lasted a few more
days, until a heavy storm blew in on the twenty-ninth.[151] As Loorz told Morgan on

---

151. At that moment an ill wind was blowing Hearst's way from another quarter. The news of
it reached Colonel Willicombe:

> This letter is for *you* unless you know that the Chief already knows that a hostile book called
> THE LORD OF SAN SIMEON written by Oliver Carlson and Ernest Sutherland Bates is
> soon to be published by the Viking Press. There is no use making him unhappy and bothering
> him about it. The article I read about it is filled with a lot of misstatements, but I am trying to
> get out our book [*William Randolph Hearst: American*] ahead of theirs which is supposed to ap-
> pear in March or April. I don't want to mess up your holiday with any additional vexation or
> effort, but I should like to get those San Simeon pictures so as to make W.R. look *very, very won-
> derful* and send them on to New York [to D. Appleton-Century Company] as soon as possible.

The writer said that, for most of the book, she already had "a very nice lot of pictures, thanks to Janet

December 27: "We had a nice fresh rain last night. Only about ⅓ inch of rain but enough to keep things green and still be very good weather for the party."

He also said that Hearst's guests seemed to be having a good time outdoors. "There is a lot of horse-back riding, hiking and tennis playing that is unusual at this time of the year."[152]

Peck and Walter Howey." From Cora Older [Mrs. Fremont Older] to Willicombe, December 27, 1935; Hearst Papers, carton 19 (under "1935 Samples"). Mrs. Older wired the Chief himself a few weeks later, her biography of him having just been published. "It was the greatest experience of my writing life," she said. From Older to Hearst, February 7, 1936; Hearst Papers, carton 20 (under "1936 Samples").

152. Among the guests during the 1935 Christmas season was the actress Paulette Goddard, who brought with her two of England's leading men of letters, Hugh Walpole and H. G. Wells. Walpole described San Simeon in his journal: "What a place!" began the colorful entry. Then he recounted that Wells "gave a great oration at dinner, saying in his whispering squeaky voice that the past hundred years in American history were nothing for Americans to be proud of, and that since 1920 Americans had behaved like idiots [in world affairs]." In response to that and other dismissals by Wells, "the Americans at table looked blue and were very polite." From Rupert Hart-Davis, *Hugh Walpole: A Biography* (New York, 1952), p. 364.

1936

Anxieties and Expectations

As MUCH AS HEARST LOVED celebrating Christmas at San Simeon, the 1935 holiday season proved to be the last he would spend there until 1938. And thus each of the two years remaining to George Loorz on The Enchanted Hill would be eerily quiet come December, although many other months would be as active as they had been in past years—not only for Loorz but for Hearst and Morgan as well.

Loorz was back at his typewriter on January 2, 1936. He produced "just a few lines" for Miss Morgan, telling her that Hearst and his entourage were about to leave San Simeon:

> Whether it is to stay away for quite a while or just break up a very large party I am not certain. Since it is a little earlier than anticipated you can draw your own conclusions.
>
> The weather looks threatening again so we may be quite uncomfortable with the little work we are doing in the [bear] grotto etc.

Hearst headed south, for on January 7 Loorz wrote to him at the *Los Angeles Examiner* with details of work they had discussed in December:

> In completing the first set of improved rooms for the help [in Hearst Camp] I am not certain just how nice you wish them. They look real nice with the new wood finish but of course would look better painted. This I will do unless you write differently. . . .
>
> I have not completed my figures on the proposed excavation below [down the road from] the Grotto. Will present them soon.
>
> If the rain, holds off another day, we will have practically all of the footings poured for the remaining columns of the Pergola. . . .
>
> Weather permitting I intend to start hauling the remaining columns right away. This will keep the White [truck] busy for three weeks without any other hauling.
>
> I approximated the cost of the original division of the grotto with grills at

$3000. This will cost more because we had to dig real deep with footings in the old fill [which] I was not aware of at the time of the estimate. Also Mr. Baldwin [the zookeeper] has wisely requested a number of drains etc that I did not include.

Hearst answered Loorz on January 9. He devoted most of his reply to the improvements in Hearst Camp, but he also said, "The added cost on the animal pits will be satisfactory."

Morgan was also one who wrote to Loorz on January 9; her concern was the next phase of work within Casa Grande:

I think we had better set out to *finish* entirely the room directly over the billiard room.

1. There is a Gothic stone doorway [in Hearst's stock of antiques] on the order of the ones alongside the mantel in [the] billiard room, that could be copied by your clever plasterer as he did there. As the windows come practically to the cornice at top and have no elaborate trim, just a Gothic moulding is needed.

Morgan's letter had three more numbered entries; they, too, specified for Loorz what else would be needed for the architectural decoration of the room. "Present plan is to be down Monday," she concluded, "unless it is a set in storm. Will be coming from Monterey."[1] She would be coming the long way around, that is, through Salinas, King City, and San Luis Obispo: the completion of the Big Sur highway still lay more than a year ahead.

Morgan, like Loorz, must have been feeling pressure from Hearst to resume work at San Simeon, even this early in the 1936 season. On January 11, the Saturday before her expected arrival, Loorz told Stolte that Hearst (who was not only sending written messages but also staying in close touch by telephone) thought "work should be progressing"—this despite nearly a week of heavy rain.[2]

---

1. Morgan owned a home on Divisadero Street in San Francisco for many years, beginning in the mid- or late twenties (p. 53, note 7). In 1934 she bought a second home at 1072 Franklin Street in Monterey, her acclaimed work for the YWCA at Asilomar (in adjoining Pacific Grove) having drawn her to that area early in her career; in fact, it was an area she had known since childhood.

Situated in the block bounded by Franklin, Cedar, Hellam, and High streets—near the Presidio of Monterey—the home was well hidden amid the pines ("Invisible," as Lynn McMurray, born in 1943, recalls from her youth). On October 27, 1937, Loorz described Morgan's property to a local realtor, Frank Binnie: "She owns only the small house and the five [undeveloped] lots on the rear street [Hellam Street] and a private entrance from Franklin St. A Mrs. Stephens I think owns the large house on Franklin [itself]." All told, Morgan's holdings when Loorz wrote Binnie were about three quarters of an acre; see also *Descriptive Guide to the Julia Morgan Collection*, p. 40 (II/01/03/18).

2. From "F.C.S. [F. C. Stolte Co.] 1936" (one of three boxes appended in 1990 to the main body of the Loorz Papers). As was stated on p. 26 in this volume, note 13, all three boxes were excluded from *The Builders Behind the Castles: George Loorz & the F. C. Stolte Co.* (San Luis Obispo, 1990).

The weather stabilized in time for Morgan to appear on Monday the thirteenth. Her visit prompted several entries in Loorz's recap notes for the room formally named Billiard Room Wing Room #1. (The narrow Billiard Room Wing in Casa Grande — or more simply the Billiard Wing — consists of the Billiard Room on the first floor and its three surmounting bedrooms. The nomenclature, though basic enough, can be confusing — witness some of Loorz's own references to these rooms in the pages ahead. "Room #1" properly refers to the bedroom on the second floor, whereas "Room #2" and "Room #3" refer to the bedrooms on the third and fourth floors. The four-story Billiard Wing connects the larger Recreation Wing — or the New Wing, as that north section was renamed in the 1940s — with the older, central section of Casa Grande.)

"Use [Spanish] corbels as selected to do the ceiling," went one of Loorz's notes on January 13 for Room #1. "Check with Mr. Williams [in the San Simeon warehouses] to see if there are plenty available."

Loorz also needed to see if there were any "beams left over from [the Gothic] Study" that could be used in Room #1. In addition, Morgan wanted him to "use [antique] stone doorway [frame] selected for the bathroom or closet and have the others [matching copies] cast of proper width." As for the matching doors themselves that Room #1 required, she had a certain "antique oak carved doorway" in mind as a "sample from which to carve new proper doors."

Loorz wrote to Hearst in Los Angeles two days later, on Wednesday, January 15. He said, "Miss Morgan has given me complete details for the room over the Billiard Room and we are already concentrating upon it." He also told Hearst, "She said you had not mentioned the bowling allies [*sic*]." Hearst planned to install bowling lanes in the basement underneath the Theater, which adjoins the Billiard Room (and which also forms the ground floor of the Recreation Wing, as it was then being called).

But the recent weather was more the subject of Loorz's letter to Hearst. "The road [up the hill] held up pretty well under the $7\frac{1}{2}$ inch rain we had in four days," he told him, referring to the deluge of the previous week. And he had this to add:

> After all that rain I drove all over the [newly surfaced] airport with my car, fast, slow, turning quickly etc and made no impression whatever. I was really surprised at this where we had so much fill in many places. Even the heavy weight of the big plan[e] should be perfectly safe.

As was also stated on p. 26, these and still later appendants are, for the most part, the only ones whose provenance I've noted in this newer book. The exceptions include items in the Morgan Collection and other holdings that I've paraphrased or quoted.

Just to be sure, though, Loorz thought they should "take the precaution to add a little more oil in these places next summer." Hearst agreed.[3]

In writing to Morgan the next day, January 16, Loorz had the latest news for her about Room #1 in the Billiard Wing. He also mentioned the bear grottos, whose partitions he was trying to complete for Hearst on the slope of Orchard Hill, a mile west of Casa Grande and the heart of The Enchanted Hill:

> If all goes well I should have the [first] grotto nearly completed [before my vacation] and perhaps he would let me wait until I returned to start dividing the next one. (He seems real anxious to get them divided and the beast removed from the top of the hill [near the Roman Pool].) However he will surely need a lot more pens or must dispose of a lot more animals for the six pens will help little.

While Loorz was tackling these and other projects for Hearst and Morgan, the new San Simeon branch of the F. C. Stolte Co. was also keeping him busy. "I have myself up to my neck in work and cant see my way clear yet," Loorz said on January 16 to his friend Bill Hollister, the County Assessor in San Luis Obispo. "On top of that I'm inviting more with the bidding on these coast schools [Cambria, Cayucos, Morro Bay], Santa Maria Hospital addition and the Lompoc Veterans Memorial building."[4] Loorz had similar words for Stolte on the sixteenth as well, telling him the new branch was working "morning, noon & night" on preparing estimates.[5]

A few days later—"Jan. 19" appears in the Morgan-Forney ledgers—Morgan went to Pasadena for the first time in 1936: her friend Edythe Tate Thompson was ready to build a house there. Very well. Hadn't Morgan resumed her pursuit of these non-Hearst accounts with gusto, now that her ill health of recent years was all but behind her?[6] And with that exception, hadn't she *always* been making such trips, over and above her efforts for Hearst?

---

3. Hearst penciled his concurring "Yes" in the margin of the letter; Willicombe sent it back to Loorz on January 19. As for a question Loorz had raised about the bear grotto, Hearst planned to return soon from Los Angeles and would address it then. Yet he wasn't at San Simeon again for nearly a month.

4. Loorz secured two of these jobs: the grammar schools in Cambria and Morro Bay, each designed by Louis Crawford of Santa Maria. But about this same time in 1936, he must have thought he'd be getting all three; on January 30 he told a friend named Harry DeHaes, "I'm the low bidder on Morro School, Cayucos & Cambria bids this week." Concerning Lompoc, see p. 206 in this volume, note 105.

5. From "F.C.S. 1936" (see note 2, above). Henceforth in this chapter, all such annotations will cite the name of the box only, as given here.

6. True, Morgan was fully active again once she got past 1933, her low point after her mastoid operations in 1932. But further on in 1936 she recounted an episode—perhaps a typical one—that occurred in Paris while she was abroad in 1934–35: her "mastoid trouble" had affected her hearing.

Absolutely, unquestionably, indisputably. Or so go some long-held beliefs, en-shrined within the Morgan myth.

In truth, it had been two years since Morgan made such a trip *without* also checking on *some* Hearst account, large or small—not since February 1934, when she went to the Monday Club in San Luis Obispo. Even then, Loorz had met her in town that day. Otherwise, a good four years had passed since any of Morgan's non-Hearst accounts lured her away from the Bay Area: to Illinois for Principia College in January 1932 and, two months later, to California's north-coast red-woods for the "Hearthstone" project.[7] In this same reverse order, two more years can be unfurled, clear back to 1930: back to the big YWCA job in Riverside and also to the YWCA job at the University of Hawaii, a smaller project that drew but a single visit (made by Jim LeFeaver in her stead). And in looking even further back—back to the late twenties at least—one can still find sizeable gaps between those trips that stood fully apart from her Hearst activity.

With Morgan slated to make another Monday visit to San Simeon (on Jan-uary 27), Loorz briefed her two days in advance on some of the problems to be solved.[8] Room #1 in the Billiard Wing posed its share, as did the Neptune Pool:

> One other consideration is that our outside pool is apparently leaking much too much. I think it is because it was empty so long it opened up at the junction of the old and new floor slabs. As soon as we know the party is not to be here for a period we can drain [it] and point up [re-grout] the marble. I say this because the house-hold have some guests coming in today and of course, they expect Mr. Hearst but have had no notification to that effect.

Morgan told Loorz during their meeting of January 27 to go ahead and drain the pool and to point up the marble as a precaution against further leakage. She also told him—according to his paraphrased notes—to "erect the remaining gar-ages and tear down the gypsie camp of miscellaneous structures near the lath house in the garden department."

This new year of 1936 would see much work of that more utilitarian kind at San Simeon. Hearst, of course, had written to Loorz about Hearst Camp back in mid-December.[9] "I am thrilled at the idea of having our camp cleaned up and

---

See Morgan to Georges Roty, July 28, 1936; Morgan Collection (in the file regarding the Phoebe Hearst portrait plaques, III/05/08/66).

7. See p. 40 in this volume and its note 30.

8. Loorz's letter is dated January 25, a Saturday—too late for it to have reached Morgan for her Monday session. He may have retained the letter and given it to her then. Or perhaps he sent it on Friday, January 24, with the date it bore being a typographical error.

9. See p. 227 in the previous chapter.

painted," Loorz said to Morgan on January 30. "I have regretted for a long time that it has been necessary to have the men live as they have."

Dick Nusbaum, an architect in the Morgan office, wrote to Loorz on February 5. Nusbaum (whose real first name was Lazer) told Loorz he was sending him "the detail drawing of doors for 2nd floor Gothic Bed Room"—meaning Room #1 in the Billiard Room Wing. "I hear that you are leaving for your vacation, soon," Dick also said. "Apparently you and I are the winter sparrows of this outfit."

LOORZ AND HIS WIFE, with their youngest son in tow, headed south on their vacation—to the same Gilman Hot Springs near Riverside that they had enjoyed in 1934. Yet they were unlucky enough to have continual rain, and then the trip was cut short by a death in Mrs. Loorz's family in Nevada.

"If I went into detail and told you everything that has happened to our little lot during this vacation," Loorz wrote Morgan on February 20, "you wouldn't believe [it]. It would be too ironical and extra ordinary." He assured her, though, that he wasn't "worried about anything." He was glad to be forced to stay home, at long last. "Instead of feeling that I'm losing my vacation, I'm really grateful that I can be at home and really take care of my own boys, without feeling that I'm shirking the job on the hill."

Loorz had a lot else to discuss, as he went on to tell Morgan in that same letter of February 20:

> Now Miss Morgan, have you ever had a chance to speak with Mr. Hearst about my work on the outside? If you think we can very frankly make suitable arrangements between us wherein I can spend just a portion of two or three days a month away from the job to look over the outside work. If finally with some such arrangement you still want me to stay on at the hill, I would like to stay. . . .
>
> Fred really wants to come down and take a lot of the responsibility of the local work on the Cambria and Morro Schools and two Santa Maria jobs.[10] That could not be for he could not give Wyntoon the personal attention it will need. Again with the contracts all signed and trades sub-let as they are the man who is running our work down here [Carl Daniels] is perhaps more capable than either of us. I should really have little to do about it.

In catching up on business after his brief vacation, Loorz hastened to pursue a lingering debt, the same day that he wrote to Morgan, February 20. He took dead

---

10. The two were the Santa Maria Sewage Plant and Santa Maria Junior College. (The latter name is obsolete; the building, however, remains on the campus of Santa Maria High School; college classes were held in it till the 1950s but have since been held at another local facility, Allan Hancock College.)

aim at W. W. Murray; for it was Bill Murray who, in San Francisco, presided over the Hearst Sunical Land & Packing Corporation and one of its foremost concerns, the Piedra Blanca (San Simeon) Ranch:[11]

> Please disregard this note if you have made a remittance of the balance on the Pico [Creek Stables] Job to the Oakland Office [of the F. C. Stolte Co.] within the past day or so. I am assuming you have been unable to make a remittance.
>
> Please feel that I understand your position in regards to making payments of large sums at all times. Even though you represent a wealthy firm, money is seldom, if ever, plentiful.
>
> However, every item has been paid in full on this job for some time and we have a good deal invested in the balance due us. We rushed the building thru at a reasonable figure with the understanding that it was a cash proposition.
>
> We are far from broke but we have a lot of good business going and it takes a lot of capital to operate it so we really need the money. Like yourselves we must collect enough to meet Income Taxes.

What a persuader! Loorz and Murray were good friends already, hence the liberties Loorz took in prodding him. (He closed with "Murray boy, please take care of us.") Who else, though, could have stood up to Hearst or Morgan, to Willicombe or LeFeaver, to Murray or any number of others the way Loorz so often did? He seemed to have the knack—the perfect knack for knowing when to attack and when to retreat. Surely Hearst alone could have stopped him cold if he was pushing too hard. Evidently he wasn't.[12]

Morgan's third and last visit in February fell on Monday the twenty-fourth. It yielded more notes on Billiard Wing Room #1 and, under "Miscellaneous," a wishful thought for good measure, one proving that Hearst hadn't forgotten how to dream: "Possibility of [Duplex] tower elevators for Doges and Deck room sections." What the Chief was eyeing were two smaller, winding staircases near the back of Casa Grande's central area, separate from and flanking the larger staircases in that part of the mansion. His thought of installing elevators in those Duplex Towers, as those smaller stairwells are called, was a fine idea. Fine for the Doges Suite, and especially for the North Deck and South Deck bedrooms, and even more so for the two Duplex suites on each side of the building. But what an

---

11. In regard to Murray, see p. 86, note 56. A letter of Loorz's on August 19, 1935, is addressed to Murray at the Piedmont Land & Cattle Co., whereas his letter of February 20, 1936, went to Murray at the Sunical Land and Packing Corporation. By 1936, the older name—Piedmont—signified a "department" within the newer Sunical entity (whose full name began with *Hearst*).

12. Loorz's bravado suited the occasion as far as Stolte was concerned. Stolte told his partner on March 15, "On the one trip to see Mr Murray, I did not make connections—he was out, so your letter was the means of getting the check." From "F.C.S. 1936."

expensive nightmare it would all have been: the tearing out, the re-designing, the re-pouring, the re-decorating. Nary a deafening jackhammer ever shattered the silence on that score.[13]

After a short stay at San Simeon in February, Hearst came back early the month after. "Attached are a couple of memos I sent up to Chief," said Willicombe to Loorz on March 7. That brief covering note evokes a distinct image. Hearst often worked alone, sometimes for hours on end, sequestered in the opulent rooms of Casa Grande—no doubt in his private third-floor suite much of the time. Even Willicombe kept the requisite distance, constantly busy all the while in his own office, not far from Hearst Camp; there he awaited the master's next summons. The two memos, at any rate, pertained to the bear grottos Loorz was working on. Hearst's unmistakable scrawl filled the right margin of the first memo: "We will turn the grizzlies into the new grottos and leave the Polars in the old ones for the present."

Loorz had spoken of "ironical and extra ordinary" events when he wrote Morgan on February 20. They continued apace for him. He next found himself practically immobilized for days on end by an ear infection. On Friday, March 13, he told Stolte, "This is the first time in my married life [since 1925] that I've actually been confined at home for more than 24 hours. It will be two weeks [this] Monday [March 16] since I left the hill."[14] With his head still throbbing, Loorz wrote to Morgan on March 13 as well:

> Though I have handled my correspondence and been on the phone continuously talking to Ray [Van Gorden], Pete [Petersen] and others of our boys on the hill, I do not feel that I have earned my salary. The trouble is non-compensative so it [is] not more than right that I should be omitted from the payroll for one week at least. That is providing they will let me go back on Monday [the sixteenth] which I am hoping. If not, I cannot expect pay for next week either. It is a big salary and I want to earn it always.
>
> I hope to see you on Monday [March 16] and decide definitely on corbels & beams for 2nd floor [Billiard Wing Room#1] bathroom ceiling and for the wood

---

13. Hearst's ideas for film projects were no less vivid, now or at any other time. Three days after Loorz made note of the Duplex elevators, Hearst expounded on subjects for motion-picture biographies. "Sir Walter Raleigh and Sir Francis Drake are spectacular characters who had much to do with the early life in the colonies. Sir Francis Drake discovered San Francisco Bay. Both participated in the defeat of the Armada." Like the remodeled Duplex Towers he visualized, the film subjects Hearst mentioned to Warner Bros.—Betsy Ross, Andrew Jackson, Davy Crockett, and several others were also named—were all "interesting pictorially." Indeed, they all exemplified "the spectacular kind." From Hearst to Jack Warner, February 27, 1936; Hearst Papers, carton 20 (under "1936 Samples").

14. From "F.C.S. 1936."

finish in the dressing room. No work is being done on these at present. How is Mr. [F. M.] Lorenz[15] coming on the doors? That reminds me I must order some olive knuckle butts to hang those doors with, also some locks and handles. I'd like to have this room in a more or less completed and cleaned state for Mr. Hearst to visit.

In correspondence with him thru Willicombe, Mr. Hearst has permitted [us] to stop work on the next grotto, has again said go ahead with the next cottage for the help and general improvement of helps quarters. . . .

Understand that Mr. Hearst is returning today or soon. Hope to have things please him so that he will appreciate that we have been doing something. I wonder how he liked our new steps and the [garden] jars on the posts at the West entrance [between the West Terrace and the Neptune Pool].[16]

Sure enough, Morgan appeared on Monday, March 16. And yet the Loorz Papers lack any recap notes from her visit. (They also lack any from her visits of March 2 and 9, which occurred while Loorz's ear was infected.) Nevertheless, Loorz usually heard the latest news on San Simeon as soon as anyone did and, quite often as quickly, the latest on Wyntoon. Stolte touched on the latter subject while writing to his partner on Sunday the fifteenth:

Last eve—[Eugene] Kower phoned—seems Willicomb[e] phoned to him, that Mr Hearst wanted the airport started and Kower passed it on to me. So far Miss Morgan has not mentioned it so I shall see her. In the meantime, I can get the costs together, and would like to get from you the description of surface, etc., used at San Simeon [on its airport].

Lathrop[17] had compiled a cost—last fall, and LeFeaver and myself had checked it. This project has become rather involved—Kower, Lathrop—(LeFeaver, Miss Morgan) and ourselves, and unless you have other suggestions, I am seeing Miss Morgan.[18]

---

15. A master woodcarver who, like the better-known Jules Suppo, was based in San Francisco and had been doing custom work for San Simeon since the 1920s.

16. This "entrance" feature was the one that Loorz first described on May 7, 1935, while writing to Mac McClure; it was the same feature that Hearst had mentioned to Morgan on April 15, 1935 (see p. 187, note 67, and pp. 188–89, note 69).

17. Most likely F. L. Lathrop, one of Hearst's attorneys. Frank Lathrop (his informal name) figures more prominently in matters stemming from the Hearst holdings at the Grand Canyon and in Mexico.

18. In a follow-up passage written on Tuesday, March 17, Stolte said, "Undoubtedly, by this time Miss Morgan has gone over the Wyntoon problems." Because Stolte had first mentioned the airport on Sunday, and because Morgan had been at San Simeon the next day, he probably hadn't been able to talk to her yet. Stolte to Loorz, in "F.C.S. 1936."

That northern estate, meanwhile, was still in its off-season, hibernating mode:

In his notes based on Morgan's visit of March 23, Loorz recorded a typical instance of her practicality, a trait she had long exhibited, in hard economic times and all others. Room #1 in the Billiard Wing provided the cue: "Can send up for floors (travertine) when truck takes busts and pedestals to Oakland." Travertine, known as "poor man's marble" in San Simeon lore, had already paved many an interior on the hill; and thus a tradition would continue. But what about those sculptures bound for Oakland? Loorz clarifed things in his final note on March 23: "Driver to take busts and pedestals to Butler S. Sturtevant, California Spring Garden Show, Exposition Bldg, Oakland. (Will be shipped tomorrow if Mr. Williams gets them all packed etc.)." Williams needed a second day, whereupon the sculptures went north for a month's showing — in an early instance of Hearst's making a museum loan (granted, a minor one) from his vast accumulations at San Simeon.[19]

As to the question Loorz posed back on February 20 — he had asked Morgan whether she'd talked to Hearst about his outside work and whether she thought suitable arrangements could be made — the letter Loorz wrote on March 24 to his brother and sister-in-law, Claude and Freda, comes about as close as any to supplying the answer: "Even though I turned in my resignation here in the face of my outside work, they have asked me to go on taking what time off I needed to take care of my own work. However, they may tire of that before long and oust me."[20] Loorz

---

Chief has told Vice President Saunders of the Southern Pacific [Railroad] that he might look around the grounds at Wyntoon, so it will be okey if he comes along [appears there] to show him around the grounds, that is all. It has been explained to Mr. Saunders that houses are closed, no accommodations of any kind.

Draft of telegram from Willicombe to Eugene Kower, March 22, 1936; Hearst Papers, carton 20 (under "1936 Samples").

19. Eight busts were involved. Some were taken from their places along the Esplanade, near Casa Grande, and later reinstalled; they remain there today. The man they were entrusted to, with a name befitting a Civil War general, was mentioned years afterward by the same Edward Hussey who once worked at Wyntoon. "Back there [at Principia College in Illinois] we had a landscape architect, Butler Sturtevant, that he [Bernard Maybeck] and Mrs. Maybeck didn't have much use for because he was a very egotistical and stuffed-shirt sort of fellow. . . . He acted like a big shot. He was a young fellow too, compared to Mr. Maybeck." See Suzanne B. Riess's interview with Hussey in *The Julia Morgan Architectural History Project*, Vol. II, p. 90.

In May 1935 Hearst lent several Spanish furnishings and decorative items to the California Pacific International Exposition, held in San Diego's Balboa Park, where the more renowned Panama-California Exposition had flourished almost twenty years before. For nearly that long in San Francisco, the M. H. de Young Museum had been displaying things from Hearst's collection, and from his mother's, too, some having first been shown at Maybeck's Palace of Fine Arts during the Panama-Pacific Exposition.

20. In writing to a man named Roy Snider the next day, Loorz was more specific in saying how long these new terms might last, namely, "for this year at least." (Snider was about to buy the Loorzes' home in Berkeley — the one whose attic once held records of the Beach House.)

also remarked that his monthly phone bill was running as high as ninety dollars on the branch-office work. "Oh me, good thing I had quite a little profit on those jobs [done in 1935]."

Hearst, after leaving the hill for a week or so, had been back in residence since mid-March. He was keeping the more humdrum projects in mind, right along with the more fascinating ones. "Mr. Hearst says to run the new help's house parallel with the others," Colonel Willicombe notified Loorz on March 27, "do not angle it back [toward the top of the hill]." As the Colonel explained, "The reason for this is in order to keep space for an extension of the incoming drive [near the south side of Casa Grande], which Miss Morgan expects to make soon."

WYNTOON HAD BEEN ON HEARST'S MIND as well with the coming of spring. Stolte, of course, had told Loorz on March 15 that Hearst wanted to get started on the airport there. Although Stolte had represented his and Loorz's company at Wyntoon for the past three seasons, Loorz was still more privy to the latest ideas Hearst and Morgan were hatching for the place. Loorz hadn't been to Wyntoon since he began working at San Simeon in 1932, and he wouldn't visit that northern estate again until 1938.[21] He was nonetheless able to spell things out for his partner on March 25,[22] saying "another banner year" at Wyntoon seemed likely for the F. C. Stolte Co.:

> Let's hope it turns out as good as last year or better with prompt payments all the way thru.
>
> I will design the bridge here for you right away [to span the McCloud River at the Bavarian Village] and make arrangements for the trusses to be built by the Summerbell Truss Co. . . .[23]
>
> Mac [McClure] gave me the sketch of the house he [Hearst] intends to build over [the bridge] and told me the length was from 82 to 84 feet, but will let me know as soon as he gets there. I took this all up with Miss Morgan. They want the bridge to be built right away.
>
> The story for the first month, which of course, will be changed, is as follows:
> 1 Painter
> 1 Foreman

---

21. See p. 189, plus its note 71.

22. From "F.C.S. 1936."

23. The arrangements were made. Stolte told Loorz on April 14 that Summerbell was "putting up the trusses and floor of the bridge" (from "F.C.S. 1936"). And the main Wyntoon account (Morgan-Forney ledgers) includes an entry under May 4 for an expenditure of $100: "Summerbell Truss Co. engr. design for bridge." See also pp. 191–92 (note 78) concerning Walter Huber's work in 1936—either on this same bridge or on a different one, farther down the McCloud River by The Gables.

12 carpenters

6 laborers

Allowance for a little plumbing & electrical work etc but no steady crew.

Total allowance of $11,000 to be spent as follows:

Approximately,

Materials	1,000	
Mill crew	1,000	hauling etc
Bridge	4,000	(Should cost less)
Repairs	500	Present bridges etc.
Turrets	2,500	Carpenters & helpers
Carving	1,500	
Misc	500	

Loorz also said that if Hearst allotted "the extra $5000" (a prospect that had apparently been considered), Stolte would "start a building for [the] help at the ranch house site" and would "do something on the Bridge house." In regard to the eventual Cinderella House in the Bavarian Village (a building for now called The Turrets), Loorz said this before he signed off on March 25:

> You know $2500 is not going to make much of a showing on the Turrets and the outline shows nothing on the other buildings at all. I know they will want other work but I would first notify them that they will not have the showing the[y] want on other work if they do.

Loorz wrote again to his partner a week later, on April 1, with precise details about the airport surfacing that had been used at San Simeon and that Stolte was contemplating for Wyntoon. "I only hope they keep up with expenses this year," said Loorz. "That would be sweet. We will need all [the money] we have and can get to operate all this work we are getting."[24]

As regarded the main office of the F. C. Stolte Co. in Oakland, Loorz was referring not only to Wyntoon but also to bread-and-butter jobs like General Pete gas stations in the Bay Area and the San Joaquin Valley. The Oakland office was tackling some bigger jobs, too. These ranged from a project right in town for Miss Morgan, the Kings Daughters Home, whose enlargement the company had secured in 1935, to some dormitories in Yosemite Valley, designed by E. T. Spencer for employees of the Yosemite Park & Curry Co.[25] Meanwhile, the San Simeon branch

---

24. From "F.C.S. 1936."

25. Morgan began her third of four follow-up jobs at Kings Daughters in October 1936. The Stolte Co. isn't mentioned in the Morgan-Forney ledgers for that job or its predecessor in 1935. But the company's own Trial Balance sheets encompass both jobs. See also p. 216, note 125. Concerning

office was landing more and more schools and other jobs around San Luis Obispo County and in Santa Barbara County. Neither office had done much in the territory that still separated their spheres of activity—in areas like Monterey County, Santa Cruz County, and San Benito County—but that would soon be changing.

Loorz spoke of his branch-office work in writing to his parents on April 2.[26] While he was at it, he also spoke of what remained his stock in trade—his work at San Simeon for Hearst and Morgan:

> The rain and government delays have held up some of the school jobs a little too much for me to make any progress or profit but I refuse to worry for they will go ahead sometime, then everything will be O.K. . . .
>
> Things are booming here on the hill again. Mr. Hearst and party are here and that means we must keep on our toes and keep lots of things moving. However, that is when I enjoy the place most so I'm not complaining. . . .
>
> We had a few days of rain and cold wind but it has been lovely for a couple of days. Weather men and old timers warn me against a coming storm very shortly so I dont know what to do. I have a crew of men way back in the hills on the [Burnett] road. If it rains real hard they'll have difficulty getting out. They have plenty to eat so it doesn't matter anyway.[27]

Loorz wrote on April 9 to yet another George in these annals—to George Edmunson, a college student in Davis, near Sacramento, who was one of two coyote hunters recruited the year before. Edmunson received some densely packed pages of fatherly advice, aimed at helping the younger man with his school work. "Now George," Loorz said as he wound down, "I could write on for hours for I enjoy it, it is a break from the routine of figures and prices and building, but I just must stop." (What a boon that Loorz so often *couldn't* stop.) This time he stopped by telling Edmunson there would be more trapping at San Simeon that summer. "I'll hold the job open until I hear from you."

Spencer and the dormitories at Yosemite (among many other buildings he designed there as the Curry architect), see *Yosemite & Its Innkeepers: The Story of a Great Park and Its Chief Concessionaires*, by Shirley Sargent (Yosemite, 1975), pp. 93, 122.

Morgan's name occasionally crops up in regard to the famous Ahwahnee Hotel—a building designed in the 1920s by Gilbert Stanley Underwood, who preceded E. T. Spencer at Yosemite. The misattribution may stem from Morgan's association with the F. C. Stolte Co. in the 1930s. It may also stem from a sanitarium she designed earlier in her career in Ahwahnee, a small town in the foothills below Yosemite National Park.

26. The date also marked the year's first trip to Wyntoon by Morgan or anyone from her staff. In this case LeFeaver went up; Morgan made her first visit there in mid-April. A couple of days before LeFeaver's trip in early April, Morgan went to the Beach House for the first time in 1936, after which she checked on the new job in Pasadena for Edythe Tate Thompson.

27. Loorz also mentioned that his two older sons, Don and Bill, would be on Easter break the following week. The grandparents could easily visualize the fun: "Our place is so centrally located and we have such attractions as the pool that other children are in the yard most of the time."

Loorz's outside jobs—which Edmunson, like many others, got to read about
—took a back seat when Loorz wrote to Morgan on April 11. He had much to tell
her about San Simeon alone, where she'd been on April 6 (preceding her second
trip that season to the Beach House). Loorz apologized; he hadn't compiled his latest recap notes.[28] Pete Petersen, his top carpenter, was in the hospital and Ray Van
Gorden had also been ill. Yet there was plenty to report:

> The panels in the [Roman] Temple [at the Neptune Pool] looked well balanced
> when raised to the member of the cap molds you indicated so John [Vanderloo] is
> proceeding with his molds for casting. The little raised member as a border adds
> a lot to the panels.
>
> We can leave the pool today, Saturday with both sets of steps leading down [to
> it from the dressing rooms] completed except for cleaning of the marble. . . .
>
> It certainly has been difficult to make any good showing with the large party
> here. We cannot do hardly anything until 10 o'clock and then have to be careful
> until 11. Of course, we work in the shop [on the slope northeast of Animal Hill]
> preparing etc but it does not show. We understand that the party is leaving Mon-
> day so we should swing into it with earnest intentions next week.
>
> Shall we plan on imitation stone [in the Billiard Wing] on the walls of the 3rd
> floor [the fourth floor: Room #3] as on the 2nd over the Billiard Room [the third
> floor: Room #2]?[29] We are not up to it [the fourth floor] but will be soon. The
> stone doorways are set completely. We are now lathing though we cannot com-
> plete [it] until we receive the sash. . . .
>
> Certain packages arrived from May Co. in Los Angeles. Peter rabbit will tell
> the tale tomorrow morning [Easter Sunday]. It is difficult to guess to whom we
> are grateful.
>
> The weather has been just wonderful and I think Mr. Hearst has enjoyed his
> visit here a lot. . . .
>
> The usual spring excitement of mosquitoes, grassing [weeds] filling washes etc
> helps to keep variety on the jobs, together with the continual helps quarters, ani-
> mal fences & quarters, gates, culverts, roads, howling coyotes and trapping. Then
> too there is the ever increasing and more than occasional hunt for one or another
> of the *Dashunds* (you know over modelled sausages). We have sounded two general
> alarms this week to round up some special pet.
>
> I forgot to mention much excitement arranging chauffeurs and cars for two

---

28. He may have skipped compiling them altogether: the Loorz Papers lack them.

29. In saying "2nd over the Billiard Room," Loorz was idiomatically on track. True, the three
bedrooms above the Billiard Room belong to what is formally called the Billiard Room Wing (or
somewhat less formally the Billiard Wing). Yet in everyday parlance—dating from Hearst's time—
the rooms are simply called 1st Over Billiard, 2nd Over Billiard, and 3rd Over Billiard. (In these
three instances, the plural variant *Billiards* has since gained equal or even surpassing stature.)

picnics this week and a rush order to have all trails cleared of branches and slides for equestrians etc. None of them small jobs when done to satisfaction.[30]

I think they intend going to Jolon today over a hastily cleared and yet muddy road (in spots). A rush to clear landing field on other side for planes to bring them back. Then, no doubt, Mac has told you that he [Hearst] sees no reason why we dont send men over right away to alter the rooms [in the Milpitas Hacienda] as intended. He told this to Mac and not to me.

Concerning the Burnett Road and the Hacienda at Jolon, Loorz wrote on April 14 to Millard Hendricks, who had been part of the Burnett crew in past seasons:

The three Barkers [Roy, Verne, and Wayne] have been out there two weeks and have the road in pretty fair shape. Only one really big slide and that just below the [Salmon Creek] gorge. I drove from the Milpitas house to the hilltop in 1 hr. 15 min. yesterday morning. Not bad eh!

Mr. Hearst and about 40 guests drove over last Saturday [April 11] for a fine Spanish picnic with 20 Spanish entertainers at Milpitas.

Hearst and his guests had "a lovely time," Loorz told Hendricks, most of them making a quick airplane flight back over the Santa Lucias rather than returning by car.

NINETEEN THIRTY-SIX was a Presidential election year, something Loorz and especially Hearst were well aware of. On April 18 the garrulous Loorz ventured into that subject in writing to Harry DeHaes, late of the San Simeon zoo staff, who was traveling in Belgium:

Well the Chief has spent a lot of time here lately. Seems to enjoy it a lot. Has been in a real good humor which is strange consider[ing] how bitter he has been with the administration as regards income taxes etc. He certainly has been hitting

---

30. Morgan had little to do with tasks and activities like those mentioned in these last two paragraphs. As a rule, such matters were the province of the Hilltop Fund, whereas her efforts came under the Hearst Construction Fund.

Yet certain efforts of hers were closely entwined with work stemming from the Hilltop Fund — indeed, so closely that four months later Loorz could write, "In accordance with instructions from Mr. Willicombe I have carefully gone over all construction etc covered by the Hilltop Fund with Miss Morgan." (Letter to A. R. Cutter, August 13, 1936; Loorz had even discussed with Morgan such extraneous pursuits as the San Carpojo Road, the subject of note 41, below.) Obviously, she had much to contribute to everyone's grasp of how projects at San Simeon had been managed since 1919, as well as how their records had been kept and their accounts balanced — regardless of the "fund."

Roosevelt hard in his editorials.[31] However, let me predict another victory for Roosevelt. Let me add, that though I differ a lot with some of the plans that have been inaugurated by this administration it has done a lot of good and can do more if given another four years. I dont think they'll put us on the rocks as predicted by their enemies.

Closer to home, Stolte was another person Loorz wrote to on April 18.[32] (If we take the go-getter Loorz at his word, he had been shirking his correspondence; he told his partner he had been "too busy to write to anyone.") A typical outpouring of details naturally ensued, beginning with news about the work at San Simeon: "I have the largest crew I've had here for a long time and on a lot of miscellaneous odd jobs that need a lot of supervising and attention." Loorz said it was "good to get back to laying out[33] and pushing again," but of course it took "time away from other things"—such as the outside jobs he also told Stolte about. These ranged from the Santa Maria Sewage Plant and the junior college building in that distant town (more than seventy miles south) to a "small cottage" in nearby Cambria, the first of many rustic summer homes the Cambria Pines Development Company hoped to build.[34]

---

31. Indeed, Hearst was both hitting and getting hit. In 1935, and especially in 1936, he was being scrutinized (and often lambasted) more than he had been in many years—and on a range of social and political issues. A survey of references to Hearst in *The New York Times* from the 1920s through the 1940s (based on the index of that paper) finds him at the apex in 1922, when he vied with Al Smith for the governorship of New York state. Not until 1935–36, when he was tangling with Roosevelt (among other adversaries), did he again prove as newsworthy; those two years also contributed numerous entries on Hearst to the *Readers' Guide to Periodical Literature*. The pendulum swung down into the early 1940s; beyond that, the man all but dropped from public view, remaining little noticed until his death in 1951. John Tebbel summarized it well in his *Life and Good Times of William Randolph Hearst* (New York, 1952), p. 368: "It should be remembered that in 1936 Hearst was a more controversial figure than at any time since 1918 [the final year of World War I], more so than he would ever be again."

Hearst's presence, however, is surprisingly faint (and sometimes non-existent) in several works on Roosevelt, the New Deal, and related subjects, just as it often is in works concerning the Spanish-American War. For example, the chapters in Albert Fried's *FDR and His Enemies* (New York, 1999) have recurrent sub-sections on Al Smith, Huey Long, John L. Lewis, Father Coughlin, and Charles Lindbergh—but none on Hearst. Nor does Hearst's name appear in the index.

32. From "F.C.S. 1936."

33. Loorz's letter to Harry DeHaes, written on this same day, explains what "laying out" meant: "Pete [Petersen, the carpentry foreman] is sick and in the hospital and I am doing all the lay-out work etc that he did."

34. Loorz had more to tell Stolte on April 18 about the small cottage: "It is figured close and our wild Swede Elof [Gustafson] is pounding like a madman to get completed by next Tuesday [April 21]. He built it practically alone in the past four weeks." As early as June 29, 1935, Loorz mentioned the prospect of building such "log cabins" through the new Stolte branch office; he did so while writing to Claude and Freda Loorz. Several of these cottages remain in Cambria; a belief like-

A few days later Loorz heard from George Wright, who had written to him from Los Angeles on April 20. Wright thought he would have been north by then on behalf of the Paddock Engineering Co., but instead he had been "shipped to Palm Springs to build a pool":

> I knocked that job out in a hurry and brought back a cost sheet that showed a damned good percentage. . . .
>
> I expect to knock off several pool jobs at Palm Springs this summer. By the time I get them built I will think back about the days on the Burnett Road in July and August and will wonder how we kept from freezing to death. At least there is no poison oak on the desert.

Dear old George, he really *had* regained his sense of humor in the wake of his dismissal by Loorz in December.

Loorz answered Wright on April 23, saying he'd be glad to see him and "lip over some dainty scandal and gossip a bit." Then he brought him up to date on the Hearst projects as well as others:

> I have the Santa Maria J. C. going strong and also the Morro School. Haven't started the Cambria School as yet for the old Government hasn't sent them any money. I wont start until someone assures me that the old long green is forth-coming.
>
> We are going again at Wyntoon. They are in the act of putting a bridge [over the McCloud River] at the [Bavarian] village. Still figuring and discussing the airport. Planned to be graded 400 x 4000 feet and paved 100 x 4000. If it takes six inches of stone to hold on that dry ash it will cost a pretty penny and Oh me is it worth it for a couple of landings a year.
>
> With all this work on the hill and my outside work George I am tied down continuously. Most every week end I take a trip around the [area and] imagine I'm checking things.

In the meantime, Colonel Willicombe (who along with Hearst would soon leave San Simeon and would not return till late May)[35] sent Loorz a typically lucid, matter-of-fact message — a reminder for us that exotic horticulture was a vital part of the hilltop's mystique. This was on April 21:

> Chief has ordered from Venezuela three cases of orchids that will have to be taken care of in a specially equipped greenhouse. I have spoken to Mr. March [Ed

---

wise remains that Hearst commissioned them. The misattribution recalls that of Morgan and the Ahwahnee Hotel (as in note 25, above).

35. Marion Davies had another picture to make at Warner Bros. in Burbank — *Cain and Mabel*, co-starring Clark Gable.

March, the head gardener] about it. Will you please arrange with him for con-struction of this greenhouse and necessary equipment to take care of these or-chids. Construction should not be delayed as they ought to be coming along within two or three weeks. If you will give me an estimate of the cost, I will get Chief's okey immediately on receipt.

Loorz scribbled a marginal note worthy of Editor Hearst: "18 x 77 —4[for] $3000." Loorz refined his estimate over the next few weeks; by then, with other needs being included, the price had nearly doubled.

Morgan arrived the same day Willicombe mentioned the orchids, April 21. She had just been at the Beach House, where a new project was getting under way: "alterations and repairs at #415 Ocean Front," as the main building was called in this latest Santa Monica account.[36] Several more trips to the Beach House awaited her in the months ahead. At San Simeon, she left Loorz with enough comments about the Neptune Pool and the Billiard Wing to yield two pages of notes—plus a third page on a new subject, the Beauty Parlor (also called the Hairdressing Par-lor).

She went to Wyntoon toward the end of April. Then came a quick return from there to the Beach House, followed by another jaunt up the coast to San Simeon. And then she was back at Wyntoon, almost immediately afterward, all in a week's time.

Mac McClure wrote to Loorz on Thursday, April 30, from that alpine hide-away. At that point, Morgan was in the midst of this whirlwind junket, this estate-hopping frenzy, every mile of it being logged for the Hearst accounts exclusively:

Miss Morgan was here once during my absence [about April 15] and also last Monday [April 27]. She seems "nervous" that things are moving so slowly and at the present rate of progress it surely looks like the Turrets [Cinderella House] would not be anywhere near ready by July 1st. However let "nature" take its course, says I, and in the meantime I am trying to save some money.

Everything else is about as usual. The weather is Spring-like but wet and rainy.

The bridge is not started yet—nor is Bridge house, or the servants' chalet. (J.M. wanted to move the Bridge axis together with all foundations now in, but gave it up when she was here—.)[37]

---

36. It was the tenth of eleven Beach House accounts altogether; the first was for 1926–28, the last for 1937–38.

37. The matter resurfaced, though, and the Bridge House foundation was moved later in the season. See Morgan to Hearst, August 5, 1936; Hearst/Morgan Correspondence, Morgan Collec-tion (mentioned on p. 268 in this chapter). See also p. 273: McClure to Loorz, September 23, 1936.

Mac's letter was en route when Loorz wrote to the ailing carpenter, Pete Petersen, on May 1:

> Things are certainly moving here on the hill. We haven't had so much activity for a long time. It is too bad you have to miss it. However, I dont want to trade places with you but I certainly would like to get away for a couple of months. I have so much that needs my attention on these outside jobs that I'd certainly like to be free from here for a while. Anyway the [outside] work is real interesting as it is progressing so actively and not dragging like most of our work here [at San Simeon].

That last sentence has a contradictory ring to it. Maybe Loorz meant that the bigger, longer-term projects on the hill were the chronically backlogged ones. In any event, he had more to tell Petersen:

> I expect Miss Morgan here today. She has promised me all the needed details for the 4th floor ceiling, [plus] all window, shutter, bathroom and shutter details for the bunch of them [2nd through 4th floors: Rooms #1 through #3 in the Billiard Wing]. I have quite a crew and it takes information to keep them going properly. I hope she likes what we have done so far.

Loorz was feeling as sorry for himself as he was for Petersen when he added, "The weather has been just grand, picnic weather every day and not time to picnic."

Indeed, Morgan's visit on May Day—a Friday that year—was no frolic for those present. Loorz's notes ran to three pages, just as they had on April 21. This time, though, they comprised even more entries; one of them under "Neptune Pool Area" posed a challenge: "Attempt to set pool lighting so that no direct rays or beams strike the pool."

As of May first, of course, Morgan was only halfway through her week-long travels. She must have completed the Wyntoon-to-Wyntoon circuit without a hitch; for on Thursday, May 7, she let Loorz know there'd be more of the same in the days ahead. "I will go to the Beach House for Monday, and will be at San Simeon Tuesday morning." That's precisely what happened. This time, before leaving the Southland to see Loorz, she checked on a non-Hearst account, the Thompson house, the one she'd begun in Pasadena a few months before.[38]

---

38. On May 27 Morgan billed her client for $262.50—a 3.5% fee based on the $7,500 the construction was slated to cost (Morgan-Forney ledgers). Morgan never charged Thompson an additional $187.50 (2.5%), as she would have if she'd sought a standard six-percent commission. She could afford to be generous now, could afford to operate, in fact, at an outright loss on certain jobs. The Hearst connection above all others provided a rare safety net.

Morgan's visit to San Simeon on Tuesday, May 12, was another corker; the result was another long recap, in which she and Loorz rounded up the usual suspects. The "Neptune Pool Area" headed the lineup. "Have John Vanderloo's crew & setters concentrate on this section trying to get it completed promptly. Make only necessary castings for work in Billiard room wing. Postpone work on outside windows [in that wing] except where forms are made and will [otherwise] be wasted."

Morgan probably had much to tell Loorz about Wyntoon as well. If nothing else, he'd just heard about that job from the plumber Jim Rankin, who'd written on May 8 from his vacation house in Ben Lomond, north of Santa Cruz where the redwoods grow:

> We finished the work to be done for the present at Wyntoon and pulled out but it won't be long before they will be ready for us again up there. . . .
>
> Fishing here is about as usual—very small and I guess an average of five inch would be about right—and to think the boys wrote me from McCloud that they were catching them twenty-four inches. I guess seeing would be believing. I do know that I had a piece of salmon that was from a fish much larger than that—but I bought it at Santa Cruz.

Loorz stayed in high gear once Morgan left the hill on May 12. Two days later, with his tongue well in his cheek, he included the following in a letter to Stolte: "I am still booming the work here but have it under control so that I dont have to worry about it as long as I hang around to answer questions about every ten minutes or less."[39]

Two more days passed; it was now Saturday, May 16. Miss Morgan spent part of the weekend at Wyntoon.

SAN SIMEON'S MANY LOOSE ENDS could be a sore subject, and we needn't look far to find someone who viewed them in that way. Colonel Willicombe wrote to Loorz from Los Angeles on Tuesday the nineteenth:

> Mr. Hearst instructs me to ask you to have the wooden beams put in place in the pergola. He would like them put in place first on the older portion, and then would like the pergola "completed in other ways and made a finished job."
>
> Mr. Keep [the orchard man] states that the grape vines are growing at such an amazing rate that it is difficult to train them without the beams; also having to

---

39. From "F.C.S. 1936."

crowd the runners together, we are losing the effect the vines would give if they
could be trained along the beams as they should be.

Your usual prompt attention appreciated.[40]

(Nigel Keep always had the pergola's best interests in mind. The year before,
he told Hearst on June 1 that since Loorz's road equipment and a supply of gravel
were nearby, it would be "a splendid thing to have the Pergola's [pathway] graveled
at this time also." During the spring, said Keep, "it gets very muddy & unpleasant
for the 'Guest Riders.'" Hearst liked the suggestion and asked Loorz to act upon it.)

Willicombe's letter of May 19, 1936, crossed with one that Loorz wrote to him
the same day:

I find it advisable for me to write to you regarding the plague of rodents we are
having here on the hilltop.

The orchard is literally crawling with the animals now coming in from the outside [the surrounding ranch] where the grass is drying up. Mr. March in the [hill-
top] garden is almost helpless. As soon as the party left and the dogs [were]
penned he put out dozens of small traps and they catch nearly 100 per day but
they are not keeping even.

They are destroying his young plants as fast as he plants them. In his lath house
they destroy 15 to 20 flats per day, that is 750 to 1000 [plants] each day.

The men that are trapping and poisoning varmint [coyotes] have them quite
under control. We do not see many tracks or signs. Would you discuss it with Mr.
Hearst and see if it would not be advisable to have these two men go to work poisoning in the fields. Perhaps the varmint were an important factor in destroying
the field mice.[41]

---

40. A separate letter from Willicombe to Loorz is also dated May 19, 1936:

Mr. Hearst instructs me to send you the attached pictures of the Detroit (Mich.) Zoological
Garden.

This park is considered one of the most interesting of its kind in the country; in fact it is
unique.

As you will note, the animals are shown in reproductions of their native surroundings.

During the season there are more than a million visitors.

Mr. Hearst will probably talk with you about the photographs when he is next at the ranch.

If he does not bring up the subject, will you kindly remind him.

Three large photographs, most likely the very ones Willicombe sent to Loorz, are preserved in
the Hearst Castle Archives.

41. Loorz, too, was his prolific self on May 19. He wrote to Hearst as well, telling him, "We are
starting the San Carpojo road work today." (Some preliminary work had been done in 1934, but
none since then.) Loorz also told Hearst, "We have the Burnett Road in the finest shape it has ever
been in, clear thru to Jolon." But as such projects went, a mere two miles of work on "San Carpojo"
(the local name for San Carpoforo Creek, hidden in one of the ruggedest canyons on the Hearst
Ranch) would be "expensive even for a narrow road." Hearst vetoed the project on May 24: "If this

A reply left Los Angeles immediately, on May 20, and it came as a letter from Hearst himself (typed, as usual, by Willicombe — in this case from Hearst's handwritten version):

Ok — bring in the executioner.

I do not think the plague is due to absence of "varmints." Every once in awhile there is a plague of something or other — locusts or grasshoppers or frogs or rats or politicians — something to afflict us.

It has been so in all recorded time — and the politicians are the worst.

If we ever get rid of them, let us institute a special Passover.[42]

With regard to the pergola on Orchard Hill, Loorz told Hearst on May 20 (in quick reply to Willicombe's letter of the day before) that he was "pleased to order the wooden beams." He went on to tell Hearst:

We have stood up all the columns we have on hand and have ordered 22 more to complete [the layout] clear around. All are plumbed and anchored. We are casting a few bird heads [for the ends of the concrete beams] each week without putting on an extra crew in the molders shop. We have already poured about 22 more concrete beams and have bird heads on hand to pour perhaps that many more.

Loorz also remarked that Nigel Keep had "the Pergola cleaner and nicer than ever."

---

road is to be expensive, it is not worth while; so please stop it." Loorz thought they should go ahead, though, prompting Hearst to pledge funds for the road on June 2: "five hundred dollars per mile, and the two miles at the gorge for one thousand dollars per mile" — to which he added, "do the best you can for that sum."

42. Edmond D. Coblentz's *William Randolph Hearst*, pp. 235–36, includes Loorz's letter to Willicombe of May 19 and Hearst's response to Loorz of May 20. See the photograph in the section following p. 326 in the present volume, showing the cursive draft of Hearst's reply (from the Willicombe family heirlooms) — an unmistakable instance of the personal, handwritten approach that Hearst often favored over direct dictation, even with a secretary as skillful as Willicombe at his command.

In the Coblentz book, Loorz's letter is the more altered of the two presented. Yet neither transcription is objectionable by the standards of a book published in 1952, aimed at a general audience.

Coblentz worked from the incoming original of Loorz's letter and a file copy of Hearst's. The Loorz Papers contain the opposite: a file copy of Loorz's letter and the outgoing version of Hearst's. From this premise, possibilities reaching beyond the Loorz Papers and similar archives can readily be imagined. Well that we should ask what ever became of all the originals Loorz sent to Fred Stolte. Or to Mac McClure. Or to numerous other correspondents — among whom was Hearst. (The Hearst Papers at the Bancroft Library include relatively little from Loorz.) The same question applies to Morgan. She may have retained too few of the originals she received and too few of her own carbon copies. But among her recipients, some old friends or colleagues (or by now their descendants) may still be holding dozens of originals, even hundreds. With correspondents as active as Loorz and Hearst and Morgan, new surfacings almost surely lie ahead.

This choice stretch of correspondence is not without its gaps. On May 26, for example, Willicombe mentioned a recent letter he'd sent Loorz, one that the Loorz Papers lack:

> Supplementing my letter yesterday about cars to be returned to ranch — only two can be returned at this time — the Buick convertible and the Chrysler — as Miss Davies is using the other Buick (starting to-day) at the [Warner Bros.] studio, and it will have to remain here until [the] picture [*Cain and Mabel*] is finished. Are you sending down for the two to go up or do you want me to arrange it at this end.

Willicombe thought there might be "some worthy fellow, not working, who could make a few dollars on this work."[43] There's no telling if Loorz knew of anyone, for his papers lack a reply as well.

HEARST CAME UP FROM the Beach House for the last weekend of the month. He wrote to Loorz on Sunday, May 31, perhaps relying on a courier for quick delivery. "I hope to see you in the morning," he said, with June 1 in mind, "but if I do not, here are a few notes":

> There seems to be an urgent demand for hot-house space.
> Mr. [Alfredo] Gomes is developing wonderful begonias, and naturally we want to see him extend his work and have better facilities.
> He would like to have a hothouse where people could see the flowers.
> Do you [can you] think of any location that would be better than where he is.
> 2. I have bought a lot of orchid cactus. Found a man who had a collection of them and pretty much bought him out.
> They will have to go into a big hothouse.

The next thing Hearst mentioned (item 3 in the sequence) sounds like the same purchase that Willicombe had told Loorz about on April 21:

> In addition to this, we have ordered a lot of orchids from South America, and when they arrive they will have to go into a large hothouse.
> So suppose we plan hothouses for awhile and make them interesting as well as useful, and put them where people can see them — not see the houses so much as their contents.

Morgan, who had been at San Simeon on Thursday, May 28, and had seen Hearst in Santa Monica on Friday — before he left for the ranch later that day —

---

43. The two Buicks and the Chrysler appear on a list dated March 6, 1936. It shows that, at San Simeon, Loorz had charge of thirty-two vehicles owned by the Hearst interests; Randy Apperson had charge of eighteen. At Wyntoon, Eugene Kower had six vehicles in his care. See unsigned [Willicombe] to W. W. Murray, July 19, 1937 (covering letter for the previous year's list, to which some additions had later been made); Hearst Papers, carton 23 (under "1937 Samples").

got a faithful version of the "hothouse" story from Loorz, plus lots of other details. Loorz's letter went out on June 3.[44]

"First and foremost," it began, "Mr. Gomez' Begonia's got the center of the stage, with Mr. Hearst and all of his guests." (The proud horticulturist was Alfredo Gomes, whose skills weren't confined to growing begonias; along with his wife, Mary, he also repaired tapestries for Hearst.) Loorz said more about Hearst in that opening paragraph of June 3:

> Though he arrived Friday evening [May 29], he had not even visited our rooms [in the Billiard Room Wing] until he visited me Monday morning at 10 A.M. We walked thru hastily as he was in a hurry to get away on the plane.
>
> It appears that Mr. Gomez [sic] gets another greenhouse right away, larger and wider. Mr. March gets one for Orchids that are apparently ordered from South America etc. Anyway the order of the day is bigger and better greenhouses.
>
> I might just add that during the two days the party was here, when we could have no traps and poison in the garden the rodents removed some 2500 small plants. It is so discouraging to Mr. March. I marvel at the number of times he has grown and replanted as fast as they are taken. . . .
>
> I got permission to use my trapping crew on poisoning and helping to stop the hordes of mice that are coming in from the surrounding fields.[45]

Loorz went on to recount for Morgan the "hasty trip" he and Hearst had made through the Billiard Wing (with its three confusingly numbered rooms) and also through the new Beauty Parlor, which adjoins that part of the building:

> He made few remarks. He liked the 1st floor [the second floor: Room #1] very well except for the light. Thot it might still be advisable to have the extra window.
>
> The second floor [the third floor: Room #2] impressed him as it did you. It had lots of light and was real nice, he stated. He liked the mantel installation very much and made no suggestion of any changes at all.
>
> The 4th floor [Room #3] had lots of light. He thot he might like the wood ceiling a little darker than the sample. We had the first coat of stain on but not all the glaze. It was just mentioned and I think when it is all pulled together he will like it.
>
> He was very much pleased with the Beauty Parlor and I told him the linoleum as designed was on the way. He thot the hair dresser should like it very much.

---

44. Loorz closed on that Wednesday morning by saying, "Some gentlemen are waiting to take this letter so that you will receive it tomorrow." But Morgan didn't see it until Friday, June 5. She'd been at Wyntoon the day before (Morgan-Forney ledgers), hence the final paragraph in the letter she wrote Loorz upon returning; see p. 257.

45. The paragraph also mentioned "Mr. Baumgartner" as being "back on the job," temporarily as part of Ed March's garden staff. Baum and his wife, Anna, were the Depression-shocked couple in Cayucos that Loorz and others helped in 1933; see p. 59.

There was still more for Loorz to tell Morgan in his letter of June 3:

> He then asked me what progress we were making on the Pergola and seemed satisfied and wanted us to keep right on until completion.
>
> He didn't have time to walk down to the [Neptune] Pool Area but asked me what we had done. Apparently he had not walked down there during the stay. He dismissed himself in haste stating he would be back again on Friday [June 5] and would go over the things more carefully. In the meantime, I was to get as much information on hothouses as possible.
>
> If you have any Lord and Burnham greenhouse catalogues that he could glance at I would appreciate them.

During 1936, and most likely right after that quick tour of the Billiard Room Wing, Hearst wrote the following to Loorz on some blank (and undated) Western Union telegram forms:[46]

> I want more light in the new rooms than Miss Morgan gives us. It will save time and money to have the lights put in at the beginning instead of later.
>
> In the lower of the three small rooms now nearing completion [Room #1] there is one lantern. There should be four or six.
>
> I do not like the table in that room. It is too big and it is poor quality. We have a great number of good ones why not use one.
>
> We should also have one or two bed side tables in *all* such rooms.
>
> We must get another window in that room no matter whether it [the resulting design] is symetrical [*sic*] or not.[47] It needs light in the day time as well as at night.
>
> Please see that there are many connections for lights in every room.
>
> This is a mania with me. I like a room that you can see your way around in.

---

46. The item may be from 1937 instead. Its content recalls a letter Hearst wrote to Morgan on May 10 of that year; see p. 319, note 53. But whereas the undated item clearly pertains to rooms in the Billiard Room Wing, the letter from 1937 is more thematic than specific.

47. This was the same window Loorz mentioned to Morgan, midway through writing to her on June 3 (p. 255). The issues of symmetry and dimness pertained especially to the east side of the room. One of its two small windows is near the northeast corner; the other window lies past the southeast corner, hidden in a dressing alcove. The proposed third window might have offset the claustrophobic feeling—akin to that experienced in a basement—but then the Billiard Wing would have looked askew when viewed from Casa Grande's east courtyard. No such change was ever made.

The more ample windows in the west wall of Room #1 are quirkishly arrayed, whether viewed from indoors or outside; one could argue that the room is architecurally more flawed than any other at San Simeon. Ironically, folklore still identifies the discordant Room #1 as Miss Morgan's room. In truth, another member of Hearst's inner circle used it for a time, no doubt with little concern about its shortcomings (it was an upgrade, in any case, from the person's former room in the Service Wing): an original key, inherited by the Hearst Castle housekeeping-curatorial staff, bore a small tag: "Mr. Willicombe's Room."

The notion that Room #1 was Morgan's room could be an old transposition, a cross-pol-

The question of light—or of excessive dimness—had cropped up before. Hearst seemed to like things brighter than Morgan did; perhaps she was more the brooding medievalist than he was, after all.

Likening Loorz's letter of Wednesday, June 3, to a "report" (which she was thankful to have), Morgan had some news and comments of her own for Loorz on June 5:

> Am glad he liked the "Beauty Parlor." You should receive the curtains today (if not already). I think they will help.
>
> Mr. Hearst plans to be back [at San Simeon] this week end but perhaps not before Sunday or Monday [June 7 or 8]—to stay a week or ten days and incidentally go to Wyntoon, so I will plan to be with you Monday.
>
> I have ideas for a greenhouse development I'd like to talk over with him—the temporary houses are becoming too prominent and we might as well plan the new units as part of a permanent scheme.
>
> Am just in from Wyntoon—(still cold and not at all like an ordinary June).

A practical, businesslike arrangement: Hearst and Morgan converged on San Simeon on Monday the eighth—ideal timing for her to get a week's worth or more of new marching orders. Not surprisingly, the Billiard Wing and the Neptune Pool dominated Loorz's recap of her visit. One entry for the pool indicated that the challenge raised in April had been met: "Mr. Hearst liked flood lighting effect. (Note—insists on these lights being on each evening at 7 P.M.—though temporary.)"[48]

Back in San Francisco on Tuesday, June 9, Morgan sent another short but vivid letter Loorz's way:

> Mr. Hearst asked last night if we did not have old wood available for the [ceiling] soffit boards of the new rooms [in the Billiard Wing]. I explained, but take it that he is not content with the "finish."
>
> Would you think it well of my hunting some old French furniture man who has done "faking" in [his] youth, to come up and just make old wood. It takes endless time and patience, and is not the right training for our carpenters.

She also said, with regard to the job up north, "We are to put a foreman on at Wyntoon and take care of the work there, but the steel should be ordered & on hand

---

lination involving ideas that arose (on paper) for a new Wyntoon Castle, after the Phoebe Hearst-Bernard Maybeck version had burned. At one point Hearst said to Morgan about Wyntoon, "This [proposed change in layout] will probably affect the character of the billiard room construction and your room above it." From Hearst to Morgan, January 21, 1931; Hearst Papers, carton 12 (under "Morgan, Julia").

48. Daylight Saving Time (discontinued after World War I) wouldn't be reinstated for nearly six more years.

before 'operations' begin."[49] What she didn't say was that in four more days she'd be back on that job.

Loorz replied on Friday, June 12. Morgan's idea of the furniture man was a good one, he said, provided she could get "the right man." He went on to elaborate on Hearst's expectations for the months ahead.

(Hearst, meanwhile, was being as unpredictable as ever; never mind Morgan's thinking he'd be at San Simeon for at least a week this time. Loorz gave her the latest before plunging into the heart of his letter: "He left last night and expects to be back again next Saturday [June 20].")

"He wants the Pergola all completed this fall and enjoyed a little ride around thru it," began Loorz's most interesting paragraph on June 12. "He said, 'See Miss Morgan about the Fair Molds for Fountains, Bulls, and Various Statuary on a grand scale, for the various points of the Pergola and especially the entrance.'"

The "Fair Molds" were the plaster models that Hearst had bought in 1935 from the old Panama-Pacific Exposition in San Francisco and that were now languishing (along with a multitude of other curios and treasures) in the San Simeon warehouses. What a nostalgic, retrogressive, almost Victorian sight their presence on Orchard Hill would have been—had his idea for using them been realized. Whereas the grounds of The Enchanted Hill itself were playing host more and more to a trendy, contemporary Art Deco theme (typified by the snow-white marble sculptures at the Neptune Pool), the Orchard Hill that Hearst imagined would have felt at least twenty years out of date from the outset—anachronistic, to be sure (like so much else he conveyed), yet deeply affective (and equally effective) just the same.

The mercurial, unpredictable Hearst was about to absent himself from California for the second half of 1936. He could thus qualify for a "nonresident" exemption from the new state income tax, which had taken effect the previous year. He had plenty of other places where he could hang his hat, both stateside and abroad,

---

49. Did Morgan mean a foreman for the steel work, such as on the bridge whose trusses came from the Summerbell Co.? Or did she mean "foreman" in a larger, supervisorial sense—more like Fred Stolte's role during the past three years at Wyntoon or George Loorz's during the past four at San Simeon? Although Morgan had already been to Wyntoon several times in 1936, the "operations" thus far may indeed have been too sluggish to suit her (a point made by Mac McClure in his letter of April 30).

Stolte told Loorz on May 20, "I am back in the Yosemite with Fred Langbehn and trying to push these jobs through so that I can be free to go up north when necessary." He mentioned Yosemite again on May 30, but not Wyntoon. And a full-page letter from Loorz to Stolte on June 1 said nothing at all about Wyntoon. However, the Stolte Co.'s Trial Balances reflect a substantial amount of work there by late spring. (All four references are from "F.C.S. 1936.")

and plenty of better ways to spend the money at stake.[50] By June 13, when Loorz wrote to his carpentry foreman, Pete Petersen (who'd left the hospital and was now taking the cure at Dr. Halder's Hot Springs in Calistoga, north of San Francisco), Hearst had an itinerary in mind for the rest of the year:

> Mr. Hearst has requested the following [for San Simeon] while he is away on his European trip:
> four greenhouses,
> two animal shelters [in the main zoo area],
> Pergola completed,
> two more helps cottages [in Hearst Camp],
> rebuilt office across the road [the hilltop driveway, west of Hearst Camp] similar to cottages,
> grotto partitions,
> widen turn-around [at end of driveway] with new concrete wall etc.
> All of this besides Miss Morgan's work and she has certainly laid out a program too large for the budget unless he increases it.

In theory, "Miss Morgan's work"—by which Loorz meant Morgan's pursuits as de facto general contractor at San Simeon—had long been synonymous with the Hearst Construction Fund. Projects outside her sphere, like the Burnett Road, had been separately handled, mainly through the Hilltop Fund. In reality, San

---

50. California's new tax law was exactly a year old now: Governor Merriam had approved it on June 13, 1935. Its provisions defined a "nonresident" as anyone who spent "in the aggregate" more than six months outside the state during a given year. Having already spent nearly half of 1935 in California, Hearst could not gain the exemption in its first year unless he left the state quickly —by July 1. A spontaneous trip within the state was one thing; but his longer journeys out of state or abroad usually involved a good deal of planning, and he didn't pursue the new exemption until 1936.

As for what he would save, *Time* magazine had glibly cited its sister publication on November 4, 1935, p. 21 (under "Taxation: Good-by to California"): "According to *Fortune* [in its October 1935 feature on Hearst and Wyntoon], Mr. Hearst's income is not $1,000,000 but around $4,000,000, and the idea of passing over a $580,000 income tax check to California was extremely repugnant to the master of $220,000,000 worth of newspapers, magazines, radio stations, cinema companies, real estate, gold mines, silver mines, cattle, chicle and forest." *Fortune* may have reported soundly enough on Wyntoon; but its trumpeting of Hearst's wealth was misleading—a theme dwelt on by the frowning Ferdinand Lundberg in *Imperial Hearst*. Hearst's salary in 1935 was an even $500,000 (still the highest in the country that year, with Mae West's $480,833 ranking second—this from a U.S. Treasury report to Congress, as conveyed by *The New York Times* on January 7, 1937, p. 28, under "Highest Salaries For 1935 Listed"). If Hearst had drawn a comparable salary in 1936, his tax obligation in California—had he chosen to stay there longer that year—would have been at least $75,000 (less any deductions or adjustments).

His earnings in a separate, non-salaried capacity (and their related taxes) may have been considerable; chances are, though, they were less than what *Time* was asserting.

Simeon had never been a perfect world. (What Loorz told Alexander Sokolow in 1932 still applied: it helped to be "somewhat of a contortionist to keep a complete, balanced record of accounts"—or in this case funds—that were as "mixed up as many of these" had become.)[51] And there would soon be a new entity, a new plot thickener, the Hearst Sunical Building Fund, overseen by Loorz's friend Bill Murray in San Francisco.

As for the wayward Hearst in mid-June, he didn't return to San Simeon on the weekend of June 20–21, as Loorz had projected. He went to Wyntoon instead, and Morgan saw him there on Friday the nineteenth. The following Wednesday, it was her turn to give Loorz the latest—on short notice. "I expected to be with you on the Hill Thursday [June 25], but instead received word today [that I] was wanted in Santa Monica instead. So will plan for *Friday* on the way up, unless something unexpected keeps me below."

She appeared as planned, on June 26, bringing a bit of Southland cheer with her: "Use marble from Santa Monica and complete the roof of the temple," as Loorz noted. The pool at the Beach House bore a likeness to the Neptune Pool, hence the suitability of some surplus material from there.

She probably savored a day at home in San Francisco, or maybe at her place in Monterey. She knew she'd soon be at Hearst's beck and call again. Come Tuesday, June 30, she flew to Arizona—to the south rim of the Grand Canyon.[52] Hearst had preceded her by a couple of days. The property he owned at the Canyon was close by, at Grandview Point.

THE HEARST ORGANIZATION, with all its divisions and sub-divisions, was a financial maze, an accountant's labyrinth, an administrative house of mirrors, as the feature published by *Fortune* in October 1935 had indelibly shown.[53] That fact is important in our trying to understand a letter like the one Loorz wrote on July 6. It went to Hearst, who by then had moved on to New York.[54] The Chief would be lay-

---

51. See p. 46. For us today the contortions would be fewer if the records Morgan kept in San Francisco of the Hearst Construction Fund still existed. Cal Poly doesn't have them; neither does the Morgan-Forney Collection. (The San Simeon copies of Hearst Construction Fund records were destroyed in 1937; see pp. 327-28, plus their notes 68–69, and pp. 405–06, note 9.)

52. The entry in the Morgan-Forney ledgers, under June 30, is unusual in its length and puzzling in its details (which cite a mere $14.50 in expenses): "Miss Morgan by airplane to Grand Canyon—airport 5.—7/3 [July 3] hotel, meals 4.50 taxi home 5—."

53. Indelibly, yes, but not very clearly. The editors at *Fortune* may have become as confused as nearly everyone else gets in plumbing the arcane depths of Hearstdom. See note 50, above; see also p. 208 in this volume.

54. Despite Hearst's absence from San Simeon through most of June, the place got some use until July 2. Things were about to change, though, as Loorz said that day to a friend in Berkeley, Irma Hall (who was hoping to see the hilltop):

ing over in Manhattan before sailing to Europe in early August—for what would prove to be the last time in his fabled life. Loorz's letter to Hearst harkened back to the one he'd written on June 13 to Pete Petersen (the one indicating that "Miss Morgan's work" usually differed from other types):

> Has there been any change in the program for the miscellaneous structures [the greenhouses, animal shelters, grotto partitions, and others that Loorz had outlined to Petersen]. . . .
>
> With Wyntoon getting more of Miss Morgan's [Hearst Construction Fund] budget, progress [at San Simeon] on North terrace steps, rails and paving,[55] and rooms in Billiard and Recreation wing[s], will slow up somewhat.
>
> Jolon [Milpitas] alterations started this date. With everything laid out quite complete and Mr. [William] Murray [of the Hearst Sunical office in San Francisco] prepared to advance funds this should all be completed within two months.
>
> Do you desire the above structures to be paid for thru the Hilltop Fund Account?

Hearst answered by returning the letter. Its margin bore a characteristic scrawl next to Loorz's question: "No let Murray pay for them."[56]

The next day, July 7, Loorz again wrote to Hearst in New York, this time about an entirely different matter:

> In dealing with Miss Morgan, looking up plans, sketches, literature and information on Spanish & Mexican buildings, I am familiar with your proposed building program in the Grand Canyon.

Just 10 minutes ago I received word from Mr. Hearst's office with general instructions to all of us as follows:

 When party leaves (that is tonight) shut the place down and discharge any an[d] all employees that are not absolutely needed. Gate keepers to be instructed to permit no visitors whatsoever. Not even relatives of workmen or my own relatives.

 This strict order is usually issued each time he leaves for a long trip but never so severely as the present one. Frankly, Irma, I think the real reason for so much excitement is that some of the guests who are here being entertained by Mrs. George Hearst were robbed of about $200.

Loorz thought Hearst would make some exceptions—if only he could be reached. However, "I think he is in the grand canyon eastward bound."

55. The largest feature of its kind on the hilltop, the North Terrace spans much of the area between the Neptune Pool and the Roman Pool; it was never finished. Loorz may actually have been referring here to the lowest (and only finished part) of the adjoining Grand Entrance. Or perhaps he meant the smaller terrace and passageway, likewise finished, between the Grand Entrance and the Neptune Pool—an area that a letter he wrote Morgan on July 14 brings especially to mind. See also p. 188 and its note 69.

56. Loorz's letter also contained a paragraph, almost telegram-like in style, concerning a short road he was building (the subject of note 41, above). "Soon be thru tough section of San Carpojo Road. Feel certain we can give you quite satisfactory road at figures or costs allowed. Can ride comfortably a half mile past last crossing at present."

Mr. Hearst I feel that I am in a position to handle that work for you as promptly, intelligently and economically, if not more so, than any other builder.

I would like you to consider my application for the work on any basis most suitable to you, namely; lump sum contract, [or] net cost plus reasonable commission or salary. . . .

Lump sum contracts are seldom, if ever, satisfactory unless complete plans, details and specifications can be prepared without any anticipated changes. I am quite certain that it is more expensive than *cost plus reasonable percentage and equipment rental.*

On open competititive contracts on the outside, from Santa Maria north thruout the state, we have been able to obtain over $300,000 of work at an average of 10% so far this year. Without the element of *gamble* we would be pleased to do the work for a commission of 5% net, if you preferred to do it that way.

Hearst's holdings at the Grand Canyon dated from 1913, the year he bought out a mining company at Grandview Point on the South Rim. Morgan built a board-and-batten cabin for him at Grandview in 1914; but he had long since envisioned a more imposing structure—a more Hearstian structure—for that property. (Mac McClure, it will be recalled, told Loorz in May 1933 that Jim LeFeaver had said Morgan's office "would have to collect for the Arizona house"—that is, for their more recent efforts, which were entirely on paper.)[57] Ultimately, Hearst's ideas for the Grand Canyon never got past the paper, but in 1936 their chances of realization had yet to be ruled out.[58]

Loorz's letter of July 7 was probably still in transit to Hearst on Friday, July 10, the morning of which found Loorz airing the Grand Canyon matter and other concerns with Stolte:

I wrote to Mr. Hearst regarding the job at Grand Canyon. I mentioned it to Miss Morgan and she thot it might be arranged but didn't state definitely. Just to make certain I wrote direct [to Hearst on July 7] and also a longer letter to Willicombe [in New York as well, likewise on July 7] about the airport and bridge at Wyn-

---

57. See p. 65 in this volume and its note 22. See also Michael F. Anderson, *Living at the Edge: Explorers, Exploiters and Settlers of the Grand Canyon Region* (Grand Canyon, Arizona, 1998), pp. 71, 72, 75.

58. For the present at least, Hearst's thoughts went beyond the architectural. One of his editors wired Willicombe at the Ritz Tower in New York: "GLOVER RUCKSTELL HEAD OF COMPANY RUNNING RECENTLY OPENED SIGHTSEEING SYSTEM AROUND BOULDER DAM [HOOVER DAM] AND GRAND CANYON SAYS HE WAS TOLD BY CHIEF AND YOURSELF [LOS ANGELES] EXAMINER WOULD COOPERATE IN PROMOTION [OF] HIS ENTERPRISE PLEASE CONFIRM." It was Hearst who replied. "Glad to help Glover Ruckstell with publicity. I thought best plan [was] to run article about Grand Canyon and Boulder Dam together with map airmailed you showing airplane view routes of Ruckstell's." From Van Ettisch to Willicombe, July 11, 1936, and from Hearst to R. T. Van Ettisch, July 12, 1936; Hearst Papers, carton 20 (under "1936 Samples").

toon. I told him we had not been asked for a bid and that we would have taken it a lot cheaper than they paid for it. It was stated carefully so as not to reflect on Miss Morgan's office.

Miss Morgan did mention it to Mr. Hearst about me wanting the job [at Grand Canyon], so she said and she thot he might get in touch with me direct. So I didn't just write without it being proper.

Frankly I like this place [San Simeon] but I'm really tired of punching the clock and no time off. Also I think I'm actually worth more money to them so why should I sit tight and wait until something nice comes my way. It is usually the result of seeking that makes things happen the way we want them to.

Fred there is a lot of smaller private work going on around this neck of the woods and I haven't the time to go out and get it. All we can take the way it is is the public jobs [like the schools] and they'll will [sic] be getting more scarce. . . .

I'm leaving for Jolon in about an hour to layout my frames etc for that job [at the Milpitas Hacienda]. They haven't made as much progress this week as I'd like but they have been fighting fires most of the time. I'd like to get that job finished in a hurry. Miss Morgan is of the same opinion and is giving me the information I need quite promptly but I still notice she is making changes.[59]

Stolte received Loorz's letter on Saturday, July 11. He answered the next day,[60] leading off with a choice bit of news about Mac McClure:

Mac left McCloud [Wyntoon] for New York to work with Mr. Hearst on the canyon project.[61] So I shall spend some extra time in McCloud. Miss Morgan finally decided that it was not necessary to send [Dick] Nusbaum to McCloud. I was there last Wed. [July 8] and the work is quite well laid out for a week or two, although I expect to go up again this Thurs [July 16].

Thus far in 1936 the work at Wyntoon had required little of Stolte's presence, despite Loorz's gung-ho thoughts about the job back in March. Stolte had kept busy the past few months with his company's work at Yosemite and on various other jobs—knowing all the while that he might need to give more time to Wyn-

---

59. From "F.C.S. 1936." Loorz sounded as if he had spoken recently with Morgan. He may have (by phone). But he hadn't seen her in person in two weeks, not since her last visit to San Simeon on June 26. In the meantime she'd not only been to the Grand Canyon, she'd also been to Wyntoon on July 8, soon after returning from Arizona.

60. From "F.C.S. 1936."

61. In this case (unlike the one mentioned in note 52), the Morgan-Forney entry is easy to grasp, except for the date (July 17). Since many of these entries were made in clusters, possibly at month's end, errors could intrude (though they seldom did). In any event: "W A McClure to Grand Canyon & New York to see Mr. Hearst." The account also shows that Mac's $308.25 in travel expenses were "refunded" in August—that is, the Hearst interests reimbursed Morgan for that amount.

toon at any moment. To judge from what Stolte was now telling Loorz on July 12, Mac McClure had recently pulled some extra duty at Wyntoon, and Dick Nusbaum of the Morgan office had come close to pinch-hitting there as well.[62]

Stolte had more to say in that letter of Sunday the twelfth, both about Wyntoon and about the issues Loorz had aired on July 10:

> Last Wed. in McCloud I told Miss Morgan that we [the F. C. Stolte Co.] would like to submit a figure on the airport whenever the job was to be started; she then said "that Mr Hearst said that we were to go ahead with air port." I believe she meant by this that WE meant her office.
>
> About the Hearst, Morgan, Loorz, Stolte, sitiation [*sic*].
>
> 1. Personnally, I would like to see you get more fun out of being in circulation again, not mentioning the value of personal attention to jobs.
>
> 2. I really believe a schedule could be worked out at San Simeon whereby you could (with a good man) handle this work say from San Luis Obispo, to start, to sort of wean them away from the present arrangement.
>
> 3. Grand Canyon job would complicate this, if you were to move there. Although if the two of us WERE ON THE LAM, this could also be taken care of.
>
> 4. I am leaving out the consideration of whether this fits in with their plans, as I feel that we can get as much work as we could take care of, in straight concrete as well as the building and general work. However, the old BLACK BUGABOO jumps up and you wonder HOW LONG WILL THIS RUSH LAST.
>
> 5. Although I would feel very badly, if we were to lose the Hearst work and Miss Morgan's good wishes, frankly I feel that you could easily make up your salary, etc; by just being near the jobs we have on hand there [in the greater San Luis Obispo area].

Stolte concluded what, for him, was a landmark letter by saying his efforts amounted to his doing "a little thinking with the typewriter which is most generally bad." To this he added: "Although as you say, you have to know what you want before you can work to get it."

Loorz probably received his partner's letter of July 12 two days later. Meanwhile, a letter dated July 13 was enroute from Hearst in New York to Loorz at San Simeon; but before it got there, Loorz may well have received Stolte's next letter,

---

62. Inasmuch as McClure and Nusbaum were draftsmen (in fact, the latter was a licensed architect), either one could theoretically have acted as on-site representative for Morgan, much as Ed Hussey had in 1933. But Stolte's paragraph brings a different image to mind, especially in Mac's case: that of a construction superintendent, a role Mac seems unlikely to have filled. A swiftly composed letter may be the culprit — the very kind that everyone in these annals was capable of producing. However, some later events point toward Mac's handling of such duties when there was no one else to assume them (see p. 373, for example, note 38).

dated July 14. Stolte reported that the "labor situation" (meaning unionized labor) was "tough in spots" and that he was therefore "sort of picking the jobs"—ideally the ones that didn't "drag too long."[63]

Before signing off on the fourteenth, Stolte had some news for his partner about Wyntoon:

> Up north, we have a fair start on the new bridge house location, will be poured the first of [the] week. I believe Miss Morgan would like to see more progress, and Mr. LeFeaver wants to cut down. Our bills run about $3000 per week and about three weeks behind.[64]

And then Loorz got the reply of July 13 from Hearst in New York. Its letterhead was an awesome roll call of the twenty-eight newspapers Hearst owned around the country, epitomizing the power and influence he still wielded—even as Roosevelt's New Deal closed in on him and his kingly way of life. As for Loorz's recent anxiety—and Stolte's, too, in his partner's behalf—it may have been mostly for naught. Hearst proved unneedful of cautious phrasing or other kowtowing. He simply wanted to continue building, albeit on what for him was a lean budget:

> I would greatly like to have you do whatever work is done at the Grand Canyon. I feel sure that you could do it to our complete satisfaction, and more reasonably than we could have it done in any other way.
>
> I have read your letters [the one to Hearst himself plus the one to Willicombe] and agree with everything you said.[65] Consequently I will write Miss Morgan im-

---

63. Back in March, Stolte had told Loorz that, with "the unions beginning to assert themselves" in the Bay Area, the "out of town work" was preferable. And as recently as July 4, he reported that some of the company's work for General Petroleum involved not only "lots of concrete and corrugated iron" but also "lots of arguments with the unions." From "F.C.S. 1936."

64. From "F.C.S. 1936." The payroll alone at San Simeon, normally drawn against the Hearst Construction Fund, had recently been that much in arrears. The Morgan-Forney ledgers show that on July 1 Morgan provided Loorz with $3,163 from her own office reserve to pay his men. She was "refunded" that amount by month's end.

65. The prolific Loorz had written Hearst two letters on July 7, plus one that same day to Joe Willicombe (as Loorz told Stolte on July 10). Of the two to Hearst, only the one about the Grand Canyon appears in this volume; the other pertained to two employees at San Simeon who weren't getting along: the head gardener, Ed March, and the begonia-tapestry man, Alfredo Gomes.

The letter to Willicombe ranged widely. It included Loorz's bold assessment of himself as "more than a $5200 a year man," Hearst having saved at least that much at San Simeon each year since 1932—"on the Hilltop Fund work"—through Loorz's effectiveness. "On [the] Burnett Road alone before I came here, records show an expenditure of around $10,000 per mile for the last two miles of road at that time." Loorz had therefore "arranged a contract for the next eight miles of much more difficult construction for a maximum of $3500 per mile which turned out a net cost to Mr. Hearst of about $3000." He went on to remind Willicombe, "Then we purchased our own equipment and built still better roads in yet more difficult construction at an average of less than $2500

mediately and urge that you be given this work to do on the basis you mention—
cost plus a commission of five percent, net.

The work at Grand Canyon must be done economically. I am not prepared to
spend a lot of money there any more than I was prepared to spend a large sum of
money for the [landing] field at Wyntoon.

I have not made any field at Wyntoon in consequence, and I would like you to
have an opportunity to estimate on that and see what you could do. Perhaps we
could get the cost down to some possible sum.

I will try to arrange all these matters by correspondence with Miss Morgan.[66]

Despite Hearst's encouraging response, inaction marked the next several
days.[67] Some confusion also cropped up to torment Loorz. Come July 25, the day
after Morgan's latest visit to San Simeon, Loorz sent her a copy of the proposal that
he had sent to Hearst back on the seventh—and that Hearst, of course, had already
reviewed. As Loorz said of the proposal in his covering letter to Morgan:[68]

I mailed it to him with this note clipped on. "If you think this is unreasonable and
not in order please send it back. I could get away from this job enough to organize
and direct the Grand Canyon work without seriously affecting the progress here
on the hill."

I hadn't the slightest idea Mr. Hearst did not connect me with Wyntoon and
Mr. Stolte. I have talked to him a lot about Wyntoon, especially the airport and

[per mile]." Loorz believed the F. C. Stolte Co. could be doing equally well for Hearst on certain jobs
at Wyntoon that other contractors were handling.

Loorz was hoping Willicombe would concur—was hoping he would "put in a good word" for
him with Hearst. Willicombe did precisely that.

66. The Morgan Collection at Cal Poly has no letters or telegrams stemming from Hearst's
second paragraph (pp. 265–66) or from this final one.

Hearst wrote another letter to Loorz on July 13, regarding the friction between Ed March and
Alfredo Gomes. Hearst shared Loorz's "good opinion of Mr. March," whom he sided with over
Gomes. Likewise on July 13, Hearst wired Loorz in reply to his proposal of July 7. And thus in his
letter about the Grand Canyon, Hearst was simply confirming and elaborating upon the news Loorz
had already received by telegram.

67. Morgan, though, remained focused on the matter. As Stolte told Loorz on July 26, she was
"in McCloud" on Monday, July 20: "Apparently she had just completed the Grand Canyon plans,
the evening before coming up." Stolte also reported that "she was still studying the problems there"
after being met at the train and before turning her attention to Wyntoon. From "F.C.S. 1936."

After appearing at Wyntoon, Morgan kept on the go: to the Beach House on July 22, a visit she
combined with her last stop in 1936 at the Edythe Tate Thompson job in Pasadena; and then up to
San Simeon on July 24, with another trip to Wyntoon just before the month ended.

68. Loorz's letter, written the morning after Morgan's visit of July 24, mistakenly bears that
same date, July 24.

the bridge, since the time you told me you had mentioned to him that I was interested with Mr. Stolte.

Also I have talked to Mr. Willicombe about "My Partner" and "my man Harry Thompson" both of whom he liked, several times.[69] I have also talked to Mr. Willicombe briefly mentioning our schools and other contracts here.

Perhaps my mention of salary might have confused him. However, Miss Morgan salary or otherwise it is all F. C. Stolte Co. I get $100 per week from you [allotted by Hearst] and Fred gets $100 per week from our company. When he got but $75 per week I put the difference of my salary in the company.[70] Frankly Miss Morgan almost every cent I possess is in the company.

I hope this helps to correct a misunderstanding and I hope you agree with me when I say that "I feel that I can be a lot of help to you on the Grand Canyon Work." I think you can save many trips down there by talking it over with me here on the hill. At other times it might be convenient for us to drive down together or from there to the nearest [railroad] station.

The confusion and misunderstanding aside, Loorz remained indispensable to Hearst and Morgan. In fact, he had spent part of Morgan's visit the previous day, July 24, at Jolon with her, a session that yielded abundant notes under "Milpitas Ranch Job."

That same session also yielded notes for San Simeon itself under the familiar headings "Neptune [Pool] Area" and "Billiard Room Wing" as well as a new heading, "Recreation Wing." With the work in the Billiard Wing well along, the adjoining Recreation Wing (whose ground-floor Theater was the only finished portion) would be the next big job tackled within Casa Grande.[71] Loorz also made some entries under "Miscellaneous," one of them saying that Val Georges, the resident ironworker at San Simeon, was "to make up a total of 15 sets of large door hinges as per antique samples for Wyntoon (For Brown Bear)."[72]

---

69. Less than a year earlier (October 10, 1935) Loorz had informed Harry Thompson, "Mr. Willicombe told me he thot you were a mighty good man and that you always got what he wanted right away and just as he wanted it."

70. See p. 152, note 89; it pinpoints the moment late in 1934 when Stolte went from $75 to $100 per week, a transition made possible by the company's success that year.

71. The Recreation Wing hadn't lain completely idle since the historic rush for Hearst's birthday in 1934. July 22, 1935, for example, found Morgan writing to Loorz about the "usable rooms over the theatre, which are to be cleaned and refurnished." Loorz's recap on October 10, 1935, included this note: "Arch[itect] to talk to Mr. Hearst about using the upper floor of the recreation wing for the use of the women of the household." A note on February 24, 1936, said work was "to continue on rooms of Recreation Wing as each one is finished," hence certain efforts Loorz began making in the current season, pending a bigger push in 1937.

72. A photograph of some of these hinges appears in Sara Boutelle's *Julia Morgan*, p. 220 — but with the woodcarver Otto Olson identified as their maker.

MORGAN WENT UP TO WYNTOON at the end of July.[73] Then on August 4 she returned to San Simeon; unfortunately, Loorz's recap notes are missing. Here is one instance, though, where the Morgan Collection at Cal Poly, archivally a very spotty player through this part of the 1930s, provides a game-winning hit. Morgan wrote to Hearst in New York on August 5 ("I am just back from San Simeon," she remarked). Indeed she was. Better yet, she gave a good many details — choice details at this juncture — on San Simeon, Jolon-Milpitas, Santa Monica, and, above all, Wyntoon. Bridge House, near the Bavarian Village at that estate, was soon to take shape; the Servants' Chalet and, down by The Gables, the Tea House were both further along. She also mentioned the muralist Willy Pogany and the work he'd be doing on Hearst's own house, Brown Bear.[74]

Morgan's letter crossed with one that Willicombe sent her from New York the next day, August 6, right before she headed north again. Following the trip to Wyntoon, she made one of her Santa Monica-to-San Simeon loops.

Willicombe's letter, like Morgan's, contains some welcome details on the under-documented Wyntoon of the moment. And it spells out the role Fred Stolte was playing there, a role that, thus far in these annals of 1936, has been uncertain, what with the "foreman" Morgan mentioned on June 9 and Stolte's own reference on July 12 to Mac McClure and Dick Nusbaum. Willicombe provided Loorz with a copy of what Morgan was sent:[75]

---

73. Pancho Estrada, graybeard majordomo and local legend (whose sole right it supposedly was to call Hearst "Weelie"), died at this time in San Luis Obispo, on July 26. Another cowboy, renowed through the silver screen, wired his condolences to Hearst in New York. "It is a great grief to lose Don Pancho whom I have known since early childhood," Hearst replied. "It makes us realize that the journey is nearing its end. But I guess by the time we get there Pancho will have the campfires burning and be ready to welcome us as always." From Hearst to William S. Hart, July 28, 1936; Hearst Papers, carton 20 (under "1936 Samples").

74. See Morgan to Hearst, August 5, 1936; Hearst/Morgan Correspondence, Morgan Collection. The parts concerning San Simeon mention the work Loorz was doing on the Recreation Wing. As for the Beach House in Santa Monica, her references to "The Great Library" and the "Help's House over the store room" bespeak a lost world, a setting whose interiors and other features can only be glimpsed through old photographs (the detached Service Wing at 321 Ocean Front is all that remains of that property).

Willy Pogany's name appears in the main Wyntoon account under January 1, 1936 (Morgan-Forney ledgers), Morgan having seen him in Los Angeles then; she evidently made the trip for that purpose alone.

75. Willicombe also sent a copy to A. R. Cutter, Hearst's controller in Los Angeles (who succeeded Alexander Sokolow in 1934). The Hearst Papers at the Bancroft Library may yet prove to have Cutter's copy, but the Morgan Collection at Cal Poly assuredly doesn't have the original letter from Willicombe to Morgan.

In addition to the $25,000 a month allot[t]ed by Mr. Hearst for construction work at San Simeon and Wyntoon, you undoubtedly know that $7,500 a month and about $750 a week additional is being expended respectively for work that Mr. Loorz is directly supervising at San Simeon, and work that Mr. Stolte is supervising at Wyntoon.

MR. HEARST WISHES TO KEEP THE TOTAL EXPENDITURE FOR ALL THIS WORK WITHIN THE $25,000 A MONTH ALLOTED TO YOU AS ABOVE.

He would like you to give it general supervision, deciding what is to go ahead and what is to be held in abeyance; of course your construction will take precedence [over that done through the new Hearst Sunical Building Fund].[76]

I have explained this to Mr. [A. R.] Cutter.[77] He says, and it seems proper, that a few weeks of the present arrangement will probably be necessary before cutting down.

Morgan and Loorz had received Willicombe's letter by August 12, when they next met at San Simeon.[78] Amid his recap notes ("Mr. Suppo to start carving on Billiard Room wing and Recreation [Wing] towers and cornices at early date" was a pipe dream), Loorz made a more pragmatic entry: the Hilltop Fund would be "closed out entirely by September 10th." This meant that certain projects like the San Carpojo Road would be scrapped. A good deal of other shifting and belt-tightening would also be taking place.

Back at San Simeon on August 26, with recent Wyntoon and Beach House visits again to her credit, Morgan had ample notes for Loorz to make on the Milpitas job at Jolon, not just on the Neptune Pool and other aspects of The Enchanted Hill. In fact, Ed March, head gardener on the hilltop, was doing some landscape work at Milpitas;[79] and Morgan's visit two weeks earlier had put Jim Rankin's name into Loorz's notes. With men like Rankin at Jolon, that job must have been like old

---

76. Willicombe may also have been alluding to work that was continuing at San Simeon under the Hilltop Fund. Thus far in 1936 roughly $50,000 had been spent from that fund on construction, maintenance, and diverse activities ranging from "Antiques & Furniture" through nearly three dozen other categories.

77. A man identified in note 75.

78. The date on Loorz's "Recapitulation" of the visit is August 11, by no means a rare typographical error in this vicinity. Morgan's latest visit to the Beach House most likely occurred then.

79. On his home turf at San Simeon, March faced a minor task, one recalling how such a stupendous place could be "the ranch" to Hearst and his friends. Under the heading "North Terrace" in Loorz's recap of August 26, this line appears: "Suggest Mr. March remove two small palms where saddle horses are tied."

home week, never mind the brutal August heat. For Loorz, March, and others based at San Simeon—and for Morgan, too—the Burnett Road provided ready access between those distant points.[80]

HEARST AND HIS PARTY, having sailed from New York on August 8, had been abroad for nearly a month when Loorz wrote to his parents in Nevada on Saturday, September 5. He told them, as he periodically did, about his efforts at San Simeon:

> Mr. Hearst is still in Europe and we do not expect him back for a couple of months. In the meantime as always we are rushing to have as much work completed for him to enjoy when he returns as is possible with the available funds. He is not spending as much as in the past, that is, on this particular place.

Labor Day was now at hand. For her part, Morgan straddled the holiday weekend by going first to Wyntoon and then, a few days later, to Santa Monica (but without stopping at San Simeon on her way home). For his part, Loorz seems (improbably) to have kept away from his typewriter until September 17, when he next saw Morgan. That morning he wrote to Louis Reesing in the Bay Area community of Menlo Park, next to Palo Alto. Reesing, a staunch freethinker, had quit as head gardener the year before in the wake of Cliff Heaton's dismissal,[81] which Loorz had also deplored:

> Let me share with you your celebration of [your] relief from serfdom, on this the 1st anniversary of your departure from this Bastile on the hill. You are not now fully aware of the anguish and mental unpleasantness you have missed during this past twelvemonth.
>
> I'm expecting Miss Morgan today [Thursday] and the usual concern regarding probable approvals and criticisms still runs thru my mind. I am more concerned this time since I learned from My Partner, via the phone last night, that she comes bearing word that construction is to shut down. He had just received such notice for Wyntoon. To what extent I cannot anticipate but I do know that I am already cut down until it is hopeless for me to try to make a real showing on this vast hilltop. . . .

---

80. Loorz himself probably used the road during these weeks as much as anyone did. Back on August 8, in writing to the San Luis Obispo contractor Ted Maino, Loorz said he had recently been at Jolon "all day"—a separate trip, perhaps, from one he and Morgan may have made there on August 4.

Maino had recently been chosen over the F. C. Stolte Co. to build Lou Crawford's Cayucos School (but see note 4, above). Maino's stature in the greater area is evident from a letter Loorz sent Stolte on June 1, 1936: "Several have asked us if we would bid the Santa Maria Federal Post Office. I think it will run about $75,000 and that will eliminate all the locals except Maino [as competitors]." Nonetheless, the Stolte Co. was eliminated as well. From "F.C.S. 1936."

81. See p. 214 and its note 121.

Business is very good here in my own business. I started another job Monday and will start another Saturday.[82] Have figures in on several more and oh boy it would really be fine if they let me out here, at least while prosperity lasts.[83]

Sure enough, the word was that both San Simeon and Wyntoon were to shut down on the first of October; also, the proposed work at the Grand Canyon was to be shelved. (Hearst had cabled Morgan from Germany at the end of August to that effect.)[84] Loorz wrote to Morgan on September 21, acknowledging that he would shut down once the month was out but with "the following exceptions":

> I will remain on to complete Jolon, to carry on the [Hearst] camp activities, supervise the use of our large amount of equipment & to supervise the erection of a Lord & Burnham greenhouse expected any day and purchased by the [Hearst Sunical] ranch building fund. One more animal shelter was to be built in the fields by this fund. Mr. Murray has no orders to stop and the Animal Department say they need it before winter. . . .
>
> I plan on keeping Ray Van Gorden, to handle the mail, and take the Bull Cook [janitor] job in camp and to answer the phone etc while I am away at Jolon etc.
>
> I plan on keeping Alex Rankin as I dont see how this place can operate without him. The man the household have cleaning pools is kept continuously busy on cleaning alone and knows little else about plumbing. As I mentioned I consider him [Rankin] the most handy all around man on the hill. . . .
>
> We will be able to use Mr. Gyorgy and helper for the work at Jolon and as you suggested whoever else from our regular men that fit in.
>
> Word comes from Jack Adams [the hilltop telegrapher][85] this morning that Mr. Hearst can be expected very very soon. Thinks he may be already on his way. Unofficial and Jack very excitable, might have no more information than you have. . . .

---

82. It's hard to say exactly what jobs Loorz meant; they were probably minor ones. By late September, the San Simeon branch of the F. C. Stolte Co. was already well along with its larger jobs for 1936—the schools in Cambria and Morro Bay, plus the sewer plant, the junior college, and a highway bridge in Santa Maria. A letter Loorz wrote on September 10 to a sub-contractor in Arroyo Grande may be pertinent: "In a very few days I expect [to have] one or two chimneys to build in small houses." One of the houses was in Cambria, the other in San Luis Obispo. From "F.C.S. 1936."

83. Reesing answered on September 24. "Yes, I did celebrate that certain anniversary," he told Loorz. "We all have our faults and virtues, but when it comes to eccentricities W R has it all over the avarage [*sic*] mortal." The embittered Reesing had more to say, little of it quotable in polite company.

84. Hearst to Morgan, August 31, 1936; Hearst/Morgan Correspondence, Morgan Collection.

85. Adams, like Jean Henry, was part of Joe Willicombe's office staff. The three of them, plus certain others, were mostly in Los Angeles during this period. Willicombe himself had returned to "the coast" (meaning California) once the Hearst party left for Europe (as he'd also done in 1934).

I have not forgotten that you would like me to complete the rail at Neptune Dressing Rooms if it is necessary to keep John Van[derloo] and one helper and Frank Frandolich on a few days extra to complete.

I'm going to town today to try to raise more plasterers for Jolon so I can bring our man back [from that job] to rush some of the small but important items [at San Simeon] thru by October 1st.

Morgan's prompt reply, dated September 23, pertained to the last week of the month:

The marble for the [Neptune] pool is promised you by the 30th but in case it arrives too late to be set [by] the 30th, please arrange for its setting in any case. This is the only exception on the construction payroll proper, it being agreed that the [management of the Hearst Camp] commissary and general overseeing [are responsibilities] you do not give up at this time, nor do I.

And then she included some further passages, equally difficult passages that no doubt made perfect sense to Loorz but that require careful reading on our part—both in our mulling over things like the old Hilltop Fund and in our trying to grasp Morgan's role in the whole madcap scheme:

As to the greenhouse and animal shelter [through the new Hearst Sunical Building Fund], I do not know, and am not in a position to judge, having nothing to do with work not formerly on "private funds."

Those last few words alluded to the Hearst Construction Fund and—presumably, theoretically—to its non-corporate, non-institutional status, a distinction riddled with complexity and contradictions. However that may be, Morgan had more to say on September 23:

If the orders stand, and funds are available, it would look as though they [the Hearst Sunical projects] could be done. I would suggest you get the confirmation from whomever placed the orders.

Her letter also included this passage: "Thinking it over, I will keep away until some time after the first, and by that time expect to hear directly from New York."

(She steered clear of that red-letter date, all right, though not by very long. She showed up at San Simeon on October 2,[86] having been at the Beach House on the first itself. Both stops were close on the heels of her latest trip to Wyntoon.)

---

86. Loorz's recap (mostly pertaining to the Jolon-Milpitas work) bore a conflated date: "Friday Oct 7, 1936." October 2 fell on Friday. Perhaps Loorz didn't type his notes till the following Wednesday, October 7.

Of course where Wyntoon was concerned, no one else could tell the tale quite like Mac McClure, who finally composed a classic for Loorz; his letter bore the same date as Morgan's recent one, September 23:

Better late than not at all—so here's the letter I intended to write all year.

According to schedule we will be out of here a week from today. This is somewhat earlier than we expected but no-one is very sorry. As far as the job goes, we will be leaving it in about as good shape as we would later. The Pinnacles (otherwise known as Cinderella House) will be nearly done but not quite. The "Chalet" (which is a building for servants quarters) is also 90% done and turned out fine, and the new Bridge House will be all framed and [its] roof papered. This later building is the one that moved across the river. Incidentally it was a great improvement to move it. We all thought it ought to have been there in the first place but it was M.D. who talked W.R. into the idea as it spoiled the down river view from the Brown Bear House (their suite).

We are curious to know just what the shut down may mean—My interpretation is that he has a bad case of jitters over European and Domestic politics.[87] Perhaps he plans a lengthy shut-down but I doubt it.

It will be interesting to know just what status the Grand Canyon job is in. As far as I know he expected it to move but then he didn't give any orders to do so.

He approved the sketches I made [in New York during the summer] and seemed to be finished with me so I wired J.M. if I should ask him anything about a definite start or get any other data but was told to come back without discussing such items—and here we are.[88] It is a peculiar set up and has possibilities for much trouble (foregoing paragraph confidential).

This ends my fourth year at Wyntoon—I hope there is not another, but it hasn't been too unpleasant. I have enjoyed the association with Fred and Harry very much and am only tired of the place and not the people.

Maybe next year will see us looking into the Grand Canyon and again may be it won't.

---

87. Jud Smelser wrote to Loorz from Salt Lake City on September 21; he'd recently heard from Mac about the pending shutdown:

You don't suppose that the hang up of the Seattle P.I. [*Post-Intelligencer*] has affected us so strongly do you? I saw a paragraph in a recent New Yorker [magazine] saying that one large town, Seattle was trying a npble [noble] experiment this fall. Trying to see if they could get along without a Hearst paper.

Struck by members of the Newspaper Guild in August, Hearst's Seattle newspaper remained closed until November. See Swanberg, *Citizen Hearst*, pp. 477, 479; see also Nasaw, *The Chief*, pp. 520, 528.

88. See p. 263: Stolte to Loorz, July 12, 1936. Mac had probably spent no more than two or three mid-summer weeks in New York, if even that many, Hearst having left for Europe by August 8. As for the telegram Mac described, the Morgan Collection at Cal Poly contains nothing of the kind.

My plans (or rather J.M.'s) are for me to take my vacation and then work in [her] office until W.R. returns. If I get some time off I may build a small house in Santa Monica. Otherwise "all is quiet on the Northern front" and I hope that the battles at San Simeon are leaving you unscarred.

Loorz soon heard from another McClure—from Maurice McClure (not related to Warren "Mac" McClure), who had just entered the College of Engineering at the University of California in Berkeley. Maurice McClure had begun working at San Simeon in 1926, first for the labor foreman Frank Souza, then for Frances O'Brien, and later still for Ada Drew, who replaced O'Brien as head housekeeper in 1932 and who, along with several other employees, was fired in 1933. Although "Morris," as he pronounced his given name, escaped the purge, he decided then and there to supplement his grade-school education (he'd never gone to high school). Instead, he went straight into junior college in Santa Maria. By 1936 he accrued enough credits for Berkeley's sake. In the meantime, he worked briefly for Loorz at San Simeon during school vacations and, most recently, for the local branch of the F. C. Stolte Co. on the Cambria Grammar School.[89] "Rumor has it that the Stolte Co. has some more work in Yosemite," McClure told Loorz on September 30. "If this is true—Congratulations! And let us hope that it proves *profitable*."

Loorz had other correspondence to catch up on just then. While awaiting Morgan's arrival on Friday, October 2, he wrote to Jud Smelser—in reply to a letter that Smelser had sent him in late September:[90]

Well things are almost maddening around here right now. The construction payroll consists of Ray Van [Gorden], Alex Rankin, the cook one waiter and myself.

On Hearst Sunical greenhouse I have Pete [Petersen], Frank Souza and Joe Galbraith.

---

89. Maurice McClure had been corresponding with Loorz since the early part of 1935. On August 14 of that year, Loorz described him to Stolte as an "excellent, hard working quiet man," reminiscent of Olin Weatherford.

The Cambria job, launched under Carl Daniels (who'd since tackled the similar school job in Morro Bay), was now being run by a builder named Frank Gendrich. In a parallel to both the Yosemite and the Cambria situations described above (in notes 25 and 34), Julia Morgan has sometimes been incorrectly named as the architect of the Cambria Grammar School.

Another misattribution involving her is especially ludicrous: that she designed the Diet building in Tokyo. Much like San Simeon, the Diet building was begun in 1919 and was worked on till 1936. Morgan, however, never got any closer to Japan than Hawaii, mainly for her work in the 1920s on the YWCA building in downtown Honolulu. (But she had nothing to do with the Royal Hawaiian Hotel, as some have thought, Walter Steilberg having worked on its revamping after World War II.) See also p. 40, note 30, for her marginal connection with the Tokyo YWCA.

90. Partly quoted in note 87, above.

On Jolon doors I have four carpenters in the shop.

Up here around the office and around the [Neptune] Pool area where we have had so much activity it is so quiet I feel like screaming. Personally I am expected to stay only until Jolon is completed unless we hear to the contrary from Mr. Hearst in the meantime. (Even the Gomez' [Alfred Gomes and his wife] have gone.)

We are starting strong at Yosemite so If you wish I could send you there [to work for the Stolte Co.]. Harry Thompson with Fred's able assistance will be Super[intendent] and is on the job today.

I had a nice letter from Mac but I dont know where to answer to. I suppose the best way would be to write thru the [Morgan] office in S.F. I would like to see him just now as I have several possibilities that we might sketch up together.

Miss Morgan will be here today and we will make that trip to Jolon etc. Wonder what headaches are in store for me. Wish things were more definite as there is certainly lots of work outside if I was free to get it.

Loorz and Morgan's trip to the Milpitas Hacienda dominated their meeting on October 2. They also spent time closer to home, as Loorz indicated by several entries under "Hilltop Miscellaneous" on his recap sheets. One such entry said, "Disconnect elevator (New one) to insure safety for present attendants and show operation to Mr. Hearst when he arrives." That had been another one of those utilitarian projects in 1936 (first mentioned in these annals in 1933)[91] — the installation of an elevator in the Recreation Wing, or the New Wing, as that north section of Casa Grande was renamed a decade later.

Following their meeting that Friday, Loorz wrote in detail to Morgan, possibly including his letter with the notes he'd made — a group of notes he misdated October 7.[92] Such discrepancies aside, his letter stands as an important summary:

The construction crew this morning is Ray Van Gorden, Alex Rankin (mostly on ranch payroll for few days) the Cook and one waiter and yours truly.

The place looks more cleaned up and completed especially around Neptune Pool than we have ever seen it.

---

91. Hearst to Loorz, December 17, 1933, refers to the newer elevator (p. 100). In contrast, Loorz to Hearst, January 30, 1934, and Hearst to Loorz, January 31, 1934, refer to the older elevator (pp. 103–05).

92. See note 86, above, concerning Loorz's recap notes of "October 7, 1936." His letter to Morgan is also oddly dated: "Sept–October 1st, 1936," as though written the day before she arrived. But the internal evidence must also be weighed: the letter seems largely based on items discussed during her visit of October 2. On the other hand, a letter from Loorz to Mrs. Frank Frandolich (who had gone to Italy to see family and friends) is clearly dated September 30; the letter is equally clear in what it contains. He began with "No doubt Frank has told you about the very unfortunate shut down of all construction work here on the hilltop tonight."

The whole crew has been paid off including their transportation. . . .

As you stated I will bring Frank Frandolich back as soon as the marble coping arrives [for the Neptune Pool area].

Frank Gyorgy and [Mickey] Brennan worked fast and a little overtime and completed placing Miss [Doris] Day's paintings on the dressing room ceiling [in one of the Billiard Wing bedrooms].[93] She said the Frieze would be shipped today [Thursday] or Friday. . . .

At this juncture Loorz referred to the work at the Milpitas Hacienda, saying he had "brot the plasterers back from Jolon last Saturday [September 26][94] and they are back there again this morning." He then resumed his account of the work at San Simeon:

Main terrace lower north steps [near the North Terrace] completed except for polishing marble risers. When too foggy to wax, waxer can spend time polishing if O.K. They look fine.

New addition on recreation wing stripped and cleaned. . . .

Placed the green tile in the 4th floor bathroom [Billiard Wing Room #3]. . . .

Iron grill placed in window outside Billiard Room hallway [facing Casa Grande's unfinished east courtyard].

Small wall between [north] duplex [tower] and recreation wing [west] tower placed and sample of tile [put] on it. Looked at it from way down the road [the main driveway] and it certainly makes the needed tie.

Loorz may have felt like screaming (as he'd told Jud Smelser on October 2), and he may have felt excessively confined at San Simeon, but at age thirty-eight (as of October 13) he hadn't lost his humor altogether. On October 6 he returned his tickets to the University of California, Berkeley, for the upcoming showdown between that school and its sister campus in Los Angeles. "I would like further to cancel my order for other tickets for this season," he said. "My reason for this cancellation is that an extended voyage to the West Indies makes it inconvenient for visiting football games."

INSTEAD OF SAILING for the Caribbean, Loorz pulled his chair back up to his typewriter. On October 10 he confirmed for Maurice McClure what the latter had heard about recently (and then had written about on September 30):

---

93. Some of Doris Day's decorative painting at Wyntoon had been exterior work on Brown Bear; done in 1934, it was work that Willy Pogany and his crew were now supplanting. Some other murals of hers from the following year, 1935, remain brightly intact: at the Monday Club in San Luis Obispo.

94. The correct date is September 26 only if Loorz did, in fact, write to Morgan on Thursday, October 1 (as in note 92); more confusingly, the Saturday in question could be October 3 instead.

We have a very fine job or jobs at Yosemite. Three three-story hotel buildings. Two of them 33-room dormitories and one two-room apartment hotel. We have a large crew on and making great headway. Wyntoon closed down so we brought Harry Thompson down to run the job and he certainly is doing his stuff.

We are also low bidders on [Hearst Radio] K.Y.A.'s new broadcasting station in S.F.[95] I figured it down here and had very few sub-[contractor] figures [available]. Therefore I had to figure nearly everything in about 24 hours. We were within $75 of the next bidder.

That hadn't been the only tight spot for Loorz lately. He went on to address the question of politics, which Maurice McClure had raised in his letter:

Believe me it has become increasingly difficult for me to express my political opinions. Miss Morgan and her office force keep feeling me out and mentioning how impractical and wasteful the present administration [in Washington] is. I make no commitments but I certainly dont make statements I dont believe.

My honest opinion is that we are going to have good times no matter who is elected. I also feel that income tax is here to stay. I also feel that the so called communists of our country except for a few radicals that we have always had are fine type men struggling to free themselves from relief and charity rolls. Quite an honorable thing I believe.

Loorz was even tardier in getting back to Louis Reesing, who'd written from Menlo Park on September 24. He finally did so on October 12:

Things are at a stand still here on the hill as you perhaps know. I have only a few men trying to get a few important things completed. When that is done It looks bad for construction. . . .

However, Miss Morgan has asked me to stand by until Mr. Hearst's return and then we'll find out definitely. That should be around the first week in November. Then I think the election will determine everything. Your guess is as good as mine.

Although construction was at a near standstill, the maintenance of the hilltop and its surroundings couldn't be ignored. A small dam on Burnett Creek, along the lower reaches of the Burnett Road, had failed during the past winter; some work

---

95. The radio station was another job that would soon involve Frank Gendrich, late of the Cambria Grammar School. On December 1, Loorz wrote to a man in Oakland named James Smith; he mentioned that Gendrich was "in charge of the KYA station on the hill above the corner of 3rd and Bayshore in San Francisco." From "F.C.S. 1936." See also Boutelle, p. 261 (cited under 1930s in the apppendix "Buildings by Julia Morgan").

needed to be done soon, lest the road itself be jeopardized. Loorz brought Bill Murray at the San Francisco headquarters up to date on October 12:

> Mr. Keep uses the road daily maintaining the [sequoia] redwood grove at Burnett [Camp] and the ranch uses the road very often going to and from between ranches [San Simeon and Milpitas]. I have mentioned this to Mr. Apperson and he agrees that it [the dam] should be repaired before winter.

Murray, knowing as well as Loorz did what Hearst's wishes would be, authorized the work through the new Hearst Sunical Building Fund.

Jud Smelser wrote back to Loorz on October 16, giving him Mac McClure's address on 6th Street in Santa Monica. "I think he is doing a hide-out but his office may have this address. He hasn't said but that is usually the way that he handles his time off." Smelser added a postscript:

> I read in a recent Time [magazine] that W.R.H. American newspaper tycoon recently purchased seventy grand of Flemish and English Art in Amsterdam. I think we have been sold down the river in the interest of art. Having always been an admirer of art I guess I shouldn't feel bitter.[96]

Loorz wrote to the Oakland plumber Jim Rankin the next day, October 17. He greeted his good friend by using his middle name, Fleming, and joked that he had taken "10 years to find out that name":

> Well I thot it wise to advise you regarding the wheres and the whyfor's around these parts. First let it be understood that no one knows anything and everybody is guessing and yours is as good as mine.
>
> However, this I can tell you. I am going to complete the Jolon job and the greenhouse. I intend to complete the heating installation but since they are a little behind in the money I have not yet asked you to go ahead. . . .
>
> As far as Jolon is concerned, that all goes thru Miss Morgan's office.[97]

---

96. *Time* published its brief reference to "William Randolph ('Buy American') Hearst" on October 12, 1936, pp. 69, 71—as part of the weekly "People" section.

97. On October 23, in writing to the coyote trapper George Edmunson (who was back in school in Davis), Loorz described the work at Jolon:

> That job has dragged out for a long time and if the special tile does not come we will not be finished until xmas. However, Otto Olson is doing a lot of carving on the doors. They are fine doors and he is doing some fine work on the carving. Just as good as the carvers we have brought in from S.F.

Loorz may have been alluding to men like Jules Suppo and F. M. Lorenz (whose *work* was what was usually "brought in," not the artisans themselves).

Murray gives the money to her and she pays it out like on Hearst Construction. . . .[98]

Well Jimmie (Fleming) business is still very very good for Fred and me and we know it has been with you. I know further that over 60 of my own relatives are far better off than three years ago. I know we are all more happy and hopeful. Then is it right that they should try to scare us so much?

Every year Jimmie are we going to let Big Business scare us to death and make us change? How can candidates be so wonderful at the beginning and so bad in the end? It just means to me that no one can satisfy them. I like this fellow Landon [Alfred M. Landon, the Republican candidate for President] but I dont think Roosevelt [is] as bad as they paint him. . . .

I'm afraid we'll have another Silent Cal [Coolidge] in the person of Mr. Landon. I think that is why they picked him. They dont want someone that does things of his own accord. . . .

Well Jimmie I know you are back on the old Elephant cart where you belong by nature and creed but give us the benefit of the doubt and please dont say we are un-American. What Motto could be more Worthwhile (if not American) than "Government for the benefit of the greater number"?

Oh Hell Jim come on down and we'll talk it over. They've got me so scared that I'm apt to vote for Landon. Also I'm certain things will go on nicely and prosperity will remain regardless for some time to come. Both are fine upright, religious, God fearing men. Roosevelt has shown that he is not a man-fearing man.

Loorz may have been wavering on the question of Alf Landon, but the Governor of Kansas had one supporter he could always count on—William Randolph Hearst. In his wishful role as the nation's soothsayer, Hearst had already made it known through his newspapers that the November election would result in a "Landonslide." He proved to be dead wrong, but the slogan was priceless.[99]

---

98. These words are a good reminder of how the Hearst Construction Fund worked. Typically, Morgan was allotted lump sums in even amounts, whose disbursement was minutely recorded. The $25,000 that Willicombe mentioned on August 6 is just one example (although this time the sum also included money for Wyntoon).

The Morgan office paid myriad expenses, large and small, through such allotments—supplies, materials, workmen's salaries, and so on. But Morgan's office staff (LeFeaver et al.) and Morgan herself were paid by other means, namely, through the commissions stemming from those expenses. Among her various jobs, both Hearst and non-Hearst, San Simeon was alone in giving rise to a separate Commission Account (summarized in Appendix B, pp. 549–50).

99. Landon was neither the weakling that Loorz described nor the puppet of Hearst, as the Democratic opposition liked to proclaim. Well into the 1936 campaign, Landon daringly alluded to—and denounced—a favorite crusade of Hearst's, one aimed at rooting out Communists and other disloyal people: "In Kansas we insist that no teacher should be required to take any oath not

A few days later—on Friday, October 23—Loorz wrote to Mac McClure at his "hideout" in Santa Monica:

> No use telling you what is going on here for it is so quiet that [it] is terrible. However, I still have a crew of a dozen or more men working on a payroll that is financed by Murray of the ranch. We are completing a greenhouse, building another shelter by the giraffe barn, and repairing the dam near Burnett. . . .
>
> I'm expecting Miss Morgan today. Glad she is coming for she hasn't been here for three weeks,[100] though I saw her two weeks ago when we bid on the K.Y.A. new [Hearst Radio] broadcasting station thru her office. By the way we are low on that at $21,000, but it was so much more money than a similar building they are just erecting in Los Angeles that they have not yet permitted us to go ahead. . . . Except for the unsightly tower the building itself is real nice. In fact it is about the neatest little unit I have see[n] come out of her office.
>
> Let me explain that, in the fact that they were given a plan of the other units that have been constructed and asked to adjust it to fit local conditions but make it look just the same as Mr. Hearst wanted them to standardize all of the stations.[101]
>
> Well they didn't want to copy the plan outright without apologies to the Architects so they wrote and explained. The L.A. Architects wrote back, "Oh dont mind just go ahead, we did the same thing we copied it from some other plans from the East."

Jim LeFeaver had got "a real kick" out of telling Loorz the story about Hearst's radio stations, as Mac learned from Loorz's letter. More important, Miss Morgan evidently took no part in the work for Hearst on those Southland stations (as of 1935, they were KELW in Burbank and KEHE in Santa Monica, but never KFWB in Los Angeles, as some have said). Why the departure from the familiar, established pattern of her involvement in virtually every project being designed or built for him in California? The answer remains at large, as does the identity— with the possible exception of Stiles O. Clements—of the "L.A. Architects" Loorz described.

---

required of all other citizens." From Donald R. McCoy, *Landon of Kansas* (Lincoln, Nebraska; 1966), p. 285.

100. Since her last stop at San Simeon on October 2, she'd been away from the Bay Area just once, on a trip at mid-month devoted entirely to the Beach House. After seeing Loorz on successive Fridays, October 23 and 30, she was at the Beach House again on both of the following Saturdays.

101. A station that wouldn't be standardized was the one Morgan designed earlier in 1936 for the Globe Wireless Co. of San Francisco (a job awarded to a builder named Tait). Globe Wireless was owned by the shipping magnate R. Stanley Dollar. But Sara Boutelle assumed Hearst was its owner, something he never had been nor ever would be; see *Julia Morgan*, p. 261 (under 1930s in the appendix "Buildings by Julia Morgan").

Morgan's non-Hearst accounts in 1936 represented twenty percent of her activity that year (p. 543 in this volume's Appendix A). Her two jobs for the Turner family in Berkeley headed the list;

ONE THING LOORZ AND MORGAN discussed during her visit to San Simeon on October 23 was his new "W.R.H. Construction Proposal," which superseded the proposal to Hearst of July 7 and which Loorz put in writing for Morgan on October 28. Loorz's new proposal called for his taking over "the complete management and financing and general supervision of construction of Mr. Hearst's work at San Simeon and elsewhere at net cost plus 10% Commission":

> It is understood that I receive no salary as a part of the cost. My full compensation for personal supervision will be a part of the commission. . . .
>
> If awarded this work it is my intention to handle it all thru our [projected] F. C. Stolte Co. Branch Office at San Luis Obispo. I will maintain a home and reside in San Luis Obispo or in the house at San Simeon as you may desire so that I will be able to give a lot of personal attention to operations on the hilltop and be able to meet you or Mr. Hearst in conference on short notice.
>
> I propose to install and keep a complete set of books and records for handling Mr. Hearst's work exclusively. This system to be similar to the present system used by your office and highly recommended by Mr. Hearst's auditors and officials. . . .
>
> Under this system or arrangement I would be free to give personal supervision to work at Wyntoon & Grand Canyon, if it goes ahead. Having worked with you and Mr. Hearst for five years [at San Simeon] I should be able to more economically execute the work on these two projects with more satisfaction and less worry to you both.

The Loorz Papers contain no reply from Morgan. Yet she and Loorz weighed the proposal over the next two weeks (during which Hearst returned to New York, after three months in Europe, and at the end of which period Morgan wrote a key letter to Hearst, dated November 11).[102]

Loorz had some important modifications for Morgan to consider on November 12. By then it was agreed that the ten-percent commission would drop to five percent (as Loorz had suggested in his earlier proposal of July 7); to offset the adjustment, Loorz would keep drawing an annual salary of $5,200.

---

the Agius residence in Petaluma was the third largest job, followed by the Globe Wireless station in San Francisco and the Thompson residence in Pasadena.

102. Even more detailed than her letter to Hearst on August 5, this missing link at Cal Poly fills a major void, a void left by too few letters of the kind Mac McClure, George Wright, Fred Stolte, and others had sent Loorz from Wyntoon in past years. Better yet, Morgan didn't tell Hearst about Wyntoon alone; she also had the latest for him on Jolon, San Simeon, and the Beach House—all of which jobs she'd visited recently. See Morgan to Hearst, November 11, 1936; Hearst/Morgan Correspondence, Morgan Collection.

The Morgan-Forney ledgers place her at Wyntoon on November 4 (for the last time in 1936); after that, she was at San Simeon on November 9 and in Santa Monica on November 10.

Loorz aired the situation in a richly detailed letter to Stolte, a letter written on the same day as the one to Morgan, November 12.[103] He began by telling his partner, "I think I will build a new home in San Luis Obispo":

> If I dont move in myself I'll let Carl [Daniels] move in and we'll have a permanent Company phone in the town. We have so much work in the town and would have a lot more if they could look up the number in their local directory and call us.

And then he divulged some key points regarding his new "W.R.H. Construction Proposal" and still other developments — the latter being of the utmost importance and comprising unexpected twists:

> After talking with Mr. LeFeaver, Miss Morgan weakened on the 10% idea and me off the payroll. She says she thinks Mr. Hearst connects me with this hilltop and superintendents salary too much that he might balk on the complete change. So she asked me to make out a new proposition including a salary and commission that would net us the 10% or about. They did not want it to sound so much like the [Frank] Hellenthal proposition [for the Beach House in Santa Monica].
>
> We talked it over at length and decided it this way. I am still to get the $5200 and live in the place [the beachfront house in San Simeon]. It is to be understood that I am free to be away directing my own business when necessary but keeping a close watch on this place [the hilltop, etc.] with another man under me. Then we [the F. C. Stolte Co.] will get 5% commission on everything [done for Hearst] and handle all the books just as she is handling them in our local [Hearst hilltop] office. The 5% commission being based upon the condition that he [will] either advance the money or pay cash in full by the 10th of each month, otherwise 7% commission.
>
> Confidentially, she has definitely decided to close her present office [in San Francisco] soon after the first of the year when she has completed what they have on hand. She expects to make no exceptions with her office force and make the break with all of them. Later on if she decides to take on something good in one room of the office she can bring back the one [person] she desires or [the one who] is idle at that time.
>
> At that time we will take over all her records etc in our [Hearst hilltop] office here where it is convenient for her and for [A. R.] Cutter of [the Hearst office in] L.A. etc.
>
> Mr. Hearst has not yet discussed his plans with her and she is not going to call him. If he doesn't send his program by Thanksgiving she intends to go back [to New York] and get it all settled definitely. She has another mission with relatives

---

103. From "F.C.S. 1936."

that would make the trip back there advisable anyway.[104] I dont think she has mentioned this to anyone but Jimmie LeFeaver and ourselves, in case something should cause her to change her mind.

I wanted to tell you the whole story so that you would know. If the arrangement is not satisfactory to you, please let me know soon so that I can correct it before it goes East to Mr. Hearst. I hope you do not object to my handling the records [of the Hearst work] here. It was her own suggestion being that I'm very friendly with Mr. Murray, Mr. Cutter, Mr. Hunter[105] & Mr. Willicombe and know their various systems so that they take my word without question. These are the various people who provide the funds and from our point of view the most important, eh? In fact, I have [had] advance funds from all of these officers and all bills paid on all the work I do direct [for Hearst]. It has amounted to nearly $100,000 already this year.[106]

Loorz devoted the rest of his three-page letter to his outside work in the greater southern area. But before he did so, he said he hoped Stolte would take all the preceding information about Hearst and Morgan as "good news." Stolte evidently did, despite the prospect of Morgan's retirement and its ramifications for his and Loorz's company.[107]

For Loorz, what was most important now, late in 1936, was Hearst's view of things—a view, no doubt, that Loorz tensely awaited. Hearst had reached New

---

104. Sara Boutelle provides a detailed note on Morgan's out-of-state travels, but the trip to New York in 1936 is excluded, perhaps because of its brevity; see *Julia Morgan*, p. 245 (note 3 under "The Morgan Atelier").

105. Since the 1920s, H. O. "Bill" Hunter of the Los Angeles office had filled in sporadically for Willicombe as Hearst's secretary; Hunter assumed those duties full-time when Willicombe retired in 1945.

106. The figure may have pertained only to work done through the Hilltop Fund and any other non-Morgan accounts. At Wyntoon, similar "direct" efforts (but on a smaller scale) were made by Eugene Kower and others outside Morgan's usual sphere—a sphere that, since 1933, had included the F. S. Stolte Co.'s efforts as the general contractor. In that regard, the Stolte Co.'s work at Wyntoon in 1936, much of it on Cinderella House, had accrued $68,311 in costs by these last weeks of the season.

107. Before 1936 ended, Morgan took some of the very steps Loorz described to Stolte. She gave one of her new accounts, the Santa Rosa Columbarium, to Dick Nusbaum. She gave another one in the greater Bay Area, the Burgess residence in Walnut Creek, to Jack Wagenet. (Both men were already licensed architects.) Wagenet wrote to Loorz on December 17. He said that he'd be starting his own practice in Oakland in January and that "by the recent turn of events in the office with the general retrenchment of the activities of W.R.H." his plans were "crystalizing into definite action." But unless Hearst truly called it quits, and Morgan did too, she wouldn't seem to be ready quite yet for Nusbaum or Wagenet to leave the nest. A letter from Nusbaum to Loorz on January 30, 1937, confirms some of her intentions (p. 293). However, Nusbaum and Wagenet were still in her employ—at least intermittently—more than a year later; see pp. 363–64: Morgan to Boyter, May 1, 1938.

York from abroad on November 2, the day before the faint dust from the "Landon-slide" was swept away by Roosevelt's decisive victory. From the thirty-third floor of his sumptuous Ritz Tower in midtown Manhattan, Hearst had wired Loorz on November 6, but not about proposals, not about politics: "Please build immediately another whole section of runways at Kennels." Otherwise, Hearst had yet to focus on the bigger picture out west.

On November 19, a week after Loorz sent Morgan his modified proposal, she wrote to him from San Francisco. Events had finally taken a significant turn:

> Mr. Hearst writes he will not be back before the middle of January, and that work can go on at San Simeon in Spring but at Wyntoon not before summer.[108]
>
> I wrote asking him as to the putting on of John Vanderloo, the Gomes [Mr. & Mrs. Gomes, to work on tapestries], and Mr. Gyorgy part time on lanterns. (No answer yet.)
>
> I am going east after Thanksgiving, will be gone about two weeks in all, and will not discuss any other questions until I see Mr. Hearst there.
>
> How is Jolon progressing? Unless much needed, I do not plan to come again until back around the middle of December.

Another turn came a few days later, as Morgan indicated in writing to Loorz on Monday, November 23:

> Mr. Hearst's plans are evidently changing — i.e. developing, — and it looks now as though he would be back around the first of the year and want to see work going on.
>
> He also says in his last letter that he wants to use Wyntoon Bridge House, Gables, etc, *early* in the year!
>
> By the time he comes, he will probably have a definite program. He suggests you *superintend* Wyntoon, San Simeon, and The Canyon.[109]

That last point was certainly good news, long-awaited news. And yet Loorz must have been wondering what the next day's mail would bring. With the quixotic Hearst as his patron, he had to be ready for anything, just as Morgan had to be.

---

108. Morgan was referring to a letter that led off with Hearst's speaking of confiscatory taxation. See Hearst to Morgan, November 13, 1936; Hearst/Morgan Correspondence, Morgan Collection. Hearst's message was originally an undictated, handwritten reply; he sprawled its penciled words over the letter that Morgan sent him on November 11 (p. 281 and its note 102) and that, so marked, was returned to her two days later. Accompanying it was Willicombe's transcription of the reply. The method closely recalls Hearst and Willicombe's handling of Loorz's "varmint" letter in May (p. 253 in this chapter, plus its note 42).

109. Hearst had made his views known once more through spontaneous, undictated penciling — applied to another letter of Morgan's that was returned to her, this time without Willicombe's intercession. See Morgan to Hearst, November 17, 1936; Hearst/Morgan Correspondence, Morgan Collection.

Loorz himself sent out a letter on Monday the twenty-third, written the day before to Stolte.[110] The partners and their families were planning to see each other soon:

> After enjoying a nice Thanksgiving with you, I hope you will be free on Friday to gallop back down to Salinas to pick up some final local bids and place the bid there with me [on the Santa Rita Grammar School] and turn in the bid at 8 P.M. Seems like a lot of energy to expend but I would like to place the bid anyway just to check up on conditions in that section of the country. We have done a lot of work and a lot of bidding down here [in the greater San Luis area] and though some of it hasn't been so successful it certainly has bee[n] worth a lot of money to get an organization together and to find out some facts and get accustomed to new conditions. I do not regret a single job, regardless.

The organization Loorz spoke of was the branch office of the F. C. Stolte Co.—the San Simeon branch—still operating out of the Loorzes' house in that distant corner of San Luis Obispo County. In less than two years the branch had done enough work around the county, and around Santa Maria as well, to be poised now with an even wider net, ready to cast it much farther afield. Loorz captured the Santa Rita job in Salinas, and it proved instrumental in his filling in the map for the company between its home base in the Bay Area and these outlying southern districts. Soon there would be other jobs up and down the long Salinas Valley in Monterey County, plus jobs in three adjoining counties.

The letter to Stolte about the Santa Rita School also contained Loorz's version of what Morgan had been saying lately about San Simeon and the like:

> You will be interested to learn that Mr. Hearst wrote Miss Morgan that work would again be resumed here after xmas and at Wyntoon on or about the first of April if the snow has cleared etc.[111]

---

110. The letter is headed "Sunday" only, but its content clearly indicates November 22 as the missing date. From "F.C.S. 1936."

Loorz wrote that day to Morgan also, answering her letter of November 19. "Jolon is getting along quite well now," he told her, the tile work being nearly on schedule. In addition, Doris Day was making good headway with her decorative painting.

"If you see Mr. Hearst [when you're in New York] and it is convenient you might mention that the kennels have been erected. I hope to complete the new set by Thanksgiving, so the dogs will again have plenty of room for a short time."

He also reported, "All other work [through the Hearst Sunical Building Fund], in case he should ask, cottages, office, turnaround, shelters and greenhouse are practically completed."

111. Loorz was loosely paraphrasing Hearst's letter to Morgan of November 13 (whose wording also appeared on her letter of November 11; see note 108). Her letter to Hearst of November 17, bearing a similar handwritten reply (as in note 109), probably hadn't arrived back in California before Sunday, November 22, when Loorz wrote to Stolte.

Loorz told his partner that Hearst therefore seemed to have no plans for "shutting down entirely."

Indeed not. As Loorz said to his parents that same day, November 22, "So the shut down was just a temporary thing like we have every winter." Two days later he told Morgan that John Vanderloo and Alfredo Gomes, along with Mrs. Gomes, were "back on the job and very, very happy," exactly as Morgan had hoped Hearst would authorize.[112] (In turn, Hearst revived the Hilltop Fund.) Frank Gyorgy would soon be back at work, too. However, Mac McClure, briefly on the scene these days, seemed to have fallen through the cracks by November 25: "Sorry to have to let Mac off but we are nearly completed with everything," Loorz commented to Jean Henry in Los Angeles, where she was operating in Willicombe's absence (the Colonel having gone east now that the Chief was back from Europe). And yet on November 30, Jud Smelser told Loorz he'd recently heard from Mac, who was "leaving for S.F. as J.M. wishes him to go to work on some stuff." On some stuff for the determined Hearst, of course. No one else could rally the troops as unstoppably, Roosevelt's damnable taxes and his renewed mandate aside.

ON THE FIRST OF DECEMBER, Colonel Willicombe wrote to Loorz from New York.[113] The welfare of the animals at San Simeon was still on Hearst's mind:

> Carey Baldwin has reminded Chief that the ape house is of cheap construction, difficult to keep at proper temperature for the young chimpanzee. As we do not want anything to happen to Mary's youngster, Chief directs me to tell you that he would like to have a new ape house built without delay. Perhaps you could airmail me a sketch and estimate and plan of location, etc.; that is if such procedure will not interfere with the new house being ready by the time the cold weather sets in. All Chief said was—
>
> "Build new ape house."

Loorz had a detailed estimate in the mail by December 7, an estimate for a well-equipped ape house at $3,500. Hearst balked at the price, which prompted him to wire Loorz on the twelfth: "DO NOT BUILD A NEW APE HOUSE RE-

---

112. Morgan wrote to Vanderloo on November 30: "You know by this [letter] Mr. Hearst sent word to ask you to go on with the casting through the winter as weather permits." Vanderloo Collection. And thus Loorz could tell Morgan on December 21, "John has cast a good deal more of the rails and posts for either side of the main wide entrance steps lower north terrace."

113. Both the San Simeon and the Wyntoon accounts in Morgan-Forney indicate Morgan left for New York the next day, December 2. (Her travel expenses were divided between those accounts.) She may have embarked, however, from Los Angeles: the Beach House account for this period indicates she was in Santa Monica on December 3.

PAIR PRESENT APE HOUSE IF NECESSARY. PROVIDE ACCESSORY HEAT FROM OUTSIDE IF NECESSARY."[114]

Yet for Loorz at this juncture the prospect of a new ape house versus a remodeled one may have seemed like little more than monkey business. More urgent matters were constantly on his mind. In writing on December 16 to the plasterer Dell Clausen, who had heard that Loorz was "thru on the hill," Loorz mentioned why he and Morgan had opted for five percent, plus the offsetting salary, on his recent "W.R.H. Construction Proposal." It had simply been "so as not to make the commission sound too big" to Hearst. Loorz elaborated for Clausen:

> She thinks I ought to continue to live here and personally supervise this place [in] what time I could spare from the others [Wyntoon and Grand Canyon] and my own business. Then I would keep a Pinch-Hitter to fill in the gaps while I'm away. This I once mentioned to you, that I had you in mind. However, I didn't mention that to her and one day she said she had just the right young fellow in mind for my right bower. A young fellow from Los Angeles. So I said nothing at least until things are definitely settled. Mr. Hearst may be displeased with the whole setup and then the rumor you're hearing might come to pass. In which case I still do not need to worry. In fact, my overhead is far too great on my private work in this district and as much as my salary is here I could do most of it [myself]. . . .
>
> My family are all quite well and happy and the wife is hoping that no more jobs come in to figure at least until after the Holidays. . . . Don, pathetically, with tears in his eyes, approached me the other evening with the remark, "All you do Daddy is Work, read the paper and go to bed."

Morgan wrote to Loorz on December 17, the day after his letter went out to Clausen:

> Am just in from New York today [Thursday] and plan to be down for Monday.
>
> We want to get the bed room [Room #1] just over the billiard room furnished. Will make a list tonight and send it to you, as well as to Mr. Williams [the warehouse manager].
>
> Mr. Hearst seemed well and cheerful, but dubious about spending any more time in California this next year than the current year.

Morgan didn't elaborate on Hearst's dubiousness, yet Loorz could read between the lines well enough. Taxation lay behind it — confiscatory taxation, as the

---

114. The Bancroft Library has a similar message; its date, content, and typography differ somewhat. "Do not build any new ape house. Do what you can with present one. Heat it additionally if necessary." From Hearst to Loorz, December 11, 1936; Hearst Papers, carton 20 (under "1936 Samples").

old warhorse liked to say. But Loorz knew by now, as well as she did, that Hearst wasn't about to roll over and play dead. Not yet anyway.

No matter what the future might hold, life went on in the bucolic realm of San Simeon, as Loorz told his parents on Friday, December 18:

> Well here it is almost xmas and things all stirring for a fine holiday season. Went to the school play last night and enjoyed it. The boys did well though poor Bill left out two verses of his piece. He did not falter, none except those that knew the piece knew the difference. But it certainly made him nervous for the rest of his parts but he made no more mistakes.
>
> Bobby still has a slight cold but is just as good as he can be. Sleeps until nearly 7:30 these mornings and is as always into everything. I think he will get a real kick out of xmas. . . .
>
> It is still lonesome here on the hilltop with only a few men but a lot of odds and ends. There is nearly as much paper work as ever and the phone rings nearly as often.
>
> We have just had a wonderful 3 inch rainfall and things are much brighter again. The farmers and cattle men around here were worried about the grass. In a day or so the grass will be up and hills all green. All we need here is rain anytime of the year and things get green. It certainly is God's country when you stop to think of it.

Morgan spent December 21 at the Beach House, rather than at San Simeon as planned. "Since you were unable to arrive today, Monday, I'll assume it is possible that you will be delayed further."[115] So began a "brief report" by Loorz, nearly three pages long, full of details for Morgan on the Jolon-Milpitas work and the re-newed efforts that John Vanderloo and others were making at San Simeon. Loorz closed with a personal note:

> The boys [Don and Bill] were real pleased with the two very appropriate cards they received from [you from] Wyoming.[116] Bill came running to show me when I got home that day. In the spirit of xmas, which is growing on them more and

---

115. The Morgan-Forney ledgers provide the best means, as usual, of pinpointing Morgan's appearance in Santa Monica. But with regard to San Simeon, the ledgers and the Cal Poly series San Simeon Financial Records (III/03/07/112) both cite December 19 for her visit—a much earlier date than the one she'd recently given Loorz (who as of December 21 had yet to see her). The discrepancy is pronounced.

116. Don Loorz still has his postcard; it shows a cowboy "leaving" his bucking bronco. Post-marked December 15 in Cheyenne, the card bears an unsigned message, which only Morgan (in her unmistakable hand) could have written: "*You* dont have to come to Wyoming to see such sights! Greetings to you & your family—." Courtesy of Don Loorz, September 29, 1999. A copy has since been added to the George Loorz Papers.

more now that they are older they each have asked if they could not send you something. I could not deny them this privilege especially since you have been so good to them.

The harried Morgan, soon to be sixty-five, was unquestionably delighted with these glad tidings from the young builder whose family she regarded as virtually her own. By those heartfelt words did a trying year stand redeemed.

1937

A Belated Reckoning

ON NEW YEAR'S DAY, Julia Morgan wrote to Don Loorz and to Bill Loorz, thanking each of them for the Christmas presents they had sent her. Her letter to Don, the oldest of the three Loorz sons, was addressed to a fifth grader who was soon to be eleven:

Once when I was younger than Bill my aunt in Boston sent me a knife for Christmas. It was the size of the one you have given me, & I was the proudest person in the house that day — Someone evidently was afraid I would cut myself & *hid it* — Nobody since ever guessed how bright a Christmas a knife could make, until you thought to send me this lovely one with a real pearl handle that *really cut* — & of a size that can go in my pocket too — Harry Thompson, at Wyntoon, cut the enclosed peach stone with a knife up at Wyntoon last summer, & perhaps I could do something on that order, only with a *cherry* stone, as were my capacity. We used to cut little baskets with handles from them, for May day.

Friends fitted up a little fir tree for me as a surprise, and I hung the lovely gifts you & Bill sent on its branches — & each night I have gone in and enjoyed looking at it & thinking of all the kind friends whose thought and affection made it so dear —.

She closed by saying, "My love to you, Don, and a share for all the family from *your friend* always, Julia Morgan."

Her letter to Bill, an eight-year-old boy in the third grade, was every bit as caring and responsive:

That is the most remarkable pencil I ever saw — If one could not think out fine things to draw with all those colors ready to just jump onto the paper, it would only mean that you forgot to include a little wee brain to fasten on top the "supply" end — Now *that would be a good idea*. Then I could just sit back and dream, & hold the pencil loosely onto the paper, & pop-pop-pop-pop- in four colors the fine ideas would all be in lovely lines & color combinations on the paper!

It is a lovely gift and I appreciate it very much, your kind note also, & the exciting Christmas card.

Little wonder that Don and Bill Loorz remember Miss Morgan as they do—not as a humorless, doctrinaire professional (though Don well recalls her "starchy" side), and, perish the thought, not as "the epitome of fierce proto-lesbiansim" that one writer called her,[1] but rather as a warm, endearing woman reminiscent of Mary Poppins (a character fondly recalled by Don from his boyhood reading).

Not long after Morgan wrote those New Year's letters,[2] the steady stream of business correspondence between Don and Bill's father and other key players resumed. George Loorz wrote to Miss Morgan on January 7, soon after her first appearance of the season at San Simeon. He had just been to Jolon (which she had yet to visit in 1937); he'd found things "looking very nice" at the Milpitas Hacienda, and he'd also seen the results of the latest storm:

> Yesterday the snow laid on the ground nearly an inch thick at Milpitas until about noon. It remained on all the hillsides and in the ravines all day. It was real cold. . . .
>
> It has been so wet and cold *here* [on The Enchanted Hill] that we haven't been able to do much. It was even too cold this sunshiny morning to place the cement finish around the marble inserts in front of the dressing rooms at Neptune Pool. Not too cold for the men but the wet cement would freeze up as soon as you spread it thin on the base.
>
> We are still making rain repairs such as additional drains, recoating roofs, opening old drains etc.[3]

The harsh weather remained a factor for several more days, as Loorz explained on January 13 in writing to Morgan again:

> Well things are going quietly on the hilltop with so very few men. It has been so cold and rainy that we haven't been able to do anything outside. It has actually been so cold that we have over 50 breaks in water pipes and Alex [Rankin] is kept real busy trying to get needed water. A lot of plants that have never suffered before have been damaged or actually ruined by the continued frost. . . .

---

1. From Paul Johnson, *A History of the American People* (New York, 1997), p. 685. The flamboyant, unquenchable Johnson thought well of Morgan and San Simeon nonetheless—and well enough, for that matter, of "the enormous, genial, and sinister Hearst." In reference to Casa Grande, Johnson called it "arguably the finest building in North America (north of the Mexican border, anyway)."

2. The two handwritten keepsakes from her are courtesy of Don Loorz, September 29, 1999, and Bill Loorz, November 27, 1989. A copy of each has been added to the George Loorz Papers.

3. Loorz wrote to Stolte on the same day, January 7. He mentioned that his annual vacation was coming up but that family obligations would intervene, much as they had during the past two years at this time. "Oh me," he said, "someday I'm going to just take two weeks and not even write a letter while I'm away."

The weather was so cold that our [Neptune] pool shrunk again leaving a place for leaking between the old and new concrete.[4] I have the boys repairing it again today. We want to have it right when Mr. Hearst gets here.

The tax-wary Hearst, absent from the scene for the past seven months, remained away till mid-February; Morgan, meanwhile, visited the Beach House on January 20 and San Simeon the day after. She followed through on having said in December that Room #1 in the Billiard Wing should be furnished.[5] "Mrs. [Augusta 'Gussie'] Redelsperger [the head housekeeper] to put towels and dainties in bathroom to make it ready for immediate occupancy," went one of Loorz's notes regarding that room. He also noted that Morgan would be buying towel bars and other fittings for the new bathrooms in the Milpitas Hacienda.

Loorz was keeping abreast of his outside work all the while, with Morgan's blessings (and evidently with Hearst's as well). Nineteen thirty-six had had its ups and downs, though, for the F. C. Stolte Co., as Loorz told his friend Jack Hall on January 25:

> We are doing quite well. In fact, we had our biggest year in 1936 but I did not do a perfect job of it. I hit a couple of tough jobs that rolled me for a few thousands. It is the first time that I let things get away from me but with a tough architect, a tough job, and relief men of the poorest caliber and myself tied down here on the hilltop it is no wonder. Fortunately Jack I had several others [jobs] down here and the partner had a lot up there so we had a very good net. In fact, Fred's greatest worry right now is to get out of income tax.

Loorz's reference to "relief men" concerned laborers on one of his PWA jobs, Santa Maria Junior College.[6] And the "tough architect" was its designer, Keith Lockard of Santa Barbara. Nonetheless, Loorz hadn't had his fill of school jobs yet, for they could yield a decent profit. The same day he wrote to Jack Hall, Loorz told the electrician Louis Schallich he was "figuring on a large school" at "$150,000 or

---

4. Most likely near the shallow end, part of which is raised on vertical piers and has a crawl space beneath it. Most of the pool basin is "below grade," the hillside having been excavated in the standard way. (Folklore, however, has it that the entire basin, even the deepest part, rests on piers "above grade.") In any case, the joining of old and new concrete dates from 1934, when Loorz and his crew enlarged the pool. The subject of leakage "where the slabs join" also appears in Loorz to LeFeaver, January 18, 1935 (p. 165); another reference appears in Loorz to Morgan, January 25, 1936 (p. 236).

5. See p. 287 in the previous chapter.

6. "Of course," Loorz had once said of that job and similar ones, "we will not do the hiring as that is done by the relief organization in San Luis Obispo" (letter to Millard Hendricks, February 25, 1936). As to the loss Loorz described to Jack Hall, most of it was on the junior college; a small highway bridge (mentioned on p. 271, note 82) caused the rest of the loss. The bridge actually stood somewhere "below Santa Maria," as Loorz told Stolte on May 17, 1936 (from "F.C.S. 1936").

so." The school was to be built in the Kings County town of Avenal, a speck on the central California map midway between Paso Robles and Fresno.[7]

It wasn't just Loorz's restlessness that drove him. He knew the future at San Simeon could cloud up as fast as the mid-winter skies he'd been mentioning. Everyone who depended closely on Hearst and Morgan, from a journeyman like Louis Schallich to a domestic like Gussie Redelesperger, needed to keep watching for the next inclement bout. On January 30 the architect Dick Nusbaum appealed to Loorz for referrals, just as his fellow Morgan staffer Jack Wagenet had in December.[8] Nusbaum was looking on the bright side as much as he could:

> I know you are aware of the changes in our office due to Miss Morgan's desire to quit her general practice in a gradual manner, keeping only the "main job" going and such others as are necessary.
>
> Miss Morgan felt that this was as good a time as any for me to get started on my own, and she has been very kind in aiding me in this.

Nusbaum's reference to the "main job" needed no explanation. The Hearst accounts, despite cutbacks and shutdowns, had constituted eighty percent of Morgan's activity in 1936. San Simeon alone had commanded more than half that amount—much of it drafting-room hours logged by Nusbaum and Wagenet. Indeed, San Simeon had generated nearly $14,000 in operating costs for the Morgan office in 1936, more than at any time since 1932 (see Appendix A). And by the close of 1936, the firm's commissions on San Simeon were about as well paid-up as they'd ever been (see Appendix B).[9] Was Morgan herself truly hoping to get out

---

7. Concerning the Avenal School, the Loorz Papers contain as many as 700 letters and related items, dating from 1939 through 1940 (the years the school was actually built). That same period yielded extensive correspondence on two similar jobs—the Washington School in Salinas and the Gonzales School, between Salinas and King City. But with minor exceptions, the precursors of these files have never surfaced: thick files, undoubtedly, on the Arroyo Grande, Cambria, and Morro Bay schools; on Santa Maria Junior College; and on other branch-office work done by Loorz and others for the F. C. Stolte Co. from 1935 through 1937.

8. See p. 283, note 107.

9. They were even more current by the time Nusbaum wrote to Loorz a month later. On January 4, 1937, Morgan received $972 from Hearst, an amount she'd billed him in August 1935. (After running about a year behind since 1933, these staggered payments came even less frequently in 1936.) Then on January 25, 1937, Morgan received a much larger amount. Comprising nine monthly billings, September 1935 through May 1936, the lump-sum payment of $9,275 was the largest she'd received on a single date since 1933 (when Hearst paid several "Special Fund" commissions; see pp. 28–29 and their note 17). The grand total for the ten monthly amounts received in January 1937 was $10,247.

Sometime in late 1936–early 1937, Morgan received a separate lump-sum payment of $9,622 —this prompted by Hearst's closing out of the Hilltop Fund in September 1936 (the same fund that, with its slate finally clean, he reopened in November 1936). The $9,622, however, had been accruing since 1932, partly from meals served in Hearst Camp to Hilltop Fund workers (apart from Morgan's

while the getting was good? One wonders. It's a question that the Loorz Papers, even when bolstered by other collections, aren't quite up to answering.

Had Hearst known of the whole prospect, he might simply have dismissed it. *What? Quit now? Come, come, Miss Morgan, things aren't really that bad, are they?*

The man was keeping busy, at any rate, with new plans, new ideas, new pipe dreams — and not just for San Simeon or Wyntoon or the Beach House. Less than a week after Loorz heard from Dick Nusbaum, Hearst was westbound by train, his mind retaining images of the Ritz Tower after the weeks he'd spent there. From Albuquerque he sent word back to Jack Hocking, a designer in New York, concerning the twenty-fifth floor of the Ritz Tower: a certain kitchen was about to get the Midas touch. That wasn't all. Hearst had plenty to say about a private railroad car he was visualizing; in fact, Paul Block, a fellow publisher, had a car that Hocking should see. Hearst asked for drawings before he turned his thoughts elsewhere.[10]

STORMY WEATHER CONTINUED in the early weeks of 1937, as Loorz told his parents soon after his mother visited San Simeon that winter:

> We have certainly had rain since you left. We had seven inches here on the hilltop in 36 hours. Roads washed out, small damns [dams on Burnett Creek] washed out and leaks everywhere about the castle. It is almost impossible to keep out water when it rains like that.
>
> Mr. Hearst is in Los Angeles and might be expected up here anytime and we must hurry to get as many leaks cleaned up and patched as possible. I certainly hope he comes soon as this place will seem more interesting. It has grown tiresome to me and I am unable to put pep into the work for myself or the men.

That was on February 8. The next day, in writing to Fred Stolte, Loorz said he wouldn't have time to "spread much bull," the mail being ready to go out. But he quickly told his partner:

> With the chief back in L.A. there is little doubt but that we will see him before long. Miss Morgan should be here in a day or so and I will try to find out anything that I can. I think she intends to call on him in L.A. soon and then come back up here to discuss plans.

---

own crews); the cost of providing those meals had been borne unduly by her Hearst Construction budget. The resemblance of the $9,622 to the $9,275 in nine monthly commissions from 1935–36 (the ones received late in January 1937) is purely coincidental. If only those two powerhouses, the Loorz Papers and the Morgan-Forney ledgers, could illuminate the matter even more. But they can't. We're left to assume that the various amounts, individually or combined, gave Morgan a much-needed shot in the arm. Enough, quite possibly, for her to rethink her plans of retiring.

10. As conveyed by Hearst to [Arthur John] Hocking, February 5, 1937; Hearst Papers, carton 23 (under "1937 Samples").

In reality, Loorz thought Morgan might not be showing up soon, for he sent her a typically detailed letter on February 10 that covered the work at Jolon and San Simeon. "Anxiously awaiting orders to put on more men and increase production," he told her. "A lot of the boys out of work and apparently not too much in site [sight] for the next month or so." Morgan replied from San Francisco the following day:

> Thank you for the "report." I don't imagine Mr. Hearst will descend at Jolon under present conditions. But I would like the furniture "distributed" so that it can be quickly put in final place. You know it always requires some shifting, however planned.
>
> Mr. [F. M.] Lorenz has 12 pieces of the 4th floor carvings [for Billiard Wing Room #3], two finished on both sides, plus the original—also all the door panels—of course no doors.
>
> He goes onto the *complete doors* for [Room #2 on] the 3rd [floor].
>
> It sounds as though the odds and ends were being caught up with pretty well. Many thanks.
>
> The curtains for the 2nd floor [Room #1] are neutral—but I could get nothing without dyeing and thought if O.K. would get Mr. Gyorgy to make a sample of the pink of the room, and bring the curtains back [to San Francisco] and have dyed. It will be much cheaper than having the fringe and material dyed separately.
>
> No word from Mr. Hearst as yet—but we can go ahead with all the work over the Billiard Room—and perhaps even get it done!

Morgan was referring here to the part of Casa Grande whose interiors she had just discussed in her letter—to the narrow stack of three bedrooms atop the ground-floor Billiard Room, the four levels together forming the Billiard Room Wing (or simply the Billiard Wing) on the north side of that main building.

The month of February saw still more stormy weather, indeed violent weather on the exposed ridge—1,600 feet above sea level—where Hearst's dream castle stood. Loorz gave Morgan a description on the fifteenth:

> We have just gone thru the worst storm and blow that I have witnessed on the hilltop. In fact, none but Mr. [Manuel] Sebastian[11] seem to be able to remember such a storm and that was in '89. Anyway it did us considerable damage Miss Morgan. It blew out glass and forced water thru sash that have never leaked before.
>
> I kept men on dipping up in the recreation wing to avoid damage down [below it] in the [ground-floor] Theater. The household stayed on duty doing the same

---

11. The proprietor of Sebastian Bros., the general store in San Simeon, and the father of Pete Sebastian (who later owned the family business).

thing in the houses and castle [proper] so that except for broken glass and even sash I think there will be no serious results.

Our chimney or flew [flue] blew off our kitchen in [Hearst] camp. Many large branches were blown off the Oaks and the garden is a mess. It whipped the vines [on Orchard Hill?] bare. The poor palms in the East Patio [of Casa Grande] never had many branches and today they have none so I wonder if they can live.

The water that comes down the chimneys alone does a lot of damage in storms as big as this one. This is particularly true in the guest houses. . . .[12]

It is not unkind for me to say that I am pleased Mr. Hearst and guests were not here during this storm.

But Hearst and the party weren't far behind. They arrived at San Simeon on February 18, having been away since June in 1936. "Mr. Hearst is here on the hill and things are going more interesting and exciting," Loorz told his sister, Iva, on the nineteenth. "It always means more work but that is just what I like. We are also having better weather for a change and we are very grateful for that."

The Depression had slowly but surely been catching up to Hearst for seven years now. The day of reckoning wasn't far ahead. And yet that incurable optimist remained full of ideas for projects, as Loorz told Morgan on February 24, soon after she'd visited San Simeon for the first time in a month:

As usual when Mr. Hearst is here he wants a lot of work done. Because financial conditions are as they appeared when you were here [most recently on February 20] I have habitually inquired about it. I find this to be absolutely necessary and to get his written approval when on his private account or the ranch account.

Ah, that vexatious matter again of accounts and, by association, funds. If "private account" is what Loorz really meant, he was speaking of the Hearst Construc-

---

12. These are the same buildings that Loorz called "the houses" in his second paragraph. This basic way of indicating Casa del Mar, Casa del Sol, and Casa del Monte—prevalent in Hearst's time—endures among the housekeeping-curatorial staff at Hearst Castle today. Yet in most other circles, the term *guest houses* (or sometimes *guesthouses*) has all but eclipsed the older form. Hearst himself was unrigid in that regard. He still called the smaller buildings *cottages* at times; and in referring to Casa Grande, he sometimes said *hacienda* (but more often simply *house*).

Meanwhile, the kingly name *Hearst Castle* (vastly better than *Hearst's Castle* or its tin-eared mate, *the Hearst Castle*) was gaining wide favor. On February 6, 1936 (once more from "F.C.S. 1936"), Stolte told Loorz about one of their employees who'd recently got to see San Simeon: Olin Weatherford was "continually remembering some of the things that make Hearst Castle so interesting." And Patience, Richard, and Johnny Abbe's book *Of All Places!* (New York, 1937) included a photograph by their father, James E. Abbe; it showed the young authors seated alone in the cavernous Refectory: "We were always the first at mealtime in the dining-room at Hearst Castle, as you can see." The Abbes visited San Simeon in this early part of 1937. Two other photographs from their trip— one of them a renowned portrait of Hearst—appear in *James Abbe: Photographer* (Norfolk, Virginia; 2000), pp. 142–43.

tion Fund, which had long been Julia Morgan's concern. He may, however, have meant "personal account," synonymous with the Hilltop Fund. Such distinctions aside, by saying "ranch account," he meant the much newer Hearst Sunical Building Fund, which was Bill Murray's concern and was better suited now to pay for things like the enlarged giraffe barn that Hearst wanted. The next passages Loorz composed for Morgan, still on February 24, can therefore be amended as follows:

> So yesterday he asked me to start right away widening the road [the driveway] from the Pergola to the [main] hilltop and get the concrete wall in [along intervening China Hill] as he mentioned before.[13] This is naturally on construction [the Hearst Construction Fund] so I mentioned that I was increasing the crew cautiously as I understood that the available funds had been reduced from last year. He said, "If Miss Morgan needs more money [in that allotment] she can ask for it for I want this wall and all the rooms in the recreation wing completed." I hope he does not change his mind.
>
> Now I know that it has not been my duty to make any inquiries regarding finances on the [Hearst] Construction account but the opportunity and the necessity was such that it was advisable in this case. I hope this meets with your approval. If not, I can only ask you to forgive me this once.
>
> He seems so anxious to have something real active going that I intended starting the shovel crew this morning. However, we are in the midst of a terrible storm and I'll have to wait perhaps until Monday [March 1].

Loorz also wrote to Jim Rankin and to Fred Stolte on February 24. He told Rankin about the upcoming work in the Recreation Wing, and then he concluded with "Anyway we are happy to have Mr. Hearst with us again, to know that he looks well and seems quite happy. He was sorry to see what havoc the frost has done to the garden but is quite reconciled to it and laughed heartily about the strange California weather." Loorz had more, though, to tell Stolte:

> Now about Mr. Hearst. He just called me up to his room [in the Gothic Suite] and announced that they had just had a catastrophe. He pointed out a broken plate glass on a storm door and laughed.

---

13. The proposed China Hill wall dated from at least 1932. It appeared that year in a list of projects Loorz sent Hearst on September 14; it also appeared in a letter Loorz sent Morgan ten days later. Another reference on October 4, 1932, found Loorz telling Alexander Sokolow about projects Hearst wanted done through the Hilltop Fund: "Then he ordered me to start widening the road [the driveway] and constructing a concrete wall around the top of Chinese Hill (the one between the present Pergola Hill and the Castle)." Not only had a few years elapsed since then, but the proposed wall had also become Morgan's responsibility through the Hearst Construction Fund. As to the name *Pergola Hill*, it crops up elsewhere in the annals, though not frequently; yet it may be as legitimate as *Orchard Hill*.

He has been in real good humor and is, of course, in the building business proper, at least in conversation. However, when Miss Morgan was here Saturday [February 20], she said he wanted things but actually had cut down the budget by more than half for both places [San Simeon and Wyntoon]. That was in accordance with a letter from New York.[14]

However, yesterday he asked me to get busy right away and do some work. I told him I had been informed that the budget had been cut and I would have to be cautious. He said, "If Miss Morgan wants more money she can ask for it, I want that [concrete wall on China Hill] done and all these rooms in this wing soon."

So if he holds to the reduced budget there will be very little at Wyntoon this year perhaps $40,000 total. Lets hope he enjoys himself so much here that he'll get the bug and build voluminously. No doubt you agree with me about it. For the present I am supposed to spend all of the budget here until you start up there then we'll split [the monthly allotments].

Hearst returned to Los Angeles the next day, February 25, or the day after.[15] Morgan was in the neighborhood, too. It's unclear, though, whether she saw him at the Beach House on the twenty-fifth; she stopped there before reappearing at San Simeon on the twenty-sixth. Either way, by the time she reached the hilltop, a letter to her from Jim LeFeaver, dated February 25, had most likely arrived as well. Its subject was one that Morgan needed to keep abreast of at every turn, both at home and on the road. Namely, the budget for money-hungry San Simeon.[16]

---

14. The nature of the letter — probably written by one of Hearst's attorneys, executives, or controllers — can easily be imagined: it alerted Hearst to danger ahead and implored him, with the utmost tact, to tread lightly in his building efforts out west.

15. Hearst had been in Los Angeles for several days in early February, right after he arrived from New York. His presence there, plus that of Marion Davies — then, now, or at both times — was prompted in part by *Ever Since Eve*, the last of four Davies films made through Warner Bros. in Burbank. As Loorz told Jud Smelser back on January 21, "pretty definite word has it that a picture will start soon."

16. If Morgan left San Francisco before receiving Loorz's letter of February 24, LeFeaver may have fielded it; he and Loorz may also have talked on the phone. As LeFeaver told her:

> George thinks that to do the road work Mr. Hearst asked for, and to have four rooms finished [in the Recreation Wing] within the next three months, we would need a [monthly] budget of $15,000.
>
> If the elevator [in the Wing] is to be finished up right away, and if the steam heating plant is to be started, he thinks nothing short of our regular $25,000 budget [per month] would make any headway.
>
> He figures that the rooms will cost a total of $10,000 apiece.
>
> We always have to remember, and as George pointed out, that four to five thousand dollars minimum comes out of the [monthly] budget as fixed operating charges [such as part of Loorz's salary], leaving only about $10,000 to work with if we get $15,000.

With regard to the Recreation Wing, prominent in LeFeaver's letter, Loorz and his men got going on that job before the month ran its course. The Wing consisted of three large floors overlying the ground-floor Theater on the north side of Casa Grande. Except for the installation of the elevator at its west end in 1936, plus some new concrete framing the same year, the Wing had seen limited work since 1934, when the crew temporarily finished several rooms for Hearst's birthday party. Masonite and plasterboard from 1934 were still in place; they were about to give way to materials befitting the grandeur of San Simeon. The second and third floors of the Wing were conventional enough spatially, but the fourth floor was more complex, with its corresponding West Tower and East Tower suites.[17] Some of the first work done in the Recreation Wing in 1937 was concentrated in these uppermost rooms. Loorz informed Morgan on Sunday, February 28, that he would have "two more carpenters on the West Tower Room on Monday." He also told her:

> I would like at least to do as much of the rough work in the East Tower as possible before we finish the West tower so we can use the elevator for the bulk of the materials, especially for mantel work and plastering.
>
> Mr. Williams is getting the rest of the Salamanca Ceiling materials out [of the warehouse] today and will have them here for me the first thing Monday morning.
>
> As mentioned to Mr. LeFeaver by phone I would like the [Persian] tile arch so I could determine the shape approximately. I know you want the [surrounding] arch shape [to be] proper & that we can adjust the tile arch to it as we did [with similar Persian tile spandrels] in the Billiard Room but it might be best to humor [adapt] to it a little if possible.
>
> If the mold under the arches and the frieze over the marble columns [in the ensemble] are to be of cast stone I would like to get started on them.
>
> I think our plasterer Dell Clausen could model these satisfactorily, what do you think? He is running a job now in Oakland but said he'd come back when we wanted him.

From LeFeaver to Morgan, February 25, 1937; Hearst/Morgan Correspondence, Morgan Collection. For their part, the Loorz Papers lack any recap notes from Morgan's visit of February 26.

17. On the first two levels over the Theater, the new rooms and suites were identified in running sequence: 1 through 3 on the second floor, 4 through 6 on the third floor. In contrast, the two rooms on the top level (the fourth floor) were already being called the West Tower and the East Tower, or 7 and 8 in the sequence. When work resumed at San Simeon after World War II, the Recreation Wing became the New Wing; most of its internal names were also revised. The level right above the Theater became New Wing 2nd Floor, comprising Rooms #1 through #4. The next level became New Wing 3rd Floor, likewise with Rooms #1 through #4. The fourth floor retained its descriptive turn, with the enlarged West Tower and East Tower suites flanking the new Center Room. But for the three floors overall, the effect of confusing names and levels — epitomized by the adjoining Billiard Wing — was helpfully avoided.

The Persian tiles (forming two spandrels, not just one) and the marble columns (which were Spanish) were things Hearst had gathered through the New
York art market, back in the palmy days before the Great Crash. In contrast, the
Salamanca ceiling was one of many Spanish examples he'd bought during that
same period, and sometimes since then, direct from Arthur Byne in Madrid. Byne,
of course—who met an untimely death in 1935—was the man who had sold
Hearst the monastery that lay behind the "big job" once proposed for Wyntoon
(and who had also sold him two other monasteries).[18]

Morgan answered Loorz on March 1, telling him, "As the ceiling for the West
Tower is not in California, Mr. Hearst agreed we had better do other rooms at this
time." She would therefore "bring down a list of the ceilings for the first floor of
rooms"—meaning those on the second floor, immediately above the Theater.
Morgan, for whatever reason, erred in saying the Salamanca ceiling was not in
California. It was in fact there, and W. R. Williams delivered it to the job that very
day, as Loorz had said he would. But first Morgan had more to say on March 1:

> Also, am not yet certain that Mr. Hearst wishes to use the remaining tile arch in
> the [West] tower room,—can also answer this next trip. The mantel can be put
> up, however.
>
> It will be a good move to get Dell Clausen back,[19] he is so obligingly handy—
> probably can do the necessary decorative work you mention. . . .
>
> It will be all right to waterproof the concrete everywhere in this wing before
> furring [preparing it for surfacing]—although the program contemplates com
> plete finish, inside and outside, this year.[20]

---

18. See pp. 68–70 in the 1933 chapter, plus their notes 27–29.

19. Loorz wrote to Clausen the next day, March 2, about the resumption of work in the Recreation Wing:

> Last week I was informed that the budget had been cut in half which certainly made me feel
> blue. However, there seems to have been a change.
>
> Therefore you can arrange your schedule to return at your convenience. . . .
>
> Mr. Hearst seems very happy to be back here and I know he would like to stay. It seems that
> [to retain his "nonresident" tax status] he will stay in California not more than three or four
> months this trip. Then he intends to come back about November to spend the holidays here.
> No doubt xmas did not mean as much to him in the hotel [the Ritz Tower] in the East.

"Xmas" also meant less to Hearst in 1936 because of Arthur Brisbane's death. It occurred on
Christmas Day.

20. Morgan wrote twice on March 1; her other letter to Loorz addressed a subject that had become perennial:

> In regard to finances, I will go over the program with Mr. Hearst, next trip, but you remember
> you were to figure out the cost of the roads, walks, etc. asked for by Mr. Hearst, and let us know
> here [in San Francisco], so that these items could be included in the report to Mr. Hearst.

The Salamanca ceiling figured in Loorz's notes of his meeting with Morgan on Wednesday, March 3. (Her last visit was just five days earlier; but Hearst had been back in residence since Monday, perhaps prompting her quick return.) "Put up three sides of antique ceiling just as dismantled with short side toward the fireplace," Loorz said of the ceiling and the West Tower. "Will adjust long side to suit then." He also noted that he was to "remove all present temporary partitions on 2nd floor and prepare to install permanent partitions" and that he was to "select antique windows for Patio side [south side of Wing] and make sufficient copies for North side."

THURSDAY, MARCH 4, found Morgan at the Beach House in Santa Monica, following up as she had twice already that winter on repairs and remodeling started the year before. More important, March 4, 1937, marked the fiftieth anniversary of William Randolph Hearst's life in newspaper publishing. His tumultuous, raucously vivid career had started in 1887 with the *San Francisco Examiner*, had embraced the *New York Journal* in 1895, and had reached out octopus-like over the following years to the ownership of newspapers around the country. Magazines, news services, motion pictures, radio interests—these as well had become part of the vast Hearst empire, an empire resting in large part on a bedrock of land and mining properties. Although Depression-battered and long in need of remodeling, this greatest of Hearst's houses—his financial house that made ostentations like San Simeon possible—still boasted an imposing facade of wealth and power.

Loorz was at the typewriter as usual on that historic day, this time writing to Frances Apperson; Mrs. Apperson's husband, Randolph, a first cousin of Hearst's, had been superintendent of the Hearst Ranch since 1934, when he succeeded Arch Parks. Loorz told Fran Apperson:

The Loorz Papers have the data; they fill a page attached to Loorz's recap notes of March 3. In making his estimate, Loorz divided a monthly figure of $15,000 among sixteen categories, from "Balustrades & Terrace Stone" to "Architects Fees." He projected $1,120 for the latter, a shade less than 7.5% (left unspecified) for Morgan's commission. (An even rate—8.0%—*is* cited in another version of the page, evidently a previous draft.) Had Hearst whittled her down by a full percentage point, or perhaps by half a point? It may never be known: the details are too elusive.

Such numbers and decimals aside, the Commission Account in the Morgan-Forney ledgers shows that in 1937, just as in past years, Morgan billed for her percentage every month, twelve times per annum, whether the job was going or not. In other words, she staggered her billing methodically (but often received her payments erratically); see note 9, above; see also Appendix B for the results of those billings. Both processes—the billing and the receiving—were completely separate from the monthly allotments that replenished the Hearst Construction Fund during the active season. Meanwhile, by 1937 the Hearst Construction Fund and the reinstated Hilltop Fund may have become stranger bedfellows than ever before; certain items in the Loorz Papers indicate as much.

Are we happy to have Mr. Hearst back and things moving again. Even though they want some things faster than available labor and materials make it possible.[21]

Among the many proposed projects is a long Spanish type bunk house for the ranch which Randy [Mr. Apperson] no doubt mentioned. It looks dandy to me, so does the cost. I hope you like it and if not I dont know what you can do about it but use your influence through Randy. Just to show my cleverness I'll sketch below what I remember of it as I glanced at it for a minute or two yesterday where Mr. Hearst and Miss Morgan had been mulling over [the drawings of] it.

Loorz made his sketch under the words *HERE'S THE EFFORT,* a sketch closely resembling the Bunkhouse — or, by formal name, the Hearst Sunical Men's Quarters — that Loorz and his crew would begin building in April.

To Randy and Fran Apperson was accorded the privilege of living in the spacious Ranch House, which Hearst's father, George Hearst, had built in the 1870s on the coastal plain below the long, sloping ridge that became The Enchanted Hill half a century later. The new Bunkhouse was slated to be built a few hundred yards away from the Ranch House. Before coming up to San Simeon on his latest visit, Hearst had written to Morgan about the proposed Bunkhouse; he suggested that it be built in the "old California style."[22] When he and Morgan conferred on March 3, they also discussed a similar building for the Jolon-Milpitas property.

---

21. Something else Hearst wanted decisive action on was the gathering of vintage photographs. He told Chris McGregor, his warehouse manager at his Bronx facility in New York:

> I want to collect ALL the old photos I can away back to 1875 [when Hearst was twelve]. I would like almost entirely stage people, and for the most part women as they are more decorative.
>
> These photos need not always be of stars. They can be of pretty girls in minor parts, or even in the chorus.
>
> I would like to go back to Alice Duning [Dunning]Lingard, Maude Branscome [Maud Branscombe], Maude Granger, Adelaide Neilson, &c, &c.
>
> They can be signed or unsigned as long as interesting.
>
> Some early photos can be had at the autograph dealers [in Manhattan], but more I imagine at regular dealers in old photos. Occasionally a collection is dispersed.
>
> Please arrange to cover all sources. Maybe you could put an ad in the papers.

From unsigned [Hearst] to McGregor, March 6, 1937; Hearst Papers, carton 23 (under "1937 Samples").

22. From Hearst to Morgan, February 27, 1937; Hearst/Morgan Correspondence, Morgan Collection. The term "old California style" came from a magazine Hearst included with his letter. Despite his penchant for anachronisms in the arts, he was speaking here of a current architectural style, one that evoked the Monterey tradition and peaked in the 1930s. Early California or the Monterey style — both terms were also used then for buildings like the Bunkhouse. Later, academics spoke of the Monterey Revival.

As usual, though, Hearst and Morgan forged their own way, produced their own variation. The Bunkhouse, unlike the two-story, balconied structures that typify the Monterey style, has a third story at one end. Still, the building unmistakably evokes that appealing phase in regional architec-

Regarding the present work on the hilltop itself, Loorz brought Morgan up to date soon after she completed her San Simeon-to-Santa Monica circuit. This was on March 9:

> With the shovel operating and the partitions coming out on the second floor [of the Recreation Wing] and some action in general Mr. Hearst seems quite happy. He comes out often and goes around with keen interest in everything.
>
> He's anxious to get us started on the concrete wall [for China Hill] and was satisfied that our program included the wall completed on the south side by the end of this year. He is going to talk to you about an entrance to China Hill and I will leave plenty of space for same until it is settled. He wants us to go right on with the grading however on the North side at this time including the terracing. He has personally gone over the terracing, approving the removal of certain trees.

China Hill, so named for the "Chinese House" Hearst planned for it in the early 1920s, was just across the hilltop driveway from the Neptune Pool. The proposed concrete retaining wall would parallel the drive, which formed a divided layout of uphill lanes on one side of China Hill and downhill lanes on the other. Though a minor effort architecturally, the wall would go far toward giving The Enchanted Hill a more dressed-up, nearly finished look. And now that Hearst had been building at San Simeon for almost twenty years, he was increasingly keen on tying up as many loose ends as possible—hence the work in 1936 on the nearby pergola, and, within the heart of the estate (and continuing more recently), the work on the Billiard Wing, the Recreation Wing, the terraces by the Neptune Pool, and so on.

Morgan, according to Loorz's recap notes of March 3, said that an artisan named John Glang was "to be brought down for antiqueing" in the Billiard Wing and, perhaps later, in the Recreation Wing. Loorz addressed that point in his letter to her of March 9:

> We wrote to Mr. Glang last week but he has not yet arrived but I suppose he had some things to straighten out before coming. I asked Mrs. Albert [Augusta Redelsperger][23] for the room he had last year and she advises that she is fully occupied. I'll make him as comfortable as I can [probably in Hearst Camp] until she can make room for him. Perhaps as soon as the party leaves.

---

ture (not the often ungainly Mission Revival of a former day, as some have thought). Good examples of the Monterey style can be seen in Paul Robinson Hunter and Walter L. Reichardt, eds., *Residential Architecture in Southern California* (Los Angeles, 1939; reissued 1998). For the sake of contrast, see also Karen J. Weitze, *California's Mission Revival* (Los Angeles, 1984).

23. Besides going by "Gussie," Augusta Redelsperger was often called "Mrs. Albert"—easily mistakable as a surname.

These are surprising lines. Had Glang stayed in Casa Grande itself in 1936, in one of the very rooms normally used by Hearst's guests? Or did Loorz mean the Service Wing—or perhaps somewhere in the Recreation Wing? In any case, the matter recalls Hearst's comment in 1933 about Martin Charles, a draftsman then in Morgan's office: "Maybe he would have enjoyed it better if we arranged for him to move into the house and be with the guests."[24] If any pampering of Glang or others truly took place, Loorz's words could provide some witness. To set such precedents, though, would seem risky—not just by Hearst's or Morgan's standards but by those of most people in those much more stratified, class-conscious times.

Loorz signed off on March 9 by telling Morgan about the Salamanca ceiling in the West Tower of the Recreation Wing. "That antique ceiling was in quite a shape and it will take quite a little labor repairing before we can actually raise it. I have sent for one more of our old Antique experienced carpenters to work with the man on it."

March 9 also found Morgan writing to Loorz. "I am thinking of coming down for Friday [March 12]," she said, "if I can get work under enough headway here." Chances are, she meant work for San Simeon or some other Hearst project. "Work at Wyntoon will not go ahead there until May,"[25] she continued, "but the ranch house sketches [for the Bunkhouse at San Simeon and the one at Milpitas] are both approved."

Morgan showed up on Saturday instead, March 13. One of Loorz's notes im-

---

24. As quoted in Loorz to Charles, June 27, 1933; see pp. 72–73. A letter Loorz sent Morgan on April 9, 1937, may add perspective to John Glang's prospects. "We have Mr. & Mrs. Gomez [Alfredo and Mary Gomes] comfortably located in 3rd floor Billiard Room Wing [to work on tapestries]. There [their] old home [in the Recreation Wing] torn down and the tile ceiling started." (The ceiling was the Sevillian example that figures later in this chapter.) Loorz's comment to Mac McClure about "special men" is also pertinent; see note 74, below.

25. Morgan had just learned that, once work resumed at Wyntoon on May 1, Hearst's monthly allotment for that estate would not be $12,500 but rather $10,000 (as opposed to San Simeon's current $15,000, likewise just approved by Hearst). See Willicombe to Morgan, March 7, 1937; Hearst/Morgan Correspondence; Morgan Collection. A combined monthly allotment of $25,000 recalls the figure Willicombe gave Morgan on August 6, 1936; see pp. 268–69.

Hearst had some other things to consider about Wyntoon during this period. A lawyer of his in New York wrote to him about that estate on March 16. Hearst's answer, "regarding WYNTOON charges," is a good one to ponder:

I am sorry, but I do not agree that managers and keepers of the property [like Eugene Kower] should be charged to me [on a personal versus company basis]. Housekeepers and servants, yes.
    Furthermore, why would it not be better to rent the property?
    The rental of a summer camp—used at most two or three months per year—could not be much.

From Hearst to Geoffr[e]y Konta, March 18, 1937; Hearst Papers, carton 23 (under "1937 Samples").

plied *practicality* all the way: "Salvage carefully all masonite [from the Recreation Wing's temporary rooms of 1934] to use in ceilings of Ranch Mens Houses [the Bunkhouse]." He was also to utilize "what doors and sash" would suit that new building.

Hearst was still on hand then. Before returning to the Beach House for the next few weeks, he sent Loorz some letters and memoranda. The one he wrote the day after Morgan's visit took the cake; its main concern was the central, cathedral-like section of Casa Grande:

> What would it cost to have the elevator—the old one—go up another story and reach the Celestial Suite?
>
> I would like to do this if not too expensive.
>
> I spoke to Miss Morgan about chimneys and flues. She agrees to everything.
>
> We will cut down the main chimney to where it was before, and during some long absence we will move the big fireplace in the living room [the Assembly Room] out a foot. That will be very advantageous.
>
> We will enlarge the flues in the new theatre wing [the Recreation Wing], and we will put in new flues for new fireplaces on first and second bedroom floors [the second and third floors of the Wing].
>
> These flues can SURELY be made right.

Although leaks had plagued many a fireplace during the recent rains at San Simeon, the tendency of these gaping structures to leave too much smoke behind was what Hearst was getting at. Indeed, the fireplace that irritated him the most—the one in the Morning Room—remained his pet peeve three years after its back-drafts had commanded center stage.[26] With that problem still in mind in 1937, he concluded his letter of March 14:

> The flue of the East Room [Morning Room] fireplace MUST positively be reconstructed all the way up. The sooner you do this the better. You can begin NOW. We will be leaving this week.
>
> Tear everything apart and put in a BIG flue so we can make the East Room fireplace like it was meant to be.

Hearst again pursued the problem of the smoking fireplace the next day, March 15:

> I would like to have a fireplace in the East Room like we have in the [adjoining] Billiard Room—a real fireplace, all open, carrying a big fire, and never smoking. To do this we need a big flue and sufficient projection.

---

26. See pp. 107 and 112 in the 1934 chapter.

It is very simple, but we cannot get it by wishing for it.
We have got to construct.[27]

The matter posed more of an inferno than Loorz alone could put out. He therefore sent Hearst's letters on to Morgan for her perusal.

Hearst soon had more to say, about other matters. On March 16, writing in one-sentence paragraphs recalling his front-page editorials, he told Loorz that he thought the bear grottos could be improved "in the following manner,—or manners":

The polar bear pits should be divided in half and the dividing line run away back to the rear wall.

That is the best way to divide the pits, and the cheapest.

[A simple sketch followed in the space provided.]

Something like the above scrawl. We can then have more bears and avoid troubles.

I think the pool in front should be filled in and concrete covered like the rest, so people can get close to the bears and see them and feed them as they can now [get] to the grizzlys.

---

27. Regarding the Assembly Room in these episodes: its fireplace had evidently been too smoky from the moment in 1937 that Hearst came back to San Simeon, February 18. In fact, the fireplace in that room had malfunctioned in the past. Loorz's recap notes from Morgan's visit of February 20 included this unusually long entry (written in his first-person voice):

Re Mr. Hearst order regarding L[i]ving Room Chimney. No restriction has been put into this flue since Mr. [George] Walker [the mantel expert before John McFadden] put it in shortly after I came here [in 1932]. He did this without our knowledge to correct the smoking of the Gothic Living Room chimney [in the same flue stack, two floors above]. I cannot account for it having worked satisfactory in the meantime. However, when they first started the fires [upon Hearst's return in February] the flues were all cold and it takes quite sometime to get them warm to the top.

Loorz and Hearst exchanged inter-office letters about the problem on March 16. Loorz's ended with these comments:

May I recall this fact? When it is cold, the fires are larger and all doors are closed tight. The flues need more air when they have less [air available to them]. The two large flues, D.R. [Dining Room, or Refectory] & L.R. [Living Room, or Assembly Room] always outdraw the East Room [or Morning Room, served by a separate flue stack] even to the point of causing a down draft [flowing from the East Room-Morning Room toward those two larger rooms]. Proof is that opening any one East Room door stops it immediately. This practice has been often and necessary since long before I came to the hilltop.

Hearst appreciated the analysis. But he remained skeptical. He said that in the Assembly Room "the fireplace NEVER smoked before, except with strong north winds." He backed off about altering that fireplace; instead, he focused on the Morning Room and the prospect (as in years past) of a full-scale rebuilding of its flue. Over the next two weeks, less drastic steps were considered, but plans for the Morning Room weren't shelved just yet. In the Assembly Room, meanwhile, Loorz re-

We will put large enough pools in the center of each of the divided pits.

We should then put a railing across like the rail in front of the grizzlys.

It is safer.

All the above is easy. Now comes the harder part.

I do not like the grizzly pits and have always thought them small.

I think all three should go clear back to the rear wall.

Thus:

[Another sketch appeared.]

I think THEIR water pools in front should be filled in and if necessary pools should be given them farther back, but I do not know that they need pools.

At any rate they can get along with small pools.

The main thing is to run these pits back to the rear wall and give the bears twice as much room.

Now comes the great question.

How much will each of these changes cost?

The postscript said, "While we are writing [waiting?] to do the above can we not dump a lot of earth over the hill opposite the bear pit [across the roadway] and cover up that ugly refuse that the workmen carelessly threw down the hill?"[28]

As for Hearst's letters about smoking fireplaces—the ones Loorz recently forwarded to Morgan—she wrote back on March 22, saying that she would be supportive:

The East room flue is exactly the size of the Billiard room flue and symmetrically placed in the flue stack. The difference is that the East room fireplace is located about 12 feet [off center] from the chimney stack, due to several changes in the location of this chimney before "your day," and consequent complications. I will see if a new chimney cannot be built some way at a less distance from the fireplace, and will go into the problem once more with Mr. Hearst and see what solution he would approve, taking the responsibility for the few days delay if necessary.

Hearst had gone back to Santa Monica by that third week of March; he wouldn't return until early in May.[29] Loorz wrote to him at the Beach House on

---

stored order by changing the fire screen—allowing better air movement and, for good measure, "a much better view of the fire itself," as he told Hearst on March 31.

28. The Loorz Papers have the original letter and the Hearst Papers the carbon copy (in carton 23 [under "1937 Samples"]). Both letters contain the two sketches indicated in the quoted text; the original and the carbon versions differ slightly from each other.

29. Hearst left San Simeon about March 17. That day, he allowed "the senior class in California History" from San Luis Obispo High School to see the hilltop; a request had been made earlier in the month to visit (according to the writer's spelling) Hearst's "magnificant castle":

Referring to your recent letter about the students in the History Class visiting San Simeon, Mr. Hearst would be glad to have them come up here, if you can arrange it, next Wednesday,

March 26, not about fireplaces but about "the old black ostrich" in the main zoo area, whose extensive acreage lay midway between the hilltop and the coastal plain.[30] The ostrich was notoriously violent and had attacked a carpenter working on the animal shelters; the carpenter, in self defense, had struck the bird dead with a two-by-four. Hearst was famous for his love of animals—witness his recent letter about bears—and for his deploring of any cruelty toward God's creatures. What on earth, Loorz must have thought, would Hearst say in this instance? His verdict soon followed:

> As long as the ostrich did not hurt the MAN there is nothing to worry about.
>
> However, we should endeavor to cure ugly birds [and animals], and I think the best way is to shoot them in the prat [with a] charge of rock salt.
>
> [Animals] are like humans—they are ugly when they [think they can] get away with it. A little severe discipline [naturally] convinces them that they can NOT get away with it.
>
> The severity is not cruel. It would have saved this ostrich's life.
>
> When the men are working in places exposed to attack, I suggest that you send a watchman along with a shot gun containing a small charge of rock salt.
>
> I think it will do the trick.[31]

Hearst added a detached line at the bottom: "$3,000 is not too much for the elevator"—Loorz having told him on March 26 that his proposed raising of the older elevator to the Celestial Suite would probably cost that much.

March 17th. As there will be some other visitors that day, it will be desirable that your party arrive at the ranch between 9 and 9:30 in the morning, which I trust will be convenient. All of the visitors will leave before noon, so that the earlier they get here the longer time they can spend.

From unsigned [Willicombe] to Betty Janssen, March 10, 1937; Hearst Papers, carton 23 (under "1937 Samples"); the file also contains Janssen's request of Hearst, dated March 5 and addressed to him at the "Hearst Hacienda."

30. As distinct from the smaller, more restricted zoo compound on the north side of Orchard Hill (housing the bears Hearst wrote about on March 16); likewise distinct from the compound at the east end of the main hilltop itself (the area called Animal Hill).

31. This typewritten letter of March 29, 1937—very likely based on Hearst's handwriting rather than his dictation—is deeply torn on its left side. My bracketed words attempt a reconstruction of the second and third paragraphs, parts of which are missing. A definitive reconstruction awaits a checking of Willicombe's carbon copy—if such a document still exists. See also p. 253, note 42.

A similar incident soon occurred in the zoo. A truck owned by an outside supplier stalled going up the hill. Another hostile ostrich went on the attack; a man named Jesse Zelda got injured, and he sued Hearst Sunical for $40,000. That summer, Joe Willicombe assured a concerned Bill Murray that Carey Baldwin, the head zookeeper, had long since restored order: the ostrich was now being used "to help hatch eggs." As Willicombe explained, "It seems the male ostrich sits on the eggs at

Morgan was at San Simeon on Monday, March 29, the day Hearst replied about the ostrich. (She'd been at the Beach House on Saturday, for the last time in 1937.)[32] As usual she conferred minutely with Loorz, who compiled two pages of notes. Some of them can be cited here under the headings as he rendered them:

CHINA HILL WALL

1. Curves at beginning near Neptune Temple to be symmetrical with Center Line thru pool axis [its cross axis].

2. Height and shape of curve to be carefully adjusted to tentative layout of stakes by Architect.

5. Wall to continue around curve at the mentioned axis line for the present and removed, if necessary when future development occurs.

BILLIARD ROOM FOURTH FLOOR [Billiard Wing Room #3]

7. Mr. [John] Glang to exercise extreme caution in antiqueing the balance of the carvings in this room. Work very much overdone. Attempt to restore some of the finer lines.

RECREATION WING

10. Ceiling of West tower very good. Exercise caution about exposed nailing.

21. Mr. Williams to hunt out tile ceiling "Sevillian" as received in 25 cases [in]

---

night and the female in the daytime." From Murray to Willicombe (who annotated the letter), July 17, 1937; Hearst Papers, carton 23 (under "1937 Samples").

32. That tenth of eleven Beach House accounts, launched in January 1936, ran through April 1937. Before it ended, some correspondence arose. Willicombe to Morgan, April 5: "Chief asks if we have in storage anywhere on Coast [American] Colonial type four-poster double bed for use at Beach House. Kindly telegraph me at [Los Angeles] Examiner." Morgan to Willicombe, April 6: "TWO DELICATE MAHOGANY FOUR POSTERS ARE IN SHASTA WAREHOUSE LOOK UNDER FURNITURE BEDS IN WYNTOON PICTURE CATALOGUE." Both telegrams: Hearst Papers, carton 23 (under "1937 Samples"). Morgan followed with a letter to Hearst on Wednesday, April 7:

> Mr. McClure [Mac McClure] is going to be in Los Angeles this week end on some personal matter, and will bring you the Wyntoon base inventory from which the photostats are made, as showing the furniture at larger scale and with the pieces not in use marked.
>
> I realize also that furniture in "The Bend" [the old Wheeler place at Wyntoon] could be drawn on as [even] the least fine are wonderful pieces.
>
> If you would like me to follow up the changes in the Beach House furniture, I will do so gladly — as it is something not easy to delegate on account of the variety of resources [inventories and other records].
>
> There is the possibility of gathering some lovely rooms by bringing together related pieces, a very light group in pear wood and painted wood or inlay — as contrasted with a group very dark and rich in tone, etc.

Hearst replied on April 15 to her "letter of April 7th regarding Wyntoon and the rooms at the Beach House." He said, "I certainly would greatly like you to follow up and make lovely rooms." And then he said, "I did [not] think I would bother you, but I am very pleased that you will do this." Both letters: Hearst Papers, carton 23 (under "1937 Samples").

1926 photo 2420. (Mr. Williams states he can locate no invoices or shipping information from which to locate same.)[33]

22. Mr. Williams says he will have no trouble finding "Blazonceil" [ceiling] or whatever it was [called] as it was received in the past two years.

24. Send back to warehouse ceiling originally selected for [Room] #4 [on the third floor][34] still crated.

MISCELLANEOUS

27. As Wyntoon will not start up until after 1st of May O.K. to spend some over $15,000 [of the present monthly budget] and get some of the Garden wall poured [on China Hill].[35]

29. Proceed to remove the brick at the top of the opening back to four inches in the East Room mantle.

31. Arch[itect] to send photographs of largest possible mantels [in Hearst's stockpile] to go into new rooms [of Recreation Wing].

Having settled on a monthly budget of $15,000 for San Simeon, the absentee Hearst was back in the building game, albeit with diminished means. In turn, he could be quick to blow the whistle. On March 31 Loorz had this to tell Carl Daniels, the head man among his local Stolte employees:

> They rushed thru plans for the [Grand] Canyon but when Mr. Hearst heard they ran $180,000 (Miss Morgan's estimate not mine) he went up in the air. Much too much says he. Sorry, for if it had run a little over $100,000 I think we would have started there May first with a bang.

---

33. Williams began managing the San Simeon warehouses in 1927. The records he inherited, compiled from 1919 through 1926, were incomplete and often amateurish. See also p. 112, note 21, and p. 132, note 52.

34. The eventual New Wing 3rd Floor Room #1 (as in note 17, above).

35. The lack of activity "up north" may explain why the Loorz Papers contain so little on Wyntoon thus far in 1937—that coupled with there being no counterpart to the previous year's "F.C.S. 1936" letter box. Consequently, players like Mac McClure and Harry Thompson are all but missing from the current cast (but see note 32, above). Fred Stolte appears in some cameos through this long pre-season for Wyntoon; he and Loorz were more apt, though, to be discussing the KYA radio station in San Francisco when they talked about Hearst-Morgan subjects. "You certainly have had some tough weather to contend with on K.Y.A.," Loorz told his partner on February 24. "Hope that [it] is not all headache and that there is at least a little [profit] left when it is over with."

Stolte gave the details when he replied on February 27. "The last six weeks have been rather bad for efficient building work, especially deep footings in mud. We had mud in one hole and hard rock for another and mud and rock for the other two, on KYA tower."

Stolte hoped to secure further work in the near future for Frank Gendrich, the superintendent on the KYA project. "There are quite a number of concrete jobs in Frisco and more coming up," he said in his letter, but he thought wood-frame construction might be better for Gendrich.

Loorz voiced a new concern on March 8. He told Stolte, "Boy if I dont get some of this school money on Morro [Bay] and Cambria before long I'll have to hock my shoes. J.C. [Junior College] at Santa Maria and all of the rest [of the branch-office jobs] are paying O.K."

With regard to the "Sevillian" tile ceiling, which Loorz mentioned in his notes of March 29, it surfaced without undue delay. Loorz told Morgan on April 2, "Mr. Williams has located the tile ceiling and is going to bring it up right away."

(Other news on April 2: Bill Murray informed Loorz that a neighboring property owner, encroached upon by the Burnett Road, had agreed to sell the disputed parcel; the matter had been simmering since September 1936. When Hearst learned about it after he got back in 1937, he wasn't pleased. "We will not buy the land at any fancy price, or exchange rights of way," he told Loorz and another employee, Roy Summers, on March 12. "We will build the road differently." He was also quick to say, "I do not see how such a mistake could have been made. It was due to extraordinary carelessness." He named Summers in particular for having been "extremely lax." Little wonder that in his letter of April 2, Murray told Loorz, "I am glad this matter is behind us, and I am sure you are also.")

On April 9, in speaking of the Recreation Wing's Room #3 (on the second floor) and Room #6 (on the third floor)[36]—between which the Sevillian ceiling was divided—Loorz could tell Morgan, "The tile ceilings are going in nicely. A little fudging here and there to make carving come out on centers etc but no damage to anything. All subject to shifting if you wish."

Loorz also told her in that letter that he could start digging the footings for the new Hearst Sunical Bunkhouse in a few more days.

THE WORK ON THE HILLTOP and elsewhere on the ranch continued briskly while Hearst was away.[37] One of Loorz's notes from Morgan's visit on April 12 proved

---

36. Room #3 became New Wing 2nd Floor Rooms #3 and #4 (which form a suite); Room #6 became New Wing 3rd Floor Room #3 (a portion of another suite).

37. San Simeon's role as a showplace also continued in Hearst's absence, hence the following letter:

> This is a memorandum regarding two small parties that are coming to the Ranch.
> They are both expected to arrive there Wednesday [April 14] by motor.
> One is coming from Los Angeles—the Rumanian Ambassador and his wife, maybe someone else with them.
> The other is coming from Pebble Beach [via Monterey and Salinas]—Prince Paul Sapieha of Poland and the Princess, and maybe someone may be with them.
> In any event take good care of them,—they are to have luncheon (if they arrive in time of course) and dinner and remain over night if they desire.
> KEEP IN MIND ALSO THAT WHILE THEY PLAN TO BE THERE WEDNESDAY, THEY MAY CHANGE THE DAY. THAT OF COURSE WOULD BE OKEY.
> So far as I know the people in one party do not know the people in the other, although they may. But if they do not, they will become acquainted.

From unsigned [Willicombe] to Albert Redelsperger, April 11, 1937; Hearst Papers, carton 23 (under "1937 Samples").

that Hearst was still thinking big, never mind his Grand Canyon worries. "Send in [to the Morgan office] complete contour [map] and location of roads and area at entrance to Pergola [on Orchard Hill] for Architectural studies of later development."[38] Hearst's long-cherished hope of reliving the Panama-Pacific Exposition of 1915 at San Simeon hadn't died; he'd aired the idea in 1936, right before he left California for the rest of the year. Once more he visualized using sculptures and fountains from that bygone event, not just on Orchard Hill but also on Reservoir Hill, across from the main hilltop.[39]

That wasn't his only incredible idea. Charles Cassou, the French sculptor whose *Birth of Venus* and other brilliant white statuary adorned the Neptune Pool, had produced a separate set of three marble groups, presided over by the Roman huntress Diana. The *Diana* ensemble was earmarked for the area adjoining the North Terrace—was standing by for that hugely scaled, dramatic feature called the North Entrance or, more fitingly, the Grand Entrance or even the Grand Staircase.[40] Hearst also meant to put stupendous fountains there.

It always helped to have plans, of course. "Try to locate complete drawings for Diana pool paving and Balustrades, presumably on job." Loorz had based that note on Morgan's visit of March 3. And now in his recap of April 12 it was this: "John [Vanderloo] to start casting ornamental balusters until plans and details are received for Diana Steps and railing etc." An infusion of cash, lots of it—more than $15,000 a month—not just more visions, not just more blueprints, would have been better still. Failing that, the *Diana* crates, stacked nearby, were sure to keep bleaching in the sun and rotting in the rain for longer than anyone cared to think.[41]

38. The recapitulation is dated "Monday April 12th (Also April 5th)." None of its thirty-five entries can readily be dated with more precision.

Morgan's earlier appearance on April 5 sounds right, since it was also a Monday. The Morgan-Forney ledgers and the records at Cal Poly cite the preceding Friday, April 2; but that date sounds unduly close to her visit on March 29. Also, since she didn't go to the Beach House again in 1937 after March 27, and since no other jobs—Hearst or non-Hearst—required her presence in the Southland or in Loorz's district on the weekend of April 3–4, a Monday visit seems all the likelier.

39. See p. 258: Loorz to Morgan (paraphrasing Hearst), June 12, 1936. Oddly, whereas Loorz's letter made Hearst sound as if he already owned the Exposition pieces, some letters from the current year suggest he had yet to acquire them. See Hearst to Morgan, March 9 and 14, 1937 (first cited on p. 175 in this volume, note 37); Hearst/Morgan Correspondence, Morgan Collection.

40. See p. 188, plus its note 69; p. 211; and p. 261, plus its note 55. On February 10, 1937, an effort preceding the use of *Diana* prompted Loorz to tell Morgan, "John [Vanderloo] is nearly completed with the casting [cast-stone work] at the North Entrance steps and Frank [Frandolich] is right behind him with the [marble] setting." As to the alternate term *Grand Staircase*, it appears on some of Morgan's drawings preserved at Hearst Castle.

41. The sculptures lay untouched there for almost twenty more years. In 1956, five years after Hearst's death, Forest Lawn Memorial Park acquired the *Diana* groups for its branch in Hollywood

Loorz stayed as optimistic as he could. What he told the former gardener Louis Reesing is a case in point. (Reesing's health had collapsed, and he lay dying now at home in Menlo Park.) Loorz wrote to him on April 12, the same day as Morgan's latest visit: "The way we have started out this year, it really looks like we are going to do more actual construction and completing than we have since I have been here." He had these details to convey as well:

> Confidentially, Louis, I attempted again to get away from this place on the first of the year. I like it [here], yes, we all like it, but I was losing on the outside more than I was making here only because I could not get away to attend to it. However, they gave me more freedom and increased my pay [to $125 a week] and told me they liked me and wanted me to stay and here I am.

The rousing part of what Loorz told Reesing must have been legitimate, for he wrote to his parents in a similar vein on April 14 (although he began by saying, "I have been terribly busy and more worried [because of problems on outside jobs] than at any time in my life"):

> There never has been a time when I have had more to do on this hill. However, I like that because I can give lots of men work (I have them [hired] already) and both Mr. Hearst & Miss Morgan are leaving me more and more to my ideas. In that way I am able to make good headway which makes everybody concerned very happy.

He told his parents in closing, "So I'll stick close to the job at least until Mr. Hearst leaves for the East. In the meantime I'm going to step on it to the extent of the money [available], in order to show him some improvement here."

Loorz wrote Morgan the next day, April 15, likewise in that spirit. "We are making headway now and everyone is happy about it," he said. "However, I fear I'll have to put on the brakes for a while as the limit is not far off." He also said, "Carpenters are making good headway on the tile [Sevillian] ceilings so I intend to start on Tarazona [another Spanish ceiling] to see if we can figure it out." He hoped she had a photograph that would make the task easier.

Morgan stuck to her recent pattern by making another Monday appearance—on April 19 in this case. In his notes, Loorz spoke of Hearst as though the great man were back in residence. He wasn't, though.[42] Maybe they'd conferred

---

Hills (not far from Warner Bros. in Burbank). The sculptures are still on display at Forest Lawn, along with some other works from the Hearst Collection.

42. Willicombe said of Hearst at this juncture: "He is talking about going to ranch today. Maybe yes, maybe no." From Willicombe to T[homas] J. White, April 19, 1937; Hearst Papers, carton 23 (under "1937 Samples"). Hearst may have been hoping to see Morgan while she was on the hill.

by phone in time for Morgan's visit, which yielded some choice entries under "Miscellaneous":

> 20. Mr. Hearst asked to move the crouching Venus to a permanent base between doorways in front of window of B House Court [Casa del Monte].
> 21. He again asks us to try the large jars up on the upper level at the West entrance [between the West Terrace and the Neptune Pool].
> 22. He also now wants the concrete wall clear around China Hill this year. I mentioned that it would take a lot of budget from Rec[reation] Wing rooms. He said no more so I dont think he will insist.
> 24. He again mentioned making the Rec. Wing baths larger but realized it would mean sacrificing a window [in an adjoining room each time] so again decided to let it go as planned.
> 25. Mentioned again his pleasure regarding the new ceilings [in the Wing] and was anxious to get the rest [installed].
> 26. Again made certain we had the [concrete] wall [on China Hill] 6ft high and seems proud of it. Now wants it about 8 ft. high on North side — Oh me.

With so much happening at San Simeon, so much hanging in the balance, this was no time for the Loorz Papers to be silent. But so they are — from the time Morgan appeared on April 19 until right after her next Monday visit on April 26. The gap resulted in a lack of recap notes for that later date, besides other losses. Among the missing: current details on the big Bunkhouse project. What a relief, therefore, to pick up the trail of that job on April 27, through a letter Loorz sent Morgan. "As mentioned yesterday the boat with our lumber aboard is [stuck] on a [sand] bar up north. This will mean a week to ten days delay." Shades of San Simeon during the era of the first builder-in-residence, Herbert Washburn — during the era even before Camille Rossi took over in 1922!

Two days later — Thursday, April 29, Hearst's seventy-fourth birthday — Loorz spread the kind of word that kept everybody hopping. He alerted Morgan, "It is rumored that Mr. Hearst & party will be here next Sunday [May 2] for a short visit." Loorz told her that he'd make the Recreation Wing presentable in case it was true — and that he'd add another hundred feet to the concrete wall on China Hill, one of Hearst's fonder projects at the moment.

The rumor was partly true, partly false. Hearst and company would soon be coming; yet their arrival on May 3 would lead to a three-week stay. In the meantime, they'd be carrying out some other plans. As Joe Willicombe told one of Hearst's executives in New York on April 16:

CHIEF WOULD LIKE ALL THE BOYS [HIS FIVE SONS] AT BIRTHDAY PARTY [AT THE BEACH HOUSE]. WILL YOU TELL

THEM? ALSO WILL YOU SUGGEST ANYONE ELSE IN EAST YOU THINK MIGHT LIKE TO COME AND SHOULD COME OUT? OF COURSE YOU WILL BE HERE AND HAVE ALREADY TOLD DICK BERLIN [OF HEARST MAGAZINES] HE IS INVITED. LET ME KNOW HOW I CAN COOPERATE. REMEMBER BIRTH-DAY TWENTYNINTH BUT PARTY SATURDAY MAY FIRST.[43]

Complete with merry-go-round, the circus party of 1937 probably ranks as the most famous birthday bash in all of Hearstiana. The Chief himself was the ring-master.

THE ODD, THE DROLL, at times the absurd are interwoven through this stretch of the Loorz Papers, just as they are through so many other stretches. "We had to build a fancy crate and ship the elephant [Marianne] to L.A. on hurried notice." The news went to Bill Murray of Hearst Sunical, conveyed by Loorz in another letter dated April 29. "Mr. Willicombe told me to do it, the Chief's orders. The cost of same will be near $140. A bit expensive but done safely and well. How many bales of alfalfa [for feed on the Hearst Ranch] would that pay for?"

Loorz mentioned the same episode in writing to Louis Reesing on May 1: "At last Louis, You have so often heard, on this hilltop about getting rid of the zoo.[44] Well the elephant was given to the L.A. zoo the other day and though she is only one animal she was a good portion by tonnage." Above all, Loorz was trying to cheer the infirm Reesing, who was in his final days and was hoping Loorz could reach his bedside in Menlo Park before the end came. Loorz tossed off some other entertaining passages for Reesing's wife, Signe, to read to her husband:

> Jim Rankin is back on the job so I have quite a little amusement. He and I get together and wave the dukes and swim along unmindful of things about us as though it were complete oblivion. It is good to get some of the old timers back and really go to town on the latest dirt. You know I was always pretty good with the shovel and I haven't decided whether it was more than a tie between us.
>
> As always in anticipation of the Chief's return it is rush here and rush there *especially in the garden.* My work is so scattered with small groups here and there that it is not difficult to keep things clean.

For Loorz and his hilltop crew, meanwhile, the Recreation Wing remained at the forefront, as his notes following Morgan's visit of May 3 indicate. (A word of

---

43. From Willicombe to Thomas J. White, April 16, 1937; Hearst Papers, carton 23 (under "1937 Samples").

44. Specifically the hilltop portion of the zoo, near the Roman Pool and the garages — the portion that Hearst had been wanting to disband for the past few years.

warning haunted the very first entry: "O.K. to proceed with present payroll but be prepared to cut down promptly when notified.") All right. Now on with the business at hand. "Cathkingceil [yet another Spanish ceiling] approved for room #2 [on the second floor],"[45] began the main entry. "Addition of one [modern] section necessary. . . . Ceiling is on hand and in very good condition as regards painting."

A further entry from May 3 began with "Show [photographs of] other mantels to Mr. Hearst for approval for other rooms." It also said, "He approved all as you selected. However, when photographs of three more came next day he liked two of them better and they are slightly smaller so all is well."[46] And then another entry, with a bit of rhyme to it: "Send sample moldings to Sam Berger from Antiques as directed for carving trim for rooms as selected." Berger, like Jules Suppo and F. M. Lorenz, was a woodcarver based in San Francisco. (Loorz's rendering of *Antiques* denotes the Antiques Department, as the warehouse operation under W. R. Williams—and, in turn, under Morgan's jurisdiction—was formally called; but the jingle is too good to bracket.)

Morgan went back to the Bay Area briefly. Come Thursday, May 6, she began a nearly week-long stint at Wyntoon, her first of any length in 1937. Mac McClure was already there; in fact, he'd been there, evidently with few others for company, since at least mid-April.[47] Maybe now the late-blooming season—delayed unlike any other since the Waterhouse and related phases began in 1933—could finally shift into accustomed gear.

At San Simeon, Hearst wrote to Loorz on May 9. His letter was about those same "Ghosts of La Cuesta Encantada" they had gone after in the Gothic Suite in 1934:[48]

> I cannot sleep in my room on account of rattlings on the roof or in the towers when the wind blows.
>
> I will have to abandon my apartment or you will have to find some way of removing these noise-makers.

---

45. The eventual New Wing 2nd Floor Room #2.

46. Swanberg wrote of Hearst's "card-index memory," which was "usually infallible" (*Citizen Hearst*, pp. 415, 466); other biographers have also described the keen mind of this lifelong collector. Yet Loorz's note suggests that even Hearst needed a photograph at times to jog his memory—just as any other mortal would have.

47. Willicombe wrote to McClure at Wyntoon on April 17 (with the same "Dear Mac" familiarity seen in his letters to Loorz). The subject was the dealer H. P. Philibosian and Persian rugs for "the recently completed PINNACLES house" (an older variant name, along with The Turrets, for Cinderella House). Hearst Papers, carton 23 (under "1937 Samples").

48. The Loorz Papers have the original letter, the Hearst Papers the carbon copy (carton 23 [under "1937 Samples"]). Before the Bancroft Library received that item, someone puzzled over Hearst's greeting of "Dear Mr. Loorz." A notation was made alongside in permanent ink: "Who?"

I have often asked your help and you have often tried to comply, but there has been no betterment. In fact, the noises seem to be worse than ever. They sound like the tin thunder in a theatre.

Please remove everything that is loose and that can possibly rattle.

Please take out the screens, and take down the bells, and take out all scaffolding and encumbrances of any kind.

We must stop these noises if we have to reconstruct the roof and the towers.

A carpenter going up on the roof for fifteen minutes some fine evening (when the wind is NOT blowing) gets us nowhere.

We will have to approach the matter thoughtfully and carefully.

Hearst then said he had "looked over the [China Hill] wall and considered the height of eight feet"; he thought that was "the RIGHT HEIGHT" for it:

We have an eight foot wall at the [Warner Bros. film] studio [in Burbank] and it is fine.

An eight foot wall here will not cut off anything worth seeing.

We will advance the planting to the wall and the high wall will be GREAT for the roses.

Hearst also wrote to Morgan then, on Sunday, May 9.[49] She wouldn't be receiving his letter in San Francisco, though, until she got back from Wyntoon later that week. In any event, Hearst reported that he'd just returned from an outing to Jolon and Milpitas. The trip helped him sharpen his thoughts about building a counterpart there to the Bunkhouse at San Simeon; first, though, he wanted Loorz and Morgan to finish the men's quarters they'd already started on the main ranch.

More important, Hearst was startled by a certain richness he encountered at the Milpitas Hacienda. He told Morgan in that same letter:

I found a great many of my fine Indian blankets [Navajo and other types] at Milpitas,—some that I had paid a thousand dollars a piece for, on the floor being further antiqued.[50]

I wish you would kindly order all the fine old blankets returned to San Simeon and put in safe moth proof storage.

We should use MODERN blankets at Milpitas. We have lots of them.

---

49. The carbon copy is in the Hearst Papers, carton 23 (under "1937 Samples"). The Morgan Collection at Cal Poly lacks the original, addressed to Morgan at the Merchants Exchange in San Francisco and presumably sent there.

50. The blankets recall those depicted by Nancy J. Blomberg in *Navajo Textiles: The William Randolph Hearst Collection* (Tucson, 1988). In fact, some may have been among the very ones she described, now owned by the Natural History Museum of Los Angeles County.

Hearst's words make it possible to identify an undated, handwritten letter that Morgan soon wrote. She sent it to Loorz, probably soon after she got back to San Francisco on Wednesday, May 12:[51]

> You probably know the Jolon [men's quarters] scheme is abandoned for a new type & location — to be built after the S.S. Ranch House [the Bunkhouse] is completed.
>
> Am sorry for the Indian rug fiasco — Hope it did not spoil the general effect of good things at Jolon.
>
> Am planning to be at S.S. Saturday [May 15] if all goes well here.

Morgan had begun designing the Bunkhouse at San Simeon in the first week of March; concurrently, she did some drafting-room work for the Milpitas version. But that outlying project was shelved by May 1, never to be resumed, despite what she'd just told Loorz.[52]

Things must have gone well enough for her at Wyntoon and then in San Francisco upon her return. For she appeared at San Simeon on May 15, as projected. It was far from the last time she'd ever be on the hilltop, yet it was the last of her visits to contribute a Recapitulation to the Loorz Papers. The first of numerous entries pertained to the Recreation Wing's "Cathkingceil," so named by the late art dealer Arthur Byne for the "Catholic kings" of Old Spain, Ferdinand and Isabella. Loorz noted, "Ceiling in Room #2 [on the second floor] to be added to by splicing out girders and adding another section of panels at either end & sides with two half girders or less, in accordance with Arch[itect]'s sketch. To mix new and old panels when installing."

---

51. Morgan wrote to Hearst as well (in a dated letter this time). She regretted that the old weavings had been "misused at Jolon." Her letter begs some deciphering, yet its general point is clear:

> Arrangement was carefully made to have the three chests containing *largely* modern rugs unpacked and the rugs cleaned and put back *until* I could get back to Jolon.
>
> In honor of your trip over, I suppose the temptation was too great not to put them down. Will see only suitable ones are used.
>
> This kind of well-intentioned mistakes is chief reason of my constant shuttle.

From Morgan to Hearst, May 12, 1937; Hearst/Morgan Correspondence, Morgan Collection. Hearst returned the original to Morgan; his handwritten reply filled the bottom of the page. And thus the Hearst Papers lack any version of her message — or his.

52. The Morgan-Forney ledgers contain a separate account for the project—separately entered, in turn, in Appendix A, p. 543 (as are the entries for "Milpitas Ranch House, Jolon" on pp. 537 and 538). The various San Simeon, Wyntoon, and Beach House accounts each year are combined in single entries; but the small Milpitas accounts are not combined with those for the Milpitas Hacienda.

Some of Loorz's other notes from May 15 went as follows:

18. Raise concrete wall at China Hill gradually up to 8 ft. height at lower end of present wall where bank is higher.

19. Be prepared to curtail total expenditure on the hilltop to about $10,000 [per month] on or about the first of June, do not cut down just now and make as much showing as possible.

20. Have Val [Georges] make some escutcheon plates for handles of Wyntoon doors that have long narrow iron hinges sent up a few weeks ago and send to Mac.[53]

Mac McClure and the others at Wyntoon made a "fine little crew," Morgan said in some handwritten notes she gave Loorz during that last interview of May 15. "Wyntoon is cut to $5000 per month," her notes also said, "finishing [Servants'] Chalet, tea house, & so far as possible, exterior of Bridge House—with present crew—The material is largely on hand." The crew she mentioned must have been small indeed: $5,000 per month signaled a steep reduction. Over the past several weeks, twice that amount had been expected for Wyntoon's relaunching on May 1; and earlier in the year, $12,500 had been expected.

In addition to Morgan's own "little crew," the muralist Willy Pogany and his helpers had arrived on the job as independent artists. They planned to decorate the walls of Angel House, the companion building to Brown Bear and Cinderella House in the Bavarian Village.[54]

---

53. See p. 267 in this volume, note 72, concerning some similar ironwork. Two other entries that Loorz made on May 15, each under "Billiard Room Wing," are pertinent here:

13. O.K. to give more ceiling lights in rooms as requested by Mr. Hearst.

14. Additional lights O.K. as above [in entry 13] in 2nd floor over Billiard Room [Room #1] but present construction does not permit of cutting new window on [East] Patio wall.

These entries no doubt allude to a letter Hearst sent Morgan recently: he emphatically said, "I like a LOT of lighting in rooms." From Hearst to Morgan, May 10, 1937; Hearst/Morgan Correspondence, Morgan Collection.

In turn, a question arises: is the undated letter from Hearst to Loorz, quoted in the 1936 chapter, p. 256, more apt to be a product of 1937? Textual and archival factors must be weighed. The similarity between what Hearst told Loorz and what he just told Morgan favors 1937. So does his telling Loorz about "rooms now nearing completion"—plus his mentioning the table he disliked in Room #1. And yet the mixup in May 1937 about rugs and blankets at Milpitas shows that rooms were temporarily furnished at times for Hearst's inspection. I chose the earlier year in compiling the *Builders Behind the Castles* in 1990; I've done the same in this volume, mostly because the undated letter surfaced amid documents from 1936, not 1937. The case remains open.

54. However, the Pogany crew would soon be asked to "suspend operations for awhile." See Willicombe to Pogany (Morgan's copy), May 21, 1937; Morgan Collection (Wyntoon file, III/06/09/05). Concerning funds earmarked for Wyntoon, see note 25, above.

ON MAY 16 SIGNE REESING wrote to Loorz from Menlo Park. "Louis gets a big kick out of your lighthearted letters," she said, "and he is looking forward to your promised visit, with a twinkle in his Eye he said: do not wait 'too long.' " Loorz stayed mostly in character in writing to Reesing two days later:

> By Golly, Louis, it looks like I'm not going to be able to get away from here without just stealing away and say nothing to anyone. We have been waiting and waiting for the party to leave and day by day they postpone leaving without even asking my permission. . . .
>
> I continue to have occasional battles with my little lady friend. So far I am ahead of the game but only because I keep a chip on my shoulder. I hate to be that way but it is sincere. I will not put up with being slighted or continue to act like a monkey on a string so each time it comes up I ask to be let out. Someday they will call my bluff and perhaps I shall regret it but who knows. You could best advise me on that score [more] than anyone else. I mean that you must have put considerable thot on the subject and honestly, do you [not] now consider that you did the very best thing when you resigned from this place with all its faults and virtues considered together?
>
> I said occasional battles for really both Mr. Hearst and Miss Morgan have been lovely to me and it is only on rare occasions that we lose our sweet dispositions. All three of us have more patience with age.[55]

His playfulness aside, Loorz was no doubt serious in saying that Morgan wore his patience thin at times, what with her merciless attention to detail and her compulsive need to accommodate Hearst's every whim. (There was also her driving need to do countless things herself, things she figured no one else could handle properly.)[56] Of course Hearst himself could be equally demanding. The previous day, May 17, he'd written to Loorz twice. One letter was about "the projection room and the dentist room" in the Recreation Wing. The other letter was more incisive. It began with "I think we have the wrong system of lighting on the tennis courts." Whereupon he followed with the usual suggestions and pronouncements.

And yet for every thunderbolt there was a gentle breeze. Hearst told Loorz on May 20:

---

55. One of the "battles" Loorz spoke of occurred recently. On May 15 he wrote Morgan, "I am terribly grieved because I have so displeased you as regards to the pipe trench at the ranch house [the Bunkhouse]." Along with pouring his heart out in detailed alibi and abject apology, he made this point: "I could not continue in my position and be happy or efficient without absolute harmony and the same combination of work and fun that we have enjoyed together."

56. The examples are numerous. For this stretch alone, see note 32, above, wherein Morgan spoke on April 7 of a specialized task that wasn't "easy to delegate." More telling, with broader implications, is her comment in early May after the "rug fiasco" at Milpitas (p. 318 and its note 51). In that

In order to finish men's bunk house on schedule, we can use men from hill top and cut down proportionately here. I want the men to have their house.

We have so much house here that we can wait.

Easier said than done, perhaps—given the need to juggle funds and accounts in such matters. But never mind those details right now; the thought was what counted.

Loorz wrote to Hearst at his hilltop office on May 22, a Saturday. He asked to be gone Monday "for urgent personal business in King City" (he had a grammar school to "sign up" there). And he needed to continue to Menlo Park—to see Louis Reesing before it was too late.

Hearst, the perennial editor, fielded a heavy influx of mail every day. Loorz heard back later that Saturday, the reply consisting of Hearst's scrawls on Loorz's original.[57] "O K to leave," went the first scrawl. "I am very sorry about Mr. Reesing," went the second. "The culverts *must* go in," went still another, despite the "present economy program" Loorz had also mentioned. Having heard that Hearst would soon be called away from San Simeon, Loorz had concluded his letter by saying, "I regret that you find it necessary to leave the hilltop, my work is so much more interesting and fun when you are here. I thank you for your cooperation, also that of Mr. Willicombe & Mr. Murray." Hearst's response to those words: "Thanks. I will be gone about a month."

Loorz saw Louis Reesing on Tuesday, May 25. It was an experience that, a week later, warranted an uncommonly serious passage in a letter Loorz sent the plumber Jim Rankin:

> I had a splendid talk with Louis the day before he died. I really must say that I en-
> joyed my visit and that the memories of that last conversation, in which he could
> not see me and could barely move his lips, will last permanently. I am pleased to
> say that he was mentally clear though slow because of weakness and dope. I am
> happy to say that though Louis had many strong convictions regarding life and
> religion in general and many of them far from conventional, he still stuck by them

---

instance she mentioned the "constant shuttle" that seemed her destined lot. She apparently meant the frequent trips and visits occasioned by the Hearst accounts. In fact, May 18, the very day Loorz wrote to Reesing, found Morgan beginning her second stint at Wyntoon in 1937; it ran through May 20.

57. The inter-office courier service was in full swing that day. Willicombe told Loorz on May 22, "I am sending you back your letter with Chief's notations, as I think this is the most comprehensive way of informing you of his wishes, rather than whipping it into the form of a letter." He also told Loorz how to go about conferring with Hearst in person that day, if he wanted to: "If you will give me a ring around two o'clock I will remind Chief to see you."

to the end. When I put the question to him his answer was, "No George I haven't changed, I still believe the same as I did, I have no regrets, I have no fear and I have no hopes."[58]

The very day Loorz was at Reesing's bedside, May 25, Hearst informed Morgan that San Simeon was in for another shutdown—a big shutdown.[59] Dire news had kept pouring in from New York. Hearst's myriad debts, many years in the accruing and epitomized by indulgences like San Simeon, had become astronomical; the creditors and stockholders could no longer be ignored. In reality, the news had been grim for at least a year—indeed, for nearly two years now with regard to ruinous tax schedules. Taxes, however, were only part of a much larger, deeper problem; they were virtually the tip of the iceberg. At almost every turn since 1935, and in many ways for much longer, the danger signs had stalked Hearst. He kept dodging them, sidestepping them, eluding them. But by no means had he been unconscious of them. He simply didn't like them.

Several items at the Bancroft Library indicate that, by now, Hearst's financial woes—and his knowledge of them—were old business. Early in the previous year, for example, "the idea of leasing the Hilltop at San Simeon" had cropped up. And exactly a year before May 1937, Hearst considered raising badly needed funds by selling "some of the articles now in the [Bronx] warehouse." He had spent close to six million dollars on the items in question; he hoped he might be able to recover much of that outlay. Earlier in 1937 itself, a similar thought can be glimpsed—that of Hearst's eyeing the Bronx warehouse again as a potential source of revenue, despite its institutional and all but inviolate status. Worded almost casually, the following lines may have been more urgent than they sounded:

Chief asking for list of things we might sell privately or work into auctions—in other words, does not see quote why we should clutter up warehouse with lot of stuff we are not going to use and which is of inferior quality and that we might get some money for by getting rid of it unquote.

---

58. Loorz to Rankin, June 1, 1937.

59. Hearst had already notified Morgan a few days earlier, as he also had Loorz, that he would soon be leaving for New York. (He left San Simeon on Monday, May 24.) See Hearst to Morgan, May 21, 1937 (coinciding with Willicombe's letter to Willy Pogany, as in note 54); Hearst/Morgan Correspondence, Morgan Collection. In regard to the shutdown itself, see Hearst to Morgan, May 25, 1937; ibid.

Another high school class from San Luis Obispo got to visit the hilltop on May 25—supremely unaware, no doubt, of the burdens Hearst had taken with him on his departure the day before. See unsigned [Willicombe] to Ida Avila, May 21, 1937, filed with Avila's request of Hearst, dated May 3; Hearst Papers, carton 23 (under "1937 Samples").

The passage, which concluded with "Kindly advise," was Willicombe's, unmistakably.[60]

Loorz already knew that Hearst had to leave San Simeon on short notice. He knew nothing of the shutdown, though, and little of the gravity of Hearst's immediate situation, until after his trip to Menlo Park.[61] "Naturally it has been quite a blow to most of our men," he told Morgan on Saturday, May 29. "Most of them already knew more about it than I did. Apparently it leaked out thru the household's copy of the letter [conveying the harsh terms of the shutdown]. My family knew all about it when I got home last night. Ha Ha this kind of news travels fast."[62]

Maurice McClure (the younger of the two men named McClure in this story) was just finishing his first year of engineering at UC Berkeley. He wrote to Loorz on May 30—without having the faintest idea of the shock waves reverberating through San Simeon. "I hope that you and 'Papa Hearst' still love each other," he jokingly said, "and that everything goes well with you up there, because after all that is really a pretty good job in spite of its drawbacks."

---

60. Telegram to C. A. McGregor, April 5, 1937; Hearst Papers, carton 23 (under "1937 Samples"). On the proposed lease, see Willicombe to Geoffr[e]y Konta, January 31, 1936, carton 20 (under "1936 Samples"); an attachment, dated January 28 [1936], refers to John Francis Neylan's views on legal and financial complexities of the subject. The passage about "some of the articles" in the Bronx facility appears in A. J. Kobler to Hearst, May 26, 1936; ibid.

61. Loorz's letter to Dell Clausen on March 2 reflected some knowledge of Hearst's strategy (at least regarding taxes) for the coming months; see note 19, above. So did Loorz's letter to his parents on April 14; see p. 313.

Insofar as that strategy included a trip to Europe, Hearst had simpler plans now; they gave rise to cheerful words just the same, like these transmitted for him:

SEND FOLLOWING NIGHT MESSAGE PREPAID TO ELLIOTT ROOSEVELT HEARST RADIO FORTWORTH TEXAS QUOTE THANKS FOR KIND MESSAGE AND WISHES ON WAY TO NEWYORK BUT NOT GOING ABROAD WILL BE BACK IN CALIFORNIA SOON GOING THEN TO WYNTOON AND WOULD GREATLY LIKE TO HAVE RUTH AND YOU VISIT US W R HEARST UNQUOTE.

From Willicombe to Jean Henry, May 28, 1937; Hearst Papers, carton 23 (under "1937 Samples").

62. There were two such letters—sent by Hearst and Willicombe to Randy Apperson, the ranch superintendent. The first letter left Los Angeles on May 25; the second letter, which superseded it, left Albuquerque, New Mexico, on May 26, while the Hearst party was enroute to New York. (And what a difference the passage of fifteen years had made: in May 1922, while returning to New York after a quick trip to emerging San Simeon, the excited Hearst wired Morgan from California and from Utah, eager to begin the structure that was now such a liability—Casa Grande. See Hearst to Morgan, May 6 and 7, 1922; Hearst/Morgan Correspondence, Morgan Collection.) Copies of the two letters from May 1937, intended for Morgan, are likewise in that archives. Her copies indicate that Albert Redelsperger, the butler, and W. R. Williams, the warehouse manager, also received copies.

Loorz took the jovial words in stride, and then he broke the news to McClure:

Now, I want to state that I personally feel that Mr. Hearst and I are still the best of friends. In fact, I must say that we had a lot to do personally together during his last visit and it was very pleasant. He became more confident and personal in all of our conversations. He would josh with me and occasionally go so far as to laugh and tap me on the shoulder.

However, Mr. Hearst and money seem to have parted company. If you were fortunate enough to read the Time [magazine] about three weeks ago you would appreciate it fully.[63] However, the fact is that the construction on the hilltop will shut down entirely for the first time. By entirely I mean we will even turn over the [Hearst Camp] commissary to the ranch. I will leave the hilltop. His instructions are that I take the best of my men and complete the large bunk house started at the ranch at a *maximum* expenditure of *not more than* $3000 per month. However, Miss Morgan and I have talked it over and my own salary and other overhead is such a large portion of this that I intend to take most of the time for my own business and a vacation, yet keep it [the Bunkhouse] going by having materials on hand and dealing with the various subs. We will see. He said it was possible that we would start up again in three months but Miss Morgan says no—not this year again.

Further drastic changes are, Albert and Mrs. Albert [the two Redelspergers: butler and head housekeeper] are to go to Wyntoon and Mr. [W. R.] Williams [is] to move into the castle to care for the antiques. At first they [the Redelspergers] were out but he reconsidered and kept them for his visit to Wyntoon when he returns in a few weeks.[64]

---

63. Loorz was speaking of "Hearstiana," a long article that *Time* printed on April 26, pp. 49–51. As recently as March 15, 1937, the magazine had been charitable toward Hearst, even admiring, in saluting his golden anniversary as a publisher (under "50 Years of Hearst," pp. 49–50). But "Hearstiana" found *Time* smugly divulging "many a Hearst publishing secret, many a Hearst businesss oddity"—a virtual dirge after the rousing waltz its sister magzine *Fortune* had once played (p. 208 in this volume). Perhaps Loorz read "Hearstiana" belatedly; if not, his relative innocence before May 28 of Hearst's predicament seems odd. Perhaps he and others simply couldn't believe the article until Hearst's actions confirmed it.

64. An allusion to the two letters from Hearst and Willicombe to Randy Apperson, the jarring terms of the first one, dated May 25, having been moderated somewhat the next day. See note 62, above. Loorz's summary for Maurice McClure in these middle paragraphs agrees closely with the second (and calmer) of the letters to Apperson—the one from New Mexico dated May 26.

Concerning Wyntoon (and San Simeon), Morgan had recently sent a key letter to Bill Murray at Hearst Sunical:

We received your letter of May 21st with check for $10,000, $5000 of which you say is "to be used for construction work at Wyntoon and $5000 for work on the Hill at San Simeon for month of May."

In the last conversation with Mr. Hearst in regard to "budget" [probably May 15], it was agreed that we were to proceed with construction work at San Simeon on a basis of $10,000

The household is reduced to nearly half. The garden department is cut to half. The orchard crew is trimmed. Two watchmen are laid off. You'll be interested in knowing that Ray Swartley, Marks [Eubanks], Dally [Carpio], Lee [Wenzlick], Charlie Harris and a few more will remain.

I have made arrangements with the ranch to have them keep Ray Van Gorden on to run the commissary up here for them and keep the remaining hands well fed.

Rather than dwell on the unexpected turn of events, Loorz devoted some intervening lines to a more workaday matter that directly concerned Maurice McClure:

Now we just this morning started a new contract on the King City School. We should be just about ready for the steel and concrete work and a lot of wrecking about the time you get out. So before I get too many local men on I'd appreciate if you would report there for work. Frank Gendrich will run the job and Elof [Gustafson] will be leadoff man. Same old Cambria [Grammar School] wrecking crew.

He then returned to the subject of the shutdown, ending his letter to McClure by saying he was "deeply grieved for such men as Gyorgy, Frandolich etc."

Grieved for the likes of Frank Gyorgy and Frank Frandolich, yes—for the older men who were to be thrown out of work by the shutdown. Loorz could be grateful now, as never before, that he had driven himself over the past two years in establishing his outside work for the F. C. Stolte Co. in the greater area. And still he remained invaluable to Hearst—and to Morgan, too, who wrote to Loorz on Tuesday, June 1, the same day he wrote to Maurice McClure. Morgan had received copies of two letters, dated May 25 and 26, which Hearst and Willicombe had sent

---

per month to end of season,—usually about Thanksgiving,— the allowance to continue two months after this date, as we always have accumulated materials bills, contract payments, etc. to pay up.

For Wyntoon, we were to go ahead on a budget of $5000 per month, this to be continued also two months beyond the stopping of actual work.

There may be later decisions—but I would say that it is not practical to try to work at San Simeon on less than $10,000 per month, given the overhead and the fact that a rounded crew [comprising diverse skills and trades] has to be collected and held together in order to make any kind of progress on the highly specialized San Simeon Hilltop work, the comment not applying to work on roads, bank walls and work of this nature.

From unsigned [Morgan] to Murray, May 24, 1937; Hearst Papers, carton 23 (under "1937 Samples," as a carbon copy that Morgan sent Willicombe). Willicombe affixed a note before showing Morgan's letter to Hearst: "On May 21 she received $5000 for this work [at San Simeon], and notice was then sent her and Mr Murray that it would not be more than $3000 hereafter." Hearst's reaction: "We will just shut down at San Simeon entirely. There appears to be nothing else to do."

Randy Apperson, the ranch superintendent. (Albert Redelsperger of the household staff and W. R. Williams, the warehouse manager, had also received copies, hence the "leak" of May 28 that Loorz mentioned to Morgan the next day.)[65] Regarding the two letters, Morgan briefed Loorz as follows on June 1:

> I read it that Mr. Hearst expects you to carry the Ranch House [or rather the Bunkhouse] on the percentage basis of Wyntoon or Grande Canyon [the Grand Canyon]. If you will do so at whatever per cent [commission] you need,—it will keep all in touch.
>
> I do *not* think Mr. Hearst intended to put this upon Mr. Apperson.
>
> Let us make this interpretation unless more direct word comes.

Some confusion was bound to accompany the big shutdown—witness Morgan's trying to clarify things for Loorz. Suffice it to say that, with Hearst and Willicombe in New York now, Julia Morgan, Bill Murray, Randy Apperson, and George Loorz were dealing with the local situation as best they could. Thus Loorz could write Willicombe on June 3 that he was "working in full cooperation" with Morgan and the others. "We fully appreciate the necessity of the shutdown," he said, "and are attempting to do so in strict accordance with instructions."

LOORZ KEPT IN CLOSE TOUCH with Morgan through the early part of June; on Friday the fourth he sent her the following details:

> The four days this week with my greatly reduced crew have been sufficient to clean up as we should properly do.
>
> I will keep on a part of the force next week and think we can leave things in shape that will please everybody concerned. By that time all of the Pergola beams will be in place and that yard [on Orchard Hill] cleaned up.
>
> The last poured section of the [China Hill] wall will be completed and cleaned up. I will have time to cover over the newly placed fields culverts to leave them safe.
>
> We will leave the Billiard Room [Wing] bedrooms completed and I think very nice. . . . All woodwork, hardware and painting will be completed. Have men polishing and waxing floors right now.[66]
>
> The recreation wing is rapidly taking shape so that we can leave things tidy and arranged to proceed without loss of time when and if they do start again.

---

65. See note 62, above.

66. Loorz and Morgan had discussed the gloomy interiors in that part of Casa Grande, a problem raised by Hearst on May 10 (as in note 53, above). Loorz told her on June 2:

> Mr. March [the head gardener] with five of his men taken away has been unable to thin out the oak tree for us [immediately west of the Billiard Wing]. I'm going up to show Mr. Williams

COURTESY OF JEAN HENRY WILLICOMBE

437

GEORGE C. LOORZ, SUPT.
HEARST CAMP
SAN SIMEON
SAN LUIS OBISPO CO., CALIF.

May 19, 1936.

Dear Mr. Willicombe:

I find it advisable for me to write to you
regarding the plague of rodents we are having here
on the hilltop.

The orchard is literally crawling with the
animals now coming in from the outside where the grass
is drying up. Mr. March in the garden is almost helpless. As soon as the party left and the dogs penned he put
out dozens of small traps and they catch nearly 100 per
day but they are not keeping even.

They are destroying his young plants as fast
as he plants them. In his lath house they destroy 15
to 20 flats per day, that is 750 to 1000 each day.

The men that are trapping and poisoning varmint
have them quite under control. We donot see many tracks
or signs. Would you discuss it with Mr. Hearst and see
if it would not be advisable to have these two men go
to work poisoning in the fields. Perhaps the varmint were
an important factor in destroying the field mice.

Very truly yours,

Geo.

OK. Bring in the executioner. I dont the plague is due to absence of "varmints". Every once in a while there is a plague of something or other — locusts or grasshoppers or frogs or rats or politicians — something to afflict us. It has been so in all recorded time — and the politicians are the worst. If we ever get rid of them let us institute a special passover.

WRH

Loorz to Joe Willicombe, May 19, 1936—answered the next day by Hearst
(through Willicombe, who transcribed the Chief's handwritten reply and
who included some small variations); see pages 252–53.

AUTHOR'S PHOTOGRAPH, 1976

AUTHOR'S PHOTOGRAPH, 1976

TOP AND BOTTOM: San Simeon's unfinished Grand Entrance.

AUTHOR'S PHOTOGRAPH, 1975

AUTHOR'S PHOTOGRAPH, 1975

TOP: The Ranch House, built by Hearst's father, George, about 1878. LEFT: Barbecue pit, Hearst Sunical Men's Quarters—more familiar as the Bunkhouse.

LOORZ FAMILY COLLECTION

AUTHOR'S PHOTOGRAPH, 1975

TOP AND BOTTOM: Bear grottos, Orchard Hill.

AUTHOR'S PHOTOGRAPH, 1975

AUTHOR'S PHOTOGRAPH, 1976

TOP AND BOTTOM: Animal shelters, main zoo area.

LOORZ FAMILY COLLECTION

AUTHOR'S PHOTOGRAPH, 1988

WARNING

DO NOT EXCEED
20 MILES PER HOUR
UP HILL
CARELESSNESS NOT TOLERATED

SAN LUIS OBISPO COUNTY HISTORICAL MUSEUM

TOP: In the main zoo area.
MIDDLE: Near the former
gatehouse, old road to hilltop.
LEFT: Animal Hill, behind Casa Grande.

SAN LUIS OBISPO COUNTY HISTORICAL MUSEUM

SAN LUIS OBISPO COUNTY HISTORICAL MUSEUM

TOP: Main zoo area. BOTTOM: Animal Hill.

STOLTE BLUEPRINT

Warren McClure, better known as Mac.

MORGAN-FORNEY COLLECTION

LOORZ FAMILY COLLECTION

TOP AND BOTTOM: Cinderella House and Angel House, Bavarian Village, Wyntoon.

LOORZ FAMILY COLLECTION

LOORZ FAMILY COLLECTION

LOORZ FAMILY COLLECTION

Matching suite of photographs, depicting Casa Grande interiors during the mid- to late 1930s
THIS PAGE: Assembly Room.
FACING PAGE, TOP: Gothic Study. FACING PAGE, BOTTOM: Library.

AUTHOR'S PHOTOGRAPH, 1990

RIGHT AND BELOW:
West corridor,
Milpitas Hacienda, Jolon.

AUTHOR'S PHOTOGRAPH, 1990

COURTESY OF *THE CAMBRIAN*

AUTHOR'S PHOTOGRAPH, 1990

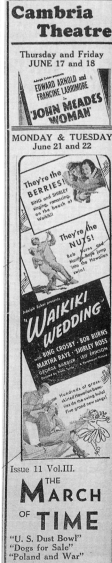

Echoes of 1937

LEFT: Advertisement for the movie that Loorz and Jim Rankin saw on June 21. ABOVE AND BELOW: Backdrops for the opening of the Big Sur highway on Sunday, June 27.

AUTHOR'S PHOTOGRAPH, 1990

AUTHOR'S PHOTOGRAPH, 1976

RIGHT: Final touches were still being added to the West Terrace (among other areas on the hilltop) in the late 1930s. BOTTOM: The young travelers and authors Patience, Richard, and Johnny Abbe, guests at San Simeon in 1937.

AUTHOR'S COLLECTION

OF ALL PLACES!

we knew that wild animals mostly run away from you anyway, with the exception of a few. But we kept seeing these shining eyes, and so we decided positively that this man we were going to see was positively no sissy.

As we went up and up we could see behind us the airport, a private one belonging to Mr. Hearst, with the lights shining through the fog. It was all very rich sort of in the fog, but we had no idea how rich until we saw what we came to in the end. The road was very slippery like all ranch roads when it is raining, so it was very exciting as we went up and up. The lights on the castle were shining through like silver and it was like going up to a castle on a cloud.

So after three and one-half miles of going up and up we landed at the castle door, and we got out in the pouring rain and went up a large white staircase full of statues, and we had never in our lives gone up such a castle stairs in our lives. But then they said, this was only the little house, but it looked very big to us. So the housekeeper then came and took us to the big castle, and we thought we were going into a cathedral. This was really some castle, fit for a King. You went in the big high door and went into a large room full of tapestries and statues and a large fireplace with

[222]

Photo by James B. Abbe

This is William Randolph Hearst and his special dachshund he calls Helen

© JOHN SWOPE TRUST

Roger Edens, MGM film composer, at the Neptune Pool (photograph by John Swope, 1938; published a year later in his book *Camera Over Hollywood*).

© JOHN SWOPE TRUST

The Beach House, Santa Monica, decked out for Hearst's seventy-fifth birthday party, April 1938 (photograph by Swope, from *Camera Over Hollywood*, 1939).

Morgan replied on Monday, June 7, saying, "I would like for us to clean up and leave the Hill this weekend—even if you have to 'bring up' help from below to do so." The Bunkhouse crew is most likely what she meant: the accounts and payrolls could be disentangled later. She also told him, "Am still planning to meet you in King City on Friday, getting off the Daylight [train] from San Francisco. I will have to go south that night from somewhere."[67]

Loorz sent her further details on June 8, among which were these: "Books being brought up to date and accounts being closed out. Records being burned as suggested. Should be able to leave hill entirely on Saturday [June 12]. Can clean up balance of mail and small accounts from my house below." So at times the woman *did* burn records: a central tenet of the Morgan myth, the Morgan mystique. (The story has long been told that she burned her office records in San Francisco about 1950.) But what prompted the little bonfire she "suggested" in 1937, and what exactly did Loorz destroy? Was it simply a matter of some housekeeping whose time had come? No, it proved to be worse. Sadly, inexplicably, it was all the Hearst Construction Fund records through 1936 (the San Simeon copies, that is), as distinct from the Hilltop Fund records (likewise the local copies), which Loorz later said he spared.[68] And thus on July 9, a month after the burning, he told Morgan he couldn't provide "the desired information for the California Unemployment Reserves Commission." He reminded her, "As per instructions we destroyed

which branch to have removed and he will squeeze in the time with his men. As you mentioned it is important that we have more light before the rooms are visited again.

67. She had to be in Beverly Hills on Saturday, June 12, to confer with Courtlandt Hill and his wife, Blanche (formerly married to Hearst's oldest son, George). The job was a consultation only. Morgan first went to the Hill residence on June 2, traveling for that purpose alone (no tie-ins with the Beach House or San Simeon, either en route or on the way back). The last of the three times she visited the Hill residence fell within a more familiar pattern, mainly detectable through the Morgan-Forney ledgers: Wyntoon on June 21, San Francisco on June 22, Beverly Hills on June 23, San Simeon on June 24. Then she went to Monterey for a less-familiar "couple of days rest," as Loorz told Mac McClure on June 25.

68. See pp. 405–06, note 9: Loorz to Randy Apperson, March 14, 1939. As for Morgan's destruction of her records in the Merchants Exchange, oral accounts of that event circulated for years and became so widely accepted that when the Morgan Collection arrived at Cal Poly in 1980, its range and richness caught nearly everyone by surprise. In turn, its presence refuted key portions of some published accounts that held sway, like the one appearing six years before the gift: "Julia Morgan's papers were destroyed by fire and she did not seem to regret the fact, having been particularly reticent to publicize herself and her work throughout her life." From Leslie Mandelson Freudenheim and Elisabeth Sussman, *Building with Nature: Roots of the San Francisco Bay Tradition* (Santa Barbara, 1974), p. x.

And yet with hindsight (especially through the Loorz Papers and the Morgan-Forney Collection), the gaps and omissions in the Morgan Collection have become painfully evident. It's less clear whether those voids resulted from Morgan's personal actions or other events.

all office records when we moved out of the office on the hill. We have only the [Hearst Construction Fund] records for 1937 which were needed to complete [the current filing with that state agency]."[69]

On June 8, meanwhile, in another letter he sent Morgan that day, he had these words to share: "It is already very lonesome here on the hill so many will be glad to leave in the next day or so. Only because they know they have to go anyway."

Then on June 9, Loorz wrote to Colonel Willicombe at the Ritz Tower, New York:

> Unless I receive further notice I shall remain in San Simeon. I have fixed my present salary with Miss Morgan on the Bunkhouse work at $200 per month. It was $500.[70] Regarding this I ask but one favor, that I be notified if resumption of construction must be given up for an indefinite period.
>
> As per Miss [Jean] Henry's phone call, I will send in figures soon on dismantling the zoo. I shall submit a separate figure on the excavation in case that is desired.[71]
>
> I wish to report that two more sections of the [China Hill] wall were poured and completed with plaster. Looks like a finished job that far.
>
> All [three] rooms over the Billiard Room completed and ready for furniture. I think Miss Morgan intends to make selections for Mr. Williams to install.
>
> All cars in good shape for Wyntoon. All new or good equipment and trucks being left operating in good shape. Two old trucks out of commission. Might be good move to abandon at least one of these if not both.

---

69. Besides writing to Morgan, Loorz also wrote to Robert Peyton on July 9. "I regret that we will be unable to furnish any [unemployment] information for 1936," he told Peyton, an accountant at the Hearst Sunical office in San Francisco. "When we moved from our office on the hilltop we brought [down] only the 1937 records and destroyed all previous records. All were burned."

70. Loorz's annual salary of $5,200 held steady through his first five years at San Simeon. At the outset of 1937 he got a long-awaited raise, an increase equating with $6,500 annually (inclusive as before of two weeks' vacation). In speaking of "$200 per month," which had been $500, Loorz actually meant for a four-week period. When he wrote to Stolte on June 15 (p. 330 in this chapter), he spoke of the new rate as $50 "per week"; he also said he'd be taking the difference of $75 per week "from the company."

71. Willicombe had written Jean Henry a week earlier, with details about bears, chimpanzees, and black panthers that would soon be leaving San Simeon. "WHEN DELIVERED OVER TO ZOOS, LET ME KNOW HOW MUCH WE HAVE DONATED (in dollars) FOR INCOME TAX PURPOSES, AS YOU KNOW." He signed off by saying, "THEN ASK GEORGE LOORZ HOW MUCH IT WILL COST TO CLEAR OFF THAT PART OF HILLTOP." From Willicombe to Henry, June 1, 1937; Hearst Papers, carton 23 (under "1937 Samples").

Certain kinds of animals were exempt from these dispersals; a brief message of a later period makes the distinction clear. "Mr. Hearst has given away all of the animals that he had in his zoo here. The only ones he has now are what might be called the field or forest animals that are not caged." Hearst had no plans to disperse them. From unsigned [Willicombe] to Earle G. Linsley, January 27, 1938; Hearst Papers, carton 25 (under "Li-Ln").

Ray Van Gorden will perhaps enjoy a few months off the hill. However, if construction is not to be resumed for a long time, if ever, I'd like you to keep him in mind for a position of his kind [bookkeeper, etc.]. They do not make more loyal, capable or efficient men, as you no doubt are aware.[72]

In the midst of the hubbub, Loorz's wife and sons left for a summer vacation in Nevada. Loorz wrote to them on Saturday, June 12, the day after he and Morgan got together as planned:

I met Miss Morgan as per schedule at noon yesterday in King City. Worked all afternoon until 5 o'clock [at the Milpitas Hacienda, Jolon] moving furniture up and down stairs etc. Back and forth all alone and I was beginning to think, oh boy, the side [the ribs] when I get thru with this.

Well we left there about 5 o'clock and headed back [to San Simeon] thru the Burnett Road. All went well until we got half way between the two dams [on Burnett Creek] and the rear end went out. It was nearly seven o'clock then and I wanted to walk on in [to the hilltop] and send a car back for her but nothing doing. She said she was a good walker and if I'd let her put her finger in my rear pocket she'd like to walk as far as she could anyway. I agreed when she promised she'd let me know when she got too tired.

As would be expected with her, she walked right straight into [Hearst] camp with me. We arrived about 8 o'clock. We walked all that distance in about 1 hour and a half. On top of that she had only a cup of coffee and a bit of pie for lunch and I had a glass of milk and piece of pie. Strange to say I was not even particularly hungry until I started eating about 9 o'clock here on the hill.

After eating and a few minutes rest (not more than 15 minutes), we started the trek thru the rooms [that concerned her in Casa Grande] up and down stairs. She insisted on calling a taxi from [Steve Zegar's in] San Luis to take her in, wouldn't let me drive her in.[73] So I followed Steve's car [down] to the ranch house [the Bunkhouse] and we got out and went thru that just before midnight.

Except for the fact that I ate a big meal with coffee so late I felt fine. Too full to sleep properly so after a restless night I got up and went out in the garden at about 5:30.

The weary Loorz signed off by telling his family, "With plenty of exercise and good habits I should be at least two years younger when I see you."

---

72. On June 1, Loorz told Randy Apperson (now charged with running Hearst Camp, plus other new duties) that he should do right by Ray Van Gorden, Jud Smelser, Alex Rankin, and other top employees: he'd be needing them. As for the versatile Rankin, Loorz said, "Let me suggest that you never attempt to entertain Mr. Hearst & guests on the hilltop without Alex or his equal present."

73. Steve Zegar operated a chauffeur service out of San Luis Obispo; Steve's Taxi, as the business was called, had counted Hearst and his guests — and Miss Morgan — among its passengers since the early 1920s. See the local booklet *A Cabbie in a Golden Era: Featuring Cabbie's Original Log of Guests Transported to Hearst Castle*, edited by Jane Sarber (n.p., n.d. [Paso Robles, 1982]).

MEANWHILE AT WYNTOON, Mac McClure, Harry Thompson, and a few others were holding down the fort on the McCloud River. (It's unclear whether Fred Stolte had spent many hours there in 1937; Morgan had been there twice in May, so he most likely had been on hand then, perhaps at other times, too; but the Loorz Papers are frustratingly thin on that point.) Loorz heard from Mac McClure three times in June. The letters were in Mac's typically graceful script, yet they were atypically devoted to humdrum details. (A painter named Fisher had argued with Thompson, who threatened to "raise hell" with Miss Morgan; and so on.) Mac concluded the first of those letters, dated June 15, by saying, "Everything else is pretty good—only waiting for the next 'surprize.'" His misspelling no doubt referred to the big shutdown.[74]

On June 15 as well, Loorz told Stolte, "We have a set of plans [to figure] on a state tennis court for the [California] Polytechnic College in San Luis Obispo." He also mentioned having agreed with Hearst to stay on at San Simeon and supervise the Bunkhouse job:

> I told him plainly that I would do this gladly in cooperation with his economy [program] if it did not last too long. If more than a few months I asked him to let me know so that I could move nearer my business and could increase the volume of my personal business. It is definitely understood that I am to be away as much as I desire on my own work to make up for the difference in loss of salary.

So Loorz had secured the terms—more or less—that he had long sought concerning his outside work. The shutdown, occasioned by Hearst's ostensible bankruptcy, had finally brought the matter to a head.

Except for the job coming up at California Polytechnic (Cal Poly), Loorz's outside work for the Stolte Co. had recently shifted north. The King City Gram-

---

74. Mac wrote his second letter on June 22; Loorz replied on June 25 (not June 26, as his typing claimed). The Fisher episode prompted him to say, "I have often differed with policies regarding the treatment of so-called special men, (Miss Morgan's men)." He had some more to divulge—or perhaps to get off his chest:

> Frankly Mac, however distasteful, I have always felt that whatever Miss Morgan wanted she got. Harry [Thompson] has had very little of this [behavior] to put up with compared to [that exhibited by] such characters as [Camille] Solon, the Gomez's [Alfredo and Mary Gomes], [John] Vanderloo, etc that we have had here. I have had to swallow my pride almost daily working with such men.

He thought Thompson deserved sympathy if Fisher was, in fact, being favored as much as some people at San Simeon were. (A year before—July 30, 1936—Loorz, in a calmer mood, asked Morgan if she had "given John Vanderloo a small raise of perhaps $1.00 per day," inasmuch as "all carpenters and special men" had been allotted "their old scales." He seemed to support Vanderloo in broaching the question.)

mar School was one example. So was the Santa Rita School in Salinas, designed by the Monterey architect C.J. Ryland. And now Loorz was figuring another job in that area, the San Benito County Hospital in Hollister, designed by two other Monterey architects, Robert Stanton and Thomas Mulvin.

Loorz told his father on June 21 that he felt as though he were on vacation. "However," he said, "they call upon me at all times even now. Yesterday, Sunday, they called me from L.A. and wanted some important papers from the hilltop files. No one else was available who knew anything about them so I had to go up and send them along." Obviously those records fell outside the bounds of the things Morgan had encouraged Loorz to burn earlier in June.

In writing to his wife and sons on the twenty-second, Loorz told them he had had a "good day of work on the job and in the office" the day before. "I had Jim Rankin come down last night [from the Bunkhouse job] and took him to the Pines [The Pines Cafe, at the Cambria Pines Lodge] for dinner and then to the movie *Waikiki Wedding* [at the Cambria Theatre]. I enjoyed Bing Crosby's songs and the show was entertaining but was strictly comedy."

Right after that, Loorz made a "hasty yet successful trip" to the Bay Area, as he told his wife in a "Friday" letter (easily datable as June 25).[75] He'd gone north to see Stolte on Wednesday, and he'd planned to see Morgan, too. "Got up early [on Thursday, June 24] and left about 10 o'clock [from Alameda] to go over to Miss Morgan's office. When I got there I learned she was down here." The mixup proved harmless. More important, it shows that Morgan was still making her periodic trips to San Simeon. She'd last been there on June 11—the day she and Loorz hiked from Burnett Creek to the hilltop. Between those dates she made her sole visit to Wyntoon that month, on June 21.[76]

Loorz wrote to his wife again, while she was still in Nevada, on Saturday, June 26. He began with a reference to the roadside fountain and marker near Big Sur —the "gratis job" he had done in the summer of 1935 for the Women's Club of Cambria:

> Tonight we have agreed to come to a Chamber of Commerce meeting or dinner [in Cambria] in honor of Gov. [Frank] Merriam and his wife. He is supposed to show up today to open up the or rather accept the Rigdon Memorial.

75. The Loorz Papers contain eight letters (all carbons, all by Loorz) dated "June 26, 1937," a Saturday. There are no letters dated "June 25, 1937." But to judge from its content, Loorz's "Friday" letter—an additional, ninth item in this cluster—clearly originated then. So did at least two of the eight: see notes 67 and 74 for one of them (which went to Mac McClure); the other one went to Morgan. Loorz must simply have mis-typed a "26" in those two instances.

76. The day before she was on the McCloud, Hearst air mailed his thoughts to her about Wyntoon. He foresaw doing some wrap-up work on that project in the weeks ahead; otherwise, things

Tomorrow the coast highway opens up and a good crowd is expected. They have asked Randy [Apperson] to be there at the opening ceremony and he has asked me to come along with him. The opening is to be celebrated somewhere about the half way point between Monterey and here. They are giving a barbecue there and I guess I should get in on it free. What a break for an old bachelor.

The Sebastians [of the general store in San Simeon] have been rushing a lot of things including new refrigerating units together so that they will be properly stocked for the anticipated crowd. I think it will help their business a lot but if they are not prepared to receive it they will make little from it. Manuel is wide awake, Pete [his son] is going ahead scornfully.[77]

Loorz followed through on June 28 by telling his family about the highway ceremony in Big Sur; the event signaled the dawning of a new era for the long-isolated coastal rim between San Simeon and the Monterey Peninsula, nearly a hundred miles north:

Yesterday [Sunday] and Saturday were very exciting days around these parts. You would scarcely know or feel the difference in San Simeon except for more traffic. However, at the [Cambria Pines] Lodge Saturday night we heard Mrs. Merriam say a few nice things of personal appreciation of the real friendly hospitality of this small community. . . . The Governor was not at this meeting but arrived at 2 A.M. that night and had breakfast there the next morning.

A short ceremony by the cross road at San Simeon at 10 A.M. yesterday where the governor cut the ribbons but made no comment. With Randy and Mr. Reid we followed the procession [up the coast] to the Rigdon Memorial where we listened to an impressive ceremony. The governor gave a nice talk as did several others. Mrs. [John] Marquart handled the program very well and made her own personal speech short. With the presence of Mrs. [Elmer] Rigdon in tears the unveiling of the fountain made it appear really as a monument to her deceased husband. Strange enough, though many might not know it, Gov. Merriam knew Mr. Rigdon well. He himself was in the Senate from Southern California in 1917 already. The governor makes a good talk and does it without notes and does it easily.

---

would have to wait till 1938. See Hearst to Morgan, June 20, 1937; Hearst/Morgan Correspondence, Morgan Collection. The timing allowed Morgan to answer him on June 22, fresh upon returning from Wyntoon and right before she left for Beverly Hills (as in note 67, above).

77. Another letter in the "June 26" group (see p. 331, note 75) went to Bill Murray. "The boys have opened the Davis road and the Marmalejo road and should complete the San Carpojo Road this next week. We will then put the equipment away and close out the account." Within the confines of the 1937 season, these projects seem almost to have sprung from the blue; they were probably minor. Still, they exemplify how hard it can be to unravel such matters. The final Trial Balance in the Loorz Papers for the Hilltop Fund, dated May 24, lists "San Simeon Roads & Gates" at $329. The final balance sheet for the separate Hearst Sunical Building Fund, also dated May 24, coincidentally lists "San Simeon Roads, Gates & Culverts" at $389.

He is a forceful talker and I feel quite favorably toward him. I think perhaps it was a very good thing for the state that he was elected [in 1934] rather than our friend [Upton] Sinclair.

About this time I was hoping you and the boys were along to hear the leaders of our state but later I was glad. We had to stop the car in a line about 1 mile long when we arrived at the picnic grounds at Big Sur.[78] We waited and waited and I finally walked on ahead to see what was happening. I found they were just starting their ceremonies on that end with another set of speeches and some rock blasting and drilling by the governor and Earl Lee Kelly.[79] I walked back to the car and had Randy park it right there and walk on back down to hear the completion of the pageant and thence to the barbecue about $3/4$ of a mile up the creek [the Big Sur River] on the opposite side from our car. As I walked back to Randy passing this long line of stopped cars I was bombarded with questions from those impatiently waiting. They would start honking their cars. There were babies and even ladies in their cars crying. Some were suffering from the heat while others were just plain hungry and tired from sitting in their cars. It was then about 2:30, they had about an hour yet to wait and had had nothing since breakfast except of course those who were fortunate enough to have taken lunches.

Well with the pageant over we went to the barbecue on tickets Randy had been given by the state Chamber of Commerce Officials. We sat with a distinguished crowd some of whom were introduced and all of us very close to the Governor where he made an even better and longer speech. . . .

. . . It was well after 5 o'clock when we got away and was nearly 7:30 when we arrived home.

Loorz concluded that memorable letter to his family by saying, "It has been real foggy here on the coast for three days but they say hotter than the devil on the hilltop." What an image that evokes: the perfumed gardens, the blinding white terraces, the shimmering Neptune Pool, the imperial castle itself lying silent in the sun under a polished blue sky, with scarcely a soul to behold the grand spectacle, as though it were the abandoned stronghold of a Persian king. And below on the coastal plain, half hidden in the gray, the string of cars plying the new road—the road named for Hearst's nemesis, Franklin Delano Roosevelt, the high priest of the New Deal.

In running past Hearst's coastal holdings in Monterey and San Luis Obispo counties, the road would diminish the sanctity of those lands from here on: a kingly private preserve, or at least its seaward edge, had in essence been nationalized,

---

78. The setting was Pfeiffer Redwoods State Park, established in 1934 and accessible until 1937 from the north only. Its present name of Pfeiffer Big Sur State Park dates from 1944.

79. Director of the California Department of Public Works.

thrown open to the masses. Hearst could reflect now on years of unchallenged lord-ship over that majestic property, some of which had been in his family since the 1860s; he could recall the heady days of his youth, when he had ridden horseback from Monterey and Carmel down to San Simeon over a mountain trail that no automobile could ever follow—until a daring highway like this one was blasted through. But if he indeed thought back, it was not from his Enchanted Hill that he did so, with this belated transition, this symbolic changing of the guard taking place below him. Instead, it was from within a palatial suite in New York—a kind of Casa Grande on Park Avenue—where he was comfortably removed from the heat and glare and clamor outside, yet hounded by the bankers and executives who were straining to save his crumbling empire.[80]

On the home front in California, the opening of the coast highway fascinated Loorz. The same day he wrote to his wife and sons, June 28, he addressed an equally long letter to his wife alone:

> There certainly is a lot of traffic by here now. A continuous line of cars just as on the other highway [U.S. 101]. The Sebastians have tripled their business I do be-lieve. They want to rush some work in on toilets as they have only the one and that not very good. I really believe a lot of work will come out of the traffic by here. It is such a long trip from here to the next service place that they should do very well. Somehow it doesn't feel so isolated as before. It seems to me that in a jaunt I can be where things are active. I know I'll keep a closer eye on Monterey from now on. Carl [Daniels] can look after things in San Luis [for the Stolte Co. branch office].

Loorz had begun that letter by saying, "Well we received another of those many surprises associated with this place. Mr. Hearst is supposed to be here Wednesday night [June 30].[81] Oh me, this will be fine for those on the Hilltop who are unhappy and still dont know what and when to do anything."

THE NEW HIGHWAY CONTINUED to hold its fascination—and Hearst arrived as anticipated—as Loorz told his sons and parents on July 1:

---

80. In other ways, life continued as it always had for Hearst during those weeks of penance in the Ritz Tower. (Forty-one stories tall and dating from the mid-1920s, the building ranked as the world's first residential skyscraper.) Soon after arriving there in June, Hearst wrote to an old friend in Santa Monica, still a titan at Metro-Goldwyn-Mayer, with whom he discussed the film industry; he did so in detail, never hinting at his financial plight. See unsigned [Hearst] to Louis B. Mayer, June 6, 1937; Hearst Papers, carton 20 (under "Mas-Mb").

81. Hearst's pilot, based at Union Airport in Burbank, got the word shortly before Loorz wrote to Mrs. Loorz. "Chief would like you to be ready with new Vultee in case he wants you to pick us up [from the westbound train] at Albuquerque or Barstow." From Willicombe to Allen Russell, June 27, 1937; Hearst Papers, carton 23 (under "1937 Samples"). Two weeks later (July 12), *Time* cited an intervening town on the Santa Fe line as the jumping-off point for Hearst: Winslow, Arizona (un-der "Hearst Steps Nos. 2 & 3," p. 26).

Cars are still going by by the dozen. I'll bet those that have business locations along the other highway certainly are noticing the loss. The Sebastians are very busy and have a fine gasoline business. Every business in Cambria is going great guns. They have to turn people away from the eating and sleeping houses and cabins. If I had a few extra thousands I would build a nice dining lodge with cabins in some nice spot between here and Monterey. It is so far between supply places that it would go well.

People who have car trouble have to send word down by other cars and that is often as much as 50 miles. So naturally they have to wait quite a while. If I was Bud Sweeters I'd certainly look around for a likely sight [site] for a service station and repair shop together with some cabins. I think with his mechanical ability he could clean up, if he got started right away before too many get into the business.

Mr. Herst [*sic*] is back on the hill. Landed yesterday in the nice new plane. I haven't seen him and will not try to unless he calls me. He may want to start something right away if he sees me. If he did I would not be able to come up and get you [boys]. I'd like to wait until I get a few of these plans [for Stolte Co. projects] out of the way. Most of the work we are figuring is around Salinas.

Hearst's return to San Simeon from his unpleasant month in New York was far from triumphal (despite the new plane), as Loorz told Morgan on July 2:

Now I haven't contacted Mr. Hearst. He knows I am here and can call if he wants me. I'll stick closely for a while so that I can be of whatever service he might desire.

However, Miss Morgan, from Randy [Apperson] I learn that Mr. Hearst is a pathetic, broken man. I dont want to bother you with this sad news. However, sad I feel that you want to know. Apparently his creditors are quite anxious to hurt him if they can. Further a government tax investigation seems eminently possible. Please let me repeat that I have heard only what Randy came down to confide in me last night.

I hope that Mr. Hearst is really not as badly off as he [Randy?] feels. We so often face difficulty with loss of confidence, oftimes needlessly so. I am so sorry for him. I am glad to hear that Randy reports Miss Davies to be very considerate of him, to be his only real comfort. They are here on the hilltop alone. She stole him away from New York as he seemed so worried and confined there that she feared he might not stand it. He was not out of the hotel [the Ritz Tower] once since he went back.[82]

---

82. In the midst of his stay, Hearst told a publishing colleague, "Cissy" Patterson, that he'd be visiting her in Washington, D.C., on June 21; he planned, through her good offices, to see President Roosevelt. But he quickly cancelled the trip, saying he'd "been laid up for two days with a bad cold" and thus was "terribly sorry and immensely disappointed." He asked for a rain check. (If secured, it was never redeemed.) See unsigned [Hearst] to Eleanor M. Patterson, June 18, 1937, and Hearst to Patter[s]on, June 19, 1937; Hearst Papers, carton 23 (under "1937 Samples"). See also Nasaw, *The Chief*, pp. 536–37, plus their note 32.

I hope further Miss Morgan that you will be provided with Funds to keep Wyntoon paid up and the Men's Quarters [the Bunkhouse] as well. I hope with things as they might be, that you will protect yourself. I know you would do all you can to help Mr. Hearst and share his burden. The truth is that all your own worries might not help him a bit. You have worried so for Mr. Hearst these many years that you should feel you have more than done your part. You should, therefore, obtain all funds due you, if possible and enjoy a little the results of your efforts.

By and large she was doing those very things—had long been doing them— right through all the pain and suffering. Yet not even Loorz was to know it. No, no, she insisted, not even he or almost anyone else—we ourselves included all these years later.

The excessively taciturn yet always well-meaning woman had been at Wyntoon when Loorz wrote his equally well-meaning letter. It would be her only trip there in July. She answered him after she got back (inexplicably dating her letter, which was handwritten, "July 7th 1935"):[83]

Mr. Hearst called me last night—unfortunately the line connection was poor & my voice extra bad on acct of a cold—He wanted a to-date line-up at Wyntoon & said he would probably not come up before the end of the month—I wrote today telling him how fresh & spring like things were, & how I hoped he would come before the heat & dust took toll of its beauty—It would do him good I am sure— there is enough activity & much he has not seen at all—It is all I can think of doing—.[84]

Loorz had said in his letter, "Please forgive me Miss Morgan, if I've been too personal. I feel free to talk this way Miss Morgan for I feel our friendship is real." She closed her handwritten reply with words of gratitude and reassurance: "Many thanks George—yes—we are *friends*."

(As for her saying there was "enough activity" at Wyntoon, Mac McClure had described things differently. Of the three letters he sent Loorz the month before, the last one, dated June 29, had said, "I suppose this job, too, will be 'folding up' before long. I look for it any day now. It seems a sad ending after the years of comparitive plenty,[85] but I will be glad to be away from it when the time comes.")

Loorz's eye for a good business prospect extended to the new highway, even as

---

83. Fortunately, Loorz saved the original envelope; it bears a San Francisco postmark from the evening of July 7, 1937.

84. Morgan's file copy of her letter to Hearst is in the Hearst/Morgan Correspondence, Morgan Collection.

85. "Comparitive" (like "surprize" on June 15) is among the misspellings found here and there in Mac's calligraphic letters.

he kept track of the Bunkhouse job and his outside work from his house in San Simeon. He wrote to his wife on July 7; she and their sons were still in Nevada:

> I hope to go up to the hill this afternoon and check up on a few things. At the same time I hope to see Mr. Hearst. I really think I will ask him if he would lease me a piece of ground near San Simeon, on the Highway for a service station. It might be mean for me to attempt to take some of the Sebastian business but this is a free country. I talked to Randy about it and he wished me luck and would certainly recommend it if Mr. Hearst asks him. He'd like to keep more of the traffic on the highway [bypass] instead of thru [the town of] San Simeon.

Loorz also wrote to Morgan then—the same day she sent him her handwritten letter—Wednesday, July 7:

> They had quite a little excitement on the hilltop during the early part of last week. Four small fires were detected close to the hilltop and put out.
>
> Conflicting stories accredit it to the heat and pieces of glass or matches in the grass, but all higher ups feel that they might have been started.[86]
>
> All watchmen have been put back on their old jobs and reenforcements have been added. Nothing further has happened. . . .
>
> They have had a few guests over the holidays [July 3–4] and not the movie crowd. Reports come in that Mr. Hearst is feeling much better again and is pleased about the California [state income tax] nine month law.[87] The governor's secretary and wife were among the guests.

He also told Morgan, "The highway has continued to be patronized at an unusual rate. No one in their wildest dreams had any idea it would be used so much. We are no longer isolated here in San Simeon."[88]

---

86. Loorz told his family on July 5, "They fear it is someone trying to scare Mr. Hearst. . . . All are quite upset about it but are now becoming quieted."

87. This was fresh news: on July 1, 1937, Governor Merriam approved amendments to the Personal Income Tax Act of 1935 (which had compelled Hearst to avoid California for at least six months in 1936). Hearst could now maintain his "nonresident" status by being out of state for a mere three months annually. Having already spent roughly nine weeks in 1937 beyond the state line (mostly in New York in January and June), he needed to leave California for just three or four more weeks before the year ended.

88. Isolation of another kind prevailed, however, with Hearst and many other Americans for whom the Great War remained a haunting memory—and for whom the prospects of "foreign entanglements" were anathema. In that regard, the title alone of Rodney Carlisle's article in the *Journal of Contemporary History* (July 1974, pp. 217–27) is enticing: "The Foreign Policy Views of an Isolationist Press Lord: W. R. Hearst and the International Crisis, 1936–41." Carlisle ended with these words about the steadfast Hearst:

> His support of a state of armed readiness as a deterrent to aggression, his fear of the Soviets as the major potential enemy, his anti-communism, his opposition to British and French overseas

Loorz's plan of running his own gas station apparently came to naught. But the letter he sent his wife on July 8 showed that soon others would be running their stations—to the benefit of the F. C. Stolte Co.:

> Oh boy, I have Carl [Daniels] and the whole gang here this morning working on everything imaginable. The demand for construction is suddenly taking wing in these parts. Besides the three jobs that go in in Salinas Saturday [July 10], we must get out sketches and figures on at least three service stations for different places up and down this [coast] road.
>
> It keeps me mumbling to myself to keep all hands posted so that we will make some fast accurate progress. No doubt we cannot lose out on all of it. I expect Cap Evans here this morning. He wants a service station, cabin arrangements and living quarters for his own family for a sight [site] just above the [Piedras Blancas] lighthouse on the ocean side.

The San Simeon branch of the Stolte Co. got the Evans job as well as some of the others Loorz mentioned.[89]

Loorz couldn't get that new highway off his mind. The scenery through Big Sur was breathtaking, and he loved to drive fast over the endless curves and grades. The sense of freedom was exhilarating. More and more he looked north, thought north, felt a homeward pull north. Soon after he got back from Nevada, where he had gone for several days to pick up his wife and sons, he had this to tell Morgan; by then it was July 21:

> I very often go to Salinas and King City now and along the new coast highway where I have a couple of small Service Stations under construction. Therefore, if you would enjoy it I'd be glad to pick you up at your place in Monterey and in two hours we would be here. If you dont make it this week why not plan it that way, or I can even call this week.

---

empires, and his willingness to cooperate with Germany in opposition to the Soviet Union were all views which earned him an isolationist label in 1936–41; by the 1950's, they formed the base on which both Democratic and Republican presidents were to formulate their policies. The consequences of those policies in Southeast Asia eventually produced an entanglement which Hearst would probably have supported had he lived into the present era.

The thought of Hearst's grappling with a crisis like Vietnam—fascinating!

89. No box of papers comparable to "F.C.S. 1936" exists for 1937. In its absence, the gas stations Loorz built along the Big Sur coast have yet to be identified (moreover, all of them may since have been replaced). They may have been in remote hamlets like Gorda and Lucia; or they may have been near Big Sur itself, where more stations were nestled along the road.

That was on Wednesday. Morgan made it down a few days later, on Monday,[90] though evidently not by the means Loorz proposed. At any rate, to get from her second home in Monterey to San Simeon in two hours, then or today, would make for a breakneck piece of driving. Loorz, still in his thirties, was no doubt happy to try. For that matter the sprightly Morgan may have been just as game.

HEARST REMAINED AT SAN SIMEON all the while—he hadn't gone to Wyntoon yet—and he naturally made his presence known to Loorz, Willicombe often acting as the intermediary.[91] July 28 brought a message about the baby giraffe. July 30

---

90. In the meantime—on Saturday—Morgan wrote to Thomas J. White, one of Hearst's top lieutenants in New York. Hearst had asked that she provide White with a copy of the "Pacific Coast Inventory"; she was thus sending him a "direct contact print" of what she called the "Pacific Coast Card Index Register." Its main compiler, she noted, had been Jim Forney (Lilian Forney's husband). See Morgan to White, July 24, 1937; Hearst/Morgan Correspondence, Morgan Collection. See also Morgan to Hearst, August 30, 1938 (regarding a copy of that inventory for Hearst himself a year later); ibid.

Better known as the "Pacific Coast Register" or simply as the "PC Register," the original compilation (preceding Tom White's copy and Hearst's as well) is a cornerstone of the Morgan-Forney Collection; at nearly 700 oversized pages, the PC Register lists virtually everything Hearst collected for San Simeon and Wyntoon, from rare books to architectural elements; it's less comprehensive regarding Santa Monica, many Beach House items having technically been owned by Marion Davies. In any case, the PC Register has had a crucial bearing on "Hearst Studies" since 1977, when Mrs. Forney and her daughter, Lynn, had a copy made for me. I shared the data with Thomas R. Aidala; his book *Hearst Castle: San Simeon* (New York, 1981) includes an appendix on pp. 235–36 whose costs, along with those in Cal Poly's new Morgan Collection, were revolutionary at that time.

91. Willicombe played that role, of course, at many other times, between Hearst and numerous people. He had recently heard from a woman who'd been at San Simeon that summer (a sister of the former Wyntoon employee Fanny Boss). The woman's letter said, "I was so distressed over Mr. Hearst's appearance that I could not keep the tears back when I looked at him. It breaks my heart to have him so worried." Willicombe's reply contained some choice details:

Mr. Hearst did look a little worn when he got here, but such rest as he has been able to get here has done him a lot of good, and he is looking and feeling better every day.

Albert and his wife [the Redelspergers] have left, and no one has been or will be appointed in their places. . . .

So that you will understand this situation, let me explain that instead of keeping a butler and housekeeper and chef here all the time, Mr. Hearst has adopted the plan of bringing up the butler [George Eckert] and chef from the Beach House [when needed at San Simeon].

A couple of maids and housemen, who will be here when we leave [for Wyntoon], will be under the direction of Mr. Williams, who will be in charge of the Hilltop.

From Phoebe H. Hill to Willicombe, July 19, 1937, and from unsigned [Willicombe] to Hill, July 22, 1937; Hearst Papers, carton 23 (under "1937 Samples"). Loorz had told Morgan on June 15, two weeks before the Hearst party got back from New York, "A complaint to Mr. Hearst by Mr. Apperson that the Redelspergers were not cooperating and would not take orders from Mr. Williams,

brought one about those persistent noises in the Gothic Suite. July 31 brought news of Hearst's concern over the safety of the remaining zoo animals. In this latest message, Willicombe painted a quick but unmistakable picture of the privacy Hearst maintained, of the distance he often put between himself and his employees and, not infrequently, between himself and his guests:

> Mr. Hearst just telephoned me to ask if you would be good enough to have all of the fences checked up to make sure there are no places where coyotes can get through to attack our animals.
>
> The presence of buzzards over the fields leads Chief to believe the coyotes may have gotten in.

Although Loorz was the man Hearst and Willicombe typically turned to in these situations, his main job through the summer of 1937 was the superintending of the Bunkhouse. In writing to Morgan about the job on August 11, he made an interesting comment regarding that normally reclusive woman: "Several people of Cambria have remarked that they were happy to see you in Cambria Pines and to seemingly enjoy it. They hope you will do it more often." The little episode may have coincided with her latest visit to San Simeon, made on August 6; in turn, Loorz may have been speaking of the Cambria Pines Lodge. Or he may have meant the cluster of buildings a mile west of downtown Cambria, a newer area called Cambria Pines in the 1930s (or the West Village in today's parlance, with Cambria proper being the East Village). For her part, Morgan went "down by plane" on August 6, according to the Morgan-Forney ledgers, and evidently back by train. Could she have flown to the landing field that was then in use near the Cambria Pines Lodge?

Air travel, at any rate, was a live topic in those mid-summer weeks. "Mr. Hearst flies to Wyntoon today." Morgan shared that news with Loorz on August 16.[92] She also said she'd be going up there the next night, the seventeeth, following which she'd meet with Loorz at San Simeon on the twentieth and discuss the Bunkhouse "if possible." It proved entirely possible. She wasn't on the road now nearly as much as she had been from 1934 through 1936. Though her trip to Wyntoon was

---

brought a prompt phone call from Mr. Willicombe to Albert [Redelsperger] and all seems well in hand at this writing."

92. Hearst spent a month and a half at San Simeon before he went north. "During this period there were 565 visitors at the ranch," his secretary reported. "Of this number 277 came there on business." Hearst's plan, therefore, was to have the resulting bills "divided up and payment made partly by himself and partly by the New York General Administrative account." From Willicombe to A. R. Cutter, August 19, 1937; Hearst Papers, carton 23 (under "1937 Samples"). Some of those visitors stayed longer than others—the usual pattern, both with business and with personal guests. On a broad average, twelve new faces appeared every day in that period.

actually her second in August 1937—she'd also gone up when the month began—
her servicing of the Hearst accounts hadn't included the Beach House since March
of the current year. And except for the Courtlandt Hill residence in Beverly Hills, a
small job she consulted on in June, her non-Hearst accounts in 1937 had yet to take
her beyond the Bay Area.[93]

She had another thing to tell Loorz in her letter of August 16; it concerned the
Service Wing in Casa Grande:

> You may not have heard that the Service Rooms, Kitchen, etc.—are not to be
> plastered at this time, but walls and ceilings of concrete and [similar] mixtures
> are to be cold water painted, rough effect [to remain] as is, and floors are to be
> leveled and smoothed up but no linoleum provided. *Because* we are to go onto the
> setting up of the stonework on exterior as soon as Ranch House [the Bunkhouse]
> and Wyntoon are paid up.

Prosaic lines for the most part. But essential ones for understanding how the
Kitchen and adjacent areas acquired their eggnog color, which covers the plain
gray bones in that part of the mansion. Outside, though, no finish work of the kind
she mentioned was ever done on the Service Wing—neither as decorative stonework to match the main part of Casa Grande (painfully expensive for the Hearst of
1937) nor even as a simpler but still effective stucco coating.[94]

Morgan visited San Simeon again about August 20 and then Wyntoon a
week after that. Between those dates, on August 25, Loorz notified the artisan Val
Georges that he should phone Morgan in San Francisco. "She has a long job for
you at Wyntoon," Loorz said, "doing iron work." But she had few other jobs there,
long or short, for anyone else.[95] Moreover, the work in the Service Wing at San

---

93. In fact, the only one besides the Hill job that would do so was the Hollywood Studio Club.
In early November, Morgan pursued some minor business at that building, which she'd designed in
the mid-twenties: $10 was entered in the Morgan-Forney ledgers. She went to the Los Angeles Exam-
iner Building the same day: another entry of $10 was duly made. Her quick swing through the South-
land came in conjuction with her last trip to San Simeon in 1937 (a familiar $35 in the ledgers). All
the while that year—since January—the Walter Schilling residence had been her largest non-
Hearst account, conveniently near at hand in San Francisco (see Appendix A, pp. 535 and 543).

94. More than two months later Morgan told Hearst that, if desired, "the setting of the new
cast and antique stone" could be done in a concentrated effort through old reliables like John Vanderloo and Frank Frandolich; the work would cost roughly $2,500 per month. See Morgan to Hearst,
November 30, 1937; Hearst/Morgan Correspondence, Morgan Collection.

95. The ironwork Loorz mentioned may have been done mostly *for* Wyntoon rather than *at*
Wyntoon, following a brief trip Georges made to that estate. Loorz told Morgan on September 12,
"Val Georges is on the job [at San Simeon] and I am putting his name on the construction payroll
[and] charging the work to Wyntoon as previously."

There was no attempt at San Simeon, meanwhile, to proceed with a job like the one LeFeaver
mentioned on July 9. He told Loorz then, "Mr. [Sam] Berger has finished the carvings for the rooms

Simeon was nothing major. The estimate Loorz sent her on August 30 gave a cost of $550—or $650 if they opted for some extra touches. Either way, it hardly signaled the return of better times; and insofar as national trends had a bearing, that same month saw a sharp downturn taking hold—the Roosevelt Recession, some were calling it—destined to reach into 1938. Only the Bunkhouse job lent San Simeon a real sense of the old kind of vitality as the summer waned.

Loorz gave Morgan an update on that building and the work in the Service Wing on September 12:

> We have practically completed the inside of the Mens Quarters [the Bunkhouse], plastering I mean. With but two days [effort] last week and a small crew. . . .
>
> On the hilltop the wash coat [in the Service Wing] has done wonders to tidy up the place. With the walls and cases cleaned up the unfinished ceilings now look quite dirty [in contrast]. . . .
>
> I feel that the clean up job you have started will while being very inexpensive do nearly as much to make the Kitchen wing clean and complete looking as a much more expensive job would have done.

All well and good. And yet a few more letters like that and even the late columnist Arthur Brisbane would be turning in his grave. No gossip, no infighting, no glamor, no intrigue? What would it take to bring those manic days back? Don't ask, Loorz and his dwindling co-workers could have said, don't even ask. For the answer was money—unthinkably more money than a fallen giant like Hearst could steer their way just now.[96]

THE BECKONING NORTH, along with Hearst's declining fortunes, prompted Loorz to relocate, as he told the plasterer Dell Clausen three weeks later. (Clausen

over the theatre. He will keep them at his shop [in San Francisco] until some convenient opportunity for you to have them picked up."

96. And yet September saw Morgan resume her third-largest Hearst account in 1937, the remodeling of the Hearst Building at 3rd and Market streets in San Francisco, done through the contractor King Parker. The project began in December 1936, sputtered early in 1937, but got back on track by Labor Day; a name long unseen in these annals, that of Hathaway Lovell, crops up on that score in October 1937.

With familiar irony, September also saw the Hearst Building's own Bill Murray briefing Hearst on a prospect of raising some badly needed funds. At stake was "the Santa Rosa (lower) Ranch," detached from the main Hearst Ranch and comprising some 2,900 acres, just south of Cambria, land on which Don Pancho Estrada was born in 1853. Another parcel of Hearst property—2,500 acres—adjoined it. Murray proposed selling the combined holdings, nearly 5,500 acres, for roughly $300,000 through an agent in San Luis Obispo. Hearst thought $500,000 could be had through the Los Angeles market. See Murray to Hearst, September 7, 1937; Murray to Willicombe, October 11, 1937; and unsigned [Willicombe] to Murray, also October 11, 1937; Hearst Papers, carton 23 (under "1937 Samples"). More decisions lay ahead; the entire acreage was sold in due course.

had shown some bona fide spunk, sorely missed of late, when he wrote to Loorz on September 23. "Give my regards to the boys, if there is any of them left around the good old '*Hilltop*.' I sure miss that big mass of concrete and steel.")[97] In replying on October 6, Loorz got some business sentiments off his chest; and then, befitting Clausen's example, he showed some of the spontaneity that usually brightens his letters:

> If this falls thru here with Mr. Hearst I am planning on moving into Monterey for permanent location. I had thot about San Luis Obispo for a long time but it is a dead place. Nothing but small buildings around this country. In Monterey I will be close to Salinas, Hollister, King City, etc. Besides I anticipate there will be lots of construction up and down this coast due to the new highway.
>
> I have gone up and down this coast so much the past month that it was easy for me to make the decision. Now that my family have become used to the sea coast I realize it will be difficult to keep them away from it for a very long [time]. . . .
>
> Drove around to King City yesterday and met Miss Morgan. Spent a very busy day rushing around furniture and curtains with her at Jolon. It looks real nice Dell. . . . We got back to the ranch bunk house about 5:30 and went over that.[98] It certainly is a nice looking building Dell. Anyway the whole day was sort of fun again.

But Loorz didn't wait for things to fall through at San Simeon. In mid-October he went ahead and negotiated for a house on Franklin Street in Monterey, near the Presidio and almost directly across the street from Morgan's property. The deal fizzled, but there were others for him to pursue in the area. As he told his parents on October 21, regarding Monterey, "In the first place it is a lovely place to live or at least I think it will be. Secondly it will be [a] good central point for me to work away from." He cited another fact in writing to his sister, likewise on October 21 — namely, that construction was "slacking off quite a bit in these parts."[99] He wasn't kidding. Through the better part of 1937, the government had tightened its New Deal spending; and around the country, the Roosevelt Recession had set in. Meanwhile, locally, Loorz's San Simeon branch of the F. C. Stolte Co. had become al-

---

97. The Morgan-Forney ledgers show that Morgan went to Wyntoon on September 24, the day after Clausen wrote his letter. She was there again in late October. But the Loorz Papers are too thin in this final part of 1937 to intersect or provide corroboration, as they once did with frequency.

98. The fast-typing (and fast-driving) Loorz can usually be taken at his word: he must have gone up the Big Sur coast and then around to King City through Carmel, Monterey, and Salinas before returning to San Simeon over the Burnett Road — a winding jaunt of at least 200 miles.

99. Loorz made a similar point on November 21, while writing to a potential branch-office employee named Ed Garbarini. "I have trampled this state in the central section from one end to the other during this past week. . . . There has been a scarcity of work for the past four months and in each district [locality] there is at least one competitor willing to take a job at near cost."

most too productive for its own good. There were only so many schools, for instance, to keep everyone busy in a rural county like San Luis Obispo, far from California's more populous areas.

Besides, Loorz wanted to "take on larger construction especially bridges" once he was "free to devote more time to it." Those words were for Ray Van Gorden, whom he wrote to in Palo Alto on October 22.

He wrote to Paul Polizzotto on the twenty-second as well; Polizzotto, a friend of his from San Luis Obispo, was traveling in Italy:

> I am still in San Simeon as you see. Have not quite finished the Ranch Bunkhouse but soon will. It is real nice looking and I'm proud to have had so much to do with it. In other words Paul there is more of me in this house than in the big one on the hill.
>
> Money is still scarce on the Hilltop and little or no work except repairs is going on. I have handled it but it hasn't been necessary for me to go up the hill very often. When I do the place seems so lonesome with no workmen around.
>
> Mr. Hearst is still at Wyntoon, Mt. Shasta [having been there since mid-August], and seems to be enjoying himself.[100] Looks like he will remain there until after Thanksgiving. Then he will have to get out of the state for a month [to complete his exemption from its income tax]. Then we hope he will return here [to San Simeon] to resume some kind of work.[101] If he doesn't then I now think my future address will be Monterey, Calif.
>
> The wife and I and boys are going to Monterey tomorrow [Saturday] to look at some old residences. I think I will buy one. Then if things blow up here at any time I'll have a permanent address and some business headquarters other than in my bag.

---

100. As always, Hearst's pleasure included being kingly and, toward those he liked or admired, indulgent and gracious. A letter he received in this part of 1937, sent from the Hotel Meurice in Paris, bespeaks that side of the man:

> I am desired by the Duke and Duchess of Windsor to say how grateful they are for the generous offer of the use of some of your houses during their forthcoming visit to America, which you have made through Miss [Alice] Head and Mr. [William] Hillman.
>
> Whilst Their Royal Highnesses much appreciate your thought for their comfort and privacy, their plans are such that they regret being unable to avail themselves of your kindness.

From T. H. Carter (the Windsors' secretary) to Hearst, November 1, 1937; Hearst Papers, carton 23 (under "1937 Samples"). Less than a week later the Windsors were forced to cancel their much-anticipated visit. Three years passed before they set foot on American soil.

101. See note 87, above; an absence closer to three weeks is what Hearst was now planning. Until Governor Merriam approved the new amendments to the tax law in July, Hearst had been planning to be gone from sometime in September through the end of the year.

The Loorzes' house-hunting trip that late October weekend bore fruit. They found a modest home in the Spanish style, quite like their home in San Simeon, but overlooking a far more historic bay. The house lay just beyond the Monterey city limits, at 203 Pine Avenue in Pacific Grove.

BACK AT SAN SIMEON, Loorz kept working on the Bunkhouse; of course, he also pursued his outside work, which continued its northerly shift. (As much as a year before, he'd begun shying from southerly prospects, such as he and Stolte had once considered; he told Carl Daniels on October 12, 1936, "It looks like there will be plenty of volume for us here [in the San Luis area] and up North without going South.") In this latter part of 1937 the Santa Cruz City Hall, for example, a handsome porticoed building designed by C. J. "Jerry" Ryland of Monterey, was coming up for bid; and Loorz was preparing to submit figures. He got the job—and went on to handle it in 1938 through what became the Pacific Grove branch of the F. C. Stolte Co.

Concerning other northern prospects, plus an eastern one, Loorz's letter to Stolte on November 11 indicated a widening map for the partners:

> Fort Bragg and Pt Arena are not far apart and it might be well to consider them more seriously if we dont land Watsonville or Porterville. Though Porterville is a splendid plan and Carl [Daniels] is anxious to go there, I fear we will not be able to beat those Valley figures. The Porterville bid goes in about 2 P.M. Whoever takes the bid there should get in touch with you so you will bid accordingly at Fort Bragg.

Loorz knew all about rock-bottom "Valley figures" from earlier in 1937: a job in the sun-bitten town of Taft, near Bakersfield, had eluded him. He and Stolte had to keep pressing, though. Things weren't slowing down for them in the greater San Luis area alone; obviously, the same was true at Wyntoon, a cornerstone for the F. C. Stolte Co. since 1933. In that first year of the cost-plus arrangement that prevailed there, Wyntoon represented almost half the company's activity. The percentage dropped in 1934 and 1936 (the figures for 1935 are missing). But the company moved ahead during those three years. It broadened its base and became less dependent on Hearst dollars. In 1936, for example, Wyntoon and the Hearst KYA radio station in San Francisco represented a fourth of the company's business; meanwhile, the General Pete gas stations and the work at Yosemite produced more than twice that amount (a combined 59.8%). And yet for Wyntoon and KYA to produce just 17.1% in 1937—Wyntoon by itself plunged from $68,311 in 1936 to $22,388—was enough to make Loorz and Stolte look farther afield than ever before. By the end of 1937 the main (Alameda) branch of the Stolte Co. tallied $218,225 in activity; the total in 1936 had been $299,741. Wyntoon wasn't entirely to blame, but that didn't make Hearst's diminished patronage any less unnerving. A new year, full of new concerns, new uncertainties, lay just ahead. Fortunately, the partners had their eggs in more than one basket. Loorz's San Simeon branch had $246,805 in activity in 1937.[102]

Morgan, who'd been to Wyntoon in the first week of November and to San Simeon in the second week, kept Loorz informed on Monday, November 15. "Latest news from the north is for an end-of-this-week departure." Hearst had been at Wyntoon for three months now. Whether she thought he'd be stopping at San Simeon is unclear. The moment was rapidly approaching for him to leave California for the rest of the year. And thus she got in a final meeting with him on November 22, held at the Beach House. Wyntoon must have been the main subject; she charged the visit to that account in the ledgers kept by her secretary, Lilian Forney.

True, Loorz had protected himself in these waning moments of 1937 by buying the house in Pacific Grove. Yet he was still biting his nails over his arrangement with Hearst. He wrote to Morgan in that regard on November 26; he began, though, on a more colloquial note:

> Indirectly I have learned that because of your ambitious farming at your home in Monterey you have been caused to suffer a lot during the past couple of weeks. If this is true then I am so sorry for I still remember the painful and awkward case of Poison Oak my wife suffered about two years ago.
>
> I have been anxious to see you and talk to you and I am really worried about my work here. Somehow I do not feel that much work will be done on the hill in the near future. Up to now I have earned my way. Next week should see the end of work at the Men's Club House [the Bunkhouse]. . . .
>
> I know now that my overhead alone is running up the cost of the Club House. I know also that my phone calls and distant trips to my outside jobs is costing me most of what I am earning here at present.
>
> As I have stated previously, I am very fond of my connection here on the hilltop. I am grateful for the privilege of working with you and Mr. Hearst. I want that connection to continue if it can be made to advantage to all of us. I would be pleased to remain here if Mr. Hearst could afford to proceed with sufficient bud-

---

102. The figures cited throughout this paragraph as "activity" are gross figures, dominated by labor, materials, and related costs. But the documents that list the figures tell nothing about profits and losses; nor do they identify cost-plus situations (Wyntoon wasn't the only one), lump-sum contracts, commission amounts, or anything of the kind. The sole exception in the 1933–37 period is Loorz's recapitulation of San Simeon branch activity, a detailed spread sheet for the year 1937. Beyond doing $246,805 "worth of work" (his frequent term for what I'm calling "activity"), the branch office made a gross profit of $11,655. Its net profit, after all remaining costs were paid, was $4,367.

get to permit me to earn my $125 per week [that applied from January through May 1937]. As it is, that would be a wasteful luxury for Mr. Hearst and I would [be] accept[ing] it as a charitable gift.

Miss Morgan, I have not written or talked to Mr. Hearst or Mr. Willicombe [about this] since construction shut down last spring. Mr. Hearst called for me once when he last spent a day here but I did not return until late that night and he flew away before I contacted him the next morning. Therefore, Miss Morgan with your permission I would like to pay Mr. Hearst a personal visit and discuss the above frankly and openly with him.[103] I assure you I will not embarrass him or encourage him to make some expenditures he cannot afford.

You will agree that our firm [the Stolte Co.] could do with a little more efficient management around the bay district. I intend that it will be one of the most efficient firms in the Bay Area. My method of bringing that about will depend upon my own place of residence. I have procrastinated too long already.

In mid-December Loorz wrote to Morgan again.[104] He was undecided about moving to Pacific Grove—he could rent out that house for the time being, if need be—and he was also thinking of moving to Oakland's neighboring town of Alameda, where Fred Stolte now lived. (In the meantime, Hearst resumed his "nonresident" status. He'd come within an inch of sailing to Honolulu with the usual party in tow, a cavalier plan for one so financially shaken; instead, he'd made a sudden about-face, opting for Manhattan and another holiday season in the Ritz Tower.)[105] The letter from Loorz to Morgan went out to her on Tuesday, December 14:

---

103. It's unclear when Hearst "last spent a day" at San Simeon—just recently, after leaving Wyntoon, or right before he went to Wyntoon in August? Loorz may have been hoping "to pay Mr. Hearst a personal visit" in Santa Monica, rather than on the hilltop, hence the unusual degree of protocol here. In any event, if Loorz didn't see him soon, his next chance wouldn't be until January.

Sometime in the fall of 1937, perhaps soon after they left Wyntoon, Hearst and Marion Davies went to Mexico, presumably to bolster his nonresident status, if only in small measure. See the Davies memoir, *The Times We Had: Life with William Randolph Hearst* (edited by Pamela Pfau and Kenneth S. Marx), photograph on p. 123. "They flew to Ensenada to avoid a tax problem," says the caption. "The San Francisco *Examiner's* plane was pressed into service."

104. By then Loorz had been the main subject of a letter she wrote Hearst. (Another subject she covered is cited in note 94.) Morgan referred to Loorz's former "$125 per week" as his "1936 salary"; however, he remained at $100 per week that entire year, according to his federal tax form. She also told Hearst that Loorz might "locate at once with his family at some central valley point." That was surely a slip—her use of *valley*—Loorz having spoken often in recent weeks of Monterey as a "central point." See Morgan to Hearst, November 30, 1937; Hearst/Morgan Correspondence, Morgan Collection.

105. For several weeks, possibly longer, Hearst had been planning to leave Los Angeles in early December, sailing on the *Lurline*. See, for example, Willicombe's letter of October 28, 1937, to Cissy Patterson (answering hers of October 23). The Colonel waxed poetic, suggesting that Mrs. Patterson,

I am sorry that I did not get a chance to see Mr. Hearst [before he left]. The reason is that I think it advisable for me to move from San Simeon so that my boys can start the next semester in their new school. I am certain you have explained carefully to Mr. Hearst regarding this, but I did want to see him personally. I am unable to decide definitely where we will move depending of course upon the amount of work that might be done on the Hill. If it were at all possible that Mr. Hearst would resume construction on a fair scale later in the spring, I would move to Monterey, where I could reach the Hilltop within 2 hours notice at any time. From where I could make at least two weekly visits with ease. Where I could conveniently keep in close touch with you.

If the proposed construction would be very small, it might be better for me to move to Alameda.

I know that this decision must be my own, for I would not put either you or Mr. Hearst in a position to feel obligated to carry on a certain amount of work because of arrangements with me. I merely mention these things as thoughts that have occurred to me in making my new plans.

It so happens that we just signed a contract for a Gymnasium at Campbell [near San Jose], [and] a City Hall at Santa Cruz. I feel that we have a splendid chance of being the low bidder on the King City Auditorium next Tuesday.[106] Monterey would be a nice center from which to manage these jobs. Of course I

---

who'd been invited to join the voyagers, "Slip out to Wyntoon" and then "Slip along to Waikiki." Hearst Papers, unnumbered box following carton 59 (under "Miscellaneous Correspondence and Clippings").

Three weeks later an attorney of Hearst's said he hoped to discuss a legal matter — "Some time before you leave for Honolulu," as he put it. From Henry S. MacKay, Jr., to Hearst, November 17, 1937; Hearst Papers, carton 20 (under "McG-McK").

Nearly a month passed; suddenly, Hearst cancelled the trip. He cabled his regrets to Honolulu, to the man whose house he'd planned to rent. "Hope for some future trip to your lovely islands, and to have the very great pleasure of seeing you." From Hearst to Chris Holmes, December 15, 1937; Hearst Papers, carton 23 (under "1937 Samples").

Hearst's return to the Ritz Tower went unmentioned in *The New York Times* — hence, nary a murmur in Swanberg's *Citizen Hearst*. David Nasaw cites some documents in the Hearst Papers from December 1937 but without mentioning Hearst's whereabouts; see *The Chief*, p. 651, notes 38–39 (to pp. 538–39 in the main text). Consequently, Hearst's trail through this period remains obscure. Another document of the hour shows that Hearst was still making *some* money, despite the liquidations and economy measures that swirled all about. "Enclosed is the check for $2,677.50 covering dividend on Tidewater stock" — an amount that was "to be deposited in Mr. Hearst's Special Account." From Willicombe to A. R. Cutter, December 18, 1937; Hearst Papers, carton 57 (under "T").

106. One of Loorz's letter boxes from this period was labeled "King City City Hall 1938." But its contents were too thin to form an archival sub-group in the Loorz Papers (like that yielded by the Avenal School and certain other jobs; see note 7, above).

Loorz mentioned the King City job in writing to Ed Garbarini the same day as he did Morgan, December 14. His words were more confident now than on November 21 (compare note 99). "We are receiving daily calls to figure more and more work," he told Garbarini, "which certainly makes 1938 look like a banner year for those with pep enough and courage enough to go out and get it."

must not forget the many possibilities offered by personal contacts with industrial heads around the Bay Area.

I must mention that one of my chief concerns holding me to San Simeon is because I have been able in no small way to take care of our mutual friends such as Frank Souza, Frank Gyorgy, Peter Petersen, [John] McFadden, Ray Van Gorden and Frank Frandolich [by giving them work]. . . .

Since the time for my change is almost at hand, I am writing my thoughts.

Loorz had indeed a big decision to make. And it was ultimately a decision that only he could make, not Miss Morgan or Mr. Hearst. Loorz's papers are too spotty over the weeks ahead to disclose when he opted for Monterey—that is to say, for Pacific Grove.[107]

But such was his decision, a decision he made at least in part because he finally learned there *would* be some work at San Simeon in 1938. As he told his old friend George Wright on January 18 of that new year, "After the first of February I can be reached at 203 Pine Street [Avenue], Pacific Grove, where our [branch] office will be located. Will run the Hearst Construction from there."

Not quite three weeks later, on February 4, 1938, Hearst sent Loorz a letter from San Simeon—that glowing letter of recommendation with which this narrative began:

I shall be very happy to have you refer anyone to me regarding the high quality of your construction work at San Simeon.

I have had the most complete satisfaction with everything that you have supervised and executed.

You have been most careful, not only about the quality of the construction, but about the cost.

I cannot imagine it possible for anyone to be more competent and conscientious, and I am glad to testify to that effect.

Some contemporaries of Loorz's have decried his pronounced ego, an ego quick to capitalize on such uplifting words—an ego second only to that of Hearst himself. So be it.[108] His rapport with Hearst was as rare as that experienced by Ar-

---

107. The question might well have been answerable—along with several more in this chapter—had a box marked "F.C.S. 1937" ever surfaced.

108. Loorz's superior had long ago defended himself. On one occasion Hearst alluded to his own salary of $500,000, justifying his means of gaining it and, in turn, the initiative and gumption of someone—like Loorz—who also strove to succeed. "They believe in compensation in proportion to service rendered," wrote Hearst, speaking of his newspapers, "and in no limit to the extent of the compensation if the extent of the service is equally great." From the editorial "The Hearst Papers Stand for Americanism and Genuine Democracy" (Sunday, April 21, 1935), reprinted in *Selections from the Writings and Speeches of William Randolph Hearst* (San Francisco, 1948; edited by E. F. Tomkins), pp. 14–16.

thur Brisbane, Edmond Coblentz, Julia Morgan, Joseph Willicombe, and precious few others in the Chief's inner circle. No begrudging of George Loorz—of his readiness, his shrewdness, and, above all, his effectiveness—can tarnish his career at San Simeon.

He treasured that letter from Hearst for the rest of his life, until he died forty years later. His wife treasured it too; and when she died in 1989, her sons found it among her personal effects, still in its original envelope.

1938

Business Not Quite As Usual

NEVER MIND THE SHOCK WAVES that had been rolling through Hearst's empire for the past several months. Now that the Chief had returned from New York after the holidays and Morgan had broached no further the prospect of retirement, construction remained a live prospect at San Simeon. Work continued on the Bunkhouse, which saw completion by the end of January 1938. And midway through the month, work resumed in the Recreation Wing of Casa Grande; with minor exceptions, nothing had been done on the hilltop itself since clear back in June.

Loorz, still on hand through the opening weeks of the new year, apologized for his "laxity in corresponding"—this while writing to Jim Rankin on Tuesday, January 18, the same day he gave George Wright the address he'd soon be using in Pacific Grove. "Not being braggadocious," Loorz told Rankin, but "the new Bunkhouse does look quite nice; especially, since we have had enough rain over the weekend to wash it good and clean, if it had been dirty."[1]

Morgan had appeared on Monday the seventeeth. In fact, she'd already been down ten days earlier, her presence coinciding closely with Hearst's return from the east. With two visits under her belt already in 1938, she and Loorz had plenty to discuss by January 19, when he wrote to her from San Simeon. (He also wrote to her on January 17, sometime after she had left the hill that Monday; but the Loorz Papers lack a copy.)[2] In his letter of the nineteenth, he emphasized the smooth tran-

---

1. In the second half of 1937, after Loorz stopped using his hilltop office and was working at home in San Simeon, he began dictating some of his correspondence. Ray Van Gorden and Conrad Gamboni (both were natives of Cambria) shared the duties; Gamboni moved to Pacific Grove with Loorz in 1938 to become his full-time secretary. Any close analysis of Loorz's letters from here on— their phrasing, punctuation, spelling—must take Gamboni's role into account. But only when applicable: Loorz continued to write many letters himself, composing them directly on the typewriter.

2. The original, however, survives at Cal Poly, even though the Morgan Collection has very few of the incoming originals from Loorz to Morgan (or carbons of her outgoing originals to him). The stray item dated January 17, 1938, is part of the series San Simeon Business Correspondence and Ephemera (III/02/07/82, under "George Loorz, 1936–1944").

sition they hoped to make to the intermittent role he'd soon be playing, more akin
to Fred Stolte's superintendent role at Wyntoon since 1933. There would also be a
supportive role for someone to play in Loorz's absence from the hilltop, equivalent
to Harry Thompson's part at Wyntoon. Loorz told Morgan that he "wanted to feel
out the selection of a general foreman [for San Simeon] a little more before taking
any definite action":

> If I were making the decision, entirely considering the job from my own point of
> view I must admit that I would appoint Pete [Petersen]. He has changed so much
> from the same man he was when I came here that I feel he will really cooperate
> with all concerned. He was considerate of [Frank] Frandolich on the Club House
> [the Bunkhouse].[3] He is so much more familiar with our [type of] work that I
> know he can do it best.
>
> However, for [someone for] you to consult with on your visits and for chance
> interviews with Mr. Hearst I think it might be a little more satisfactory with
> [John] McFadden.

There were other points to consider, other pros and cons regarding the two
men. With respect to McFadden, for instance, "He has a lot to learn particularly
about our woodwork and antiques in general."

The choice, in any case, involved a meeting of Loorz's mind and Morgan's.
"Whatever decision we make I will protect you Miss Morgan." Loorz further assured her, "I'll take responsibility of the decision and soften it to the best of my ability." He also said he wanted "to make the decision public not later than Monday"—January 24, that is, when she'd most likely be appearing next. That way he
could smooth out any wrinkles before he moved to Pacific Grove. He planned to go
on the last weekend of the month.

---

3. After the big shutdown in 1937 Loorz had made room for Frandolich on the Bunkhouse job,
which Petersen also worked on. As Loorz told Morgan on June 26 that year:

> I am still using Frank Frandolich as the only laborer on the job. He likes it a lot and is so happy
> that at least for the time being he doesn't have to move [from his house in San Simeon village].
> I am paying him $5.00 per day as against $4.00 I was paying laborers he replaced [$4 being the
> old hilltop scale of many years' standing for unskilled construction help]. The work is not hard
> for him but rather good for him. At his age I cannot expect him to wield a shovel as fast as the
> boys he replaced but considering everything I think the above is fair to both Mr. Hearst and
> Frank. At least he is happy.

> On the other hand, Loorz assured Morgan, he had "kept Frank Souza [the labor foreman] un-
> til the last hour possible" at that tenuous stage in 1937. "At $9.00 [per day] he would be far to[o] ex-
> pensive as an ordinary laborer [on par with Frandolich] and only finish carpentry remains [for
> someone like Petersen to do]. When we come to the cement finish [at the Bunkhouse] I'll bring him
> [Souza] back if he wishes."

On Tuesday, February 1, Loorz officially hung out his shingle at his new address on the Monterey Peninsula. That same morning found Ray Van Gorden writing to him from Hearst Camp on The Enchanted Hill:

> Well Miss Morgan was on the job yesterday. I was surprised at about noon by a phone call from the gate that she was on her way up. The wind was just howling and the rain was coming down in sheets. She was up with Pete [Petersen] for a couple of hours and went back to San Luis at about 5 P.M. Even John Vanderloo didn't get to see her. This morning everything is quiet and the storm is over until possibly tomorrow or the next day. I heard over the radio last night that the San Simeon [Big Sur coast] road had a big slide and was closed indefinitely. You got through just in time but it wont be so handy to come down weekly all the way around [on Highway 101].

Van Gorden was optimistic, though, that the state maintenance crews could soon reopen the coast road. (Hopeful words like those can still be heard today during soggy winters.) But why he was surprised to see Morgan is another matter. Stiff weather or not, Hearst was back home now and would be staying for several weeks. Morgan had resumed her familiar Monday pattern: even in 1938 her Hearst accounts would represent no less than three quarters of her total activity.[4] At a glance, one could say that the dark clouds of 1937, to say nothing of those from previous years, had never materialized, that the sun had shone unchallenged through it all, that the Great Depression and the steepened taxes and the shrunken budgets and the disruptive shutdowns and all the other annoyances had never occurred. This was merely at a glance, though—a quick, illusory glance.

Loorz got mired in domestic bliss while the highway got mired in rocks and mud. "We are so upset with painters, plumbers, carpenters, etc. that I am not going to the Hilltop this week, even though I had previously planned on being there Fri-

---

4. Morgan's work on the greater Hearst accounts had averaged eighty-three percent of her total activity over the past five years, 1933 through 1937; see Appendix A. The drop in 1938 was an obvious result of Hearst's slowdown. Morgan partly offset the deficit through the largest of her non-Hearst accounts that year, a house in Piedmont for Allan Starr and his wife. Or did she? In reality, Morgan pursued the job at a conspicuous loss. In 1938 alone, her $2,384 in operating costs for the Starrs was well off the break-even pace; in 1939 she accrued $1,319 in costs. Her grand total for 1938–39 of $3,703 was more than twice the $1,780 she earned in commissions. Most likely, the Starr job found Morgan falling back on her Hearst safety net, which enabled her to perform at her own pace, on her own terms. One can only hope the Starrs were appreciative.

To view the matter another way: since Morgan's commission of $1,780 reflected "7% of actual cost" (Morgan-Forney ledgers), her $3,703 in expenses would have been right on track—if the house had cost $52,900 to build. But the Starrs paid their contractor and his "subs" $25,432, not $52,900. Morgan's expenses were 14.6% of that smaller figure, a much higher commission than she could possibly charge.

day." It was already Thursday when he notified Morgan in that manner, February 3. In the process he thanked her for "the kind thoughts" she'd sent him from San Luis Obispo earlier in the week (part of a letter that never turned up in the Loorz Papers). He also told her that some information he received from Pete Petersen—who'd become the on-site man over John McFadden—squared with what she said in her letter from San Luis, so all was well.

A brief message from Hearst to Loorz, dated February 7, 1938, sounds enough like a tale of yore—as though Loorz had never moved and was still near at hand—to seem a vestige of times gone by. Yet the date is clear, the context right: "Will you kindly have me a couple of dozen more electric light caryatids cast so I can continue the lighting along the terraces in front of [west of] house C [Casa del Sol] and along the north balustrade." Only the last two words need further deciphering. Did Hearst mean the balustrade along the north end of the West Terrace? Or the one encircling the north end of the Neptune Pool? Then again, maybe he meant the balustrade closer to the unfinished Grand Entrance. All three areas have twin-headed lamp standards in grayish cast stone, familiar to everyone who has seen The Enchanted Hill. Loorz no doubt knew exactly what Hearst meant. Yet without further "Recapitulations" (none of them postdates May 15, 1937) and similar items to guide us, we're forced to make guesses.

Meanwhile, Loorz's stand-ins took an honest stab at compiling their own recapitulation. On February 7, during her latest Monday visit, Morgan left Petersen some notes for Room #2 on the Recreation Wing's second floor. Ray Van Gorden typed them up; they appeared in a letter he sent Loorz the next day.[5] Concerning the old Spanish ceiling (the "Cathkingceil" from Arthur Byne), "Use frieze boards on side walls, and make new ones [to match] for between corbels." Another entry said, "Mr. Williams will bring up all of small corbels we have. If not enough, please ask John Vanderloo to cast extras [in plaster of Paris]."

Five more entries were incorporated in Van Gorden's letter—too incorporated, really, the whole group being all but buried in a dense paragraph. If only a new series of recaps had emerged in 1938, on par with Loorz's often personalized, sometimes humorous notes from 1932 through 1937. But such was not to be.

Van Gorden had some further things to say on February 8. In regard to Morgan, "She seemed to be in wonderful spirits and spent quite a lot of time with Pete." He also said, "It seems there has been a change and everything comes and goes

---

5. The letter is misdated "February 7th. 1938." Van Gorden began by telling Loorz, "As you probably know, Miss Morgan was here yesterday," an unmistakable reference to Monday the seventh, not Sunday the sixth. Other internal evidence also points toward February 8 as the correct date.

direct from Mr. Hearst rather than through the Hearst Sunical Land & Packing Corp. as before [in 1936 and 1937].[6] I know Mr. Willicombe called her about her allowance for her budget yesterday." Van Gorden also had this to tell Loorz:

> Mr. Hearst isn't very active these days, especially since the weather has been so miserable. He shows up for his lunch around 3 or 4 o'clock and then for dinner at about 9. I haven't seen him around the grounds for over a week. There hasn't been any complaints as yet as to noise.

Chances are, the "noise" was that chorus of odd sounds — those Ghosts of La Cuesta Encantada — that still bedeviled the Gothic Suite at times.

Loorz also heard from Morgan, who likewise wrote to him on February 8, fresh from her trip the day before:

> Mr. Hearst agreed on the use of material for #2 Room [in the Recreation Wing] as per sample set up in place — even as to color decoration. . . .
>
> Mr. Hearst, as foreseen, was not satisfied with the progress [at San Simeon] and suggested taking off the Wyntoon carvers [in San Francisco] and applying all the small funds onto this work.[7]
>
> I explained we would be both artistically and financially losers to do so — but would take off enough to give an extra carpenter for the ceilings, etc.

In addition, she elaborated on something Loorz would be reading about in Van Gorden's letter of the same date:

> As to setup:— We are no longer a part of "Sunical," but are to work directly under Mr. Hearst as employer. I imagine the best way will be to have Ray take care

---

6. In designating the 1936–37 period, I've alluded (as perhaps Van Gorden did) to Bill Murray's prominence in those years and, in turn, to the Hearst Sunical Building Fund. However, as Van Gorden surely knew, that short-lived account had been terminated by 1938. As Loorz told his wife and family on June 19, 1937 (while they were in Nevada):

> I have a lot of records to complete as they want me to close out that Hilltop Fund [reinstated late in 1936] as soon as possible. . . . By that time [July 10] I hope to be able to close out the Hearst Sunical Bldg fund also. That is the fund provided by the ranch [Bill Murray's office] but not the [new and even shorter-lived] Bunk house fund. That will then leave only the Bunk house fund and there will be little left for me to worry about.

7. Budgets, allotments, new schemes for saving money and juggling accounts — these were as much on Hearst's mind nowadays as ever; indeed, more than ever after the rude awakenings of 1937. The end of that year found him discoursing, at times bitterly, almost feverishly, on some odd byways of these subjects, even with regard to his beloved San Simeon. "I am getting out of the ranch entirely and storing my things," he stamped his foot at one point. "Now let the institution see what they can rent the house for unfurnished, and to people who will pay the upkeep and be desirable tenants." As quoted in Willicombe to Konta ("Supplementary Message"), December 5, 1937; Hearst Papers, carton 23 (under "1937 Samples"). David Nasaw cites some related passages from the same period (and the same archives) in *The Chief,* pp. 538–39.

of all the insurance and make out the pay checks, sending them up here for signa-
tures. It is hard to tell what work will go on and to what extent, but it does not look
as though there would be much done this year.

She and Loorz and certain others had been under the Hearst Sunical wing for
the sake of the Bunkhouse mainly, the job that had dominated the second half of
1937, done through Bill Murray in San Francisco. On the surface her "Sunical"
comment means nothing more than that. (The job, however, had not relied on the
Hearst Sunical Building Fund, which ceased in July 1937—despite the Bunkhouse's formal name being the Hearst Sunical Men's Quarters. Instead, a new
entity had provided the means, the so-called Bunkhouse Fund.)[8] Morgan herself
had been little involved in most Hearst Sunical projects, often akin to those done
through the Hilltop Fund, such as road work and giraffe barns. And thus to be "directly under Mr. Hearst as employer" wasn't a new approach for her; it closely resembled on a smaller scale the days when the Hearst Construction Fund reigned
supreme. But there was this crucial difference: Hearst no longer ruled with im-
punity, free to foist expenses on "the company." From now on he'd be spending
"personal" dollars—insofar as his corporate overlords could make the distinction
stick.[9]

Loorz got off a letter of his own on February 8. It went to Hearst, thanking
him for the enviable recommendation of four days earlier—the one in which the
young builder, still in his thirties, was applauded for being "competent and conscientious." Loorz used the moment to tell Hearst, "I expect to be on the Hilltop,
Thursday, February tenth."[10]

---

8. Or by its own formal name, the Hearst Sunical Men's Quarters Fund; see also note 6,
above. "Hearst Sunical" crops up in yet another guise—pertaining to a new fund or account—on
p. 366 in this chapter: Loorz to the McCloud River Lumber Co. (May 8, 1938).

9. Hearst's foremost regent, "Judge" Shearn, had recently spelled things out, with specific regard to Hearst's activities in California:

It is the duty of the Board of Directors of Hearst Sunical [Land & Packing Corporation] to
make sure that all items of expense incurred in connection with Wyntoon and San Simeon,
which are not, in the judgment of the Board, true and proper items of corporate expense, be
charged to Mr. Hearst and forwarded to the General Auditor of American Newspapers, Inc.
[in New York], with which Mr. Hearst maintains a running credit, for proper entry and reim-
bursement. . . .

It is of course in Mr. Hearst's interest to keep all expenses, both company and personal, as
low as reasonably possible and I know that you will cooperate to this end.

From Clarence J. Shearn to Edward H. Clark, December 16, 1937 (contained in Clark to
Hearst, December 23, 1937); Hearst Papers, carton 23 (under "1937 Samples").

10. Van Gorden's misdated letter of February 8 (see note 5, above) alludes to a more casual
arrangement between Loorz and Hearst than probably applied. Van Gorden told Loorz in a post-

LOORZ'S VISIT THAT DAY, his first since moving north, deserved a quick re-counting. Stolte got to hear about it when his partner wrote to him on February 12:

> I had a splendid interview with Mr. Hearst in the midst of a terrible storm and many leaks. He was in good spirits and seemed pleased to talk things over with me. He took me away from the guests in the Living Room [the Assembly Room] and we sat down in a corner by ourselves and talked things over. When I arrived on the job there was a painful excited letter about conditions in general but as you see it had all died down by the time we talked.

If the rain could seep through, why not someone's correspondence with Hearst? It almost sounded as if the letter had been posted in plain view. That un-doubtedly hadn't happened. Yet Loorz clearly was still in the know, still implicitly trusted.[11]

Morgan was on the job again on February 14, the Monday after Loorz was there. She had much to tell him by Tuesday, partly about the Recreation Wing, partly about inclement weather:

> I asked again that no one be taken off this crew [in the Wing] for repair work ex-cept "immediate disaster" response. I asked Ray Van Gorden to keep the storm damage labor and material on a separate sheet each week—amounts to be reim-bursed by Mr. Willicombe on our voucher. . . .
>
> It was fortunate we held off the order on the steel [window] sash above the the-atre [for the rooms in the Wing], as Mr. Hearst orders them all to be double, open-ing in, similar to the steel sash in "C" house. This eliminates screens.

Before signing off, she also said that Nigel Keep would be moving up in the world. He'd be getting the house vacated by the Loorzes in San Simeon, complete with backyard pool. Keep's old place, closer to the warehouses and scarcely more than a wooden shack, was marked for demolition.

Colonel Willicombe wrote to Loorz that same day, February 15. He knew that Thursday the seventeenth was apt to be Loorz's next visit. He wanted him to talk

---

script, "I phoned Mr. Willicombe the next day after our telephone conversation. He took your phone number and said if Mr. Hearst ever wanted you to come down he would get in touch with you."

11. In its Hearst/Morgan Correspondence, the Morgan Collection at Cal Poly has a tran-scribed copy of a letter from Hearst to Loorz, dated February 10, 1938—the Thursday on which Loorz appeared—but no version of that letter exists in the Loorz Papers. Hearst's letter marveled at the ferocity of the winter weather on The Enchanted Hill and called for measures to combat it, lest the buildings be unusable in the wind and rain. (Both collections, the Morgan and the Loorz, have earlier letters of Hearst's that addressed the same matter, his stays at San Simeon having shifted more toward the non-summer months ever since the late twenties.) Hearst made an unmistakable point at this moment in 1938: he regarded Wyntoon as a summer place and San Simeon as a winter counterpart.

with Hearst about two things the Chief was considering for the Neptune Pool—a "watershed roof on colonnades" along with "flood lights on corners of colonnades."

The first of those ideas may well have dominated when Loorz showed up. For the weather bore down with renewed vengeance. So much so that Van Gorden's words on Friday, February 18, came as no surprise when Loorz received them in Pacific Grove: "It is raining and blowing like hell here today." Fortunately, "A little water in the switchboard room at the Telegraph Office [is] the only complaint to this hour, 2 P.M." Loorz could visualize each drop. Had he not moved north, he'd be grappling every day with monsoonal conditions at San Simeon.

But in writing to Morgan on February 19 ("another trip to San Simeon and another storm weathered"), he indicated that he and Hearst had, in fact, discussed both matters regarding the Neptune colonnades (or the "pavillions," as the term is sometimes misspelled in these papers):

> Mr. Hearst has been noticing the pools of water on top of the pool pavillions and asked about a shed roof or something. When I explained that it was only because the drains were up about $2\frac{1}{2}$ inches to receive the finish marble roof and that all would drain then, he asked that inasmuch as we had the materials on hand couldn't we put those roofs on as soon as weather permitted. The answer, of course, is simple but in the meantime I asked Alex [Rankin] to unscrew the drain tops if possible without dismantling [them] and let the present water out.

The simple answer, presumably, was that Hearst couldn't afford the intensive labor required, despite having enough marble for the job. Loorz had more to report:

> He wanted you to think over the simplest method of installin[g] flood lights on the posts on top of the pavillions. He stated [that] the ones we have look and are temporary. He thot part of them could flood the temple and the other part the cascades and statuary group [*The Birth of Venus*]. He thot enough and preferable [preferably] reflected light would light the pool.
>
> He mentioned also that a few of the statues in front of the Castle (The seasons) etc should be set on simple permanent bases at an early date. His general remark [was] that it seemed like a small outlay would really make these items look completed.[12]

---

12. Two months later, while writing to Morgan, Hearst himself clarified the main subject of Loorz's paragraph. "Make bases and finish foundations on those four statues—SPRING-SUMMER-AUTUMN-WINTER—that are on either side of the stairways on the plaza [the Main Terrace] in front of the big house." From Hearst to Morgan, April 9, 1938; Hearst/Morgan Correspondence, Morgan Collection. The sculptures, long since removed from that area, are visible in several period photographs (some of them published).

Loorz touched on one more subject in wrapping up his report for Morgan. He assured her, "All hands seem to know what is wanted and are making progress on the ceiling [in Room #2] and recreation [wing] rooms in accordance with your instructions."

Another Monday visit by Morgan (February 21) led Ray Van Gorden to provide Loorz with another follow-up letter (February 22):

> Miss Morgan was here yesterday as per schedule, but since I was down to John's [John Vanderloo's mold shop, past the Roman Pool and Animal Hill] most of the afternoon, I did not get to see her. Suppose she was well satisfied with the progress as the boys say she spent only a short while up in the Rec. Wing Rooms. She must have spent some time with Mr. Hearst as she wasn't in the Archt's office [by the Service Wing].

Before Morgan returned a week later for the last Monday in February, tragedy struck. Two British subjects, Lord and Lady Plunket, were invited to the hilltop. They got no closer than the airstrip Loorz enlarged in 1935. Although the plane carrying them belonged to Hearst, it missed the fogbound runway and crashed, killing its pilot and the Plunkets.[13]

Jud Smelser, the waggish but steadfast insider, gave Loorz a rare glimpse of one person's response. He wrote on Sunday, February 27; the accident had occurred on Thursday:

> M.D. [Marion Davies] fainted in the picture show [in the Theater] last night, or passed out, I'm not sure which. She has really taken the crack up of the plane quite severely and has been in semi-hysterics on and off but then all of the Douras family [her real surname] are good at dramatics but I really feel that she is genuinely upset and hasn't the ability to control her emotions as we of the sturdy pioneer stock can do. It is rumored that W.R. plans to fly south to the funeral of the Plunket's and it is also rumored that he has grounded the rest of the planes for some time but I won't be able to verify these rumors until Monday [February 28] when I go after the mail and can talk it over with Pete Sebastian [at the general store in San Simeon].

---

13. Hearst called the accident "inexplicable." He said that the pilot "was competent," that he "had always passed every government technical test and requirement" and that he "had been physically examined the day before the accident occurred." The plane itself "was in perfect condition." Hearst could only conclude, "We do not know how or why" the accident happened. "We are overwhelmed with grief at the loss of our friends." From Hearst to the London Telegraph [newspaper], February 25, 1938; Hearst Papers, carton 25 (under "Lo-Lt").

Apart from current press coverage, followed by years of oral versions (heard locally and in Hollywood circles), accounts of the Plunket tragedy didn't appear in books for more than thirty years. The one in Fred Lawrence Guiles, *Marion Davies* (1972), pp. 300–02, was evidently the first. Davies herself was quoted on the subject in *The Times We Had* (1975), pp. 208, 210.

Loorz didn't mention the Plunkets or the crash when he answered Smelser on March 1. Yet he left no doubt of what prompted the quip, "Glad to know that you still rely on Pete Sebastian for verification."

In reality, the tragedy left few unaffected. "I neglected to mention the following when I saw you yesterday — too much airplane accident." Loorz had had those words for Morgan, whom he saw on Sunday, February 27, evidently in Monterey before she left by train for San Luis; his letter on Monday the twenty-eighth had coincided with her visit to the hilltop.[14] As for the "following" that he still needed to give her: mostly details concerning the Recreation Wing.

For the time being, this was a handy arrangement for these key players. Loorz stuck with his Thursdays at San Simeon, just as Morgan did with her Mondays.[15] Between those days, they met in Monterey (or perhaps in San Francisco) at least once or twice during this period. Sunday, March 13, for example, found him telling her, "Since I did not visit you last week end and our phone conversation was short, I did not mention drain covers." More dismal weather, more leaks and messes. "Perhaps Mr. Williams told you of a most unusual flood in the library [on the second floor of Casa Grande]. If not this is how it happened":

> During the heavy storms dirt got onto the drains in the [bell] towers and there was many inches of water standing on each level when Mark [Marks Eubanks] climbed up to make an investigation. He opened the drains and so much water spilled out of the leaders onto the porches outside of the Library, that dirt covered drains [clogged drains] here also failed to carry the water away and it backed up and over the door sills into the library and down the stairways [behind the Library].

Unbelievable! Water running over the teak floors and Persian carpets in that glorious room, with few but the ancient faces on Greek pottery to bear witness? Indeed, it happened. And there was more, much more, as Loorz kept telling Morgan on March 13:

> Also during this heaviest of rains the dirt covered [clogged] drains at the Celestial doors caused the water to back up and over the sills or thru the weepholes and onto the rugs as always. . . .

---

14. Morgan may have missed seeing Hearst on February 28. It was about then that he and Miss Davies went south for the Plunkets' funeral; but the latest round of wet weather prevented their attending the pilot's funeral, likewise held in the Los Angeles area. See *The Times We Had*, p. 210.

15. In writing to his parents on March 13, Loorz described his current pattern, along with telling them that "the weekly trip to San Simeon" had its drawbacks. "However," he went on to say, "the Hearst work combined with the work I have and will get near Cambria will make it worth while. I go down every Thursday and return Friday evening."

As to the drains in the towers. The dirt was largely debris from broken light bulbs and perhaps shades blown down. However, just so you'll know, mainly because it has been common practice to drop old bulbs to these levels when replacing with new ones on the tower. I have had them cleared up many times.

All told, Loorz had more than two pages of "storm damage" and other news to relate. Morgan couldn't have been pleased. Nobody could have. "From Mr. Williams and Mark[s]," he informed her at one point, "Mr. Hearst was aware of the accidental flood and nervously ordered prompt correction, hence my promptness in ordering same."

Amen, she must have said.[16]

THE LOORZ PAPERS, so essential to our grasp of events at San Simeon, start thinning out on that subject in March 1938. The Morgan Collection at Cal Poly and the private Morgan-Forney Collection help bridge the gaps. Both the former and the latter (each confirms the other here) indicate that, throughout March and April, Morgan held religiously to her pattern of visiting San Simeon each Monday. And by itself, the latter collection—the Morgan-Forney—indicates that after the third Monday in March and the second one in April, she continued south to Santa Monica. A new job there for Hearst and Davies, yielding the small "Garden Terraces" account (the last of eleven for the Beach House), had begun in the winter and would run through the spring.

That's welcome knowledge, to be sure. And yet the interpretive, explanatory, at times sharply slanted words that Morgan and others wrote—Loorz so often being the effusive one—provide a vital link, a connective tissue whose absence can make for a starved and limping organism, a documentary body in dire need of replenishment. Loorz's letter to Jim Rankin on March 29 offers some much-needed sustenance, no matter how bland:

> Miss Morgan has informed me that it will be okay to order the necessary pipes and fittings for roughing in the tower bathroom of the Recreation Wing. She insists, however, that you mail her office a copy of the order with the costs thereon. With the limited budget it is necessary that we know exactly where we stand at all times.
>
> We will now be able to let Alex [Rankin] proceed with the installation. He will

---

16. In the letter that Loorz sent his parents on March 13 (the same one mentioned in note 15), he had Pacific Grove in mind when he said, "Like all the rest of California it has been raining most of the time since we arrived." He also said, "I like to think that all this rain, in spite of the damage and lives lost means millions of dollars to California. For the previous few years, last year excepted, it has been too dry in this State."

be able to keep ahead of us with the help of one of our laborers for drilling concrete and handling his material.

Considering the crew on the job, Jim, we feel that we are making real progress.

The *small* crew is what Loorz meant, the *minuscule* crew. Pete Petersen, Frank Frandolich, John McFadden, Ray Van Gorden, John Vanderloo, Alex Rankin — there weren't many more now on the hilltop's daily roster. In addition, a few subcontractors and other outside workers still came and went sporadically.

The flow of letters remained sporadic, too.[17] Loorz finally dispatched a good one to Morgan on Saturday, April 30; it followed one of their weekend meetings, most likely held in Monterey:

> After our discussion last Sunday regarding the requests of the carpenters for the ten dollar [daily] scale, I thought it best to meet their demands without hesitation at this time.
>
> However, when I told them in a group that we would pay the $10 scale beginning next Monday [May 2], I said that we were doing it to avoid friction at this time. I also informed them that they [Hearst et al.] were seriously considering the transfer of the present budget from San Simeon to Wyntoon. I told them, further, that we have been working to the limit of the budget provided; therefore, if work was to continue at San Simeon, and the budget not increased, one man would have to go [be laid off] to take care of the advances. . . .
>
> I concluded the conversation by telling them that when San Jose, Salinas, and the general wage scale of the Northern district was $10 [per day] we would be in favor of that scale. In this case, the Bay Area is the only spot in the State where that [high a] scale exists.
>
> I advised them that inasmuch as there was now an active local union in San Luis Obispo County, we would, hereafter, set our scale at $1.00 above that of their local scale because of the inaccessibility of the Hilltop. We are now paying one dollar more than the present $8.00 scale.

---

17. Cal Poly has a relative rarity from this period: a letter from Hearst to Morgan in early April (a portion is quoted in note 12, above). He also mentioned the China Hill wall of 1937 (he hoped to extend it). More important, he said the general business climate seemed better now (despite the recession of 1937–38 and its crippling of the stock market in March). Therefore, the work they'd resumed at San Simeon could keep going. See Hearst to Morgan, April 9, 1938; Hearst/Morgan Correspondence, Morgan Collection.

In this same stretch, the Loorz Papers have a letter from Loorz to Stolte dated April 14, a Thursday. "As I mentioned on the phone last night, I'll be in San Simeon this afternoon, Cambria tomorrow [to check on some work there]. Then I have promised to drive the family over to Yosemite to see some snow. It will be a fast trip in order to get back for school Monday." Loorz said something else that stemmed from his lingering ties to the southern region. "The bid goes in tomorrow night on Santa Maria and I think we have a good figure."

Back when Loorz gave Morgan his long rundown on flood damage (March 13), he'd also told her that Pete Petersen thought the job was "hardly worth while," thanks to "no Saturday work, increased expenses etc." Although Petersen had "no intentions of walking out," he still let Loorz know he might be seeking better prospects.

And thus the final passages in Loorz's letter to Morgan on April 30 are as follows — in further summation of his talk with Petersen and the other men:

> Their reaction was pleasant. They understood and I am certain would not have walked out on us; however, the fact that we met their requests for the time being pleased them.
>
> I mentioned to Pete the possibility of moving him and his boys [his co-workers] to Wyntoon. I asked him not to mention it to the boys, because except for Otto Olson, I do not think it advisable to take the others to Wyntoon.
>
> He was pleased at the opportunity and knew his wife would be glad to move for a change. However, he wondered if he might lose the San Simeon house [across the street from Loorz's old home], in case he returned to San Simeon.
>
> I advised him that I thought we could pay him $12.00 per day at Wyntoon. Considering his [rent-free] home, that would be less than he received at San Simeon [in total compensation], but it is so difficult to reduce wages once high.[18]

The next day was May 1, a Sunday preceding yet another weekly appearance by Morgan at San Simeon. Her successive Monday visits — made through most of January, all of February, all of March, all of April — would continue with May 2 and 9 before finally skipping a beat. (No sign of her on May 16, and then a reappearance on the following Monday, May 23.) Long before that, though, back on May 1 itself, she wrote a telling letter headed "S.F. Train." Otherwise, she left it undated. But both the letter and its postmarked envelope were saved by the recipient, Elizabeth Boyter, who'd been in New York the past several years and who now hoped to find architectural work in California through Morgan, her old mentor and employer. Miss Morgan brought Miss Boyter up to date:

> Good draughtsmen are beginning to be in demand again. I know of none unemployed. So you will probably fall on some good opening. Am only sorry I cant say — "come right home," to us.

---

18. Petersen and his wife, Elsie, lived in the "duplex" in bayside San Simeon, the only one of the Spanish houses on the north side of the street. (Loorz's sons can't recall which side of the unit, east or west, was the Petersens'.)

Besides what Loorz told Morgan on December 14, 1937 (some excerpts appear on pp. 348–49), he mentioned Petersen in particular: "Actually I think he needs the work less than any of the others, for he has saved." He had saved a great deal, in fact, or was somehow blessed with sufficient means. In recent years he'd been making short-term loans to Loorz (starting with $1,000 twice in 1935, fol-

Jack Wagenet, Dick [Nusbaum], Ray Carlson & Warren McClure — (outside man) are still holding on — mostly on very reduced Hearst work, widely spread out.[19] It may finish with this year, although S.S. will not be, — never will be, — completed. There is a smattering of very small work for very fine old clients — & that is all. But one can never guess what is around the corner & we were born optimistic.[20]

So was Hearst, God knows. If not, the dark side of what Morgan told Boyter would have been even gloomier.

Morgan's letter, of course, falls outside the George Loorz Papers. But what better company for it to keep at this juncture? For their part, the Loorz Papers contain a letter from Jim Rankin on May 4 — in belated reply to the one Loorz sent him on March 29. Rankin touched on several points of mutual interest and concern:

George I havent been in San Simeon for so long, that I know it wont look the same since you have moved away — but here is hoping that we may all be there again some day as before. . . .

I haven't even been over to the [Morgan] office for a long time and it seems no one over there even J.M. knows much about the future of that work [for Hearst] either North or South —

I thought it rather strange on receipt of your letter [as] regards the work in the recreation [wing] going ahead — to receive a phone call shortly after from Mr LeFeaver stating he had a copy of the letter and to do nothing about it — [21] When I asked the reason he said they didn't know which way the wind was blowing — so that was all he could say and I havent heard anything since.

---

lowed by $2,000 in 1936). These were to help Loorz launch the new San Simeon branch of the F. C. Stolte Co. As of 1938, the two friends were still financially involved — amicably, by all indications.

19. See p. 283, note 107; see also p. 293: Nusbaum to Loorz, January 30, 1937. At the end of 1937, when Morgan wrote to another woman she had once employed, Dorothy Wormser Coblentz, she mentioned that year's "office adjustments" (in reference perhaps to changes that had involved Wagenet, Nusbaum, and others since 1936). Excerpts from Morgan's letter appear in *The Julia Morgan Architectural History Project*, Vol. II, pp. 123, 124.

20. From Morgan to Boyter, undated (but with its envelope postmarked May 1, 1938); Elizabeth M. Boyter Papers, Bancroft Library.

The letter also mentions Charlotte Knapp. She was another woman who'd been part of Morgan's "office family" and who, within the past week, had done some spot work for the firm: seven hours of follow-up drafting devoted to the Kings Daughters Home in Oakland. By then the F. C. Stolte Co. had completed its part of "Additions to Laundry," as the job was called in Morgan-Forney. (This was the third of four Kings Daughters jobs Morgan had between 1924 and 1941; the Stolte Co. had the contract on the second and the third ones, the Men's Building and the Laundry; see p. 216, note 125, and p. 243, note 25.)

21. Not only the Morgan office but also Ray Van Gorden had received copies of the Loorz-Rankin letter of March 29. Rankin's comment on May 4 prompted Loorz to tell him five days later, "It *was* a funny change to my order regarding the recreation wing. Miss M. was so certain it was okay the day before [March 28]. I wondered myself; that is why I sent a copy to the office."

Rankin also said he'd seen Harry Thompson several times lately. But when he said, "I think he is now on a pretty good job," he didn't mean at Wyntoon or any-place else for the Stolte Co. No, things had changed for no-nonsense Harry. He'd left the fold for good.

Ray Van Gorden wrote to Loorz the same day Rankin did, Wednesday, May 4. His tidings were of the more enticing kind, a welcome break from construc-tion news alone:

> Mr. Hearst and Miss Davies arrived at 5 P.M. yesterday and Bill & Randolph [two of his sons] & wives at about noon. They are all that are here for the present. That surely was some party they had at Santa Monica [for Hearst's seventy-fifth birth-day on April 29]. 300 guests in all—it seemed about all the picture colony of Hol-lywood besides his newspaper men [were there].

He also told Loorz, "Miss Morgan was in extra good humor this last Monday. Maybe it was because she thought the carpenters are now satisfied."

WYNTOON AND MCCLOUD —those names were increasingly on everyone's lips. Loorz hadn't been there since 1931.[22] He'd seen plenty of photographs, though, pored over plenty of drawings, read just as many letters, heard even more fish sto-ries and tall tales. By this time in early May, free of the daily grind at San Simeon and well settled in Pacific Grove, he was ideally equipped to check on Wyntoon for Hearst and Morgan. Northward he went at their behest.

He spent two days there, probably May 5 and 6; immediately afterward, he went down to San Simeon to see Hearst. Both episodes got his correspondence flowing.[23] Back in Pacific Grove by Sunday, May 8, he wrote to Eugene Kower, who was well into his fourth year as full-time caretaker at Wyntoon. He also wrote to Mac McClure, now in his sixth year there, albeit on a seasonal basis.

Loorz told Gene Kower, "I had the extreme pleasure of reporting to Miss Morgan, Mr. Willicombe and Mr. Hearst the splendid condition in which I care-fully observed Wyntoon.[24] The place shows evidence of careful management, even with a small crew." Both Hearst and Willicombe thought that Kower had things

---

22. See p. 189 in this volume, note 71.

23. Jud Smelser, San Simeon's head chauffeur and utility man, wrote to Loorz on May 6. "Everything seems to be doing nicely here except the coffers," he said. "God only knows what hap-pened to them of late they almost seem to be non-existent." He also mentioned some of Hearst's five sons. "Two of the boys are here now. Randolph and Bill Jr. They are giving the cars hell as usual." And then he said, "It looks like Wyntoon soon. Guess I'll never get to Pac. Grove."

24. Morgan, however, was not at San Simeon (as Hearst and Willicombe were) when Loorz gave his report. She had last been there on Monday, May 2, and would next appear on the following Monday.

"well in hand" and that he was "particularly qualified for the position." It wasn't "*Blarney*," Loorz assured him. "I talked to each separately and I believe their remarks most sincere."[25]

And yet Loorz and Kower weren't old friends. They'd just met in person for the first time. In contrast, the letter Loorz wrote Mac the same day fell squarely within the tell-all tradition:

> Mr. Hearst was pleased to hear that we are doing something at Wyntoon. He wants it to go faster, however, and is willing to stop any department at San Simeon to do more up there. I see that we can look forward to an increased budget for the time being at least. From the intonations in his voice I gather that he is making this budget with an ill-afforded gesture. Frankly he did not look too happy and well to me. Perhaps the reaction from an exciting party [in Santa Monica] on his birthday [the weekend before], together with the various and sundry ramifications that always accompany such parties. . . .
>
> Mr. Hearst would like the two front towers [on Angel House in the Bavarian Village] promptly but does not care if we dont even start those on the rear.

Earlier in his letter, Loorz had told Mac he didn't think Bridge House would see any renewed efforts in 1938. "However, one never can tell with this organization."

Loorz wrote to the McCloud River Lumber Co. on May 8 as well, spelling out some new arrangements in the wake of his trip north—and his follow-up trip that had taken him south:

> We are resuming construction at Wyntoon on a small scale this year and will therefore be purchasing various materials.
>
> From Mr. Kower, you will know that the F. C. Stolte Co. will not handle the work this year. Though I own half that company, I will manage the work as Superintendent of Construction, as an individual.
>
> For economical reasons the small amount of work will be handled by transferring our San Simeon Crew.
>
> To make certain there will be no mix-up in the billing etc. kindly keep all records entirely separate from the Hearst Sunical Account or the W. R. Hearst Private [Account] which will exist during Mr. Hearst's anticipated visit.
>
> This [new] account will therefore be known as the W. R. Hearst Construction [Account] c/o Geo. C. Loorz. Please send invoices in triplicate to Wyntoon. Invoices will be checked and approved, if correct, and sent to Julia Morgan, Arch's office in San Francisco for payment.

---

25. Kower wrote back to Loorz on May 12. He said in part, "Am naturally pleased that chief is satisfied—thats my job—and handing on the good word is not the usual—Thanks."

There it was in a nutshell—a summation of how the work at San Simeon had long been pursued, a simple blueprint (despite the multiple accounts or "funds") for the approach they'd now be using at Wyntoon. It meant, of course, that the cost-plus days were over, the days involving Fred Stolte and the company he and Loorz still owned. In lieu of that previous arrangement, George Loorz would be reprising his former role at San Simeon on a new stage, a much smaller stage, to be sure, flanked by a much smaller cast.[26]

No more Stolte Co. at Wyntoon also meant no more Harry Thompson. Jim Rankin's letter of May 4 had intimated as much. Loorz answered it on May 9:

> Yes, Jim, I always have liked Harry very much. I even enjoyed working with him [at San Simeon, for instance, in the early thirties]. I understood his blunt, yet honest, statements he is addicted to making at certain times. Harry's efficiency and loyalty is beyond question; his honesty likewise. He is not masterful in the art of soft soap, the one reason he was not called back to Wyntoon, so far as I can see.[27] Give him my kindest personal regards when you see him.

Mac McClure, by writing to Loorz on May 10 (in reply to his letter of May 8), continued the renewed dialogue:

> I am glad to hear that Earl [Tomasini] is coming.[28] He was here during the party last year and knows the place etc., and we like him.

---

26. An undated note of May 1938, written to Loorz by his secretary, Conrad Gamboni, is headed "Bid on Wyntoon Sash." It suggests that Stolte may have appeared briefly on the McCloud that year. "Mr. Stolte wants you to talk to him before letting this work [windows for Angel House]." Gamboni also reported, "He says that they can be carted up there for about $50-$60—He will bring back a load of our stuff."

Months later—October 2—Stolte told Loorz, "I think it would be a good idea to get our [remaining] equipment from McCloud. We could use a lot of it now, especially the saw and the wheelbarrows etc." But it's unclear if Stolte himself or anyone else went north for that purpose. By then, the windows Gamboni mentioned had long since been delivered. The year-end Trial Balance for the Alameda office cites $35 in costs next to "McCloud," for which $55 was collected. That tiny but profitable job was the sole instance of any work for Hearst by the Stolte Co. in 1938 (as contrasted with Loorz's independent work).

27. Thompson could only have gone back, though, on independent terms, there being no provision in 1938 for anyone, not even Loorz, to work at Wyntoon on behalf of the F. C. Stolte Co.

28. Loorz's letter of May 8 had alerted Mac that Tomasini would be en route from San Simeon—in the course of which he would "bring up the very fine [iron] lamp Standards that Val [Georges] made." Loorz was sure that Tomasini, who had been with him for "a long time and was a good worker," would cooperate fully with Mac and with Gene Kower.

Loorz also mentioned Tomasini in writing to Morgan on May 10. "You will recognize him from his work on the Hill and at Jolon, and as watchman last summer at Wyntoon. He worked for a long time as helper for [John] McFadden, Dell [Clausen], and for another mason we had on the hill."

[Willy] Pogany's men were back for a day last week to do some touching up on their pictures [the exterior murals in the Bavarian Village]. They thought they would all be back for a Summer's work soon![29]

Since Mac didn't mail his letter until Wednesday, May 11, he got to add a postscript: "A letter from Miss Morgan this A.M. [dated May 10] mentions an itemized program both here and at San Simeon. Under the circumstances, I think we had better keep the laborer who is helping Tony Vietti plus Earl Tomasini."

Morgan also wrote to Loorz on May 10. Her similar words probably arrived in Pacific Grove the next day, coinciding with Mac's receipt of her letter.[30] (She, too, received a letter on May 11 — from Loorz, likewise dated May 10. "Missed you Sunday," went his opening, an allusion most likely to their Monterey connection. "Mr. Hearst apparently pleased with starting work at Wyntoon." Enough so, said Loorz, after his recent trip to the hilltop, for him to suggest that Hearst "would prefer shifting all activity from San Simeon" for Wyntoon's sake. However, "From his remarks I conclude there is little or no hopes of an increased budget this year.")

Morgan's letters of May 10 stemmed from her own trip to San Simeon on Monday the ninth. The one to Loorz went as follows:

It is decided that

1. Gyorgy is to paint at San Simeon all summer.

2. John Vanderloo and an apprentice helper, and Frank Frandolich and helper, are to cast and set stone at San Simeon all summer.

3. Ceiling and mantel work [in the Recreation Wing] is to stop with this week at San Simeon.

4. [Pete] Petersen, plus those you arrange to send, are to go up as soon as possible to Wyntoon.

5. Enough more stone men are to be employed as needed to make all possible advancement on the two front Sleeping Beauty house [Angel House] turrets, and front entrance, — and from there go onto Bridge [House] gate.

---

29. The artist Willy Pogany first appears in the annals of Wyntoon in 1935; he and his crew did their major work on Brown Bear and Cinderella House in the summer and fall of 1936 (when Hearst was gone from California). See the "Hearst" feature in *Fortune* (October 1935), p. 44. See also Hearst to Morgan, September 18, 1935; Morgan to Hearst, August 5, 1936; and Morgan to Hearst, November 11, 1936 — all in the Hearst/Morgan Correspondence, Morgan Collection. The same archives has Willicombe to Pogany (Morgan's copy), May 21, 1937, in the separate Wyntoon file (III/06/09/05). Sara Boutelle's chapter on Wyntoon in *Julia Morgan* includes color photographs of the Pogany murals; so does Sally Woodbridge's article in *Architectural Digest* (January 1988).

30. Morgan's copy of her letter to Mac was probably in her files once — if the original was typewritten. (The letter she also wrote Loorz suggests it was.) But in the surviving papers that form the Morgan Collection, the carbon version of what she sent Mac is nowhere to be found. Nor is her carbon of what Loorz received.

6. Mr. Hearst says bridge will have to be raised this Fall, which means looking out for necessary changes in the footings of the Bridge [House] gate.[31]

7. Thinking it over, if carpenters can be up early in week, they can start right in on turret framing [on Angel House], propping up, or cantering out, until stone work is [put] up.

8. I will go up when sure the workers are up there.

But why the emphasis now on Wyntoon? The question poses itself in mid-narrative. The answer is simple, fundamental, unignorable. Because Hearst knew he could stay there—and, never forget, because he also knew he could *build* there, thus indulging a ceaseless passion—more affordably on his "personal" account than he could at San Simeon.

Loorz got back to Mac McClure on May 14, discussing the game plan for Wyntoon. An early passage in that Saturday letter shows that nicknames can be confusing: "In addition to stone work, Mac should be very useful since he can do anything from running the crusher to electrical work." The sentence wasn't mispunctuated or lacking some words. John *McFadden* was the man in question, not Warren *McClure*. Luckily, it's a fine point that seldom arises.

"As it now stands," Loorz continued, "I don't expect to come very often. You will enjoy Miss Morgan's weekly visit starting early next week." (Sure enough, she finally broke her Mondays-at-San Simeon pattern. She didn't go there on May 16; instead, she went to Wyntoon on Wednesday, May 18, her first trip north during the new season.)

There was more for Loorz to tell Mac—Mac McClure, of course—in his letter of Saturday the fourteenth:

By the time this reaches you, [Paul] Catelli and [John] McFadden should be on the job. They can start the other tower and the entrance [for Angel House]. Pete [Petersen] and Otto Olson should arrive some time Monday [May 16], as well, to start tearing out in preparation for the towers and entrance piers.[32]

Personally, I would not have sent the carpenters until the stone work was a little

---

31. As the brackets indicate, Morgan's capitalized *Bridge* in this sentence and the preceding one (#5) refers to Bridge House; the lower-case *bridge*, earlier in sentence #6, refers to an actual bridge, which adjoins Bridge House and spans the McCloud River.

32. Van Gorden confirmed the men's departure from San Simeon when he wrote Loorz on Tuesday, May 17: "Pete, Mac & Otto [Petersen, McFadden, and Olson] left Saturday as per schedule." In turn, Mac McClure told Loorz: "Olsen [Olson], McFadden and Catelli arrived this morning." Mac probably wrote that line on Monday, May 16, the men's first day on the job; yet he misdated his letter May 12. He had some other news just the same, concerning Angel House: "Roof covers are being removed also the plaster piers at either side of front entrance." Mac also told Loorz, "The river is about a foot higher and rising due to heat and rainy weather."

farther on, but I had no choice in the matter. Mr. Hearst is very anxious to get the towers up quickly and get at the Bridge House, and J.M. insisted on the men "right now."

"Laid off al[l] but five men at San Simeon," Loorz also told Mac on Saturday. He didn't specify who did the laying off, but John Vanderloo, Ray Van Gorden, and Frank Frandolich were among the survivors:

> This brings San Simeon to a standstill, except—I am to get a crew on immediately and repair the Jolon road [the Burnett Road]. It was too rough on a picnic last Wednesday [May 11].
>
>   Mr. Hearst was in excellent spending fetter and in high spirit in a brief but enjoyable interview Thursday evening, oh me![33]

Loorz spent his usual night away from home after seeing Hearst. For he also said to Mac, "Bill Murray jumped me yesterday in San Simeon [on Friday, May 13] about the two men we understood Mr. Kower was to pay."[34] Along with conveying that and other last-minute details, Loorz signed off by saying, "Just received a set of the Angel House plans. Will send you my suggestions regarding the framing early next week."

Morgan wrote to Loorz on Thursday, May 19, saying she was "just in from Wyntoon":

> It was necessary to take out the stone-work done,—no strength in the mortar and shape lost for lack of cutting, etc., due to each man working according to his lights.
>
>   I put McFadden in charge of stone work, to lay out however [by whatever means] with Petersen, which looked as though it would work.

Her next passage, though probably well-enough intended, must have stung a bit:

> Your third floor roof, etc. drawings came while I was there. Don't bother with any more as you haven't the facts in detail. In this case the hip does not come onto the opening but onto the untouched front plate.

---

33. "Certainly Sunical must pay for this work," Hearst declared, "which is necessary, as the roads are almost impassable." Those were his words for Willicombe, who relayed them to Loorz on May 16. The cost was slated to be $1,500. Hearst also thought Sunical should pay for a small maintenance job on Orchard Hill.

34. Mac's letter to Loorz of "May 12" (the misdated one in note 32) confirms that Gene Kower made the payment in question. Loorz was compliant when he replied on May 18. He had to tell Mac, though, "I fear it would complicate matters to ask Miss Morgan's office to do this [reimburse Kower], and I want to be certain that we start off with the proper system." He knew well of what he spoke (and perhaps Mac did, too)—from years of dealing with tangled accounts at San Simeon.

She closed by telling Loorz, "Progress is going to be very slow and will not re-quire more than far spaced visits." And then she commented, "Weather was fine and the place as a whole looks very well."

True, she wouldn't go north again till late June, but she had some other visits to make right away. It was Thursday when she wrote Loorz from San Francisco; she'd be at the Beach House on Sunday and at San Simeon on Monday.

Before she made that southern loop, Loorz heard from Mac McClure; his letter was headed "Wyntoon Fri—May 20th 38" and began with a reference to Morgan:

> The lady visited us on Wednesday, as you probably know. She was just so-so and made us tear down one corner turret [on Angel House] which was entirely up. The stones didn't have the "right feeling." She put McFadden in charge of the stone masons and after she left he told me, just as Tony [Vietti] did, that it was almost impossible to get results from the old castle rock pile [salvaged after the Maybeck-Phoebe Hearst structure burned in 1930].—So we are digging into the old quarry that the Bend material [for the Charles Wheeler place] came from. Also we are to make a concrete core for the turrets which Pete and Olson are now framing. She seemed particularly anxious to get them cutting into the corners on second & third floors.
>
> I was disappointed to learn you would not be up again unless absolutely neces-sary. Your visits would have been bright spots in a dull summer.
>
> Apparently, she will be giving us her close personal supervision. It doesn't look to me like the work is going to progress as fast as expected. The stone work, care-fully cut and fitted as she desires will take plenty of time. The bridge entrance has considerable ornamental work. The idea now is to bring John Van der Loo [Vanderloo] up and cast it here.
>
> Be discreet in quoting me to J.M. also better not let on that you have heard the news before she tells me. You know the reactions.

The renewed pen pals, Loorz and McClure, wrote to each other on May 23, the same Monday that found Morgan at San Simeon after being in Santa Monica. Loorz led off by telling Mac, "You can be assured that I shall be extremely cautious in quoting you to J.M.":

> It now appears that she will handle the job herself [exclusively through her office], so I will have very little to do with it. I think this is her choice. Frankly, I would rather have nothing at all to do with it than to be connected as I am. I think that is is [sic] only because of Mr. Hearst's suggestion that I am in the picture at all.
>
> Saw Mr. Hearst Thursday [May 19] and had a very pleasant two hours with him. Asked a lot of questions about progress at Wyntoon. Mostly which I could not answer intelligently. Sorry that I told him the stone work of one tower was nearly ready for carpenters. . . .

Why they put a concrete core in the turrets [of Angel House] is beyond me. You could use it for an anchor to hold down, for certain, [but] it will take no weight with the cantilever condition that exists. I am only remarking, Mac, as I have nothing to say about it.

Loorz said in closing, "Have to appear in San Luis as a witness in the ostrich deal tomorrow. How I dread that — especially, when I have so much to do."[35]

Mac's letter to Loorz, also dated May 23, mentioned the work being done by Pete Petersen and John McFadden. Mac further reported, "Forney and Rounds are here going over the antique situation and the expectation is that they will be here a week or two."

H. C. Forney, better known as Jim Forney, was the husband of Lilian Forney, who had been Morgan's secretary since 1924. (The Forneys were roughly the same age as Loorz and McClure.) Jim Forney had been synonymous with one of Morgan's extra-architectural efforts in recent years — the improved cataloguing of Hearst's art collection at San Simeon and Wyntoon.[36] C. C. Rounds (Charlie Rounds informally) had succeeded Chris McGregor as head of the Hearst warehouses in the Bronx. Following Hearst's loss of face and financial autonomy in 1937 — his abdication, as some were calling it — Rounds became a central figure in the juggling about and, increasingly, the liquidation of almost countless objects owned by Hearst. Rounds had more lists and schedules, more inventories and appraisals to contend with now than most museum curators ever see in a lifetime.[37]

---

35. Loorz was referring to the civil suit filed by Jesse Zelda in 1937; see p. 308, note 31.

36. Several entries in the Morgan-Forney ledgers reflect Jim Forney's travels and other activities related to this work. Forney spent time at San Simeon, for instance, in the fall of 1935; he also went to New York once, late in 1936. Between those dates he was at Wyntoon more often, and then again in 1937. Certain other trips weren't recorded, like the one to Wyntoon that Mac McClure mentioned at this point in 1938.

37. Things had changed immensely in such matters in just a year's time. In the spring of 1937, while Chris McGregor was still at the Bronx helm, he informed Hearst that *The New Yorker* wanted to publish "a short piece about the warehouse." McGregor seemed pleased, yet Hearst was plainly aghast. He made sure McGregor knew it:

No kidding, — but I am surprised that you should submit the suggestion of the NEW YORKER Magazine to write up our warehouse. Tell them positively NO, and do not give them any reason for the NO. The warehouse belongs to the International Studio Art Corporation [a Hearst subsidiary], and that corporation does [not] want any short pieces or long pieces or any other kind of pieces in the NEW YORKER.

Just between you and me, in the present state of things such an article would be merely an invitation to some red nut to come around and start something. For a little round ball could be fired through a window and go off with a loud noise and a lot of damage.

Let us now not boast of our wordly possessions. Get me?

From McGregor to Hearst, May 15, 1937, and from Hearst to McGregor, May 19, 1937; Hearst Papers, Carton 23 (under "1937 Samples"). Hearst's point at that juncture was well taken for a few

His resident counterpart at San Simeon was the crotchety, often small-minded W. R. Williams. Jim Forney, as Morgan's bright and able proxy, provided more fitting company for Rounds. In turn, Forney's appearances at Wyntoon and San Simeon in a touch-and-go, post-climactic year for Hearst like 1938 proved that Morgan was just as entangled in this part of Hearst's life as she'd ever been. It was a rare burden for any architect to bear, yet an irresistible and compelling one.

Jim Forney and Charlie Rounds weren't the only jugglers in this circus that was Hearstdom. Morgan's other Jim—Jim LeFeaver, still part of the office "family"—wrote to Loorz on May 25, revealing how much of a high-wire act the efforts at Wyntoon had become:

> You apparently overlooked our inquiry about the six day week which the men are working there. If they went up there [from San Simeon] with the understanding that they were to work six days per week, of course we will have to continue on that basis, but we will have to make adustments somewhere else. If, however, no arrangement to that effect was made with them, it will probably be more satisfactory to stick to the now standard five day week.
>
> It certainly will enable us to come nearer maintaining our present number of employees with the budget available.

How puny *was* the allotment from Hearst? The annals don't say, the records are too thin. But with hairs like these being constantly split, it couldn't have been much. San Simeon's $15,000 per month in the first part of 1937—and even the much smaller amount that Wyntoon was getting then—seem positively royal compared with what now prevailed.

Loorz and Mac exchanged letters again on May 27. LeFeaver's message had reached Pacific Grove, and Loorz hastened to tell Mac about the preferred five-day week.[38] Mac shared a different brand of news. He told Loorz, "A letter from J.M. Wed [May 25] said that Mr H would be up alone late in the week (she didn't say what week) and that the party would be up in 3 weeks or so. No further word on the subject."

By all indications, Hearst stayed put at San Simeon.

---

more days; after that (as his financial crisis began boiling over), most bets were off. The warehouse's address in the South Bronx gave the article its title: "387 Southern Boulevard." *The New Yorker* ran it in "The Talk of the Town" section on November 6, 1937, p. 15.

38. The lean budget at Wyntoon meant that Mac had more to do than draw plans; he was also helping to steer the ship. Examples include his letter to Loorz on May 10 (pp. 367–68), in which he further said, "Earl [Tomasini] hasn't arrived yet, but will turn up soon, no doubt. I have thought up several jobs he can do so will keep him busy." Loorz's reply of May 14 (pp. 369–70) began on that note. "You are exactly correct in using Earl as you mentioned [mainly on stone and concrete work]. . . . Use him to best advantage wherever you think best."

But initiative could have a price, as Mac told Loorz on May 11. "The salary question for Tony

RAY VAN GORDEN wrote to Loorz on Tuesday, June 7. He had the latest news for his friend, straight from the hilltop, where Hearst had spent most of his time in 1938—despite a dreary winter, a shocking plane crash, and a dearth of funds:

> Mr. Hearst and all the party left here at 4 P.M. yesterday. Marks [Eubanks] said he was going to Chicago and from there probably on to New York. They didn't leave a check for the [Burnett] road work but will probably send it in due time.[39] I thought Miss Morgan would surely be here yesterday to see him, but she didn't show up. Mr. Williams received a letter from her and she told him she didn't think she would be here.

Van Gorden also spoke of some work being done then on the Italian cypresses, those midnight-green, columnar trees that accentuate the grounds near the Neptune Pool and the Grand Entrance. The height of the trees required an old-fashioned approach—the use of scaffolding:

> Jake [Alfred Jacobson] moved [the scaffolds] up by the Dressing Room[s] yesterday, although there are still two more trees on the lower north terrace. The tree man says this is a permanent job—that the wire [used to bind the cypresses] will not break and that it will last for years and all that will have to be done in the future is trim the trees [to the wire hooping].

Loorz wrote to Jim LeFeaver in San Francisco on that same late-spring Tuesday, June 7:

> Please note that I am more than willing to make the trip [to Wyntoon] at any time. For economical reasons the expense of such trips is to be considered with our present limited budget. I have no desire to go unless I can actually be of service. . . .
>
> You will be interested to know that the ranch [the Hearst Sunical office] refused to allow the budget for the road work that Mr. Hearst requested.

Hearst therefore planned to make a series of "personal payments accordingly."[40] Loorz signed off by telling LeFeaver, "Have been hoping to see Miss Mor-

---

[Vietti] and his local helper is still unsettled. Kower has received no O.K. from Murray yet. I hate to start advancing funds from my own pocket to keep them going."

39. In fact, Willicombe had already sent Loorz the first of six monthly installments ($250 each). He did so on June 4, commenting that Hearst would be "reimbursed later by the Sunical Land & Packing Company."

40. The payments, whether personal or corporate, would be the monthly amounts of $250 (as in note 39). The new twist here wasn't that the road work might not take place (it had already started, through a newly revived Hilltop Fund) but rather that Hearst might not be reimbursed (he eventually was). On the other hand, Bill Murray of Hearst Sunical had approved company payment of the "Cypress Tree Scaffold Job"—the hilltop project that involved Jake Jacobson and that Ray Van Gorden mentioned to Loorz on June 7.

gan here in Monterey some week end. Will try to get up to S.F. this week before going South [to San Simeon again]."

Mac had an update for Loorz on June 10—the kind that sounded as though, somehow, life would just keep inching along:

> Everything is going smoothly enough up here. Progress is very slow but surely as much as one could expect from a small crew. I believe it will take the whole summer to complete the turrets new entrance [on Angel House], and Bridge [House] gateway—I mean, with tiles in place—stucco and timbering etc.

When Loorz answered on Monday, June 13, he had other things to say about those same projects at Wyntoon:

> Mac, would [you] please caution the boys to mark on their [time] cards the job that they are on as well as the kind of work? So far as I know, there will be but two jobs [to report]; Angel House and Bridge Gateway. We have assumed that you have done no work on the Gateway, as yet, and have charged all to Angel House.

And then came this passage in Loorz's letter to Mac, part of which sounds more serious than it was (the episode did not involve Morgan herself):

> Talked to Miss Morgan yesterday via telephone for the first time in over a month. Was very sorry to hear about the automobile accident. I only heard about every fourth word so I still know little about it.[41]

Loorz didn't dwell on the matter. He skipped ahead. It remained for this next passage to dominate his letter of June 13:

> You will be interested to know that I have a small budget for repairing the Jolon road. Other things at San Simeon very quiet. I only hope Frandy [Frank Frandolich] doesn't go to sleep, fall, and hurt himself while he is waiting for John [Vanderloo] to cast stone. Mr. Hearst told me to set a number of statues [newly made

---

41. Mac gave an account of things while writing to Loorz on June 18 (beyond the excerpts further on in this chapter):

> The accident you partially heard about was this: While Rounds and Forney were here, Kower was to provide them with a car which R could drive (J.M.'s arrangement). On Sunday [June 12?] they decided to take a trip out toward Birney [Burney] Falls (Kower's suggestion). On way back the car decided to leave the highway and try to dislodge a big stump which was alongside which caused an immediate depreciation in the car value of $387 and several aches and pains to Rounds and Forney (none serious). The alarming development was that W.R.H. cars are not insured against anything but liability and that R & F are expected to fork over $387. . . . Anyway it was a very expensive trip.

It's unknown whether Rounds and Forney heard Mac's opinion — or acted upon it: "If I were they I believe I would refuse to pay anything."

cast-stone lamp standards] on the west terrace. This would be work for Frank, but I certainly would not proceed without consulting J.M. Her attitude yesterday was that the setting was too expensive even to consider at this time.

He took a new tack when he wrote to Mac again two days later; by then it was Wednesday, June 15:

> Fred and I were discussing our future plans for expansion Sunday and decided that it was quite possible for us to use your services to advantage to both of us. This, of course, assumed [assuming] the Hearst work would stop.
>
> On the heels of this assumption comes word from Miss Morgan late last night that all Hearst work would shut down about the end of the month. . . .[42]
>
> No doubt, Miss Morgan will advise you of the impending shut-down, so I ask that you wait for her word before notifying the other men.

Loorz wrote to Morgan on the fifteenth also. She had asked him to join her at San Simeon the following Monday, June 20; he said he'd be glad to. "Why can't you plan on spending the weekend in Monterey and on driving down with me early Monday morning?" Then he described the drive down the Big Sur coast—more realistically than he had when the highway first opened and he was burning rubber every mile: "I usually leave around seven which puts me in San Simeon about nine-thirty."

He had a final line for Morgan, one that hit the nail straight on the head. "I am not at all surprised about the shut-down, in fact, I have marvelled how Mr. Hearst has continued as he has."

Morgan made sure Mac got the official news of the shutdown. "We are to finish by July 1st or so," he confirmed when he wrote back to Loorz on June 16. "Of course we will not be finished and will do well to get the frames set and walls & roofs sheathed and papered. Tiling or half timbering is out of the question."

---

42. Morgan herself had received the news about a week after the Hearst party left California for points east. From an unspecified place (most likely the Ritz Tower, New York), Willicombe wired a "night letter" to Jean Henry in Los Angeles:

> Do not send July remittance to Miss Morgan and do not send any more [money] unless you hear from me otherwise.
>
> 2. Chief has requested her to finish all work [her work at San Simeon and Wyntoon, as distinct from separate pursuits like the Burnett Road] and do nothing further after June thirtieth.
>
> 3. Tell [Al] Russell [Hearst's pilot] that Chief has instructed Charlie Mayer [of the *San Francisco Examiner*] to sell small plane and trimotor and lay up Vultee.
>
> 4. We leave tonight for Baltimore, Maryland, Belvedere Hotel. Will keep you informed.

From Willicombe to Henry, June 12, 1938; Hearst Papers, carton 26 (under "Henry, Jean"). The telegram had a fifth entry as well, pertaining to a back payment of $5,000 that Hearst planned to make to an art dealer.

Following that comment, Mac alluded to Loorz's last letter. "You were right on presuming that the [latest] work was all on Angel Ho[use].—All we have done on Bridge Gate was to dig a hole (and fill it in again)." And then came a paragraph in the best McClure tradition, one of those that we're so much the richer for having:

> I suppose you saw the big newspaper spread about the Hearst Realty—subdivision and sale of Triunfo Ranch north [by west] of L.A. [near Thousand Oaks and Lake Sherwood], etc. Lots of work for somebody in building roads and laying in utilities etc.

"Incidentally," he told Loorz in closing, "Miss M's note [about the shutdown] said that it would be better for you to notify the crew here so I have not spilled the beans yet."

MORGAN THANKED LOORZ for offering to drive her to San Simeon on Monday the twentieth. She began with such words on June 16. But she also said she wouldn't be needing a ride—she'd be "coming up the other direction." Coming up from where, though? From San Luis Obispo, following the usual train trip down the Salinas Valley? Perhaps that's all she meant. She had last been to Santa Monica in late May and wouldn't be going there again in 1938. On the other hand, having just started the preliminary, drawing-board warm-ups on a new job for Hearst and Miss Davies, she needed to check the building concerned—the Cosmopolitan bungalow, still at Warner Bros. in Burbank (after its move from MGM in Culver City in 1934). Even though Davies had left the silver screen in 1937, Hearst's film company, Cosmopolitan Productions, remained active; and the bungalow remained one of its prime assets. Morgan's role stemmed from Hearst's hopes of finding a new home for the bungalow (in concert with his seeking a new studio to associate with in his post-Warner phase, which would soon be upon him). Several months later, the transition would entail another awkward, improbable trucking of the bungalow—from Burbank back through Cahuenga Pass to the Beverly Hills side of the Los Angeles area.[43]

Morgan was in Burbank on June 22, two days after the Monday she and Loorz spent at San Simeon.[44] Perhaps her plans changed after she wrote him the previous

43. Because of its multiple addresses (more than just the well-known ones in Culver City and Burbank), the Cosmopolitan bungalow has been assigned to "Los Angeles" in the summary section of Appendix A, p. 535. The bungalow's specific addresses in 1933–34 and in 1938–39 appear on pp. 541–42 and p. 544 of the same appendix.

44. The date June 22 is from the Morgan-Forney ledgers. Tuesday, June 21 seems likelier, though, for her visit to Burbank: the day after she was at San Simeon on June 20 and two days, not just one, before she appeared at Wyntoon on Thursday, June 23.

Thursday, June 16. In any event, she had told Loorz that they'd be discussing Wyntoon, not just San Simeon, when they met on Monday, June 20. (At the very least, she wanted to "get the work begun on the Angel House completed.")

Pending those things, more news from the firing line — or *lines*, since it came from both ends of the spectrum. Ray Van Gorden compiled a full page of details for Loorz on Friday, June 17, in time to reach him before he went south:

> I'm very sorry to advise that Mr. William's [*sic*] men broke a Marble Statue, I think, beyond repair yesterday. They were moving it in the big Ford Truck and it got away from them, I suppose when they were unloading it at the Temple [by the Neptune Pool]. This is only a supposition, however, although I did see the statue and it is pretty much broken up. I'm sure it will be a blow to both Miss Morgan and Mr. Hearst. . . .[45]
>
> I have been keeping plenty busy helping both John and Frandy [John Vanderloo and Frank Frandolich] but that is just what I like. We have everything completed on the West Terrace with the exception of two Caryatids [cast-stone lamp standards] and have one of those made. There are still two more Pedestals and Caryatids [in those same designs] to be made for the entrance to the Colonnades [at the adjoining Neptune Pool]. We have been having lots of trouble with our glue due to this hot weather. It cracks and then makes a bum job. Frandy repaired the column and says he has plenty [of] work ahead.
>
> Miss Morgan told Frank Gyorgy about the shutdown on the 1st of the month. I'm sorry but I suppose it cant be helped. She explained that Mr. Hearst had to make good his dividend [payment to stockholders] on his Hearst [Consolidated] Publications and needed all his spare cash. No doubt you know all about it.

The counterpart of Van Gorden's letter came from Mac McClure at Wyntoon; Mac wrote it on Saturday, though, June 18; and thus Loorz wouldn't have seen it before he went to San Simeon on Monday:

> Miss Morgan's last letter [possibly the same "note" Mac mentioned on June 16][46] indicated that by reducing the crew we could keep on another week or so and fin-

---

45. Eddie Shaug, part of the warehouse crew under Williams, liked to recount how Frank Frandolich came to the rescue on such occasions — perhaps even involving the large coat-of-arms sculpture in Hearst's Gothic Study, installed by Loorz's men in 1934 while Hearst was in Europe. The sculpture supposedly got damaged, to everyone's horror. But "Frandy" Frandolich allayed their fears. "I fix, I fix," he promised in his strong Italian accent; and so he did. (And so Shaug regaled me in the 1980s, impersonating Frandy's voice and his twitch-eyed gestures. But the subject of the broken sculpture at the Neptune Pool didn't come up.)

46. Hearst Castle has latter-day copies of numerous letters kept by Mac McClure. The originals date mostly from 1939 and are still privately held by relatives of Mac's in Michigan, his home state. No letter resembling the one he mentioned in June 1938 is among the copies (but see notes 65 and 66, below, for a different item from that year). The Castle's copies are known as the War-

ish all the new work—tile, timbering, plaster and all. I doubt very much if this can be done even if we work all next month—She will be here next week and may see this for herself.

This shut-down is for at least the rest of the year, they tell me—and I presume it includes S.S. (excepting Gomez of course [Alfredo Gomes, the tapestry repairman]). I wonder just how much longer this can operate, and I hope the Chief dosn't [*sic*] expect J.M. to supply schemes and sketches for new work during the interval.

Mac's postscript said, "Miss Morgan told us to work Saturdays for the remainder of the time 'To make the men feel better' hence the longer hours on time cards."

Nothing like Loorz's old recap notes exists for his trips to San Simeon in 1938. Consequently, the things he and Morgan discussed on June 20 can only be surmised: the West Terrace quite likely, maybe even the Italian cypresses, for which Jake Jacobson was still building scaffolds to hold the tree trimmer. And the broken statue: something may have been said about that. The one thing they unquestionably dealt with was a project in Casa Grande—the insertion of antique sculptures in the end walls of the Assembly Room. Loorz mentioned the project to Morgan two days after he saw her.[47] But Van Gorden, while writing to Loorz on June 24, was the one who really did the story justice:

> That job in the Assembly Room has turned out to be quite a job. Frandy and I have been sweating blood trying to make some headway. I think after we have the first one [of a matching foursome] in place the remainder will come a lot easier. Nick Yost is in San Francisco, Eddie Shaug had to go to Wyntoon and Leonard Leach is now on the mail job so you can imagine [*sic*] how much help we will receive from them.[48] It is quite a job even to bring those statues [circular marble

---

ren McClure Papers, despite their physically derivative status—their content, of course, being the thing that counts.

47. Writing from Pacific Grove on June 22, he told her he was "back in the office this morn," following which he discussed some bookkeeping details. Then he turned to the big job in the Assembly Room:

> After uncrating the first marble panel [one of the sculptures], Frank [Gyorgy or Frandolich] found 1½" variation in the thickness of the marble between the top and the bottom. By phone, Frandolich insists that the furring and mold would not cover, so I permitted a slight chiseling of the concrete [wall] near the bottom.
>
> The others [the remaining sculptures] do not vary so much so we may not have to chisel.
>
> As our general practice has not been to chisel concrete, I hesitated to make the above decision. To avoid delay in this case, an emergency, I advised them to proceed.

48. Yost, Shaug, and Leach worked mostly under W. R. Williams in the San Simeon warehouses. (Williams still managed that division—called the Antiques Department—but since 1937

reliefs] into the Assembly Room. We have to cut all the anchors and then unrivet the cleats and change them into their new position [thus imbedding the sculptures in the walls]. It all takes a lot of time.

The four reliefs were huge "medallions" in Italian marble. Hearst had bought them through the London market the previous year,[49] right before his art collecting—along with so many of his other extravagances—lapsed into hibernation. Van Gorden, meanwhile, was no Old World artisan. Yet he was able-bodied and quick-witted enough to improvise, as he'd been doing all season; besides, there were few others on hand to help the wizard Frandolich at this crucial moment. Sweating indeed! The job couldn't have been attempted in a more high-profile, strategic spot. The slightest error could have been fatal, not just in the installation phase but also in the precise finish work afterward. Decorative stucco-and-mortar covered the wall spaces where the reliefs were chiseled into place. That existing surface and any new stucco being used would need to blend perfectly. Hearst and his guests would notice the two workmen's efforts (aided by Frank Gyorgy and John Vanderloo) every time they used the great room from then on. And Morgan would be especially hawkeyed about it.

THE CHIEF HIMSELF would be passing judgment soon enough. He was back in California now from the east, back where he could stay a step ahead of the lawyers, the bankers, the yes men, the no men—or at least where he could breathe some fresh air while trying. Mac McClure was prompt in keeping Loorz apprised of events at Wyntoon.[50] Sunday, June 26, was a good time to write, before a new week began on the McCloud:

> Mr H and a party of about 8 arrived Thursday morning [June 23]—Miss M was on the same train but didn't know it.[51] Mr Hearst spent some time looking over the work [on Angel House], which all passed more or less except the front en-

---

he'd also been running the Household Department on the hilltop.) Among Yost and his fellows, one or more of them figured in the recent mishap at the Neptune Pool, described by Van Gorden on June 17 (p. 378).

49. Specifically, through the Victor Rothschild sale at Sotheby & Co. in April 1937, a renowned dispersal that also enriched Hearst's collection of antique silver.

50. Pending Mac's inside details, Loorz already knew that Hearst was back at Wyntoon; he had just written to Willicombe there the previous day, June 25, about the Burnett Road. Rather than pose a direct question, Loorz made an assumption: "Because of the latest shut-down of other construction work on July 1st, there might be no more funds forthcoming on this road account."

He was wrong. The Burnett job would continue. A follow-up letter to Willicombe on June 30 began by saying, "As Mr. Hearst has decided to continue the road work, we will expect a remittance of the next $250 during the first part of July."

51. See note 44, above.

trance which is to be quite elaborate—carved stone moldings and capitals. It will take weeks to do it. Pete [Petersen] has had me write to Ray Van G for stone hammar [hammer] which we will use with compressor now here.

Miss M. said W.R.H. wanted the Turrets[52] and entrance finished completely and maybe foundations for bridge house. With 2 carpenters for a crew it will take time especially as it takes about half of each day providing the office force [Hearst and Willicombe's staff] with shelves, hooks, holes, screens and other miscellaneous items.

Mac wrote Loorz a follow-up note the next day, Monday the twenty-seventh (preceding a rare Tuesday for this period that Morgan spent at San Simeon). Mac said, "I wrote to J.M. today asking her if we can send a load of stones down to S.F. and have the molds and carved capitals made there—Pete says we can hardly do them here with hand tools."

June gave way to July by the end of that week.[53] But the code word *shutdown*, long muttered, maligned, and at times misspelled, failed to apply just yet at Wyntoon—or at San Simeon. The situation figured in a long letter that Loorz wrote Pete Petersen on Sunday, July 3:

Well things change every day, dont they? It looks like you might be up there quite a while now. Miss Morgan thot it would be three or four weeks yet to do what Mr. Hearst still wants to do. However, I know as long as he is there you will have so many things to do besides work on the Angel House that you wont be able to accomplish much. . . .

The old Hilltop is certainly lonesome. All the boys who still live on the hill have to ride [by car] to the ranch [the Bunkhouse probably] for their meals. I dont think it will last long for many of them. I think it would be much nicer to shut

---

52. Mac was referring to some turret-like features on Angel House—not to The Turrets (Cinderella House), for which another obsolete name was The Pinnacles.

53. On Friday, Willicombe wrote to Phoebe Hill, a sister of Fanny Boss; the year before (p. 339, note 91), he had allayed Miss Hill's concerns about Hearst's well being, as he also did at this point in 1938:

I know it will be a ray of light to you to learn that Mr. Hearst is feeling fine. He is certainly in remarkably good health, especially with all the cares and worries of business that he is carrying. It would have done your heart good to have seen him today with his blue sport shirt and feather-decorated Alpine hat and sporty English gray trousers, stepping around Wyntoon, writing editorials, directing some misguided editors and publishers, straightening out his architect on some angle of the construction work, and generally inspiring and pepping up everybody within sight or ear-shot.

From Willicombe to Hill, July 1, 1938; Hearst Papers, carton 24 (under "Hi-Hn"). Morgan had no doubt left Wyntoon by then, a week having passed since her appearance on June 23, and she wouldn't reappear till July 11; Mac McClure must have been the "architect" Willicombe mentioned.

down entirely for quite a while until he [Hearst] could get enough ahead to really do something worth while. The way it is, no one can depend upon anything and few are happy as a result.

It looks like I'll get the $250 per month on the [Burnett] road account until we get it cleaned up, at least to Davis [Flat]. I wish it would stop for I will not take anything for the little I do after the first of July and I will not turn Mr. Hearst down. Even if I get nothing now I fell [feel] that I have been well paid in the past. . . .

Pete, I think Miss Morgan is well satisfied with your work. She hasn't said much but when she doesn't complain then I know things are O.K. You know Pete she is not one to pat anyone on the back very much. She feels appreciation without voicing [it]. We need only to be thotful and wide awake to interpret her inner self.

In his letter of July 3, Loorz also touched on the recent fortunes of the F. C. Stolte Co. (Loorz freelanced, in essence, at San Simeon and Wyntoon in 1938. And now that the KYA radio station had been finished, the Stolte Co.'s current efforts fell almost entirely outside the Hearst-Morgan sphere. Moreover, the company had not been involved in any of Morgan's other projects—her non-Hearst work— since 1936–37, when it handled the second of its two Kings Daughters jobs for her in Oakland.)[54] As Loorz told Petersen, "Some of the work we took on last fall is not checking out so well [yielding a profit] now that we are completing [it], but all of the work we have done this year has and is checking out very well, so we cannot complain."[55]

On July 5, Loorz wrote to Joe Willicombe at Wyntoon. The individual role played by Loorz in 1938 (with some help from a few Stolte employees) stood behind the activities he mentioned, hence his allusive use of the editorial *we*:

Please advise Mr. Hearst that after July 1st I will not be on any of his payrolls. However, I wish to assure him that I will continue to supervise the [Burnett] road improvements as economically as I know how. I will merely keep in touch on my

---

54. See note 20 in this chapter. The company's next non-Hearst job for Morgan lay a year ahead—the Parsons residence in Monterey, handled by Loorz through his Pacific Grove branch.

55. Loorz told his parents a week earlier, June 26, that the Stolte Co. still had "a lot of work" and that some of the jobs were "working out better":

I expect within the next few months we will be able to take work at a nice profit. We expect to finish the year out as good or better than last year and that [situation] was fine. This new Spend-lend program of the government is right up our alley.

Spend-lend (also called lend-spend) was Franklin Roosevelt's antidote to the recession of 1937–38: deficit spending rather than a balanced budget. The PWA alone got nearly a billion dollars.

regular visits to my other work in San Luis Obispo County. As the budget is small, I cannot work a crew continuously. I am using my own men to do this work.

Further, though we [the F. C. Stolte Co.] have no real authority over the present work at Wyntoon we are assisting in the purchases, payrolls, etc., for the convenience of Miss Morgan and the men on the job. We will continue this service as desired until the work ceases.

Predictably, he also asked Willicombe to tell Hearst that, in the future, the company hoped to be involved again "in proposed construction."

If nothing else, Loorz and others could keep up their correspondence until the moment came. Mac McClure did his part by writing on July 6. "I thought I would bring you up to date on developments here," he told Loorz that Wednesday:

> Mr Hearst was clamoring for action and Miss M., finally let us enlarge the crew and arranged to have the carved [stone] work done by Cardini in S.F. The front entrance design [for Angel House] as finally approved is elaborate and expensive. We had to remove all the work we had done and put in additional footings. . . .
>
> I received a roll of plans of the [Cosmopolitan] studio bungalow alterations last week with instructions to hand the "roll" to Mr H. I did so and he immediately spread it out for me to work over. I am doing it now but with some trepidations.
>
> Mr. Pogany, the mural artist, is here with a crew to finish the Cinderella House. . . .[56]
>
> . . . From appearances it looks like several weeks more of activity here. Mr H looked at me rather accusingly the other day saying, "When are you going to start putting up carving" (interiors). I answered "Whenever you say."
>
> P. S. Have scarsely heard a word from J.M.

Signs of Morgan, written or otherwise, may indeed have been "scarse" lately. But she'd be appearing in person within a few days—come the Monday lying just ahead.

Loorz answered Mac's letter on the Friday before she arrived. "Thanks a million, Mac, for the report on Wyntoon. It sounds like prosperity has returned." Then he remarked, "It is really funny, my present connections with the Hearst organization. I'm meddling with your work up there and doing some road work at the ranch. I have no authority and I am on no pay roll. Call me what you will."

Prompt mail service permitting, Morgan would also have heard from Loorz before she left for Wyntoon; he wrote to her, as he did to Mac, on Friday, July 8.

---

56. Willicombe's letter to Pogany of May 21, 1937 (listed in note 29, above), indicates that Angel House had been slated for Pogany's work shortly before that date. Its murals remained on hold more than a year later. See also p. 319 and its note 54.

That daring job at San Simeon was the main topic—that job in the Assembly Room for which the men had been sweating blood:

> In case you did not visit the hilltop this week [she hadn't, and she wouldn't be there till August], you will be interested in the developments. Frandy set the last of the placques [the marble reliefs in the corner walls] while I was there Wednesday, [and] he will go down and set the remainder of the heads [the cast-stone lamp standards] at the lower terrace and [is] expected to be completed by Friday night [July 8].
>
> The carpenter had a few hours left of work on the frames [for the marble reliefs]. He had them altogether and was fitting them so that John [Vanderloo] would have little trouble setting them.
>
> John was keeping up with the carpenter in the plaster patches [on the Assembly Room job] and completing the few [cast-stone] heads at the same time.
>
> Frank G. [Frank Gyorgy] was well along with the gilding of one [frame]. With the other three completed, he can do them all at the same time. It will take him two or three weeks before they will be all finished.
>
> We removed the large scaffold [for the installation job] and Mr. Williams's is going to proceed with his cleaning. He was very anxious to get started as he has only two men and expected it would take them several weeks to clean properly. The frames are very light and can be set without making dirt.
>
> All else very, very quiet.

The silence aside, the Assembly Room job was too important, too impressive to drop from the record without further comment. Loorz gave it a proper sendoff on July 19, in another letter to Morgan:

> The frames are gilded and in place and look fine. John did the last of the pointing-up today [the dovetailing into the stucco-and-mortar finish]. Frank Gyorgy will touch up John's patches tomorrow.

Everyone's performance on that job was masterful, as millions have since witnessed.[57] Loorz had some final things to tell Morgan:

> Between times John has completed heads [for the lamp standards] on the lower terrace. He is now making a few extras. To the best of my knowledge all of the

---

57. The medallion-like reliefs have carved their own niche in San Simeon lore: each relief, goes the story, weighs a full ton, a bone-crushing two thousand pounds. In truth, each of them weighs at least several hundred pounds. And if they're indeed as thick as eight inches, as certain records say (in contrast to the chisel-wary Loorz references), a weight closer to fourteen hundred pounds apiece would apply. Geometry aside, pictures of the reliefs in their former setting (the ballroom of the Rothschild mansion at 148 Piccadilly, London) convey a sense of lightness and delicacy, not one of

work you requested us to complete is now finished. John has the impression that you wanted to continue on heads. I understood a few extra was all you desired at this time.

If you prefer that work to stop before your next visit please let me know by phone, Monterey 8115, and I will deliver the message.

As you know, things are very quiet on the Hill.

Morgan's reply was prompt and brief. She told Loorz the next day, "There are enough heads done for the present and I think all work should stop with this week." She also acknowledged how much he'd been helping her (departing from the portrayal Loorz gave Pete Petersen on July 3). A simple line did the trick: "Many thanks to you."

ONE LIFE DISRUPTED by the lack of work at San Simeon was that of Lo On, a Chinese cook. On June 25 Loorz had written to On's countryman George Wu, saying, "I suppose Lo told you that he quit on the hill. The men go down to the ranch now for their meals." Loorz also recounted, "Lo told me he was going to start a small Chop Suey joint in Cambria. If he does, I hope he makes good."[58]

Nearly a month later—July 20—Lo On wrote to Loorz from Elko, Nevada; he had found work with the Western Pacific Railroad and was cooking for 115 laborers at every meal. He told a poignant story stemming from recent events in the Sino-Japanese War:[59]

I am sorry I didn't see you before I leave the Camp. I have told Mr. Ray Van Gorden to give my regards and say good bye to you. I left the Hill Top Kitchen in the

---

heaviness and mass. See, for example, Gerald Reitlinger, *The Economics of Taste: The Rise and Fall of the Objets d'Art Market since 1750* (New York, 1963), photograph following p. 64.

58. Chinese immigrants had lived in and around Cambria since the late 1800s, mainly as seaweed farmers. A small Chinatown — or "Chinese Center" by name — was in the heart of Cambria (with traces remaining today), close to the house Loorz helped Frank Souza build in 1935. Lo On had a restaurant in Berkeley about 1940; it didn't last long.

59. On's letter, and one dated October 28, were written for him by a fellow railroad cook. Since its outbreak a year earlier, the Sino-Japanese conflict had caught Hearst's periodic attention. On December 12, 1937, the Japanese sank the American gunboat *Panay* in China, a callous, prophetic act that preceded Pearl Harbor by four years — virtually to the day — and that confirmed Hearst's deep suspicion of the "Yellow Peril." (He would have been mid-ocean on the *Lurline* when the *Panay* sank — had he not cancelled his tax-dodging trip to Hawaii at the last minute.) His editorial in the *San Francisco Examiner* on December 14 called for preparedness more than for retribution (as cited in Rodney Carlisle's "Foreign Policy Views of an Isolationist Press Lord," pp. 222–23). But before 1937 ended Hearst was using strident words: "Japan is an aggressive, belligerent, militaristic, ambitious and impudent nation, intoxicated by its continual success in predatory warfare." From a signed editorial headed "The Japanese Menace," published on December 30 and partially reprinted in Tomkins, *Selections from the Writings and Speeches of William Randolph Hearst*, pp. 282–83.

evening of June 15 to Cambria. I stay there one night and next day and went to San Luis Obispo then I went to San Francisco by train to my sister's house meantime my sister show me a letter from my house in China. My home was destroyed by Japanese bombs I feel very depressed. So I don't feel like going back to Cambria to open the Chop Suey house, the business condition is very bad for me and I lost lots of money.

Loorz answered on July 29, sending his reply to On's railroad camp in Nevada:

Sorry to hear that your home was destroyed during the time of stress in China, Lo On, but I know that you are like all of your people and will not give up even though the odds may be great against you. I, and the world as a whole, look upon the bombings with great distaste. However, Lo On, no matter what the Japanese might do, they will never be able to conquer the Chinese people because your people has had a civilization and culture of a very high order in the past and will again in the future. The invading countries might annex much of the Chinese territory, but it will always be China, even though ruled by another nation. This because the Chinese want to be, and will be, a distinct nationality.

Things are very quiet on the Hilltop, as you know, but if it should ever start again when I am connected with it, you will hear from me.

And so Loorz remained the confidant, the dear friend—and even the father figure sometimes—to a wide array of correspondents, from a draftsman as highly placed as Mac McClure to a cook as humble as Lo On.

Loorz wrote to Hearst at Wyntoon that same day, July 29. The crew working on the Burnett Road was near the summit and would be reaching Davis Flat in another week. "This will also bring us at the end of our July budget," said Loorz:

If you intend continuing in August, I would be pleased to receive the August budget soon. It will be convenient and economical if the boys can go right on.

With the hot weather coming on it is quite an advantage to have the road open as far as it is to combat possible fires.

One of "the boys" was the versatile Ray Van Gorden. He wrote to Loorz on July 30. His words showed that the crew was farther along than Hearst had just been informed.[60] "We are now about a half mile down little Salmon Creek," Van Gorden said. "The road doesn't seem to be so bad and we are making pretty good

---

60. Loorz had based his report of July 29 on a previous letter from Van Gorden, dated July 26 and containing details that were changing quickly. "We are now on the other side of the cattle pass on top of the mountain," he told Loorz at that juncture. "Not yet to the summit, however. We ordered a new blade for the Dozer this morning as the one on it is about worn out."

headway. The big culvert right on the other side of Davis Flat was out entirely. Vern [Verne Barker][61] pushed it up in place and filled in the gulch."

Van Gorden also told Loorz, "It has been good and hot over Burnett way and one surely earns his money in that country. All the equipment gets so hot that you can hardly touch it."

Someone else who wrote to Loorz on July 30 was Willicombe. "Your letter of July 29th [the one to Hearst] puzzles me," said the Colonel, inasmuch as "the road work was not affected by the Hilltop construction shut-down." Therefore, the latest allotment of $250 would soon be arriving.[62]

And thus with the back-country job continuing, Van Gorden had more news for Loorz on August 3:

> We are about one mile down the canyon from Davis Flat now. We are just about to a very bad place which is all washed out. Vern thinks it will take a day to repair it providing we can get the dirt without shooting [dynamiting]. He says this place has gone out every year so you probably know where it is. It has been more than hot down that canyon.

In the wake of the shutdown, Van Gorden had become a commuter based in Cambria, his native town. Nonetheless, "I have the typewriter, stationery, and everything here at home and do all the office work from here [payrolls for the hilltop caretakers, and so on]."

Through most of the Burnett job, Van Gorden kept the descriptions flowing Loorz's way. "We put in all of Friday drilling and shooting to get by that bad place in the road." He mentioned that on Saturday, August 6. "Expect much better going from the Creek Camp to the [Nacimiento] River." That was three days later—the day after Morgan visited San Simeon for the last time in 1938. But with the exception of Van Gorden's steady voice, the sounds emanating from San Simeon were growing fainter and fainter.

As for Wyntoon, Morgan's footsteps were heard there only once in recent weeks, back on July 10. August would likewise find her making just one trip north. (Hearst, meanwhile, had been staying in the Bavarian Village since June, follow-

---

61. Although Barker's first name more often appears as *Vern* in these annals, *Verne* was the correct spelling.

62. Willicombe wrote to Loorz again a few days later, elaborating on the Burnett situation. He said in part, "You will remember in our correspondence also that we referred to the Hilltop work and I stated that the CLOSING DOWN of the work on the Hill would not interfere with the arrangement for the road repair work." From Willicombe to Loorz, August 5, 1938; Hearst Papers, carton 57 (under "Li-Lz"). Despite the welcome existence of this carbon copy (the Loorz Papers lack the original), the Hearst Papers have few other items from 1938 that interleave with Loorz items, whether by date or in subject matter.

ing his return from Chicago and points east.)[63] With her monthly visit coming up, Morgan wired Loorz in Pacific Grove on Thursday, August 18; she did so from San Francisco: "CAN YOU BE AT WYNTOON SUNDAY FOR THAT DAY ONLY. I WILL GO ALSO."

It was August 21 that she had in mind, and Loorz chimed in. Their presence there, plus some of what occurred, can be glimpsed from a letter that Willicombe wrote Morgan a day later, on Monday the twenty-second. The way he delved into the matter that follows—no mention of Hearst's wishes or even any allusion to them—seems unlike the Colonel:

> Mr. Pogany stopped me to-day outside the office here and said that he made another examination of the plaster on river side of the Sleeping Beauty House [Angel House] and found so many cracks—which he has marked with pencil—that he had reached the conclusion that that kind of p[l]astering would not do for his work.
>
> Also he said that the ideal plaster was that which is now on the front of the house.
>
> As this appeared to reverse his statements when he and George Loorz and I discussed the matter—when Mr. Pogany declared that he could take care of any kind of surface, no matter how rough, and that the finish of the river side of the Sleeping Beauty House was OK—I told him that I would write you and Mr. Loorz (to whom I am sending a copy of this letter)[64] and that Mr. Loorz would not [re]do the plastering until you both and Mr. Pogany had agreed upon exactly the kind of plaster that would be satisfactory. ALSO I TOLD HIM TO TALK WITH MR. [LOUIS] HILL HERE TODAY ABOUT IT—AND I TOLD MR. HILL TO TALK WITH HIM.[65]
>
> Undoubtedly you or Mr. Loorz will want to take the matter up further with Mr. Pogany.

---

63. In that early part of the summer, Hearst had viewed his imminent prospects differently. On June 27 Willicombe told a man named S. O. Johnson that Hearst would be pleased to see him at Wyntoon. "Will be here for the Fourth [of July] but only two or three days afterwards." Hearst Papers, carton 24 (under "Jo-Jz"). Elsewhere in his letter to Phoebe Hill on July 1 (note 53, above), Willicombe told her, "We have been at Wyntoon only a few days and are planning to leave here in another week or ten days"; he further indicated that Hearst would be making another trip to the East Coast. But as Willicombe also said to Miss Hill, Hearst's plans in that regard were "not definite." Hearst Papers, ibid. (under "Hi-Hn").

64. Hence its existence in the Loorz Papers. The original itself, which Willicombe sent Morgan, is not in the Morgan Collection at Cal Poly. The Loorz Papers also contain a travel invoice that Loorz submitted to Morgan after he got home; he, like Pogany, had also examined the plaster, as the wording on his invoice specified: "Plaster Inspection."

65. Louis Hill's name appears in the Loorz Papers as early as 1932. It crops up repeatedly in 1935, Hill having been a Stolte plasterer on Morgan's job for Edward Bull in San Francisco and, likewise in that city, on the remodeling done by the Stolte Co. for Claude and Freda Loorz. Hill was

The Loorz Papers start thinning out in such matters by late August. It's a blessing, therefore, that a typically vivid letter of Mac McClure's dates from September 1, not long after that episode at Wyntoon. Loorz was on the receiving end:

> About two weeks ago Mr. Hearst asked me to electrify the [German and other] tile stoves in the Cinderella house.
>
> I told him that considerable work was required before we could do that as that house is on a temporary line from another set of transformers and is already doing all it can stand and that to install the heaters we would first have to install the transformers in the now empty vault. I wrote all this to Miss Morgan but had received no reply [until August 27].[66]
>
> Today he was a trifle upset to find nothing done and said to go ahead and *do* it and not bother Miss M — and [he] decided to call you up — thinking, I suppose, you were still in charge. —
>
> Outside of this little flurry things are fairly quiet. Pogany was sent home (for the season at least) the Tuesday [August 23] after you were here.
>
> We dont know what our program is, if any, during Miss M's absence (she sails to Europe in a week as you no doubt know).

Undoubtedly Loorz did, just as he surely knew that almost four years had passed since her last trip abroad. But his papers are too quiet at this interval to confirm either point.[67]

---

also a plasterer on the Theta Chi Chapter House, a Stolte job in Palo Alto for the architect Will Corlett.

Morgan mentioned Hill when she wrote to Mac McClure on August 26 (the sole letter from 1938 in the Warren McClure Papers at Hearst Castle, the research copies described in note 46, above). See also note 66.

66. Morgan replied on Friday, August 26 (the same letter referred to in note 65); it probably reached Mac the next day. In any case, her letter makes his use of *had* more decipherable (lest *have* be construed as his real intention). Besides mentioning Louis Hill and tile stoves on August 26, Morgan also commented on the matter that Willicombe had aired a few days before: "The plaster question does not sound so very settled!"

67. Two days before Mac wrote Loorz, Morgan informed Hearst that she'd soon be leaving San Francisco. She'd be sailing to Europe through the Panama Canal. She especially hoped to visit Sicily; it would be her first time. See Morgan to Hearst, August 30, 1938; Hearst/Morgan Correspondence, Morgan Collection. Sara Boutelle gives an itinerary in *Julia Morgan*, p. 245 (note 3 under "The Morgan Atelier"). "To Saint Louis for the Principia College commission. To New York, then to Sicily, Venice, Siena, Florence, and Switzerland." The Cal Poly holdings don't reveal whether Morgan changed her plans after writing to Hearst. If she sailed from New York instead, she may have stopped at Principia on her way there. More likely, though, her trip to St. Louis in January 1932 is what Boutelle caught wind of, connecting it with 1938. See p. 15, note 24, and pp. 18–19, note 4, both in this volume.

A separate letter from Morgan to Hearst on August 30, 1938 (also at Cal Poly), pertains to the Pacific Coast Register, a massive inventory she sent to him at Wyntoon; see p. 339 in the 1937 chapter, note 90.

LOORZ AND VAN GORDEN were among the few scribes who stayed active in these final weeks of the summer. Their letters indicate that portions of the Burnett Road still awaited attention, long after the heavy winter had gripped the area. Loorz learned about his friend's progress (and Verne Barker's as well) through a letter dated August 31, in which Van Gorden told Loorz:

> We are now about 1 mile from the Gabillon [Gabilan] Corrals [between the Na-cimiento River and Jolon] and if they have opened the road to there from the other side [the Jolon-Milpitas area] we will be to the end tomorrow. If not it will take us another couple of days although we do not know how bad it is. Vern thinks there was a cloudburst on the other side of Naciemento Bridge [*sic*] as the road was very bad there for about three miles. All the culverts washed out and wash-outs along the road. It is some hot over in that country—the sun beats down with a vengeance all day.

Van Gorden included some news from the cooler side of the Santa Lucias:

> There isn't much activity in this neck of the woods [the Cambria-San Simeon coastal area] with the mine closed down as well as the Camp [on the hilltop]. With the election over Cambria will now lie down and die. They added another teacher to the High School Faculty, however [in Cambria].[68]

Van Gorden was not only a native of the Cambria-San Simeon area but also a descendant of one of its founding families. Loorz, drawing upon his six years of full-time residency on the "North Coast" (as that part of San Luis Obispo County is still called), sounded almost as native in replying on September 4:

> I am a little like you are about Cambria and its slow death. However, I think with the increased use of the road [the coast route to Monterey] which is inevitable they will gain as much as they lose from local industry. However, again, no town is as nice that is dependent upon transients as upon local industry.

The recent news on the Burnett job allowed Loorz to bring Hearst up to date; he wrote to him at Wyntoon, also on September 4 (misspelling some place names, much as Van Gorden had):

> The road crew tied into the Jolon Ranch road at the Gabillan Corrals during this last week. . . .
> The portion of the road that suffered most on the Jolon side was the washing

---

68. The mine may have been a quicksilver operation, such as the Oceanic Mine, yet no clo-sure of that or any other local mine seems to have occurred in 1938; the closure may have been an earlier one that still applied. The election was the California State Primary, which took place on August 30, the day before Van Gorden wrote to Loorz. Local and county offices were at stake; so

out of culverts east of the Naciemiento River Bridge. Nearly every one of these culverts were washed out. In nearly every case a tree or other obstruction blocked the culverts. This emphasizes the importance of patroling the road during the stormy season.

Van Gorden had some further descriptions for Loorz on Wednesday, September 7, right after Labor Day weekend:[69]

We are leaving the river tomorrow [the Nacimiento] and there are a number of slides along [the route already traversed] that we just moved enough to get through on our way out [to the heart of the job]. We will make a pretty good job of it as we go along [while returning to the coast].

In other words, Van Gorden and Barker needed to tie up some loose ends, some details that remained from earlier in the process of opening and repairing a remote country road.

Van Gorden added a postscript for Loorz: "They have discontinued the mail service to the Hill. Mr. Hearst must be broke."

HIS FINANCIAL WOES ASIDE, Hearst left Wyntoon by late September — in favor of San Simeon. From here through December the Loorz Papers are too spotty to pin down Hearst's daily whereabouts. But he'd pulled up stakes at Wyntoon for now; that much is clear. The crew itself, from Mac McClure on down, soon disbanded in his wake.

It remained for the Beach House alone to alternate with the hilltop as Hearst's preferred address. Despite its white-elephant status, San Simeon may have seen

---

were bigger ones (in November, Culbert Olson went on to wrest the governorship from Frank Merriam).

69. September 7 also found Morgan writing to Hearst, apparently right before her trip. Santa Maria de Ovila — the monastery slated for the "big job" at Wyntoon in 1933 — had become one of Hearst's salable assets. He had asked for some existing sketches or drawings, by Bernard Maybeck or by her; she wasn't sure which, thus her letter. (He meant Maybeck's sketches in colored chalk.)

Referring to "Mt. Olive," a code name for the monastery when it left Spain in 1931, Morgan seized the moment on September 7. She waxed poetic: the old building would make a fine museum, she said; and other massive, architectural things she and Hearst had thought of using with it would also qualify. These included the Bradenstoke barn. Besides touching on financial details (there were costs to recoup from years back), she got even more poetic before closing. "I have always hoped the castle [the monastery] would some day go up on that lovely coast Point you showed me above Santa Monica." Premonitions of the Roman villa built by J. Paul Getty in Malibu! See Morgan to Hearst, September 7, 1938; Morgan Collection, Santa Maria de Ovila file (III/06/09/09). See also Willicombe to Morgan, September 10, 1938; ibid.

Hearst had property near Tuna Canyon, five miles up the coast from the Beach House. See Betty Lou Young, *Pacific Palisades: Where the Mountains Meet the Sea* (Pacific Palisades, California; 1983), p. 148.

more of him and his guests in the fall of 1938 than Santa Monica did.[70] Either way, Hearst knuckled under in dear old California. His charade of making himself a "nonresident"—whether through six months of absence or just three—was confined to the years 1936 and 1937. In 1938, and from then on, he abandoned the ploy.

A man of seventy-five now, Hearst busied himself, as he always had, with the running of his newspapers. Although his empire was in a virtual receivership, he'd retained editorial control of his papers; more than anything else, he was a newspaperman at heart. However, all manner of his assets, sometimes even newspapers, had been partly or, in some instances, entirely liquidated by this time, more than a year having passed since his grim comeuppance in New York in June 1937. And though he'd left Wyntoon for the moment, he wasn't out of the woods entirely. Indeed, he wouldn't be out for a good long while.[71]

Hearst's convertible assets included thousands of art objects—among which were the ones Jim Forney and Charlie Rounds were scrambling to identify and keep straight. After sleuthing about Wyntoon earlier in 1938, Forney and Rounds entered the maze called San Simeon.

Van Gorden referred to those two men in a letter he wrote Loorz on October 4. He also mentioned Jud Smelser, who'd been with the Hearst party all summer at Wyntoon and who was now on duty at San Simeon. Van Gorden began, though, by telling Loorz:

> I was surprised on my return [from a recent trip to Los Angeles] to find that Mr. Hearst had stayed here since you thought he was going back to Wyntoon. I know how his plans are subject to change over night, however.[72]

---

70. In this part of 1938 or perhaps a few months earlier, Aldous Huxley and his wife were guests at San Simeon; Huxley's novel *After Many a Summer Dies the Swan*, a keenly satirical takeoff on Hearst's life, appeared in October 1939. The exact timing of the Huxley visit is unclear in accounts of the subject; see, for example, Frank Baldanza's article "Huxley and Hearst" in the *Journal of Modern Literature* (September 1979, pp. 441–55), which, to thicken the plot a bit more, relates that the Huxleys "spent at least one weekend at San Simeon."

One of the characters in Huxley's novel bore an unmistakably familiar name: Dr. Obispo. Fearful of being too libelous, Huxley changed another character's name before publication: Virginia Dowlas, an allusion to Marion Davies (and her real surname of Douras), became Virginia Maunciple; but Jo Stoyte, allusive of Hearst, remained as chosen. Neither Baldanza's article nor any other writings about Huxley explain the coinage of the name *Stoyte*. But we needn't look far to spot a possible source, however unlikely: *Stoyte*, with its *y* changed to an *l*, becomes *Stolte*.

71. W. A. Swanberg provides a useful overview of the liquidations in *Citizen Hearst*, pp. 483–93. Lindsay Chaney and Michael Cieply probe the subject repeatedly in *The Hearsts: Family and Empire—The Later Years* (New York, 1981; see index listings on p. 403). So does David Nasaw in *The Chief* (see index listings on pp. 668–69).

72. August Wahlberg, who by now had replaced Joseph Yelinek as Hearst's valet, recounted that Hearst flew from Wyntoon to San Simeon for a rare family reunion with his estranged wife, Millicent, and their five sons. Nasaw, after reading Wahlberg's testimony (Hearst Castle oral-history

Before writing to Loorz, Van Gorden had gone from Cambria up to the little town of San Simeon to get the mail; that's when he bumped into Smelser:

> I saw Jud while there — he was hauling around the men that are inventorying the antiques. Among them [was] Forney who I met in Cambria just before I left for L.A. [the week before]. He seems a nice fellow and says some pretty nice things about you. He and [Alfredo] Gomes seem to be real friendly. . . .
>
> . . . Mr. Forney was telling me that Mr. LeFeaver is now working for the Fair [the Golden Gate International Exposition in San Francisco][73] and that his wife [Mrs. Forney] is all that Miss Morgan has in her office.[74]
>
> He was of the opinion that Mr. Hearst might never start [building] again but when I told him that Miss Morgan had written me[75] that he probably would start in the spring again providing his business continued to improve, he said he meant that he would never start on a large scale. He is probably only guessing like the most of us must do.

Now that Morgan had left for Europe as early as September — a month that, in past years, had typically found her still at Hearst's beck and call — and now that her office had too little work to sustain even a fixture like Jim LeFeaver, her architectural practice seemed on the verge of ending. In reality, it was just on hold until she returned. Even in 1938 she remained closely entwined with Hearst while she was abroad, undoubtedly more so than with any other client still on her active list.[76]

---

collection) and after interviewing Randolph Hearst, one of Hearst's twin sons, placed the rendezvous in "the summer or fall of 1938"; see *The Chief*, p. 547, plus the photograph in the section following p. 464. The same picture appeared previously in *The Hearsts: Father and Son*, by William Randolph Hearst, Jr., with Jack Casserly (Niwot, Colorado; 1991), in the section following p. 112.

73. Back on January 31, Loorz's friend Armand Brady mentioned the Exposition. He sent Loorz an application for its "Principal Construction Engineer," a job paying $500 per month; Brady knew Loorz was well qualified and urged him to apply; he also said he'd try "pulling what few strings" he could in Sacramento, his home base. Loorz answered on February 8, right after moving to Pacific Grove, saying he was flattered by the thought. "However, Armand, I hope to do a lot better than $500 a month this year and be my own boss most of the time."

74. In telling Hearst about her trip to Europe (as in note 67, above), Morgan ended by saying, "The office will have a smaller staff for the winter than usual, but a carefully chosen one." See Morgan to Hearst, August 30, 1938; Hearst/Morgan Correspondence, Morgan Collection.

75. No correspondence of 1938 between Morgan and Van Gorden survives in the Morgan Collection; some items from earlier years are extant, however.

76. An occasion arose for Morgan's secretary to correspond with Hearst's secretary. "Miss Morgan has written us that if you have a possible purchaser for the Wyntoon Mt. Olive [monastery], and you need explanations of material and its use, etc., she will gladly return [from Europe] upon receipt of a cable, any time." From unsigned [Lilian Forney] to Willicombe, November 1, 1938; Morgan Collection, Santa Maria de Ovila file (III/06/09/09). Morgan was able to continue traveling. Good thing, or Don Loorz would be a postcard poorer: she sent him one after seeing the island of Malta (mailed on December 7 from Messina, Sicily).

Despite LeFeaver's absence, the Morgan-Forney ledgers show that at least two jobs required

Loorz was at San Simeon at least once during October 1938, the last time he was there till the following year. All the while he was hard at work building up the Pacific Grove branch of the F. C. Stolte Co., as he had been ever since he moved north during the winter. "As usual we have been rushing," he told his parents on October 8. "However, we now have some $300,000 worth of work. This includes a fine home [at] $60,000 near the Del Monte Hotel in Monterey and four schools."[77] He also told them, "We enjoy a real reputation as being one of, if not, the biggest contractors in the middle part of this state."

As October progressed (a month that saw Loorz turning forty), he kept in limited touch with a San Simeonite or two — Nigel Keep, Ray Van Gorden — but otherwise Hearst's lack of building activity put a damper on the mail.[78] An exception marked the end of the month. It came as a letter from an uncustomary source, John McFadden, the all-around carpenter, stone mason, and electrician. He wrote to Loorz from Cambria on October 30:

> I got in a weeks work about the middle of the month on the hill overhauling the tennis court lights to the satisfaction [of] Mr. Hearst, but there seems little chance of my getting much work from there but an occasional job is quiet a lift.

Certainly he meant *quite*. And certainly Mc Fadden wasn't alone in wondering about new prospects, now that the Wyntoon campaign of '38 had been scrapped.

In that regard, Mac McClure was recalling now what Loorz had told him back on June 15, namely, that he might fit into the Stolte Co.'s "future plans." Loorz

---

drafting through the fall of 1938; Ray Carlson may have worked on both. The new house for Allan Starr in Piedmont had been in design for most of the year. The Hearst Building in San Francisco was a bigger job. Its remodeling began late in 1936, yet things didn't hit their stride until September 1937; then the job ran steadily, continuing throughout 1938 and lasting till the first part of 1939.

77. Loorz gave "the kidlets" (Claude and Freda Loorz in San Francisco) a detailed analysis on October 30:

> At present we have the following [jobs]: Salinas School $41,000, San Lucas School [in the Salinas Valley, south of King City] $70,000, King City City Hall $41,000, Cunningham Residence in Del Monte $60,000, Monterey High School Alteration $10,000, Shandon School [east of Paso Robles] $30,000: besides a few miscellaneous small jobs (Private). We have not quite completed the two jobs we have at Polytechnic College in San Luis Obispo.

He gave Claude and Freda some further details, briefer but equally important: "Fred has done pretty well up there also. . . . He hasn't as much in volume but he makes more money."

78. A letter from Willicombe to Loorz, dated October 3, 1938, and sent from San Simeon, can be added to the list. "Thought of you the other day when I drove through Pacific Grove on [the] way from Wyntoon," wrote the Colonel. "It's a nice little town. You know how to pick 'em." The letter helps to pinpoint Hearst's whereabouts; combined with other evidence, it suggests that the Hearst family rendezvous during the summer or fall (note 72, above) took place earlier rather than later in that period.

had also said then, "Mac, you at one time stated that you would enjoy living on this [Monterey] peninsula. As soon as possible, let's get together and discuss our program."[79] Three months later Mac's name cropped up again; it did so when Fred Stolte asked Loorz on September 12, "Does Mac [Mc]Clure still seem interested in your plan for him?" Stolte thought Palo Alto might be "an excellent location" for a draftsman of his caliber.

By November 9, therefore, Mac had several things to tell Loorz; he wrote from an address in the Brentwood part of West Los Angeles:[80]

> When I passed through San Francisco a month ago, I gave Fred a call and he told me briefly of the plan to be carried out at Palo Alto. At that time I told him of the proposed remodeling of the [Cosmopolitan] studio bungalow here [in the Los Angeles area], which was to be carried out this Winter.
>
> I promised J.M. I would do this [pursue the bungalow project] before she left and it looked fairly certain at that time. Nothing has developed on it, however, and according to Frank Hellenthal it is more or less shelved.

Hellenthal still served as Loorz's counterpart, in essence, on Hearst-Morgan jobs around the Los Angeles area; in recent years, most of those had been at the Beach House. Mac had more to tell Loorz in his November letter:

> The program, as far as I am concerned, with Hearst work is most uncertain. Presumably there will be some work done up North next Summer, but if it is to be done on the cramped budget of last season, I don't want to be involved. As you know W.R.H. was not especially satisfied with results [on Angel House, etc.].
>
> At present, I am not on salary, and consider myself free to look for other connections, which I must soon do. I should like very much to hear more details of what the work at Palo Alto would include.

Mac planned to visit that part of the Bay Area soon for a closer look. In fact, he'd been wanting to "build a small studio type duplex or triplex for income," and he supposed Palo Alto might be as good a locale as any.

JUD SMELSER WROTE TO LOORZ from San Simeon on November 14. His appetite for intrigue had often colored his letters. He proved just as determined now to

---

79. Most of what Loorz told Mac on June 15 appears on p. 376 in this chapter. The passage used in this present context is from an elided paragraph.

80. Its number was 11758 San Vicente Blvd., denoting a small yet upscale commercial space to this day. Julia Morgan later spoke of Mac's desire to "try out his shop experiment." See Morgan to Hearst, June 9, 1939; Hearst/Morgan Correspondence, Morgan Collection. Fifteen years after that, Mac had an antique gallery, which was combined with living quarters, in downtown Santa Barbara — as listed in *Polk's Santa Barbara City Directory 1954* (Los Angeles, 1954), p. 341, and in the same publisher's directory for 1955, p. 344.

give Loorz an inside glimpse, a glimpse of life on the hilltop in these little-known times. Were they indeed times of loneliness, of decline and melancholy? They tend to impart that feeling when we look back. Perhaps it was merely that the voices from before—Hearst's, Morgan's, Loorz's, plus those of several other people— were too quiet to remind us that San Simeon's heyday wasn't entirely a bygone thing.[81] Smelser, in any case, had some ordinary details to include for Loorz:

> I wonder if you remember who it was you had out from S.L.O. [San Luis Obispo] to cover the pool tables [in the Billiard Room] and what the approx. cost was including his transportation? I've got J.W. [Joe Willicombe] interested in this one & he asked me to get prices. So if you will answer pronto I'd be pleased for I wish to strike while the iron is hot. . . . Gene Shannon claims he can do the trick but stated he wouldn't be interested in coming up to do it. Silly isn't he? Cries hard times then refuses a job for fear he'll lose a couple of neck trims some morning.
>
> Estelle [Forsythe] & I enjoyed our hour with you folks [in Pacific Grove] & hope to repeat sometime with more time with you & perhaps chow as you so generously offered in a weak moment.
>
> However I hardly know when I'll ever get away again [from San Simeon] as Al Berger has gone now and I have that 24 hr. responsibility [of chauffeuring] along with all the crappy little Filipino (spelled how?) errands he W.R.W. [W. R. Williams, now head of the household][82] hands me thru each evening in order to show me I rate not with him & he is the big shot. I've never given him the satisfaction of a complaint out of me yet which hurts him like Hell, I hope. You know the Thunder of Silence is greater than the Power of Words. And added to all this Steve [Zegar, of Steve's Taxi] seems to be out & [Garner] Lovell does all the [shuttling to and from San Luis for the] Daylight Trains & I the night trains.[83] J.W. pays me

---

81. Despite Hearst's continued use of San Simeon from 1938 through 1940, the usual tendency has been to compress those years. Having known, for instance, that another war lay close ahead, most biographers and other writers have rushed through this period, drawn toward larger events.

True, Hearst and his associates were leaving fainter traces of themselves now. Big groups of guests and gala parties were nearly unheard of—too expensive, above all, and perhaps too disruptive for an aging man. Or so the story goes. And yet weren't there still twenty-four hours in a day and, of those, seven in a week? Of course there were. Things still *happened*; the world hadn't ground to a halt. But, yes, what *had* slowed greatly was the outpouring of written words, the voices rising from paper, forming a chorus in the best moments. Without them, a sense of blandness and boredom can easily take hold—or worse, a sense of emptiness.

82. Smelser's correct spelling of *Filipino* alluded to some household employees under the fuss-budget Williams, most notably Dalmatio "Dally" Carpio, the head chef.

83. Garner Lovell (unrelated to Hathaway Lovell, a colleague at times of Loorz and Morgan) was drawn from Joe Willicombe's office staff in Los Angeles. It was probably Smelser, though, who shuttled the guest that Willicombe named in a brief message. "Please give Chris Jensen the reservation for lower berth to Los Angeles that I telephoned for tonight, and charge to Mr. Hearst's account.

separately for that[duty] which WRW doesn't know yet and last night due to engine trouble with the S.P. [Southern Pacific] I didn't get back here until 5 A.M. If
my strength holds up I'll have a bit of spending money by Xmas. Counting tip[s]
I made 8.50 extra last night which I wouldn't want any one to know around here
before WRW gets a nephew or son-in-law on the job.

Smelser's postscript said, "Jack Adams [the telegrapher] seems to be gone for
good. Very mysterious. They installed a teletype for wires [telegrams and similar
media]."

In the past, a letter like Smelser's would have won a full page in reply, maybe
more. But Loorz claimed on November 17 to be too busy to answer in proper style.
He'd write later, he promised.

The next day, Ray Van Gorden wrote to Loorz from Los Angeles, where he
was "trying to rustle a job":

This town beats them all for climate especially this time of the year. The days are
perfect although it is a little chilly at night.

I phoned Mr. [H. O.] Hunter the other day as regards a job on the Examiner
[the Hearst morning paper] and he told me to come over and he would introduce
me to Mr. [E. W.] Hedland but thought it would be better if I would have Mr. Willicombe write him in my behalf. I dont know just what I could do there but think
that 18 years service for Mr. Hearst [at San Simeon] should count for something. . . .

Haven't seen any of the Hearst Camp bums around. Dont know where they
hang out but I know it isn't around Broadway or Hill [in downtown Los An-
geles]. . . .

P. S. I thought you were a wizz on the typewriter but some of these women
around here could lay you in the shade.

This time Loorz answered promptly. He told Van Gorden on November 19
that if "a real big job" he was figuring came through, he could use him to "take
care of the time and materials." Pending that, he had some news for Van Gorden
about Pete Petersen, who had seen the Loorzes in Pacific Grove. "He is in no hurry
to go to work," Loorz said of the financially stable Petersen.[84] "In fact, he's looking
around for some little business or farm but hasn't made up his mind yet. Says he
cant stay in San Simeon much longer."

I have given him his ticket." From Willicombe to Ticket Agent (Southern Pacific Depot, San Luis
Obispo), December 1, 1938; Hearst Papers, carton 24 (under "Ja-Jn").

84. See note 18, above. On October 30, Loorz told Petersen that, together, they might "figure
and build some good big job" on which Petersen could get foreman wages plus half the profits. "That
is providing you helped in the financing," Loorz also said.

Not without working for Hearst, that is, an arrangement allowing Petersen's further use of the picturesque house he'd occupied for several years.

At the end of November — on Monday the twenty-eighth — the perpetually busy Loorz found time to answer Mac McClure, whose letter about Palo Alto and Wyntoon and the Cosmopolitan bungalow went back almost three weeks. Playing fast and loose with events that fall, Loorz told Mac, "I didn't know you and the gang had left Wyntoon until a few days before I got your letter [of November 9]." He had actually known since at least October 20.[85] Nonetheless: "Jud drove up [from San Simeon] with Mrs. Forsythe and told me about it. Even Pete didn't write and of course I haven't seen anyone else." Loorz continued by saying:

> Anyway I'm sorry I didn't answer sooner but please believe that I have been rushed like h—. We now have over $400,000 worth of contracts in this little branch office and Fred has about $150,000 up there [in Alameda]. . . .
>
> Mac I think things are on the up and will be for a few years. I was only depending upon one or two years of good times but now I see more ahead. If you can build up your funds as I've built mine in a short space of time you'd not be in a hurry to go back to Wyntoon next summer.[86]

He still thought, as Stolte did, that Palo Alto could hold some promise for Mac.

Right after that, Van Gorden wrote from Cambria, having just returned from Los Angeles; his letter to Loorz went out on December 1, a Thursday.[87] Van Gorden had seen an old friend of his from San Simeon's earlier times — none other than Camille Rossi:

> I was out to visit the Rossi family at Glendale last Saturday afternoon and they have a wonderful home. He is working for the Gov't in an office on 8th & Figue-

---

85. Loorz's letter to Petersen of October 30 (note 84, above) sounded more precise about dates and details. "I never knew until 10 days ago when Ed [Sullivan] came up that you were back from Wyntoon." (Sullivan was Loorz's brother-in-law and was part of Nigel Keep's orchard crew at San Simeon.) "Mac did not write to me and no one else did," Loorz explained to Petersen. "I thot certainly you would drop in or write me a note when you left there."

86. Overall, the foundation of Loorz's prosperity since February 1932 had been his high salary from Hearst, coupled with rent-free living in San Simeon through January 1938. The "short space of time" Loorz mentioned is harder to define; he may have been counting from mid-1935, the period of his branch-office work for the Stolte Co. His gross earnings, through Hearst and Stolte combined, ran as high as $10,400 in 1936 and $11,674 in 1937. It was partly for that reason that Loorz informed his partner on September 5, 1938, "Now Fred I have decided to leave myself off of the payroll entirely for the balance of the year." The issue was taxes and the like, not altruism. Come 1939, Loorz reported a Hearst-Stolte gross for himself of $5,398 in 1938.

87. Loorz most likely received a letter from Lilian Forney the day before Van Gorden's arrived; hers was dated November 30. After some words of business (regarding "final Wyntoon bills to

roa [in Los Angeles] and when he started there were 56 in the office and now there are but 8 and 3 more are to be let go before the 1st of the year and he is afraid he might be one of the 3. He has had some pretty tough sledding and is now trying to make some connection to go into business. . . .

I was also up to see Mr. Hunter who introduced me to Mr. Hedland who does the hiring at the Examiner. They were both surprised there was no more construction going on at Hearst Camp, they both asked about you and how you were making it in your business and I told them of all the jobs you were doing which made them sit up and take notice. I think they are in the habit of seeing men that leave the Hearst Organization starve to death.

The upshot of it all was that Van Gorden didn't find work at the *Examiner*— or at any other place in Los Angeles:

By the way, I wrote a letter to Mr. Willicombe asking him for a letter in my behalf to Mr. Hedland. I waited around for a week for it but he never answered. I know I would have a better chance of getting one from Mr. Hearst but there isn't any way one can get past Willicombe.

One could, of course, with a name like Loorz or Morgan. The overlooked Van Gorden was simply too low on the totem pole this time, just as the rank-and-file usually were, no matter how noble their motives. The thought of Hearst's inaccessibility is humbling, sobering (whether it was willful on his part or not). On top of that, Willicombe could make himself equally remote and impregnable. The buck could stop right there, stone cold on the Colonel's desk, without ever reaching Hearst's level.

Pete Petersen and another good friend of Loorz's, Frank Souza, were luckier at the moment. Loorz had told Souza in late November that if he joined the union in Salinas, he could work as a labor foreman for Loorz's branch of the F. C. Stolte Co. The pay would be adequate: nine dollars a day.[88] Souza declined. "I thank you a million times for the offer of a job," he answered on December 6, "but at the present I have a contract on a fence for the Hearst Ranch, which will not be completed

---

be paid"), Mrs. Forney told Loorz: "You probably know Miss Morgan is in Europe—had a letter from her from Venice yesterday. She seems to be enjoying her vacation immensely!"

88. For perspective, the amount promised Souza can be compared with the eight- to ten-dollar rates Loorz summarized for Morgan on April 30 (p. 362 in this chapter). Loorz's own earning power provides too high a benchmark. But what he said to Anna Baumgartner on June 25—for the sake of her husband, Ernest ("Baum" in these annals)—shows that Souza could have done much worse. "I believe they are paying only $2.50 [per day] and board to the new men they are putting in the garden [at San Simeon]." Therefore, Loorz told her, "It would be unjust for me to give any encouragement for work on the Hilltop, even if Nigel Keep desired to employ 'Baum' [in the separate Orchard Department]."

before the first of the year." After that, though, Souza would have "nothing in view" and would like to work for Loorz.

As for Petersen, Loorz had high hopes of luring him north for one of the many jobs the branch office had secured. Petersen mulled it over; and after he got back from a trip to Los Angeles, he learned that Hearst had summoned him — to do some kind of woodwork or carpentry.[89] Writing didn't come easy for Petersen. When he gave Loorz the news on December 14, he left out the details.

Even Loorz had to read between the lines. "I gather from your letter that you are working on the hill again." Thus began his reply of December 18. "I am glad for that is so much better than loafing," he joshed. "You never were very good at the latter anwyay."

Loorz took a last stab at luring Petersen. His letter went on to say, "Remember Pete if I get this job on Dec. 27th you still have first chance at it." But he assured his friend, "You can do as you wish."

Then he offered some words that spoke not only for himself and Petersen but also for everyone else in their uncommon circle. "Maybe they will start up with a small crew on the hill again. We never can tell."

---

89. A minor job that may still have been pending was the improvement of the dog kennels. Norman Johnson, who ran that department, projected an outlay of $125 to do the work, $45 of it being for a week's worth of carpentry (at $9 per day). See Johnson to Willicombe, November 11, 1938; Hearst Papers, carton 24 (under "Jo-Jz").

1939

Never Say Die

L OORZ'S LETTER TO PETE PETERSEN—the one dated December 18, 1938 —had been written on a Sunday. Loorz had done the honors himself (rather than impose on his secretary, Conrad Gamboni), probably having been glad to keep his fingers limber. He was still a writer, still a man whose words sought the eye, not just the ear. For that matter, he'd done his own typing the next day, too, December 19, despite its being a Monday. The resulting letter, like the one to Petersen, had also gone to San Simeon—to Joe Willicombe. Loorz had begun by telling the Colonel, "I will hastily note the important things to be taken care of this time of year on the hilltop."

Loorz may have been fielding a request from Willicombe, or maybe he just felt like being helpful. His papers are too scarce at this juncture to provide the answer. At any rate, the past two winters had been fierce, and he knew perfectly well what Hearst, Willicombe, and everyone else at San Simeon might soon be facing. He filled a page with details on installing storm sash, checking and cleaning drains, and re-caulking certain windows. He didn't tiptoe down his list. Willicombe needed information, not coddling. "See that all dampers are open in fireplaces not used much," Loorz emphatically said. "Damaging smoke has resulted in the past when fires were built with closed dampers. This happened in the Doges [Suite] once."

His last point concerned the need for "pointing up" (re-grouting) the tile decks on the lowest, ocean-facing level of Casa del Mar. Some little rooms in that vulnerable spot, where Hearst's valet usually stayed, had leaked every year but had managed to remain livable. "Complete correction always was too big for the budget," Loorz noted—right before he signed off with his customary "Cheerio."

Yes, that old bugaboo the budget had cramped Hearst's style in many situations, and not just since the doomsday year of 1937.

But things were surely tighter now in the era of "personal" versus "company" funds. Loorz and Nigel Keep had kept in touch through the late part of 1938, mostly about improving Keep's pride and joy, the pergola on Orchard Hill; they continued writing in the early weeks of the new year. Keep's handwritten letters are a challenge to read, more so than any others in the Loorz Papers. (One could easily mistake them for the scribbles of a madman.) Yet they prove to contain some solid nuggets amid the curlicues and other eccentricities. "Doubtless Geo," he wrote on January 30, 1939, "you know Ed [Sullivan] left us, I had straight orders from the office to reduce wages from 100 to 80 [dollars per month][1] and that cut Ed would not stand for." Sullivan had denounced Keep, had called him a hypocrite, had held him liable for what occurred. But Keep, who'd gone to bat for Sullivan many times and was deeply hurt by the outcry, described himself to Loorz as being *"absolutely guiltless."* In fact, Keep had also been ordered to lay off two other men, not just reduce their wages. "Economy rule from N.Y. & S.F.," as he put it.

Loorz was indeed aware that Sullivan had left San Simeon; the man was Grace Loorz's brother. Sullivan had headed straight to Pacific Grove when he fell out with Keep. Loorz hammered out a full-page response on February 1, knowing that Keep's feelings and sanity were at stake. "First few people know Ed's short comings as well as I do. Second, no man can change my opinion of you and your sense of fair play because I have seen with my own eyes":

> You may rest assured Nigel that you are still one of my dearest and sincerest friends and I'll be the first to tell you when I change my mind. I really value your friendship Nigel more than you know.
>
> Frankly Ed merely mentioned that he refused to take the cut and that is that. I think Nigel he knows that without your continued support he would have been out long ago. I know also that ever since I have known him he has always found fault with his superiors after he has been with them for a while. This includes me Nigel as well as Louis [Reesing], Ed March and yourself.
>
> I continue to employ him first because he is my brother-in-law, secondly because he really is a good and careful workman. He has always more than earned his money while working for me. I know he did with you or you would have discharged him long ago.

---

1. Hearst's employees were paid on a weekly, half monthly, or monthly basis. The pay scale Keep spoke of recalls the one Loorz mentioned to Anna Baumgartner midway through 1938 (p. 399, note 88). Later that year, a local man with the rare name of Doris Ingles complained that, for ranch hands and related help, Randy Apperson had "cut the wages from $70 to $50 [per month]." See Ingles to Willicombe, October 31, 1938; Hearst Papers, carton 24 (under "I"). Sometime the following year Willicombe asked Hearst if Albert Redelsperger—who along with his wife, Gussie, had left Hearst's employ midway through 1937, had been rehired (at the Beach House) early in 1938, but had since been dismissed—could get a letter of recommendation to go with his final wages. Hearst said Redelsperger could, for he was "a good man." Willicombe's query ended with "I PRESUME NO OBJECTION TO PAYING HIM FOR THE FULL HALF MONTH—$55." Hearst Papers, carton 27 (under "Hearst Memorandums 1939").

So let it be that way Nigel and I think it is for the best for all concerned. I only hope Randy [Apperson, still the ranch manager] and you will believe me that I have never had any sympathies with Ed's bolshevistic ideas. His is only talk so I have put up with it.[2]

Keep, having received Loorz's letter on February 2 ("kind and soothing," he called it), wrote a brief reply that evening. The rough weather of the past two winters hadn't materialized after all, at least not yet:

Rain since 2 pm & its raining hard now, well we need it—10" below normal for the season. . . . Pkd 40 doz[en] oranges today, frost did us NO damage, but just bet[ween] 10 & 11 am we had quite a snow storm & it is (the snow) still on Pine Mountain.

A white mantle on the nearby peaks is always a sight to behold: even at those higher elevations, it doesn't last long. Hearst and his party missed seeing it that Thursday. For as Keep also reported, "W R H in S. Monica since Monday [January 30]." He may have been at the Beach House earlier in the month, too.[3]

During Hearst's latest absence from San Simeon, Mac McClure went up to the hilltop from Los Angeles. He arrived the day before the snow did, February 1.[4] Morgan wasn't back from Europe yet. But with Mac's appearance on behalf of her

---

2. Loorz, like Keep, had also gone to bat for Ed Sullivan at times. An episode in 1936 stands out. On November 28 of that year, Bill Murray of Hearst Sunical asked Loorz why an employee was using Hearst Camp stationery; Sullivan, writing under that letterhead, had got in touch with a company that proved to be an advertiser in the Hearst papers, causing "considerable embarrassment." Loorz wrote to Murray twice to mend fences (both times on November 30, 1936).

In writing to his parents on February 13, 1939, Loorz mentioned that he'd sent Sullivan "on a trip with the truck to Shandon," a remote town east of Paso Robles where a school job was under way; Sullivan, though, had been late in returning because of "a little truck trouble." All the more time, perhaps, for John Steinbeck's presence, which pervaded the long road through the Salinas Valley—as it still does today—to nurture those "bolshevistic ideas" that Sullivan harbored.

Loorz urged his parents in that February letter to visit Pacific Grove soon; he proved for a moment to be as observant as Steinbeck himself, though not as graceful. "You ought to come now for the Spring winds will be coming in before long. When they do we are good for two months of wind every afternoon the same as at San Simeon."

3. The Bancroft Library has letters addressed to Hearst in Santa Monica then, sent by people who often knew his whereabouts. See for example H. S. MacKay, Jr., to Hearst, January 23, 1939; Hearst Papers, carton 27 (under "MacKay, H. S."). Other letters of MacKay's, plus some memos in the Hearst Papers, indicate that Hearst remained in Santa Monica through early March. His presence there also figures in "Dusk at Santa Monica," a cover story published by *Time* (March 13, 1939), pp. 49–56.

4. The date appears both in the Morgan-Forney ledgers and in the Cal Poly series San Simeon Financial Records (under III/03/07/115: "Morgan's Fees and Expenses, 1939"). The entries differ, however, in other details. The Cal Poly version was typed in June 1939 from the earlier Morgan-Forney version (which was handwritten as usual, but too unclearly in this instance).

office, a fledgling new season of Hearst activity was now under way. Actually, her staff had produced some final details in January for a Hearst project other than San Simeon or Wyntoon, namely, for the Sunical headquarters in San Francisco. The push to remodel the Hearst Building at 3rd and Market streets dated from 1936 and 1937; the job had been in fuller swing, though, throughout 1938, remaining so even after Morgan went abroad.[5]

THE FIRST HINT of Morgan's return to action in 1939 lies in the Morgan-Forney ledgers, buried as deep as an entry can be. "Miss Morgan to L.A." That's all Lilian Forney noted for March 18 of the new year—in a section of undesignated, mostly unspecific entries headed "Office." The date, in any case, fell on a Saturday; yet whether Morgan saw Hearst or Frank Hellenthal or someone else is unclear. What's much more discernible, thanks to the regular account sheets for San Simeon, is that she appeared on the hilltop by Monday, March 20. She was also there the next day; in fact, she didn't get back to San Francisco until mid-week.

She wrote to Hearst the following week, on March 29.[6] And then the next day she wrote to Loorz, likewise from San Francisco:

> A gay Christmas Greeting from "the Boys" [Loorz's three sons], candle on it & Holly too— reached me with just as much a load of pleasure at the kind thoughtfulness just before leaving Sicily in March, as though it had arrived as it should have by all calculations, at Christmas proper! "Mail" was the least well managed part of an interesting winter—Thanks to Don, Bill & Bob.
>
> I did not want to write anyone until I had a chance to pick up my own ideas— even if unrelated [to what clients or others were presently doing]—I find I must keep busy—have too much strength & too many ideas to drop out of an active life—Just how & what it will result in is not yet clear.

---

5. Morgan came much closer to balancing costs on the Hearst Building, even at just a six-percent commmission, than she did on the Allan Starr residence of 1938–39 at seven percent. The Hearst interests paid $96,223 for the work done on the Hearst Building by King Parker's company and various sub-contractors. Morgan collected $5,773—$823 less than the $6,596 she accrued in operating costs. (Comparisons: had the job commanded $109,933, her costs would have equaled six percent; or if she'd charged 6.85% of $96,223, she would likewise have broken even.)

During Morgan's six-month absence in late 1938-early 1939, her office accrued nearly $1,300 in costs on the Hearst Building ($500 of it being for Walter Huber's engineering services). The Starr job in Piedmont produced more than $2,000 in office costs through the same period.

6. The Hearst/Morgan Correspondence at Cal Poly has two letters closely following the trip in March; both are from Morgan to Hearst. The second letter, dated March 29 (a copy went to Mac McClure), addressed in fair detail something Morgan touched on only briefly when she wrote to Loorz on March 30: the proposed work in Casa del Sol. The Warren McClure Papers at Hearst Castle include three letters from the same week; their main subject is also Casa del Sol. At least two years earlier Hearst conceived a similar revamping of all three houses, not just the aforementioned one; see Hearst to Morgan, March 14, 1937; Hearst/Morgan Correspondence, Morgan Collection.

Mr Hearst looks much better than I had reason to expect, & will, am sure, make the grade [recover financially] & surprise everyone. However, I think only repairs & minor things will be done anywhere this year, although a remodeling of House "C" [Casa del Sol] is on the boards "if not too expensive"—If you hear a call at Monterey, beyond greetings, it will be to ask you to drop over & check my ideas as to this cost—I do not think it can be done at what Mr Hearst would or could consider a "not too expensive" base.

It will be interesting to hear how family, work, etc has been these [past few] months—Please give my affectionate regards to the family one & all—.[7]

A woman of sixty-seven now, Morgan sounded as eager as ever to resume work. And yet conditions had often been grueling over the years, right down to the present almost. The partial retirement she'd visualized in 1936 (discouraged by Hearst's perseverance since then, along with his numerous catch-up payments) may have posed a likelier, more attractive prospect now than ever before.[8] It remained too soon to say, though.

Morgan's letter to Loorz, dated March 30, coincided with one that Loorz himself wrote to Alex Rankin, the jack-of-all-trades son of the Oakland plumber Jim Rankin:

With the pleasant association we have had together for seven years, it is too bad to bow our heads and work without further thought of each other. . . .

Mr. Willicombe calls occasionally and Mr. Apperson needs information from time to time so that I keep in fairly close touch with the Hilltop.[9]

Every now and then, an enquiry comes up that sounds like work is anticipated but I doubt very much that it will happen this year.

---

7. Morgan's letter to Loorz of March 30, 1939, is one of five from 1938 through 1940 that surfaced in December 1997. All but one (Arch Parks to George and Grace Loorz, November 29, 1938) proved germane to this newer book; the group has since been added to the George Loorz Papers at the San Luis Obispo County Historical Museum.

8. As was stated in the 1937 chapter (pp. 293–94, note 9), Morgan received multiple payments at the outset of that year. They amounted to nearly $10,250, and they pertained strictly to her Commission Account for San Simeon; by June 1937 she received close to $8,800 more in back payments for the same account. (The exact total—$19,039—appears in Appendix B.) In addition, likewise regarding San Simeon, Morgan received nearly $12,400 in 1936–37, both through a belated reconciling of the Hilltop Fund and through periodic "refunds"; she made good headway in 1938 as well. (Meanwhile, from December 1936 through June 1938, she received commission payments and refunds for Wyntoon of roughly $8,500.) See also notes 33 and 37, below.

By the end of 1939, on the other hand, Morgan vacated "1135," as her office in the Merchants Exchange had been known for years. She took smaller (and presumably less expensive) quarters on the same floor in Room 1107, her second and final address in that grand old building on California Street. Both Walter Steilberg and the Morgan Norths alluded to the move from Room 1135, though not with much precision. See *The Julia Morgan Architectural History Project*, Vol. I, p. 141, and Vol. II, p. 178.

9. In Randy Apperson's case, Loorz had written to him on March 14 about San Simeon's poultry unit. "I have searched through what records I have, back and forth," Loorz told him, "and have

We [the F. C. Stolte Co.] still have a good deal of business and expect a fairly good net return for the year. We [the Loorz family] are all completely satisfied with our home here on Monterey Bay, so, what more can we ask?

Before Rankin had time to answer, Loorz hastened to write Morgan on Monday, April 3; he and his family had been to the Golden Gate Exposition in San Francisco over the weekend, and Morgan's recent letter reached him that morning:

Yes, Miss Morgan, we have no complaints whatever to make with the volume of business we have been so fortunate to have this year. We [the Pacific Grove branch] have other contracts on hand, at the present time, to carry us nicely for the next six months. They range from a fine home ($65,000 in Del Monte Fairways) to a $100,000 sewer disposal plant in Carmel, and five or six schools in between.[10] In the Alameda office [under Fred Stolte] they are doing mostly service station work. I believe they have six or seven under construction at present and are still coming in fast. These are not so interesting as they are profitable.[11]

I will be delighted to have you call me at your earliest opportunity when you are in Monterey. If the preliminary estimate [for the proposed work at San Simeon] is not in order at that time, I would, at least, like to visit with you.

I hear from the boys [such as Frank Gyorgy], that were with us on the Hill, quite regularly; mostly through visits from one or the other. Daily I think of writing to them but somehow think of something else more important to do. This is wrong for I value the boys as friends and hope to keep them as friends.

---

not been able to find the sketches or the estimates on the Mallard Duck Ponds that were proposed in 1933 or 1934." He also told Apperson:

If I could remember the approximate length of the winding pond proposed, I could refigure it very quickly. Though we destroyed [in 1937] all of the records under the Hearst Construction [Fund], I did preserve those in connection with [the] Hilltop Fund or Mr. Hearst's personal work through me.

Along with those sobering words, Loorz had more to tell Apperson on March 24, 1939. "I made another search through my records and found a rough note that had been given to Mr. Hearst." It spoke of duck ponds that would cost about $800, but Loorz had yet to find more data. He speculated, "It may be that the sketch is still on the shelf in the construction office on the hill."

10. The "fine home" was the Cunnigham residence, mentioned to Claude and Freda Loorz in the fall of 1938; see p. 394, note 77. The Carmel Sewage Plant was a newer job, begun in February. No further schools had been started yet in 1939; but in Salinas itself there were actually two such jobs, the Washington School and Salinas Junior College.

11. Besides doing further work in 1939 on "General Pete" stations in northern California, the Alameda office handled several jobs for the Mohawk, Richfield, Seaside, and Signal oil companies. Associated Oil was an even better customer, for which Stolte's Alameda office built stations in the Bay Area, in Sacramento (where it also built a General Pete), and in towns as far north as Ukiah and Eureka. However, the Shell Oil Company was by far the foremost gas-station account in 1939 —good for more than a dozen jobs, mainly around the Bay Area. Meanwhile, Alameda's largest job that year was the gymnasium it built at Castlemont High School in Oakland, superintended by Frank Gendrich.

We have driven past your home here many times and thought of you since you have been away on your trip. We are more than happy to know that your trip has given you new strength and ambition.

On the subject of San Simeon, Morgan had left out some key details in her letter of March 30. She hadn't told Loorz that she and Hearst discussed a good deal more than House "C" earlier that month. Indeed, a proposal to improve the East Room, harkening back to the days of grand gestures and seemingly boundless means, wouldn't be laid at Loorz's doorstep for two more months.[12] She and Mac McClure would wrestle with the problem till then—with the age-old problem of the East Room (or Morning Room) fireplace and the smoke and ashes it spewed. Hearst still hoped for corrections, despite the strain they would put on his non-corporate purse.

Mac stayed on at San Simeon after Morgan's visit in late March. April 16 found him going to Los Angeles, possibly to see Hearst, who'd recently left the ranch (but who might not have remained at the Beach House long, pending a trip he'd be making out of state).[13] Morgan herself headed south on April 21. This time, though, her main business was of the non-Hearst variety. "Travel Miss Morgan Los Angeles Cemeteries," went Lilian Forney's first entry on a new account page, the subject being the so-called Darbee Mausoleum. Mrs. A. H. Darbee of San Francisco had retained Morgan, along with Bernard Maybeck, to design a burial ground of the highest order. San Francisco's neighboring city of Lawndale (renamed Colma in 1941) was the proposed setting for what would formally be known as Western Hills of Memorial City. The job would be the first Morgan-Maybeck collaboration since Principia College. Mrs. Darbee's tastes were as nostalgic as

---

12. The proposed work was first described by Morgan in a brief list headed "East Room Changes," dated April 4, 1939. It was superseded by a longer, more detailed list she compiled for Mac McClure on April 10 and then sent to Loorz about May 31 (pp. 413–14 in this chapter); the shorter list of April 4 may have gone to Loorz at the same time.

13. A telegram from Bill Hearst, the second of Hearst's five sons, went to "Pop" in California on April 17 but was rerouted to Chicago the next day; Hearst Papers, carton 27 (under "Hearst, W.R. & Family"). A week later, April 25, Bill Hearst wrote to Joe Willicombe at the Belvedere Hotel in Baltimore; Hearst Papers, ibid. By April 29, Hearst and his party were at Cissy Patterson's home in Washington, D.C., the setting for his seventy-sixth birthday. (Patterson had assumed full ownership of Hearst's Washington papers in January, the morning *Herald* and the evening *Times*, publishing them from then on as the combined *Times-Herald*.)

A photograph of Hearst's birthday gathering—the Chief is seated center front, surrounded by Willicombe and several other men, but not by Mrs. Patterson or any other women—has appeared in at least two books, both times dated incorrectly. In *The Hearsts*, Lindsay Chaney and Michael Cieply cite 1937 (photo 14, following p. 160). The Marion Davies memoir, *The Times We Had*, cites 1938 (p. 203). The proper date appears in a contemporary, typewritten caption, attached to a copy of the photograph owned by Willicombe's heirs.

Hearst's, as deeply anachronistic; she foresaw a tribute to Maybeck's Palace of Fine Arts from the old Panama-Pacific world's fair, only grander and more dramatic. Morgan began her part of the drawings soon after she returned from Los Angeles.[14]

In the meantime, also on April 21, Loorz wrote to a friend he'd made in the early days on the Burnett Road, King Walters. Walters had written from the San Fernando Valley town of Van Nuys on April 16. "I see where they are going to open up the Sherwood Lake Tract," he told Loorz, "and do quite a bit of road work. I would like very much to get in on it, as it is near where we have bought our home." The land he meant was the Triunfo Ranch property, close to Thousand Oaks and sold by the Hearst interests in 1938 (as Mac had noted on June 16 that year).[15]

"I am sorry I cannot give you a hint on the Tract you mention," Loorz wrote in reply. "Frankly," he told Walters, "I do not believe Mr. Hearst has a thing to do with it though it is done under his name."

Loorz also said, "I still keep in touch with the Hilltop through enquiries from Mr. Hearst and Miss Morgan. Until more money is raised, I feel that there would be little more work done. How times have changed!"[16]

---

14. Maybeck is said to have designed additions in the 1930s to Woodlawn Memorial Park, one of Colma's many cemeteries, and one not far from the Darbee property. (Cypress Lawn Cemetery, where Hearst was buried in 1951, is even closer.) All these parcels are within the Colma city limits, not within those of neighboring South San Francisco, to which the Morgan-Maybeck project has sometimes been assigned.

The Julia Morgan Collection, Environmental Design Archives, has a "Preliminary Prospectus of Western Hills of Memorial City, Incorporated." The foreword makes a bold assertion. The project would "not only outrank in conception, design and function anything in Northern California" but would also "compare favorably in general interest with the Arlington Memorial in Washington, D.C., or other of the all-too-few famous burial places of the world." Mrs. Darbee, however, owned some forty acres in Lawndale-Colma, a parcel half the size of the Woodlawn facility and a fifth the size of Cypress Lawn (as they presently stand). The Arlington National Cemetery was already ten times greater than the Darbee acreage before the Morgan-Maybeck project was conceived—a project regarded, no doubt, as one emphasizing quality over quantity. (Arlington now comprises more than 600 acres.)

15. See p. 377 in this volume. See also Carol A. Bidwell, *The Conejo Valley: Old and New Frontiers* (Chatsworth, California; 1989), pp. 38, 42.

16. On April 23, Loorz wrote to an old friend in San Francisco named John McKee. "After seven years at San Simeon directing Mr. Hearst's construction," said Loorz (evidently including 1938 with the 1932–37 period), "it is quite a pleasure to be back in a live community":

One reason for locating here [in Pacific Grove] and not back in Berkeley was to be near the Hearst estate. That has been a profitable contact. However, with the turn of financial events in his regards I have little hopes for much more if any work. There is still the desire, however, since I get an occasional inquiry from him. Maybe he can come back.

He also told McKee, "Right now the F. C. Stolte Co. has more work than any contractor south of San Jose. We are not the biggest but are aiming at becoming the best." It all amounted to "quite a

RAY VAN GORDEN had been missing from the annals all year. On May 4 he reappeared in top form; Loorz received two pages of tightly packed details, sent from Cambria. ("The old town has just about folded up," Van Gorden remarked in the early going.) Some of his further news regarded mutual friends of theirs, plus other matters:

> Frank Gyorgy is getting pretty anxious for something to turn up and Mrs. Gyorgy is much more so. I was down there [at their place in Cambria] cleaning the lot and kidded them along some. John Vanderloo still has hopes of the camp opening and isn't worrying a bit. . . . I haven't seen [Frank] Frandolich but they tell me with Louisa [his wife] working occasionally, he has a strangle hold on that wolf.
>
> Babe Souza [Frank Souza] is as busy as a bee — he has another ranch leased in green valley [Green Valley, between Cambria and Harmony] as well as a crop of sugar beets there. . . . He is also building fence for the real estater that is selling off the Hearst Property [the nearby Santa Rosa Ranch].[17] They are having quite a time selling off the land even if it is cheap. It is all offered on a cash basis only and there dont seem to be much cash around at the present time. I heard yesterday that the deal with Link Luchessa [a prospective buyer] had fell through altho I doubt if it [is] so. . . .
>
> Conrad [Gamboni, Loorz's secretary] told me that you had listened in on Hitler's speech in the early hours of the morning. . . . I think he and Poland are going to get together on their differences, but will France and Italy do the same by theirs? They are doing a very good job of keeping the whole world stirred up in such a way that no country can make any progress. I think business would pick up in this country at this time if it wasn't for the war scare. . . .
>
> The Camp [on the hilltop] is entirely deserted at the present time as far as the guests are concerned. I saw Mr. [W. R.] Williams (and he looks well) at the High School program [in Cambria] the other night and they are now getting off at 2:30 in the afternoon for a welcome change. They say Mr. Hearst will go directly to Wyntoon on his return from the East. Link [Luchessa] said a 15 million [amount] had come into the kitty here of late that wasn't expected so I guess Mr. Hearst feels like he can strut his self again. Damon Runyon had an interesting article about him a few days ago.[18] Probably you read it. One has to give him [Hearst] credit for being a loyal American, first, last and all the time.

---

step from a farmer boy in Lovelock [Nevada]," in Loorz's view. To which he added, "I'm not saying whether it is up or down."

17. Prospects for Santa Rosa's sale had been aired in some correspondence of Hearst, Murray, and Willicombe a year and a half earlier; see p. 342, note 96.

18. Most likely in Runyon's daily feature column, "The Brighter Side," which ran in the *San Francisco Examiner* and other Hearst morning papers.

In the wake of that, Loorz sent out an undated letter, marked "Tuesday" only — this during a thin stretch when his words and everyone else's were much too scarce to treat casually. (At the time, of course, he wouldn't have been worried about it.) Loorz probably wrote soon after Van Gorden did, perhaps on May 9. Some of what he told his recipient, Pete Petersen, sounds reassuringly familiar:

> Had a nice visit with Miss Morgan a few weeks ago. It looks like things will be real slow getting started again on the hilltop. However, one rumor came to the effect that Mr. Hearst got hold of some $15,000,000 which should pull him out of the dumps. Lets hope the rumor has some portion of truth to it. One cannot believe many stories about Mr. Hearst.[19]

Whereas Ray Van Gorden, Frank Gyorgy, and John Vanderloo were hunkered down in Cambria, awaiting Hearst's call to arms, a small group of their compatriots still lived closer to where the action might resume. And thus Loorz's final line for Petersen: "How is Elsie [Pete's wife], Louisa [Frandolich], Frandy and the rest of the San Simeon natives?"

Morgan herself, likewise awaiting the call, had started another job outside the Hearst sphere — aside from the mausoleum for Mrs. A. H. Darbee in Lawndale-Colma. James Parsons and his wife were planning a home in Monterey. They chose Morgan as their architect; she in turn had Loorz start the bidding process, and by late May his local branch of the Stolte Co. was on board as her builder. In the meantime, Hearst had been back on the coast since early that month. Rather than make a beeline for Wyntoon, as some had thought he would, he dug in for several weeks at San Simeon. In mid-May, Morgan stopped by to see him before heading south on a job they'd barely started the year before, the remodeling of the Cosmopolitan bungalow.[20] By now the structure had been dismantled again (echoes of

---

19. The fifteen-million figure recalls the article "$15,000,000 Worth" that appeared in *Time* the year before (March 14, 1938), p. 39. The amount was the purported value of antiques and related items Hearst "had decided to sell or otherwise dispose of," representing two thirds of his art holdings. (If acts of factual transference were still occurring more than a year after this brief but influential story was published, no one should be surprised.)

Cissy Patterson's purchase of Hearst's Washington papers in January 1939 (note 13, above) offers no basis for that superheated rumor — lest anyone assume so — her outlay having been a small fraction of fifteen million dollars.

Another possible tie-in involves "the Canadians" who supplied Hearst with newsprint and who said there would be "no more credit after March 25th." From H. S. MacKay, Jr., to Hearst, March 13, 1939; Hearst Papers, carton 27 (under "MacKay, H. S."). With that same period in mind, John Francis Neylan later claimed to have "exposed the newsprint companies drive for a fifteen million dollar steal." See Neylan to Hearst, March 8, 1944; ibid., carton 39 (under "New-Nh").

20. Under "May 14 & 16," the Morgan-Forney ledgers report "Travel Miss Morgan — to S.S., to L.A., back to SS & SF." This entry in the bungalow account provides the only evidence that Morgan was at San Simeon that month. Otherwise, the March 20–22 entry in the San Simeon account

1934) and moved from Warner Bros. in Burbank to a new studio address, that of Twentieth Century-Fox in Westwood, just outside the Beverly Hills city limits. Bearing Hearst's latest wishes, Morgan made the first of numerous trips in 1939— there were sixteen all told—to work with Frank Hellenthal on a partial, greatly modified re-erection of the bungalow. The latest plot twist was that Hearst was merely storing the segmented structure on the Twentieth Century lot.[21] Yet another setting, featuring a small house on Benedict Canyon Drive in Beverly Hills, would be absorbing selected parts from the bungalow assemblage. The house belonged to Marion Davies and was close to her better-known place on Lexington Road.[22]

(repeated in the Cal Poly series San Simeon Financial Records, as in note 4, above) would indicate she was never on the hilltop later that year. To its sole credit, the Cal Poly version includes "May 21 Los Angeles to San Simeon" for Mac McClure, an entirely plausible entry that occurs nowhere in the Morgan-Forney ledgers.

21. Hearst and Darryl Zanuck, head of Twentieth Century-Fox, were associated now through Cosmopolitan Productions, whose "label" appeared on such movies from 1939 as *Young Mr. Lincoln* and *The Story of Alexander Graham Bell*. This last deal of its kind for Hearst was short-lived, expiring in February 1940. A subsequent news item explained how such arrangements worked (Hearst didn't "produce" those films in the usual sense); see "No Renewal Between 20th-Fox and Hearst's Cosmo Pix in Prospect," *Variety* (weekly edition of March 27, 1940), p. 5—partially cited in Louis Pizzitola, *Hearst Over Hollywood: Power, Passion, and Propaganda in the Movies*, p. 372 (plus note on p. 492). Pizzitola assumed the bungalow went from the Fox lot to 910 Benedict Canyon when the Hearst-Zanuck deal lapsed in the winter of 1940 (instead of being moved there several months before).

Bob Board, collector extraordinaire of Marion Davies items, has a clipping dated March 1939 about the bungalow's move that year "from the Warner lot via Cahuenga Pass to the Twentieth Century-Fox lot," a job "costing $15,000." The event foreshadowed the resumption in May 1939 of the Cosmopolitan bungalow account (Morgan-Forney ledgers), whose entries through the summer and fall correspond with Frank Hellenthal's use of bungalow material at 910 Benedict—a project pursued mainly, if not entirely, in 1939.

Nevertheless, certain portions of the bungalow were still being stored at Twentieth Century as late as 1942. On June 4 that year, Miss Davies wired Ella Williams: "I am giving Rose [Douras] my bungalow dressing room for her birthday. Take her to the studio and have her look at it and put her name on it [claim it] if she likes it. This will save me money." (Bob Board Collection.)

22. In *Julia Morgan*, Sara Boutelle cites the bungalow under 1937—as a "demolished" structure—and with a job number as high as 780 (in the appendix "Buildings by Julia Morgan," p. 262). With further regard to job number 780, see Nancy E. Loe, *Descriptive Guide to the Julia Morgan Collection*, pp. 62, 74, 82; Boutelle's appendix is partly based on Loe's catalogue. Meanwhile under 1939 (likewise in "Buildings by Julia Morgan," p. 262), Boutelle correctly associates 910 Benedict Canyon Drive with a "Marion Davies house and pool" but assigns the address to Santa Monica, a city lying a few miles southwest of Beverly Hills.

The house at 910 Benedict—loosely synonymous with the bungalow—and the house at 1700 Lexington Road are in the same part of Beverly Hills. In fact, the two streets intersect, and the houses so numbered are around the corner from each other. The Lexington house is larger than its neighbor on Benedict Canyon. Miss Davies and her mother bought 1700 Lexington in the mid-twenties, about the time Hearst moved Cosmopolitan Productions from New York to California; see Guiles, *Marion Davies*, pp. 140–41. Later, Davies added 910 Benedict Canyon to her real estate holdings in the greater area (presumably sometime before—perhaps long before—portions of the bungalow were used in the house at that address).

Hearst, meanwhile, took up a project that may have been brewing for several months, one that Loorz and Nigel Keep's letters had hinted at as 1938 drew to a close. And now on May 16, with the days getting long and Hearst feeling ripe for action, Keep sent a new page of hieroglyphics to Loorz:

> I am writing Geo to see if you can give me the name & address of—as Mr Hearst says "OUR usual surveyor," he wants a surveyor to survey for a Pergola round China Hill & I dont know who our *usual surveyor* is, so lets know what you know, all well here, but weather is miserable, cold & foggy with a water shortage, 1¼″ coming over the weir & thats every drop thats coming in at the spring on P Mt [Pine Mountain]. . . . Planted 800 more Pines this spring. On ridges opp[osite] Bear grotto.

The skies had rained themselves out after two wet winters—that much was evident from Keep's letter. And the trees he mentioned: without such features, the outlying portions of The Enchanted Hill wouldn't be half as enchanting. It's surprising to learn how late in the game some of this forestation work was being done. Right now, though, Hearst had a more exacting, technical project in mind. That was Keep's big concern.

Loorz answered on May 19. He told Keep that the surveyor Hearst spoke of was I. J. Boyd of Atascadero (a man involved in the earliest work on the Burnett Road). Yet Loorz wasn't sure if Dick Boyd (as he was more often called) could be easily reached:

> If you are unable to make contact with him and Mr. Hearst was agreeable, I would be pleased to come down some weekend and with the assistance of one of your fleet-footed younger men, I am certain we could run a contour map of China Hill, upon which we could lay out a purgola [*sic*] to the most suitable location.

Keep's reply, dated May 24, said that Loorz's letter had been placed "before the chief," with these results:

> Quote "Please get in communication with Mr. Loorz. I am sure he could do the job perfectly & if he is willing to" Unquote —.
>
> So Geo can you come sometime within the next 2 weeks, as the chief said—"of course I want to be here when Mr Loorz surveys it," and I expect the chief to be away at Wyntoon after 2 weeks.

Loorz assured Keep on Thursday, May 25, that he would be down soon to do the survey. "In fact," he said, "there is a possibility that I might be able to make it next Monday," the twenty-ninth of May.

THE JOB TOOK PLACE a bit later instead, with Loorz appearing over the weekend of June 3–4. The trip was his first to San Simeon since October. When he got back to Pacific Grove on June 5, he wrote to Mac McClure, who'd been on hand both days to help.[23] Mac would not only be remaining at San Simeon; he would also be going to Wyntoon shortly. No one was better suited to be Hearst's designer-in-residence.

Loorz wrote a longer letter to Morgan while the typewriter was still warm, likewise on Monday, June 5:

> I just returned this noon from two days on the hilltop. I went down in answer to a request from Mr. Hearst thru Mr. Keep. He wanted me to run a survey of China Hill and layout a narrow Pergola Pathway around the [same] hill. It is too far for him to walk to the present one [the pergola on Orchard Hill] and walking on China Hill is now nearly impossible. He always walks around the hill [China Hill] now on the road [the divided driveway] which is both dangerous and not too pleasant. I'm certain it was just another air castle but enjoyed the two days in the sunshine and really worked hard to complete [the survey] so I could come back this morning.

He'd begun his letter with an apology: he hadn't answered her about "the proposed change in the East Room." Morgan had sent him a list a few days before — an excerpt, to be exact, from a letter she'd written Mac as early as April 10.[24] Why she'd waited this long to get Loorz's view is unclear. The East Room-Morning Room problem wasn't one that could be quickly assessed. And thus Loorz told her on June 5, "First I have had to think a lot about it for frankly I could not estimate it properly. Second I have been away for most of the time for four days [mostly on the survey]."

The excerpt Loorz saw had begun with these words of Morgan's: "Am sorry," she'd told Mac in April, "but it is not possible to quote ahead with any sureness on

---

23. Loorz's letter includes a passage that invites some visualizing of Mac's routine and whereabouts during his local stints for Hearst and Morgan. "I tried to phone you from San Simeon as I drove thru this morning about 10 A.M. [heading up the coast to Pacific Grove] but you had just left and were not yet at the office or your room [on the hilltop]." Loorz also mentioned some specifics from the weekend survey. The proposed work on China Hill, or at least a component of it, was evidently what he meant in signing off, "However, all agree it is a now forgotten issue."

24. The Hearst/Morgan Correspondence at Cal Poly has Morgan's file copy of what she sent Mac on April 10. The excerpt Loorz received lacked only the first paragraph (it dealt with unrelated things). In writing to Mac on May 31, Morgan mentioned the "outline" (the excerpt-list) that she was sending Loorz; Hearst Castle has a copy of her letter in its Warren McClure Papers; the Morgan Collection at Cal Poly does not. For their part, the Loorz Papers contain the excerpt-list plus an older, briefer, similar list of Morgan's, cited in note 12 of this chapter.

remodeling. Each change Mr. Hearst inquires the cost of, seems to require practically all trades—[concerning] for instance, the Morning Room—." She'd also provided Mac, and now Loorz all these weeks later, with a detailed list:

1. *Concrete driller and labor.* Skillful concrete drill man to remove the walls behind fireplace, and the chimney over the [adjoining] men's dressing room and the various walls, also to cut new door under Billiard Room stair to men's toilet [in a small room near the dressing room proper].[25]

2. *Plumber* to remove plumbing fixture lines and fixtures.

3. *Carpenters* to take out ceiling of men's room, [plus] doors, joists, studs, etc. and to reframe for and put up new panel of East room [or Morning Room] ceiling.

4. *Stone masons* to take down the mantel and the two doorways and take up the three little marble floors and fill in toilet room door.

5. *Electrician* to take out present wiring and rewire.

6. *Plasterer* to replaster new section and patch at new toilet door.

7. *Millwork and carving* "down below" [in the workmen's shops beyond Animal Hill] to furnish the new section of ceiling.

8. *Carpenters* to put up above.

9. *Marble work* "down below" to furnish material for new section of floor to match that of Morning Room.

10. *Marble man* to set the above.

11. *Painter* [to decorate] New ceiling panel walls and retouching.

12. A man in charge to coordinate all the above.

Loorz had those twelve points in mind when he told Morgan on June 5, "My guess is that it will cost between $15,000 & $20,000. 'Tis honestly only a rash guess with a tendency to play safe and to include all possible costs."[26]

He also said he'd avoided mentioning the subject when he was at San Simeon on the survey; he hadn't even looked at the room. He must have known she was less than thrilled with the prospect. For the excerpt from April 10—coming from the letter she'd originally sent Mac—included this line, too: "We will have to pay [the workmen] the same transportation and time lost for their short stay as we would for the whole season."

In other words, the arrangements would be involved, expensive, impracti-

---

25. The Men's Dressing Room comprises a small toilet room and a detached washroom. The washroom is between the East Room-Morning Room and the Billiard Room. The toilet room is tucked between one of the large staircases in Casa Grande's central section and a smaller staircase (Morgan's "Billiard Room stair") that leads to the North Duplex suites.

26. Loorz was right in saying "guess" in two places here. Morgan had done the same on May 31 (when she wrote to Mac, as in note 24). "I can only make a guess," she said of the Morning Room, "Mr. LeFeaver likewise." By the same token, "George's also would be more or less of a guess."

cal—and to judge from her tone, almost foolish. Not only that, but she'd made a point that was one she'd emphasized several times through the years: the need to engage "practically all trades" for work this varied and, in nearly every respect, this specialized. Petersen and Frandy and a few other local holdouts couldn't do it alone. No, all the boys would have to pitch in; yet several of them like Dell Clausen, Alex Rankin, and John McFadden had left the area, had been forced to commit themselves elsewhere. And what about the "man in charge" that she spoke of? The chances weren't good just now of reassembling a full crew of top-notch men, especially for a limited tour. The chances of making the whole enterprise affordable were even worse.[27]

Loorz's letter to Morgan of June 5 was a long one, and besides saying more about the weekend survey, he also put the East Room-Morning Room situation in broad perspective for her:

> Though I worked late both Saturday and Sunday I took time in the evenings to visit John Vanderloo, Frank Gyorgy, Frank Souza's family (Frank was out), Mrs Frandolich as her Frank is in the City and has perhaps called on you and all the rest of our many mutual friends that were with us on the hilltop [in years past].[28] Needless to say all visits were very brief but enjoyable.
>
> For the sake of our mutual friends I would love to see some work start at San Simeon. However, this particular job in the East Room might include many many headaches. When completed Mr. Hearst would have a beautiful large room but I think the fireplace would still smoke. I feel that this [the smoking] is why the alteration is considered. I say this with conviction Miss Morgan for with big fires in all fireplaces and unfavorable winds around the Recreation [Wing] tower from

---

27. A prime example of Morgan's stance in such matters dates from seven years before, concerning the Celestial Suite. "The bath rooms can be usable any time, but are not completed—so many small items each of a different craft and of necessary sequence. However, they promise to be well worth the effort." From Morgan to Hearst, June 28, 1932; Hearst Papers, carton 15 (under "Morgan, Julia").

Morgan North, Miss Morgan's nephew, referred to work at San Simeon that required many skilled hands concurrently. He was speaking more of earlier years, when the work was on a larger scale, yet his observations are also pertinent here; they're also at their most informed and insightful on such points (unlike too much of what he said about his aunt's finances). See *The Julia Morgan Architectural History Project*, Vol. II, p. 182.

28. The last of the "Franks" Loorz described had indeed called on Morgan in San Francisco. "Frandolich was in today," Mac learned from her letter of Friday, June 2 (Warren McClure Papers). She and that old Italian artisan talked about some finishing touches for the Main Terrace on the hilltop; these concerned the "four Seasons" sculptures that Hearst and others had discussed in 1938 and that still needed attention (see p. 358, plus its note 12). As Morgan said of Frandy and that job in writing Mac on June 2, "He could do them [the decorative pedestals] with a helper & there is plenty of stone on hand." But she told Mac to plan on redoing the sketches he'd already prepared for the job: in a year's time, they seemed to have been misplaced.

the North [side of Casa Grande, the East Room] will not be [favorably] affected by the alteration.[29] Fewer ashes might blow back for there will be less flat portion for them to accumulate on but the smoke is another thing.

I am honestly interested but must admit my inability to supply exact information. Wish we could talk it over in detail together.

He signed off on a most unusual note: "I have even considered the total labor costs of finishing such rooms as the Deck rooms and the Duplex's." Heaven only knows what he meant by that. All those rooms—the North Deck and South Deck, plus the four Duplex suites—had long been finished on the inside. Was he alluding to their rough exteriors? Otherwise, that part of Casa Grande hadn't been a concern in more than three years, not since Hearst had a notion of putting elevators in the nearby stairwells.[30]

The outcome, simply put, was that none of these ideas or proposals in 1939 ever took wing—the East Room, China Hill, Casa del Sol—none of them. Retrenchment, in fact, was more like it at San Simeon. A small note dated June 10, typed by Willicombe for Hearst to see, pertained to "the abandonment of the indoor pool":

> One of the men (Shaug) who is evidently familiar with such matters, and has worked around pools, says that the metal pipes have become corroded and may be useless when the pool is put back into use. Shall I ask Mr Williams to check on this and report to you?

The note bears a thickly penciled "Yes please" in Hearst's hand. Above it, "Rankin" appears in Willicombe's hand.[31]

EVER SINCE HEARST began using personal funds for the work he *could* afford, Willicombe's secretarial load had taken on some new accounting duties. An example was the work in 1938 on the Burnett Road, for which Willicombe had disbursed

---

29. Unbracketed, this part of Loorz's sentence makes little sense: "the Recreation tower from the North will not be affected by the alteration." Yet even with heavy bracketing, the thought he meant to convey is hard to pin down. His relatively few letters that survive as originals—his outgoing versions, that is, versus his carbon copies that abound in the Loorz Papers—suggest he was more partial to marginal addenda than he was to methodical, interlinear corrections of missing words or unclear phrasing.

Hearst eventually closed off the fireplace with a simple but decorative iron plate, made by Val Georges. The plate was removed in 1986.

30. See pp. 238–39 in the 1936 chapter.

31. The unaddressed, unsigned note is filed in the Hearst Papers, carton 27 (under "Hearst Memorandums 1939").

monthly payments to Loorz. Humdrum, yes, but important if we're to understand a development in June 1939 that involved Mac McClure, one that Loorz wouldn't hear about (from Mac himself) for a few more weeks. Pending that, Morgan had some things to tell Loorz about a small job at San Simeon; the date was June 13:

> Please take care of [paying] Otto Olson and send the bill for time, expense, etc., directly *without percentage* [architect's commission] to Mr. Willicombe. I will explain why when I see you.
>
> The locks [whose installation would follow Olson's work] will not be here for some time yet as [they] only leave the factory after the 15th. Then get from Mr. Willicombe the order to send him back [to San Simeon] to put them on.

Loorz complied by sending Willicombe a statement on June 20 for "Locksets and Repairs," a carpentry job by definition and one that took Olson about sixty hours. The statement went to San Simeon, where the Hearst party had been for nearly two months:

> In accordance with Miss Morgan's suggestion I am enclosing our bill for the work done by Otto Olson recently on the hilltop [May 23–June 1]. Note that we have billed only for the net cost.[32]
>
> If you wish Otto back [on behalf of the Stolte Co.] to place the locks when they arrive please phone or write. Of course, if Pete [Petersen] is in San Simeon you may want him [instead, as an independent workman].

Since everyone was walking on eggs, Loorz tried to make perfect steps. He went on to tell Willicombe:

> Please be frank and advise me if you think it would be in order for me to bill for my expenses and services in connection with the two days surveying I did recently on China Hill.
>
> In consideration of my past pleasant connections with the organization I will not bill for my services unless it is definitely in order.

On June 20 as well, Loorz sent Morgan copies of his letter to Willicombe and the invoice for Olson's work—"self-explanatory" items, he said. (This way she would know which of them was being kinder toward Hearst. She had Loorz beat by a mile, for she never charged Hearst for her drafting-room time and certain

---

32. The amount—$78.40—was part of a slightly larger $84.75 next to "W. R. Hearst," as recorded in Loorz's monthly ledgers for his Pacific Grove branch of the Stolte Co. The $78.40 portion was paid in July 1939. The balance due of $6.35, denoting the only other work for which the company billed Hearst that year, remained unpaid; in 1940 it was rolled over with other stray amounts into "Old Jobs" (and thus its individual trail was erased).

other costs that San Simeon gave rise to in 1939.)[33] Loorz also mentioned the Parsons job in Monterey; Morgan had done so in her letter of June 13 and would do so again on June 22. He closed on the twentieth with these paragraphs, which sounded like the Loorz of yore:

> It has been so long since we have seen you Miss Morgan I hope you will have time to take a Sunday ride thru Carmel and have lunch with us this next week end, if you come. We are particularly anxious to hear more about your European trip. The wife and I certainly enjoyed the last time we talked about it.
>
> The seemingly smallest experiences, like "catching the wrong train" are strangely amusing now. At the time they perhaps were very unpleasant or upsetting.

June had another ten days to go. Right before it ended, Hearst and his party finally pulled up stakes at San Simeon and headed to Wyntoon, evidently for the

---

33. Those costs stood at $1,641 by year's end (see Appendix A). About sixty percent of that figure stemmed from familiar categories: drafting-room time, travel, and overhead. The remaining part stemmed mostly from Morgan's inventorying of some Hearst items called the Oriental Collection, an activity that required her renting an adjacent room in the Merchants Exchange from July through October—Room 1136, her office having long been in Room 1135. (In 1937 she had rented Room 1140 for some concentrated work on the Pacific Coast Register and similar records.) Her rental of Room 1136 in 1939 recalls her permanent move that year from Room 1135 to Room 1107, whose exact timing is unknown; see note 8, above.

Meanwhile, cash flow seemed a minor problem for her. In the first quarter of 1939 she received $1,371 in commission payments on the San Simeon account; most of it pertained to 1938, the remainder to 1937. By the end of 1938, Hearst had paid Morgan $426,472 in commissions since 1919, $744 less than the $427,216 she had billed him through those twenty years (see Appendix B, pp. 549–50). The $1,371 he paid in 1939 put him ahead of the pace for the first time since 1924 (by $627). The Commission Account was never marked "closed," yet no further entries were made after March 1939.

Her "Refunds" account (a separate entity) indicates she received $862 from Hearst in 1939 to offset travel costs and certain other expenses ($219 pertained to 1938, $643 to 1939). Together, the $1,371 in commissions and the $862 in refunds totaled $2,233, surpassing her $1,641 in annual operating costs by $592. This is fast-and-loose accounting, of course. Better assessments await a full auditing of the Morgan-Forney ledgers, whose San Simeon pages are the most complex of all. (For one thing, roughly $27,000 that Morgan received in refunds from 1924 through 1940—pertaining to San Simeon—needs to be reconciled with her $262,715 in operating costs for that job in those seventeen years; see the introduction to Appendix B, pp. 546–49.)

Unmistakably, though, Morgan wasn't nearly so bad off as many have said she was. She kept close watch on such matters at all times. A statement she sent Hearst on June 1, 1939 (for refund rather than commission purposes), included a matter-of-fact comment: "We have made no charge for overhead or personal services [regarding the $427 at stake], but we find that hereafter it will be necessary to make a charge for the overhead that is clearly involved." See the file "Morgan's Fees and Expenses, 1939"; Morgan Collection, Cal Poly (III/03/07/115). See also Morgan to Hearst, June 9, 1939; Hearst/Morgan Correspondence, ibid. (in which one of Morgan's paragraphs mentioned the "necessity of keeping track of expenses" and in which another one included "I could have had no

first time since the fall of 1938. Mac McClure was part of the northerly shift. Pete Petersen would soon be following suit, much as he had when the boys from San Simeon relocated there the year before.

MAC WROTE TO LOORZ from that northern estate on July 10,[34] beginning with "Mr. Hearst wants some work started here, on a small scale. I don't know how long it may last but I expect a month or more—possibly all Summer":

> What I want to know is, what chance is there of borrowing Otto Olson to work with Pete—(2 [men] only)?
>
> Mr. Willicombe tells me that the two carpenters will be housed and fed with other help on the place.

Then came the heart of Mac's letter, a passage stemming from the personal versus company approach that Hearst was coming more and more to grips with. Mac gave the essential details—and between his lines, Loorz could undoubtedly read a good deal more:

> Since you were at San Simeon [in early June], an arrangement was made between W.R.H. and Miss Morgan, whereby, my salary and any other expenses would be handled directly by Mr. Willicombe. As this is working out it means that construction work is being handled independently [through Hearst's personal account] which I am sorry to see but is none of my arranging as you well know.[35]

Not only that, but Morgan herself was out of the current picture at Wyntoon, except as a facilitator for which she charged no fees; she wouldn't figure there as an architect for hire again until 1942 (and then just briefly, almost insignificantly).[36]

---

profit in these years and I have not wanted it"—words almost begging to be misconstrued). The matter resumes on p. 446 in this volume, note 36).

34. One of the five letters from 1938 through 1940 that surfaced in 1997 (see note 7, above). All of them have since been added to the Loorz Papers at the San Luis Obispo County Historical Museum.

35. Hearst and Morgan's recent discussions about Mac can be inferred from two letters in the Hearst/Morgan Correspondence—Morgan to Hearst on June 9 and June 12, 1939. Although a neighboring item, Hearst to Morgan on June 10, doesn't mention Mac, it includes Hearst's view of the bigger picture. "But circumstances demand the most limited possible expenditure on my part," he said to Morgan about the 1939 season. "In fact, for the rest of the year I must not contemplate anything of any consequence." Morgan knew better than to take Hearst too literally; his undying urge to build is obvious from what Mac told Loorz exactly one month later.

36. An item or two in the Hearst/Morgan Correspondence, Cal Poly, plus some items in the Warren McClure Papers at Hearst Castle and also in the Vanderloo Collection, provide a sense of Morgan's absentee role at Wyntoon in 1939: she strived to help Mac and other key people, right through the summer and fall. Her role three years later belongs to this volume's 1941–44 chapter.

Otherwise, after June 12, 1939, the main Wyntoon account lapsed; this was the big Waterhouse account that Morgan began in the fall of 1932 and that reflected so much of the activity on the McCloud from then until late in 1938.[37] The services of Fred Stolte, Harry Thompson, and others in the F. C. Stolte Co. had proved un-needed after the 1937 season; even George Loorz, still working independently as construction superintendent for Hearst and Morgan through the first half of 1938, had gone off the payroll by July of that year. And as of July 1939 there was no room at the inn for Miss Morgan either—except at the place called the Cosmopolitan bungalow.[38] At Wyntoon itself, Mac was the only one of the higher-ups remaining, short of Hearst and Willicombe themselves.

---

37. San Simeon was the only job for which Morgan kept separate track of commissions and of refunds. The Waterhouse account in Morgan-Forney includes a section of "Wyntoon Receipts," in which entries for those two kinds of payments—earnings at 8.5% and reimbursements for certain costs—are closely intertwined. Before that main Wyntoon account lapsed in 1939 (a step short of being "closed"), Morgan collected $1,477 in commissions and $174 in refunds; all of it pertained to 1938.

The Waterhouse and its fellow accounts need to be carefully audited. (Morgan's work at Wyntoon in 1942 yielded a separate account, not applicable here.) And yet once audited, the Wyntoon accounts of 1924–39 won't be so revealing as the San Simeon data of the same period: two of those Wyntoon accounts—mostly for 1929–32, one of them minor—contain the usual cost entries (totaling some $11,300) but no lists of payments or commission rates.

Some guarded observations can still be made. Four of the Wyntoon accounts, dominated by the wide-ranging Waterhouse example (which includes The Gables for 1933–38), show that, through the foursome alone, Morgan collected about $55,500 in commissions and refunds. That was against operating costs slightly greater than $48,300 (representing eighty-one percent of the $59,624 cited for Wyntoon costs in Appendix A, p. 534). She did better than break-even business, though not dramatically so. The deep pockets of San Simeon, lined with expensive materials and workmanship, far exceeded those of Wyntoon. Presumably, the two under-documented Wyntoon accounts (the remaining nineteen percent, or $11,300 of $59,624 in operating costs) would do little to affect the general trend, even if more data turned up.

It's surprising, then, that Morgan herself named Wyntoon as having cost more than a million dollars to build—perhaps half again the $700,000 or so that Hearst is likely to have spent (an extrapolation at 8.5% from the six accounts cited above). See the list of projects in Sara Boutelle's *Julia Morgan*, p. 243. In responding in 1946 to the AIA survey that Boutelle cited, Morgan named the Phoebe Hearst Gym, the Honolulu YWCA, and the Berkeley City Club in category (b): "Three Projects Costing from $300,000 to $1,000,000." Category (c) allowed for three projects also, those "Costing Over $1,000,000." San Simeon unquestionably belonged there; and Morgan, pressed for space, may simply have shrugged in listing Wyntoon as well. If Hearst had spent that much on Wyntoon, Morgan's quiet prosperity would have been even greater.

38. On Saturday, July 8, two days before Mac wrote to Loorz, Morgan included these words in a letter she sent to Mac: "Will be out of the hospital Monday, go south with my sister Monday night, but will surely be back in harness [in San Francisco] by Thursday [July 13]." Morgan explained that she'd had "a sudden recurrence of one of the old troubles which wasted this week [of July 2–8] entirely." From the Warren McClure Papers.

Morgan's trip south—cited as July 10 in the Morgan-Forney ledgers—included her fourth

Mac signed off on July 10 by telling Loorz, "Wyntoon looks nicely after a light Winter. Mr. Hearst is 'itching' to start something, but to date it is nothing larger than a barbeque oven which Eddie Schaug [Shaug] and I are making!" He added a straightforward postscript concerning the helper that Petersen would be needing: "If not Otto perhaps you can suggest another who could work with Pete. Work will probably be re-framing in Angel House so need not be [a] finish carpenter."

Loorz answered Mac on July 12. He dictated the letter, the likeliest reason for its somewhat stiff, formal tone. Nonetheless, its content has much to tell us:

> I am sorry that you have asked for the loan of Otto Olson. From a selfish point of view I prefer to keep him; especially, since I have gone out of my way releasing other men [from the Pacific Grove branch] in order to keep him.
>
> However, my former connections with Mr. Hearst makes me feel it advisable to let you have him.
>
> Please let me know when you want him and what you will pay him. He should get $10.00 per day and board.
>
> I hope the new arrangement [described in Mac's letter] works to the satisfaction of all concerned.

Mac lobbed the ball right back into Loorz's court; it was just a day later now, July 13:

> Many thanks for your offer to send us Otto but do not do so if you need him. We can get someone else and as I said it was only if by chance you did not want him for awhile.
>
> Pete arrived last evening and for the time being we will get along with a local helper. The present work will consist of re-framing in Angel House.
>
> I understand that the locks are at San Simeon now. If you care to send Otto down there for a day or so to install them sometime before Sept 1st, it would be a good deed.

Writing in longhand as usual, Mac offered another postcript, virtually a trademark of his style. He had some "bad news" to share with Loorz, who he knew would be sympathetic, never mind the business mood of his last letter: Al Horn, Hearst's projectionist, "cracked up his car and himself night before last." Horn had shattered one of his legs and would be out of commission for months to come.

---

visit of 1939 to the Cosmopolitan bungalow. (She'd also gone there twice in late June, right before she entered the hospital, perhaps for her mastoid condition; she would check on the bungalow three times again in July alone.) Despite her recent bout with ill health, Morgan faced the subject of mortality straight on. Her trip of July 10–11 produced a concurrent entry of "Travel L.A." in a ledger besides the Cosmopolitan one — namely, in the one begun in April for the Darbee Mausoleum.

AS THE SUMMER of 1939 went on—and as Europe moved closer to an upheaval far surpassing the Great War of Loorz's youth—Angel House and other projects at Wyntoon left barely a trace in that builder's papers. Pete Petersen broke the silence on August 15. He told Loorz, "We are still working here but how long?" Loorz had written to him in early July at San Simeon, and yet Petersen had already begun heading north; the letter had gone in circles before reaching Wyntoon weeks later. Despite learning why Petersen had delayed so in answering, Loorz caught the uncommunicative bug and remained silent till August 28. The loss is entirely ours, not theirs (foretelling the frustrating gaps we'll almost surely leave those who follow in our less writerly, less documentary footsteps). "Say Hello to Mr. Willicombe for me," Loorz offered when he finally wrote back. "Hope Mr. Hearst and all the gang are well and enjoying themselves."

In the meantime, a small collection of related papers—the Vanderloo Collection—helps bridge the gap in the late summer of 1939.[39] Julia Morgan, John Vanderloo, and Mac McClure exchanged some brief but welcome letters, beginning with one that Mac wrote from Wyntoon on August 4; it went to Vanderloo in Cambria:

> We only needed *four* of the Urns and bases for the front of the house [Casa Grande at San Simeon]. However if the six you mentioned are already cast we can use the extra pair elsewhere.
>
> If you can get along by yourself we will try and not add another to the pay-roll. If you need a helper once in awhile perhaps Mr Williams can lend Marks [Eubanks] or someone else.[40]

Although Morgan got in on the exchange, the surviving letters in the Vanderloo Collection are too spotty to provide a full sense of the latest developments; it appears, at any rate, that Vanderloo was casting some decorative features for Wyntoon as well as for San Simeon. As she told him in mid-August:

---

39. The earliest letter in the Vanderloo Collection dates from 1930, the latest one from 1945. One item dated December 6, 1938, is a copy that John Vanderloo made of a letter he wrote to "Colonel Willicombe" at San Simeon. It concerned "the cost of making [cast stone] light standards, similar to those which are used on the balustrade, steps, and wall around Roman Greek Pool"—in other words, the Neptune Pool. After Miss Morgan arranged for Vanderloo to do the work—akin to his and Frank Frandolich's previous efforts in 1938—Hearst told her it would have to be stopped. (So said Vanderloo; but since Morgan was in Europe throughout the fall that year, he must have been speaking of earlier decisions.) The letter provides a glimpse of a little-known episode in the work at San Simeon.

40. Vanderloo Collection. The managerial side of Mac's work is more evident in this short letter than in most others in this volume.

That was a lot of material to have handled, and am only sorry it had to be stopped off [brought to a halt] — for Wyntoon.

We will hope it will be "on again" when the people return to the Hill.[41]

Vanderloo replied on August 20; the stoppage he spoke of was different from the one now affecting Wyntoon; he must still have had things to do for San Simeon. "I will continue this work and will try to finish by the end of the Month," he told Morgan. "In case you want me to *stop*, I will do so promptly on receipt of your orders."[42]

He was given sufficient rein to complete things. On September 19 Morgan told him cheerfully, "I saw Mr. McClure at McCloud Saturday [September 16] and he said you were about through." Vanderloo was a personal favorite of hers, a man for whom these closing words of Morgan's were more than merely polite: "I hope other work will come up — one never can tell."[43] That's as far, though, as the Vanderloo Collection goes in recreating events from 1939.

Wyntoon was still seeing action in late September. The trail provided by the Loorz Papers resumes then; they disclose that, through Morgan, Mac McClure requested the services of Otto Olson once more, or of Jake Jacobson if Olson wasn't available. Loorz had Olson working in hot country — on the Avenal School, northeast of Paso Robles. The Morgan office appealed to Loorz in Mac's behalf on September 22, not knowing that Loorz (as he told Morgan three days later) had "contracted for a church that has a grand antique walnut wainscot throughout the chapel." The job was in cooler, pine-enshrouded Carmel and had Olson's name written all over it. But Loorz, wanting to be as compliant as Morgan, sent Olson to Wyntoon anyway. The small mixup led to an apology from her on September 27.

---

41. Morgan's letter is dated August 15, 1939; Vanderloo Collection.

42. From the series San Simeon Business Correspondence and Ephemera; Morgan Collection (III/02/07/86, under "John J. Vanderloo, 1939"). Without the perspective provided by like-dated items in the Vanderloo Collection, this solitary letter at Cal Poly is a contextual orphan — a classic instance of how all such collections, small or large, are often interdependent.

43. Vanderloo Collection. The date of Morgan's presence at Wyntoon in September is confirmed by this letter. The Morgan-Forney Collection (Cosmopolitan bungalow account) cites the preceding date only, September 15, suggesting she was enroute then to see Hearst and Mac on the sixteenth.

A week earlier — September 9, 1939 — Morgan told Hearst, "Anything else I can do for the rest of the year at Wyntoon, please allow me to do without any question of commission." As quoted by Boutelle in *Julia Morgan*, pp. 230, 232 (from a letter she saw in the Hearst Corporation files, New York). By itself, and despite its familiar theme, the letter is another contextual orphan; but it's less of one now alongside items in the Vanderloo Collection and the Warren McClure Papers. Morgan may have been alluding to something as simple as her part in John Vanderloo's recent efforts.

Minor details, faint echoes of livelier times—almost reduced to a whisper now. All it took, though, was a solid letter or two, like the ones Loorz and Mac exchanged later in the fall, to bring the good times back.[44] Loorz led off with some passages in the old tradition on November 1:

> Hope the work is going along nicely and that there will be no winter shut down. What are you working on mostly? Was Willicombe sice [sick] and away on leave? How is Mr. Hearst? Does that move [movie] star, what's her name actually visit Mr. Hearst's estate? You know who I mean. I have heard so little about the outfit of late that I'm entirely out of touch.
>
> Saw Miss Morgan a couple of weeks ago and she said she had been up there once. Didnt have much to say. Mentioned you were working on the Bend [the old Wheeler place][45] as well as the Angel House. She looks better since her sister [her sister-in-law, Mrs. Parmelee Morgan] passed away. She was terribly run down there for a while going to L.A. once or twice a week. She still goes to

---

44. The Warren McClure Papers include a "Sunday" letter of Morgan's from this period, identifiable as one written either on August 20 or, more likely (through a Morgan-Forney collation), on October 8. "Am just in from Tahoe," she told Mac, referring to the Else Schilling house that she'd begun during the summer.

Morgan had originally told Mac about that new job on July 8 (in the same letter quoted above in note 38). Besides mentioning Wyntoon, her week in the hospital, and the trip she'd soon be making south, she had waxed eloquent at that moment, exactly three months before her letter in October:

> It sounds [with regard to Hearst work] as if you would be kept busy! If by any chance not, Miss Schilling has bought a really interesting piece of property on the Lake at Tahoe & I'll get you to go up & locate the main trees & area of building site. It is practical[l]y bounded on the two sides by little streams, has a clean narrow sandy beach along the lake, lovely fine trees & a wood [forest] floor covering of tiny strawberrys like one finds in Swiss high lands & masses of lovely fine wild flowers. I thought we could do something with much stone, natural timbers —some plaster fresco in gables (Miss Day) & a little carved banding inside.

Morgan's intentions in early July of building that way (and of using Doris Day) came to pass in nearly every detail; see Boutelle, pp. 160, 162. But Mac remained too busy at Wyntoon to take part; instead, Morgan sent Ray Carlson to Lake Tahoe on July 15; she herself went there four times in 1939, the last trip preceding her letter of October 8 by two days.

On that "Sunday" in October (the only date Morgan gave the letter), she also told Mac, "I am going south tonight." Her destination would be the Cosmopolitan bungalow in Beverly Hills—for the fifteenth time in 1939. She made a final, account-closing trip there on October 28.

45. The McClure Papers contain references to The Bend on August 17 and, more substantially, on October 11 and 27; the earlier date in October applies to a typewritten letter from Hearst to McClure. The McClure Papers also contain a handwritten letter from Hearst (left undated, but flanked by items from August 24). "The curse of the bend is the darkness," he told Mac that time, sounding a perennial note. "We have got to let in all the light we can—and do it *everywhere*. . . . We must have a greater feeling of light and airiness."

visit the little girl [her niece, Judith Avery Morgan], to make her think there is really still someone who cares.[46] How many of us would inconvenience ourselves that much.

All our family are very well and quite happy. Our business is still holding up but we cant land any new work. I think it will be better after the Ham & Eggs fail (will they).[47] However, they have lots of oil business [gas stations] in the Alameda office [of the F. C. Stolte Co.]. It is profitable and prompt with pay. We should check out with a banner year. However, if more larger work doesn't turn up here I will be tempted to move into richer and more fertile fields.

Say Hello to Pete, Otto and all of the gang for me. Tweek Judd's nose [Jud Smelser's] if you are on speaking terms at the present writing. . . . Tell him if he knows of any ripe scandal just give a buzz and let us in on it.

Mac answered promptly, on November 4, with a classic of a letter rivaling those he had written a few years earlier when Wyntoon was at its height. He began with a reference to the work he and Loorz had done at San Simeon in early June:

It was good to hear from you after a long time—I guess the last time we had a visit was the day spent gathering fox tails on China Hill!

It has been quite a long Season here. For me at least, it has amounted to as much as other years. We started in on Angel House in July but were soon switched to The Bend where quite a nice alteration job is in progress.

Mr. Hearst has been quite contented—I think —He would like a little more action but he is getting all we can produce with 3 carpenters, 3 stone masons, and two laborers.

Jas. Rankin and Co. were called in two weeks ago to rough plumb a remodeled wing at The Bend and also to put in the pipes for steam heat. Jim is away just at present but will be back soon.

Mr. H., has been jumping around with his program, even more than usual. One day it is one thing and the next day another. I think he tries to get more out of us by heaping on the work. As it now stands, we will spend the rest of this year getting, what is now under way, closed in for the winter.

---

46. In a working vein, Morgan's visits to the Southland had been frequent enough in recent months. (Except for including some Darbee business on July 10, as in note 38, a dozen such trips that she'd made since mid-July dwelled on the Cosmopolitan bungalow.) It's unclear whether those same trips found her pursuing the personal matters Loorz spoke of.

47. Yes, they would. The original Ham and Eggs pension scheme (also spelled Ham 'n Eggs) had been defeated in 1938—in the same election, ironically, that saw Culbert Olson unseating Frank Merriam as governor. A year later the Ham and Eggers had gained a special election, but their proposal failed on November 7, 1939, for the second and last time. See Kevin Starr, *Endangered Dreams: The Great Depression in California*, chapter 7 (pp. 197–222).

Miss Morgan came up the one time [that Loorz mentioned on November 1] to check items on the [Cosmopolitan] bungalow I think.[48] She had little to say about the work here. I have been more or less in touch with her right along and write to her for information now and then.[49]

All in all this year is no better and no worse than usual. The whole outfit is "screwy" and the best thing one can do is to not let it "get" you down. We will probably close in a month or six weeks and then I plan to run back to Detroit for the holidays, but will be back on the coast early in 1940.

Hope to see you soon —.

P.S. You ask is [if] Col W was sick — He & Jean H. [Jean Henry] were married two weeks ago in Reno!

Thanksgiving and Christmas in 1939 found Hearst and his party holding fast at wintery Wyntoon, where, with one brief exception, they'd been staying since July.[50] And then right after Christmas they finally headed south, dividing their time around the New Year's weekend between San Simeon and the Beach House (Marion Davies would be all of forty-three come Tuesday, January 3).

But even though San Simeon, not Santa Monica, was the address Hearst would favor for the next several months, a new pattern had emerged in 1939. Overall, it would dominate the first half of the 1940s: long stays at Wyntoon, as long as and at times longer than those Hearst had accorded San Simeon in the late 1920s and for so much of the 1930s. It meant that the Christmas he'd spent at San Simeon in 1938 would be his last on the hilltop until 1944. And by then the war — the Greater War that eclipsed the Great War of a bygone day — would be nearly over.

---

48. Morgan went to Wyntoon on bungalow business in mid-September (the Morgan-Forney ledgers indicate the main subject of the trip, the Vanderloo Collection its on-site date; see note 43, above). The trip was her only one to that estate in 1939, for any purpose. Besides mentioning the bungalow when she wrote to Mac McClure on July 8, she also mentioned it to Mac on July 25 and to Hearst on August 24 (McClure Papers). Those papers also have Mac's reference copy of a letter dated October 16. The original, from W. R. Williams at San Simeon, went to an unrelated Williams in Beverly Hills (Westwood actually) — to Ella Williams of Cosmopolitan Productions, headquartered now in its post-Warner days at Twentieth Century-Fox.

49. Despite having almost twenty letters to Mac from Julia Morgan — many of them invaluable — the Warren McClure Papers have no copies of the letters he sent her. With regard to 1939, Cal Poly has none of the items Mac mentioned (postdating the spring of that year), neither his originals to Morgan nor the copies she once kept of the things she sent him.

50. The first nine or ten days of September were the sole departure from the norm before the holiday season. Hearst may have gone east in that late-summer interval (if so, it was a little-known trip). "I heard you were in Chicago [at the Drake Hotel] and I want to send my greetings and best wishes." Those were a colleague's words, sent from New York, where he hoped Hearst would also be going. But Hearst was nearly back at Wyntoon by then, and the letter caught up with him there: "Forwarded from Chicago," noted Willicombe upon its arrival. See Paul Block to Hearst, September 8, 1939; Hearst Papers, carton 27 (under "Block, Paul").

1940

Endings and Beginnings

FOR SAN SIMEON AND WYNTOON the 1940s offer fewer letters or other documents bearing on those two subjects—fewer items, that is, than the 1930s do, that shimmering period in the Loorz Papers. Of course the Hearst Papers, the Morgan-Forney Collection, the Julia Morgan Collection at Cal Poly, and still other holdings are important supplements, at times indispensable ones. With their continued help the Loorz Papers can provide a recounting of 1940 itself; in its best moments the story rivals the annual chronicles running through 1939. In that respect 1940 belongs more with its predeceding years (as in 1932–40) than with its succeeding ones (as in the next chapter's 1941–44 or the final chapter's 1945 and beyond).

The long-established trend, though, has been to race forward from 1940, or even from some previous year, to the far side of World War II—to 1945 and Hearst's resumption of efforts at San Simeon. Intervening years like 1942 and 1943 get swept along in the same swift tide. Hence the need here to slow down, slow down (and, where feasible, to fill in the gaps). The earliest months in 1944, for example, lie nearly fifteen hundred days ahead of their counterparts in 1940. For that matter, Pearl Harbor lies well ahead, halfway between the present moment and the dawn of 1944. (However, Hearst's return to San Simeon in 1944, on hold since the first half of 1941, didn't occur till the eve of 1945.) As for the letters, the memos, the telegrams that Hearst and Morgan—and Loorz and others—produced all the while: granted, there are fewer than before on San Simeon, Wyntoon, and all such subjects once dominated by the Loorz Papers. Yet there had to have been more items, substantially more, than today's surviving examples.

The ironic result is that, except for 1940 itself, and despite their being closer to our own time, the 1940s are less known (perhaps permanently) than the 1930s and, quite often, even less so than the 1920s.

IN HEARST'S LONG ABSENCE from San Simeon in 1939, a sense of status quo may have descended on the place. If so, the situation changed abruptly. Ray Van

Gorden, writing from Cambria on January 2, 1940, had some late-breaking news
for George Loorz:

> Mr. Hearst sort of made a cleaning up to Camp, they say. Let Mr. [W. R.] Wil-
> liams and all his force go — all but Nick Yost and Marks [Eubanks]. He [Hearst]
> figures on staying at Santa Monica, where he now is, but you know how long
> he will stay there. Jud [Smelser] is back on the Hill again but doesn't know what
> his future is. . . . Suppose Mac [Mc]Clure is in Los Angeles. Received a nice card
> from Miss Morgan at Christmas.

In addition, Van Gorden ventured some thoughts that a man in Loorz's position had to hope were realistic:

> In spite of the letdown in PWA [pending its dissolution], I think 1940 will be a big
> building year. Lots of money was made in the last 4 months of 1939 and will [also]
> be in 1940 which will naturally effect [affect] the building industry.[1] I see where
> Los Angeles already has a 76 million dollar program.

Loorz tarried a while in answering. When he did, he invoked the same unde-
fined "they" that Van Gorden had; this was on January 12:

> They report that Mrs. [Edna] Caulkins has charge on the hilltop now. Is [Nigel]
> Keep still there? Of course he is but has he any crew at all left? Does it all come
> under Randy [Apperson] now?
>   If you find out where Mr. Williams moves to, please let me know I would like to
> write to him. Suppose Jud is still on the hill [as a chauffeur].

Since Van Gorden had clearly stated that Jud Smelser was back — back from
Wyntoon with the party, that is — Loorz probably meant that he supposed Smelser,

---

1. Loorz summed up 1939 for his friend Phil Smith, last seen in these annals in 1934, on January 11, 1940 (misdated 1939). The allusion was to both offices of the Stolte Co. — Alameda and Pacific Grove — when Loorz told him: "During the course of the past year we have constructed some
$700,000 worth of buildings, sewers, disposal plants, schools, oil stations and warehouses etc." (The
combined gross for the two offices in 1939 was closer to $900,000.)

Smith, having heard about a sale of horses on the Hearst Ranch, got the lowdown from Loorz
at the same time:

> I was certainly sorry you did not get down [from Fort Bragg] when the Arabians were sold.
> They went much better than they expected. However, they still have many finer animals and
> will no doubt be advertising another sale later on.
>   I too love horses and always enjoyed being around the fine Stallions Mr. Hearst had. I rode
> quite a little while down there but not since coming up here.

"I do most of my local work in Carmel," Loorz said in closing. "Should really have bought
there instead of here."

a key employee, had survived the shakeup, just as he safely assumed Nigel Keep had.

Loorz also reported that he'd "signed up a couple of small jobs" in the greater Monterey area. Though he wasn't "too worried" about the jobs' limited prospects, he did say that his overhead—mostly fixed operating costs—posed a momentary burden.[2] "However," he told Van Gorden, "there is really more stirring now than there has been at any time I can remember at this time of year. All of it private work."

January 19 found Loorz writing to Pete Petersen, who, thanks to the increasing gaps in the Loorz Papers, had last been visible during the summer. The same goes for Otto Olson. Loorz had planned to use Olson on the remodeling of the Carmel Community Church, and yet for Morgan's benefit (and even more for Hearst's) he'd let Olson go up to Wyntoon to help Petersen and Mac McClure. A brief passage Loorz included for Petersen on January 19 brought the sequel up to date. "Otto certainly came in handy on the church. I wished you had come straight down with him [from Wyntoon, when efforts ended there late in 1939]. However, with a few more days it should be under control." In reality, the church Loorz was speaking of, where work had begun in October, required a few more months to complete.

Meanwhile, on January 17, two days before Loorz wrote to Petersen, Morgan went to San Simeon to confer with Hearst (who'd returned from the Beach House about as quickly as Van Gorden had guessed he would). Morgan had been on the road three weeks earlier; she'd gone to Los Angeles, not for Hearst's sake but for that of F. C. Turner, a client of hers who owned several buildings in Berkeley on Bancroft Way.[3]

---

2. Loorz spoke further of 1939 in writing to another old friend, Jack Hall, on January 14, 1940 (likewise misdated 1939, as was the letter to Phil Smith). Loorz mentioned "a year of ups and downs" (the "ups" had prevailed). He also told Hall, "With a good big overhead I did not net so much but with both offices we should be able to split 30 grand for our wages and good luck. To me that is a lot." The $30,000 exceeded Loorz and Stolte's net personal earnings: Loorz declared a salary of $6,000 on his tax return for 1939, his first year since 1932 to show no income from Hearst or Morgan. Nonetheless, Loorz and Stolte were both prospering now, especially Stolte. As Loorz told Carl Daniels on February 18, "Fred took out over $22,000 of his [credit in the business, as the partners called it] and invested it in real estate."

3. The largest of the F. C. Turner accounts in the Morgan-Forney ledgers, dated June 1939 through September 1940, comprises "a new store building on Bancroft Way, Berkeley" and its adjunct, the Black Sheep Restaurant (which still dominates the complex, hence the name used in Appendix A, pp. 534 and 545). The complex, catty corner from Morgan and Maybeck's Phoebe Hearst Gym, has since been altered and is now called the Turner Building. See Boutelle, *Julia Morgan*, p. 262 (under 1938–41, of which 1938 properly applies to the neighboring but separate Turner Laboratory Building that no longer stands). Early in 1940, meanwhile, Morgan did her final work for the Darbee Mausoleum in Lawndale-Colma. Jim LeFeaver also worked on the project. So did Walter Huber, who wrote twice to Mrs. Darbee in the spring of 1940 (Morgan Collection [Earl and Wright

But her trip to San Simeon, where she hadn't been in eight months, was both a homecoming and, as things ultimately turned out, a farewell. By all indications it was the last time she ever set foot on The Enchanted Hill.[4]

So much for hindsight, though, and for backward glances that no one then had any reason to make. Such conceptions are much more ours to contend with. It was now January; and along the coast, especially at higher reaches, it was a month that brought its share of rain, as it still does today, sometimes torrentially. Morgan had been back in San Francisco for a few days when the hilltop took a stiff beating. A plea for help went out from Hearst's exotic stronghold, not to Loorz in Pacific Grove or to Morgan herself (although her name came up). It went instead to Bill Murray at Hearst Sunical in San Francisco; he replied to Joe Willicombe on January 25:

> Immediately on receiving your telephone call last night as to the leaks at the Hilltop, I got in touch with Miss Morgan's office and spoke to Mr. LeFeaver. He told me that the County Roofing Company [County Roof Service] of San Luis Obispo has done considerable roofing work for Miss Morgan at San Simeon, and that they would be the best onces [*sic*] to contact.
>
> I thereupon telephoned Mr. Apperson, and told him to arrange with this concern to have a man at San Simeon this morning (Thursday) to make the necessary temporary repairs, and in addition give us an estimate on the work that should be done to make the roofs in question water tight.[5]

Company portion], II/03/04/36–37); Huber also wrote to Mrs. Darbee in May 1942. By then, Morgan and Maybeck's efforts had long been shelved (Bernard Maybeck retired in 1941) and the war had intervened.

4. If she was ever there later, the Loorz Papers, the Hearst Papers, the Morgan-Forney Collection, the three Julia Morgan collections, and all other known holdings are unanimous in their textual silence. In the visual realm, Hearst Castle has more than 8,000 architectural drawings from the Hearst-Morgan era. Those produced in the 1940s await further identification as her work versus that of Mac McClure, Ray Carlson, or other draftsmen; some examples may contain notations or other clues as to her whereabouts then.

Right before Morgan saw Hearst in January 1940, she billed him for $12.30, the final amount in her Refunds account. She received his payment two weeks later but did not mark the account "closed" (just as she didn't with the Commission Account in March 1939—or with the main Wyntoon account in July that year). Normally, the absence of "closed" in any of her accounts meant the door was still open for business.

As for the $27 in Appendix A, p. 545 (rounded off from $27.27 to reflect San Simeon's accrued costs for Morgan in 1940), it stemmed from $25 for the trip to see Hearst, plus $2.27 for supplies used in inventory work.

5. From Murray to Willicombe, January 25, 1940; Hearst Papers, carton 31 (under "1940 Samples"). The County Roof Service was synonymous with James Quaglino, who in 1935 had helped Loorz and the architect Lou Crawford to become associated (p. 182, note 55). Typically, Jud Smelser had included these words about Quaglino while writing to Loorz on February 27, 1938: "Charlini or

Routine matters, to be sure: they proved there was nothing new under the sun at San Simeon—climatically. The preventive and corrective measures were of a new breed, though, dependent now on someone like Bill Murray more than two hundred miles away. In the days when a construction boss like Loorz and workmen of various trades were close by, Willicombe could have saved himself a long-distance call.

Loorz got a late-breaking weather report from Nigel Keep, dated February 1 —and a good deal more in the process:

> Well you can just thank the rain for this "Billet doux" [love letter] cause there's lots of mud in the Pergola & Orchard, & as I'm not a duck & dont care for mud & water, I am inside. However none of us are squaking cause it IS wet, needed it very badly, since Jan 1 we have had 28" of rain, that should pep up Pine Mt Spring which all thru June [1939] to Jan ran only $^3/_4$" over the weir [at the reservoir], however, we watered only necessary trees & those with a spoon. Cost only 2 Pine trees from want of water—garden [on the hilltop proper] didnt suffer, water in Lily Pool [on the Main Terrace] got a trifle green, but that helped to feed the fish. Things are very quiet round here, but with only one explosion, when WR— Williams [that is] & wife were politely asked to move on, They have gone to San Luis Obispo & gossip says, he is going into the photo business but would imagine that is muchly overdone in S.L.O., I see the stakes round China Hill [from June 1939] & wonder why, when & How that is to be done IF EVER.

But things like leaks and mud and rainfall totals weren't even mentioned by Loorz in a long letter he wrote Morgan on February 8, as they might have been in past years. Instead, his letter was intimate, introspective, and richly detailed in other ways. Evidently it was about the last of its kind that he ever sent her (and in the Loorz tradition of "rushing," it was a quickly typewritten one that omitted some punctuation):

> It has been so long since I have seen you that I am anxious to hear from you again. After our many years of most pleasant association I honestly miss it. Just for fun I'd like to visit with you if you have time and will let me know the next time you come down [to Monterey]. If I come up there soon, which is likely I'll make it a point to call on you.
>
> The family are quite well and happy and have more than we need, in fact more than we have ever had. Just the same we lived too long with the friends of the hill-top connections not to long to see them.
>
> In fact, I have Frank Gyorgy with me. He has worked for me steadily since be-

---

Carlini or ———ini didn't show up yesterday, Saturday, and hope he comes tomorrow [on roof repairs] for it looks like rain today. . . . Come to think of it I believe that name was Qualinini."

fore xmas. I think he called on you over the holidays. His work is so much better than the local painters. I have been able to have him gold leaf quite a little on two different jobs.[6]

Otto Olson came back to me the day he finished at Wyntoon and I have him carving daily. We put a very nice Antique carved walnut wainscot in the Nave of the little church we are doing in Carmel. As usual we have had to stretch and squeeze and I dont know what I would have done without him. I still have three other boys that we [had] with us on the hilltop.

From Nigel Keep and others I learned of Mr. Williams dismissal. It was too bad for it will not be easy for him to make headway in San Luis. I am honestly sorry for his own sake and Mrs Williams but I breathed a sigh of relief for Sandy [Nick Yost].[7] It was really cruel the way he was abused, especially the past year or so. I still have the greatest regards for Mr. Williams honesty, his ability, his morality and his sincerity, but I could never account for his disagreeableness to those under him. Of course we see the faults in others more than in ourselves.

I admit that I have shown conceit and selfishness but I tried to [give] the other fellow some consideration. I thot I succeeded in part at San Simeon.

Anyhow I'd love to talk with you. We have two or three small jobs to start and when the competition gets a little less keen I'm confident we'll have more big jobs with a profit.[8]

The subject of drips and seeps wasn't about to go away that easily, even if Loorz hadn't mentioned it to Morgan. Willicombe had further news for Bill Murray on February 15:

Chief instructed me to tell you:

"The leaks are a little worse than they were before the people came that Mr. Murray sent to fix them—not much worse, but just a little worse.

"I will see what we can do with our own people, or what little help we can get here; or else I will have Miss Morgan come down.

"It will not cost much, but I think I will do it myself and try to get it done right."

In speaking of doing it himself, Hearst didn't mean he'd be climbing a ladder or wielding a hot mop. He meant he was ready to foot the bill personally, rather

---

6. Early in 1940 Loorz was helping his brother and his sister-in-law, Claude and Freda, with their place in San Francisco, as he had in the past. He told them on January 22, "If you'd like to have Frank Gyorgy come up for a few days to get you started correctly, I could spare him." He fumbled the next line but still made his point about Gyorgy: "As a brother of mine I think he would take $6.00 a day."

7. Nickolas Yost (not *Nicholas*) became manager of the San Simeon warehouses in January 1940, taking over when Williams was fired. Yost stayed on until 1956.

8. Loorz's letter is among the five from 1938 through 1940 that surfaced in 1997 (as first cited in the 1939 chapter, notes 7 and 34). All five have since been added to the George Loorz Papers.

than lean on Big Brother — on some part of the greater corporation — to do the honors. It was that same question that had cropped up in recent years with the Burnett Road and certain other projects: who pays?

Murray was flabbergasted — and probably glad he'd never had to fill Camille Rossi's or George Loorz's shoes, not to mention Julia Morgan's.[9] He got back to Willicombe the next day:

> I cannot understand why the leaks are worse now than they were before they were fixed. The people I engaged to do the repair work are the same people who did the roofing at San Simeon under Miss Morgan's supervision.[10] I am communicating with them today to check into this matter. There is no reason why they should not do good work, and we will not pay them until they do.[11]

The problem lodged itself deeply in Hearst's psyche. (His part of Casa Grande, the third-floor Gothic Suite and the Celestial Suite above it, was where the faulty repairs had been concentrated.) Indeed, such matters may have led to the expounding he did for a man at the *Los Angeles Examiner*:

> Incidentally, the weather in the whole Northern Hemisphere is growing warmer. The Northern ice cap is melting. The glaciers in Switzerland are disappearing.
>
> These things are not due to the Japan current. They are due to those long and little understood glacial periods.
>
> Probably the Northern Hemisphere will continue to grow warmer until the North Pole is temperate and the animals which now inhabit the temperate zones wander over it. The frozen bodies of such animals as the Mastodons are now found meshed in Arctic ice.[12]

---

9. Thirteen years earlier to the very month — February 1927 — San Simeon was awash in similar conditions, as it had been and would be at mid-winter in certain other years. But the trials of 1927 are especially memorable, thanks to the Morgan Collection at Cal Poly; it has letters on the subject between Hearst and Camille Rossi, not just between Hearst and Morgan.

For 1940, that same archives has a letter about Rossi himself, whose efforts to get ahead had gained Willicombe's attention. Willicombe wondered if Rossi was truly qualified for a certain post as an engineer — but since Rossi had never been a "shrinking violet," his assertiveness came as no surprise. See Willicombe to Morgan, January 25, 1940; Hearst/Morgan Correspondence, Morgan Collection. The résumé that Maurice McClure showed Loorz in June 1940 (note 22, below) indicated that Rossi, whom McClure gave as a reference, was "presently employed with the U.S. Army Engineers."

10. Murray meant the County Roof Service (which he called the County Roofing Company in writing to Willicombe on January 25). Mentioned in the Loorz Papers as early as 1932, Quaglino's firm had been a sub-contractor on the Bunkhouse job, for example, in 1937.

11. From Murray to Willicombe, February 16, 1940; Hearst Papers, carton 31 (under "1940 Samples").

12. From unsigned [Hearst] to Warden Woolard, February 26, 1940; ibid.

Hearst loved good slogans for his newspapers, many of which he coined. Unfortunately, no one had come up yet with *global warming*.

THE CHIEF WAS IN SANTA MONICA when even soggier news arrived from the north end of the state. On February 28, Murray wrote up the details that Hearst and Willicombe had just received from him; his letter went to Willicombe:

> Confirming my telephone conversation with you today, I received the following telegram from Mr. Kower at McCloud.
> "River in extreme flood Gables bridge only one left Water flowing one and a half feet deep across river group [Bavarian Village] lawn in front of building with only Brown Bear first floor still nine inches out of water Moving furnishings upstairs and doing everything else possible River still rising."

Murray had tried to reach Gene Kower and his wife by phone, but the connection was dismal. Still, he'd managed to convey a message from Hearst: "remove if possible the precious things out of the buildings into the Gables or to some higher point where they would be safe from flood damage."

And yet as Murray related, "Mrs. Kower told me this would be impossible to accomplish at the moment; that the only possible way of protecting the contents of the buildings was to move them to the upper stories."[13]

Murray and Willicombe were on the phone again the next day, February 29, a conversation that Murray likewise confirmed in writing:

> I received a second telegram from Mr. Kower at Wyntoon, reading as follows:
> "River down four feet Weather clearing Gables bridge apparently safe Water entered Angel and Cinderella houses only Approximately 7 inches deep Have all rugs out and washed Am drying [and] oiling bottoms and legs of furniture which shows very limited damage Kept one tranformer [basement] vault dry and will get temporary power for lights and pumping as river lowers We then can survey electrical damage Installing circulating heater in Cinderella fire-

---

13. From Murray to Willicombe, February 28, 1940; ibid. The message from Hearst, incorporated in the letter, appears in Murray's own words.

February 28 also found Loorz writing to Stolte — on more agreeable business. "Fred I havent seen so much proposed private work in my life," said Loorz. He went on to tell his partner, "Would like to see you and go over the many projects and my present plans. It begins with staying here [in Pacific Grove] instead of moving north [back to the Bay Area]." Furthermore, he told Stolte he was joining "the Monterey Country Club," the least expensive and yet "most popular Club on the Penninsula [*sic*]." Loorz had a basic idea: "Dont expect to play golf, just want to meet many people who dont even know me."

place Much work to be done to grounds River group [damage] due [to] cutting effect [of river] and tons silt and debris deposited Will send pictures promptly."

Murray tried to remain cheerful through it all. "I am very glad that the storm has abated," he told Willicombe, "and that the river has receded, and altho it is too bad that any damage should have been done, we are fortunate that it is not worse."[14]

Gene Kower sent Murray a detailed letter on March 3. Nearly twelve inches of rain had fallen, he said, between February 22 and 29—on top of a snow pack from previous storms. The flooding began late in the evening of the twenty-seventh. Earlier that day the McCloud River reached a height that, in 1937, had almost equaled a level attained in the 1880s; and by 11 P.M. the water surpassed both those heights. Then it began to recede. Kower and his main helper, Cal Shewmaker, kept some pumps going full blast till 1:30 in the morning. They stole a few hours' sleep, hoping the McCloud would keep dropping, knowing they were powerless to turn it back if it didn't. They awoke to find that two of Wyntoon's three bridges were gone (the ones at the Bavarian Village and down at The Bend; the intermediate one at The Gables had stood). As Kower said of those darkest hours on February 28, "The river instead of continuing to fall had risen an additional two feet in [the] night and continued rising till 11 A.M." He had still more to tell. The place was a mess: roads, trails, lawns, buildings—much of Wyntoon was entombed in mud or had washed away. "First job this morning was to move all Brown Bear furnishings to 2nd floor. Nothing could be done about Cinderella 1st floor." And so on with other descriptions that appalled those who could visualize the scene.[15]

Hearst asked the obvious question. Was he properly insured? Alas, he wasn't. Murray explained to Willicombe on March 8 that Hearst's policies on Wyntoon protected him against a long list of possibilities besides fire ("tornado" and "riot" were among the least likely). "Flood or rising waters" didn't figure at all. Better coverage had to be secured before the river set a new mark; in the meantime, Murray knew there was little else anyone could say: "The flood damage at McCloud this year was most unusual."[16]

---

14. From "Bill" [Murray] to Willicombe, February 29, 1940; Hearst Papers, carton 31 (under "1940 Samples").

15. See Kower to Murray, March 3, 1940 (a copy of the letter accompanies Murray to Willicombe, March 4); ibid.

16. From Murray to Willicombe, March 8, 1940; ibid.

TWO WEEKS LATER, March 16, Loorz mentioned the flood while writing to Pete Petersen:[17]

> Suppose you heard that the [uppermost] Bridge at Wyntoon washed out. Logs got in front of the bridge and the whole flat [at the Bavarian Village] was covered with two foot of water. A good deal of damage was done but mostly mud.
>
> Mac went up to look things over. He said he didn't think Mr. Hearst could afford to go to Wyntoon this year. That sounds funny.

It does indeed without Bill Murray's letters and Gene Kower's report at hand. How Hearst managed (with many people's help and through many dollars spent) to dig back in at Wyntoon in 1940 is a story all its own — one that the Loorz Papers barely touch on.[18]

Loorz's letter of March 16 had some more news for Petersen. "Business looks good here and I sort of wanted to talk it over with you":

> Also I am figuring a job for Mr. Hearst in Los Angeles. If I get it I would like to have you run it for me. I would give you Otto [Olson] and any other good men you might want.[19]

The job in Los Angeles proved to be some remodeling of the Marion Davies house in Beverly Hills — involving the larger house at 1700 Lexington Road,

---

17. About this same time — Tuesday, March 11 — the Governor of California, Culbert Olson, got in touch with Hearst and arranged to meet him right away at San Simeon; Hearst made notes on the incident the next day:

> The Governor (Olson) telephoned from Santa Barbara (yesterday) and again from Santa Maria that he wanted to see me and would like to stop on his way north at the ranch.
>
> I of course received him as courteously as possible.
>
> We had quite a discussion last night and again this morning.
>
> I do not think either one of us convinced the other, and he is departing this afternoon, convinced I think that we just belong to different schools of thought, and cannot very well reconcile our ideas.

Hearst planned to send Clarence Lindner (publisher of the *San Francisco Examiner*) a more detailed account. From a transcription of Hearst's notes, as relayed to Lindner and also to the attorney Heinie MacKay, March 12, 1940; Hearst Papers, carton 31 (under "1940 Samples").

18. The Hearst Papers and related holdings at the Bancroft Library are perhaps the best hope of fleshing out that story. A few good letters could be enough to do it.

19. Loorz wrote to Morgan on March 16 also. The letter is his last one to her in the Loorz Papers (his last *surviving* one, that is):

> We were very sorry you felt too bad to enjoy that Sunday afternoon with us. We hope you will, Please, tell us when you can arrange to be with us again. We had planned a drive thru the back roads from the Drive [the 17 Mile Drive, from Pacific Grove to Carmel through Pebble Beach]. There are so many wild flowers there now that it is simply grand.

around the corner from the smaller one at 910 Benedict Canyon Drive (where portions of the Cosmopolitan bungalow had recently been used). Loorz provided more details — "It is raining like the devil," he began — in a letter he wrote his parents on Saturday, March 30:

> We finally landed a couple of jobs. A small home here in Pacific Grove and an alteration on Miss Davies old home in Beverly Hills. They took a figure from the man [Frank Hellenthal] who has done most of Mr. Hearst's work down there since I was down there in 1928 [on the Beach House job]. Well they thot he was a bit high on this one and called me in to figure [it] and I got it.[20] I intend to start it Monday [April 1]. Hope this rain lets up before that.

The Davies job had materialized with good timing. "It has been slow getting started this year," Loorz also told his parents. "No P.W.A. is the reason."

On April 10 he referred once more to that offspring of the New Deal, that frequent godsend for him since 1935, when he launched the branch office of the F. C. Stolte Co.; this was in writing to his sister, Iva, and her family:

> We have some work but still not enough to cover my overhead. However, I have faith that things will break again just as they did last year and the year before etc. I must admit that there is no P.W.A. to fill the gap as there has been in the past. My hope now is that some real healthy private business will develop that will do the trick. In the meantime hold everything.

He also mentioned the new job he'd begun for Hearst and Miss Davies down south:

> We are doing a nice alteration to Marion Davies old home in Beverly Hills. I have to go down about every two weeks and that costs about $40 per trip without salary. It is a [lump-sum] contract so I may not come out as I should. It is difficult

---

The second (and last) paragraph contained a more telling passage:

> I know also Miss Morgan that you come down here for relaxation and that dinners and such inter[r]upt that restfulness you get otherwise.

He assured her, therefore, that the Loorzes would be patient until she truly felt like socializing. "We want you only when it will really be enjoyable to you."

20. The efforts at the Beach House resulted in Loorz's being "down there" in 1927 also; see pp. 6–7 in this volume and their notes 11–12. As to Hellenthal, who'd been Morgan's builder on the 910 Benedict Canyon job in 1939 and who bid on 1700 Lexington in 1940, the Morgan Collection has some items of his stemming from those closely related jobs (filed under "Marion Davies Residence," III/06/09/04). The Hellenthal items are dated September 14, 1939, and March 15, 1940.

operating economically so far away. I have a good foreman there and a good supervisor but that is double overhead.[21] One [such man] is hardly good enough to
operate alone.

The "Beverly Hills job" was likewise on Loorz's mind when he wrote on April
14 to Charlie Badley (still a close friend in the Bay Area, though for some time a
minor presence in these annals). Loorz also mentioned Maurice McClure—
as distinct from Mac McClure, who was seven years older than "Morris" McClure
(as the pronunciation went) and unrelated to him.[22] Loorz hoped Badley would
encourage the younger McClure and his wife, Hazel, to join the Pacific Grove employees for "a company barbeque at Big Sur," to be held a week later. "Hope it
doesn't rain," Loorz remarked. (The event went off without a hitch. As Fred Stolte
said to Loorz on April 29, "You must have had quite a crowd at the picnic, and lots
of eats etc.")

With the Marion Davies job, it's one thing to identify the foreman and supervisor Loorz told his sister about on April 10. Yet it's quite another thing to identify
the architect. Julia Morgan was no doubt involved, at least in part: the Morgan
Collection at Cal Poly has sketches and drawings of hers that pertain to the job,

---

21. Pete Petersen was obviously one of those men. Since Loorz had told him on March 16 regarding that job, "I would like to have you run it for me," the supervisor's role would seem to have
been Petersen's (recalling 1938, when Loorz preferred him to John McFadden for the position of
"general foreman" at San Simeon). Whether that's what happened in Beverly Hills—whether Petersen was actually the foreman, not the supervisor—the identity of the second man remains unknown.

22. Maurice McClure, a month away from his degree in civil engineering at UC Berkeley, assumed that the Stolte Co. had no place for him currently. In telling Loorz on April 29 about his "recent hurried search for employment," McClure mentioned his approach:

> In filling out applications, I have stated that I have worked for the Stolte Co. under your super-
> vision for the years 1933–1939 inclusive during school vacations. . . . These statements stretch
> the truth a little, but I have found them necessary in view of the claims of other men seeking
> similar positions.

McClure knew full well, as Loorz also did, that 1933 had been a crucial turning point: having
nearly lost his job at San Simeon (when Ada Drew and others were swept out in the "housecleaning"
that year), McClure had decided to resume his education, dormant since grade school. Loorz liked
"Morris" and had unexpected news for him on May 3, 1940:

> Maurice, we are starting a $35,000 job at Camp McQuaide in Watsonville next Tuesday and
> we would be glad to have you work with Elof [Gustafson] on that job, if you so desired. The job
> consists of sewer lines, a small sewage disposal plant, four latrines.

McClure decided not to work there; instead, he sent Loorz his new résumé on June 15: "In line
with your suggestion, I intend to become a registered engineer at the earliest convenience." McClure
gave his years of work under Loorz as "1933 to 1940" and those under Camille Rossi (whom he always admired) as "1926 to 1933," likewise a padded span.

1939 being the only date on any of them. The time lag isn't the point. For construction in one year to be based on drawings from the previous year is nothing new, in her case or anyone else's.

What's puzzling is that no ledger of Morgan's exists for the Davies job—a job carried out by Loorz in a year that saw Morgan itemizing her "Distribution of Expenses" to the last penny, as she and her staff had methodically done since 1924.

True, 1940 was the last year for which those comprehensive sheets in the Morgan-Forney Collection were compiled (or from which they've survived). In contrast, the individual account ledgers, on which the year-end tally sheets were based, continued past 1940—unevenly, though, from the first of 1941 onward. (Thus does Appendix A, pp. 531–45, devote itself to the seventeen previous years only, 1924–40, whose annual "Distribution" data are complete and whose corresponding job ledgers, although at times less complete, are still abundantly detailed; at the very least, all the job names and their total operating costs appear on those seventeen summarizing sheets.)

Concerning the Davies-Beverly job—whose precursors in 1925–27 and 1929 *are* identifiable in Morgan's ledgers[23]—at least two possibilities present themselves. The first is that Morgan's work in 1939 on the nearby 910 Benedict Canyon project (which absorbed parts of the Cosmopolitan bungalow) may have been combined with drafting and other efforts she allotted 1700 Lexington Road, likewise in 1939. If so, her use of a single account ledger (the bungalow ledger) for two related jobs would have been unusual, though not unheard of. At any rate, she entered $1,479 in operating costs in the bungalow ledger for 1939. Fully half that amount was for travel. The other half stemmed mostly from drafting-room time and office overhead.

A second possibility may be this: Morgan started the architectual part of the Beverly job on Lexington in 1939, and then Mac McClure took over and stayed with the project into 1940. Hearst, of course (in behalf of Miss Davies), was probably making changes up to the last minute in March and April—and even later—changes that someone had to carry out. Mac was the best candidate.

It's also possible that Morgan worked on the Beverly job in 1939, and in 1940 as well, but that she never charged Hearst (or Davies either). The prospect seems unlikely, though, if for no other reason than a documentary one. Namely, when Morgan did gratis jobs for clients, she still kept a running ledger that closely reflected her efforts, no less so than when she strove for a profit. (Some of this same unlikeliness applies to the second possibility, the one involving Mac McClure.)

---

23. Each occurrence in Appendix A of "Marion Davies Residence, Beverly Hills" pertains to 1700 Lexington Road; see pp. 534, 537, 538, and 539.

One of the few guesses, therefore, that's worth venturing is that her trip to San Simeon in January *probably* included "Beverly" business. Without Mac or Loorz or the Morgan-Forney data to guide us further, we're left to wonder. The dimness, the ironic obscurity that typifies so much of the Hearst-Morgan saga in the 1940s, remains unbrightened on that sunny knoll in Beverly Hills, known as 1700 Lexington Road.

THE MONTH OF MAY could well have seen Hearst re-establishing Wyntoon as his main address—had it not been for all the mud and misery. The trend toward longer stays there, easily discernible as of 1939, would probably have resumed in 1940 after he laid over at San Simeon and the Beach House. Instead, Gene Kower and his crew up north needed extra time before welcoming the Chief home. How they dug out, how they bridged the river, how they kept the costs from skyrocketing is hard to say. Until more documents surface, either in the Hearst Papers or elsewhere, the answers will be out of reach. The crew must have made good headway, though, for Hearst finally settled in at Wyntoon in 1940, albeit on the late side (in what may have been a second try). And once he got comfortable, he stayed right through December.

As for San Simeon, "Imagine that they have been keeping you quite busy with all the company on the Hilltop." If only we had some sense, any sense, of who "the company" were.[24] Our wistfulness aside, those words went to Marks Eubanks, San Simeon's resident electrician and maintenance man, Loorz having dictated a brief reply to him on May 23. (Where was Jud Smelser all the while?)

Eubanks had sounded out Loorz three days earlier.[25] Plainspoken fare for the

---

24. Apart from noting that Hearst may have invited more business associates in 1940 than he often had in earlier years, one can almost say more easily who "the company" *weren't*. Among them: the novelist and mystery writer Frances Crane, who described the time she and her friend Alice tried to gain admittance, either in 1940 or not long before. (Unlike most who've recounted being at San Simeon when Hearst was living, the two women drove down from the north, by way of Carmel and Big Sur.) They thought a letter of introduction, which Frances was overdue in redeeming, might open the gates for them. "It's the kind of letter that gets you a pass," a cowboy agreed after the women drove onto the ranch and caught his eye. "Only there ain't anybody here to give y'all a pass," he elaborated. "There ain't nobody at the castle now, anyhow, but caretakers." From Frances Crane, "My Visit to San Simeon," *The New Yorker* (April 5, 1941), pp. 37–38.

25. In the meantime, Hearst sent Bill Murray an impassioned letter; the tug-of-war between personal and corporate resources was still in play. Hearst sounded almost as though he weren't writing from San Simeon, yet that's where he was holding forth:

If the folks in the East want me to live at San Simeon, or are willing for me to live there, they must make it possible for me to live there.

They have cut my salary down to one-fifth of what it was [from $500,000 to $100,000]— and what it ought to be — they refuse to let me have the money that is actually mine, but which

most part: the tennis court at the quaint little school in old-town San Simeon needed work; Eubanks thought Loorz might have some suggestions. He aimed higher, though, in another matter:

> If you readily see Frank Georgie [Gyorgy] would you please ask him what he used to put on the alabaster shades [for lamp standards on the hilltop] to preserve them — don't go out of your way to do this if he is not handy — for I know you are a busy man these days — and I can get his address and write to him.

In offering best wishes to Loorz and his family, Eubanks said, "you see San Simeon misses you all in more ways than one." In answering on May 23, Loorz told Eubanks he was "contemplating on coming down Saturday [May 25] and staying over for the Rodeo [in Cambria]." He assured him he'd give the school "a looking over" if he made the trip.

No matter what was, in fact, going on up at 1,600 feet, up where Hearst and his party were steeped in the hilltop's springtime beauty — no matter how tight the budget and how worrisome the future — a trip out of state was now in the offing. That much is known. (April 29 had marked Hearst's seventy-seventh birthday, the first he'd celebrated at San Simeon since 1934 — that much is also known.) He still had some trips to Mexico inside him; they would take place soon enough. Apart from those, his trip to Chicago early in June 1940, a minor excursion in a life rich with travel, may have marked his last measurable absence from California. The event is barely known — no mention in *The New York Times*, or by any of his biographers — in short, another of those non-events virtually, as voiceless as the tree whose fall was silent, there having been no one nearby to hear it.[26]

---

they have tied up in some kind of complication; they refuse other funds which should be allotted to me, and which in total amount to over a million dollars.

Having deprived me of income, they must realize that I have not the funds available to pay unnecessary charges of the character we have been discussing.

If they will put my salary back to where it was, and release the funds that are properly mine, I will make the payments demanded. But I cannot otherwise.

I am not being perverse or obstinate.

I simply must have conditions which will permit me to live economically.

From unsigned [Hearst] to Murray, May 22, 1940 (together with a draft dated May 19); Hearst Papers, carton 31 (under "1940 Samples"). Hearst had been trying to cut costs all year. Willicombe told Murray on March 28, "Chief says that if Mr. [W.B.N.] Brookes [of the New York office] is disturbed about the chicken farm here, you are at liberty to shut it up as far as he is concerned." But Hearst didn't see why the poultry operation couldn't be put on "a self-supporting basis," said Willicombe, "charging him for what he uses, the Ranch for what it uses, and selling what you can outside." Hearst Papers, ibid.

26. The Hearst Papers at the Bancroft Library, the best source of these overlooked episodes (though still an under-processed collection), may have other stateside examples from these later

Hearst was returning to the coast when Morgan wrote to John Vanderloo in Cambria on June 15. (She had written to that artisan three months earlier; concerning San Simeon, she'd been the bearer of disheartening news: "I hope work can be resumed this summer but it may again not be possible. I'm sorry to say so!") In the meantime, she and Vanderloo had failed to connect in Monterey, a rendezvous they'd long been hoping for. Her letter of June 15 began on that note. Then she quickly alluded to two current jobs, the house she'd begun for Else Schilling in Lake Tahoe the year before and a store-restaurant complex for F. C. Turner in Berkeley; she dwelled at greater length, though still allusively, on the building that she and Maybeck had been designing all the while for Mrs. A. H. Darbee in Colma but that had since hit a snag. Morgan also had some clearer, more familiar words for Vanderloo about Hearst and the like:

> How sorry I am to have missed that long looked forward to visit of you and your family to Monterey!
>
> My own work has been in [and] out of town work, Tahoe [Schilling], Berkeley [Turner], down the [San Francisco] peninsula [Darbee],—with the development of one fine project [the Darbee Mausoleum] these world conditions have halted the financing of [it].[27] I had hopes for all of those [artisans like Vanderloo] of San Simeon groups [of workmen], as there is much ornamental & decorative design involved. Now that [the Darbee project] is in a future none can even guess as to.
>
> I do not believe there will be a re-newal of Mr Hearst's projects for some time. You can speculate as well as any one. I do think trained & capable people will be at a premium before long again—Ornamental work will have different types of sculptural forms and will tend to larger, more centralized and grouped, rather than spread, over-all uses—as was popular twenty years ago—but will require expert craftsmen just the same. It is the next four months that will make decisions harder than ever—for the wisest and most informed people cannot guess how all our future will be affected.
>
> Not a cheerful letter, John. But I think we *can* be cheerful & thankful for the comparative safety of our present [situation in the world]. If I can provide any definite advice, do not hesitate to ask it.

---

years. The trip to Chicago was probably for corporate business—not for something like the Republican National Convention, held in June as well but in Philadelphia, a non-Hearst city. (And it was too soon for the Democratic Convention, anathema to the Hearst of this era but slated for more accustomed territory—Chicago.) See also p. 509, note 14.

27. Morgan's handwritten wording and punctuation are often problematic; in the second half of this sentence, her intended syntax could possibly have been "—with the development of one fine project [that] these world conditions have halted the financing of." Either way, she could only have meant the Darbee commission. Nothing else she worked on in 1939 or 1940 fits the context or the description.

She signed off, "With fondest remembrances to all your dear family and hopes you will find a satisfactory outlet [for your skills]—."[28] Vanderloo no doubt could have done so, yet he might have to leave isolated Cambria now that San Simeon's prospects were more remote than ever.

When Hearst got back from Chicago in late June, he relied as before on San Simeon. Wyntoon remained unusable till mid-July. On the workaday front, Loorz wrote to Fred Stolte during this period; some of what he reported on June 21 touched on familiar turf:

> Beverly Hills [the Davies job], McQuaid [Camp McQuaide, north of Monterey near Watsonville][29] and Gonzales [the school in that Salinas Valley town] are checking out much better than we figured. That is unusual for jobs figured as close as they were. That is all I can point to with pride for this half year. . . .
>
> Miss Morgan has another plan out for figures down here but didn't call us. I told her we lost on her last one [the Parsons residence in Monterey], in fact, all of them, so she rightfully thinks we are not interested. However, $11,000 is normally a very good house and should be O.K. She let a small one to a small Carmel contractor and word comes that he is not figuring this one.[30]

A letter to Pete Petersen on Tuesday, July 2, had an impressive look, conveyed by the address Loorz typed above the greeting:

P. H. Petersen
1700 Lexington Drive,
Beverly Hills, Calif.

---

28. Vanderloo Collection. The earlier letter from Morgan, dated March 11, 1940, is in the same collection. For a variant reading of Morgan's second paragraph on June 15, 1940, see Victoria Kastner, *Hearst Castle: The Biography of a Country House*, pp. 197, 208–09, wherein Morgan's allusions to the Darbee project in Colma have been taken to mean San Simeon. In regard to the Schilling job at Lake Tahoe, Morgan had gone there as recently as June 4, her first trip there since the fall of 1939; she made a final visit in July 1940.

29. The job at Camp McQuaide (as in note 22, above) was separate from, and much smaller than, the big job Loorz landed there a few months later (mentioned further on in this chapter).

30. A house by Morgan for Emma Wightman Pope and her husband sounds like the one that wasn't being figured. Another house, the "small one" Loorz mentioned, may have been designed for a client named Sarah Oddie (whose name also appears in the Morgan-Forney data in 1932).

As for houses besides the Parsons residence on which the Stolte Co. lost money, they could only have been jobs in 1934 or 1935—such as the work for Mrs. Selden Williams in Berkeley or for Edward Bull in San Francisco—there having been no Morgan-Stolte residential jobs, except those for Hearst, from the mid-thirties until the Parsons job in 1939. But see p. 152, note 89: Loorz to Weatherford, December 7, 1934, in which Loorz spoke favorably of Morgan's "various jobs." Not quite a year later, though (October 19, 1935), Stolte told Loorz that the Bull job had been "one of those tough ones" and that (as he further said on November 17) Morgan had requested several "extras"—items over budget by $500, for which the partners might be unwise to charge.

June 1940 also found Morgan, along with Ray Carlson, working on the "proposed mezzanine

Loorz meant Lexington *Road*, of course, and his message followed close on the heels of a telephone conversation he'd just had with Petersen:

> Sorry not to have come down before this but I see no reason to be there.
>
> Now that you have the approved detail of the mantel you can go ahead with that and keep ahead of the painters [such as James Vickery] as much as possible. I hope everything else is in order. Hope the painters arent stalling too much.
>
> As per my wire Miss Davies O.K'd the extra painting on the exterior walls and Patio Walls. Also the bleaching of the hallway, which I think was a mistake.
>
> She will not go ahead with the kitchen alteration of the stairway from [room] #3 to #4 etc. May get some more work in the garden but not at this time. I think she will go ahead with the signal system at the other house [910 Benedict Canyon] but not at 1700.
>
> We expect to be down on the 5th [Friday], in fact we may arrive on the 4th. Will see you then.
>
> I just phoned you so all the above is old stuff to you. I thot I waited long enough to talk to Mac but not luck.
>
> As I said by phone, remove and carefully crate the fine mantel and have it stored at the Beach House. Order your materials and construct the new mantel as soon as possible. Tell the painter to go ahead with the painting of the Patio and exterior garden walls clear around. Try to do it with the one coat job if possible.

"Old stuff" this may have been to Petersen, yes. But in the absence of the telegram Loorz mentioned, and with the Loorz Papers getting spottier through this period, words like these that may once have seemed extraneous are worth their weight in archival gold.

A letter that Loorz sent to San Francisco, likewise on July 2 and written for "the kidlets"—Claude and Freda Loorz, his brother and sister-in-law—sounds as if it had followed the letter to Petersen.[31] "Well we expected to come up that way over the 4th but now it seems advisable for me to go to Beverly Hills. The job there is about to be finished and I am needed." Loorz's wife and their three sons would be going too. (The clout of that era's dollar comes to mind here. Loorz also told Claude and Freda, "The boys [Don, Bill, and Bob, now fourteen, twelve, and five] have been working about three hours per day. Pay them 25¢ per hour.")

---

floor" for the Merchants Exchange building in San Francisco, a small job involving Walter Huber as well; Morgan's firm also did some drawings for that building in 1930 (Morgan-Forney ledgers).

31. The day before—July 1, 1940—Hearst's acreage and buildings at the Grand Canyon became government property. The transfer (or "land grab," as some believed) stemmed from condemnation proceedings, begun in earnest nearly a year before and foreshadowed by other dealings in 1938. The Hearst Papers contain numerous items, filed in three or more cartons (27, 30, and 31 for

Some three weeks later, on July 20, Loorz not only told Stolte that the Pacific Grove branch was "very busy" and was "making a little money at the present time," he also mentioned specific details that could be pertinent. "With eight small houses going and as we are architects as well it takes a lot of time and work. Have four more [houses] to start as soon as we get plans and loans thru."

As we are architects as well. Could Loorz's use of local designers like Jerry Ryland, based in Monterey, help explain Morgan's absence from the Davies job in 1940? Or was Mac McClure's presence (to which Loorz alluded when he wrote Petersen) enough to carry the day? It may have been.

MISS MORGAN, at any rate, wasn't thinking of Loorz's houses in the Monterey area or the Davies job in Beverly Hills when she wrote to Willicombe at San Simeon; it was August 2, a Friday:[32]

> Mr. [Herbert] Fleishhacker and one or more others are coming in on Tuesday morning to see what Mt. Olive [Santa Maria de Ovila] photographs and information are here. Mr. Fleishhacker said Mr. Hearst had offered it [the monastery] to the city Art-Park-Museum Commission [of San Francisco], but they would need to know more about it, see pictures, plans, etc., and have an idea as to the erection cost as an addition to the deYoung Museum before answering. They think of it evidently as a building to be viewed from the outside—and [a] complete [one].
>
> If it is in order to show what data remains in the office,[33] please let me know just what Mr. Hearst proposed to give them, and in what way, so that I may cooperate. Please make this very clear.
>
> You can reach me Sunday at Monterey between twelve and one o'clock. Monday I will be out on some work [in Carmel][34] and back in San Francisco too late to reach.

The ancient Spanish monastery, once slated for Wyntoon and fully warranting its "big job" stature in the Loorz Papers of 1933, had reposed all the while

---

starters). Michael Anderson's book is also pertinent; see *Living at the Edge: Explorers, Exploiters and Settlers of the Grand Canyon Region*, pp. 72, 75.

32. The letter is part of the Santa Maria de Ovila correspondence file; Morgan Collection (III/06/09/09).

33. Plenty of items were still on hand; but Maybeck's colored sketches had left the office two years before, at Hearst's request, and there may have been other departures. See Morgan to Hearst, September 7, 1938, and Willicombe to Morgan, September 10, 1938; Morgan Collection (III/06/09/09). In contrast, Willicombe to Morgan on September 21, 1938, mentions items that her office was getting back; ibid.

34. Most likely the house for the "Doctors Pope" (Emma Wightman Pope and her husband, as in note 30, above). See Boutelle, *Julia Morgan*, pp. 143–44.

in San Francisco, with storage provided by the Haslett Warehouse Company.[35] Hearst and Morgan (and Willicombe, too) had corresponded since 1938 about the monastery and its fate.[36] The details are numberless; suffice it to say that Morgan and her main draftsman in 1940, Ray Carlson, soon rolled up their sleeves on "Mount Olive"—and kept them rolled up for the next year and a half. Later still, Morgan and Walter Steilberg, whose name also crops up in the 1940–42 phase, would tackle the monastery challenge with the utmost gusto. But for now, that's jumping too far ahead—all the way to the other side of World War II. Meanwhile on this side, Morgan began a new account called "Park Museum" (as in Golden Gate Park); it ran from August 1940 to July 1944. However, the final instances of drafting-room time for the Park Museum, as opposed to lesser aspects of the job, date from March 1942.

(In Appendix A, p. 534, "Santa Maria de Ovila," the proper name of the monastery, comprises the so-called Mount Olive account of 1931 along with the 1940 portion of the Park Museum account. Hearst owned the monastery until May 1941; but since no Distribution of Expenses sheet exists for that year in the Morgan-Forney Collection, Appendix A confines itself—for the sake of completeness—to the years 1924–40. For 1940 itself, Morgan is assumed here to have done her Park

---

35. One brief letter, from back in 1938, is enough to suggest that Hearst was still paying top dollar for that space. "I am enclosing check for $1,083.20, being payment of storage charges on things belonging to Mr. Hearst in your warehouse for the months of January and February." From Willicombe to S. M. Haslett, Jr., April 6, 1938; Hearst Papers, carton 24 (under "Has-Hd"). The file contains other letters of the same period, on the same subject; they all elicit groans.

36. Some of the letters are mentioned on p. 391 in the 1938 chapter, note 69; see also note 33, above. But a letter Morgan sent Hearst in 1939 is the one that opens Pandora's box on the monastery question:

It might be well to say that you have been asked to pay for no unexecuted work for many years back, in fact before we made the working drawings for Mount Olive at Wyntoon. You realize thinking back the many projects we have developed together, that I could have had no profit in these years and I have not wanted it.

Could have had no profit, that is, on *unexecuted work*—on something like the museum once planned for the Berkeley campus, 1927–30. Morgan's $1,422 outlay on that proposal (Appendix A, p. 535) must be viewed against a backdrop of San Simeon, The Great Provider—no matter how much she deserved to be paid. See Morgan to Hearst, June 9, 1939; Hearst/Morgan Correspondence, Morgan Collection.

"Mount Olive"—the Santa Maria de Ovila monastery—thickens the plot considerably. Morgan accrued $2,758 on that account in 1931; most of that amount, $2,353, was refunded by year's end. But $405 stood in arrears. Fifteen years later she marked the front of the account: "NOTE NEVER PAID 1946." Its bluntness jumps out from the Morgan-Forney ledgers; and yet the amount was $405, not the $15,000 that her nephew, Morgan North, later claimed. See his testimony—much of it insightful, some of it contradictory and misinformed, all of it well intended—in *The Julia Morgan Architectural History Project*, Vol. II, pp. 157 *ff.* (especially p. 201 for the overstated debt). See also note 37, opposite.

Museum work on Hearst's behalf, not for the city of San Francisco, as was later true.)

The "very clear" information Morgan sought from Willicombe on August 2, 1940, has yet to be found. Hence another trail grown cold, another enticing but elusive lead. The Morgan Collection at Cal Poly (whence comes the letter to Willicombe, plus similar items) contains some notes Morgan compiled on August 20. But until the mid-forties are upon us, Cal Poly has little else to divulge about the story of Santa Maria de Ovila.[37]

The Loorz Papers are nearly as mum through these late-summer weeks of 1940, regardless of the subject. However, Nigel Keep wrote on August 20, telling Loorz, "Things very quiet on the Hill. Jack Steiner in chg [charge], with Mrs. Frandolich [working] 3 days a week to catch the spiders, & reset the mouse traps." Otherwise, spottiness seems epidemic now in *all* the archives that have shaped this book.

There's one other exception, and a good one at that. Mac McClure wrote to Loorz on August 20, as Nigel Keep did, the same day that Morgan made her "Mount Olive" notes. The Hearst entourage had finally moved back to Wyntoon,[38]

---

37. Morgan's notes of August 20, 1940, command a single page in the Santa Maria de Ovila file; Morgan Collection. The page is headed "Mt. Olive" and is impressive in scope: Morgan projected nearly $20,000 in office costs for one year's full-blown pursuit of the re-erection job, or nearly $30,000 for eighteen months. However, she marked the page "File" and, right under that, "But Not Used."

The Park Museum account attained no such heights. The office costs were $417 in 1940; $4,017 in 1941; $756 in 1942. Appendix A, with its 1924–40 range, combines the $417 from 1940 with Santa Maria's $2,758 from back in 1931 (yielding $3,175 for those two years).

If Hearst failed to pay the $417 from 1940, his debt of $405 from 1931 (note 36) increased to $822. In 1941 Morgan accrued $841 in new costs during his final five months of ownership; the remaining $3,176 in 1941 came after he gave the monastery to the city of San Francisco. (If the city indeed "bought" the monastery from him for $10,000, as some have said—or even $30,000, according to others—it was neglible after the storage charges he'd been paying; see note 35.) All told, therefore, Hearst's arrears on Santa Maria de Ovila for 1931, combined with those for 1940–41, may have been $1,663 (plus any interest one might assess).

The entire matter is cursed by insufficient data. The identically named Morgan collections at Cal Poly and in the Environmental Design Archives, the Hearst Papers at the Bancroft Library, and the Morgan-Forney Collection don't provide enough information. True, more probing into San Francisco's municipal records needs to be done. Better yet, if the documents of Morgan's (and Walter Steilberg's) that the M. H. de Young Museum once had were to resurface, the matter would invite a sweeping update. But for several years now the whereabouts of the de Young items have been unknown. See also pp. 516–17 in this volume, note 30.

38. Some of Hearst's top men thought he should remain at Wyntoon for a while, safely removed from process servers during a period of legal as well as financial grief. See, for example, Martin Huberth to H. S. "Heinie" MacKay, Jr., September 13, 1940 (within Heinie to Willicombe, November 7, 1940); Hearst Papers, carton 30 (under "MacKay, H. S., Jr."). David Nasaw cited the Huberth-MacKay letter of September 13, yet without realizing that Hearst was already at Wyntoon; see *The Chief*, p. 550, plus its note 21.

where Mac's services were in demand as usual. The good news is that his letter survives. The bad news is that Loorz's doesn't (he'd been in touch earlier, sometime before August 20). All the more reason for Mac to have the floor here:

> I'm terribly sorry, but I can't see how I can possibly do the work you sent up. We are trying to get organized and all of the necessary Full sizing [large drafting tissue?] is needed right away to order the mill work. On top of this Mr Hearst has me going on the usual schemes, sketches etc—The ordering of material, phone calls, and time reports are all mine to do. Last night I received an order for a grand re-furnishing jamboree which is taking place today. All of this to show you that I just haven't the time left to give [to Loorz's work] much as I would like to do so.

It can't be known what Loorz had requested—perhaps sketches or details for one of his jobs around Monterey. Although Mac had to beg off on that score, he shared some further news before he finished (although he never said anything about the flood damage or what had been done to correct it):

> We are just about organized here now. [Jim] Rankin and two helpers,—[Pete] Petersen, Nackler [Carl Nakler] and Cuzlock(?) [Pete Kruslock] are the carpenters and [Frank] Pellando[39] and helper are building a chimney.

Naturally there had to be a postscript; and though it's not one of Mac's best, it still provides a glimpse of that fairytale realm on the once-swollen McCloud:

> The Hollywood Light Fixture Co (Mr Lutton) told me it would cost nearly as much to polish the D.R. [Dining Room] fixtures [in the The Gables] as to silver plate them.

Loorz must have responded, yet once more his papers bear no trace. And thus the range and the extent of what he saved from years past, from as early as 1932, stand out all the more boldly by 1940.

THE PARK MUSEUM in San Francisco and a small alteration at the Oakland YWCA were foremost on Morgan's agenda come September. Leaving Ray Carlson at the drafting helm, Morgan opted for a replay of September 1938: she chose that month in 1940 to make her next voyage through the Panama Canal. But she allotted herself less time on this occasion, and she didn't cross the Atlantic to Europe. Instead, she was gone for a month; Havana was among her ports of call; the

---

39. Formerly at San Simeon, Pellando was a less-gifted stone mason and marble setter than Frank Frandolich. His name appears next to "Spanish Tile" in the account for 910 Benedict Canyon Drive (Morgan-Forney ledgers, 1939). In the Loorz Papers, Pellando's name appears as early as 1932.

trip ended in Baltimore, Maryland. (It's another of those overlooked episodes, on par with Hearst's trip to Chicago in June.) Morgan kept a log of the journey in a minuscule hand. Her final entry, dated October 17, referred to the *Baltimore News-Post*: "Wyntoon pict. in the local Hearst paper!"[40]

Coincidentally, Mac McClure wrote to Loorz from Wyntoon the next day. Would that Mac's pen had never run dry, but his letter of October 18 is the last of its kind to be found in the George Loorz Papers:[41]

> Thought you might be interested in the state of affairs up here. We are still work-ing—finishing up the rooms at The Bend, building fountains and drawing plans by the acre.[42]

> W.R.H. is peevish at times because we are too slow—He expects our crew of 5 to do 15 men's work and his ideas are as intricate as ever. Recently he mentioned the 1700 Lex[ington] job as being economical and speedy and thought we might do likewise up here—What is your reaction on that? I would be more than pleased if it could be worked out. You know the draw backs as well as I, but a big one would be persuading Sunical [Bill Murray's office] to pay for anything (They pay us now).[43]

> I often wonder how you made out on the last payment on the Bev Hills job [at 1700 Lexington]—hope you got it promptly. Anyhow, they [Hearst and Marion Davies] were well pleased with the job, I am sure.

Mac's next paragraph warrants a close reading. It pertained to Hearst and, following that, both to Loorz himself and to the larger entity of the F. C. Stolte Co.:

> I haven't tried very hard yet to sell him on the idea—If by any chance you weren't interested I certainly wouldn't want someone else.

---

40. From the series Travel Memorabilia; Morgan Collection (I/05/02/07, whose notes "Pan-ama Canal and Havana" and "Baltimore" are ostensibly separate but were made on the same trip). The trip is absent from Sara Boutelle's list; see *Julia Morgan*, p. 245 (note 3 under "The Morgan Atelier").

41. Mac continued writing, as one would expect—and as the Hearst Papers, the Morgan Col-lection, and the Shewmaker Collection all attest; in the Loorz Papers themselves, the typewritten sig-nature "W. A. McClure" appears on some carbon copies made in 1942, products of Mac's wartime employment with Stolte Inc. The more typical handwritten example from Mac to Loorz in October 1940 is one of five letters that surfaced in 1997 (as in note 8, above).

42. Regarding progress at The Bend, the Shewmaker Collection has two letters from L. Cardini (of The Sculptors Work Shop in San Francisco) to Mac McClure, dated September 12 and 25, 1940. Both letters pertain to mantels Hearst wanted for "1st floor Pink room" and for "2nd floor Blue room" (penciled in Mac's hand on the earlier letter).

43. In other words, Hearst was no longer using "personal" funds for such expenses, or so the distinction seems to have it. But without further data these nuances, fine points, and allusions are often more bewildering than enlightening. For a year like 1940 the Hearst Papers are probably the best hope in such matters for taking up where the Loorz Papers leave off.

Mac concluded by saying, "This year's work will apparently go on for 6 or 8 weeks more." And then a final allusion to Hearst: "He doesn't know I am writing to you."

This last letter of October 18 also contained a postscript—squarely in the "Mac" tradition. It referred in part to the efforts the Hearst interests were still making to raise desperately needed capital: "You knew that $2\frac{1}{2}$ millions worth of the Milpitas ranch has been sold to the government didn't you (The money went to the corporation)."[44]

Loorz answered on October 22. His opening paragraphs addressed the topic Mac had been so allusive about on the eighteenth—the part about "the idea" Mac had only whispered to Hearst:

> Glad to hear from you and many thanks for the tip about the work [presumably for Hearst, most likely at Wyntoon].
>
> I would be interested in the work, but wonder if the time in which to complete the remainder of the work would be [too] short for me to make the necessary contacts?
>
> We are very busy now and perhaps we would not be able to give quite the service that they [Hearst et al.] would expect. However, we feel that we could handle it very nicely for all concerned.

Undoubtedly they could—the Pacific Grove branch, that is, perhaps with extra help from some of Fred Stolte's men in Alameda. (This assumes that Mac thought Hearst should dispense with his do-it-yourself program, that he thought Hearst should be approaching Wyntoon in the same way he and Miss Davies had done things in Beverly Hills—namely, by relying on a good contractor, preferably Loorz, to whip The Bend and other projects into shape.) In any case, Loorz had indeed been busy, as he spelled out for Mac in that same letter of October 22:

---

44. Two days before Mac's letter, the *Los Angeles Examiner* sought permission to run an Associated Press story on the sale. "CONGRESS RECENTLY APPROPRIATED $2,000,000 TO FINANCE ACQUISITION OF 154,000 ACRES," it said in part. Hearst scrawled "OK" on the teletyped inquiry. From [R. T.] Van Ettisch to Willicombe, October 16, 1940; Hearst Papers, carton 31 (under "Van Ettisch"). The government acquired other properties in the Jolon-Milpitas area for military use; the grand total, inclusive of the Hearst portion, was roughly a quarter million acres.

Hearst had seemed indifferent toward Milpitas earlier in the year (the Grand Canyon fight had raised his hackles a good deal more). Bill Murray wrote Willicombe at the outset of 1940:

> As you know, we constructed an airport at the Jolon headquarters to facilitate Mr. Hearst's visits there. I understand that the airplanes are no longer going to be used, and I write to inquire whether it is in order for us to abandon the airport at this location, and relieve us of the expense of keeping it up.

Willicombe shot back a one-liner: "Chief says it is all right to abandon the airport at Jolon." From

We were fortunate enough to land a $450,000 govt. job out of Watsonville [Camp McQuaide, some twenty miles north of Monterey]. We were only $4900 low on it and feel that we have a good job. Have been given $50,000 worth of extra buildings to date [at Camp McQuaide] and have a hunch that there will be more before we leave the site. In addition, we have around $100,000 worth of residences [private, non-government work] under construction or ready to go in the next few weeks. Needless to say, they are keeping us busy as bird dogs. I have been spending a lot of my time right on the jobsite of the Govt. Job.[45]

Yes, I read about the Milpitas Ranch sale. Understand that a tent camp will be built down there by the Govt.

Sorry to report that we have not received final payment on 1700 Lexington — or even any encouragement. However, I am going to make another appeal in the next day or so.

The appeal worked, as evidenced by some news Loorz shared with Pete Petersen a few weeks later.

FRANKLIN DELANO ROOSEVELT won an unprecedented third term on November 5. Hearst, predictably, had supported Wendell Willkie, though "without enthusiasm."[46] Unpolitical events were much likelier to bring a smile to Hearst's face these days; in that respect, Morgan struck the perfect chord when she wrote to him on November 6, the day after Roosevelt's historic victory. She spoke of her recent trip:

> The ship on which I was meandering again, stopped in Baltimore Harbor and the first newspaper up the gangplank had the very pretty picture of the unveiled Bear Fountain [at Wyntoon] with you and Marion both looking so well and so happy — I was delighted.[47]

Murray to Willicombe, February 5, 1940, and from Willicombe to Murray, February 7, 1940; Hearst Papers (both under "1940 Samples").

45. Comprising almost a thousand items (some 850 of which are correspondence), the Camp McQuaide file is the largest of the *processed* ones surviving from Loorz's years in Pacific Grove; the Camp Roberts items from 1941 are more extensive but, as of 2002, still awaited full processing.

On the big job at Camp McQuaide, Ray Van Gorden was appointed "head book-keeper, time-keeper and materials clerk," as Loorz informed him on October 6, 1940.

46. As observed by Nasaw in *The Chief*, p. 555. Typifying a trend among Hearst biographers — that of allotting relatively few pages to the man's final years — W. A. Swanberg made even briefer reference to Willkie in *Citizen Hearst*, p. 524. John K. Winkler was in less of a rush; he gave the matter its own paragraph in *William Randolph Hearst: A New Appraisal* (New York, 1955), p. 283. But three years before Winkler, John Tebbel skipped Willkie altogether in *The Life and Good Times of William Randolph Hearst*. A charismatic figure who died prematurely in 1944, Willkie has long been undervalued and almost forgotten.

47. Morgan's reference to Miss Davies by her first name only is seldom met with (at least in written sources).

> On the way back, in Arizona I came upon a little relative of Fraulein [Hanna] Gaertner's bear [the one produced by that sculptor for the fountain]—only older in spite of his bright new eyes. I thought you might like him [as depicted, perhaps, in something Morgan enclosed].
>
> I cannot say how much I have appreciated your "In the News."[48]

November 6 also found Bill Murray of Hearst Sunical writing to Loorz. The subject was the Milpitas Hacienda, the compound near Mission San Antonio that had just been sold, along with thousands of adjoining acres.

> We have at Jolon a supply of [so-called] Spanish tiles, originally purchased to be used for Mr. Hearst's personal suite at the Jolon headquarters [the Hacienda]. However, this plan was later changed, and the tile was never used.
>
> Miss Morgan's office tells me that the tile manufacturer has gone out of business, and suggests that you might be able to use this tile in the construction work you are doing.
>
> I have asked Mr. [Charlie] Parlet to send you samples of this tile.[49]

Loorz's answer of November 11 showed that his priorities were of a different kind:

> About the Spanish tiles. I'm afraid that there is not much demand for them right now, but I'll look into it and let you know if I can use them.
>
> I would be interested in a bulldozer, roller, shovel, and crusher which are at San Simeon, however.

While thanking Loorz for his reply, Murray aired the matter once more; he evoked, in turn, a parting image of Jolon-Milpitas and its switch from Hearst ownership:

> We have to know immediately whether or not you can use them [the tiles], as we have to vacate the premises by December 1st. Therefore, if you can't give me a definite answer on this, we will have to dispose of them elsewhere.
>
> As to the other items you mention, [which] you might be interested in, the only thing we have for sale at the moment is the rock crusher, and if you are sufficiently interested in this equipment, I will be open to a bid on it.

That final letter of Murray's about the "Spanish" tiles went forth on November 15, a day that also found Loorz writing to Pete Petersen at Wyntoon. "Well, we

---

48. From Morgan to Hearst, November 6, 1940; Morgan Collection (in the separate Wyntoon file, III/06/09/05). "In the News" was the front-page column Hearst had begun writing for his newspapers earlier in 1940; see Nasaw, pp. 558–61; Swanberg, pp. 494–96. A photograph of the "unveiled" fountain appears in Bill Hearst's memoir, *The Hearsts: Father and Son*, in the section following p. 112 (either the same picture Morgan saw in Baltimore or one taken the same day).

49. Parlet succeeded Randy Apperson as superintendent of the Hearst Ranch in 1963.

just received the final payment on the Davies Job so I am enclosing [a] check in the amount of $230 in appreciation of your efforts." The amount was apparently a bonus, something Loorz often paid his top men on jobs that proved successful. (His year-end profit-and-loss sheet lists the "Marion Davies Res." at $24,864, of which $3,227 was the net profit; proportionately, it was one of Pacific Grove's best showings in 1940.)

Loorz brought Petersen up to date in customary form. "We are busy as a bull in fly time. Lot of Govt. building down this way." He meant the half-million-dollar job at Camp McQuaide, of course. He also referred to the private homes in progress.

And thus his closing thoughts: "Pete, as soon as you get through up there [at Wyntoon] contact us as we will be able to put you to work at once. Would like to have your whole gang [of fellow workmen] as things look promising down this way."

Petersen answered on November 29,[50] writing from Wyntoon in his broken, almost illiterate hand; yet that didn't keep him from giving an insider's view:

> I am glad to hear that you have recived the final payment from 1700 Lexington Rd. it sure was a long drawn out job. it is about the same here build it up today and change it to morrow special [especially] the paint job. James Vickery [late of 1700 Lexington] is doing the work. I am glad to hear that you have lots of work down ther how about men? but in regard to comming down there it is hard to say when Mr. Hearst will say stop joust heard that he will stay til after Christmas and as for Mr. McClure well I would not let him down here on the job. We have only a verry few men here but as soon as we get time here then I am going to take a trip down and see you.

---

50. In the interval between Loorz's and Petersen's letters, Joseph P. Kennedy visited Hearst at Wyntoon; his second son, the future President, accompanied him. "Jack and I had a great time at Wyntoon and they couldn't have been nicer to me at the house at the beach [the Beach House in Santa Monica] for which I am very grateful to both you and Marion." See Kennedy to Hearst, November 26, 1940, in Amanda Smith, ed., *Hostage to Fortune: The Letters of Joseph P. Kennedy* (New York, 2001), pp. 492, 493–94. The Davies memoir, *The Times We Had*, mentions the November visit but conflates it with one made in the summer of 1940 by Joseph Kennedy, Jr. (pp. 219, 222, 224). See also Hank Searls, *The Lost Prince: Young Joe, The Forgotten Kennedy: The Story of the Oldest Brother* (New York, 1969), p. 165.

The role of Joseph Kennedy, Sr., in "saving" Hearst during the crisis that boiled over in 1937 has yet to be fully ascertained. At one extreme lies cloying praise of Kennedy's genius in the matter, as in John H. Davis, *The Kennedys: Dynasty and Disaster 1848–1983* (New York, 1984), pp. 75–76. At the other extreme lies vile contempt. "Within a short time he demonstrated he was nothing more or less than a stock market manipulator," recalled John Francis Neylan in writing to Hearst. "In January and February of 1937 it was plain to me that the Kennedy schemes were ruining you, and I protested. . . . In June of 1937 you came to a realization of what Mr. Kennedy was." From Neylan to Hearst, March 8, 1944; Hearst Papers, carton 39 (under "New-Nh").

In closing, Petersen said he hoped Loorz and his "familie" were in "good helt."

James Vickery, the painter whom Petersen mentioned, lived in Glendale, near Los Angeles; before working at Wyntoon, he may have been known to Hearst and Miss Davies through their connections in that area, perhaps through Frank Hellenthal.[51] "Vic" Vickery and Loorz hit it off well in 1940. In December they exchanged some letters concerning the short-term job in Beverly Hills and the open-ended one up north. Unlike Petersen's statement on November 29, Vickery's to Loorz on December 6 was this: "I just returned from Wyntoon where I went to do some touching up!!! It lasted five weeks, but they are fine people." Vickery wrote those words in Glendale on a Friday.

Most likely on that same day, Nigel Keep read a letter from Loorz, sent from Pacific Grove to San Simeon and dated "Thursday Dec. 5th." Keep learned about the big job near Watsonville—the Camp McQuaide project. Loorz was now saying the job would "run over $500,000 considerable." A far cry from any PWA school! More important, vastly more important, Europe was embroiled in its second year of war. Camp McQuaide typified Roosevelt's new breed of huge-scale federal spending, geared toward preparedness, mobilization, and the nation's defense. "All of it must be done in 90 days and that is something," Loorz explained to Keep. "I have campled [camped] right on the job coming home only about every other night." With luck, he said, he'd be able to complete things by the deadline of January 2, never mind the holidays:

> Also Nigel I am pleased to report that it looks like it is going to check out very good. It even looks like we might make our anticipated 10%. That is a lot of money for us Nigel and I am planning already on nice bonuses and xmas gifts for the complete organization. You see, if I had kept all we have made in this little business and not given so many bonuses I would have had quite a few sheckles [shekels]. In fact, I might have been able to retire as you can and could have for these many years past.

Loorz had more news and lightheartedness to share with Keep. Ed Sullivan, for example, who'd felt compelled to leave San Simeon and its low wages nearly two years before, was "still working every day and studying singing at night."

Had Loorz been clairvoyant, he could have closed on a more urgent, more sobering note: a dark and infamous event lay just a year ahead now, nearly to the day.

---

51. Vickery seems not to have worked on the Davies-Beverly job as a Stolte employee but rather as a sub-contractor. The painter Frank Gyorgy, on the other hand, had been a "Stoltean" for a year now, part of Loorz's Pacific Grove roster. An invoice dated December 17, 1940, lists Gyorgy as having painted at the new Cunningham residence in Del Monte, a neighborhood in Monterey.

LOORZ FAMILY COLLECTION

LEFT: Loorz and his
three sons at the Marion
Davies job, 1700
Lexington Road,
Beverly Hills, July 1940.
BELOW: C. J. Ryland's
Santa Cruz City Hall
(F. C. Stolte Co., Pacific
Grove branch, 1938).

AUTHOR'S PHOTOGRAPH, 1990

The Bavarian
Village, Wyntoon
RIGHT: Brown Bear.
BOTTOM: Angel House
and Cinderella House.

COURTESY OF JEAN HENRY WILLICOMBE

LOORZ FAMILY COLLECTION

MORGAN-FORNEY COLLECTION

AUTHOR'S PHOTOGRAPH, 1976

TOP: The Bavarian Village: River House.
BOTTOM: The Chicken House (San Simeon's poultry unit) kept
the Beach House and especially Wyntoon supplied in the early 1940s.

LOORZ FAMILY COLLECTION

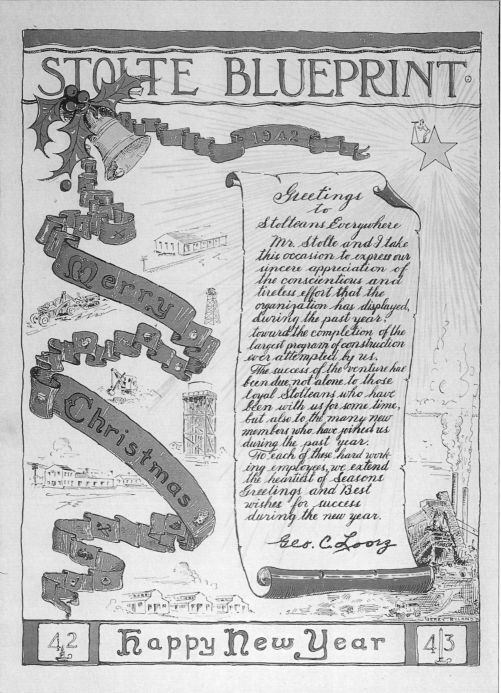

STOLTE BLUEPRINT.

1942

Merry Christmas

Greetings
to
Stolteans Everywhere
Mr. Stolte and I take
this occasion to express our
sincere appreciation of
the conscientious and
tireless effort that the
organization has displayed,
during the past year;
toward the completion of the
largest program of construction
ever attempted by us.
The success of the venture has
been due, not alone to those
loyal Stolteans who have
been with us for some time,
but also to the many new
members who have joined us
during the past year.
To each of these hard working employees, we extend
the heartiest of Seasons
Greetings and Best
wishes for success
during the new year.

Geo. C. Loorz

42 Happy New Year 43

Wartime prosperity: the second issue of Stolte Inc.'s new company magazine.

LOORZ FAMILY COLLECTION

STOLTE BLUEPRINT

VOL. 4　　　　　　　　FRIDAY, JUNE 22, 1945　　　　　　　　NO. 1

U.S. ENGINEERS
FAIRFIELD-SUISUN
ARMY AIR BASE
MORRISON-KNUDSEN CO. INC,
AND
STOLTE INC.

Sunset over the Pacific Theater.

STOLTE BLUEPRINT

RIGHT AND BOTTOM:
The sure hand
of Bill O'Malley,
Stolte cartoonist
and cover artist.

LOORZ FAMILY COLLECTION

GEORGE C. LOORZ   F. C. STOLTE

LEFT AND BELOW: The high command at work and play.

STOLTE BLUEPRINT

Buy a Home in
SUNNY SITKA!

All over Alaska you will see billboards of the men pictured above. Their names are four and five letter household words.

WHY? Because these men have solved the housing crisis. Rome would never have burned if it had been built out of Peerless lumber, and these public spirited citizens got an idea from that. Right now, at Sitka, they are constructing 10,000 igloos prefabricated by nature and guaranteed not to burn down. Certain insurance brokers are furious.

Fred Stolte and George Loorz saw a need and froze onto it. They will not be thawed out by other envious contractors who were all too quick to see the beauty of working 24 hours a day in summer, and sleeping the rest of the year.

BUY NOW! It is not too late to purchase a home in this project. Materials are available; the snowfall was heavy in Sitka last year. You, too, can soon be sitting around a seal oil lamp, chewing your blubber, and thanking the arctic wind for such men as George and Fred.

DON'T WAIT! Call CEntigrade 0001, or FAhrenheit 0002, and tell us you are coming. Bring your blowtorch with you, of course, for heating is done by blowtorch at Sitka, and is not in the specifications. Also, since transportation is by husky dog team it would be well to lay in a case of salmon: the dogs never bother customers who feed them.

See you in Sitka

SMKBDHDHRNCBAFWPPPP COMPANIES · (A Joint Venture)

PAGE 23

STOLTE BLUEPRINT

Maurice McClure, construction superintendent
at San Simeon, 1945–48.

San Simeon Chatter

By Hazel McClure

The $200,000.00 San Simeon Airport is nearing completion. The landing strip has been in use for six weeks. The lighting, under the supervision of Mark Eubanks, Hearst electrician, and the hangar which is being constructed by Paul Gatschet and his crew are the only two unfinished items.

The Recreation Wing is progressing nicely. Frank Frandolich and Carlo Bianchi are still carving away at the stone windows. Al Hayden is progressing nicely with the plastering. Otto Olson with the able assistance of Gustav Buck, Ed Miller, and others has installed the antique ceilings on the third floor and is working on the fourth floor ceilings. Thomas E. Adams, electrician, finds that usually he could be twins to good advantage. John McFadden has finished laying the tile floor in one large room and has another well under way.

Gerald Franklin and his small crew are beginning to believe that repairs and maintenance at the ranch could easily be a life time job.

We just finished laying seven miles of oil mix road from San Simeon to the Hilltop and believe me, those of us who drive automobiles over this road shouted for joy when we saw that bit of construction finished before the rains started.

Our painter, Harold O. Tomlin, somehow manages to keep Mr. Apperson, Buck Dyer, Mr. Keep, Mr. Reed and Mr. Hearst happy. He knows how to make his seconds count.

Jimmy Rankin, plumbing contractor, and his crew with the assistance of Roy Evans and his labor gang have installed new waterlines to the Poultry Plant and Ranch House and are now installing one to the new airport. This, plus a new sprinkling system at Pico Creek Stables, steam heat and plumbing installations in the Recreation Wing and the hours of maintenance required of the plumbers forces "Jimmy" to stay young.

Warren McClure and Ray Carlson of Mr. Hearst's Architect's office are kept quite busy getting out plans and details for the Recreation and Service Wings. "Mac" is really kept busy since he also directs Mr. Hearst's work in Los Angeles and Wyntoon and we never know when a new day starts whether he will be on deck or has disappeared during the night to one of the other locations. Faithful Ray is always here, however, to give a suggestion here, lend a helping hand there and make himself generally an asset.

Meet the Stolteans at San Simeon

Upper Left: (1) A group of Stolte Stalwarts at Simeon. Top row, left to right—Paul Gatschet, Roy Evans, Otto Olson. Bottom row, left to right—John MacFadden, James Rankin, Maurice Mclure. Upper Right: (2) Maurice and Hazel McClure. Center: (3) The Hangar crew, who have been doing such an excellent job on the new hangar. Bottom: (4) The Stolte Staff at San Simeon. First row, left to right—James Rankin, Hazel McClure, Maurice McClure, John McFadden, Paul Gatschet, Roy Evans, Otto Olson. Second row — Wm. Lough, Gerald Franklin, L. G. Warren, Geo. Masse, Chas. Krenkel, Wm. Simpson, Russell D. May, Harold O. Tomlin, Earl Sheids, Rudolph Barrios, "Val" Georges, Carlo Bianchi. Third row—Jimmy Anderson, Harvey Gilroy, Max Steiner, Carl Canolls, Felix Valles, Ray Johnson, Gene Peterson, "Gus" Cosso, Theodore Rathbun, Kenneth Hitchcock, Clark Silacci, Erwin M. Haugen, Vincent B. Morris, Al Hayden, Frank Wyman, Norman Rotanzi, Ernest Minetti. Fourth row — Geo. Atchison, Emmitt Perkins, Ira A. Moore, Galli Bardine, Chas. Ghezzi, John Galbraith, Gustav Buck, Ed Miller, Robert Stratton, John Albee, Thos. E. Adams, Wm. McCowen, Bradford Caligari, Livio Villa, Frank Caligari.

LOORZ FAMILY COLLECTION

LOORZ FAMILY COLLECTION

Wyntoon TOP: The Gables (burned 1944). BOTTOM: The Bend.

LOORZ FAMILY COLLECTION

LOORZ FAMILY COLLECTION

Two views of The Bend
ABOVE: Chandelier salvaged
from the Wyntoon Castle
fire of 1930.
LEFT: Frank Gendrich,
construction superintendent,
1945–48.

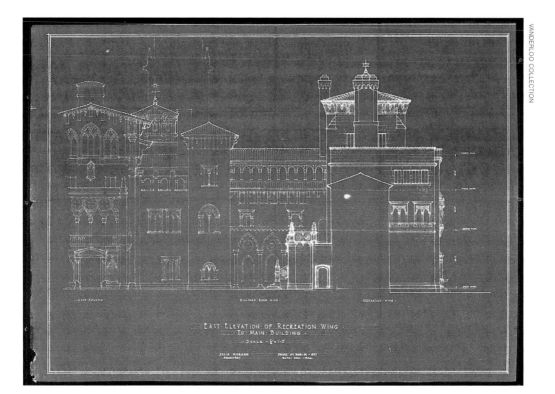

VANDERLOO COLLECTION

EAST·ELEVATION·OF·RECREATION·WING
·TO·MAIN·BUILDING·
·SCALE·⅛"·1'·0·

JULIA MORGAN
ARCHITECT

AUTHOR'S PHOTOGRAPH, 1975

AUTHOR'S PHOTOGRAPH, 1974

AUTHOR'S PHOTOGRAPH, 1975

TOP: Unfinished concrete exterior of the Service Wing, Casa Grande.
BOTTOM: Southeast from China Hill.
FACING PAGE, TOP: One of four such elevations by Julia Morgan, December 1936.
"Recreation Wing" pertains only to the right third of the drawing; the middle third
shows the connecting Billiard Room Wing and the North Duplex Tower;
the left third shows part of Casa Grande's central axis (see map on page xxiii).
FACING PAGE, BOTTOM: South elevation, Recreation Wing (or the "New Wing,"
in reference to its postwar enlargement and completion).

LOORZ FAMILY COLLECTION

BISON ARCHIVES

Two loggias, shown years before they were enclosed with glass in the 1940s RIGHT: Casa del Mar, San Simeon. BELOW: 1007 N. Beverly Drive, Beverly Hills.

BISON ARCHIVES

BISON ARCHIVES

The Beverly House, 1007 N. Beverly Drive
TOP: Old stonework ensemble, erected in the late forties at the swimming pool.
BOTTOM: View from the pool toward the main house.

AUTHOR'S PHOTOGRAPH, 1975

AUTHOR'S PHOTOGRAPH, 1988

TOP: Remnants of the pergola, Orchard Hill.
BOTTOM: Reminiscent of times gone by: the new pier at
San Simeon Bay, built shortly after Hearst's death.

Loorz couldn't be expected to have known that, though, or even to have sensed its coming. Neither could Keep. In theory, meanwhile, the economy had stabilized after the Roosevelt Recession of 1937–38. But rural, isolated San Luis Obispo County was one of many places where the hard times of an entire decade still imposed a serious grip; in fact, had begun to affect a second decade. Keep and a few other stalwarts like John Vanderloo had to remain hopeful that Hearst would rally somehow and come to their aid.

A revival like that could enhance Loorz's life, too—seldom a dull moment with Mr. Hearst in full harness. Loorz had implied as much in the long letter he'd sent Miss Morgan back in February. For the time being, then, optimism still counted. Besides, the season was at hand, prompting Loorz to bid Nigel Keep adieu with the utmost flourish. "To you my friend—CHEERIO."

1941–44

You're in the Army Now

FOR THE FIRST TIME EVER, Hearst stayed at Wyntoon through the holiday season and right into January, in fact, right into February and early March. So did Mac McClure, along with Pete Petersen. In sending Petersen a quick letter on February 20 of that new year, 1941, Loorz resorted to a technique we can be glad he rarely used—handwriting:

> Enclosed $60 for interest June 1st [1940] to Jan 1st [on a business loan Petersen made to Loorz].
>
> We have had a good year Pete & I really dont need your funds. I can return it anytime. . . .
>
> Saw Miss Morgan today & she said you were still at Wyntoon. I thot you surely would be away by this time or I would have written sooner.
>
> Give my regards to Mac, Mr Willicombe & all my friends sorry not to say more but you know we hurried contractors.

Petersen's reply bears an errant "Feb. 18" (or else Loorz's letter is the misdated one). Either way, Petersen said "thanks for the check" before he offered a disclaimer: "I am not much at whriting but here goes." Having said that, he went on to tell Loorz:

> I am glad to hear that you have lots off work wish that I wear down there to [I]t is verry tiresome to work here and the pay is just so so There is only Nick Neaklar [Carl Nakler] and myself working here Mac is fine to work for and Mr. Hearst I have only seing once sins New Year Mr. Hearst is going to Mexico next Monday [February 24] what for I do not know but I hope that he will close up shop here and tell me to get the hell out off here and if he does well what you have [have you] got to offer.

Petersen had more to say a week later, on February 25, telling Loorz that the crew was working indoors (in The Bend) on the steam heating system—however, "cant get men to come up here," he said of the understaffed conditions. Hearst, meanwhile, seems to have delayed in heading to Mexico; for Petersen added, "I dont know how long Mr. Hearst will stay here hope not to long and also that when he goes that he will close up the works here."[1]

That lonesome carpenter wasn't the only disgruntled employee. As Loorz said while replying on March 2, "Mac too doesn't seem to be too happy up there. Tell him we will get at his estimate this coming week." (Mac was designing a small house in San Luis Obispo, one that he hoped to build on spec through Daniels & Loorz, a recent venture of Loorz's in addition to his branch-office work in Pacific Grove.)[2]

Loorz had more to tell Petersen, befitting a winter whose moisture would soon break records:

> The rain has been so consistent that we have made little or no progress on our jobs. It certainly is expensive but nothing can be done about it. Will have to wait for the spring to make more money.
>
> If they finish with you up there and you feel like [it] come right on down with your whole ganga [*sic*] and we can very likely use them all. . . .
>
> Otto [Olson] lost some time during the past week for the first time for a long long time. Too much rain for outside work and we had not enough inside work for all the men.

So it was business as usual, at least by a wet year's standards. All the more reason for Hearst to go south—a long way south—not just to his Babicora Ranch in the state of Chihuahua, a good two hundred miles below El Paso, but clear down to Mexico City. He and Marion Davies, plus the requisite group of friends, sojourned in that country through most of March 1941; two of Hearst's sons and

---

1. Petersen's two letters of February 1941 were in response to two letters from Loorz, of which only the one dated February 20 is extant. If Loorz's other one were at hand, an errant date that seems present among the existing letters might be easier to pin down. As things stand, this harmless riddle is unsolvable.

2. Established in February 1940, Daniels & Loorz foreshadowed a larger "family" of Stolte enterprises; see also notes 20, 21, 22, and 47 in this chapter. (Earlier, the short-lived Dell Clausen Co.—formed by Loorz, Stolte, and Clausen in September 1938—had pointed the same way.) To clear the air before he and Carl Daniels set forth, Loorz wrote Daniels a blistering letter on February 18, 1940, five days before they drew up documents for their new venture. "Even Lou Crawford who like[d] you very much preferred to have Frank Genrdrick [Gendrich] than you [overseeing a job]"—this because Daniels was considered "one of the most careless superintendents" on the circuit. Daniels shaped up in a hurry.

As for Mac McClure's connection with Daniels & Loorz, Loorz had thanked Mac on February 18, 1941, for submitting plans for the spec house. "Inasmuch as we are now doing some work in San Luis," Loorz told him, "I would be glad to give you a figure on this plan." Coincidentally or not, the Daniels & Loorz balance sheet for an earlier period, January 1941, includes "McClure Job" at $416.

their wives rounded out the party. Willicombe, though, stayed behind in Los Angeles.[3]

Morgan, for her part, embarked on a year that, for the first time since 1923, would leave an incomplete record, as would every year from now until her retirement. The outline of her workload from here on can be established well enough; the specifics are what tend to be lacking. She was active nonetheless in 1941 from New Year's onward. The Park Museum project resumed in early January (and after May, when Hearst gave Santa Maria de Ovila to San Francisco, the monastery became by far the most active of her current accounts). Starting in February, the Society for the Protection and Education of Russian Infant Children — she'd never had a client with a longer name — was on her drafting boards through July. That was a hometown job, a San Francisco job, as was the Park Museum. So were some alterations she began in January for the Volkmanns, old friends of hers, and, across the bay in Oakland and likewise that winter, some work for the Kings Daughters Home, where she'd relied twice on the Alameda office of the Stolte Co. in recent years.[4]

The heavy rains in 1941 were a blessing in dry areas that seemed a world away from the coast. On March 28 Loorz told Bill Kimes in Avenal, where the Pacific Grove branch had completed a school and where the heat and dust had yet to reappear, that he'd try to stop by to see the profusion of wildflowers. He sounded much more like his old self in also telling Kimes, "Yes, we are keeping quite busy." Loorz gave some details: "We are finishing up some $700,000 worth of contracts at Camp

---

3. W. A. Swanberg, whose chronology of Hearst's life has long been foundational, cited *Shirt-Sleeve Diplomat* (Chapel Hill, North Carolina; 1947), one of several memoirs by Josephus Daniels, American ambassador to Mexico from 1933 to 1942. In *Citizen Hearst*, p. 498, Swanberg summarized pp. 353–55 in Daniels, thus relaying details that might have gone unnoticed by Hearst researchers for years to come. In addition, Swanberg drew from other knowledge — unattributed this time yet entirely credible — in naming the film director Raoul Walsh as part of the Hearst-Davies entourage.

Living royally on the trip, Hearst at one point summoned his dentist from Los Angeles; on March 29 Dr. Brownson used the office of Dr. Iberri, a Mexican dentist. Iberri, who stood by "until four thirty in the morning awaiting the arrival of Mr. Hearst's train" [from the interior of Mexico], hoped to collect $200 for his services. "I did not think that my fee would seem high to a patient who has sufficient means to have his own dentist come from Los Angeles to Chihuahua." From Jorge Iberri M. to Edward Ardoin [Jr., Hearst's agent in El Paso], April 24, 1941; Hearst Papers, carton 35 (under "1941 Samples").

4. From January through May 1941, when Hearst still owned Santa Maria, Morgan accrued $841 on the Park Museum account, versus $3,176 from June through December; see note 37 in the 1940 chapter. The "Russian Children's" account (its shorter name) accrued $628 in office costs in 1941; Morgan received a "token payment" of $100 in 1945. The Volkmann job accrued a budget-ignoring $297; Morgan collected $163 — seven percent of $2,335 in total construction costs. The Kings Daughters job, identified merely as "sign" (perhaps a decorative feature), accrued $308; but no further record exists. (All such data come from the Morgan-Forney account ledgers.)

McQuaide, Watsonville; have $60,000 at the Presidio of Monterey; $300,000 at Camp Roberts, San Miguel; $25,000 at Camp San Luis Obispo; in addition to quite a sum of private work." Things were "checking out very well," he commented, and the company expected "another good profitable year."

Three days afterward—on the last day of March—it was Mac McClure's turn to elaborate; he did so while Hearst was still gone, producing a handwritten report on the "Status of work at Wyntoon." It wasn't directed to anyone by name (yet Hearst's files became its archival home):

> The construction crew now numbers five instead of the two we had when Mr Hearst left. These comprise a stone mason, marble setter, our original two carpenters [Petersen and Nakler] and an extra carpenter who can do some carving.
>
> Most of these men have joined us during the past two weeks.

Mac included details on rooms in The Bend—the Gothic room, the red room, the green room were the extent for now of their simple names—and then he alluded to what most likely was the flood damage of the year before:

> We located a carpet layer in Oregon who has laid the salvaged Bend carpet in the Brown Bear halls and on the stair case.
>
> The stone mason, who was needed for altering the Bend chimney [Frank Pellando?], has also been working on a walk from Bear house to the office. This is a small part of the general scheme of a walk arround [sic] the village area.[5]

About the only difference, at the standard fast glance, between 1941 and the past several years is that Mac and the crew were off to the races sooner than usual at Wyntoon (1935 still holding the record for early starts thus far).

WHEN HEARST CAME BACK from Mexico, he went to San Simeon. He stayed just briefly—Wyntoon became his main address again by early or mid-May—and so whether his seventy-ninth birthday was observed on the hilltop, or perhaps at the Beach House instead, is another detail that awaits discovery.[6] And yet one thing is clear about the April-May period in 1941: once Hearst left San Simeon that spring,

---

5. The unaddressed report is dated "Mar 31st 1941" and is signed "Warren A. McClure"; Hearst Papers, carton 32 (under "McA-McC"). The file contains further items by Mac from the 1941 season at Wyntoon.

6. For the early part of April, Hearst's whereabouts are indicated by a letter to Joe Willicombe, sent to San Simeon by someone who usually knew the score—the Los Angeles attorney Heinie MacKay. He told Willicombe in a postscript, "I am sorry to have missed you the other day at San Simeon. I understand you bought a Ranch at Santa Cruz [actually in Carmel Valley, near Monterey]. There is nothing like being a farmer. I congratulate you." From Heinie [H. S. MacKay, Jr.] to Willicombe, April 8, 1941; Hearst Papers, carton 35 (under "MacKay, H. S., Jr.").

he didn't use the place again for more than three years, not till the final weeks of 1944.

Long before that, though—in 1941 itself—Nigel Keep wrote to Loorz from San Simeon on April 23 (with no fewer than four full-sized pages, containing enough hieroglyphs to make anyone squint):

> I met Frank George [Gyorgy] . . . up here he is painting some iron grill work in big house, its rusting badly in fact the whole fabric of the big house needs lots of attention, but, I'm "busted" [says Hearst] so it just cant be done. Help shortened down once again. . . . we had about 58" [rainfall] on the Hill top & was the Road [the driveway] bad. I never saw so many earth slides & faults & on the N Pergola [on Orchard Hill], where you & I had so many furious arguments about the Bank sloughing in well it is as I *said* it would do, the banks now kiss the Pillars in many places—[for] once you were dead wrong.

"The Burnett Road is impassable," Keep also said, thanks to "slides & more slides."

At least the Hearst interests wouldn't have to reopen the road the way Verne Barker and Ray Van Gorden had in 1938. Everything beyond the Santa Lucia summit was now government acreage, encompassed within the huge buyout of Hearst and other property owners in the fall of 1940.

Frank Gyorgy, whose work Keep mentioned, wrote to Loorz from San Simeon on Wednesday, April 30, exactly a week after Keep did. (Since Hearst's birthday in 1941 fell on Tuesday the twenty-ninth, he may have done his celebrating midway between those letters.) In any event, what Gyorgy told Loorz contains some important clues:

> I am enclosing time cards for the week ending May 1st [however, Friday and Saturday fell on May 2 and 3] also ship[p]ing bill for gold [leaf] from Fuller [W. P. Fuller & Co. in San Francisco]. [Will] try to finish as soon as possible, there would be surely enough work here for some time. Since the party left here it feels like living in a cemetery what a difference now and when the [work] was going on the hill top.

Gyorgy was sending those cards to Pacific Grove, to Loorz's branch office of the F. C. Stolte Co.—which acted as contractor on this small job for Hearst in 1941, just as it had in 1939, when Otto Olson helped install some new locks.[7] (In 1940, Pacific Grove would most likely have acted as contractor, too, had Hearst done any work at San Simeon then; instead, the much larger Davies job in Beverly Hills is what kept the Hearst-Loorz connection alive and well that year.) The difference,

---

7. See pp. 417 and 421 in this volume.

though, between Olson's small job at San Simeon in 1939 and the one Gyorgy did two years later is that Morgan wasn't involved this time.[8]

On May 1, 1941, one day after Gyorgy wrote Loorz, Lilian Forney made what proved to be the final entry in Morgan's ledger of the main San Simeon account—the big account that, unlike all her others, large or small, could be traced from as far back as 1919. "Blue Print (S.S. plot plan for Oscar Lawler, L.A.),"[9] went the entry, with a notation of "67" next to it. Mrs. Forney meant sixty-seven cents, not sixty-seven dollars, the faintest whisper of an ending to page upon page of substantial entries. Yet it was an ending by default rather than by design. The word "closed" never appeared below the entry, as so often occurred with the common lot of Morgan's accounts.[10]

Although Hearst dug in at Wyntoon about then—for a much longer stay than he could possibly have foreseen—some of his people, even some prominent ones, weren't always current on where he was holding court. "Please instruct to have Chief's papers sent here instead of San Simeon and oblige." Those were Willicombe's words on June 21, sent belatedly to Harry Bitner of the *Pittsburgh Sun-Telegraph*, part of the Hearst chain since 1927.[11] When it was all said and done, the Chief was still an editor, a publisher, a newspaperman—as much at seventy-nine as he had ever been.

---

8. Furthermore on the 1941 job, Conrad Gamboni wrote to Gyorgy at San Simeon on May 9. "Geo. [Loorz] was the one that mentioned the gilding to Willicombe so go ahead with it as he wants. . . . Fix them up [Hearst et al.] the way they want, Frank." Willicombe told Bill Murray about the job on June 19; in fact, Hearst Sunical was in line to pay for it outright, rather than Hearst himself, who would then be reimbursed (as he was with the Burnett Road work in 1938):

Chief instructs me to send you the enclosed bill from F. C. Stolte Co. for necessary maintenance work at La Cuesta Encantada ordered by Chief, regarding which Chief says:
   "The exposed iron work all over the place was rusting and rotting. It had to be painted and, where gilding originally was, regilded."
Chief says the bill of $688.64 is OK for payment.

Unfortunately, the Trial Balances for the Pacific Grove branch in 1941 are missing from the Loorz Papers; should they ever surface, $688.64 will probably appear next to "W. R. Hearst" or a similar entry.

9. Lawler, renowned in the Los Angeles legal community, was another of Hearst's attorneys, though not part of Heinie MacKay's firm, Flint & MacKay. A similar and perhaps identical plot (or ground) plan in the Morgan Collection, Cal Poly, is reproduced in Boutelle, *Julia Morgan*, p. 202.

10. The date of that final entry, May 1, coincided with the first public showing of *Citizen Kane*—at the RKO Palace in New York. Supposedly a pre-release print had been sent to Hearst at San Simeon in early February, but the film cans were returned unopened. See Robert L. Carringer, *The Making of Citizen Kane* (Berkeley, 1996 [revised and updated edition]), p. 115. Hearst was at Wyntoon, of course, in the opening weeks of 1941, pending his trip to Mexico.

11. Hearst Papers, carton 32 (under "Bi-Bk"). Other Bancroft items suggest Hearst had gone north well before Willicombe wired Bitner. Nick Yost wrote to Willicombe at Wyntoon on May 13

THE SECOND HALF of 1941 found Morgan shifting into overdrive on the Park Museum. Hearst's gift of Santa Maria de Ovila had come in May; and by early July, Morgan and her small staff immersed themselves in that project (mainly drafting-room time at this stage) for the rest of the year and on through the first quarter of 1942. Midway through 1941 she wrote to Mildred Stapley Byne in Madrid, the widow of Arthur Byne, who'd secured the monastery components for Hearst and whom Walter Steilberg had worked with at the importation site in 1931. Morgan believed deeply in Santa Maria's prospects as a medieval museum. Hence her reliance through the early forties, as much as budgets and gathering war clouds permitted, on Steilberg's expertise. Her friendship with Mrs. Byne was another important link with the past.[12]

For George Loorz, meanwhile, those tons of ancient stone in Haslett Warehouse couldn't have been further from his mind. On August 4 he told his friends Cleo and Dick Vreeland, for whom his branch office had built a house in Burlingame, south of San Francisco, "I was called to Camp Roberts about three weeks ago and have been unable to get away. The job is so large and so rushed that it keeps me going from six to six six days a week. I get home for Saturday night and Sunday."[13]

---

and May 27. In the second instance he warned that "Morland Hall" (or rather Norland Hall), an old building Hearst had imported from England that lay dismantled near San Simeon's bayside warehouses, "should be moved or have a fence built around it, as the turist's are packing it off piece by piece, and it is impos[s]ible to keep an eye on it all the time as it is so close to the road." Hearst Papers, carton 34 (under "X-Y").

On June 22, 1941, Charles Lindbergh and his wife arrived at Wyntoon, where they remained through June 24; they stayed in Cinderella House. Lindbergh's account of Wyntoon is among the best ever published. See *The Wartime Journals of Charles A. Lindberg* (New York, 1970), pp. 505, 507–10. Lindbergh was probably never at San Simeon—in 1927 or in any other year—despite what Fred Lawrence Guiles said in *Marion Davies*, p. 198, a portrayal I accepted in *Hearst's Dream* (San Luis Obispo, 1989), p. 68. The esteemed biographer A. Scott Berg made no such claim in *Lindbergh* (New York, 1998).

Nor after recounting Lindbergh's visit to Wyntoon in 1941 did Berg say (rightly so) that Lindbergh was at Wyntoon a second time, in 1943–44. But Louis Pizzitola said he was in *Hearst Over Hollywood*, p. 404 and its note on p. 496, *The Times We Had* (the often vague Davies memoir) having proved misleading, along with a passage in David Nasaw's biography, *The Chief*, p. 563.

12. The Morgan-Forney Collection has Mrs. Byne's reply of July 30, 1941. It appears on Morgan's stationery, transcribed from the incoming original; however, the collection lacks a copy of Morgan's outgoing letter that prompted the exchange. The reply, in any case, indicates that the women talked about the Santa Maria monastery and other buildings the Bynes had purveyed to Hearst. The two women also mentioned the sale at Gimbel Brothers department store in New York, where since January 1941 thousands of Hearst's books and art objects had been on sale. (The event went on to become widely publicized and frequently ridiculed.) Though Mildred Byne was three years younger than Morgan, she died suddenly at the end of 1941.

13. Loorz also told the Vreelands about some leisure time he'd be spending near San Jose. "The F. C. Stolte Co. are giving a picnic at Uvas Dam in back of Morgan Hill—west [of that town],

Camp Roberts, twenty-five miles northeast of San Simeon, put Loorz back in the greater neighborhood, despite the indirect routes that lay between him and the coast (no more Burnett Road, storm ravaged or not, to provide a handy shortcut). Sometime early that August—he forgot to date his letter—Loorz wrote to Hearst at Wyntoon:

> I finally found time last Saturday to go to the Hill with Mr. Apperson and look over the equipment. The equipment has quite naturally deteriorated rapidly because of rusting and lack of use.

The equipment comprised the same items Loorz and Bill Murray discussed in November 1940. As for Loorz's trip in August 1941, it marked the first time he'd been up "on top" in two years, since he and Mac tramped around on China Hill while surveying for a new pergola. A distant memory, though. Roosevelt's push toward further mobilization was what prompted Loorz to act, not Hearst's thoughts about a new pergola. Loorz had two trucks and six other things in mind, the big-ticket item being a steam shovel his men could use at Camp Roberts to excavate the rock they needed for concrete aggregate.

Willicombe gave Loorz the word on August 14. "Mr. Hearst instructs me to tell you that the price of $2,950 offered by you for the equipment on Hilltop at San Simeon—as listed in your letter—is satisfactory, under all the circumstances, and your offer is accepted."[14]

---

on Sunday, August 10. There will be about 250 us of present. A lot of the boys you know from Cambria will be there." He urged the Vreelands to join the fun. "Come early, stay late. Bring a smile and a bathing suit."

14. Two days later Morgan had words of her own about San Simeon. John Vanderloo, one of her favorite artisans on that job, had inquired again about prospects there; she answered him in Cambria, where he still lived despite a lack of work on the hilltop in recent years:

> It would indeed be a pleasure to say I thought we could go back onto San Simeon soon—but I could not. Last winter was so unusually mild I imagine from Mr [Mac] McClures reports that Mr Hearst has a wrong idea of it as an all year possibility. He still has an urge to build where [wherever] he is, & probably will do something on his return to San Simeon—but there is so much necessary repair, need of roofs & windows in finished sections etc. I imagine the available funds will not do much of new works.

From Morgan to Vanderloo, August 16, 1941; Vanderloo Collection. Her letter is provocative throughout. The mild winter (in its temperatures perhaps, surely not in its rainfall); the reports from Mac (indicating her continued involvement, in guiding spirit at least); Hearst's vain hope of working through the winter months at San Simeon (seldom attempted in earlier years); her list of maintenance needs (confirming that Gyorgy's recent efforts had indeed been called for)—obviously she was more attuned than the surviving documents can begin to tell us. Just as obviously, though, she had no idea Hearst wouldn't be back at San Simeon for more than three years. Then again, he had no idea either.

So far so good. Getting those things across the Santa Lucia Range, especially the big shovel, wouldn't be easy, though. Armed with a permit from the Division of Highways, Loorz prepared to have the Burnett veteran Verne Barker and another man do the honors. That was the whole idea in 1941 — being prepared, as in *preparedness*, a theme Hearst had been harping on in his newspapers for months on end. Lord knows what former projects of Hearst's owed their grandeur and might to that rusty shovel. A new life awaited it under the scorching sun on the Monterey-San Luis Obispo county line. There it could do its part, however small, in fending off a contagious war.[15]

A LETTER THAT LOORZ wrote from Camp Roberts on August 22, 1941, is arresting in its informality. "Dear Jean and Joe," it began, the recipients being none other than Colonel Willicombe and his young wife, the former Jean Henry whom he'd married two years before. "We enclose a rough sketch of your revised home," Loorz told them. The setting was on the godlier side of the mountains, where the Willicombes had bought a place in Carmel Valley; it wasn't far from Loorz's home base in Pacific Grove. Just the same, when Loorz explained that "the total cost might be as much as $17,000 at the present price range," the Willicombes gasped.

"That $17,000 settles it," the Colonel replied from Wyntoon on August 25, "and we have decided to wait until prices come down." The price was "far and away" beyond their reach, he added — "yet we would like to have the kind of house and place that you have worked out."

The Willicombes remained hopeful, and Loorz thought of ways to economize. "The $1500 cut on original estimate looks good," the Colonel told him a month later, "but Jean and I have some other ideas that we think will cut it still more, and we will send them to you in the near future." However, there was more to consider than just the house. As Willicombe also told Loorz, "No objection to gravel road in any event."

Willicombe's letter was dated September 22. Earlier in the month a friend of Hearst's — actually, a former ward of his mother named Phoebe Hearst Brown — saw some sights firsthand that far surpassed anything $17,000 could buy, even in those days when a dollar was a dollar, as people like to say. The episode began with Hearst's telling Miss Brown, "Have telegraphed Mr Apper-

---

15. The Loorz Papers contain myriad items on Camp Roberts, few of which got processed before the San Luis Obispo County Historical Museum received the Loorz bequest in 1990. The museum has since processed much of the "Roberts" material; more remains to be done, both on that subject and on certain other Stolte projects of the early 1940s. Pending that, a misattribution can be cited: the Camp Roberts acreage has sometimes been thought of as former Hearst property.

son, Superintendent of San Simeon Ranch, to permit you to drive up the hill and see place on your motor trip."[16] Those words by themselves aren't terribly surprising: the absentee Hearst let someone take a peek at the hilltop in the off-year of 1941. What *is* surprising is the casual yet convincing account the woman gave of her trip; it sounded more like something composed in nineteen *thirty-one*. She wrote to Hearst a week after hearing from him:

> Many thanks for allowing us to go up the hill & see San Simeon. The gardens look lovely, with the begonias in full flower—the castle has a slightly hollow sound without the hum of occupancy, but it was in beautiful order & fun & a great privilege to see it again.
>
> The herds on the way up seem very much at home & have increased & multiplied past my memory. I was charmed to discover that however strange an emu may look, at heart it's just a rather large chicken—each emu invariably crossed the road at our approach with the sole object, apparently[,] of getting to the other side.[17]

Hearst had to have been pleased with the letter from Phoebe Hearst Brown, so full of praise and a sense of contentment. But on the opposite side of the Santa Lucias, where no emus or buffalo roamed, people had humbler things to mull over.

---

16. Hearst to Brown, September 2, 1941; Hearst Papers, carton 32 (under "Brown"). The name Phoebe Hearst Brown recalls that of another ward in these annals, Phoebe H. Hill, whose middle initial probably stood for Hearst.

17. Brown to Hearst, September 10, 1941; ibid. A list from this period by John Connelly, the main zookeeper at San Simeon in 1941, is uncommonly precise—for a post-climactic year like the present one or for any time since Hearst began stocking his zoo in the 1920s:

37 Tahr	8 Yak
12 Kangaroo	3 Water Buck
185 Fallow Deer	1 female Eland—One horn
45 Axis Deer	2 female Barasingle Deer
5 male Blackbuck	5 Water Buffalo
12 Bison	12 Camel
54 Elk	1 female Gnu
15 Zebra	1 male Blesbok
16 Sambar Deer	2 female Goat
54 Aoudad Sheep	23 Emu
11 Oryx	1 male Ostrich
1 female Nilgai	1 male Rhea
2 male Ibex	3 Cassowary
19 Llama	

Connelly's list, dated April 1, 1941, is in the Hearst Papers, carton 31 (under "An-Aq"). By this time the bear grottos on Orchard Hill had been vacated for nearly four years, as had Animal Hill, near the Roman Pool (except for the kennels). The remaining zoo was confined to the lower slopes of the Hearst Ranch and comprised species that, for the most part, could graze freely and fend for themselves.

Loorz, writing from Camp Roberts on October 3, had these words for Dave Condin, a former employee on that job who was soon to be drafted:

> I feel confident that in the years to come you will always look back with a bit of pride in the fact that you were in the service during this period of emergency, even though we may not actually enter the war.

He also told Condin, "We have approx. 220 instead of 500 men and things are far less active than when you were here." As a result, "It is still not pleasant working under conditions wherein we cannot get materials to really complete many of the buildings." Hearst's crew up north, still inching along at Wyntoon under Mac McClure, could have seconded that last point, never mind the financial constraints that were also to blame.

Unseen behind closed doors on the McCloud, beyond the proper range of a plumber, a carpenter, a marble setter, or any other tradesman, Hearst kept up with his writing, his masterminding, his entertaining. Willicombe juggled endless duties, secretarial and other, as he always had, even as the country moved closer and closer to the brink.

All the while, the absurd played its role, just as it, too, had always done. On November 28, the day after Thanksgiving in 1941, Willicombe sent disheartening news to Phillip Appling, who'd been running the Chicken Ranch—the poultry unit at San Simeon—for the past two years (Hearst's thoughts in 1940 of abandoning that operation having come to naught). "The soup chickens ordered on November 14th arrived last Saturday [the twenty-second] and they were literally NOTHING BUT SKIN AND BONES":

> Please be sure to have some meat on the chickens and if you haven't any except these emaciated specimens, let me know and we will get them somewhere else.
>
> The friers that we received were not plucked properly. They were full of feathers. A little more care in this direction will also be appreciated.[18]

Episodes like these, outranked by others far more pressing, were part of life at isolated, fairytale Wyntoon. And then came December 7 and its electrifying news from the mid-Pacific.

People living near the coastline itself felt especially vulnerable after Pearl Harbor. Hearst didn't have to fear for his safety in that sense; he'd been sequestered deep in the forest for a good six months or more.[19] When he finally emerged for the

---

18. Hearst Papers, carton 31 (under "An-Aq").

19. There can be no question of Hearst's whereabouts on the "date which shall live in infamy." The Hearst Papers provide hard evidence throughout late November and early December in registered postmarks, "Wyntoon" letterheads that Hearst and Willicombe used, telegram and teletype

first time about two months later, he did so in favor of a brief stay at the Beach House, not at San Simeon.

In fact, to judge purely from correspondence—too often a deceptive approach when the Loorz Papers or any other collection runs this thin—December 7 left scarcely a mark on the radar screen. Loorz and Randy Apperson exchanged letters in late December 1941 (about the pier at San Simeon Bay) without saying boo about Pearl Harbor. Then on December 29, a man named J. L. Petty wrote to Loorz from Cambria; good thing he dated his letter, for its content seemed oblivious of what had happened three weeks earlier in Hawaii:

> With all the activity in most communities we are, no doubt, located in the most quiet [one]. Very quiet past season and nothing during past month, with outlook [that the] same will continue.
>
> With nothing to do and [to] have something coming in for living I have been working a part of the time at Oceanic Mine [a few miles east of Cambria], however this is not steady and working conditions are poor. I am writing to you with view of getting to work where I can be of use and make something for the family to live on.

Loorz's reply to Petty, dated December 30, gave better evidence finally that the world was indeed a bigger place:

> I regret that you happened to have selected the most quiet locality on this very active coast.

---

datelines, and many kindred details; moreover, the circumstantial evidence is abundant. Ideally, they all bear noting, since tradition too often has placed Hearst at San Simeon on December 7. A few examples must suffice.

Heinie MacKay, who knew where to reach his man, wrote to Hearst at Wyntoon on December 1, 1941; the subject was Hearst's "income tax loss on the Grand Canyon property," following the government's takeover the year before (carton 34 [under "Huberth, Martin"]). Lt. Thornton wrote from Camp Roberts on December 2. He assumed Hearst was just across the Santa Lucias then: could some homesick personnel, asked Thornton, visit the hilltop during the holiday season? Willicombe conveyed the answer, but not until December 30: "Mr. Hearst instructs me to inform you that your letter, forwarded to him here from San Simeon, was received too late to make it possible for you and some of your men to make a one-day recreational trip to the ranch" (carton 35 on both items [under "1941 Samples"]). Richard Berlin of Hearst Magazines in New York, as much an insider as Heinie MacKay, wrote to Hearst at Wyntoon on December 4; the subject was *Motor*, the oldest periodical in that division of the empire (carton 34 [under "Berlin, R. E."]). And so on over the next few days, Sunday the seventh included.

On a teletype from MacKay to Willicombe on December 9—concerning gifts, taxes, and contributions, not the debacle in Hawaii—Hearst applied his familiar pencil: "I want to give my Indian blankets to the Los Angeles Museum. Please find if they want them. They are the best collection extant" (carton 35 [under "MacKay, H. S., Jr."]). The museum proved amenable; and Hearst made numerous gifts to that institution over the next several years, starting with Navajo rugs and related textiles in 1942.

With the new emergency status on the coast I feel confident that Cambria will soon see some activity. . . .

We have just now opened a[n] office in San Luis Obispo and have as a start the sewage disposal plant, the Union hall building and the finishing touches on the USO Building there. We hope to have more in a short time.[20]

The rain, however, was "practically halting work." The refrain couldn't have been more familiar, in peacetime or in war. Still, Loorz gave Petty his solemn word in closing: "You can be sure I will not forget you."

Loorz also made up for having skimped on current events in his recent letter to Apperson. "Randy, don't let any of those Japs land and take you fellows." By the time he said that, it was January 7, the dawn of this country's first full year in the global war.

THE CREW AT WYNTOON in 1941 had included Earl Tomasini, who hailed from the coastal hamlet of Cayucos, just down the road from San Simeon and Cambria. He told Loorz on January 5, 1942: "We closed at Wyntoon on Dec. 21 and it seems like maybe there will be no more construction there in the future, so am rather anxious to get started somewhere else." Loorz was Tomasini's best hope. As for Hearst, nothing short of Pearl Harbor and its aftermath had been enough for him to order an old-style shutdown at that estate. Even then he'd be watching for the first chance to put some men back to work there.

A greater sense of how things had gone at Wyntoon can be gained from Loorz's next letter to Pete Petersen, dated January 9, the second Friday in 1942:

> Otto [Olson] was in for a few minutes the other days [*sic*] and said you had a long steady run this [past] summer. Talked to Alex Rankin last Saturday [January 3] and he told me a lot that his Dad [Jim Rankin] had told him. From Mac and Jim and Otto it seems that working for them now [Hearst et al.] is not as pleasant as it used to be. At that it still must be alot better than running around over the country as carpenters have to do for us. Very few of our boys have been able to be home much during the past year.

January 9 also found Loorz writing to his close friend Charlie Badley:

> Work is coming out so fast it is astonishing but certainly not surprising. The thing I have difficulty in doing is adjusting my thots so that I can select wisely the jobs

---

20. In writing to a man named Ed Chew on December 28, 1941, Loorz referred to the company's "various home and field offices." The office stemming from the San Luis Sewer Plant and other nearby jobs was of the former kind: "We have just opened a home office in San Luis Obispo."

we should try for. . . . When I got word that we might have to wait a long time and even might have to shut down the San Luis Job [the sewer plant, begun the day after Pearl Harbor] to wait for steel because of LOW Priority, I must change my program.

Confidentially It looks like we will have to work further from home. Except for small jobs that continue to come out here and at Camp Roberts the most of the proposed work in our field (San Jose to Santa Maria) is of the lower Priority type. I did so want that kind, permanent construction, keeping the men employed longer in one spot, less figuring etc. Just a bit of the old "Laziness" returning.

Pete Petersen commented on some of those points in his unique, scribbling style. "Running around the country from job to job is no picnick," he said on January 15; "it is a pretty hard time now having anny trouble getting material not on goverment work." His was also a scrambled style. Yet his meaning was clear enough. Among other implications: even the hands of a titan like Hearst were tied for the time being. Morgan was also feeling the pinch, or at least was about to. (She was also about to be seventy, as of January 20.) True, the Park Museum account was still active and would remain so through March 1942; but then it would slow to a crawl and would finally lapse altogether, not to be reinstated (superseded actually) until after the war.

In gearing up for more federal work like that which he'd done at Camp McQuaide and Camp Roberts, Loorz had to recruit more men, from common laborers to estimators and beyond. Maurice McClure, former San Simeonite and Stoltean too, had tried his luck elsewhere after graduating from Berkeley in civil engineering, class of 1940. Well and good; all in the name of broader experience. But the time had come now for Loorz to get "Morris" back. On February 6, 1942, he told McClure (who was working for Kyle & Company in Stockton), "I hereby, therefore, declare myself to be on open search for your services":

I will not take time to tell you in detail of the progress of our little firm during the past two years. Briefly, we completed over three million dollars worth of work in 1941. I had the extreme pleasure of handing out over $25,000 in bonuses at Christmas (5 [thousand] each to Conrad [Gamboni] and Bob [Harbison] for a start).

I have in our employ at present three more engineers, only one of them with considerable experience. I pay him $5,000 a year. Last week I returned from Los Angeles where I contacted another engineer [Russell Quick] who has been with

---

But whether home or field, the San Luis office did not become a full-fledged branch of the F. C. Stolte Co.

Bechtel and Co. (*6* companies) [the renowned Six Companies conglomerate] for
about 8 years. . . . I know he would come at the right salary, but could offer only
$7,000.[21] I must be a little cautious at least about my overhead.

Cautious indeed. Five thousand dollars, seven thousand dollars; this was serious pay. (And to think that when Loorz started at San Simeon, a decade earlier to
the very week, his salary stood at $5,200—in one of the worst years of the Depres-
sion. He had capitalized on his rare good fortune, just as the tight-lipped Morgan
had.) Loorz had more to tell Maurice McClure on February 6:

With this personnel properly directed we should be equipped to handle EFFI-
CIENTLY a volume of work like we had last year or like we hope to do this year.
We have under contract now, well over $300,000 worth of work to start with. We
are in the midst of negotiating a two million dollar proposition. In this deal, of
course, we will combine [in the Six Companies tradition] with one other contractor.

That other party may in fact have been a Six Companies member, namely, the
Morrison-Knudsen Company of Boise, Idaho, with which the Stolte Co. would
soon be aligned on at least one of its jobs.

McClure answered on February 10, 1942, leading off with a choice passage
about the energetic, irrepressible Loorz: "I have observed with amazement and admiration, the growth of the small 'tail' of the Stolte Company. Now that tail appears
to be wagging the entire dog." You bet, was his point; he wanted in on the fun. In
fact, he told Loorz, he'd be honored to have $300 a month—$3,600 annually:

---

21. Loorz had written to Russell Quick just two days before, on February 4, 1942. Quick replied on February 23, calling Loorz's offer "very generous" but saying he'd be remaining with
Bechtel. Loorz tried once more on February 25. "I did not mention, I think, Russ, that we have recently decided to issue stock and thereby permit six of our employees to become actual members of
the firm. Certainly you would have been granted this privilege." He also told Quick that, in keeping
with the expansive times, the two of them might want to form "a new company" of their own. This
apparently posed no conflict. As Loorz explained, "I personally control an Electric firm [Del Monte
Electric Company], a Plumbing firm [Monterey County Plumbing Company], and a small contracting firm [Daniels & Loorz], outside the F. C. Stolte Co." See also note 47, below.

But Loorz still considered himself a "small-fry," and not with any false modesty. Bechtel and
other firms who'd combined as Six Companies on huge jobs were the true giants of the Far West
—they'd built Hoover Dam, no less. And so when the Stolte Co. had been invited in October 1940
to join the Northern California Chapter of Associated General Contractors (founded by the late
Warren Bechtel himself), Loorz had asked for a Class "C" rating, rather than a Class "B" or, on top
of the heap, a Class "A" rating. (He didn't realize how soon that highest rating would apply to the
Stolte Co., yet the firm still wouldn't be building anything as stupendous as Hoover Dam.) For perspective, see Donald E. Wolf, *Big Dams and Other Dreams: The Six Companies Story* (Norman, Oklahoma; 1996). See also Joseph E. Stevens, *Hoover Dam: An American Adventure* (Norman, 1988).

It would be clearly understood that a revision of salary, either upward or downward, could be effected as the change of business conditions warranted. These are not normal times. Many commodity prices have already risen to 140 or 150% of their pre-war level.

Details, details. McClure and Loorz made their pact, and yet Hazel McClure was losing sleep. "Golly George," she said in an undated letter that month, "I'm so afraid that Maurice will be called into the Army. You see here [in Stockton] he had been deferred because he was in charge of defense." A teacher by trade, Hazel had this to say also: "We have decided that where he goes I, too, must go, so I am going to ask my school board to release me." She remained fearful, though, that after she left, her husband would be drafted and she'd be an unemployed war bride.

Not to worry, said the confident Loorz. As he told Hazel McClure on February 18:

> Very definitely, Maurice will be on defense work. Last year ninety-five percent of our work was defense work and this year may be nearly a hundred percent.
>
> I regret that I cannot tell you exactly where Maurice will be [working] until I talk with him. If he were here now I think I would put him in charge of the San Miguel Sewer job [north of Paso Robles]. This will last at least 3 or 4 months. However, if we are lucky on [securing] the Marysville job [north of Sacramento], I would need every experienced man to help direct and manage. I would certainly take him there with me. He would do even better than his present salary. There would be no question about his being deferred when the Draft Board was notified of the responsible position he would have.

The McClures took a deep breath, just as Loorz had done when he left for San Simeon ten years before. They never looked back.[22]

WHEN THE SAN SIMEON BRANCH of the F. C. Stolte Co. was in existence (succeeded by Pacific Grove in 1938), Loorz had looked for work as far south as Lompoc at one point, but without success. He and Fred Stolte had even hoped to gain a toehold someday in the Los Angeles area, once more without success. The distance had simply been too great. The Marion Davies job in 1940 had been a pronounced

---

22. Dave Condin, part of Loorz's crew at Camp Roberts and now, in 1942, a Navy ensign back east, got an update from California at this point. Loorz informed him on Saturday, February 28, "One more engineer, Maurice McClure, long time with our organization, is returning tomorrow." Condin also learned that Loorz and Carl Daniels had "decided that private work will be too little in the next few years to be worthwhile." (The firm of Daniels & Loorz, established in 1940, had thus been disbanded.) "Therefore," Loorz told Condin of Daniels, "he has returned to this organization and is one of our best estimators and superintendents."

exception—an aberration almost, despite its happy outcome—the sole instance thus far of any work having been done by the company below the San Luis or Santa Maria areas.[23]

Early in March 1942, the Los Angeles office of Defense Public Works (DPW) reached Loorz by telegram in Pacific Grove: would the company like to bid a job in Lompoc? Six months earlier Loorz had passed up a much larger job in Santa Ana, southeast of Los Angeles. That confirmed his northern leanings, as did his response to DPW on March 9:

> Thank you for your invitation to bid on the Type "A" Recreation Building at Lompoc, California.
>
> We would be pleased to bid but we were low bidder on a $1,500,000 project at Pittsburg [west of Stockton] last week and are putting in $6,000,000 worth of bids at Marysville tomorrow so we would not be able to do your project justice.

The next day, Loorz told Randy Apperson much the same: 1.5 million in new federal work was about to become 7.5 million, provided Marysville came through. (It soon did.) "Therefore," he told Hearst's cousin, "our feet are way off of the ground and we are soaring in the clouds." Loorz wondered, though, if the good fortune would continue: "we are expecting to come down out of these clouds one of these days and will be surprised if it doesn't occur."

It didn't occur any time soon, so far as piling up more work was concerned. But there were plenty of headaches to offset the prosperity; in matters of payment, the government could be nearly as slow as Hearst had been at his most overburdened. Loorz shared some details on May 26, 1942, with Harold McBroom, the Stolte office manager in Alameda:

> As to collections, they are not too good. After taking a note down to the bank today, we will have some $448,000 borrowed on the Marysville Job, $200,000 on the Jap Camp and about $41,000 outstanding on old notes. I have been whittling

---

23. Regarding Lompoc, see p. 206 in this volume, note 105; a small job that Loorz's San Simeon branch did in 1937 was nearly as far south, in the rural town of Los Alamos. A "Report of Contracts on Hand" in the Loorz Papers (dated November 8, 1940) includes a residence in Santa Barbara along with similar jobs on the Monterey Peninsula; however, the "Santa Barbara" listing probably denotes a street by that name in Seaside, a town next to Monterey.

Still, Loorz was casting an occasional eye southward. On February 4, 1942, he wrote to Ray Van Gorden, who was in Los Angeles and, momentarily, working outside the Stolte fold. Loorz predicted, "If we do anything in Los Angeles it will not be worked up to the point of opening an office with help [clerical employees like Van Gorden] for at least 3 or 4 months or more." Loorz certainly wasn't looking as far south, though, as Lt. George Cully suggested that winter while writing from the Canal Zone. (The young officer was another "Roberts" alumnus, like Dave Condin.) "Say Mr Loorz," Cully said on January 8, "how about you getting a hook into this building program down here? You could really get your hooks into some nice cold cash if you want to."

at the old notes and if payments should come in as expected, I hope to have them all paid off within the next couple of weeks. We have lots of possibilities of collections, only hope they materialize.

The "Jap Camp" Loorz mentioned—formally called the Japanese Induction Unit in his papers—was a component of the Marysville contracts he'd recently landed. Technically, the camp was one of twelve "assembly centers" in California, as distinct from the state's subsequent and more infamous "relocation centers" at Tule Lake and Manzanar.

The slurs, the euphemisms, and the hysteria aside (common during that era, not just among patriotic builders), Loorz and hundreds of other men had jobs to do that yielded good pay while imposing new ways of life, at times disagreeably. "Geo. has only been home twice since March 15th and inasmuch as his family is spending the summer vacation with him at Marysville I do not expect to see him again for awhile." That was Conrad Gamboni writing from Pacific Grove on June 16, his recipient being an old friend in his hometown of Cambria.

Gamboni's letters are what keep the Loorz Papers going at this juncture; Loorz himself had little time in a pulsating year like 1942 to write to anyone. Come July 31, Gamboni answered Robert Stanton and Thomas Mulvin, the Monterey architects for whom Loorz had built the San Benito County Hospital in Hollister:

> Thank you for the invitation to build the Fort Ord School. However, Mr. Loorz has instructed us not to take any more work for awhile.
>
> We have over ten million dollars worth of contracts in the northern part of the state and Mr. Loorz has transferred most of his personnel and equipment to that sector.

A new job that had helped the company reach those heights—ten *million* in contracts!—was the Sierra Ordnance Depot near Honey Lake, just west of the California-Nevada state line and a few miles off the main road from Reno to Susanville. On August 28, Gamboni sent the company's insurance agent a list of employees on the Sierra job and other projects. It was like old-home week, a resounding roll call of "the boys." Elof Gustafson, Ray Van Gorden, Millard Hendricks, Frank Gyorgy, Carl Daniels, Olin Weatherford, Maurice McClure—even that wag of an attorney, Armand Brady. Farther down the list, a draftsman's name on a Stolte job in Chico appeared, Jerry Ryland, whose superb Santa Cruz City Hall seemed as retrograde now as anything at San Simeon or Wyntoon.

Close to Ryland's name was that of a newer man, identified as "Draftsman, Sierra." He was none other than Warren McClure.

MAC'S VERY PRESENCE on the Sierra Ordnance job confirmed that progress at Wyntoon was on hold. Hearst may have had a drone or two chipping away at The Bend—if so, the details have yet to arise—but he couldn't make any real showing without Mac, even if he had plenty of materials stockpiled. Thus far in 1942, Hearst had called Wyntoon home, except for brief trips to Los Angeles in February and to San Francisco in March. He'd spent his birthday at Wyntoon—that was unprecedented. So was his having brought Nigel Keep up from San Simeon to fight a lopsided battle, that of establishing orchards and other plantings in a rugged climate. For the most part, Hearst stayed put at Wyntoon through the late spring and into the summer, although his exact comings and goings have yet to be nailed down.[24]

Hearst could do with some renewed (or even increased) nailing of his own by now. In Mac's absence he turned to Miss Morgan. She went up to see him on Labor Day; she also made single trips in October and November. The "Angel House" account in the Morgan-Forney data cites those trips; it likewise cites the eighty-five hours she spent in the fall of 1942 at her drafting table for Wyntoon's sake. She billed Hearst in three installments. He paid in good time. A grand total just shy of $340 was the extent of it all; and the account lapsed after his final payment reached her office in December. It was a quiet, quiet ending to the years she and Hearst had devoted to Wyntoon. She most likely never saw the place again.

Back in September when she first met with him about Angel House, she'd taken care of a separate matter (which gave rise to a small account of its own): the supplying of plot plans and photostats of San Simeon, Wyntoon, and the Beach House. These went to the Hollywood office of Hearst Sunical, a satellite of Bill Murray's headquarters in San Francisco. Here again it was a minor episode, one involving a few hundred dollars that Morgan had no trouble collecting. Its importance is that, with respect to San Simeon, 1942 became a date of record—namely, the ostensible last date of her activity on that job, conveyed in future documents as "1919–1942."[25] Obviously, though, she hadn't done a lick of work at San Simeon in

---

24. The whereabouts of Hearst in the first half of 1942—as in much of 1941—can best be determined through the Bancroft holdings. In addition, *Time* magazine mentioned his being in San Francisco that winter (under "Hearst's Third War," March 23, p. 40) but wrongly assumed he'd gone there from San Simeon. His two birthday files in the Hearst Papers (carton 38) are well stocked; they include a greeting from Camille Rossi in Florida. An earlier item, sent to Wyntoon on April 9 by the insider Harry Crocker, mentioned the Military Ball to be held in Los Angeles (carton 35 [under "1942 Samples"]). Hearst and Miss Davies showed up, he in evening wear, she in a California National Guard uniform. See Swanberg, *Citizen Hearst*, photo 41, facing p. 239; two photographs in Pizzitola, *Hearst Over Hollywood*, facing p. 279, were taken at the same event in 1942.

25. Those dates appear in the Morgan Collection, Cal Poly, in its series San Simeon Financial Records, under "Cost of Construction, 1919–1942" (III/03/07/119). Another series at Cal Poly, the renowned one comprising the Hearst/Morgan Correspondence, has a similar list of expenditures

1942, not even *in absentia* (except for supplying the plots and photostats). Nineteen forty-one had been equally blank (except for $0.67 in expenses), and so had the previous year, save for the one trip in January 1940—the trip to the hilltop that, much like her current ones to Wyntoon, would probably prove to be her last.

September 28, 1942, a date falling between the first two of those Wyntoon visits, found Conrad Gamboni providing the War Production Board in San Francisco with some big numbers. The WPB had sought from the Stolte Co. "the exact amount of reinforced steel rods" already used on certain jobs and about to be used on others. The figure exceeded two thousand tons (about 4.2 million pounds), close to half of it slated for the Sierra Ordnance job. Ten years earlier the West Terrace at San Simeon had absorbed a tiny fraction of that tonnage. And thus an improbable but useful comparison: imagine seventy West Terraces, each about a hundred feet long and many of them being built concurrently. That's the scale the F. C. Stolte Co. was operating on (with regard to the company's concrete work alone) as it approached the first anniversary of Pearl Harbor.

Times had changed so much, though, that the old kept giving way to the new at a stunning pace. September 28 also found Gamboni writing to the Bank of America and other parties:

> This is to advise that on October 1, 1942, Stolte Inc. will be used as our corporate name. F. C. Stolte Co. has been dissolved and Stolte Inc., a new corporation, has been formed which will take over all of the assets and has agreed to assume all of the outstanding obligations of F. C. Stolte Co.
>
> The same Board of Directors represents both corporations.

In a nutshell, Fred Stolte and George Loorz would remain partners. Yet from this moment forward the financial intricacies of a company this large, this expansive are well beyond the scope of the present book; moreover, the records are lacking after 1944. Suffice it to say that Mr. Stolte and Mr. Loorz and certain other key players were reaping benefits from years of hard work and dedication—plus a little help from Father Hearst, not just from Uncle Sam. As Armand Brady told Gamboni sometime late in September 1942 (he didn't date his letter), "I did not get back to Reno [from the big Sierra job] until late Monday nite as I had to chase Fred down on his new ranch some twelve miles out of Stockton. Needed his signature on some papers."

---

dated 1919–1942; it goes with a letter from Morgan to Hearst on February 20, 1945 (III/01/07/75). A third series concerning San Simeon has more of the same under "George Loorz, 1936–1944" (III/02/07/82); its 1919–1942 items are with a letter from Morgan to Bill Murray on November 9, 1944 (probably intended for a file on Murray, not Loorz). See also pp. 501–02 in the next chapter, plus their note 3, and pp. 547–49 in Appendix B.

For his part, Loorz was easy to find then. Gamboni told a former employee, Cecil Murphree, on October 5, "George is as busy as two bird dogs with that Sierra Ordnance job. He works ten hours a day on record and another seven or eight off the record, six days a week and on Sunday I imagine he is still working." Murphree could easily visualize the action when Gamboni added, "Bob [Harbison], Jim Butler, Elof [Gustafson], Joe Galbraith, Kay Crowley and practically the whole gang are up there."

Mac McClure was still among them, as another list of Gamboni's showed on November 5, 1942.

Later that month, right after Thanksgiving, Gamboni heard from Loorz himself. Business and tax matters galore: Loorz wanted to be sure that the company knew exactly where it stood and that its records would bear up under the government's closest scrutiny. Back in February, when he tried to recruit Russell Quick from Bechtel, he had told him: "We feel positive that you and Mrs. Quick would fit into this picture and enjoy living in your own home on the Monterey Peninsula." And then he'd added, "Later developments of the Company might require a location in a larger city—we hope not."[26] Alas, that moment was fast approaching. Loorz had griped at times about his move from San Simeon to Pacific Grove: it had been too cautious a strategy, the Bay Area had always been his destiny. The fact was, however, he'd fallen deeply under the spell of places like Carmel and Monterey; Hearst's proximity had been a major influence, and Loorz had ultimately been glad of that and how it had shaped his life. In short, he liked his autonomy, his independence in Pacific Grove; his partnership with Fred Stolte wasn't perfect—he knew that few things in life were—yet the two oddly matched men had thrived, frankly, on lording it over their respective turfs. And thus when Loorz went on to tell Gamboni, "I realize that a central office in and around the Bay Area would be the solution of many difficulties," it wasn't with any gleefulness that he spoke. That was purely business, with life itself taking a back seat; and the prosperous, almost giddy juggernaut called World War II was the ironic cause. Therein lay his not-so-veiled message.

Nonetheless, Loorz polished off that same letter of November 27 with some solid details on the Sierra Ordnance work:

> The job itself, (the original contract), is finishing up nicely and except for paving, we should have it ready for occupancy by December 15th. The balance of the work, (extras), should be completed by February 1st [1943]. Our completion date on the job, of course, is February 16th, so we should have no trouble at all. At the

---

26. Loorz had voiced the same sentiments about the Monterey area two years before, to the very month; see note 13 in the 1940 chapter. He had also done so in the late 1930s.

end of next week we should be able to cut down at least 500 men, and another 300 the following week, and 200 the following week, leaving us an excellent crew of selected men to complete the job under most uncomfortable weather conditions. This makes no difference where good men are involved.

He closed with a passage that could readily have served in letters of years gone by, back when Hearst and Morgan held the purse strings and Wyntoon's or San Simeon's fate (or even the Grand Canyon's) was dangling with uncertainty:

There have been rumors from above to the effect that considerable more work is anticipated here and that we are in line for it. Until we get the contract I refuse to take Santa Claus too seriously.

Gamboni, the native Cambrian for whom the Monterey Peninsula was urban enough, knew he'd also have to head north if Loorz and Stolte gave the word. He struck the most realistic yet positive note he could when he answered Loorz on November 30:

The hardest thing will be to establish a definite policy and procedure and then for both this [office] and the Alameda Office to adhere rigidly to it. A central office would probably make things somewhat easier, but with a definite policy and procedure I believe that the same results can be attained with not too much hardship on anyone.

He also applauded Loorz. "Glad to hear that the job is shaping up so nicely," the job of course being the one at Sierra:

All say it was quite a feat of organization and cooperation among everyone. Don't rumors fly thick and fast. I heard from an *impeachable* and *unreliable* source that we were in line for the large tunneling job from Marina [near Monterey] to Tokio via the Solomons, New Guinea, and other Jap points. Don't breathe it to a soul.

Loorz had trained his man well in the fine art of balderdash. He had also kept him guessing. "We enjoyed the Stolte Blueprint very much," Gamboni said a moment later. "It was a complete surprise to us." *Stolte Blueprint* was a corporate magazine, privately produced to mark the recent debut of Stolte Inc. and, above all, to celebrate the company's rousing success in the building industry. With the groundwork laid, the issues appeared intermittently over the next several years. The surviving copies are an invaluable resource.[27]

November 30, 1942, fell on a Monday. Gamboni's letter to Loorz was a long

---

27. The copies of *Stolte Blueprint* on which this volume relies are courtesy of Don Loorz, May 29, 1990, and November 10, 1999.

one and a good one, too; writing it was a good way for its author to start a new week. In San Francisco, meanwhile, Julia Morgan had likewise found a good way to get moving. She boarded a train that Monday, but not for Dunsmuir, nor for San Luis Obispo or Los Angeles, though she passed through both. No, she was heading out of state and across the border—to El Paso, Texas, and then down to Chihuahua, Mexico, down to the enormous ranch called the Babicora. She'd be conferring there with Hearst.[28]

KING FEATURES SYNDICATE, presided over by the bon vivant Joseph Connolly, was a cornerstone of Hearstdom; Damon Runyon, for instance, a favorite writer of Hearst's, reached an audience well beyond the Hearst newspapers alone, thanks to the good offices of King Features. On December 21 in New York, Joe Connolly wired another Joe—as in Joe Willicombe, the Colonel—stationed in Los Angeles at the close of 1942 while the Chief was away. (Connolly already knew that messages could be forwarded to Hearst from El Paso, but he hoped to make more direct contact.) "HAPPY CHRISTMAS TO YOU JOE," said Connolly on the twenty-first. "PLEASE LET ME KNOW WHERE MR HEARST WILL BE ON CHRISTMAS EVE." Colonel Willicombe replied that same day. "Chief now at Geneve Hotel [the Hotel de Genève], Mexico City. He will either be there or at Babicora Ranch, which is near Chihuahua [City], on Christmas Eve, so far as I can ascertain." Willicombe had more for Connolly on December 22. "Chief still at Hotel Geneve, Mexico City. Will note [not] return to Babicora until after New Year's." Ah, but this was vintage Hearst: as much as ever, the man with the changeable mind. Willicombe gave a further update on Tuesday, December 29. "Please note that Chief will be in Los Angeles Friday [January 1, 1943]. All communications should be addressed to him there in care of Los Angeles Examiner."[29]

28. A datebook of Morgan's for 1946 is in the Morgan-Forney Collection; tucked into it are notes and letters from other years in the forties. One such item—typewritten—lists Morgan's trips to Mexico, beginning with the one that commenced on November 30, 1942; next to that, a notation of "Train" appears in her hand. Another hand, that of Lilian Forney, made the first entry in the new Babicora Ranch account: "Travel Miss Morgan" under December 1942, with a mere $58.50 listed as its expense.

In *Citizen Hearst,* Swanberg gave no account of what for Hearst was his second and final trip to Mexico in the 1940s. But Harry Crocker of the *Los Angeles Examiner* provided a glimpse of the coming event. He told Hearst well in advance that, because of commitments, he'd fly to El Paso in the wee hours of December 5, in time to join the group that morning as it left for the Babicora. "I am looking forward greatly to the trip," said Crocker, "and, as the day approaches, I grow more and more excited to see the ranch." From Crocker to Hearst, November 12, 1942; Hearst Papers, carton 35 (under "1942 Samples").

29. Connolly to Willicombe, December 10 and 21, 1942, plus Willicombe to Connolly, December 21, 22, and 29, 1942; Hearst Papers, carton 38 (under "Connolly, J. V."). Louella Parsons touched on the allure of Mexico City during this period in *The Gay Illiterate* (New York, 1944), p. 141.

Morgan's whereabouts aren't as readily traceable. She's known to have written to Bernard Maybeck and his wife during the trip. Replying from their little mountain retreat in Twain Harte, northwest of Yosemite, the Maybecks asked in puzzlement: "Why are you in El Paso?"[30] Good question. If Morgan had peered into a crystal ball, she'd have known that two more trips to Mexico awaited her on the new Babicora Ranch account. And after that, she'd be going to Mexico twice again (both times for her own sake, with one of the trips including Guatemala). As for Hearst himself, who still had more than eight years to live, he seems to have remained in California from here on.[31]

Upon getting wind of Hearst's recent travels, or of Morgan's for that matter, Loorz and the boys may simply have shaken their heads in mild disbelief. Government work kept pouring in as 1943 took hold; a life as rarefied as Hearst's had to seem almost fictional. On a more earthbound level, Stolte Inc. turned down another architect that Loorz had worked with before, Charles Butner of Salinas. Gamboni conveyed an increasingly familiar message on January 11, this time regarding "labor camps in Stanislaus County":

> We appreciate receiving [the] invitation to bid and intended submitting a figure. However, we were just recently awarded a $4,000,000 Housing Project in Alameda and did not feel that we could do justice to you or ourselves at this time.[32]

An equally familiar message went forth on January 13, 1943; however, this was another one of those from that other world, from that place that was close enough geographically yet so remote in its workings. "Chief asks that you kindly send him a young white male deer, which he would like you to kill and dress." Willicombe's

---

30. Annie and Bernard Maybeck to Morgan, January 9, 1943; Morgan Collection (I/07/02/32). The Maybecks also told Morgan, "Had a note from Mrs. Darbee who's clerking in her store." About thirty years later, Morgan North recalled that wealth from the Tillamook Cheese Company (and from a "smell-less violet" that florists liked) had once been slated to make the Darbee Mausoleum a reality. And yet Mrs. Darbee herself lived "in a little hovel over a store across from where the cable winding house of the California Street Cable Railway was [in San Francisco], and had a little florist store underneath which her son ran." From *The Julia Morgan Architectural History Project*, Vol. II, pp. 188–89.

31. Concerning Morgan, the dates of her trips, plus notes on modes of travel, are in her datebook for 1946 (as in note 28, above); Morgan-Forney Collection. Sara Boutelle was right in specifying that Morgan made three trips to Mexico in Hearst's behalf, but she cited 1941, 1942, and 1945; the correct dates are 1942, 1943, and 1944. See *Julia Morgan*, p. 245 (note 3 under "The Morgan Atelier"). Concerning Hearst, a quick trip he made past the state line in 1946 may be the sole exception to the California rule; see p. 509 in this volume, note 14.

32. Gamboni's letter was addressed to the Guayule Emergency Rubber Project in Los Angeles, not to Butner (who as the designer of record was sent a copy). The Washington School in Salinas, built by Loorz's Pacific Grove branch a few years before, was a Butner design; so was the San Ardo School, between King City and Paso Robles (a job Loorz had watched but seems not to have gotten).

voice, unmistakably; Randy Apperson was on the receiving end. Hearst also wanted "half a beef" as well as "any suitable lamb." Apperson was to ship the meats to 415 Ocean Front in Santa Monica, the street address of the Beach House.

In that same letter, Willicombe made a final request: "Will you kindly ask Nick Yost to pack up the bathing suits on the Hilltop and send them to Chief at 910 Benedict Canyon [Drive], Beverly Hills."[33]

Now *that* was a new angle. The house at 910 Benedict was where parts of the Cosmopolitan bungalow had been used in 1939. True, the house had a pool, too, hence the swimsuits. But the most surprising thing is that at this juncture in 1943, Hearst and Miss Davies were planning to *live* there. It's an oddity because 910 Benedict is about as plain a setting, about as middle-class an environment (by Hearst's kingly standards) as one could ever imagine him choosing. Even in that era Benedict Canyon carried a good deal of traffic, the street being a link between Beverly Hills and the San Fernando Valley. And unlike the old Davies place at 1700 Lexington Road, which commanded a pleasant knoll, the neighboring Benedict place sat on a perfectly flat lot, almost hugging the street (as it still does today, little having changed except for the heightened traffic).

Maybe this short-lived interlude, during which Hearst made some further use of the Beach House also, was his way of rationing or economizing or biting the bullet for a while. He and Miss Davies never stayed at 910 again after the first part of 1943. Why they chose to be there at all (aside from avoiding wintry Wyntoon) has yet to be determined; for starters, the larger place at 1700 Lexington must have been unavailable for their use.[34]

---

33. Willicombe to Apperson, January 13, 1943; Hearst Papers, carton 38 (under "Apperson, R. W."). A week earlier in Pacific Grove, Conrad Gamboni thanked the San Jose Steel Company for its generosity during the Christmas season: "In these days of food shortages and rationing those Santa Clara pears are a greatly appreciated gift" (Loorz Papers, January 6). Apperson also received word about San Simeon during this period:

> Two young women who were telephone operators at Wyntoon have informed Chief that they will be in San Simeon shortly and have asked him if they might go up the hill and see the place. Chief has told them that it will be all right for them to do so. So will you kindly see that they get by the gate. It would be nice also if you would let Eddie Shaug take them up, as he knows them. He can show them around, including a little of the inside of buildings.

From Willicombe to Apperson, January 20, 1943; Hearst Papers, ibid.

34. References to 910 Benedict Canyon appear in Hollywood literature, though not widely; but the existing ones suggest that many people knew the Cosmopolitan bungalow had come back "over the hill" from Warner Bros. in Burbank (whence it had gone after its fabled reign at MGM in Culver City). The earliest book to lay claim may well be *The Whole Truth and Nothing But*, by Hedda Hopper and James Brough (New York, 1963), p. 188. Fred Lawrence Guiles missed the cue entirely in *Marion Davies* (1972). Richard Meryman had some inkling in *Mank: The Wit, World, and Life of Herman Mankiewicz* (New York, 1978), p. 282, yet not enough to avoid associating the bungalow with

A letter that Randy Apperson sent Hearst on January 22 fits more conveniently within familiar, accustomed bounds:

> I dont suppose you are particularly enjoying this kind of weather we are having at present; but you should see it here at the ranch. In the past 48 hours, we have had only 6½ inches of rain, and a gale of wind. I have never seen the Arroyo La Cruze [Arroyo de la Cruz, west of the hilltop] as high, since I have been here [1934], as it was yesterday. Fortunately, it has dropped considerably.
>
> I am glad to say, the Hilltop has weathered the storm with no damage so far. The range [the grazing land] will benefit greatly, after this supply of rain, and it should be a good year for the stock.[35]

Blood may have been thicker than water. But in these lean and lonesome times, Hearst held his cousin answerable for all of San Simeon: the ranch work, the caretaking of the castle — the whole operation. Apperson was being more than just newsy when he said things were okay. He was whispering a prayer for continued good fortune.[36]

THE NEW STOLTE JOB in Alameda was mentioned in a letter of Gamboni's on February 5, 1943. In replying to Chuck Osborne, a recent Stolte employee who'd written from Long Beach, Gamboni began with "Glad to get your [post]card and know that the war will be terminated sooner now that you are in it":

> Carl [Daniels], Ray Sutton, and a bunch of the gang are at the Hotel Del Monte [in Monterey] remodelling it for the the Navy Pre-Flight School. About a $150,000 cost-plus job.

---

a "Benedict Canyon estate." Charles Higham mentioned 910 Benedict in *Merchant of Dreams: Louis B. Mayer, M.G.M., and the Secret Hollywood* (New York, 1993), p. 338. He was preceded by Gary Carey, who'd given a fuller account in *All the Stars in Heaven: Louis B. Mayer's M-G-M* (New York, 1981), p. 264. Carey described 910 Benedict as "the former Marion Davies dressing room/bungalow which had been carted from Metro to Warners before reaching its final resting place in Beverly Hills." In *Hearst Over Hollywood* (2002), p. 404, Louis Pizzitola drew upon Meryman's "estate" reference of 1978, a description surpassing the modest home at 910 and its surroundings.

As to the tie-in with Mayer: Hopper and Brough, Carey, and Higham apparently didn't know that Hearst and Davies lived at 910 briefly; Meryman and Pizzitola did. At any rate, Carey and Higham were the most specific in recounting that Mayer, upon leaving his wife in 1944, moved to 910 Benedict and called the place home for several years. Hearst wrote to "Louie" at that address on November 8, 1947; Hearst Papers, carton 42 (under "1947 Samples").

35. From Apperson to "Cousin Will," January 22, 1943; Hearst Papers, carton 38 (under "Apperson, R. W."). Willicombe wrote to Apperson on that same day: "Please send Chief as quickly as possible to 910 Benedict Canyon Road [Drive], Beverly Hills, four turkeys." He continued, "Chief also asks that you send him a list of the poultry available at San Simeon." Hearst Papers, ibid.

36. Or as Apperson himself later said in a different context, "Inasmuch that Mr. Hearst holds me accountable for the Hilltop, I feel it is only proper that I also be advised of the things that are

Geo. [Loorz] and Bob [Harbison] are now at Alameda on the $4 million dollar housing project. Elof and Maurice are finishing up at Sierra Ordnance.

Carl Daniels, veteran of the Arroyo Grande School (plus other San Simeon and Pacific Grove projects that now seemed nostalgic), had been among the minority: the men who'd held down the Stolte fort in the Monterey area while so many of "the gang" went to places like Pittsburg, Marysville, and especially the bleak surroundings north of Reno for the Sierra job. A recent assignment for Daniels had fallen outside the government mold: a resumption of work in Carmel Valley for Jean and Joe Willicombe (who were soon to be parents). The details are scarce. But at this moment, smack dab in the middle of the war and with the Loorz Papers scraping bottom, those limited data provide vital links between the Hearst and Loorz camps. Without such links 1943 has a vague, rootless status, making it a year that's lost somewhere between the thirties decade and the postwar period. Daniels and his crew squeezed a small job in edgewise for the Willicombes, from late in December 1942 through the middle of January 1943. It cost less than a thousand dollars; the $17,000 Loorz mentioned in 1941 had been cut to the bone (either that or the records of other remodeling never surfaced). Later on in 1943, Loorz wrote to the Willicombes about the work:

> I am enclosing some papers for your records. You will note on the March 22nd billing [for the December-January work] that we have stated there would be a charge for the installation of [the] heater. This ran around $80 but I misplaced the bill so I am not including same.
>
> However, in appreciation of the many past favors and courtesies and for those I might ask in the future, I want you to disregard these billings altogether.[37] We are pleased to have been able to accommodate you.
>
> I hope you are enjoying that lovely Carmel Valley sunshine.

Except for yielding that letter to the Willicombes, the Loorz Papers are too quiet to keep speaking for the first half of 1943. The Hearst Papers and other sources are stronger voices through this stretch. (Indeed, the Hearst-Morgan correspondence in Cal Poly's Morgan Collection regains its tone and volume

---

requisitioned to go [up to Wyntoon]." From Apperson to Estelle Forsythe, October 9, 1944; Hearst Papers, carton 40 (under "Apperson, R. W.").

37. It's unclear whether "billings" pertained to the itemization of both in-house and subcontracted expenses dated March 22, 1943 — their total amount being $857.14 — or whether Loorz was also alluding to other phases of the job. In any event, Loorz didn't send the March 22 invoice to the Willicombes for nearly six months, not till September 8.

here after a long silence, yet mostly with regard to the far-removed Babicora project.)[38]

The Hearst Papers, for example, contain a letter that Randy Apperson wrote Hearst on February 22; he mentioned the same War Production Board that, five months earlier, Conrad Gamboni had provided with figures on steel rods (the term *rebar* was still to come). San Luis Obispo County had conducted a "scrap drive," said Apperson, and the Hearst Ranch had proved abundant. "In addition to 224,000 pounds of scrap metal, we also contributed 2,000 pounds of rubber—a remarkable contribution, I think." An old airplane engine wound up in the pile. And somewhere in all that junk there must have been scraps from a derelict truck—perhaps from a few of them—on which Rossi or Loorz, or maybe Williams, had hauled astounding loads up the hillside.[39]

Hearst was delighted. But rusted paint cans and other castoffs (standard rubbish on old ranches) weren't enough to sustain his accustomed style. "Our meat supply will be exhausted by the end of next week," wrote Willicombe to Apperson on March 22. "Chief would like you to ship another half beef, so that it will arrive at 415 Ocean Front (Santa Monica) first part of next week—say Monday the 29th." He also said, "You can send that young deer with this shipment"—evidently a newer deer than the one he mentioned to Apperson back in January.[40]

The rationing of that era affected everyone. Although Hearst had his ranch to keep him supplied with choice meat and other products, gasoline was another matter. Willicombe to Apperson, March 28, 1943: "Chief instructs me to ask you to do your utmost to help Nick Yost get a 'B' gas rationing card." Apperson was to "go to the extreme limit," if necessary, making it known that Yost was "employed by Hearst Sunical, which is engaged in an essential industry." Beef cattle must have

---

38. The Hearst/Morgan Babicora Correspondence at Cal Poly comprises eleven monthly files for February through December 1943, plus a single file for 1944; a few other files in the Morgan Collection also pertain to Babicora. Meanwhile, that collection has some stray items of this vintage (like the Maybecks' letter in note 30); their authors' voices should also be heard. Marion Suppo, for example, wrote Morgan on January 15, 1943; her father, Jules, had done a great deal of custom woodwork for San Simeon and other projects in the past. Yet even in 1943 there were signs of continuity: "Daddy is so pleased over the work he's doing for you. He is never happier than when he has something interesting to work on" (I/07/02/37). Suppo's recent efforts may well have stemmed from Morgan's three trips to Wyntoon late in 1942.

39. See Apperson to Hearst, February 22, 1943 (plus attachment from Camp San Luis Obispo, dated February 17 and bearing Hearst's penciled comments, made with future publicity in mind); Hearst Papers, carton 38 (under "Apperson, R. W.").

40. Willicombe to Apperson, March 22, 1943; Hearst Papers, ibid. "Glad you enjoyed the editorial page feature on scrap," Willicombe also said in that letter. "It was well worth while." His reference was to the salvaging Apperson had done on the Hearst Ranch.

been what he meant. (Yost's main job, however, was to care for the art-ladened warehouses.) Just the same, Steve Zegar in San Luis Obispo—of Steve's Taxi in earlier annals—was a "rich and influential citizen," declared Willicombe, a man whose help Apperson might want to seek.[41]

Next came that yearly high spot, a milestone this time—the Chief's eightieth birthday. Apperson learned that Hearst wanted more than fifty pheasants, mallards, and other poultry sent from the Chicken Ranch at San Simeon. "I telephoned to save time," Willicombe explained on April 23, "as they must arrive NOT LATER THAN WEDNESDAY, APRIL 28th—CHIEF'S BIRTHDAY, AS YOU KNOW, BEING ON THE 29th."[42]

Down south, Hearst's activities in 1943 ran the gamut, as much as Loorz's did up north; but Hearst, despite his age, was still leading the historical, ultimately archival pack. As expressive as ever, he used that trait to convey wisdom one minute and its opposite the next, invoking an old man's prerogative. On May 6 he wrote to "Cobbie"—Edmond D. Coblentz—an editor of long standing who was now at the *Call-Bulletin*, Hearst's evening paper in San Francisco:

> I have a strong feeling that the Japanese will raid our Coast cities soon—maybe any day, and I think the Coast papers [Los Angeles, San Francisco, Oakland, Seattle] should take very exceptional measures to extinguish fires in the building [in each city] and in the neighborhood of the building, and should have some fire drills and regulations to go into effect if the raid occurs.
>
> The chances that our building would be actually struck are small, but the chances that it would be caught in a general conflagration are very large, and it is time we were making complete preparations for such a catastrophe.[43]

---

41. Hearst Papers, carton 38 (as in notes 39 and 40).

42. Ibid. *Time* provided coverage of the event in Santa Monica under "Hearst is 80" (May 10, 1943), p. 50, as did Louella Parsons in *The Gay Illiterate*, pp. 97–98. See also Bill Hearst's memoir, *The Hearsts*, p. 168 (in which Wyntoon figures as the setting).

43. Hearst Papers, carton 38 (under "Coblentz, E. D."). Fears that the Japanese might attack the West Coast were no longer rampant in May 1943, the pivotal Battle of Midway having occurred the previous June. However, an American scholar, fluent in Japanese and conversant with arcane documents and sources, has offered this account:

> According to the distinguished [Japanese] military historian Ikuhiko Hata, late in 1944 a group of naval officers led by Lieutenant Commander Daiji Yamaoka seriously entertained the prospect of launching a suicide strike in California. Some three-hundred chosen men of the "Yamaoka Parachute Brigade" were to be transported across the Pacific on several mammoth submarines and landed in the vicinity of Santa Barbara. They were then to shoot their way into Los Angeles via Santa Monica, wrecking havoc with the Douglas and Lockheed aircraft factories and taking as many lives as possible before their own annihilation. Training for this operation began in December 1944 but was halted in May 1945 with the selection of a new target, the Mariana Islands.

Perhaps he needed to get away again, needed to remove himself to a distant, neutral place like Mexico. He and Miss Morgan had been corresponding about the Babicora Ranch since they returned to California early in 1943. In fact, on April 13 she asked what they ought to call the house—the hacienda really—that they were visualizing there. Its elevation was a good deal higher than its counterpart at San Simeon, airborne enough at 1,600 feet (not to mention Wyntoon at almost twice that height). No, the Babicora was clear up in the clouds—7,500 feet above sea level. "The Clouds," therefore. That should be its name. Morgan got the message in a letter from H. O. Hunter, Willicombe's relief man and successor-in-waiting; it went out from Wyntoon on May 28. Willicombe himself had notified Morgan on May 24 that Hearst had left for Wyntoon the night before.[44]

So the Chief had finally gone north, and he wouldn't be going south. But Morgan would—on June 4. This time she'd be flying to Mexico City. From there she'd be doubling back to Chihuahua's capital, a good nine hundred miles to the northwest, with nearly two hundred miles waiting to be traversed between there and The Clouds.[45]

MORGAN WAS STILL IN MEXICO when Jim LeFeaver's name cropped up again in the Loorz Papers. From Alameda, Loorz sent a memorandum to several employees on June 18, 1943. He advised them that "all purchases of every type made for the Monterey County Plumbing Co. will be placed through J. H. LeFeaver, who will act as purchasing agent." LeFeaver, of course, had been indispensable to Morgan through the twenties, the thirties, even into the opening moments of the forties. But in 1942 he had finally left the fold, just as Mac McClure had done in his arrangement with Hearst. As it was, LeFeaver's work for Morgan after 1938–39, following her trip to Europe that fall and winter, had been increasingly spotty, done

From John J. Stephan, *Hawaii Under the Rising Sun: Japan's Plans for Conquest After Pearl Harbor* (Honolulu, 1984), p. 169. Indeed, a plan that diabolical would strike much too close to home for Hearst's comfort, yet it's ludicrous to assume he had any more than vague suspicions of such prospects.

44. The Hearst/Morgan Babicora Correspondence at Cal Poly contains "The Clouds" reference (under III/06/09/23); see also the preceding folder in that series.

45. Morgan's list of travels to Mexico (see notes 28 and 31, above) is marked "Plane" and also "auto" next to the "June 4, 1943" entry, indicating the date she left on this second trip for Hearst (Morgan-Forney Collection). The remaining details come from the Morgan Collection (III/06/09/23). Morgan told Hearst on May 20 that his "suggestion of flying to Mexico City" would make her trip "very simple." He commented to her on May 28, "By the way, there is to be a plane service from Chihuahua to the [California] Coast, so we can soon fly from Los Angeles to Chihuahua and from Chihuahua to the ranch [the Babicora]—all in a day."

For this second trip, it's not known if she covered the great distance between Mexico City and the Babicora by "auto" or some other means.

mostly (perhaps entirely) on an independent consulting basis. He prepared the estimate in 1940, for example, on the Darbee Mausoleum, destined never to be built.
He did another estimating job for her in 1941, aimed at re-erecting the old Spanish
monastery Hearst had given to San Francisco.[46]

As to the Monterey County Plumbing Company, it didn't require LeFeaver's
presence in the Monterey area. Known by its initials MCPC, Monterey County
Plumbing began as an offshoot of the old F. C. Stolte Co.; it remained one in relation to the new company, Stolte Inc. (Its "offshoot" status meant that George Loorz
and Fred Stolte owned MCPC separately from their main corporate holdings.)
Loorz was the one who established MCPC before Pearl Harbor, before that event
and the war's escalation in 1942 ended the agreeable life he'd known in Pacific
Grove.[47] At this mid-point in 1943, when the Loorz family was preparing to move
to Alameda, part of MCPC was also being shifted north. Stolte Inc. established
a new branch office in Monterey as part of the transition, replacing the one in Pacific Grove (namely, the Loorzes' home); MCPC would still be represented
in that local area, just as Stolte Inc. would. Jim LeFeaver would be pursuing his
MCPC work from the main Stolte headquarters, which themselves were about to
be moved—but only a short distance, from Alameda to adjoining Oakland.[48]

The greater Hearst connection stayed alive that summer through continued

---

46. See note 80, below, on LeFeaver as estimator. In his wartime work for the Monterey
County Plumbing Company, Jim LeFeaver became one of the boys. E. J. Rockee of the main Stolte
office wrote to him on October 19, 1943, as "Mr. Errol Flynn LeFeavor." After dispensing with business, Rockee signed off as "Your friend and Stalin's."

47. When he wrote to Ed Chew back on December 28, 1941 (note 20, above), Loorz mentioned
MCPC and other components of his and Fred Stolte's growing network. He told Chew, "You are
aware perhaps that we have now five very busy offices,—Stolte Company of Alameda, Stolte Company, Pacific Grove, Monterey County Plumbing Company, Monterey, Del Monte Electric Company, Pacific Grove, and Daniels & Loorz, Carmel." (And yet on October 10, 1941, while writing to
a man named Kloeckner, Loorz said of the Daniels & Loorz venture: "We operate entirely separate
from the F. C. Stolte Co." Loorz spoke likewise to Russ Quick on February 25, 1942; see note 21,
above.) What Loorz meant in these situations, as Don Loorz explained to me, is that certain entities
like MCPC were owned jointly by George Loorz *and* Fred Stolte outside the corporate realm, not
within it as subsidiaries.

The main change since 1941, besides the dissolution of Daniels & Loorz in 1942, had been the
formation later that year of Stolte Inc. as a new corporation. MCPC still existed as an offshoot when
Loorz moved north in 1943, and so did Del Monte Electric; but unlike MCPC, part of which also
went north, Del Monte may have remained purely a branch-office appendage.

48. The move from Alameda meant that Fred Stolte would no longer be operating from his
home in that city, just as Loorz would no longer be operating from his home in Pacific Grove. The
transition was part of the expansion, the upgrading, the maturing that followed the establishment of
Stolte Inc. almost a year before. Fred Stolte's home remained in Alameda, the same city where Loorz
now lived.

work, albeit minor, done by Stolte Inc. for Jean and Joe Willicombe; on July 21, for example, Conrad Gamboni wrote about the survey of their property in Carmel Valley.[49] The Colonel himself was now seventy and had been making a slow but steady transition toward retirement, one that defined him as the "executive secretary" whereas Bill Hunter (H. O. Hunter officially) was the unadorned "secretary."[50] For the Willicombes, and for Hearst as well, whose finances were improving, Stolte Inc. was clearly the builder of choice if the war were to end and the private sector were to resume construction with real vigor.[51]

But in 1943 that moment was still a long way off. On September 1, Loorz spoke of being utterly steeped in government work—this while writing to his friend and former employee Cecil Murphree, now an Army sergeant:

> We are quite busy right now. We are finishing two Housing Project jobs in Alameda and have a new project just starting, also in Alameda. We have several jobs at Moffett Field [near Mountain View and Sunnyvale] and McClelland Field [McClellan Air Force Base in Sacramento]; a job at Pittsburg; a bridge for Western Pacific R.R. [Railroad] at Sierra Ordnance; WAVE Barracks at Mare Island [near Vallejo]; jobs at Vallejo and more at Sierra Ordnance.
>
> Elof is still at Sierra Ordnance. Ray [Van Gorden] is back in Los Angeles with

---

49. Gamboni's letter went to Lee Perry, a Stolte employee based in Sacramento at the moment along with Carl Daniels. Gamboni needed Perry to call the Willicombes and tell them how to locate their property line.

50. Examples of Willicombe as "executive secretary"—no such distinction applied before he and Bill Hunter began overlapping—are scattered through the Hearst Papers of the early and mid-1940s. See, for instance, Willicombe to Delmar J. Brent, November 18, 1941 (which includes, "Mr. Hearst has no position open for a confidential secretary, but did advertise recently for a stenographer and assistant to the writer [Willicombe?]," a position that since then had been filled); Hearst Papers, carton 35 (under "1941 Samples"). See also Willicombe to Herbert O'Conor (Governor of Maryland), February 21, 1944; ibid., carton 39 (under "Oa-Og").

51. The summer of 1943 figured later that year in a letter by Walter Steilberg, who since 1942 had been a civilian engineer for the Navy in Alaska; he told Julia Morgan the following on December 26, 1943:

> I know that even though you are well, you can not be entirely happy without a lot of work to do; and when I was in S.F. last July the private practice of architecture seemed to be just about closed out for the duration [of the war]; even those who like [Gardner] Dailey and [Will] Corlett were reported as having much work were operating on a shoe string with almost no office force.

From the series Personal Correspondence in the Morgan Collection, Cal Poly (I/07/02/36). Morgan's spotty records for 1943 show that, beyond the Babicora account, only two others were active then, the Park Museum account and the Vincent account of 1940–46 (the latter known only from a loose note in her 1946 datebook). Each of those non-Hearst accounts was a small producer in 1943. In 1942 the Park Museum had been her largest account of any kind, Hearst or non-Hearst (even at just $756 in operating costs).

his wife. Caulkins [L. H. Calkins] is on the new Housing Project in Alameda. The Pacific Grove office, including Conrad, Miss Hildebrand and Miss Gordon, are now here in Oakland in our new plant [on San Leandro Street].[52]

"We certainly hope you are transferred to the West," Loorz told Murphree in closing, "preferably the San Francisco-Oakland Bay Area."

Loorz was calling that area home again, nearly a dozen years after he'd left Berkeley in 1932 for a season's work at San Simeon. He'd spoken many times of how he should go back to the East Bay, of how he needed to be closer to the action. Pacific Grove had proved a welcome surprise, an unexpected high point. But now that interlude was also slipping into the past. His wife and sons had completed their part of the move. The oldest son, Don, would be a senior at Alameda High School.

In writing from the new main office in Oakland on September 7, 1943, Loorz said that Stolte Inc. had "constructed some $12,000,000 of work during 1942." He so informed Captain R. E. Hancock, who had charge of construction at Camp Parks, over toward Dublin, Pleasanton, and the Livermore Valley—not far from where Phoebe Hearst's old Hacienda del Pozo de Verona had become the Castlewood Country Club. Loorz asked to be included in Hancock's "list of eligible contractors":

> We employ, continuously, from 1,000 to 3,500 men and have licensed engineers, licensed architects, draftsmen and estimators in our personnel, as well as superintendents and foremen especially fitted for this type of work. The company owns general construction equipment valued at approximately $200,000 and can handle every phase of construction work.

Indeed they could: the immediate need at Camp Parks was merely to build two recreation units, a job that Stolte Inc. could knock out blindfolded. It was another prospect at Camp Parks, however, the enlargement of its Navy hospital, that Loorz told Captain Hancock about a week later, things having suddenly changed by September 15:

> Please be advised that due to developments in the past twenty-four hours, we feel unable to place a bid on the above project [the hospital], even though our estimate is complete.
>
> This firm has been "drafted" by the U. S. Engineers to start work immediately on a large project involving many buildings in a bombing range out of this State and, therefore, all available personnel and equipment will be shifted immediately to this project which must be completed by October 31st.

---

52. The plant was at the extreme south end of Oakland, on the corner of San Leandro Street and 85th Avenue, a mile or so from the city limits of the adjoining town, San Leandro. And thus a

And so Loorz was going back on the road, together with a convoy of workmen. Their destination was the gigantic Nellis Air Force Range, served by the mining town of Tonopah. That jumping-off point lay 250 miles due east of Oakland — out in Nevada past Yosemite and Mono Lake, with the job itself concealed in the desert vastness untold miles away.

ALTHOUGH STOLTE INC. had its own engineers, architects, draftsmen, and the like, Mac McClure ceased to be one of them in 1943. The first big phase of the Sierra Ordnance job had been completed early that year. Whether Mac stayed on for any of the subsequent work is unknown; whether Hearst lured him back or Mac tired of the Stolte regimen is also unknown.[53] By late spring, at any rate, Hearst had dug back in at Wyntoon; his life there in 1943 can be glimpsed through the Hearst Papers at the Bancroft, a life comfortably lived despite the constraints of wartime. Once more he had San Simeon's own Nigel Keep on hand, as had been true the year before.[54] And now that Mac was also on hand again, some construction could be done, no matter how piddling. Miss Morgan, long since back from Mexico, not only stayed current with Hearst on Babicora matters, she also kept up on the prog-

---

minor misattribution, occasionally heard at Hearst Castle in years past: "Some of this place was built by the Stolte Co. from up in San Leandro." Or words to that effect.

53. Mac's early discharge from the company service — honorable, no doubt — recalls something Morgan said about him before the war. She told Hearst, "I know him well enough to realize that he does not like too long confinement to our city office and so use him on outside work as is possible." From Morgan to Hearst, June 9, 1939; Hearst/Morgan Correspondence, Morgan Collection.

54. The Hearst Papers have much to reveal about life at Wyntoon in the summer of 1943. On July 10, Willicombe asked Randy Apperson for extra bed linens from the hilltop stock; he specified enough to furnish a small hotel. A letter from Apperson to Willicombe on July 28 likewise showed how dependent Wyntoon could be on San Simeon's bounty:

> The meat and poultry order will be shipped Friday [July 30] and arrive at Dunsmuir Saturday according to the Express Company. There will be no roasters for a while as the chickens are not quite old enough for roasting, but the others will be shipped.
>
> As to the corn we will do the very best we can for the Chief. We have some golden bantam planted and can supply some of this for his use, but due to the very limited help situation I am not too sure about the beans and other corn as it is late [in the season] and help is so scarce.

Willicombe spoke of Hearst in telling Apperson on August 10, "He understands the difficulties you are under with regard to help, but you will please him greatly if you can and will supply some of these farm products." Willicombe added, "Real good stuff is getting scarcer every day."

Shortly before that, Willicombe informed Apperson on August 6 of an enviable arrangement: "Chief has told Mr. Charles Mayer of the San Francisco Examiner that he may bring a party of friends to San Simeon the weekend of August 28–29." Mayer's group may have had the place all to itself. (Hearst Papers, carton 38 on all these July and August excerpts [under "Apperson, R. W."].) Hearst also allowed an Army colonel from Camp Roberts to visit the hilltop a month later and, before his appointed date, some Navy cadets from Monterey. See Willicombe to Apperson, September 11 and 24, 1943; ibid.

ress at Wyntoon, such as it was. Perhaps she acted once more as a facilitator or sounding board, somewhat as she had in 1939. Mac's letter to her on September 29, 1943, recalls some aspects of that earlier year:[55]

> I thought you might be interested to know how much (or rather how little) was going on up here.
>
> Practically everything has been "side-tracked" except for a little stone building for wood storage between Pat's house [an employee's quarters][56] and the Bear House. It is 12′ x 17′ and as far back toward the River Bank as practical. I am enclosing rough sketch.
>
> There is one carpenter and helper and one stone-mason. The "crew" is supposed to be finishing the Bend room but there is little time left after the usual daily repairs and adjustments called for.
>
> I told Mr. Hearst about the plumbing fixtures and he is agreeable to use those on hand. There is no immediate need for them, however. The Bend Room has fixtures [awaiting it] if we get that far.
>
> Mr Hearst asked about Mrs [Doris] Day's painted shutters some time ago. I finally found four nice ones and have them nailed on office wall.

Mac's letter postdates its nearest counterparts in the Hearst Papers by two years (1941) and those in the Loorz Papers by three (1940).[57] Mac took kindly to writing, just as Hearst, Morgan, and Loorz did; and thus the very *survival* of this item from 1943 is the remarkable thing, far less so its initial existence. Unexpectedly, the letter came to light in Cal Poly's files on the Babicora project, an unrelated but concurrent subject. (This may explain the letter's presence in the Morgan Collection when so many others like it on Wyntoon are long gone.)

Above all, we'd be cheating ourselves if we didn't partake of Mac's writing and a glimpse of Wyntoon whenever and wherever they turn up. Mac had more to tell Morgan on September 29—in a dramatic departure from how his letter began:

> You may have read the Examiner account of the plane crash here. It came in very low over the [Bavarian] village with apparent engine trouble and crashed about two miles up Angel Creek canyon. We all tried to reach it but the fire was intense and country very inaccessible.

---

55. From the Hearst/Morgan Babicora Correspondence; Morgan Collection (but filed with the December 1943 items in III/06/09/30).

56. Pat (last name unknown) was mentioned by Gene Kower in his letter to Bill Murray of March 3, 1940, describing the McCloud River in flood that winter (p. 435). A longtime fixture at Wyntoon, Pat was a caretaker's helper for the Bosses, then the Kowers, and finally the Shewmakers.

57. One such item from 1941 appears on p. 459 in this chapter; see also its note 5. For the examples from 1940, see pp. 447–48 and 449–50 in that year's chapter. Exceptions to the specified (handwritten) examples in the Loorz Papers are the typewritten letters dating from Mac's stint at Sierra Ordnance; see p. 449, note 41.

Four men were killed and one bailed out, unharmed except for minor injuries. The survivor wandered in the next morning. It created a lot of excitement here and a state of normalcy has not been reached yet.

The forrest fire ignited by the plane was controlled quickly and is completely out.

The crash occurred at 11:30 P.M. last Friday [September 24].[58]

Cal Poly's files on Babicora contain three other letters from Mac. The one he wrote Morgan on November 18 starts off by saying, "There are some mantels [on paper] and a floor plan of Babicora coming down to you, which Mr Hearst wanted me to draw up." His next letter, written to her on December 12, includes this line: "Several days ago Mr Hearst brought up the Mexcian ranch house again." And Mac's last letter in this series, December 21, begins with his telling Morgan, "I am sending you (a roll) with a floor plan of Babicora showing a portion of new building tacked on to the present ranch house, which Mr Hearst asked me to draw up and send to you."[59] Mac was unquestionably involved in Babicora's evolution, not just in the work at Wyntoon, a subject likewise covered in the three letters. It's hard to say what's more uncanny through this stretch: the way Mac continued juggling Hearst's and Morgan's ideas, on par with episodes of long past, or the very fact that 1943 was providing the stage for this little-known drama.

The Hearst-Morgan letters on Babicora are too much their own entity, too far afield in substance, to be properly aired here. Occasionally, though, their content dovetails with events and details touched on earlier in this book. On November 17, for example — still in 1943 — Hearst said to Morgan, "Perhaps we should also get some tile pictures such as we set in the wall of the bungalow at Beverly Hills."[60] He was speaking of 910 Benedict Canyon Drive, a reference to the work Morgan and others, such as the artisan Frank Pellando, had done there in 1939.[61]

Hearst resumed his 1940s pattern (broken only in 1942, when he went to Mexico) of spending the holidays at Wyntoon. He didn't plan to remain there from late in 1943 right through the winter and spring of 1944, yet that's what it came

---

58. The aircraft was an Army transport plane that had taken off in Reno, bound for Seattle on a training flight. All four victims were Army personnel, as was the lone survivor (although some reports mentioned a sixth man as well, said to be a sailor who had stowed away on the flight).

59. The November letter is in III/06/09/29; the two December letters are in III/06/09/30. The last of them should be compared with Marion Suppo's letter of nearly a year before (note 38, above). Mac told Morgan on December 21, "Thanks for the information regarding the availability of Mr [Jules] Suppo. We may not need him. Our local carver [Romolo Rizzio] wants to try one head for Mr Hearst's approval and will apparently be quite hurt if we send the work to S.F. [to Suppo's workshop]." Mac also touched on the Rizzio-Suppo situation in his letter of December 12.

60. Hearst/Morgan Babicora Correspondence (III/06/09/29).

61. See p. 448 in this volume, note 39.

to: a round robin, four-seasons' layover on the McCloud, actually comprising a good eighteen months all told, from May 1943 through November 1944. Bill Murray of Hearst Sunical recalled the heart of that period when, in 1958, he wrote that "on one occasion" Hearst stayed at Wyntoon "for a full year through a very heavy winter."[62]

Mac McClure also stayed close to the hearth after 1943 ended. The Hearst Papers contain a memo dated February 8, 1944, composed by Bill Hunter in his less adroit though competent style (Willicombe's shoes being impossible for anyone to fill). Hunter quoted Mac on the recent progress at Wyntoon:

> Mr. McClure says the delay in completing the room at Bend is due to the fact that the men are diverted from that work.
>
> "Recently," he said, "we had to make some wardrobes for the Bear House, which occupied the men ten days.
>
> "There has been the wood shed and the office reconstruction,[63] and the wall under Cinderella House.
>
> "Those things are largely responsible for the delay, although those [types of] rooms always take a long time.
>
> "In the past, however, when we had 15 men we could use some [of them] for this other work, but with only two men we have to stop the work on the room when they are diverted.
>
> "Also there is a lot of work done, such as carvings, already fabricated, but not put up."[64]

Dating from a week later that same winter, 1944, a shorter memo of Hunter's suggests there was now an extra man or two on the job. "CAL SHEWMAKER

---

62. W. W. Murray, "Wyntoon," *Siskiyou Pioneer* (1958), p. 19. As of December 21, 1943, Murray's "heavy winter" had yet to take hold. The last paragraph in Mac McClure's letter to Morgan on that date (Hearst/Morgan Babicora Correspondence: see p. 491 plus its note 59) began with "The weather remains unseasonably mild. No snow has appeared yet and grass is still green." Mac also told her, "There doesn't seem to be much indication [on Hearst's part] of any trip South but a change in the weather may alter things."

Sure enough, Hearst told State Senator Jack Tenney a month later, "We are coming down from here shortly as the winter is getting too severe" (January 18, 1944; Hearst Papers, carton 40 [under "Te-Tg"]). But despite Hearst's saying he'd be glad to see Tenney in Los Angeles, he never made the trip.

63. Mac McClure to Miss Morgan, November 18, 1943: "Wyntoon goes on much the same as ever. At present, an addition is being made to Col. Willicombe office (on river side). It is rather sizable and means plumbing and heating changes. Fortunately, we were able to get some help from McCloud, temporarily." Hearst/Morgan Babicora Correspondence; Morgan Collection (III/06/09/29).

64. Although it's dated "2-8-44," the memo is unaddressed and unsigned. The style is clearly Hunter's. Hearst Papers, carton 40 (under "Hearst Memorandum[s] 1944").

[chief caretaker, successor to Gene Kower] ASKS IF MR BUCK, THE HEAD CARPENTER, MAY USE THE BROWN BUICK TO GET HIS MEN BACK AND FORTH WHILE WORKING AT THE BEND—ALSO TO GET THEM TO MEALS." Hunter also noted, "CAL WILL SUPPLY THE GAS." The rationed gas, that is. "OK," went the Hearstian scrawl in approval.[65]

Rationing prompted the master secretary himself, Colonel Willicombe, to unlimber his guns on April 2. He had appealed to the Office of Defense Transportation in Medford, Oregon, on March 18, hoping to secure an "additional mileage-motor fuel allotment for the second quarter of 1944." He found he had to be more emphatic. What he said on April 2 evokes some compelling images of Hearst the working man, Hearst the editor and executive who always had more to do than simply dream about Old Mexico, even though he was almost eighty-one:

> Our trucks are used in the operation of Mr. Hearst's business as a newspaper publisher. It is necessary to make daily trips to Dunsmuir and occasional trips to Mt. Shasta [the town of Mount Shasta] to pick up express—such as proofs, layouts, drawings, and dummies in connection with the publications of his various newspapers and periodicals; also in carrying luggage for business men who have appointments with Mr. Hearst. In addition our trucks haul newspapers, magazines, office supplies, mail, also food for his employees as well as for himself and business associates.

Willicombe reminded the agency that Dunsmuir, the "nearest railroad point," was situated "twenty-five miles from Wyntoon where Mr. Hearst conducts his business operations."[66] He didn't let on that Wyntoon was also a place where

---

65. February 14, 1944; ibid. Another memo in the same carton and folder says, "Mr. Buck, one of the carpenters, would like to borrow one of the books in the library at the Gables—'Clothes Make the Pirate.' He saw the book when he was working in there and would like to read it." Hearst gave permission. The otherwise undated memo was later marked, "Ret'd to Gables 4/11/44."

After years of liquidations and dispersals, Hearst was eager to do more than just build. He stood by, though, when the New York office passed on acquiring a parcel next to Pico Creek Stables in San Simeon, valued at roughly $7,000. See Willicombe to Apperson, February 21, 1944, and Apperson to Willicombe, February 23, 1944; Hearst Papers, carton 40 (under "Apperson, R. W."); see also the memo dated "2-17-43" [1944], ibid. (under "Hearst Memorandum[s] 1944").

66. Both items (March 18 and April 2, 1944) are in the Hearst Papers, carton 39 (under "Oa-Og"). Between those dates, a woman appealed to Hearst for employment as a feature writer but was turned down. The verdict brings his concerns of May 1943 back to mind (see note 43, above):

> Mr. Hearst instructed me to thank you for your letter of March 23rd and to say that we might call upon you later, but that for the present we are awaiting developments dependent on Japanese invasion of India, as we think England will have to put the Pacific war first if India is invaded.

From Willicombe to Adeline Gray, March 31, 1944; ibid. (under "Gra-Grd"). The only part of India

Hearst still entertained friends and certain other people who weren't there on business.

Morgan left for the Babicora again right before Willicombe submitted those appeals; it was her third and final trip to Chihuahua in Hearst's behalf. She went at least part way by plane, as she had the previous time.[67] On June 15, 1944, she spoke of "having spent the last two months wandering around down there," this while bringing Hearst up to date on conditions in Mexico. In that same letter she confirmed that a report Bill Murray had submitted on Babicora was sound. Yet the project had reached an impasse; unbeknownst to all concerned then, it would not be getting back on track. Morgan also told Hearst on June 15, "You ask for our charge [levied by her firm] on the Babicora work, which is difficult to do following fixed schedules." Therefore, she said, "If $1500 seems to you overcharging, kindly send only what [amount] below that would seem fair, and a receipted bill will be returned to you."[68] Hearst must have been satisfied; he paid the full amount a week later. Morgan recorded some small costs for July (less than seven dollars), whereupon the Babicora Ranch account lapsed at that midpoint in 1944.[69]

AS A WRITER, GEORGE LOORZ was quickly dropping from view in 1944. As a builder, though, he would reappear soon enough; we needn't worry about him or about Stolte Inc. Loorz was still adept at "rushing" and the company still had its government work, which kept everyone as busy as the proverbial bird dog.

But with the rarest exceptions, the Loorz Papers—the *surviving* papers, that is—are about to cease, just as suddenly as they began back in 1932. Few letters, telegrams, or memoranda exist to break the archival silence from 1945 onward. (Never mind the almost deafening noise that stemmed from prosperity and wartime mo-

---

legitimately in question was the extreme northeastern part—the territory of Manipur, bordering on Burma—not the vast subcontinent proper.

67. Morgan's list of travels to Mexico (as in notes 28, 31, and 45) gives a departure date of March 13, 1944; her hand notation of "plane" appears alongside.

68. All excerpts from Morgan's letter of June 15, 1944: Hearst/Morgan Babicora Correspondence; Morgan Collection (III/06/09/24). The Morgan Collection also has a letter from Flora North, dated May 30, 1944, and sent to Morgan in Mexico; Mrs. North hoped Miss Morgan wouldn't be "so swamped with work" after returning from the trip (I/01/01/24).

69. The Babicora ledger in Morgan-Forney is sparse enough to suggest the job was almost trifling: it shows just $197 in expenses such as telegrams and blueprints, but it has no entries for drafting-room time. The only entry that hints at a larger undertaking is $378 for travel expenses, accrued on the second trip (1943) and separately paid or "refunded" outside the $1,500 Morgan later collected (thus bringing the total she received to $1,878). Overall, the files at Cal Poly are more detailed, more indicative of how involved the Babicora job actually became at its height. (But not so detailed as to reveal, for instance, that Hearst was using 910 Benedict Canyon early in 1943. Hearst's and Willicombe's letters to Morgan on Babicora matters appear repeatedly on *Los Angeles Examiner* stationery; her outgoing letters are addressed in kind.)

mentum.) One of the very last items, dated November 20, 1944, is headed "CON-STRUCTION OF RADIO BUILDING AT POINT SUR LIGHT STA-TION—ANTICIPATED DELAY IN DELIVERY OF MATERIALS." The greater Monterey area, bordering on former Hearst Country, was still a Stolte toe-hold; indeed, more than just that. Not long after the war ended, the company's Monterey branch would build the Big Sur Lodge, a stone's throw from where Loorz and Randy Apperson had attended the highway opening in 1937.

To back up, though—still within 1944. If not Loorz, then Hearst and Mor-gan, especially Hearst: they can carry the archival flag for the moment. July 18 of that wartime year found the Chief writing to an unexpected party, the Colonel. Joe Willicombe liked to taste the fruits of retirement when he could, but he wouldn't be home free for another year. Hearst told the briefly absent Willicombe that they should transfer their main West Coast office, with all its files and records (of which the Bancroft Library boasts certain portions only), from Los Angeles to San Fran-cisco. "It will be more easily reached by you [from Carmel Valley]," said Hearst, "and also by me [from Wyntoon]."[70] By itself, this development is of no great importance—simply a practical matter, although it reminds us how northerly Hearst's life had become. Such a transfer, however, seems never to have been made.

The summer of 1944 marked the beginning of Hearst's second full year at Wyntoon. There's no telling how differently history might now be writ if not for what happened on August 22. It was a Tuesday, an ordinary day by all accounts. Fire is a constant threat during the dry season in forested areas, but the blaze that ruined The Gables came from within; faulty wiring caused it. Though the building wasn't a complete loss (its gutted shell stood for years to come), it may as well have been. Gone was the dining room, where Hearst and his guests had convened, much as they had (and would again) in the sole dining room that Casa Grande provided at San Simeon. Gone, too, were the library and other strategic rooms, plus numer-ous guest quarters. "It was an awful calamity," wrote Willicombe on August 26, an-swering one of many consoling letters.[71] Apart from the loss of art objects, wrought iron, carved woodwork—the usual Wyntoon attributes—daily convenience and tradition were also lost. The billiard room in The Bend, farther down the river

---

70. John Tebbel gave as good an account of Willicombe's status in the mid-1940s as can be found in print. "Even after his supposed retirement, he came up twice a week to his San Francisco office from his home in Carmel Valley, and there he kept a knowledgeable finger on the pulse of the whole San Francisco area." From *The Life and Good Times of William Randolph Hearst*, p. 292. Hearst to Willicombe on July 18, 1944, is from the Hearst Papers, carton 40 (under "Will-Wilz").

71. Willicombe to John Coffin in New York (prompted by Coffin to Hearst from Montreal, August 24, 1944); Hearst Papers, carton 39 (both items under "Coa-Cok"). Tebbel cited 1943 as the date of the fire; *Life and Good Times*, p. 293. Boutelle cited 1945 in *Julia Morgan*, p. 230 (the accompa-nying picture shows The Bend, not The Gables); see also p. 247, note 4, in Boutelle.

from The Gables, became the improvised dining room on which the Bavarian Village now depended. If not for the war, Hearst would probably have bid Wyntoon a quick good-bye. Instead, he and the party toughed it out for three more months.

Morgan was willing as usual to do what she could. "Mr. Murray telephoned that he located a good man through Miss Morgan to check on the electrical system here." It was September 14 by then. "OK," scrawled Hearst on an unsigned message from Hunter. "We can put him up at the Bend."[72]

They couldn't do much other putting up, though—not by preferred standards. "It is impossible for us to have visitors," Hearst told Helen Clark Park on October 20; Mrs. Park was an old friend who'd asked him for an appointment. "We are burnt out," he bluntly explained. "We have insufficient help and insufficient accommodations and are planning to leave here ourselves."[73]

Another month passed before he made good on that forecast. And when he finally did, he did so with suitable flair. Thanksgiving, by Roosevelt's decree, now fell on the fourth Thursday in November; for 1944 that meant Thursday the twenty-third. Hearst probably observed the holiday at Wyntoon before he left, evidently on the weekend. By Saturday, November 25, the word was being transmitted far and wide to his editors: the old man's mail and newspapers were no longer to be sent to Dunsmuir or Mount Shasta for delivery to Wyntoon. No, the Chief was heading south—to San Simeon, entourage and all, the war and the rationing and the various other drawbacks be damned. He couldn't know it at the time, nor could anyone else, but he would never see Wyntoon again.[74]

That's not to say, though, that he'd lost interest in the place. He certainly hadn't. Wyntoon was still one of his sacred possessions. The day after Thanksgiving itself, he learned that the War Production Board had approved his application to

---

72. Hearst Papers, carton 40 (under "Hearst Memorandum[s] 1944"). The man Morgan recommended, Harry Blohm, may have been the same one that Hearst later found wanting: "Tell Mr. Murray the electrician that had charge of the work at Wyntoon is a complete washout and we should not have anything more to do with him." Quoted by Hunter on December 21, 1944; ibid.

73. Hearst Papers, carton 39 (under "Cl-Cn"). Mrs. Park had written to Hearst on October 17, 1944; ibid.

74. The question of when Hearst returned to San Simeon in the mid-1940s runs parallel to the one regarding his whereabouts on December 7, 1941: misconceptions and false itineraries abound. The Hearst Papers have specific evidence of his move from Wyntoon. See, for example, Neville to Forsythe, November 26, 1944, in carton 39 (under "Nea-Nev") and Van Ettisch to Hunter, November 27, 1944, in carton 40 (under "Van Ettisch"). The evidence of his staying put at San Simeon through December 1944 is also specific. In fact, with scattered exceptions the hilltop remained his headquarters, his principal address for two and a half years after he left Wyntoon—until the well-known date of May 1947, which marked his final departure from San Simeon.

Meanwhile, the Hearst Papers contain very few documents from the first several months of 1945. But Hearst's preponderant use of the hilltop through that stretch can be sufficiently charted by other means.

spend $20,000 on construction at Wyntoon. He'd long wanted to replace the tin-kering there, just as Mac McClure had, with a more concerted effort. This was the first real breakthrough in at least three years. Bill Hunter, the secretary whose memo brought Hearst the good news on that Friday, November 24, posed a ques-tion in turn. "Shall we go ahead and arrange to put Mr. Loorz's men on the ranch [Wyntoon] payroll? Mr. Loorz is willing."

Hearst was also willing. "Yes," he said in economical reply.[75]

SO LOORZ AND STOLTE INC. were back in the picture, even if the Loorz Papers no longer were. Or to be more exact, no longer *are*. The increased activities of Stolte Inc., and of Loorz in turn, were generating new records that, despite their extensiveness, have since been lost. And thus the Loorz Papers as we know them — originally filed in the quaint old letter boxes by George Loorz himself, as well as by Conrad Gamboni and Ray Van Gorden — are the records that reached an abrupt end late in 1944. In this same present-tense mode, the Hearst Papers are about to drop from view: the years 1945 and 1946 — which were once extensive, no doubt — are thinly represented at the Bancroft. In contrast, 1947 comprises dozens of files.

All the more reason, then, to include items from December 1944, that month in which Hearst had Christmas at San Simeon for the first time since 1938. Equipped with new funds for Wyntoon, he went ahead in 1944–45 with plans that had been gestating there since Mac McClure returned in 1943 (when some minor building had also been done); plans had also been gestating since 1942, when Mor-gan went there on her Angel House account; for that matter, they'd been gestating since 1941 and even earlier, with carpentry and other work being done each season by pocket-sized crews. If, in fact, during the war itself there was a protracted time when no such efforts were made, it would only have been in 1942 or early in 1943 — if even then. An old craftsman or two could have been tinkering for Hearst even while Mac was at Honey Lake on the Sierra Ordnance job. At any rate, Bill Hunt-er's memo of December 1, 1944, pertained to The Bend, as did the larger-scale work that Loorz and Stolte Inc. were about to tackle at Wyntoon, even as Hearst dug in at San Simeon for what became a lengthy stay:

> Neither Mr. McClure nor Mr. Shewmaker wants Romolo [Rizzio], the wood carver, to work at Wyntoon.
>
> Mr. McClure says he is a wood carver, and that is all, and there is no work for him there.
>
> In addition, his health is very bad and he is liable to have a stroke any time. . . .

---

75. Hearst Papers, carton 40 (under "Hearst Memorandum[s] 1944").

It is the general impression that he is pretty well fixed financially.

Mr. Shewmaker suggested that if you merely want to pension him, it would be better to leave him in San Francisco, as he would be just a liability at Wyntoon.[76]

Hearst's reply, which Hunter requested, has yet to turn up. The other memos of December vintage are too spotty to put the December 1 item in clearer perspective.[77] Were Mac and Cal Shewmaker simply trying to shut down for the winter? If so, how should the $20,000 figure and Loorz's willingness be assessed?

One of Hunter's memos dates from the last day of 1944. "Mr. Rankin arrived this afternoon. He expects to be here [at San Simeon] three or possibly four days." That was the plumber Jim Rankin, of course (whose name had also figured in Hearst and Morgan's Babicora dealings). Hunter finished the memo by asking Hearst, "Do you want to see him about anything?"

This time, Hearst penciled a reply. "Yes. I would like very much to see him. Perhaps Mr. McClure could come up before Mr. Rankin leaves."[78] The meaning of "come up" can be analyzed. A plausible hunch is that Mac was in Los Angeles for the holidays, or possibly for a longer off-season break, a familar pattern in earlier years. Hearst wanted to confer with him as well as with Rankin. But about Wyntoon? San Simeon? Both places? A letter three months later from Loorz to his oldest son, Don—one falling outside the George Loorz Papers—suggests that

---

76. Hearst Papers, carton 40 (under "Hearst Memorandum[s] 1944"). On pensioning and the like: Hearst made provisions selectively for certain people. The Loorz Papers contain an example from back on May 15, 1941. A workman named Bill Martin told Loorz, "Now after being in San Jose Hospital for 10 days (thanks to Mr Hearst & Murray) I am now in a convalescent home, and expect to be out in a couple of weeks." Martin hoped Loorz could use him at Jolon, where the Stolte Co. had a job on the new Hunter Liggett Military Reservation. In answering on May 19 that year, Loorz cautioned Martin about the extreme heat in the Jolon district—"not too encouraging for a convalescent man to work in."

77. In a completely separate vein, a letter from the editor of the *New York Mirror*, a Hearst tabloid, gives a distinct impression of The Enchanted Hill in the period right after Hearst returned there from Wyntoon:

> As a first-time visitor to San Simeon, I cannot help but tell you what a rich experience it was for me. You have created there something of complete and enduring beauty. You have shown that the wonderful artistry of man is—as all true artists intend—something to be lived with for its daily inspiration. I am sure all who have known the pleasure of San Simeon's hospitality must feel as I do.

From Glenn Neville to Hearst, December 17, 1944; Hearst Papers, carton 39 (under "Nea-Nev"). About two weeks later, Frank J. Taylor of the American Merchant Marine Institute wrote to Hearst, addressing the letter to him at Wyntoon—an oversight reproduced without comment in Tomkins, *Selections from the Writings and Speeches of William Randolph Hearst*, pp. 742–43.

78. Hearst Papers, carton 40 (under "Hearst Memorandum[s] 1944").

Wyntoon was the main subject on the table when Hearst and Rankin met, most likely with Mac also in attendance.

Despite the brevity of the December 31 memo (both on Hunter's part and on Hearst's), its content is strikingly different from many similar communications of former times. In those examples, Hearst's reply would often refer to Miss Morgan, who perhaps could "come down." Had she conceded the field to Mac by the eve of 1945? She may have in large part (in ways reminiscent of 1939). But she was by no means out of the picture, in spite of Babicora's inactive status for the past several months. On December 20, 1944, she billed Hearst for $500; it applied to recent plans for one of his buildings that she'd last worked on in the 1920s, the Post-Enquirer newspaper plant in Oakland. (Hearst had been approached in 1943 about parting with the Oakland paper; Willicombe had conveyed Hearst's unwavering response: "positively none of our papers is for sale." Indeed, in November 1944 Hearst remarked to a fellow publisher, Walter Annenberg, about conditions that had also prevailed for some time in a closely related field: "all magazines seem to be doing very well these days . . . everybody is prosperous.")[79] Just the same, the new Post-Enquirer job through Morgan was evidently stillborn, though not before Jim LeFeaver prepared the estimate for her, as he'd done a few years earlier on the Darbee Mausoleum and the Park Museum.[80]

Hearst paid Morgan the full $500 on January 10 of the new year, 1945. Her records show that in 1944 he had been her only measurable client; three quarters of the $2,000 she'd billed him had been for the Babicora account, the rest of it for the Post-Enquirer Building.[81] She still had her office in the Merchants Exchange

---

79. See Lester J. Clarke to Hearst, November 13, 1943, and Willicombe to Clarke, November 16, 1943; Hearst Papers, carton 39 (under "1943 Samples"). See also Annenberg to Hearst, November 7, 1944, and Hearst to Annenberg, November 27, 1944; Hearst Papers, carton 41 (under "1944 Samples").

80. LeFeaver's estimate on the Post-Enquirer job commanded $50, whereas the Darbee estimate added $172 to the running tally on that larger job (Morgan-Forney ledgers). LeFeaver's name doesn't appear in the Park Museum account. Several years later, though, Walter Steilberg said that in 1941 LeFeaver estimated the work entailed by Santa Maria de Ovila, following Hearst's gift of the monastery to San Francisco. See Steilberg to Herbert Fleishhaker [Fleishhacker] and Walter Heil, January 23, 1950; Morgan Collection (III/06/09/09). See also Steilberg to James Cook, June 11, 1959; Steilberg Collection, Environmental Design Archives. The pertinent dates and events in both letters reflect Steilberg's memory working at full power.

81. Both the Babicora and the Post-Enquirer payments were compensatory dollars, not commission dollars. Some other examples of that distinction are touched on in Appendix B, pp. 531–33. Hearst's payments on the KYA radio project of 1946 were also compensatory; see p. 512, note 19. Things may, in fact, have changed in such matters since the prewar years; see pp. 418–19, note 33, for that period; see also pp. 446–47, notes 36 and 37.

Meanwhile, under the name "Mr Vincent" for the period 1940–46 (as in note 51, above), Morgan recorded just $2.75 in expenses for 1944.

(granted, a smaller office since the end of the thirties). Come the summer of 1945, she'd be heading to Mexico and Guatemala (flying, no less), yet she wouldn't be making the trip for Hearst's sake.[82]

How did she manage? The answer couldn't be simpler. She reached under her mattress, as it were, drawing again and again on her substantial earnings from Hearst to replenish her purse—to pay for travel, to pay her office rent, to pay for her homes in San Francisco and Monterey, to pay her secretary and other help, to pay for gifts and assorted generosities, which in past years had included staff bonuses. She lived long enough to spend practically every dollar. But as of January 1945, when she turned seventy-three, she still had twelve years to go.

All the while she'd been solvent, very solvent, a burden to no one. She'd also been waiting, waiting—waiting for her big chance, which no longer had anything to do with San Simeon or Wyntoon. She seems to have given up those ghosts. Her heart had long been set on something else instead, on the old monastery in San Francisco, Santa Maria de Ovila, the former Park Museum account that had finally lapsed in 1944. The revival of that project, along with its bona fide pursuit and an ample budget that might be hers after the war ended—*that* had endured as her most compelling dream.[83]

---

82. "Aug. 27, 1945 to Guatamala [*sic*] and Mexico" is the fourth of five entries for travel in the years 1942–46 (1946 datebook, Morgan-Forney Collection); a notation of "plane" goes with the 1945 entry.

83. Morgan had clung to hope each time the subject came up. "Dr. Heil [Walter Heil, Director of the M. H. de Young Museum] said he has to appear before the finance committee of the Board of Supervisors at 4 P.M. today and doesn't know how long that would take. Said he could come down to see you after that, or he will be out at the Museum tomorrow [in Golden Gate Park]." From Lilian Forney to Morgan, September 28, 1944; loose note in Morgan's 1946 datebook, Morgan-Forney Collection. In the meantime, effective July 1944, the old Park Museum account gained its last entry.

1945 and Later

Episodes and Epitaphs

SANTA MARIA DE OVILA had been on Morgan's mind since at least 1938, when Hearst began taking steps toward its disposition. More than six years later—on February 5, 1945—she wrote about the monastery to Walter Steilberg; he was still a structural engineer with the public works division of the Navy in Kodiak, Alaska, where he'd been assigned shortly after Pearl Harbor. Morgan thought so highly of Santa Maria's prospects that, with Steilberg's help (and *only* with his help), she felt certain they could recapture the spirit of the Middle Ages—indeed, more effectively than had been done in New York with The Cloisters, under the auspices of the Metropolitan Museum. That was a bold claim to make. Alas, there were funding problems, she told him; and a delay till "the *second year after* the close of the war" could now be expected—unless private money were to materialize beforehand.[1]

Morgan also stayed in touch with Hearst through these waning months of the war. February 20 found her writing to him twice at San Simeon. In one letter she bemoaned his loss of The Gables at Wyntoon, an event six months in the past that she'd found inexpressible ever since.[2] In the other letter, she spoke of the financial maze she'd been working through at Bill Murray's request, an effort showing

---

1. The handwritten letter (retained by Morgan or returned to her) is from the series Personal Correspondence at Cal Poly (I/07/02/36, though not listed in the *Descriptive Guide*). Dorothy Wormser Coblentz, formerly of Morgan's office, said in 1974 of Santa Maria's potential, "It would have been cloisters to out-cloister all cloisters"—a building "more beautiful," that is, than its counterpart in New York. From *The Julia Morgan Architectural History Project*, Vol. II, p. 129.

Morgan's letter to Steilberg originated on the same day that *Time* published "Hearst *Redivivus*" (February 5, 1945), pp. 63–64. "Hearst is making money again," the article began. It also noted that he had recently "moved back into his feudal barony of San Simeon, which had been dark for three years." The only thing lacking was that *Time* didn't specify three *and a half* years.

2. Morgan's letter about The Gables is from the "Hearst Warehouse Files" in New York; see Sara Boutelle's acknowledgements in *Julia Morgan*, p. 248. The date February 20, 1945, made Boutelle think the fire occurred that year; see p. 495 in the present volume, note 71. She cited two additional Morgan letters from the New York files (June 5 and 13, 1945); both concerned other subjects and were sent to Hearst, who presumably was at San Simeon (*Julia Morgan*, p. 215).

that roughly 4.7 million dollars had been spent on San Simeon from its inception. Oft-quoted in recent years, the figure pertains to Hearst's expenditures through Morgan (primarily stemming from the Hearst Construction Fund). The figure excludes any of his expenditures through the Hilltop Fund or other disbursements that fell outside her bounds. Still, 4.7 million dollars represents the lion's share of his outlay on construction at San Simeon, measured from 1919 to the eve of World War II.[3]

Despite these distinctive matters involving Morgan, the first half of 1945 is frustratingly sketchy. It's a godsend, then, that a certain letter from George Loorz to Don Loorz survives;[4] written in Alameda on a "restful" Sunday at home, March 18, it was sent by Loorz to his son at Fort Benning, Georgia, where the young Army draftee, now nineteen years old, was enrolled in Officer Candidate School:

> Warren McClure called me an hour ago from McCloud. Mr. Hearst asked him to have me come up and look over some more alterations that he intends doing. So as soon as I can get train reservations I'll make that trip. Right now I dont prefer the work but the war work may stop abruptly any day and we will need all the work we can get. I cant afford to burn down anything now and repent later.

Although Mac had returned to Wyntoon in recent months, Hearst was holding fast at San Simeon, despite what the usual quick wording in Loorz's letter might imply.

Come April, Hearst and Marion Davies did, in fact, leave the hilltop to go north, but San Francisco was their destination, not Wyntoon; their trip overlapped

---

3. Cal Poly's Hearst/Morgan Correspondence has Morgan's other letter of February 20, 1945, in which she told Hearst about the 4.7 million dollars. It was addressed to him at San Simeon—one of several indicators of his whereabouts at this point, helping to offset the thinness of the Hearst Papers for 1945. See also the Personal Correspondence series in the Morgan Collection (I/07/02/29): a letter of May 26, 1945, from Hearst to Morgan appears on La Cuesta Encantada stationery, addressed to her home at 2229 Divisadero Street, San Francisco.

The list of expenditures from 1919 to 1942 first appeared in Thomas R. Aidala, *Hearst Castle: San Simeon* (1981), appendix on pp. 235–36. An astounding revelation at the time, fresh on the heels of the Morgan Collection's debut at Cal Poly, the new data have long since become old data, widely disseminated through the public tours at San Simeon. (True, Aidala erred in saying, for example, that "laborers received about $1 per day"; overall, though, his appendix has weathered the years well.) Victoria Kastner has amplified the 1919–1942 data to include 1.3 million in construction costs for the postwar period (as recalled by Maurice McClure in 1981); see *Hearst Castle: The Biography of a Country House* (2000), pp. 206–07. But a fuller accounting of Hearst's expenditures—based on hitherto unsuspected factors, like the Hilltop Fund—lies years ahead. Indeed, its time may never come: too many records are missing. See the introduction to Appendix B in this volume, pp. 546–49.

4. The letter (first mentioned on p. 498) is courtesy of Don Loorz: while reading the last part of this book in manuscript, he was inspired to dig deeper in his personal files than ever before. Don uncovered not only the item from March 18, 1945, but also the one from October of that year, quoted on p. 504 in this chapter. He rushed copies of both letters to me on January 2, 2002.

with the United Nations conference in the city by the bay. They were back on the hill in time for Hearst's eighty-second birthday on April 29. It was the first one he'd observed there since 1940.[5] April also marked the full-fledged retirement of Joe Willicombe. Bill Hunter was fully in stride already as the main secretary, a demanding job that required steady help from Estelle Forsythe (whom Jud Smelser mentioned as far back as 1938).[6] Yet in matters of construction and the like, either at Wyntoon under Mac McClure and the Stolte forces or at San Simeon itself, the records are too spotty through this stretch to be of much further help.

Everything changed, though, by the late summer of 1945. Oral accounts and reminiscences run thick from then on, the gist of them being that Hearst plunged back into the building game at San Simeon—with emphasis on the Recreation Wing of Casa Grande—once the war was completely over. It's true; he did; he'd been poised in readiness for weeks, maybe for months. And he did likewise at Wyntoon, which all the while had lent itself to smaller-scale work as it was, more so than San Simeon had. (The prevailing view, however, has long been that he did nothing at *either* estate until the war ended—a more plausible thought in San Simeon's case, given its type of construction—whereupon large crews got right to work at both places, never mind the planning and logistics that such overnight efforts would require. For San Simeon, the view coincides neatly with the erroneous belief that he didn't return there from Wyntoon until the summer of 1945.)

Morgan chose that very moment, August 1945, to embark on her trip to Mexico and Guatemala; if only we knew what arrangements she and Hearst had made.[7] Naturally he had Mac McClure to depend on. George Loorz, meanwhile, had become an absentee player where San Simeon was concerned. Day by day, that distant job and the equally distant one at Wyntoon were now in the able hands of defense-work veterans like Maurice McClure, Frank Gendrich, and dozens of others that Loorz and Fred Stolte delegated from Oakland.

Exceptions to such rules are always welcome. About mid-October, Loorz got

5. David Nasaw knew that Hearst and Miss Davies were at San Simeon before they went to San Francisco in April 1945; see *The Chief*, p. 582. Earlier, though, he adopted a prevalent view in saying that "Hearst celebrated the nation's victory over Japan by returning from Wyntoon with Marion to take up residence at San Simeon" (p. 580).

6. See p. 396 in this volume. Forsythe's name appears with increasing prominence in the Hearst Papers from the early 1940s onward. For a brief period in 1946, a young man named Roland Dragon provided clerical support; long afterward he said he had been Hearst's private secretary that year (and for part of 1947 also), a claim that Hunter and Forsythe would have found startling.

7. She left on August 27, according to the list of travels in her 1946 datebook; see p. 500 in the previous chapter, note 82. A postcard from Cecilia Graham, dated August 30, was too late to catch the departing Morgan: "If you have not already flown away I want to send a 'Bon Voyage' from your friends at Lake Tahoe. . . . Have a beautiful trip. All success in finding what you are after!" Morgan Collection (I/07/02/21).

off another letter to his son Don, who was newly commissioned as a second lieuten-
ant and had recently gone to the Philippines. Loorz omitted the date; but in mentioning his recent birthday (Saturday, October 13, when he turned forty-seven), he
set the stage for recounting events that took place sometime in the following week.
Among them was this episode:

> I went to the office [in Oakland] the next morning to work while I waited for the
> fog to lift here and at San Simeon so that I could fly down for an appointment
> [with Hearst] about more work at the airport etc. I was both confused and busy
> until it looked a bit favorable about 3 P.M., still bad in in [*sic*] San Simeon, but I
> was so anxious to go, we flew down [the pilot was Vic Voight of Stolte Inc.], cir-
> cled Pine Mountain but could not get down thru the dense fog, had to return
> quickly to King City to land just at darkness. Maurice and Hazel [McClure]
> drove over to get me arriving at about ten [P.M.] (He is San Simeon Superinten-
> dent, she is [the equivalent of] Ray Van Gorden there, mess hall and office). We
> arrived back in San Simeon a little after one [A.M.] and I went up to my room at
> Appersons' (Randy had warned Maurice that I was to come there [to the Ranch
> House] and if I failed he would be very angry at me). He left the light on, I walked
> in quietly and to the room but they heard me, he stepped to the door of his room
> and said "hellow fellow," very happily, she [Fran Apperson] shouted from her bed
> "Hello Georgie." I went promptly to bed, got up first, ate breakfast with them and
> off to business. However, he [Randy] wanted lots of things done like, a new equip-
> ment shed, road from S.S. to ranch yard oiled and a few things on the hilltop on
> ranch accounts [revolving funds], then he stayed with me all day, excusing him-
> self when I had my interview with Mr. Hearst and waited to take me back [to
> King City?] so I could fly away promptly at 4 P.M. or before so I could land, which
> I did, just before dark in Belmont [near San Mateo].[8]

His description sounds like a homecoming, as though Loorz hadn't been to
San Simeon since before the war—perhaps not since the time he and Randy Apperson looked at old equipment on the hilltop back in the summer of 1941.

Likewise in that first autumn of the postwar era, the magazine *Stolte Blueprint*
contained invaluable details on both the Wyntoon and the San Simeon jobs that
Stolte Inc. was handling for Hearst. In an unsigned article, the *Blueprint* of October
31, 1945, reported the following under "Cast Stone Shop Opened":

> Stolte Inc. is gratified to announce establishment of a cast stone and plaster shop
> at our 85th Avenue Yard [on the corner of San Leandro Street in Oakland].
> Here, under the guidance of Superintendent Fred Jurgewitz, an experienced unit

---

8. Courtesy of Don Loorz, January 2, 2002 (see note 4, above).

of artisans will model, mold, and cast a wide variety of objects both useful and ornamental.

Fred's initial task will be the creation of ornamental plastics for the Hearst estate at Wyntoon. In addition to this, however, he will be open to orders from the general public—in fact, is keenly interested in expanding the use and appreciation of this type of work.[9]

That same fall issue of the *Blueprint* contained some newsy tidbits by Chuck Carlen, who touched on Wyntoon (among several other subjects) under "Who's Where?":

Frank Gendrich left the Berglund job at Napa in the capable hands of Messrs. Langbehn and Winterholder, and hied him to Wyntoon where, from his letters, one judges the trout make swimming almost impossible. We're glad to see Bill Gatschet up there along with Morris Adams.

Elsewhere in his column of October 31, Carlen also touched on Wyntoon's southern counterpart, where work had kicked into high gear after the war ended in August. He included some names—John McFadden's, most notably—that hadn't appeared in the annals for a long time:

San Simeon has called a slew of Stolte indefatiguables [*sic*] south: Maurice and Hazel McClure, John D. McFadden, Peter H. Petersen, Gerald E. Franklin, Dewey O. Trout, Robert L. Simons, Otto Olson, Roy Evans, Ralph Layman, Earl Tomasini, and Valentine Georges.

All like the job, and they think Mr. Hearst pretty generous in affording the Stolte crowd the use of the Roman pool.

A drawing by the staff cartoonist, Bill O'Malley, appeared next to the "Who's Where?" column. It showed two men marveling at a huge basin of water, which towered over them and some nearby trees: "When Mr. Hearst orders a birdbath he ain't woofin'!"

The *Stolte Blueprint* of December 21, 1945, contained articles on both San Simeon and Wyntoon. Hazel McClure contributed the one on San Simeon. Her husband, Maurice (who was unrelated, of course, to Mac McClure), could well be proud of his title as construction superintendent on that job: the torch had been passed to him by Loorz, a man he had long revered. Hazel's article was entitled "Life Fit for a King at San Simeon Estate":

Stolteans from various jobs are more and more heading for the Hearst estate at San Simeon. They've heard tell by now of how every day is finished off by a swim

---

9. As was mentioned on p. 477 in the previous chapter, note 27, the copies of *Stolte Blueprint* consulted for this book are from Don Loorz's collection.

in the magnificent Roman plunge, heated to 80 degrees; of how employees are later invited to attend Mr. Hearst's private theater where a show is given nightly.

We've discovered low gear in order to wind our way through the zebras, yaks, oryx, kangaroos, camels, emus, llamas, and many other animals that roam freely over the hills.[10]

As for personalities: Snuffy Layman is happy with his new loader. Otto Olson is still rushing to get 12 hours work into 8. John McFadden, in charge of electrical and stonework, is a handy man indeed. Roy Evans, he and his family well again, is getting those well known Stolte results.

Frank Wilson is pushing an eight-inch pipeline from the new reservoir on the Hearst ranch to the town of San Simeon for fire protection. Bill Igo is handling the pipe when the dozer is down.

Maurice McClure has his eye on the 73 dachsunds in Mr. Hearst's kennels. And him with two cocker spaniels already and the promise of a great dane next spring!

As for myself, I'm in the kitchen doubling for cook and helper who up and left us. Not boasting, you understand, but I drew and cut up 15 chickens and had them in the pan the other day in an hour and 20 minutes.

The pictures adjoining the San Simeon article showed Hazel McClure at the Neptune Pool, Gerald Franklin at the tennis courts, and Maurice McClure at Casa del Sol—all of them looking perfectly at home in their glamorous surroundings. A healthy dose of humor and good fun characterized each issue of *Stolte Blueprint*, and Hazel's article fell squarely within the tradition.

The companion article in that *Blueprint* of December 21, 1945, was entitled "Wyntoon Has a Heat Wave in the Snow"; the author was identified as "Mr. X-mas":

It seems that one of our best men—a fellow named Morris Adams—was shaking like a palsy patient on one of the cold afternoons we've been having recently. Frank Gendrich felt sorry for him and told him to build a little fire in a firepot for himself and the other boys.

---

10. Furthermore, many animals (or their offspring) had long been roaming freely outside the zoo acreage itself. In 1930 a fire trapped some of them in a canyon below The Enchanted Hill. Cowboys knocked the fence down; yet after the danger passed, the men could never round up all the animals that had fled; hence the Barbary sheep (aoudads), the African pygmy goats, and certain other tenacious species that have flourished ever since on rocky slopes and summits, often miles from the old zoo. This account was shared with me in 1973 by Walter Warren of San Simeon Creek, a rancher (now deceased) whose family holdings still harbor numerous descendants of the Hearst zoo.

The fire figured several times in the Hearst/Morgan Correspondence of August 1930 (Morgan Collection), even though nothing was ever said about missing animals. However, Bill Hearst reported "no animals hurt" when he cabled his father that summer in Germany, telling him about the fire (undated telegram in the Hearst Papers, carton 11 [under "1930 Samples"]).

He did, but the fire didn't seem to warm him. Nobody knows what he did next to build up the fire. All any of us know is that suddenly the whole building felt like it was ablaze.

The building wasn't—but Morris was. What we saw of him, though, was a streak of fire as he zoomed past us in the direction of a snowdrift. When we pulled him out the seat of his pants was missing; the seat of his underwear was gone; part of his understanding was even impaired. . . .

It has snowed heavily here in the past 24 hours so that there are now about two and a half feet of snow on the ground. The roads are hard to navigate, since they are mostly steep and narrow.

Frank Gendrich, for example, slid into a ditch on his way down to the Bend this morning. With the help of a lot of the fellows, like Gustav Buck, Bill Gatschet, and Morris—whose arms are all right—we finally got the pickup back on the road. On the next trip Frank walked.

Gendrich, formerly of San Francisco and San Luis Obispo, superintended the work at Wyntoon throughout the postwar period. He had been a Stolte regular since 1936, when he built the Cambria Grammar School while based in San Luis.

Stolte Blueprint was "published periodically" by Stolte Inc. "in the interests of its personnel"—as many as six times in its peak year of 1943. Two issues appeared in 1944, three in 1945, and then two again in 1946. Single year-end issues appeared in 1947 and 1948.

IN THE MIDST OF THAT SPAN a knowing voice spoke once more; on April 29, 1946, George Loorz wrote again to his son Don, who was back on active duty in the Philippines after a stint in New Guinea. Well into his long letter, Loorz included a paragraph that, from our vantage point today, pulls the curtains back on the Hearst saga as never before:

I am flying to San Simeon in the morning. Mr. Hearst and Marion bought three fine estates in Beverly Hills, one $250,000, one $110,000 and one $63,000. They now want us to start remodelling same but I fear C.P.A. [the Civilian Production Administration] will not permit it and I hate to tell him so. He celebrated his 83rd birthday today. I do hope he enjoyed it and that he is in [a] fine mood tomorrow.[11]

---

11. Courtesy of Don Loorz, October 2, 1999. "I told you about business," Don's father also said in that letter, "it is terrific." Stolte Inc. had "nearly $6,000,000 of private work and about $3,000,000 [in government work] to complete at Fairfield." The Fairfield-Suisun Army Air Base was a joint venture with Morrison-Knudsen, one of the founding members of Six Companies.

An unrelated yet concurrent matter: Morgan's 1946 datebook contains a tucked-in letter from Bjarne Dahl, Jr., written on May 1, 1946, soon after he turned sixteen. (His father, after working for Morgan on the Honolulu Y in the 1920s, had remained in the Hawaiian Islands to pursue architecture through other employers; but see p. 198, note 91. Bjarne, Jr., born in the Islands in 1930, stayed

We can easily visualize Loorz's bypassing King City this time and using the Hearst landing strip of the 1930s, one soon to be outclassed by a much larger strip that Stolte Inc. built later in 1946. We can also imagine the cramping of Hearst's style by the CPA, the new federal agency charged with "reconversion" to a peacetime economy, an agency that ceased operating by the end of 1946. As for Hearst's recent birthday, we can read all about it in *Newsweek*, which covered the event in its next issue.[12]

But *three* estates in Beverly Hills? The well-known story is that Miss Davies bought *two* estates in 1946, the second one only after Hearst, who was starting to fade, vetoed the first one as a place for his convalescence, as an urban refuge from San Simeon's remoteness. The most prominent of the three, at any rate—bought like the others at fire-sale prices that cursed such properties—was the former Milton Getz residence at 1007 N. Beverly Drive. What a steal! The "Beverly House" was a mansion on the Hearstian scale, an imposing yet sumptuous Mediterranean example that stood on several hilltop acres. (Gordon Kaufmann had designed it in the gilded twenties, before doing his better-known work on Hoover Dam and before designing Santa Anita Park, the new racetrack Hearst and his friends visited in 1935.) The old Davies home that Loorz's crew had remodeled in 1940, nearly a mile away at 1700 Lexington Road, was a minor building compared to the Getz residence; and the still-smaller house at 910 Benedict Canyon (where Louis B.

---

with Morgan in San Francisco for several months in 1942.) Nonetheless, Sara Boutelle's interview with the elder Dahl and his son in 1975 includes some misleading statements; see *The Julia Morgan Architectural History Project*, Vol. II, pp. 145–55. For example, the father said that Camille Rossi, whom he called his "good friend," worked at San Simeon for twenty years. More important, the father invoked the Morgan myth by saying of the woman behind it: "And every Christmas she divided up all her dividends with all her employees. She didn't keep anything for herself; everyone was her big family." Miss Morgan did, in fact, pay periodic bonuses, as the Morgan-Forney data attest; but Bjarne Dahl (or his son) would have known as little about her finances as the Morgan Norths did, probably even less.

12. "The Seer of San Simeon" (May 6, 1946), pp. 62–64. Morgan remembered his birthday; under April 26, her 1946 datebook says "wrote to WRH—mailed 27th." And then on the twenty-ninth itself: "WRHs Day." More accessible, the *Newsweek* article is one of the prime examples of Hearstiana hailing from these later years; it includes a brief interview with "the Seer" himself.

Among books in the Hearstiana field, a rare portrait of the man and his castle—in fact, better than rare, more like priceless—stems from a trip to the hill by Ludwig Bemelmans right before the war ended, back in March 1945. The result was his satirical yet humane and perceptive "Visit to San Simeon," a chapter in *To the One I Love the Best* (New York, 1955), pp. 151–72. From late wartime as well (the exact date is unknown), a less artful but still uncommon account appears in *My Parents: A Differing View*, by James Roosevelt with Bill Libby (Chicago, 1976), pp. 191–92. Franklin and Eleanor's oldest son had his own views indeed. Ludwig Bemelmans, speaking of dinner at San Simeon, said the food was "mediocre and badly served." James Roosevelt, speaking of lunch during his separate visit, said it was "fabulous."

Mayer now lived) was utterly outclassed. The Beverly House was a place to be reckoned with.[13]

Cutting through federal red tape and paying lip service to his encroaching mortality, Hearst the perennial builder did well for himself on three fronts in 1946: at San Simeon, at Wyntoon, and at one or more of the new places in Beverly Hills. Of these far-flung locales, San Simeon was what he called home for the entire year, except for some quick trips that he made to the Los Angeles area.[14] By having been on The Enchanted Hill almost continuously since late in 1944, and by remaining there till the spring of 1947, he set records for protracted stays; they far surpassed the five months he logged in 1934–35, after his return from Europe, or his long stay in 1940, the year Wyntoon got flooded.

In this twilight period, as much as in the heyday of the 1930s, the proximity of youth helped sustain him. Enthusiasts like Hazel McClure were as vital to the

---

13. Of Hearst's biographers from 1952 to 1961 (Coblentz, Tebbel, Winkler, Swanberg), John Tebbel led the way in describing 1007 N. Beverly Drive; see *The Life and Good Times of William Randolph Hearst* (1952), pp. 10–13. Tebbel barely touched on "three [other] large houses" that Miss Davies owned, evidently in the same town (p. 16). It remained for Fred Lawrence Guiles in *Marion Davies* (1972), pp. 328–29, to mention "a seven-acre estate on Lexington Road in Beverly Hills, only two long blocks from her first mansion in California [at 1700 Lexington]." The new place on Lexington cost $250,000, said Guiles, a price Loorz mentioned; but Hearst disliked "its closeness to the street," hence the purchase of the Milton Getz place on Beverly Drive for a paltry $120,000 (pp. 329–30). Loorz's closest figure is $110,000. Guiles said nothing about a third newly bought property.

Meanwhile, Guiles said the Beverly House was "off Benedict Canyon" (it's actually off Coldwater Canyon Drive, another major traffic artery). Guiles may have had some inkling of 910 Benedict Canyon Drive: that small property is close to the street, as is an equally small place at 1501 Lexington Road, the address he didn't identify but said was "two long blocks" from the old Davies place at 1700. He was thinking, though, of a big place, not a small one.

The confusion worsens. The seven-acre place is catty-corner from 1700 Lexington, perched high above the entire block (the address would probably be 1601 Lexington if a driveway were present). Hearst's own *Los Angeles Examiner* identified (or misidentified) the seven-acre place—the former Walter McCarty residence—as 1501 Lexington (May 5, 1946, Part I, p. 12; from Marc Wanamaker, Bison Archives). That address, 1501 Lexington, is one that crops up in the Hearst Castle architectural drawings (which were once held at Cal Poly). Thus did 1501 come to Sara Boutelle's attention; she cited it in *Julia Morgan*, p. 262 (under 1946).

In sum, from Loorz's letter, the Guiles book, and other sources, Hearst and Davies can be said to have bought the big Getz place on N. Beverly, the equally big McCarty place on Lexington ("1601"), and the much smaller unnamed place a block away on Lexington (1501)—all in 1946 for $423,000, according to Loorz's figures. See also notes 22 and 25, below.

14. The late Ann Miller (Rotanzi) Lopez, head housekeeper for many years on the hilltop, told Louis Pizzitola that Hearst "took a day trip by plane" to Las Vegas in 1946; see *Hearst Over Hollywood*, p. 428. The subject never came up in the numerous conversations I had with Mrs. Lopez when I worked at Hearst Castle (or in those I had with her former husband, the head gardener Norman Rotanzi). But I'm not surprised that accounts of the flight got lost in a welter of other details about Hearst and San Simeon.

Chief as were his beloved Marion and their inner circle of friends. The summer of 1946 found Mrs. McClure in top form, cheerily addressing her fellow Stolteans on August 20 in the latest issue of *Stolte Blueprint*—in a single paragraph several hundred words long, peppered with ellipses and headed "San Simeon Spotlight":

Our "Castle" reporter tells me that . . . Excavation, paving and grading operations at the new airport are being handled by Roy Copley formerly of the Fairfield-Suisun gang. He is ably assisted by such old timers as "Galli" Bardine, Roy Epps and "Stubby" Walker. Verne Barker returned to the old haunts recently and installed a rock crusher which had also made little ones out of big ones at this site in 1932. . . . A newcomer to the airport fold and doing nicely with the grade stakes is Sherman Eubanks, son of Marks Eubanks, Hearst old timer in Electrical Maintenance. . . . Otto Olson, carpenter foreman, who began wrestling antique ceilings for Mr. Hearst back in 1923 is at it again in the Recreation Wing doing his best to keep Mr. Hearst from pulling his (Mr. Hearst's) hair out. . . . We are proud to announce that John McFadden is still with us altering fireplaces and chasing down hot electrical wires. . . . Frank Frandolich, another Hearst old-timer is doing a bang-up job setting antiques and cast stone windows. . . . Paul Gatschet, formerly of Uncle Sam's Navy is doing a splendid job keeping "Buck" Dyer, dynamic new manager at the Hearst Stables, out of our hair. . . . Gerald Franklin, new to some of the Stolte gang, handles the miscellaneous jobs at the Ranch and at the airport. . . . Roy Evans, Hearst and Stolte old-timer, wishes he were twins or maybe even more when it is 100 degrees in the shade and he is trying to be with twenty-five or thirty laborers scattered over forty square miles. We take our hats off to Roy. No matter how thin you spread him, he can "take it." . . . Stan Kister and his gang come down occasionally to re- establish damaged control points for our grading operations at the airport. . . . Ray Humphrey, formerly of Marysville and Jap camp fame, popped in Monday for the purpose of dismantling, moving and reconstructing a hangar [from the old airport] containing about 7,800 square feet of floor space. . . . The ancient Oak tree is about ready to travel to its new home under the able direction of Charlie Todd. This giant, combined with its ball of earth, concrete perimeter and necessary lagging, weigh[s] about 450 tons. It is being moved about thirty feet to allow room for an addition to the Service Wing of the castle. . . .[15] Warren McClure has just returned from a much needed vacation, if you can call a three-day weekend a vacation, and is once again bending over the drafting board in an effort to keep the details ahead of that speedy Stolte pace. . . . Our chef, George Atchison, is still with us and doing an

---

15. Regarding the tree: Maurice McClure had first worked at San Simeon in the 1920s, under the labor foreman, Frank Souza. He and Souza kept in touch over the years; they both did likewise with their old superintendent, Camille Rossi. Through his McClure-Souza connection, Rossi returned briefly to the hilltop in 1946—to consult on the oak-moving job near the Service Wing.

exceptionally good job feeding about ninety construction men. . . . Our plumbing contractor, James Rankin, is with us again for a few weeks. Although he takes very good care of us in his absence through his assistants, George Masse and Max Steiner, the place always takes on new life and zest when he appears. . . . "Val" Georges, ornamental iron genius of long standing in the Hearst employ is still with us and trying ever so hard to finish the Loggia of "A" House [Casa del Mar][16] in spite of being swamped with repairs etc. . . . Gustav Paul Buck, one of our Wyntoon right hand men last fall is now with us at San Simeon rolling out mill work for the Castle-Recreation Wing.

In the meantime, regarding July 1946, images of Julia Morgan regain focus on the historical screen. After returning from Mexico and Guatemala the previous fall, she had spoken on November 6, 1945, of a job that was well in progress: "I do not expect to go to San Simeon through this winter."[17] A simple comment, a very telling comment. Her highest hopes were still those of resuming work on Santa Maria de Ovila. Nonetheless, she'd done some minor work around the Bay Area since then, the California Crematorium in Oakland being her foremost account before the summer of 1946. At that point she waived designing a house at Lake Tahoe for a woman in Piedmont. But she did accommodate Else Schilling, whose Tahoe house she'd designed right before the war, by starting in early July on a group of student apartments called Prospect Court. That was in Berkeley, a job that would involve Walter Steilberg toward the end of 1946. On July 15 Morgan received the best possible news, both for herself and for Steilberg: funds would soon be available for the monastery project. Work began in August and September "under City appropriation" and was going full blast by November. The old Park Museum account had finally given way to an account for the Museum of Medieval Arts.[18]

---

16. Upon returning to San Simeon late in 1944 Hearst and Miss Davies set up housekeeping in Casa del Mar, making limited use of the Gothic Suite in Casa Grande (or even none at all) from then until 1947. A similar glassing-in of the exposed loggia at 1007 N. Beverly Drive also dates from the postwar period.

17. Earlier in that same letter, written to Mrs. John Vanderloo, Morgan had told her:

It has taken two weeks + to shake off the troubles caught in Mexico, partly because it was their winter, very cold wet and probably full of the just right kind of germs to like me. But in another week or two [I] expect to go again week ends to Monterey for the "Woods" need a friendly hand badly — and it is always a rest to be in sight of the water, & to hear the pine trees rustle.

The letter is the final one of those from Morgan in the Vanderloo Collection, dating from 1930 to this last example in 1945.

18. Dorothy Wormser Coblentz, who had worked for Morgan in the 1920s, recalled Morgan's asking her long afterward (at an unspecified date), "Do you think you could do the landscaping for the model that I'm doing of the monastery?" The context of Coblentz's recollection favors the Medieval Museum phase. Coblentz went on to cite "this period of the model" as the time when Morgan altered "two old houses on Divisadero [Street]" that she'd bought for her own use (number 2229

During that same July, Morgan also started some work for Hearst, well within the Bay Area mode she was clearly favoring. Hearst Radio KYA, whose facility the F. C. Stolte Co. had built a decade earlier, was considering a new site by 1946— up on Twin Peaks, overlooking San Francisco. Jim LeFeaver was involved; so was Phillip Joy (as a new draftsman), another member of Morgan's inner circle whose father, Thaddeus, had been dead now for nearly four years.[19]

Beyond the Hearst Radio prospect and other local pursuits of the day (recorded in the Morgan-Forney holdings),[20] the Morgan Collection at Cal Poly has sketches and related items stemming from the Beverly House, the new Hearst-Davies property at 1007 N. Beverly Drive. Two items are dated. September 14, 1946, appears on a blueprint, whereas a much later date, October 17, 1947, appears on a drawing. That's the easy part. Determining how and to what degree Morgan affected that job is a good deal harder. Was she merely acting as a consultant, a sounding board, an arbiter, an advisor? Quite likely she was, a limited role that never required her presence in Beverly Hills—or even at San Simeon to confer with Hearst.[21] True, some of the sketches are unmistakably in her hand. Others

---

and the unmapped 2231, both formerly identified as 2211). See *The Julia Morgan Architectural History Project*, Vol. II, pp. 111, 112. (The major work at 2229 Divisadero, not merely its occupation by Morgan and some tenants she had, may have postdated by several years her acquisition of 2211 Divisadero, as that duplex property was once numbered; the alterations may also have postdated some earlier, lesser efforts she made at that address; see p. 53 in this volume, note 7.)

19. Thaddeus Joy died on December 3, 1942, at the age of fifty-nine; Morgan had just left on her first trip to the Babicora. For several years she had steered some small, manageable work his way, things he could do at home in Berkeley; he never overcame the illness he contracted in 1929 (see p. 45 in this volume, plus its note 38). In 1946 itself, Hathaway Lovell died. "Hatch" was only forty-six.

The KYA radio project seems not to have gone far. Morgan accrued $605 in expenses by the end of 1946, paid in full by Hearst in January 1947.

20. In her 1946 datebook, Morgan made an entry under September 28: "letter from Mr. Easton regds. San Antonio Mission." She responded on September 30. Prominent in Santa Maria and Santa Barbara, Robert E. Easton and his wife had known Morgan for years—since at least 1925, when she and Mrs. Easton began conferring about the Minerva Club that Morgan designed in Santa Maria. Unfortunately, the Easton Collection at UC Santa Barbara contains no Easton-Morgan correspondence from 1946 (or any other year). As to Morgan's purported role in restoring Mission San Antonio, it must have been minimal if it occurred at all: most work of that kind took place too late in the forties to include her.

21. However plausible it may be that Morgan was at San Simeon between January 1940 (her last recorded visit) and May 1947 (Hearst's final departure), no sources tapped for this book can place her there (but see p. 430, note 4, for a potential exception). Maurice McClure said she was never present between August 1945 and January 1948, a period extending well past Hearst's departure; anyone who spoke with the clear-minded, reminiscing "Morris" in the 1980s (as I did several times) was told as much. Hearst Castle taped some of his recollections on September 13, 1981; see "From Laborer to Construction Superintendent," p. 13, transcribed from an interview by Metta Hake. McClure also said that 1.3 million dollars were spent on postwar construction at San Simeon (p. 7).

are more apt to be Mac McClure's work or that of another draftsman.[22] Yet there's nothing remotely akin to a "Beverly House" account in Morgan-Forney (nor do accounts exist for the other properties that Hearst and Davies had recently bought in Beverly Hills).

Such matters aside, and despite her overriding passion for the Santa Maria monastery, Morgan left San Francisco in late October 1946 on yet another trip to Mexico. She went by train this time. Queretaro, San Miguel de Allende, Guadalajara, Mazatlan—all are mentioned in the datebook she kept that year. She was gone less than a month; in fact, her purpose may partly have been to study old masonry construction, befitting the monastery's ancient stonework. To do so in Mexico was cheaper and faster than to travel to the war-ravaged Old World. Either that or she'd simply developed a yen for Spanish Colonial and Latin American culture in its architecural and other guises. Her stop in Havana, Cuba, in 1940 comes to mind. And of course her Babicora travels had occurred in the interim. Similar episodes and destinations awaited her in the years still ahead.[23]

Morgan had been back from Mexico for a month or so when the next issue of *Stolte Blueprint* appeared. Dated December 20, 1946, the magazine provided a forum once more for Hazel McClure. This time her column was conventionally paragraphed, and yet its heading was as Stoltean as ever—"San Simeon Chatter":

> The $200,000 San Simeon Airport is nearing completion. The landing strip has been in use for six weeks. The lighting, under the supervision of Mark[s] Eubanks, Hearst electrician, and the hangar which is being constructed by Paul Gatschet and his crew are the only two unfinished items.

---

22. The Morgan Collection, Cal Poly, has a sketch by Mac McClure of the gatehouse at 1007 N. Beverly Drive, unsigned yet (thanks to his accompanying words) unmistakably in Mac's hand. The sketch is filed, however, with items pertaining to 910 Benedict Canyon Drive (V/03/22/11).

23. Typifying Morgan's Hispanic interests, which Hearst shared in a period when few other designers or collectors were like-minded, her Christmas gift to him in 1943 was *Old Architecture of Southern Mexico* (by Garrett Van Pelt, Jr.; Cleveland, 1926)—a "beautiful book," Hearst said while thanking her on January 12, 1944. Cal Poly has the original letter (I/07/02/29). The Hearst Papers have the carbon copy but, along with it, the original "Miss Morgan" calling card, inscribed "WRH. from JM. with affectionate greetings"; carton 39 (under "Hearst, W. R.—Christmas [1943]").

Further instances of Morgan's zeal for things Hispanic, reinforced above all by Santa Maria de Ovila's prospects, are evident in both the Park Museum and the Medieval Museum ledgers. In June 1942, Dawson's Book Shop in Los Angeles supplied "Byne ceilings," probably *Decorated Wooden Ceilings in Spain*, by Arthur Byne (New York, 1920). Four other entries in 1942 refer to the London bookseller John Tiranti, whose name also crops up in October 1946; the new Medieval Museum account was in force by then. A letter from the Tiranti shop—dated September 12, 1946, and tucked inside Morgan's datebook of that year—most likely equates with the October entry in her ledger. If so, she paid $60.45 for *España: Sus Monumentos y Artes . . .* (Barcelona, 1884–91), a set of twenty-four volumes on Spanish cities and provinces. (All references here: Morgan-Forney Collection.)

The Recreation Wing is progressing nicely. Frank Frandolich and Carlo Bianchi are still carving away at the stone windows. Al Hayden is progressing nicely with the plastering. Otto Olson with the able assistance of Gustav Buck, Ed Miller, and others has installed the antique ceilings on the third floor and is working on the fourth floor ceilings. Thomas E. Adams, electrician, finds that usually he could be twins to good advantage. John McFadden has finished laying the tile floor in one large room and has another well under way.

Gerald Franklin and his small crew are beginning to believe that repairs and maintenance at the ranch could easily be a life time job.

We just finished laying seven miles of oil mix road from San Simeon to the Hilltop and believe me, those of us who drive automobiles over this road shouted for joy when we saw that bit of construction finished before the rains started.[24]

Our painter, Harold O. Tomlin, somehow manages to keep Mr. Apperson, Buck Dyer, Mr. Keep, Mr. Reed *and* Mr. Hearst happy. He knows how to make his seconds count.

Jimmy Rankin, plumbing contractor, and his crew with the assistance of Roy Evans and his labor gang have installed new waterlines to the Poultry Plant and Ranch House and are now installing one to the new airport. This, plus a new sprinkling system at Pico Creek Stables, steam heat and plumbing installations in the Recreation Wing and the hours of maintenance required of the plumbers forces "Jimmy" to stay quite young.

Warren McClure and Ray Carlson of Mr. Hearst's Architect's office are kept quite busy getting out plans and details for the Recreation and Service Wings. "Mac" is really kept busy since he also directs Mr. Hearst's work in Los Angeles and Wyntoon and we never know when a new day starts whether he will be on deck or has disappeared during the night to one of the other locations. Faithful Ray is always here, however, to give a suggestion here, lend a helping hand there and make himself generally an asset.

Would that all the other years in San Simeon's annals—even those in the 1930s that yielded the best of the George Loorz Papers—had been as effectively summarized by Hazel McClure. Her tongue-in-cheek style and infectious optimism aside, her columns are truthful and reliable, plausible to the last detail; for these virtually "missing years" of the late 1940s, they're indispensable. She left few important points unmentioned, few pertinent names unrecited. In that regard, the absence of George Loorz and Fred Stolte in her reports can be easily explained:

---

24. More than a decade earlier (July 30, 1934), King Walters had asked Loorz if he was "still contemplating the paving of the road from the castle to San Simeon." In his reply three days later, Loorz explained that the budget-depleting Neptune Pool was too much of a priority just then: "Now as to the road I know nothing will be done this year."

the partners were masterminding their company's operations from Oakland, the Hearst projects at San Simeon and Wyntoon being just two of many jobs for Stolte Inc. in this period.

As for Morgan's absence in *Stolte Blueprint*—she seems never to have been mentioned, from its first issue onward—her marginal or even slighter role in Hearst's pursuits at San Simeon, Wyntoon, and in Beverly Hills couldn't be more conspicuous.[25] In turn, the great majority of the postwar designs for those places should be credited to Mac McClure—to that under-heralded draftsman whom Hearst liked "better than anyone in Miss Morgan's office," as Loorz had ventured in 1933, Mac being the one who knew Hearst's "likes and dislikes best."[26] Mac's longevity could mean only that, all these years later, he was no less esteemed by the demanding Hearst. The task of succeeding Julia Morgan, master architect, was a thankless one, an almost impossible one, yet the equally self-effacing Warren McClure had made the transition as smoothly as any mortal could have.

THE BUYER'S MARKET that delivered the Beverly House to Hearst and Miss Davies on a silver platter had its down side for them, too. The Beach House became the sacrificial lamb. Late in 1946 they were about to sell the main compound at 415 Ocean Front (in a deal excluding the separate service unit at 312 Ocean Front). But the Hollywood producer Hal Roach, who had "intimated a cash offer" of half a million dollars for "the big house," proved to have lost interest; and Donald Douglas, speaking for the Douglas Aircraft Company, said "the big house was too rich for their blood as they were now in a period of retrenchment and pulling back after their heavy war contracts."[27] Hearst and Davies had to feel lucky when a different buyer came forward, paying as much as $600,000. It was that party, Jo-

---

25. The identification of Morgan with Hearst's postwar efforts in Beverly Hills relies on a group of drawings at Cal Poly, pertaining to 1007 N. Beverly Drive (V/06/A06/04); see pp. 512–13, plus their note 22.

The tangle of addresses and details that awaits unraveling (as in note 13, above) will require more than putting 1501 Lexington Road (plus "1601" Lexington) in proper perspective. The Hollywood archivist Marc Wanamaker, for instance, thinks that further portions of the Cosmopolitan bungalow were used on the old McCarty property, across from the original Davies residence at 1700 Lexington Road. (The McCarty "1601" place, it turns out, is correctly identified as 1000 Cove Way, a side street off Lexington where the McCarty driveway begins its ascent; the probable bungalow portions are at 1010 Cove Way.)

26. See p. 64 in this volume: Loorz to Harry Thompson, May 10, 1933 (regarding the new work that would soon begin that year at Wyntoon).

27. See Martin Huberth to Hearst, December 27, 1946, plus attachments of December 11, 1946, and January 9, 1947; Hearst Papers, carton 49 (under "Real Estate"). The Roach and Douglas excerpts are from Huberth's paraphrasing of what the two men said.

seph Drown, who renamed the place Ocean House and converted it to a private club.[28]

Change was everywhere at hand by now, early in 1947—just as always in Hearst's life; nothing new about that. He was quickly getting older and frailer, though, and his days at San Simeon were numbered. Building continued on the Recreation Wing (or the New Wing, as it was increasingly being called),[29] that north side of Casa Grande where Loorz and Pete Petersen and others had left off in 1938, that section where work had resumed in high style in 1945 before cresting in 1946. Work also continued on the projects Hazel McClure had described in *Stolte Blueprint*. But just like Douglas Aircraft, Stolte Inc. had wartime headiness to retrench from. Loorz and Stolte remained solidly prosperous, even though 1946 was the last year to see multiple issues of the *Blueprint*. For our purposes, it means precious little reportage exists for 1947, whose sole issue of the magazine appeared at Christmastime. And by then Hearst had been off the hilltop for several months, his convalescence at the Beverly House having begun an unbroken stretch that ended in 1951.

After Morgan dispensed with several small jobs in 1946—the last time she had a varied workload—she focused on a single job as the year ended, the Museum of Medieval Arts in San Francisco (or informally the "Medieval Museum"). In fact, from January 1947 onward, the city-funded work on Santa Maria de Ovila was her only account, large or small. It ran through July that year; and those seven months yielded about $10,200 in operating costs, two thirds of it for Walter Steilberg's services. The account lapsed as of August, never to be revived.[30]

---

28. The selling price appears in Swanberg, who cited "Providence *Journal*, Jan 3., 1960" in *Citizen Hearst*, p. 513. On the illegitimacy—indeed, the non-existence—of "Ocean House" as a name for the Beach House before Drown bought it, see p. 6 in this volume, note 9. A year before Martin Huberth wrote to Hearst (note 27, above), Parke-Bernet Galleries held an auction in New York—"Fine Colonial and Early Federal Furniture . . . Property of Miss Marion Davies; Removed from Her Beach House at 415 Ocean Front, Santa Monica, Calif." The sale took place on December 7–8, 1945. Hearst and Davies sent certain other items from the Beach House to San Simeon, where some remain today.

29. *New Wing* may have had few adherents in 1947 (besides members of the Stolte crew, who may have coined the name, as Don Loorz recalls), yet it was the one destined to endure. Nick Yost formalized the usage through the master inventories he compiled in 1949. But Norman Rotanzi, who continued as head gardener long after Hearst's last hurrah at San Simeon, liked to put things this way: "That ain't no *new* wing." True, it wasn't a newly built structure but rather one that was newly remodeled and, in certain details, newly finished for the first time.

30. A final entry, dated October 1 and thus falling outside the January-July period, was for $400 payable to Steilberg; hence roughly $10,600 in various expenses for 1947 overall. According to the Medieval Museum ledger, Morgan received $9,000 from the city appropriation; she seems to have received no payments, either from Hearst or from the city, on the old Park Museum account. The figures (all from Morgan-Forney) can thus be analyzed as follows:

And yet Morgan herself didn't lapse. She left San Francisco that very month —August 1947—for a voyage around South America. (She got home in December, having had a marvelous time; sadly, though, the South American trip and a less-familiar trip she made to Europe in 1948 have been conflated—have been portrayed, that is, as a single, connected episode; and in the process, a pernicious tale regarding her mental health has become part of the Morgan myth.)[31] When she sailed in August 1947, Hearst had been housebound in Beverly Hills for three months. Despite *his* worsened health (physical, not mental), work was still under way on the hilltop and likewise at Wyntoon. Those projects were two spheres of ac-

---

A. Morgan's expenses on Santa Maria from 1940 through 1947 (Park Museum and Medieval Museum combined): $17,612 in costs, minus $9,000 in payments ($8,612 left unpaid).

B. Her expenses from June 1941 (post-Hearst ownership) on the Park Museum plus those on the Medieval Museum: $16,771 in costs, minus $9,000 in payments ($7,771 left unpaid).

C. Her expenses in 1931 on the Mount Olive account, plus those on the Park Museum and Medieval Museum accounts, each in their entirety: $20,369 in costs, minus $11,353 in payments ($2,353 from Hearst in Mount Olive "refunds" and $9,000 from the city; for a grand total of $9,016 left unpaid).

Until further records surface, the $9,016 in arrears is the closest one can get to the $15,000 that Morgan North spoke of; see the 1940 chapter, notes 36 and 37.

31. Sara Boutelle said Morgan "failed to return to the ship at the appointed time and was, as a consequence, not permitted ashore at the next port"—this with respect to her "1947 freighter voyage to Portugal and Spain"; see *Julia Morgan*, p. 242; plus ibid., p. 245, note 3 (entry for 1947, which includes the Azores).

Morgan left a stream-of-consciousness account, a lengthy travelogue that mentions the Equator (Pacific side), Chile, the Straits of Magellan, Argentina, Uruguay, Brazil, Trinidad, and Venezuela, followed by the Panama Canal, Baja California, and, finally, Los Angeles. She spent time in Buenos Aires, Montevideo, and other coastal cities; she went inland, too. She often omitted dates and place names: some future editor faces a demanding text, as in the passage that follows, evidently regarding Buenos Aires:

All Saints day, a Saturday [November 1], thought Sunday because open field between cemetery walks on Hill, *filled* with flower sellers, people of every kind, with the loveliest flowers of all kinds of colors, sizes, varietys ever seen + more—Men, women & children further on, shops closed, & general air of a special Sunday—At Zoo, very few visitors—My old grey egret bird looked at me more friendly—Going back was lost as to FK[?] car! rescued by a kind young couple in auto—! & taken to a car stop! Funny head waiter & [his?] choosing most suitable dishes for me! The wise one in (green cup & saucer) breakfast room who always explained he had no bread on time (with gestures)! Pleasant place, kindly services & fellow guests—very much appreciated.

From "Diary of Trip Around South America, 1947"; Julia Morgan Collection, Environmental Design Archives. In 1974 Morgan North said of his aunt, "She got lost in Spain. She forgot where she was and forgot where her ship was." See *The Julia Morgan Architectural History Project*, Vol. II, p. 173. Boutelle's conflation (possibly North's as well) stemmed from two things: a poor reading of Miss Morgan's lighthearted account (whose nearly illegible "FK car" suggests the *Falkanger*, her ship) and the faint knowledge North conveyed of the trip in 1948—a trip otherwise missing from the book *Julia Morgan*, which also lacks the personal, non-business trips of 1940, 1945, 1946, and 1950.

tivity Morgan no longer watched—insofar as she'd been watching them at all—
or rather three spheres if Beverly Hills is included.[32]

Soon after Morgan got home, Frank Gendrich wrote a "Letter from Wyntoon" that appeared in the single issue of *Stolte Blueprint* for 1947, the "Christmas
Issue" dated December 25:

> The Wyntoon crew is quite small at the present and there is not much of a story
> to be told, but the following might be of some interest to the Stolte fishermen
> anyway.
>
> It's about the big one, a "Dolly Varden" trout 28 inches long, which did *not* get
> away. . . .
>
> As this job is nearing its completion, I want to thank the Ranch Superinten-
> dent, Cal Shewmaker and his crew for the splendid assistance and cooperation
> extended to us during construction. . . .
>
> And last but not least, let's extend our sincere thanks to our architect, Mr. War-
> ren McClure, under whose able guidance and assistance we were able to do an-
> other Stolte job well, indeed.

An unsigned article entitled "San Simeon News" appeared in that same *Stolte
Blueprint* of December 25, 1947:

> There is very little to report from San Simeon in view of the fact that we have a
> very small crew at the present time.
>
> Work on the Service Wing has been temporarily discontinued and Paul
> Gatschet, who was in charge of the construction of that wing, took his crew and
> departed to the Fairfield-Suisun Army Airbase to work with Elof [Gustafson] on
> the Hospital.
>
> John McFadden, Frank Frandolich, Otto Olson, Gustav Buck and Wm.
> George are still buzzing away, trying to complete the finish work in the Recre-
> ation Wing. Jerry Franklin is still with us, handling miscellaneous jobs at Ranch
> and Hilltop.
>
> Roy Evans, our labor foreman, with a crew of almost zero is still with us and
> finds plenty of activity to engage in.
>
> Mr. [Camille] Solon, the interior decorator,[33] departed recently to complete
> some decorating in his own home in Mill Valley. We are hoping for his quick re-
> turn to our fold.
>
> Ted Rathbun, our blacksmith, is learning that his trade embodies untold types
> of activity never before dreamed of. Ted is able to "take it" however, and we never
> hear a murmur of complaint.

---

32. See notes 13, 22, and 25 in this chapter.

33. Solon's murals in the Center Room (between the East Tower and West Tower suites of the
New Wing) are reminiscent of those he painted in the 1930s in the Gothic Study.

Ray Carlson is still handling the architectural work here, while Warren Mc-Clure divides his time between the Los Angeles [Beverly House and possibly other Hearst-Davies jobs] and Wyntoon jobs. The "grapevine" tells us that Warren McClure is going to take a much needed vacation to Detroit, Michigan, and other points East in the very near future.

That "near future" wasn't long in arriving. The other McClure—Maurice McClure—recalled that January 1948 was the final month of any work at San Simeon, at least under Stolte auspices.[34] Wyntoon also shut down before long. The year-end *Stolte Blueprint* for 1948 provided a hint of what happened next. In the article "Work Starts on New Oakland Public Library," Lee Perry reported the following, though without giving specific dates:

Dirt is flying as construction of the new Main Library for the City of Oakland moves into high gear. . . .
Chosen to "supe" the project is Frank Gendrich who, since Wyntoon, has been champing at the bit for a big and beautiful one. Well, here it is, Frank. Go to it: we're all either ahead of you or behind you; either pulling for you, or pushing you; but knowing the job will be in good hands.

In the meantime, earlier in 1948, Morgan began using a new datebook, a leatherette keepsake with a gold-embossed "Julia Morgan" on the front cover and "Stolte Inc." on the back, a personalized gift from the company. Her notations indicate she served on a jury in Sacramento from April 27 to May 10; in the midst of that period she made this entry:

Dont know which day but Geo Loorz & Mr Stolte "called" on me at the Senator [Hotel]—said "very busy"—had [branch] office in Sac[ramento] etc. Said Mr H not off floor (2nd) for full six months past [in Beverly Hills]. Putting in an elevator so he can do so—.[35]

Should she be taken at face value? Had she truly lost sight of Hearst as completely as her words imply? Evidently so.[36] His eighty-fifth birthday, which oc-

---

34. "From Laborer to Construction Superintendent," pp. 4, 6, and 7; see also note 21, above.
35. Morgan-Forney Collection. A contract from the Otis Elevator Company, dated August 22, 1947, specifies that the elevator would be "in complete running order" by November 18 (some six months after Hearst had left San Simeon that year). See S. M. Cronk to Georjean Rehr [Rehn], September 2, 1947; Hearst Papers, carton 42 (under "1947 Samples"). Georjean Rehn began working as a secretary at San Simeon early in 1947, under Bill Hunter and Estelle Forsythe. Yet another secretary, Richard Stanley (also known as Waldo Stanley), was likewise prominent in Hearst's final years.
36. At the outset of Morgan's leisurely voyage in 1947, her ship stopped in Los Angeles Harbor for several days in early August before continuing toward South America. She had time to visit her YWCA buildings in nearby Long Beach and San Pedro; she also visited the main part of Los Angeles but didn't get to see her Hollywood Studio Club. Through it all, she said nothing in her travelogue (note 31 in this chapter) about Santa Monica or Beverly Hills, nor anything about Hearst.

curred in this period (she herself was now seventy-six), his efforts through Mac Mc-
Clure to improve his surroundings as usual—such things fell outside her daily
concerns now, more than they ever had before. One has to wonder if Joe Willicombe's death that summer is something she heard about promptly.[37]

But she hadn't declined physically as much as Hearst had. Nor had she lost her
zeal for life. By summer's end in 1948, she was traveling again, sailing to the Old
World for the first time in ten years, a trip whose identity has been conflated with
that of her voyage to South America in 1947 or, more often, ignored altogether.
"Miss Morgan is in Europe and will not return until some time in November."
Thank God for that shred of evidence. Lilian Forney conveyed the news on September 22, while writing to an acquaintance of Morgan's in Monterey.[38]

Two months after Morgan got home, Bill Murray of Hearst Sunical wrote to
her at the Merchants Exchange; by then it was January 21, 1949. She was still paying office rent, despite not having plied her trade for a year and a half—not since
July 1947, when the Medieval Museum was shelved. That may have been her ratio-
nale: keep the faith while waiting for work to resume on the monastery.[39] Surely she
hadn't hung on in Room 1107 for Hearst's sake or even to help Mac, who was still at
work in Beverly Hills. Bill Murray, in any case, knew she had files on Hearst's collecting that went beyond anything Nick Yost, Charlie Rounds, or anybody else had.
Yost was updating the San Simeon inventories; Murray hoped that Morgan could
have Lilian and Jim Forney burrow through her correspondence with Hearst,
"from year one through 1938."[40] She no doubt complied.

Morgan's trail can be traced a bit further. On March 21, 1949, she thanked

---

37. The prolific Herbert Bayard Swope thought the Colonel's passing deserved notice:

My sympathy goes to W.R. on the death of Joe Willicombe. I knew him when I was a young
reporter in New York. I am not writing directly to your Dad because you, or someone else, told
me he did not like letters of sympathy. Fortunately, he has had occasion for few, and I hope that
record will remain unspoiled. If, however, you think it would please him to know I had this
thought of him, you may, if you care to, forward this note to him.

From Swope to William Randolph Hearst, Jr., August 2, 1948; Hearst Papers, carton 42 (under
"1948 Samples"). Bill Hearst marked the letter "Send to Pop."

38. Mrs. Forney to Clyde A. Dorsey (City Manager, Monterey), filed with "General Correspondence" regarding Morgan's home in that city; Morgan Collection (II/01/03/18).

39. Under "Newspapers Clippings re Santa Maria de Ovila, 1941" (III/06/09/08), the Morgan Collection at Cal Poly has items from other years also, some from as late as 1948. The adjoining
file on Santa Maria (III/06/09/09) has four letters from Walter Steilberg; two are directly to Morgan,
two are copies of letters to other people; all four date from 1950 (see note 80 in the previous chapter,
concerning the one dated January 23).

40. Morgan-Forney Collection.

Carl Daniels of Stolte Inc. for trimming the trees at her place in Monterey. In writing to him, she spoke of "some 47 years of very active work" that she'd done—in other words, since 1902, when she came back from the Beaux-Arts in Paris and began practicing. However, if she was truly still active—professionally active—in a year like 1949, the evidence has yet to turn up.[41]

Another voice at this juncture is just as familiar, just as welcome. Mac McClure wrote to Cal Shewmaker at Wyntoon on May 17, 1949; he did so from 1007 N. Beverly Drive, his main address during the two years Hearst had lived there:

> Things here are the same—no better and no worse. Apparently the boss is "holding his own."
>
> Did Bob Harbison [of Stolte Inc.] come up this year for his annual fishing expedition?—I rarely hear from any of the Stolte person[n]el except for an occasional letter from Bob. Once in a while I get a note from [Jim] Rankin and also from Nigel Keep—otherwise the contacts are few and far between.
>
> Bill Murray and [Martin] Huberth [of the Hearst Corporation] have been here but I did not see them. I guess they had other things to think about besides me.

Any such letter of Mac's deserved a postcript, in 1949 as much as in years gone by. "Jud [Smelser] is still more or less laid up with his broken arm, living on unemployment insurance and his Mom's old age pension apparently!"[42]

A year or two earlier, Mac may have heard from—indeed, may have seen in person—several Stolteans, quite possibly Loorz among them. To install the elevator Loorz and Stolte told Morgan about would have required skilled workmen. Equally exacting, if not more so, was the re-erection of an Italian palazzo ensemble—arches, columns, capitals, bases—at the outdoor swimming pool. (A perfect job for Frank Frandolich or his equivalent.) The carved stone ensemble came from Hearst's architectural stock, still replete with paneled rooms and the like, even after years of dispersals in New York. In a presentation recalling the Roman temple and flanking colonnades at the Neptune Pool, Mac and his crew relied on old techniques and sleight-of-hand to make the stonework a proper tribute to the Hearst-

---

41. Morgan to Daniels on March 21, 1949, and a reply from Daniels the next day are in the same file as Lilian Forney's letter of 1948 (note 38); Morgan Collection (II/01/03/18).

42. Shewmaker Collection. Mac used *Los Angeles Examiner* stationery on this occasion. Thirty years later—on August 12, 1979—Mac wrote to Cal Shewmaker's widow, Nellie, mentioning Bill Murray, who had died recently, as had Bob Harbison, one of Loorz's best friends. "Bob H's death was a particular shock to me too," said Mac. "I always thought of him as a kid, which he was when he first came to Wyntoon. Both Bob and Geo Loorz were hard workers and put too much in their efforts to get ahead. It doesn't pay to over work."

Morgan approach. Location scouts have been entranced by the assemblage ever since, as epitomized by its appearance in *The Godfather* and other films.[43]

Morgan went abroad again at the outset of 1950. Walter Steilberg wrote to her in Mazatlan, Mexico, in mid-January and then in the Canal Zone two weeks later. In each instance that old passion of theirs, the Medieval Museum, urged him to make contact even while she was traveling. "As the enclosures indicate," he told her in the second letter, "there is again some activity with reference to the Museum project." A great deal of money—"about $800,000 with which the project might be started"—seemed as though it might materialize.[44]

It didn't; and in that same year, 1950, Morgan finally left the Merchants Exchange. She'd already retired in the normal sense in 1947. And thus in her lingering use of that building until 1950, she resembled a professor emeritus who maintains an office on campus—never mind that in her case she had to pay dearly for the privilege. Rents and leases in such buildings could be steep.[45]

Nineteen fifty was also a pivotal year for George Loorz. Unlike the aging

---

43. See Charles Lockwood and Jeff Hyland, *The Estates of Beverly Hills* (Beverly Hills, 1984), pp. 18–25. The assemblage appears sometimes in magazine ads as well.

44. In writing to Robert M. Clements, Jr., in 1975 about Santa Maria de Ovila, Edward Hussey cited a letter of Steilberg's to Morgan in Mazatlan (January 18, 1950). The Hussey-Clements document is a highly important one, since the subsequent Steilberg Collection at EDA lacks a copy of the January 18 item and certain others Hussey listed; the Hussey-Clements document is reproduced in *The Julia Morgan Architectural History Project*, Vol. I, pp. 333–36.

The Morgan Collection, Cal Poly, also lacks the letter of January 18 (the one Steilberg sent to Mazatlan), but it has his letter to Morgan in the Canal Zone, dated January 30, 1950 (III/06/09/09). The same file includes a letter from Steilberg to Morgan dated November 1, 1950 (of which EDA, atypically for this stretch, has a copy). Although mostly about the monastery, the November letter also speaks of the time when Morgan was "enroute to Spain," evidently meaning her trip to Europe in 1948 (a voyage that may or may not have included Portugal and the Azores).

45. "At the request of the American Institute of Architects in 1957 I wrote this brief outline for the A.I.A. Archives in Washington." So noted Walter Steilberg on his two pages about Miss Morgan, following her death that year; see *The Julia Morgan Architectural History Project*, Vol I, pp. 135a-135b. "Retired 1950," he said of her; the date signifies her vacating the Merchants Exchange. In turn, Steilberg's letter of November 1, 1950 (note 44), went to her in "San Francisco." The EDA copy has "2229 Divisidero" (his spelling) in a separate address line, indicating that the original went to Morgan's home, not to the office she'd relinquished by then; however, the original letter (which is at Cal Poly, III/06/09/09) has no street address at all.

Cal Poly also has "Payroll Records, 1916–1950" (II/02/03/34). The items, however, are from two years only, 1915 and 1916; the similar sounding *fifteen* and *fifty* may have got confused.

This leaves Sara Boutelle's account, persuasively set forth in *Julia Morgan*, p. 241, that 1951 was the year Morgan retired. Boutelle made no reference to Steilberg's date of 1950 or to any earlier one, found in some sources. She relied implicitly on Otto Haake, a man who told her he had struck the match when it came time to destroy most of Morgan's records. Be that as it may, Boutelle's dates were repeatedly off by a year or two, sometimes more. If her account involving Otto Haake can simply be moved back—from 1951 to 1950—the world can rest easier, pending further progress in the unraveling of Morgan's final years.

Morgan, he was still in full harness; fifty-two is all the older he would be come October. He was elected president that year of the Northern California chapter of Associated General Contractors, the organization that Warren Bechtel—Dad Bechtel, he'd been called—had founded back in the twenties, when Loorz was studying at Berkeley. Loorz's new position with AGC was one brimming with prestige. His career at Stolte Inc. had more than twenty years to go. So did Fred Stolte's.

And then there was William Randolph Hearst, the great enabler, the man who had had such a profound effect on Morgan's career and on Loorz's, too. Eighty-seven as of April 1950, he hadn't much time left. Yet it's inspiring to see how nimble minded he remained, even in his physical decline that kept him all but housebound in Beverly Hills; at least he could gaze out on the Italian palazzo fragments that Mac and, most likely, some of the Stolteans had assembled at the swimming pool—a scene unmistakably inspired by the Neptune Pool at San Simeon. Hearst's mental acuity stayed intact almost until the day he died in 1951. He was eighty-eight by then.[46]

Morgan died in 1957, soon after her eighty-fifth birthday. Marion Davies died in 1961, prematurely at age sixty-four. Jim LeFeaver, the next of those otherwise long-lived players to pass on, died in 1969 when he was eighty-four, followed by Walter Steilberg in 1974 at age eighty-eight. And then came George Loorz's turn, in 1978. He had just turned eighty but should have lived longer, despite the night blindness he'd developed: standing after dark near parked cars, he suddenly stepped in front of one that was moving. Fred Stolte was still living then; he died at the grand old age of ninety-three in 1983. Mac McClure was also alive when George Loorz died; a year older than Loorz, Mac lasted until 1985, when—like Hearst and Steilberg—he died at the age of eighty-eight.

THE MORGAN-FORNEY COLLECTION and several other archives, public and private, have supplemented the George Loorz Papers in many parts of this book. Be-

---

46. On May 21, 1951, for example, Hearst authorized "THE SALE OF THE PROPERTY KNOWN AS 1501 LEXINGTON ROAD, BEVERLY HILLS"; he so informed R. F. McCauley at the Hearst Corporation headquarters in New York. On June 27 he asked Benjamin McPeake in London to allow Marjorie and Huntington Hartford the use of St. Donat's Castle, which the Hearst interests still owned. On July 2 he notified Howard Handleman in Tokyo, "MISS MARION DAVIES DID NOT REQUEST TO HAVE CAPTAIN HORACE BROWN, JR., INVESTIGATED. . . . WILL YOU LET ME KNOW THE OUTCOME OF THIS MISTAKE." And on August 11, 1951, three days before he died, Hearst asked Sam Day at the *New York Journal-American* to give Red Skelton and his wife, plus the writer Gene Fowler, some good publicity. "I WOULD APPRECIATE IT VERY MUCH," he said. All such messages stem unmistakably from Hearst's wording, no matter how faint his voice had become. Hearst Papers, carton 43 (under "McA"; under "1950–60 Samples"; under "Haa"; and under "Da").

yond these supportive, often corroborating items, some even newer examples occur in the Shewmaker Collection, which has letters of Mac McClure's from as recently as the late 1970s and the early 1980s. Two of these are especially pertinent to the period covered in *Building for Hearst and Morgan*.[47] Mac was eighty-five when he wrote the first of the two letters, dated December 21, 1982. His recipient was Nellie Shewmaker, the widow of Cal Shewmaker, who succeeded Gene Kower in 1942 as the caretaker of Wyntoon. Mac typed the letter; it contained several misspellings and other irregularities; fortunately, none of them lessens the value of the words that follow:

> Soon after I arrived at San Simeon in Jan 1929 [1930] news arrived that the Phoebe Hearst Castle at Wyntoon had been totaled by a fire said to be of electrical source. The building was being remodeled slightly so that Mr. Hearst could visit it although he was at Santa Monica at the time. I recall how little the fire seemed to upset anyone. I learned afterword that it meant the fun of a new project.[48]
>
> I had come to Los Angeles in 1922[49]—hoping to get movie studio work in designing historical architectural work in which I had some proficientry. I did not get far but did get access to Mr. Hearst through Mr. Thad[d]eus Joy who was Miss Morgan's assistant. I recall working on a big Beverly Hills, house in Old English Tudor style[50] which pleased Mr. Hearst and I was later sent to San Simeon where I arrived on the date to the castle fire at Wyntoon [January 18, 1930].
>
> The relationship between Mr. Hearst and his architect was unique. His knowledge of art and style was enough to enable him to control to a great extent. Miss Morgan had the ability to steer projects into reasonable channels. Even so, Mr.

---

47. Copies of both letters were sent to me on October 2, 1989, by Maurice McClure, who in turn had received copies of the letters from Shirley Shewmaker Wahl in 1988. Though unrelated to Mac McClure, Maurice McClure (likewise deceased now, as is Mrs. Wahl) maintained a lively interest in Mac and several other people mentioned in this book. Before she died in 2001, Mrs. Wahl lent me copies of further items for this book, all of them from the Shewmaker Collection.

48. Such as the work done in 1930 and 1931 on The Gables, some of it involving the F. C. Stolte Co. Mac may also have been alluding to a subsequent phase — to the prospect of using the old Spanish monastery at Wyntoon.

49. Mac was twenty-four or twenty-five then (he was born in August 1897). As early as 1916, he was listed in *Polk's Detroit City Directory* as a draftsman; he was next listed, again as a draftsman, in 1923–24 (combined half-year listings began with the 1920–21 edition). Thus he may have gone west as early as 1922 — in what may have proved a false start. Jud Smelser claimed to have known him since about 1924, apparently having met him in Los Angeles, Smelser's home town; see p. 188 in this volume, note 68.

50. The original Davies residence at 1700 Lexington Road, on which Morgan had an account ledger for 1925–27 and then for 1929 (the year Mac began with her). It was the same house that Mac, Loorz, and Petersen worked on in 1940. A photograph of the house during its Tudor phase, possibly predating Morgan's first efforts, appears in Charles Lockwood, *Dream Palaces: Hollywood at Home* (New York, 1981), p. 205.

Hearst wanted a draftsman's designer at hand whereever he was. At San Simeon he spent a part of every day in the architect's offices sometimes late at night, working out his idea with me.

Hard times and coming war time pinches made the San Simeon program greatly curtailed but it never stopped completely. The plans turned out were mostly all for Wyntoon.[51]

The big development was the purchase of a ruined monastery in Spain [Santa Maria de Ovila] which wa[s] brought to San Francisco at great expense — finally to be abandoned where the unreality of the situation dawned on all concerned.

The Bavarian Village of Old German architecture provided living quarters and the purchase of the Bend property a mile down river gave something new to work on.

In 1946–47 work on the Bend main building began to take shape. Mr. Hearst's health began to cause anziety — Miss Morgan felt that she could no longer maintain her office in San Francisco which she closed.[52]

It was her arrangement to transfer my employment to the Hearst payroll.[53] I think it was the winter of 1947 that the Bend main building was re-constructed from the foundation up by the Stolte Co. contractors of which George Loorz had been construction sup't at San Simeon. It was hard to get away from Beverly Hills [1007 N. Beverly Drive] for me to travel north very often but the results were pretty good. Of all the buildings this one [was] primarily the design of W. R. Hearst. I regret that his failing health prevented him from seeing it. He did approve the photos.[54]

Miss Morgan did not see it either.

You asked about Willie Pogany. He was a big time artist — He may have been with M.G.M. but usually in N.Y.C. The Pogany [mural] project [in the Bavarian Village at Wyntoon] took all the budget money one summer.[55]

---

51. Concerning San Simeon, the context here is the first several years of the 1930s; the work (with the most minor exceptions) surely *did* stop at that southern estate in 1939 and did not resume until 1945.

52. Mac had a date closer to 1947 in mind, not one as far ahead as 1950. Either way, he was viewing Morgan in that sense through a Hearst prism, never hinting at Santa Maria de Ovila's importance in her final years.

53. The arrangement dated from 1939, foreshadowed by events in 1938. Except for working at the Sierra Ordnance Depot in 1942–43, Mac may never have been a Stolte employee (any more than Morgan ever was), not even during the big push on Hearst's part in years like 1945 and 1946. Ray Carlson's status during the immediate postwar period also needs further defining. Once part of Morgan's regular office staff, Carlson would be invisible in that late period if not for *Stolte Blueprint*.

54. Hearst also did not see the completed New Wing at San Simeon; however, he saw photographs of it, much as Mac recounted his having seen those of The Bend.

55. The summer and fall of 1936 come the closest to the period recalled; however, other types of work besides murals were done then, as they were in other "Pogany" years. Mostly its own entity, Pogany's work may have dominated a certain *fund*, akin to the Hilltop Fund at San Simeon.

Doris Day preceded Pogany's time. I believe she is still living in San Francisco. My writing is not what it used to be.—neither am I as I had a light stroke a year ago—Still can manage but not too good.

Mac's declining health had reduced his graceful script of former years to a tortured scrawl, in which he wrote the second of those vivid letters; this one went to Nellie and Cal Shewmaker's daughter, Shirley Shewmaker Wahl, on December 17, 1983; Mac was eighty-six by then but still willing "to answer questions." In writing to Mrs. Wahl, he told much the same story as in the first letter but with some variations and additional details:[56]

I came to California in the 20's, hoping to get work as a set designer. My previous efforts were that of architectural draftsman in the Detroit area. I didn't land a studio job but did meet Julia Morgan's assistant who was engaged in building an annex to Miss Davies Beach house in Santa Monica. Thad Joy was this assistant and [it] was through him I joined Miss Morgan's staff and agreed to go to San Simeon when the Santa Monica job ended.

I arrived at San Simeon in Jan 1930. I had very little to do with the Castle [Casa Grande, etc.] but from the start began working on schemes for re building the Wyntoon Castle which burned in the same month of Jan 1930.

It was also the year of [or rather following] the great financial crash [of Octo-

---

56. The letter Mac wrote to Nellie Shewmaker on August 12, 1979 (a long one, partly cited in note 42, above), contained some information that didn't resurface in Mac's letters of 1982 and 1983:

Do you remember when the Kennedy family were at Wyntoon? The 3 boys John, Robert, & Ted were with their Dad and Mother and stayed several days. It may have been before your time.

Was Mac speaking of a visit besides the one by Joe Kennedy, Jr., in 1940 and, later that year, the one by Joe's father and John F. Kennedy? (See p. 453, note 50.) Perhaps, but the travels of that family seem too richly documented for Mac alone to be citing a *third* Kennedy trip, especially one so well attended. In any event, Mac ended his long, tightly handwritten letter on a more plausible note:

Bill Murray handled a difficult job during those last years very well. Sunical Corp provided the funds for the construction work and it was difficult to keep Mr Hearst on a low expense level. The Gables fire [1944] gave some insurance money which helped finance the Bend rebuilding. I always regret[t]ed that Mr H did not get to see the Bend after it was finished. After Mr H got to Beverly Hills he failed in health very fast. There was no building program during the last year [1950–51?].

Ever the devoted pen pal, Mac wrote to Nellie Shewmaker on several other occasions in the late 1970s and early 1980s (besides those cited in these pages). As to building activity at 1007 N. Beverly Drive shortly before or after Hearst died in August 1951, Guiles said that Eleanor Boardman "moved into the gatehouse" in 1950; see *Marion Davies*, pp. 338, 358; see also note 22, above. In 1952 an esteemed Southland architect did some work for Miss Boardman at that address, presumably on the gatehouse. See *Wallace Neff 1895-1982: The Romance of Regional Architecture* (San Marino, 1989), unnumbered p. 133.

ber 1929] which cramped expenditures for continuance [of] work even with seeming endless money supply but there were insurance funds to work with for a Wyntoon replacement.

About this time Mr. Hearst bought the Spanish monastery, or the usable parts, at least. It was an impulsive buy and a disaster as far as usable material for a Wyntoon new castle. The idea was solely to get Wyntoon going again, but the program began to look like a too grand and time consuming fiasco and the monastery was abandoned. Before it was entirely given up, it was agreed to have Bernard May-beck have a hand in the project. Maybeck was a celebrated S.F. Architect who had been Phoebe Hearst's Architect for the original Wyntoon building. He was also the mentor for the young Julia Morgan who was a friend of Mrs. [Phoebe] Hearst and did considerable work at Pleasanton [on Mrs. Hearst's Hacienda del Pozo de Verona]. In any case I well recall the Sunday in '30 when Miss Morgan brought Mr. Maybeck to S.S. who produced a role of chalk drawings on brown wrapping paper of a fairy tale castle to be built on the old castle site. Years later some of these brown paper sketches were found by your mother in the Angel House.[57] Nellie [Mrs. Wahl's mother] will know what I am talking about.

Anyhow we know that the big castle schemes were abandoned in favor of a Ba-varian Village on the Waterhouse property which could be built rather quickly (and relatively economically) and so it was. Then The Bend came into view and efforts to convert the building there to usable condition — summer of 1933 as I re-call [Hearst bought The Bend in 1934].

After The Gables burned [August 1944] there was a new source of insurance money and The Bend project became bigger. The present Bend looks rather grand scale compared to the Bavarian Village which are "frame" wooden buildings.

I regret that Mr. Hearst never saw the completed Bend. Neither did Miss Mor-gan to my knowledge.

Thad Joy, whom I mentioned, had a lot to do with the San Simeon project also the early work at Wyntoon [after the fire of 1930] such as the first re-build of the Gables to provide a "headquarters" provision. Unfortunately Joy died early in the game a few months after I arrived.[58]

San Simeon is truly Miss Morgan's monument — Mr. Hearst's also. People comment on the religious indications by the architecture and decorations. The

---

57. Other Maybeck sketches of this type and vintage are among the Hearst Castle collection of architectural drawings, which number in the thousands all told (and are dominated by Morgan's work and that of her own draftsmen).

58. Joy was debilitated enough after 1929 to have died in essence long before 1942; his death that year may have gone almost unnoticed. How else to explain this great a lapse in Mac's keen memory? (But see note 56, above.) In any event, Mac must have regarded the F. C. Stolte Co.'s work on The Gables from 1933 onward as a "second re-build," the first one having been right after the big fire in 1930.

dining room [the Refectory] and the [Gothic] study on 3rd floor indicate this particularly.

It was a handicap to be tied down by "hard times" lack of funds. Mr. Hearst never seemed to be able to accept the fact that 16 men could not produce what 60 did in the good old days.

George Loorz had been dead a few years when Mac McClure wrote those letters. Had he still been alive and had he, too, heard from Mac in this reminiscent way, we can easily imagine his having concurred — can easily imagine his having replied in his vibrant, unencumbered style, "That's just how it was Mac and you told it better than anybody could." We can also imagine his having signed off as he so often had in writing to his many, many friends over the years — with that warm-hearted "Cheerio" they all knew was distinctly his.

Afterword

BIOGRAPHERS AND HISTORIANS sometimes regard correspondence as a poor witness or, worse still, as a misleading one. Their point is well taken, for in its weaker moments the act of letter-writing admits of bias and prejudice, of hyperbole and even outright fabrication. How prone were George Loorz and his fellow correspondents to such weaknesses, to the deceptive mingling of fact and fiction? Notably little on the whole. Another strong suit: insofar as letters speak for themselves—and too many that get into print do not—hundreds of passages from the Loorz Papers are uncommonly eloquent. Yet even those better-written words require their share of explaining, of deciphering and interpolating, as numerous pages in *Building for Hearst and Morgan* have shown.

Omissions and gaps are a different matter. The loss or destruction of certain letters or other documents can pose problems that no amount of supplementary data can solve. This is the frustrating nature of the game, true not only of the George Loorz Papers at times but also of related manuscript holdings. It's certainly true of Cal Poly's Morgan Collection for the years covered in this book; it's also true of the Hearst Papers in the Bancroft Library and, furthermore, of that great missing link called the Morgan-Forney Collection. Nonetheless, these and some additional holdings have provided telling corroboration for the Loorz Papers—much as the latter could for those holdings in future books about Hearst and Morgan, about San Simeon and Wyntoon, or about any number of kindred subjects.

Should not *all* such archives be consulted from here on? Of course they should, both the ones in public repositories and those in other hands (most of which private sources are now sufficiently approachable).

And thus I offer a literary-historical call to arms—having been preceded by Morgan North, who in 1975 spoke "To the Historian" in his last of three interviews with Suzanne Riess. My version of such a call goes like this:

> To my fellow editors, researchers, and aficionados, too (as North himself might have said more broadly a generation later). Make use of as many sources as possi-

ble, for together the Loorz Papers and all similar holdings, well known or obscure, are unrivaled in their field. Approach each of them with gratitude (for the miracle of their existence) and with admiration (for the richness of their contents), seeking not so much to declare one of them superior—always a tempting thing with the Loorz material—as to bask in the rare light they all reflect from times gone by. Strive in turn to be worthy mirrors, aiming those reflections toward the years ahead. It's the least we should do. We'll be the better for it today; and if posterity remembers us even half as fondly as it now can the Chief and Miss Morgan and Loorz as well—plus Fred Stolte, Mac McClure, Joe Willicombe, and all the others whose voices live on—we will have justified our efforts, many times over.

In his own credo of 1975, Morgan North touched on several key points. Among them: "The economics are not good, because the cost of doing this [the cost, that is, of writing a truly competent book on Julia Morgan] would be quite substantial; and although I think it would be possible to find a publisher, I don't think they would be climbing all over knocking people's doors down, trying to get the manuscript." Amen, with regard either to Miss Morgan as a main subject or to George Loorz, Hearst himself having the only surefire name in their circle.

It remains for readers of this volume to decide how well I've answered a call like Mr. North's, not to mention the newer, broader one I've just posed. In the meantime, there can be no question that without the unwavering support of friends and colleagues—among them John Porter, Lynn Forney McMurray, Will Hearst III, and, above all, Bill Loorz—I could never have come within a mile. What I said back in 1990 in my original preface still applies: I'll be forever grateful.

TAYLOR COFFMAN

Morgan North's comments for historians are from The Julia Morgan Architectural History Project, *Vol. II, pp. 237–40.*

Appendix A

Julia Morgan's Work for William Randolph Hearst and Other Clients, 1924–1940

The three account ledgers in the Morgan-Forney Collection contain hundreds of loose-leaf pages, all of which are unnumbered and many of which have entries on both sides. More than a thousand sides exist, comprising a varied assortment of fronts and backs of pages. The smallest jobs command a single, front-sided page only. But many of the jobs have a separate title page, whose back gives a typewritten record of commissions or other payments. One or more pages of itemized entries follow, governed by the size of the job. The main San Simeon account has about 120 pages, the main Wyntoon account about twenty-five, and nearly all the non-Hearst accounts fewer still. No matter their range, though, the pages following the title-recap page are handwritten (true of so many pages in the ledgers, whether a given account has a title page or not). That factor alone insures that the eventual editing of these documents will require painstaking care.

In most cases the account ledgers disclose what it cost Morgan to pursue and, quite often, carry out a given job (thus bringing commission payments into play)—in short, her operating costs, her expenses accrued in practicing architecture. Some of the recap pages spell out the "job history" involved. A good example stems from her work on the unrealized Darbee Mausoleum; a typed entry dated November 27, 1940, was made several months after that account had begun to lapse:

> [Pertaining] To actual expense incurred, excl. of any personal serv., in preparation of prelim. plans and estimates for the development of grounds & bldgs of Western Hills of Memorial City, Inc. Lawndale [now Colma], Cal. from Apr. 1939 to date—Drafting, engineering & gen. office exp., blue prints, photostats, mounts, supplies, etc.

Morgan's total charges stood at $1,944.50, which Mrs. Darbee paid in four installments over the next few months. (Had the job gone ahead, Morgan's commission on building costs would probably have been her sole remuneration; ideally, that amount would have surpassed the $1,944.50 and all other operating costs yet to come.) As it stands, the record of the aborted activity on the Darbee project makes for a simple, open-and-shut case.

Another clarifying example—and one also regarding a project that never gelled for Morgan—stems from a job that, intermittently in the 1920s, found her accruing a substantial sum of $4,507 in drafting and related expenses. These warranted payment in the same way that the Darbee expenses later would, inasmuch as no offsetting commission was imminent:

> For services rendered in connection with proposed San Carlos Borromeo Church at Monterey, charges being actual cost of preparing architectural and structural plans and specifications.

Here again the recap sheet is straightforward and to the point. So is the recap of 1929 for a job in San Francisco that, in contrast, reached fruition for Morgan and thus yielded commission dollars as her sole mode of payment. In 1923 she began taking up where a much earlier architect had left off—this time in behalf of the Ladies Protection & Relief Society:

> In full for services in connection with extension of elevator and additions and alterations to building at 3400 Laguna St.

Examples like these help illuminate those jobs that have minimal recap sheets, or sometimes none at all. Other recaps give brief but vital details that appear nowhere else in the ledgers, as in this instance for one of the Wyntoon accounts:

> To services in connection with additions to Gables alterations to China House, taking down masonry walls of Castle [after the recent fire], minor changes at farm house, etc. at Wyntoon, in the spring and summer of 1930.

In all such instances, whether Hearst or another party was the client, Morgan accrued certain expenses in plying her trade: costs such as draftsmanship, blueprints and photographs, travel and on-site consultation, general office overhead, and still more. That's the foremost thing that her ledgers disclose. Very often they also indicate whether her earnings were non-commission, compensatory dollars (as with the Darbee Mausoleum and the San Carlos Church) or commission-only dollars (as with the many jobs that included actual construction). The ledgers less often disclose the total cost for a client or builder to complete a project based on her designs.

With regard to San Simeon, the plot thickens fast. Complexity becomes a byword, beyond anything found in the various non-Hearst situations, indeed, beyond that which is found in all the other *Hearst* situations. A perusal of the main San Simeon account—as distinct from the lesser San Simeon accounts, some as brief as a single page—raises more questions than this book on the Loorz Papers can answer. Nothing short of a full audit and its detailed analysis will ever suffice. Consider salaries, for instance. Rarely do Morgan's ledgers show what a given draftsman was paid to prepare drawings for a job; aside from recording anonymous drafting-room time, the ledgers seldom serve that purpose; nor do they double as payroll records. And yet an exception was made for Morgan's secretary, Lilian Forney, whose *entire* salary from December

1925 through July 1938, pertaining to Hearst and non-Hearst jobs alike, was declared as part of the main San Simeon account. So were Hathaway Lovell's earnings for his on-site role in the late twenties. (Theoretically, it made little difference *what* Morgan chose to include in her San Simeon ledgers: she relied mostly on commission-only dollars from Hearst, not compensatory ones of the Darbee or San Carlos type.)

Nonetheless, the unusual salary entries can't be handily dismissed. The ones on behalf of Mrs. Forney and Hatch Lovell amount to some $26,220—roughly a tenth of San Simeon's commanding $262,715 on p. 534 (a sum reflecting both the main account for that job and lesser brethren like the Bunkhouse and Chicken House accounts cited in Appendix B). Should the $26,220 be "backed out" to yield an adjusted figure ($236,495) that's more in keeping with the nature of many accounts in the ledgers? If so, San Simeon's all-encompassing 37.4% on p. 534 would become 33.6% (of $703,048). But first the $703,048 would need to be reduced by $26,220 and would thus become $678,828, of which San Simeon's scaled-down $236,495 would become 34.8%; in turn, the grand Hearst total of $418,703 on p. 536 would become $392,483, equating with 57.8% (of $678,828). And so the intricate process would continue, through dozens of shifting figures and percentages.

No, the best approach for now is to "follow copy" and leave the Morgan-Forney data as they stand, steeped in their own logic. (In completing this book on the Loorz Papers and, specifically, Appendix A, I had to abandon my attempts to adjust *all* the ledger figures from a gross stature to a net "refunded" stature—among other possible adjustments.) Plenty of accounts besides those for Hearst projects have their own oddities; in short order, pending a full-scale audit and further scrutiny, confusion would reign if one tinkered too much.

Thus do some words offered earlier in this book bear repeating: the Morgan-Forney data can be endlessly analyzed, their salient points emphasized, their finer points compared and pondered. They still portray Julia Morgan as an architect who, from the mid-1920s through the late 1930s, was uncommonly in step with William Randolph Hearst and, indeed, more beholden to him than to any other client or patron.

Throughout the following twelve pages, all figures have been rounded to the nearest whole number; the results are deemed accurate within one dollar. All percentages have been rounded to the nearest tenth of a full point. Related accounts, epitomized by the multiple San Simeon, Wyntoon, and Beach House examples, have with rare exceptions been grouped under single headings. Certain jobs from the first half of Morgan's career, such as Asilomar or the Katherine Burke School, gave rise to follow-up efforts in the second half, hence their inclusion on pp. 534–35; the figures cited for them apply strictly to the period from 1924 through 1940.

JULIA MORGAN'S LARGEST ACCOUNTS, 1924–1940
Reflecting $652,859 (92.9%) of $703,048 in total operating costs,
as stated on her annual "Distribution of Expenses" sheets
and reconciled with the job-ledger entries they summarize
The ∗ symbol denotes a Hearst account in each instance

∗	1.	San Simeon	$262,715	37.4%
∗	2.	Wyntoon	59,624	8.5
	3.	California Crematorium, Oakland	28,333	4.0
	4.	YWCA Building, Honolulu, Hawaii	27,367	3.9
	5.	Principia College, Elsah, Illinois	22,731	3.2
∗	6.	Beach House, Santa Monica	21,662	3.1
	7.	Berkeley Women's City Club	20,675	2.9
	8.	YWCA "Residence" Building, San Francisco	19,449	2.8
∗	9.	Phoebe A. Hearst Memorial Women's Gym, Berkeley	15,451	2.2
	10.	Margaret Baylor Inn, Santa Barbara	14,934	2.1
	11.	YWCA Building, Long Beach	12,475	1.8
	12.	YWCA Building, Riverside	11,996	1.7
∗	13.	San Francisco Examiner Building	9,721	1.4
	14.	YWCA "Studio Club," Hollywood	9,399	1.3
	15.	Native Daughters of the Golden West, San Francisco	7,232	1.0
	16.	Selden Williams Residence, Berkeley	7,048	1.0
∗	17.	Hearst Building, San Francisco	6,596	0.9
∗	18.	George Hearst Residence, Hillsborough	6,454	0.9
∗	19.	Oakland-Post Enquirer Building	5,998	0.9
∗	20.	Marion Davies Clinic, West Los Angeles	5,927	0.8
	21.	Tooker Memorial School, Oakland	5,474	0.8
	22.	Ladies Protection & Relief Society, San Francisco	5,125	0.7
∗	23.	Milpitas Hacienda, Jolon	5,115	0.7
∗	24.	Marion Davies Residence, Beverly Hills	3,980	0.6
	25.	YWCA Buildings, Asilomar, Pacific Grove	3,890	0.6

	26.	Black Sheep Restaurant Complex, Berkeley	$3,830	0.5%
	27.	Allan M. Starr Residence, Piedmont	3,703	0.5
*	28.	Santa Maria de Ovila (Spanish Monastery)	3,175	0.5
	29.	Hamlin School, San Francisco	2,906	0.4
	30.	Chinese YWCA Building, San Francisco	2,659	0.4
*	31.	Cosmopolitan Bungalow, Los Angeles	2,469	0.4
	32.	Japanese YWCA Building, San Francisco	2,321	0.3
	33.	Bellshire Housing Project, San Francisco	2,244	0.3
*	34.	Los Angeles Examiner Building	2,187	0.3
*	35.	Hearst Radio KYA Facility, San Francisco	2,146	0.3
	36.	Western Hills (Darbee Mausoleum), Lawndale-Colma	1,945	0.3
	37.	Walter Schilling Residence, San Francisco	1,880	0.3
	38.	Santa Barbara Recreation Center Gymnasium	1,879	0.3
	39.	San Carlos Borromeo Church, Monterey	1,843	0.3
*	40.	Hearst Radio KUP Facility, San Mateo	1,831	0.3
	41.	Turner Medical Building, Berkeley	1,827	0.3
	42.	American Legion Building, Marysville	1,780	0.3
	43.	Delta Zeta Sorority House, Berkeley	1,743	0.3
	44.	YWCA Building, University of Hawaii, Honolulu	1,732	0.2
	45.	Katherine Burke School, San Francisco	1,701	0.2
	46.	B. W. Reed Residence, Oakland	1,678	0.2
	47.	H. H. North Apartments, Berkeley	1,607	0.2
	48.	Homelani Columbarium, Hilo, Hawaii	1,526	0.2
	49.	Else Schilling Residence, Lake Tahoe	1,454	0.2
*	50.	University of California Museum, Berkeley	1,422	0.2

SUBTOTAL	$652,859	92.9%
San Francisco County Nurses ($1,420) and all remaining non-Hearst accounts	47,959	6.8
Grandview Point, Grand Canyon ($759) and all remaining Hearst accounts	2,230	0.3
TOTAL	$703,048	100.0%

Summary I

The 17 largest Hearst accounts	$416,473	59.2%
The 33 largest non-Hearst accounts	236,386	33.6
All other accounts (Hearst and non-Hearst)	50,189	7.2
TOTAL	$703,048	100.0%

Summary II

All Hearst accounts	$418,703	59.6%
All non-Hearst accounts	284,345	40.4
TOTAL	$703,048	100.0%

NOTE: Several of the accounts on pp. 534–35 begin in the earliest years covered by the Morgan-Forney ledgers, 1919–23; a few accounts that begin in the main years, 1924–40, extend into the latest years covered, 1941–47. Two accounts—San Simeon and the California Crematorium—touch on all three periods, albeit lightly on the last one. But the lack of Distribution of Expenses sheets for the earliest and latest years precludes their full recounting.

Some observations can still be made about those flanking periods. A further $95,429 stems from twenty-one of the fifty accounts named above; 51.2% of it ($49,313) was San Simeon's doing, almost entirely in 1919–23, a mere $51 in costs having occurred in 1941–42. This boosts "the mother of all accounts" to $311,977 for 1919–40 (or to a slightly higher $312,028 for 1919–42, its full recorded span). The Santa Maria de Ovila monastery produced the next highest increase, $17,194 (for a total of $20,369 when combined with its 1924–40 stature); the gain came strictly in the 1941–47 period. The Long Beach YWCA carried $11,740 into 1924 (thus yielding $24,215 for 1923–25).

Those three accounts—San Simeon, Santa Maria de Ovila, and Long Beach—command 82.0% ($78,247) of the $95,429 accrued in the flanking years. A further 13.0% ($12,445) of the $95,429, all of it predating 1924, comprises the American Legion Building in Marysville, the Los Angeles Examiner Building, the San Carlos Borromeo Church in Monterey, and the Ladies Protection & Relief Society in San Francisco.

If added to the 1924–40 total of $703,048, the $95,429 from the flanking years puts $800,000 within easy reach. Because many accounts from 1919–23 are missing (and perhaps some from 1941–47 are also missing), a grand total closer to $900,000 in itemized costs seems plausible for 1919–47 overall. All such amounts are historical; their equivalents today range from eight to thirteen times greater, as noted on p. xxvi.

ANALYSIS OF ACCOUNTS, 1924–1940
The Hearst accounts are itemized annually, followed by a summary
each time of all other accounts (whose largest one is identified
and whose portion of the non-Hearst total for the year is cited)

1924
Hearst: $26,263 (48.8%) of $53,860 overall

San Simeon	$21,744	40.4%
Phoebe A. Hearst Memorial Gym, Berkeley	3,237	6.0
Los Angeles Examiner Building	703	1.3
San Francisco Examiner Building	576	1.1
Wyntoon	3	0.0
	$26,263	48.8%
YWCA Building, Long Beach ($7,517) and all other non-Hearst accounts	27,597	51.2
TOTAL	$53,860	100.0%

1925
Hearst: $27,683 (41.0%) of $67,516 overall

San Simeon	$14,850	22.0%
Phoebe A. Hearst Memorial Gym, Berkeley	7,589	11.2
San Francisco Examiner Building	4,185	6.2
Marion Davies Residence, Beverly Hills	996	1.5
Los Angeles Examiner Building	39	0.1
Milpitas Ranch House, Jolon	24	0.0
	$27,683	41.0%
YWCA Building, Honolulu ($8,111) and all other non-Hearst accounts	39,833	59.0
TOTAL	$67,516	100.0%

1926
Hearst: $31,559 (46.6%) of $67,719 overall

San Simeon	$19,455	28.7%
Phoebe A. Hearst Memorial Gym, Berkeley	4,308	6.4
Beach House, Santa Monica	3,937	5.8
Marion Davies Residence, Beverly Hills	2,539	3.8
San Francisco Examiner Building	961	1.4
San Francisco Call Building	297	0.4
Milpitas Ranch House, Jolon	62	0.1
	$31,559	46.6%
YWCA Building, Honolulu ($13,306) and all other non-Hearst accounts	36,160	53.4
TOTAL	$67,719	100.0%

1927
Hearst: $38,845 (56.7%) of $68,510 overall

San Simeon	$32,585	47.6%
Oakland Post-Enquirer Building	3,736	5.4
Beach House, Santa Monica	1,564	2.3
Phoebe A. Hearst Memorial Gym, Berkeley	313	0.5
San Francisco Examiner Building	269	0.4
UC Museum, Berkeley	227	0.3
UC Auditorium, Berkeley	109	0.2
Marion Davies Residence, Beverly Hills	27	0.0
San Francisco Call Building	15	0.0
	$38,845	56.7%
California Crematorium, Oakland ($9,482) and all other non-Hearst accounts	29,665	43.3
TOTAL	$68,510	100.0%

1928
Hearst: $45,137 (63.0%) of $71,671 overall

San Simeon	$36,453	50.9%
Beach House, Santa Monica	3,729	5.2
Oakland Post-Enquirer Building	2,261	3.2
San Francisco Examiner Building	1,307	1.8
Wyntoon	1,234	1.7
UC Museum, Berkeley	148	0.2
Phoebe A. Hearst Memorial Gym, Berkeley	4	0.0
UC Auditorium, Berkeley	1	0.0
	$45,137	63.0%
California Crematorium, Oakland ($7,229) and all other non-Hearst accounts	26,534	37.0
TOTAL	$71,671	100.0%

1929
Hearst: $42,366 (68.2%) of $62,155 overall

San Simeon	$25,062	40.3%
Beach House, Santa Monica	8,122	13.1
Wyntoon	4,185	6.7
Milpitas Hacienda, Jolon	2,676	4.3
UC Museum, Berkeley	1,041	1.7
George Hearst Residence, Hillsborough	727	1.2
Marion Davies Residence, Beverly Hills	418	0.7
St. Donat's Castle, Wales, U.K.	134	0.2
Oakland Post-Enquirer Building	1	0.0
	$42,366	68.2%
Berkeley Women's City Club ($7,838) and all other non-Hearst accounts	19,789	31.9
TOTAL	$62,155	100.1%

1930
Hearst: $30,033 (60.6%) of $49,557 overall

San Simeon	$18,957	38.3%
George Hearst Residence, Hillsborough	4,363	8.8
Wyntoon	4,280	8.6
Milpitas Hacienda, Jolon	1,335	2.7
Beach House, Santa Monica	792	1.6
Los Angeles Examiner Building	301	0.6
UC Museum, Berkeley	5	0.0
	$30,033	60.6%
Berkeley Women's City Club ($11,368) and all other non-Hearst accounts	19,524	39.4
TOTAL	$49,557	100.0%

1931
Hearst: $30,943 (50.1%) of $61,780 overall

San Simeon	$19,718	32.0%
Wyntoon	4,125	6.7
Santa Maria de Ovila Monastery, Spain and San Francisco	2,758	4.5
Marion Davies Clinic, West Los Angeles	2,172	3.5
Los Angeles Examiner Building	951	1.5
George Hearst Residence, Hillsborough	825	1.3
Beach House, Santa Monica	254	0.4
Milpitas Hacienda, Jolon	140	0.2
	$30,943	50.1%
Principia College, Illinois ($15,435) and all other non-Hearst accounts	30,837	50.0
TOTAL	$61,780	100.1%

1932
Hearst: $24,329 (58.7%) of $41,475 overall

San Simeon	$19,502	47.0%
Marion Davies Clinic, West Los Angeles	3,179	7.7
Wyntoon	1,024	2.5
George Hearst Residence, Hillsborough	262	0.6
Beach House, Santa Monica	242	0.6
Phoebe A. Hearst School, Washington D.C.	120	0.3
	$24,329	58.7%
YWCA "Residence," San Francisco ($7,121) and all other non-Hearst accounts	17,146	41.3
TOTAL	$41,475	100.0%

1933
Hearst: $20,606 (78.9%) of $26,127 overall

San Simeon	$11,192	42.9%
Wyntoon	8,819	33.8
Marion Davies Clinic, West Los Angeles	276	1.1
Los Angeles Examiner Building	183	0.7
George Hearst Residence, Hillsborough	55	0.2
Cosmopolitan Bungalow, Culver City	32	0.1
Grandview Point, Grand Canyon, Arizona	27	0.1
Beach House, Santa Monica	22	0.0
	$20,606	78.9%
Bellshire Housing Project, San Francisco ($2,240) and all other non-Hearst accounts	5,521	21.1
TOTAL	$26,127	100.0%

1934
Hearst: $19,931 (86.7%) of $22,988 overall

San Simeon	$11,913	51.8%
Wyntoon	6,171	26.9
Cosmopolitan Bungalow, Culver City	892	3.9
George Hearst Residence, Holmby Hills	418	1.8
Marion Davies Clinic, Los Angeles	300	1.3
Beach House, Santa Monica	139	0.6
George Hearst Residence, Hillsborough	73	0.3
San Francisco Examiner Building	25	0.1
	$19,931	86.7%
California Crematorium, Oakland ($1,770) and all other non-Hearst accounts	3,057	13.3
TOTAL	$22,988	100.0%

1935
Hearst: $21,346 (83.8%) of $25,477 overall

Wyntoon	$10,495	41.2%
San Simeon	7,001	27.5
Hearst Radio KUP Facility, San Mateo	1,487	5.8
San Francisco Examiner Building	1,303	5.1
Beach House, Santa Monica	956	3.7
Milpitas Hacienda, Jolon	65	0.3
George Hearst Residence, Hillsborough	39	0.2
	$21,346	83.8%
Homelani Columbarium, Hilo ($1,097) and all other non-Hearst accounts	4,131	16.2
TOTAL	$25,477	100.0%

1936
Hearst: $24,851 (79.8%) of $31,153 overall

San Simeon	$13,842	44.4%
Wyntoon	6,963	22.4
Beach House, Santa Monica	1,501	4.8
Grandview Point, Grand Canyon, Arizona	732	2.4
Hearst Radio KYA Facility, San Francisco	690	2.2
Milpitas Hacienda, Jolon	500	1.6
Hearst Radio KUP Facility, San Mateo	344	1.1
San Francisco Examiner Building	166	0.5
Hearst Building, San Francisco	86	0.3
George Hearst Residence, Hillsborough	27	0.1
	$24,851	79.8%
Turner Medical Building, Berkeley ($1,064) and all other non-Hearst accounts	6,302	20.2
TOTAL	$31,153	100.0%

1937
Hearst: $17,881 (85.8%) of $20,851 overall

Wyntoon	$6,764	32.5%
San Simeon	5,924	28.4
Hearst Building, San Francisco	2,295	11.0
Hearst Radio KYA Facility, San Francisco	1,439	6.9
San Francisco Examiner Building	451	2.2
Milpitas Hacienda, Jolon	399	1.9
Milpitas Ranch Men's Quarters	292	1.4
Beach House, Santa Monica	227	1.1
George Hearst Residence, Hillsborough	80	0.4
Los Angeles Examiner Building	10	0.0
	$17,881	85.8%
W. Schilling Residence, San Francisco ($1,860) and all other non-Hearst accounts	2,970	14.2
TOTAL	$20,851	100.0%

1938
Hearst: $12,934 (75.1%) of $17,223 overall

Wyntoon	$5,560	32.3%
Hearst Building, San Francisco	4,134	24.0
San Simeon	2,849	16.5
Beach House, Santa Monica	177	1.0
San Francisco Examiner Building	128	0.8
Cosmopolitan Bungalow, Burbank	66	0.4
Hearst Radio KYA Facility, San Francisco	17	0.1
George Hearst Residence, Hillsborough	3	0.0
	$12,934	75.1%
Starr Residence, Piedmont ($2,384) and all other non-Hearst accounts	4,289	24.9
TOTAL	$17,223	100.0%

1939
Hearst: $3,202 (37.5%) of $8,546 overall

San Simeon	$1,641	19.2%
Cosmopolitan Bungalow, Beverly Hills	1,479	17.3
Hearst Building, San Francisco	81	1.0
Wyntoon	1	0.0
	$3,202	37.5%
Darbee Mausoleum, Lawndale-Colma ($1,533) and all other non-Hearst accounts	5,344	62.5
TOTAL	$8,546	100.0%

1940
Hearst: $794 (12.3%) of $6,440 overall

Santa Maria de Ovila Monastery, San Francisco	$417	6.5%
San Francisco Examiner Building	350	5.4
San Simeon	27	0.4
	$794	12.3%
Black Sheep Restaurant, Berkeley ($2,983) and all other non-Hearst accounts	5,646	87.7
TOTAL	$6,440	100.0%

For the period after 1940, no annual Distribution of Expenses sheets exist; without them, the corresponding job ledgers can't be properly reconciled. Appendix A is therefore confined to the seventeen years starting in 1924 (but see the note on p. 536, concerning the years 1919–23 and 1941–47).

Appendix B

Julia Morgan's Commission Account:
San Simeon, 1919–1939

The eighteen pages bearing the "Commission Account" for San Simeon stand out boldly in the Morgan-Forney ledgers. In contrast, the parallel "Wyntoon Receipts" for 1933–39 run a distant second at just five pages; and the untitled recaps of the largest non-Hearst jobs, like the Berkeley City Club or the Honolulu Y, are shorter still. The ratios make sense: San Simeon dominated the latter half of Morgan's career. The job may have exhausted her sometimes, yet it enriched her—monetarily at the very least—in ways that no other job ever did. She can be remembered for having paid periodic bonuses to her office staff at the Merchants Exchange; for having accepted certain jobs on which no architect could make money; and, in what leisure time she took, for having traveled farther and, overall, more frequently and more creatively than was common in her day.

Morgan could have done those things only if she had been prosperous—which she was, because of Hearst above all.

True, she allowed most people to think the opposite (the Morgan Norths among them, and often George Loorz as well). Such was her right, her choice, her prerogative. It suited her breeding and temperament; it discreetly defined her place in the world.

How significant was the $115,893 she cleared on the San Simeon job from 1919 through 1939? (It drops to $115,815 when her minuscule costs of $27 in 1940 and $51 in 1941–42 are included: a mere $78 stemming from activity that did not lead to commission payments.) The adjusted amount—$115,815—is the difference between Appendix A's $312,028 in total operating costs (noted on p. 536, a sum including her draftsmen's hours and most other office expenses tied to San Simeon) and the commission receipts of $427,843 cited here in Appendix B. In assessing what Morgan made, we can venture for starters a broad twenty-one-year average (for 1919–1939) of $20,373 in gross annual proceeds and $5,515 in net annual profit. The net figure recalls Loorz's salary at San Simeon, an amount paid not through Morgan's Commission Account—as were the in-house salaries of people like Jim LeFeaver, Dick Nusbaum, and Jack Wagenet—but jointly through the Hearst Construction Fund and the Hilltop Fund.

Hearst not only defrayed his share of Morgan's staff time and overhead in San Francisco, he also paid her nearly $31,000 in "refunds" during these years, inclusive of the 1940–42 period. All such payments were over and above the $427,843. Better yet for Morgan, as of 1923 (a pivotal year) both the commissions and the refunds were segregated from San Simeon's time-and-materials expenses that Hearst covered through his monthly allotments—through his lump-sum replenishing of the Hearst Construction Fund. From 1919 onward, for that matter, the more he provided, the more she eventually collected. The evidence is irrefutable: Morgan made money as Hearst's architect, especially on the high-priced work that prevailed at San Simeon. Her good fortune was too precious to squander in loose talk or conspicuous consumption of her own devising.

More arithmetic can be done with her $427,843 in commissions. As a gross figure (before disbursement, taxes, and so forth), it represents 8.5% of $5,033,447, extrapolated from her rate for most of the period from 1919 through 1939. But come the mid-1940s, when her office and Bill Murray's compared notes on San Simeon's total cost (for 1919–1942), a smaller figure is what they reckoned with—$4,717,077, soon rounded to $4,717,000. Her $427,843 represents 9.1% of that amount, with or without the $77 tacked on (this isn't to suggest, though, that her rate with Hearst ever went that high).

Obviously, all such figures and percentages, whether real or imaginary, are in a similar league.

The highest figure ($5,033,447) exceeds the next highest one ($4,717,077) by $316,370. However, $316,370 is an arbitrary, perhaps meaningless figure, there being no reason to increase the well-established 4.7 million by that particular sum, despite the likelihood that five million dollars is closer to what Hearst spent on San Simeon before the war (irrespective, as both Tom Aidala and Victoria Kastner have pointed out in their books, of art objects and architectural antiques). In fact, the prewar amount could be closer to 5.5 million, especially if we regard most of Morgan's commission dollars as byproducts of 4.7 million, not as intrinsic parts of it. The moral is that, in amplifying the 4.7 million figure—imperative now that Morgan's earnings, the Hilltop Fund, and still other factors have gained greater focus—we should measure our steps in tens of thousands of dollars and, at the utmost, in hundreds of thousands. (In that spirit, the 1.3 million that Maurice McClure said Hearst spent on construction after World War II—separate once more from expenditures on art objects and the like—seems too high a figure to leave unquestioned. If the new airport cost about $200,000, could the other projects of 1945–48 truly have cost almost six times as much? Perhaps they did.)

Morgan designed two buildings for San Simeon whose construction costs are precisely known; however, those costs fall outside the list she and Bill Murray refined in the mid-1940s. In addition, her earnings on the two buildings fall outside the Commission Account and its $427,843. And yet who would want to exclude the Chicken House (the poultry unit) and the Bunkhouse from the 1919–1942 list? The list includes the missionesque warehouse on San Simeon Bay, built by the general contractor W. J. Smith; the list also includes the houses that Loorz and Pete Petersen and Pancho Estrada and others lived in, likewise entrusted to Smith. Why not buildings closer to the heart of the Hearst Ranch—buildings we may have thought lay between the lines of Morgan and Murray's list? Why their exclusion?

Apart from the Hearst Construction Fund projects at 8.5%, Morgan got six percent ($1,682) for the Chicken House, on which Hearst spent $28,028 (excluding his separate "plus" payment to Smith as the cost-plus builder). Morgan also got six percent ($1,764) for the Bunkhouse, which cost Hearst $29,406 (but which was done through Loorz, not Smith). Such factors aside, neither building fitted Murray's accounting requirements in the mid-forties. The Chicken House, dating from 1930, owed its existence to the Piedmont Land & Cattle Company (a fund by that name may once have existed). The Bunkhouse, hailing from 1937–38, was beholden to the newer Hearst Sunical Land & Packing Corporation (by way of the so-called Bunkhouse Fund, not the Hearst Sunical Building Fund). Confusion, contradiction, uncertainty: in the absence of complete records, such impressions are bound to occur.

Morgan (through Camille Rossi, not through Smith or Loorz) also built the main reservoir—the big one on Reservoir Hill—for $27,874 in 1931. This time her rate was the more-familiar 8.5% ($2,369); nonetheless, it too falls outside her Commission Account; and thus her $1,682 on the Chicken House, $1,764 on the Bunkhouse, and $2,369 on the reservoir exceed the $427,843 by a combined $5,815. To make matters stickier, the reservoir appears on the 1919–1942 list, despite having been (like the Chicken House) a separate Piedmont Land & Cattle project. More to ponder, more to puzzle over.

Meanwhile, Hearst spent $114,202 on the Milpitas Hacienda in 1929–31, another job yielding Morgan six percent (and one also involving W. J. Smith). Hearst spent a further $14,268 on it in 1935–37, this time relying on Loorz instead—presumably, as before—through a Milpitas Fund or its equivalent. Morgan again got six percent ($7,708 total on Hearst's outlay of $128,470 in the two phases, with her share naturally being well outside the bounds of her Commission Account). Most would agree that the Milpitas Hacienda should contribute no more than a footnote to the 1919–1942 list: the place wasn't just geographically removed; the Hearst interests had sold it in 1940. But if the reservoir job of 1931 is to be included, the Chicken House and the Bunkhouse seem deserving of the same treatment, quite apart from the details of Morgan's earnings and the names of the builders involved. Those two structures represent $57,434 (plus a shade more in cost-plus terms) that Hearst spent beyond the familiar 4.7 million, an amount recalling annual expenditures through the Hilltop Fund—whose progeny are likewise excluded from the list.

The Loorz Papers are the best source on that subject. (If there were comparable Rossi Papers for the 1920s, they might disclose some earlier building funds that remain unknown.) In any event, Loorz's records show that $44,161 was spent in 1934 through the Hilltop Fund and $63,563 in 1935, the only years for which a complete tally exists. Seven months' worth of 1933 is discernible ($19,334); so are eight months' worth of 1936 ($50,710) and five months' worth of 1937 ($3,842). The outlay through the shorter-lived Hearst Sunical Building Fund is fully traceable in the Loorz Papers: $25,604 was spent in 1936–37. The total for the known expenditures through the Hilltop and Hearst Sunical funds comes to $207,214. For perspective, the amount is $21,310 more than $185,904—the price tags on Milpitas (both phases), the Chicken House, and the Bunkhouse combined.

Morgan's role in the use of those two funds was limited. And their pertinence to the 1919–1942 list is limited, too (though not so sharply). Indeed, many a Hilltop Fund or Hearst Sunical project intersects with things that Morgan and Murray focused on in the forties, with lasting improvements (not just maintenance tasks) both on the hilltop proper and elsewhere—the very kinds of features that, along with The Enchanted Hill itself, constitute what can justly be regarded as *San Simeon*.

———

The list below embodies the standards established for Appendix A: all figures gravitate to the nearest whole number, each being accurate within a dollar; likewise, all percentages denote the nearest tenth of a point.

	AMOUNT BILLED		AMOUNT RECEIVED		PAID UP
1919	$1,000	(1,000)	$1,000	(1,000)	100.0%
1920	6,000	(7,000)	5,000	(6,000)	85.7
1921	16,000	(23,000)	15,000	(21,000)	91.3
1922	40,000	(63,000)	18,500	(39,500)	62.7
1923	32,655	(95,655)	50,663	(90,163)	94.3
1924	26,872	(122,527)	34,014	(124,177)	101.3
1925	26,010	(148,537)	20,254	(144,432)	97.2
1926	31,650	(180,186)	27,105	(171,537)	95.2

APPENDIX B

	AMOUNT BILLED		AMOUNT RECEIVED		PAID UP
1927	$39,863	(220,049)	$37,103	(208,639)	94.8%
1928	44,784	(264,834)	40,370	(249,010)	94.0
1929	30,114	(294,947)	37,483	(286,493)	97.1
1930	26,303	(321,250)	18,191	(304,684)	94.8
1931	20,363	(341,613)	19,908	(324,592)	95.0
1932	20,060	(361,673)	18,520	(343,112)	94.9
1933	15,891	(377,565)	19,615	(362,727)	96.1
1934	14,979	(392,544)	15,665	(378,392)	96.4
1935	12,814	(405,357)	12,644	(391,036)	96.5
1936	13,292	(418,650)	9,797	(400,833)	95.7
1937	6,880	(425,530)	19,039	(419,872)	98.7
1938	1,686	(427,216)	6,600	(426,472)	99.8
1939	0	(427,216)	1,371	(427,843)	100.1
TOTALS		$427,216	$427,843	[+$627]	94.4%*

Average paid-up status over the twenty-one years

Bibliography

The following entries refer to sources besides the George Loorz Papers at the San Luis Obispo County Historical Museum—sources either mentioned along the way or, more often, actually cited or quoted, mostly in the footnotes. The entries include page numbers from *Building for Hearst and Morgan*. Preceded by the initials BHM, the numbers pertain to the main text of this volume, to its notes, or to both, as the occasion warrants. These bibliography-as-index listings overlap at times with the index listings on pp. 562–81; in fact, some of the archival listings on pp. 551–53 are more comprehensive than their counterparts in the regular index.

A. ARCHIVAL AND RELATED SOURCES

Author's Collection. BHM 23

Bernard Maybeck Collection. Environmental Design Archives, University of California, Berkeley [College of Environmental Design]. BHM 2, 7, 15, 40, 55, 68, 71, 86, 179

Bison Archives; Marc Wanamaker, Los Angeles. BHM 509, 515

Bob Board Collection. BHM 411

Coffman, Taylor, comp. "The George Loorz Papers: Storage List and Finding Aid." [Cambria], 1990. BHM 2, 26

Descriptive Guide to the Julia Morgan Collection [Nancy E. Loe, comp.]. San Luis Obispo: California Polytechnic State University, Special Collections Department, n.d. [1985]. BHM 31, 32, 65, 104, 186, 233, 411, 501

Edward Bright Hussey Collection. Environmental Design Archives, University of California, Berkeley [College of Environmental Design]. BHM 2, 39–40, 75, 76

Elizabeth M. Boyter Papers. The Bancroft Library, University of California, Berkeley. BHM 2, 18–19, 62, 65, 76, 172, 283, 364

Everingham, Carol J., comp. "Dateline: San Simeon 1919–1939: A Chronological Development of Ideas, Plans, Drawings, and Actual Construction Starting in 1919 at the William Randolph Hearst Estate in San Simeon." [San Simeon: Photocopied for private distribution], 1981. BHM 31, 32

Hearst Castle Archives, Hearst San Simeon State Historical Monument. BHM 68, 171, 252, 392–93, 430, 509, 512, 519, 527

James Rankin & Sons Records. The Bancroft Library, University of California, Berkeley. BHM 2, 9, 45

Julia Morgan Collection: The Bancroft Library, University of California, Berkeley. BHM 2, 40, 430

Julia Morgan Collection: Environmental Design Archives, University of California, Berkeley [College of Environmental Design]. BHM 2, 46, 52, 55, 68, 69, 87–88, 408, 430, 447, 517

Julia Morgan Collection: Special Collections & University Archives, California Polytechnic State University—San Luis Obispo. BHM 2–3, 12, 14, 15, 16, 20, 26, 28–30, 31, 32, 33, 35, 41, 46, 47, 53, 55, 65, 70, 82, 86, 90, 104, 107, 114, 117, 118, 121, 125, 131, 135, 138, 140, 151, 160, 161, 164, 175, 186, 187, 189, 191, 199, 208, 226, 235–36, 249, 260, 266, 268, 271, 273, 281, 284, 285, 288, 298–99, 302, 304, 312, 317, 318, 319, 322, 323, 327, 331–32, 336, 341, 347, 351, 357, 358, 362, 368, 383, 388, 389, 391, 393, 395, 403, 404, 410–11, 413, 418–19, 426, 429–30, 433, 437, 445, 446, 447, 449, 452, 461, 474–75, 479, 482–83, 485, 487, 489, 490, 491, 492, 494, 499, 501, 502, 503, 513, 515, 520–21, 522, 529, 547–48, 549

Loorz Family Collection. BHM 2, 5–6, 7, 9–10, 18, 151, 159, 171, 189, 212–13, 217, 222, 288, 290–91, 393, 498, 502, 504, 507. See also *Stolte Blueprint* in section B

M. H. de Young Memorial Museum, San Francisco (division of the Fine Arts Museums). BHM 69, 447

Morgan-Forney Collection. Privately held by Lynn Forney McMurray. BHM 2, 3, 6, 7, 8, 11–13, 28, 29–30, 31, 35–36, 41, 45, 50, 56, 63, 65, 68, 69, 75, 82, 85, 91, 95, 104, 120, 122, 123, 129–30, 131, 132, 135, 136, 139, 143, 149, 151, 180, 183, 185, 191, 193, 196, 198, 203, 206, 208, 209, 211, 216, 218–19, 235–36, 242, 243, 249, 250, 255, 260, 263, 265, 268, 279, 280–81, 286, 288, 293–94, 301, 312, 318, 327, 339, 341, 342, 343, 353, 364, 372, 377, 393–94, 403, 404, 405, 410–11, 418, 420–21, 423, 424, 425, 426, 429, 430, 439–40, 443–44, 446, 447, 448, 458, 462, 474–75, 478, 479, 485, 487, 494, 499, 500, 502, 503, 507–08, 511–12, 513, 516–17, 519, 520, 523, 529, 531–50

Riess, Suzanne B., ed. *The Julia Morgan Architectural History Project.* Berkeley: University of California, The Bancroft Library, Regional Oral History Office, 1976. Volume I, "The Work of Walter Steilberg and Julia Morgan," etc. BHM 12, 45, 55, 63, 69, 74, 75, 76, 83, 84, 87, 522

———. *The Julia Morgan Architectural History Project.* Berkeley: University of California, The Bancroft Library, Regional Oral History Office, 1976. Volume II, "Julia Morgan, Her Office, and a House." BHM 12, 13, 40–41, 63, 68, 75, 76, 82, 241, 364, 405, 415, 446, 479, 501, 507–08, 511–12, 517, 530. See also North, Flora D., in section B

Robert E. Easton Collection. Department of Special Collections, Davidson Library; University of California, Santa Barbara. BHM 512

Shewmaker Collection. Privately held by the estate of Shirley Shewmaker Wahl. BHM 2, 86, 159, 449, 521, 524–27

Vanderloo Collection. Privately held by Judy Bellis. BHM 2, 47, 286, 419, 422–23, 426, 442–43, 463, 511

Walter T. Steilberg Collection. Environmental Design Archives, University of California, Berkeley [College of Environmental Design]. BHM 2, 69, 522

Warren McClure Papers. Privately held by Robert and Claudia Rhode (reference copies in the Hearst Castle Archives, San Simeon). BHM 2, 378–79, 389, 404, 413, 419, 420, 423, 424, 426

William Randolph Hearst Papers (77/121 collection). The Bancroft Library, University of California, Berkeley. BHM 2, 3, 15, 18, 20, 26, 27, 28, 29, 32, 33, 35, 37, 38, 42, 45, 47, 57, 65, 70, 77, 86, 99, 113, 116, 118, 138, 139, 140, 177–78, 231, 239, 240–41, 254, 257, 262, 268, 287, 294, 302, 304, 307–09, 311, 313, 314–15, 316, 317, 322, 323, 324–25, 328, 334, 335, 339–40, 342, 344, 347–48, 355, 356, 359, 372, 376, 381, 387, 388, 396–97, 400, 402, 403, 407, 410, 415, 416, 426, 430, 433, 434, 435, 436, 440–42, 444–45, 446, 447, 449, 450–51, 453, 458, 459, 461–62, 465, 466–67, 474, 478, 480, 481–82, 483, 484, 487, 489, 490, 492, 493, 495, 496, 497, 498, 499, 502, 503, 506, 513, 515, 519, 520, 523, 529

B. BOOKS, JOURNALS, MAGAZINES, NEWSPAPERS

Abbe; Patience, Richard, and Johnny. *Of All Places!* New York: Frederick A. Stokes Company, 1937. BHM 170–71, 296

Aidala, Thomas R. *Hearst Castle: San Simeon.* New York: Hudson Hills Press, 1981. BHM 339, 502, 547

Aikman, Duncan. "A Renaissance Palace in our West." *New York Times Magazine* (July 21, 1929; Part V of *The New York Times* Sunday edition), pp. 10–11. BHM 81

Allen, James B. *The Company Town in the American West.* Norman, Oklahoma: University of Oklahoma Press, 1966. BHM 96

Anderson, Michael F. *Living at the Edge: Explorers, Exploiters and Settlers of the Grand Canyon Region.* Grand Canyon, Arizona: Grand Canyon Association, 1998. BHM 262, 445

Aslet, Clive. *The Last Country Houses.* New Haven and London: Yale University Press, 1982. BHM 55

Baldanza, Frank. "Huxley and Hearst." *Journal of Modern Literature* (September 1979), pp. 441–55. BHM 392

Bemelmans, Ludwig. *To the One I Love the Best.* New York: The Viking Press, 1955. BHM 171, 508

Berg, A. Scott. *Lindbergh.* New York: G. P. Putnam's Sons, 1998. BHM 462

Bidwell, Carol A. *The Conejo Valley: Old and New Frontiers.* Chatsworth, California: Windsor Publications, 1989. BHM 408

Blomberg, Nancy J. *Navajo Textiles: The William Randolph Hearst Collection*. Tucson: The University of Arizona Press, 1988. BHM 317

Boutelle, Sara Holmes. *Julia Morgan: Architect*. New York: Abbeville Press, 1988 (revised and updated edition, 1995). BHM 8, 13, 14, 40, 52, 53, 65, 68, 79, 87, 95, 96, 130, 132, 133, 139, 149, 151, 159, 170, 189, 199, 208, 219, 267, 277, 280, 283, 368, 389, 411, 420, 423, 424, 429, 445, 449, 461, 479, 495, 501, 509, 517, 522

Byne, Arthur. *Decorated Wooden Ceilings in Spain*. New York: G. P. Putnam's Sons, 1920. BHM 513

Carey, Gary. *All the Stars in Heaven: Louis B. Mayer's M-G-M*. New York: E. P. Dutton, 1981. BHM 481

Carlisle, Rodney. "The Foreign Policy Views of an Isolationist Press Lord: W. R. Hearst and the International Crisis, 1936–41." *Journal of Contemporary History* (July 1974), pp. 217–27. BHM 337–38, 385

Carlson, Oliver, and Ernest Sutherland Bates. *Hearst: Lord of San Simeon*. New York: The Viking Press, 1936. BHM 109, 126, 230

Carringer, Robert L. *The Making of Citizen Kane*. Berkeley: University of California Press, 1985 (revised and updated edition, 1996). BHM 461

Carter, Randolph, and Robert Reed Cole. *Joseph Urban: Architecture, Theatre, Opera, Film*. New York: Abbeville Press, 1992. BHM 6

Chaney, Lindsay, and Michael Cieply. *The Hearsts: Family and Empire—The Later Years*. New York: Simon and Schuster, 1981. BHM 392, 407

Clements, Robert M., Jr., "William Randolph Hearst's Monastery." *American Heritage* (April/May 1981), pp. 51–59. BHM 69, 208

———. "Wyntoon—1930." Excerpt under "Morgan, Julia" in Alison Sky and Michelle Stone [eds.]. *Unbuilt America: Forgotten Architecture in the United States from Thomas Jefferson to the Space Age*. New York: McGraw-Hill Book Company, 1976. BHM 69, 208

Coblentz, Edmond D., ed. *William Randolph Hearst: A Portrait in His Own Words*. New York: Simon and Schuster, 1952. BHM 33, 125, 253

Coffman, Taylor. *The Builders Behind the Castles: George Loorz & the F. C. Stolte Co.* San Luis Obispo: San Luis Obispo Historical Society, 1990. BHM 5, 8, 26, 233, 319

———. *Hearst's Dream*. San Luis Obispo: E Z Nature Books, 1989. BHM 462

Crane, Frances. "My Visit to San Simeon." *The New Yorker* (April 5, 1941), p. 37–38. BHM 440

Crowther, Bosley. *Hollywood Rajah: The Life and Times of Louis B. Mayer*. New York: Henry Holt and Company, 1960. BHM 149

———. *The Lion's Share: The Story of an Entertainment Empire*. New York: E. P. Dutton & Company, 1957. BHM 149

Daily Variety. "Hearst Quitting California" (September 30, 1935), pp., 1,3. BHM 221

———. "Story Favoritism Blamed for Hearst-Metro Break, Sending Davies to WB" (November 1, 1934), pp. 1, 3. BHM 143

———. "Why I Am Leaving California, by W. R. Hearst" (October 23, 1935), pp. 1, 4.
    BHM 221

    See also *Variety* in this section

Daniels, Josephus. *Shirt-Sleeve Diplomat.* Chapel Hill: The University of North Caro-
    lina Press, 1947. BHM 458

Davies, Marion. *The Times We Had: Life with William Randolph Hearst.* Edited by Pam-
    ela Pfau and Kenneth S. Marx. Indianapolis and New York: The Bobbs-Merrill
    Company, 1975. BHM 171, 347, 359, 360, 407, 411, 453, 462

Davis, John H. *The Kennedys: Dynasty and Disaster 1848–1983.* New York: McGraw-Hill
    Book Company, 1984. BHM 453

Edmonds, Andy. *Hot Toddy: The True Story of Hollywood's Most Sensational Murder.* New
    York: William Morrow and Company, 1989. BHM 228

España: Sus Monumentos y Artes — Su Naturaleza e Historia. Barcelona: Daniel Cortezo y
    Compania, 1884–91. BHM 513

Farley, James A. *Behind the Ballots: The Personal History of a Politician.* New York: Har-
    court, Brace and Company, 1938. BHM 33

———. *Jim Farley's Story: The Roosevelt Years.* New York and Toronto: Whittlesey House
    (McGraw-Hill Book Company), 1948. BHM 33

*Fine Colonial and Early Federal Furniture: Georgian and Other Important Silver; Old Crown
    Derby, Worcester, Rockingham and Other Table Porcelain; Property of Miss Marion Davies;
    Removed from Her Beach House at 415 Ocean Front, Santa Monica, Calif.* New York:
    Parke-Bernet Galleries, 1945 (catalogue for a "Public Auction Sale" held on Decem-
    ber 7–8). BHM 516

Fortune (magazine). "Hearst" (October 1935), pp. 42–55, 123–62 *passim.* BHM 79,
    208, 259, 260, 324, 368

———. "Hearst at Home" (May 1931), pp. 56–68, 130. BHM 81

Fried, Albert. *FDR and His Enemies.* New York: St. Martin's Press, 1999. BHM 247

Freudenheim, Leslie Mandelson, and Elisabeth Sussman. *Building with Nature: Roots of
    the San Francisco Bay Tradition.* Santa Barbara and Salt Lake City: Peregrine Smith,
    1974. BHM 327

Gebhard, David, et al. *A Guide to Architecture in San Francisco & Northern California.*
    Santa Barbara and Salt Lake City: Peregrine Smith, 1973. BHM 25

Gudde, Erwin G. *California Place Names: A Geographical Dictionary.* Berkeley and Los
    Angeles: University of California Press, 1949. BHM 25

———. *California Place Names: The Origin and Etymology of Current Geographical Names.*
    Berkeley: University of California Press, 1998 (fourth edition, revised and enlarged
    by William Bright). BHM 25–26

Guiles, Fred Lawrence. *Marion Davies.* New York: McGraw-Hill Book Company, 1972.
    BHM 81, 90, 116, 183, 359, 411, 462, 480, 509, 526

Hart-Davis, Rupert. *Hugh Walpole: A Biography.* New York: The Macmillan Com-
    pany, 1952. BHM 170, 231

Hearst, William Randolph, Jr., with Jack Casserly. *The Hearsts: Father and Son*. Niwot, Colorado: Roberts Rinehart Publishers, 1991. BHM 393, 452, 484

Higham, Charles. *Merchant of Dreams: Louis B. Mayer, M.G.M., and the Secret Hollywood*. New York: Donald I. Fine, 1993. BHM 481

Hopper, Hedda, and James Brough. *The Whole Truth and Nothing But*. Garden City, New York: Doubleday & Company, 1963. BHM 480, 481

Hosmer, Charles B., Jr. *Bernard Maybeck and Principia College: The Historic District*. Elsah, Illinois: Principia College, 1988. BHM 15

Hunter, Paul Robinson, and Walter L. Reichardt, eds. *Residential Architecture in Southern California*. Los Angeles: Southern California Chapter, The American Institute of Architects, 1939 (reissued as *Residential Architecture in Southern California, 1939: Mediterranean to Modern* [Los Angeles: Hennessey & Ingalls, 1998]). BHM 303

Huxley, Aldous. *After Many a Summer Dies the Swan*. New York: Harper & Brothers, 1939. BHM 392

James Abbe: Photographer [text by Terence Pepper]. Norfolk, Virginia: Chrysler Museum of Art, 2000. BHM 296

Johnson, Paul. *A History of the American People*. New York: HarperCollins Publishers, 1997. BHM 291

Kastner, Victoria. *Hearst Castle: The Biography of a Country House*. New York: Harry N. Abrams, 2000. BHM 29, 35, 101, 443, 502, 547

Leuchtenburg, William E. *Franklin D. Roosevelt and the New Deal, 1932–1940*. New York: Harper & Row, 1963. BHM 3

Lewis, Oscar. *Fabulous San Simeon: A History of the Hearst Castle*. San Francisco: California Historical Society, 1958. BHM 155

Life (magazine). "A Unique Tour of San Simeon" (August 26, 1957), pp. 68–84. BHM 21–22

Lockwood, Charles. *Dream Palaces: Hollywood at Home*. New York: The Viking Press, 1981. BHM 524

———, and Jeff Hyland. *The Estates of Beverly Hills*. Beverly Hills: Margrant Publishing Company, 1984. BHM 522

Loe, Nancy E. *Hearst Castle: An Interpretive History of W. R. Hearst's San Simeon Estate*. Santa Barbara: Companion Press, 1994. BHM 97, 221. See also *Descriptive Guide to the Julia Morgan Collection* in section A

Longstreth, Richard W. *Julia Morgan: Architect*. Berkeley: Berkeley Architectural Heritage Association, 1977. BHM 13

Lundberg, Ferdinand. *Imperial Hearst: A Social Biography*. New York: Equinox Cooperative Press, 1936. BHM 126, 195, 259

McCoy, Donald R. *Landon of Kansas*. Lincoln, Nebraska: University of Nebraska Press, 1966. BHM 279–80

McCusker, John J. *How Much Is That In Real Money? A Historical Commodity Price Index for Use as a Deflator of Money Values in the Economy of the United States*. Worcester, Massachusetts: American Antiquarian Society, 1992 (second edition, revised and enlarged, 2001). BHM XXVI

McKeen, Rose. *Parade Along the Creek: San Luis Obispo Memories of the 1920s through '60s.* San Luis Obispo: Privately published, 1988. BHM 35

McMurry, Enfys. *Hearst's Other Castle.* Bridgend, Wales: seren, 1999. BHM 55

Maher, James T. *The Twilight of Splendor: Chronicles of the Age of American Palaces.* Boston and Toronto: Little, Brown and Company, 1975. BHM 13

Merritt, Frank Clinton. *History of Alameda County California.* Chicago: The S. J. Clarke Publishing Company, 1928. BHM 8–9, 222

Meryman, Richard. *Mank: The Wit, World, and Life of Herman Mankiewicz.* New York: William Morrow and Company, 1978. BHM 480–81

Mesic, Julian C. "Berkeley Women's City Club." *The Architect and Engineer* (April 1931), pp. 25–34. BHM 52

Mitchell, Greg. *The Campaign of the Century: Upton Sinclair's Race for Governor of California and the Birth of Media Politics.* New York: Random House, 1992. BHM 155

Murray, W. W. "Wyntoon." *The Siskiyou Pioneer* (Yreka, California; 1958), pp. 13–20. BHM 86, 492

Nasaw, David. *The Chief: The Life of William Randolph Hearst.* Boston and New York: Houghton Mifflin Company, 2000. BHM 6, 55, 61, 227, 273, 335, 348, 355, 392–93, 447, 451, 462, 503

Newsweek (magazine). "The Seer of San Simeon" (May 6, 1946 ["The Press" section]), pp. 62–64. BHM 508

Newton, A. Edward. "A Tourist in Spite of Himself—At the Hearst Ranch." *The Atlantic Monthly* (October 1932), pp. 461–67. BHM 81

The New Yorker (magazine). "387 Southern Boulevard" (November 6, 1937 ["The Talk of the Town" section]), p. 15. BHM 372–73
See also Crane, Frances, in this section

The New York Times. "Hearst Importing a Spanish Cloister." December 14, 1926, p. 1. BHM 69
———. "Highest Salaries for 1935 Listed." January 7, 1937, p. 28. BHM 259
———. "Threat to Call Hearst. California Income Tax Bill Author Assails Publisher." April 20, 1935, p. 17. BHM 202–03
———. "Topics of the Times: Precept and Practice." December 27, 1932, p. 12. BHM 43–44
———. "Topics of the Times: War with Spain." May 3, 1935, p. 18. BHM 125–26
See also Aikman, Duncan, in this section

North, Flora D. "She Built for the Ages." *Kappa Alpha Theta Journal* (Spring 1967), pp. 9–11. BHM 13, 40

Older, Mrs. Fremont. *William Randolph Hearst: American.* New York and London: D. Appleton-Century Company, 1936. BHM 11, 33, 101, 126, 230–31

Packard, Robert T., and Balthazar Korab. *Encyclopedia of American Architecture.* New York: McGraw-Hill, 1995 (second edition). BHM 8

Parsons, Louella O. *The Gay Illiterate*. Garden City, New York: Doubleday, Doran and Co., 1944. BHM 478, 484

Pavlik, Robert C. "'Something a Little Different': La Cuesta Encantada's Architectural Precedents and Cultural Prototypes." *California History* (Winter 1992/93), pp. 463–77, 548–49. BHM 175

Perkins, Hayes. "Here and There: An Itinerant Worker in the Pacific Northwest, 1898." Introduction by Carlos A. Schwantes. *Oregon Historical Quarterly* (Fall 2001), pp. 352–76. BHM 97

Pizzitola, Louis. *Hearst Over Hollywood: Power, Passion, and Propaganda in the Movies*. New York: Columbia University Press, 2002. BHM 97, 411, 462, 474, 481, 509

Polk's Detroit City Directory (editions for 1916 and 1923–24). Detroit: R. L. Polk & Co., 1916, 1924. BHM 524

Polk's Santa Barbara City Directory (editions for 1954 and 1955). Los Angeles: R. L. Polk & Co., 1954, 1955. BHM 395

Reitlinger, Gerald. *The Economics of Taste. The Rise and Fall of the Objets d'Art Market since 1750*. New York: Holt, Rinehart and Winston, 1963. BHM 384–85

Richey, Elinor. *Eminent Women of the West*. Berkeley: Howell-North Books, 1975. BHM 13, 87, 138

Robinson, Judith. *The Hearsts: An American Dynasty*. Newark, Delaware: University of Delaware Press, 1991. BHM 8, 64

Roosevelt, James, with Bill Libby. *My Parents: A Differing View*. Chicago: Playboy Press, 1976. BHM 508

St. Johns, Adela Rogers. *The Honeycomb*. New York: Doubleday & Company, 1969. BHM 159, 171, 206

Sanchez, Nellie Van de Grift. *Spanish and Indian Place Names of California: Their Meaning and Their Romance*. San Francisco: A. M. Robertson, 1914. BHM 25

Sarber, Jane, ed. *A Cabbie in a Golden Era: Featuring Cabbie's Original Log of Guests Transported to Hearst Castle*. N.p., n.d. [Paso Robles, California: Privately published, 1982]. BHM 329

Sargent, Shirley. *Yosemite & Its Innkeepers: The Story of a Great Park and Its Chief Concessionaires*. Yosemite, California: Flying Spur Press, 1975. BHM 244

Searls, Hank. *The Lost Prince: Young Joe, The Forgotten Kennedy: The Story of the Oldest Brother*. New York and Cleveland: The World Publishing Company, 1969. BHM 453

Sinclair, Upton. *I, Candidate for Governor: And How I Got Licked*. Berkeley: University of California Press, 1994 (facsimile reprint of original edition [Pasadena: The Author, 1935]). BHM 155–56

Smith, Amanda, ed. *Hostage to Fortune: The Letters of Joseph P. Kennedy*. New York: Viking, 2001. BHM 453

Starr, Kevin. *Endangered Dreams: The Great Depression in California*. New York and Oxford: Oxford University Press, 1996. BHM 125, 155, 425

Steilberg, Walter T. "Some Examples of The Work of Julia Morgan." *The Architect and Engineer of California* (November 1918), pp. 39–107. BHM 13

Stephan, John J. *Hawaii Under the Rising Sun: Japan's Plans for Conquest After Pearl Harbor.* Honolulu: University of Hawaii Press, 1984. BHM 484–85

Stevens, Joseph E. *Hoover Dam: An American Adventure.* Norman and London: University of Oklahoma Press, 1988. BHM 470

Stolte Blueprint (magazine). "Cast Stone Shop Opened" (October 31, 1945), p. 7. BHM 504–05

———. "Letter from Wyntoon," by Frank Gendrich (December 25, 1947), p. 10. BHM 518

———. "Life Fit for a King at San Simeon Estate," by Hazel McClure (December 21, 1945), p. 10. BHM 505–06

———. "San Simeon Chatter," by Hazel McClure (December 20, 1946), p. 9. BHM 513–14

———. "San Simeon News" (December 25, 1947), p. 10. BHM 518–19

———. "San Simeon Spotlight," by Hazel McClure (August 20, 1946), p. 11. BHM 510–11

———. "Who's Where," by Chuck Carlen (October 31, 1945), pp. 2, 11. BHM 505

———. "Work Starts on New Oakland Public Library," by Lee Perry (December 25, 1948), pp. 4, 30. BHM 519

———. "Wyntoon Has a Heat Wave in the Snow," by Mr. X-mas (December 21, 1945), p. 11. BHM 506–07

Swanberg, W. A. *Citizen Hearst: A Biography of William Randolph Hearst.* New York: Charles Scribner's Sons, 1961. BHM 117, 125, 149, 165, 208, 227, 273, 316, 348, 392, 451, 458, 474, 478, 515

———. *Luce and His Empire.* New York: Charles Scribner's Sons, 1972. BHM 117

Swing, Raymond Gram. *Forerunners of American Fascism.* New York: Julian Messner, 1935. BHM 195

Tebbel, John. *The Life and Good Times of William Randolph Hearst.* New York: E. P. Dutton & Co., 1952. BHM 6, 126, 247, 451, 495, 509

———, and Sarah Miles Watts. *The Press and The Presidency: From George Washington to Ronald Reagan.* New York and London: Oxford University Press, 1985. BHM 126

Time (magazine). "Dusk at Santa Monica" (March 13, 1939 ["The Press" section]), pp. 49–56. BHM 403

———. "$15,000,000 Worth" (March 14, 1938 ["Art" section]), p. 39. BHM 410

———. "50 Years of Hearst" (March 15, 1937 ["The Press" section]), pp. 49–50. BHM 324

———. "Hearstiana" (April 26, 1937 ["The Press" section]), pp. 49–51. BHM 324

———. "Hearst is 80" (May 10, 1943 ["The Press" section]), p. 50. BHM 484

———. "Hearst *Redivivus*" (February 5, 1945 ["The Press" section]), pp. 63–64. BHM 501

————. "Hearst Steps Nos. 2 & 3" (July 12, 1937 ["The Press" section]), p. 26. BHM 334

————. "Hearst's Third War" (March 23, 1942 ["The Press" section]), pp. 40, 42. BHM 474

————. "People" section (October 12, 1936), pp. 69, 71. BHM 278

————. "Taxation: Good-by to California" (November 4, 1935 ["National Affairs" section]), p. 21. BHM 259

Tomkins, E. F., ed. *Selections from the Writings and Speeches of William Randolph Hearst.* San Francisco: Privately published, 1948. BHM 349–50, 385, 498

Vanderbilt, Gloria Morgan, with Palma Wayne. *Without Prejudice.* New York: E. P. Dutton & Company, 1936. BHM 169

Van Pelt, Jr., Garrett. *Old Architecture of Southern Mexico.* Cleveland: J. H. Hansen, 1926. BHM 513

Variety (weekly edition). "No Renewal Between 20th-Fox and Hearst's Cosmo Pix in Prospect" (March 27, 1940), p. 5. BHM 411

See also *Daily Variety* in this section

Vidor, King. *A Tree is a Tree.* New York: Harcourt, Brace and Company, 1953. BHM 21

Villard, Oswald Garrison. *Some Newspapers and Newspaper-Men.* New York: Alfred A. Knopf, 1923. BHM 125

Wadsworth, Ginger. *Julia Morgan: Architect of Dreams.* Minneapolis: Lerner Publications Company, 1990. BHM 149

Wallace Neff 1895–1982: The Romance of Regional Architecture [Andrea P. A. Belloli, ed.]. San Marino: The Huntington Library, 1989. BHM 526

Walsh, Raoul. *Each Man in His Time: The Life Story of a Director.* New York: Farrar, Straus and Giroux, 1974. BHM 103

Warner, Jack L., with Dean Jennings. *My First Hundred Years in Hollywood.* New York: Random House, 1965. BHM 143

Warren, Charles S. *History of the Santa Monica Bay Region.* Santa Monica: A. H. Cawston, 1934. BHM 144

The Wartime Journals of Charles A. Lindbergh. New York: Harcourt Brace Jovanovich, 1970. BHM 462

Weitze, Karen J. *California's Mission Revival.* Los Angeles: Hennessey & Ingalls, 1984. BHM 303

Winkler, John K. *W. R. Hearst: An American Phenomenon.* New York: Simon and Schuster, 1928. BHM 81

————. *William Randolph Hearst: A New Appraisal.* New York: Hastings House, 1955. BHM 451

Wolf, Donald E. *Big Dams and Other Dreams: The Six Companies Story.* Norman and London: University of Oklahoma Press, 1996. BHM 470

Woodbridge, Sally B. *Bernard Maybeck: Visionary Architect.* New York: Abbeville Press, 1992. BHM 68

————. "Historic Architecture: Wyntoon." *Architectural Digest* (January 1988), pp. 98–103, 156. BHM 87, 368

Woon, Basil. *Incredible Land: A Jaunty Baedeker to Hollywood and the Great Southwest.* New York: Liveright Publishing Corporation, 1933. BHM 81

Young, Betty Lou. *Pacific Palisades: Where the Mountains Meet the Sea.* Pacific Palisades, California: Pacific Palisades Historical Society Press, 1983. BHM 391

Index

The first number cited below—27n—indicates a reference confined to the footnote section of that page, on par with all other "n" listings. By itself, 27 would indicate the main text and *possibly* that page's footnote section as well. But no double entries—such as 27, 27n—occur in the index. In contrast, entries like 27–28 indicate either the main text on adjoining pages or a text-footnote combination on those pages, whereas 27–28n would apply strictly to the footnotes involved.

Building for Hearst and Morgan was designed by Jeff Clark of Wilsted & Taylor

Publishing Services. The text was digitally composed in Baskerville.

Printed and bound by Edwards Brothers, Ann Arbor, Michigan.